KINGDOM
in the
WEST

The Mormons and the American Frontier

VOLUME IV

MELISSA BURTON CORAY KIMBALL

Melissa Kimball was one of four women who accompanied the Mormon Battalion from Council Bluffs to San Diego. Melissa Coray Peak in the Sierra Nevada commemorates the contributions of this American heroine to the opening of Carson Pass in 1848. Her first husband, former Sgt. William Coray, died of tuberculosis at Great Salt Lake City in 1849. She is pictured here as the wife of Nauvoo Legion General William H. Kimball in a previously unpublished photograph from about 1860. *Courtesy, Paul H. Kimball.*

Army of Israel
Mormon Battalion
Narratives

Edited by
David L. Bigler
and
Will Bagley

THE ARTHUR H. CLARK COMPANY
Spokane, Washington
2000

Maps by David L. Bigler
All rights reserved including the rights
to translate or reproduce this work or parts
thereof in any form or by any media

THE ARTHUR H. CLARK CO.
P.O. Box 14707
Spokane, WA   99214

LIBRARY OF CONGRESS CATALOG CARD NUMBER 99-086550
ISBN-0-87062-297-8
ISBN-0-87062-274-9 (entire series)

Library of Congress Cataloging-in-Publication Data

Army of Israel: Mormon Battalion narratives / edited by David L. Bigler and Will Bagley.
     496 p.   cm. —(Kingdom in the West ; v. 4)
   Includes bibliographical references and index.
   ISBN 0-87062-297-8 (alk. paper)
     1. United States. Army. Mormon Battalion. 2. Mexican War, 1846–1848—Regimental his-
tories—United States. 3. Mexican War, 1846–1848—Participation, Mormon. 4. Mormons
—Southwest, New—History—19th century. 5. Mexican War, 1846–1848—Campaigns—
Southwest, New. 6. Mexican War, 1846-1848—Campaigns—California. 7. Southwest, New
—History, Military—19th century. 8. California—History, Military—19th century.
I. Bigler, David L., 1927–   II. Bagley, Will, 1950–   III. Series.
E409.5.172A76   2000
973.6'24—dc21   99-086550
                                                                                CIP

FOR CASSANDRA MARGENE BAILEY BAGLEY,
LAURA BLEIWEISS, AND PAM COPIER.

CONTENTS

ILLUSTRATIONS

MAPS

ACKNOWLEDGMENTS

We can only begin to recognize a few of the people who assisted in compiling this book. The staffs of the following institutions helped locate many of the original manuscripts presented in this volume: the Bancroft Library; the California State Library; the California State Archives; the California Historical Society; the Utah State Historical Society; the Utah State Archives; Special Collections and Manuscripts at the University of Utah's Marriott Library; Special Collections and Archives at the Merrill Library, Utah State University; Special Collections and Manuscripts at the Harold B. Lee Library, Brigham Young University; Special Collections at Gerald R. Sherratt Library, Southern Utah University; the Pioneer Memorial Museum of the International Society, Daughters of Utah Pioneers; the Henry E. Huntington Library; the Missouri Historical Society; the Library & Archives of the Reorganized Church of Jesus Christ of Latter Day Saints; the Mid-Continent Public Library of Independence, Missouri; the Feldheym Library of San Bernardino, California; the National Archives; and the Library of Congress. We owe a great debt to the staff of the Historical Department and Library of the Church of Jesus Christ of Latter-day Saints for their untiring assistance. We would like to acknowledge the special help of librarians and archivists Alan Barnett, Barbara Bernauer, Peter J. Blodgett, Kelly Bullock, Ann Buttars, Annette W. Curtis, David B. Gracy II, John R. Gonzales, Bonnie Hardwick, Jeffery O. Johnson, Walter Jones, Patricia Keats, Gary F. Kurutz, Sue McDonald, Edith Menna, Ronald E. Romig, Janet Burton Seegmiller, William Slaughter, Gregory C. Thompson, Ronald G. Watt, Bradford Westwood, David Whittaker, Val Wilson, and Sibylle Zemitis.

Historians Lyndia Carter, D. Robert Carter, Charles Cresap, Lorin K. Hansen, Robert K. Hoshide, Paul Hutton, Kristin Johnson, Janet Lecompte, Ben Lofgren, Brigham D. Madsen, Tom Mahach, Michael Marquardt, Susan Payne, D. Michael Quinn, Eugene A. Rose, Will

"Bud" Rusho, and the late Harold Schindler shared time and materials with us, greatly extending our understanding of the battalion's place in Western and Mormon history. Terry Cook contributed her knowledge of Stephen Watts Kearny and the conquest of California, and John Hutchinson of the Marshall Gold Discovery State Historic Park provided helpful information on the discovery of gold in California. G. Ralph Bailey has given us access to documents in his collection. Legendary booksellers Curt Bench, Rick Grunder, Ken Sanders, and Sam Weller have provided us not only with books and documents, but also with much-appreciated time and expertise. Friends G. J. "Chris" Graves and L. Louise Jee added to our knowledge of the trail near Warner's Ranch, and Steve Covey contributed information on early southern California ranches.

Descendants of battalion veterans have greatly assisted our work. April S. Hancock shared her transcriptions of the writings she edited in *The Life of Levi W. Hancock*. Lula DeValve supplied us with her transcription of the Thomas Dunn journal. Steve Berlin helped us track down material by his ancestors, George W. and Fanny Taggart. Connie Edholm provided us with extracts from the Charles Brent Hancock diary. Carmen Smith shared her knowledge of the trail and the "Lost Well." Barbara S. Lateer gave us a Capt. J. D. Hunter letter, while Andrew D. Crews provided a picture of his ancestor, Robert Whitworth. Robert Cole shared Daniel Tyler material with us. John J. Riser's family graciously permitted us to use parts of his previously unpublished memoir, including his important description of opening the Salt Lake–Los Angeles wagon road. Carl Larson's data base of battalion soldiers has been a tremendous help.

Todd I. Berens, B. Carmon Hardy, Michael W. Homer, Melvin C. Johnson, Michael N. Landon, William P. MacKinnon, Floyd A. O'Neil, and Kenneth N. Owens have reviewed all or parts of this book. They merit special thanks for sharing their time, sources, transcriptions, suggestions, and insights. Once again John Alley's remarkable editorial skills have proved invaluable to us. Publisher Robert A. Clark's patience and support have been a constant throughout the project. We are proud to represent one of the many contributions of Clark, his family, and The Arthur H. Clark Company have made to the cause of Western history.

We must recognize an old friend, Norma Baldwin Ricketts, who for many years has graciously shared her private archives and unmatched knowledge of the battalion's story with us. We should also note the many problems her definitive narrative history, *The Mormon Battalion: U.S. Army of the West, 1846–1848,* has solved for us. Her book relieved us of the need to compile detailed rosters of the battalion and its many off-shoots, and her comprehensive bibliography has allowed us to list only the few items she missed and the sources and manuscripts we consulted. Her exhaustive survey of Latter-day Saint sources and her faithful representation of the soldiers' perspective freed us to address the larger military, political, and cultural issues that are so intertwined in this remarkable story. We have made a conscious effort not to duplicate material presented in her book, and readers should consult her volume for elements they find missing in this one, particularly rosters. She has ably summarized several of the diaries and journals—notably those of William Coray and Henry Boyle—that we surely would have used had she not made such an undertaking redundant.

Many might presume that Mrs. Ricketts' comprehensive survey and able summary of some of the best battalion sources would have stolen a march on our book. Fortunately the depth of this event's documentary history is so great that even with the addition of this volume, much work remains to be done. The battalion's Indian relations and the winter its detachments spent at El Pueblo merit detailed studies of their own. We have tried to select the most essential of the well-known accounts and the best of the overlooked, obscure, or hard-to-find sources—letters, journals, recollections, military reports, and government documents—and hope readers will find that these diverse sources tell a compelling story.

While we attempted to survey all known primary sources on the battalion, we have not seen every available record. We consulted only a few of the Mormon Battalion pension files at the National Archives, and the appearance of many previously unknown diaries, letters, and reminiscences in the last decade suggests that significant new sources will continue to come to light. We hope that this study will draw attention to the wealth of material available for future studies of the Mormon Battalion and the Army of the West. We especially want to encourage further publication of battalion narratives, and hold out hope that the future will bring forth discovery and publication of some of the great "lost" battalion narratives, including those of William Coray, James Ferguson, John Forsgren, and John G. Smith.

We must finally recognize the support of our wives and families. They have waited patiently for their husbands and fathers who have long been lost in the past, following dusty tracks along the Arkansas and the Rio Grande, the Gila and the San Joaquin, the Truckee and Mary's River, and the Sweetwater and the Platte, but always pointed toward home.

David L. Bigler   Will Bagley
Roseville, California   Salt Lake City, Utah
November, 1999

EDITORIAL PROCEDURES

This collection of Mormon Battalion documents attempts to represent faithfully the original records in a readable format. With noted exceptions, these transcriptions preserve the grammar, spelling, and style of the originals. Capitalization follows that of the source except that the first letters of sentences and of personal names are capitalized; where the case used in the manuscript is ambiguous, we follow standard capitalization. We added periods to the ends of sentences. Where a writer employed commas in the place of periods, they are converted to periods, but otherwise we maintained the punctuation (or its absence) of the original. We have done our best to produce transcriptions that are as accurate as possible, but this arduous task does not encourage any claim to infallibility.

We generally preserved the dating style of the source. Where the writer omitted the year in journal entries, we inserted it in brackets on the first and fifteenth days of the month or as needed to make dates easy to identify. We use "*sic*" sparingly, where the item in question is especially significant or could be mistaken for a typo. Brackets enclose added letters, missing words, and conjectural readings. [Blank] indicates a blank space, while other bracketed comments, such as [*tear*], note physical defects in the manuscript. We placed interlined insertions in their logical location in the text. Abbreviations A.M. and P.M. are set in small caps, but maintain the punctuation and capitalization of the original text. Underlined text is italicized, while crossed-out text is rendered as ~~strikethroughs~~.

The Journal History of the LDS church, a daily "scrapbook" of Mormon history consisting of journals, minutes, letters, and articles extracted (and expurgated) from church records by Andrew Jenson, is cited as Journal History. Materials from the extensive battalion sources held at the Archives of the Historical Department of the Church of Jesus Christ of Latter-day Saints in Salt Lake City, Utah, including the Brigham Young Collection, are cited as LDS Archives.

The material is organized into chapters, sections, and documents. Each document contains an abbreviated heading identifying the source and its location. Full citations for these items, including manuscript numbers, are found in the bibliography.

Footnotes cite published sources by author, title, and page number. Where available, newspaper citations are to page/column: 2/3. The bibliography contains a complete listing of all the books, articles, newspapers, journals, and manuscripts referenced in the footnotes. We have italicized book titles and put article, thesis, and dissertation titles in quotation marks. Manuscript citations appear in plain text without quotation marks. Quoted material from the sources reproduced in this volume book is not footnoted, though it is sometimes cross-referenced. Where biographical information is drawn from standard references, such as Bancroft's "Pioneer Register" from his *History of California*, Larson's data base, Jenson's *LDS Biographical Encyclopedia*, or Thrapp's *Encyclopedia of Frontier Biography*, we have not always provided detailed citations. Except when used as adjectives, ages are given as numerals.

The editing strategy outlined above is in some cases modified, as in portions of the Levi Hancock journal, to give a better sense of the original. Those who want to see the text in its true form are encouraged to visit the libraries and archives preserving these documents. Holding such remarkable artifacts in one's hands is quite literally touching the past. Perhaps nothing speaks as eloquently of this forgotten but fascinating military enterprise as the humble, worn daybooks that record in simple but splendid detail these westering pilgrims' progress. We trust that their stories tell a compelling human tale, and that our readers will find the journey worthwhile.

INTRODUCTION

"History may be searched in vain for an equal march of infantry," said Lt. Col. Philip St. George Cooke in his famous Order No. 1 commending the Mormon Battalion for its epic march in 1846 from Council Bluffs, Iowa, to San Diego and Los Angeles to claim California for the United States. Yet this historic journey across the Southwest during the War with Mexico was but one of the reasons this command holds a unique place in U.S. military annals as well as in the larger story of America's western migration during the nineteenth century.

Unlike other American military outfits, the five hundred members of the battalion, with fewer than ten exceptions, were recruited from the same religious body.[1] Almost all belonged to the Church of Jesus Christ of Latter-day Saints, popularly known as the Mormons, a controversial millennial movement founded in 1830 at Manchester, New York, by Joseph Smith, Jr., who claimed to be an American prophet. In faith they made up a homogenous corps whose members marched to a radically different drummer than any other military unit that ever served in the American armed forces.

Moreover few, if any, of the Mormon "volunteers" really wanted to enlist in the first place. Almost to a man they were reluctant to leave their families, entrusted only to God and the care of others, in what they perceived as an open wilderness. Most deeply resented being asked to serve a country that had failed to preserve their personal security and religious freedoms. Thirty-seven-year-old New Yorker Albert Smith expressed the general bitterness when he protested, "For government to mak[e] Such a demand when we ware driven from our homes & Posse-sions & were scattred upon the plains from Nauvoo to the Mosurie [Missouri] river was more Cruel than the Grave."[2]

In contrast to the thousands of other young men who flocked to the

---

[1]Norma B. Ricketts established that the battalion consisted of exactly five hundred men. For her detailed rosters and analysis of the unit's composition, see Ricketts, *The Mormon Battalion*, 279–90.

[2]Journal of Albert Smith, 2 July 1846.

colors in 1846, Mormon Battalion members answered to a church call, not to the voice of patriotism. They volunteered out of obedience to the leaders of their faith. Throughout their service the majority gave their first loyalty to their church and the leaders it had placed over them, not to the U.S. Army or its officers. Most of them served for only twelve months. While other Americans, usually outnumbered and long-since forgotten, fought bloody battles deep in Mexico, they never fired a shot in combat with an enemy of their country.

Yet this battalion, perhaps the most unusual body of men ever to serve in America's armed forces, holds a singular place not only in Western history, but also in the larger annals of the republic. Between 1846 and1848 its members played pivotal roles in events of such magnitude that they continue to shape the nation's destiny and the lives of its people. Their story is often told as a celebration of a religious epic, with an oddly triumphal parochialism that views the episode as part of Utah's rather than America's story. This study seeks to place the larger political and military role of the Mormon Battalion in the context of the history of the American West.

For sixteen years prior to its enlistment, the millennial faith to which its members belonged had seen no peace. Frontier forms of American democracy had proved inadequate to cope with a dynamic religious movement that acted as one according to the dictates of heaven. Conflict in Missouri broke out in 1831 when the prophet Joseph Smith, Jr., revealed that Jackson County was the land of Zion and its frontier seat, Independence, was the place to build New Jerusalem for the gathering of God's chosen people in the Last Days. Fighting flared across seven western counties over the next eight years until the Mormons were finally expelled from the state in 1839.

That year the citizens of western Illinois gave food and shelter to the suffering remnants of Israel that streamed across the Mississippi River from Missouri. Some fifty miles north of Quincy, Illinois, on a quiet bend of the river, they created an exotic city-state named Nauvoo "the beautiful," which became over the next four years one of the largest cities in Illinois. The sovereign Mormon metropolis was unlike any other urban center in western America.

The new city's charter, won from state legislators with the promise of unanimous Mormon political support, allowed Joseph Smith and his followers to establish an independent theocracy within the state of Illinois. As described by Governor Thomas Ford, it was "a government within a government, a legislature with power to pass ordinances at war with the laws of the state; courts to execute them with but little dependence upon the constitutional judiciary; and a military force at their own command."[3] Incompatible with other forms of democracy, such a society could never exist free of conflict on the American frontier.

Justified or not, fear spread among other settlers in Hancock County as the powers of government at Nauvoo became centered in one man. Most alarming to neighbors was the Nauvoo Legion, a semi-private military force that grew under compulsory enlistment to number some four thousand, armed and uniformed, and nearly half the size of the U.S. Army. At its head stood Lt. Gen. Joseph Smith, who also wielded the powers of mayor, head of the city council, and chief justice of the municipal court. Nauvoo became a self-governing city-state, above the reach of county or state law, and a sanctuary for counterfeiters and wrongdoers.[4]

Amid growing opposition from the outside, dissenters within the faith sparked a crisis that led to the fall of the Mormon prophet and his city. Rejecting the theocratic system and the revealed doctrine of polygamy, some of Smith's senior associates published the first and last issue of an opposition newspaper, the *Nauvoo Expositor*. At Smith's direction, the city council ordered the offending sheet destroyed. His action set off a series of events that climaxed in the murder of the prophet and his brother, Hyrum, on 27 June 1844 in the jail at Carthage, Illinois.

Unable to live in peace with its neighbors and dogged by a federal court's indictment of many of its leaders for counterfeiting, the Mormon church early in 1846 began its exodus from the United States. The faithful headed west to establish the Kingdom of God in the Rocky Mountains, in what was then a remote corner of the Mexican province of Alta California. That same year, James K. Polk, one of the nation's most important if little-recognized presidents, deliberately or not goaded Mexico into firing the first shot of the Mexican War by stationing a small American army on a disputed strip of land at the mouth of the Rio Grande. The provocation was the first step toward his larger goal

[3]Ford, *A History of Illinois*, 2:66.
[4]Godfrey, "Crime and Punishment in Mormon Nauvoo," 195–222.

to annex New Mexico and the territory he coveted most, California, to the United States.

When it came to the latter prize, the president feared Mexico less than he did Great Britain and the designs this old adversary might have on the Pacific. With one eye on the British, on 2 June 1846 Polk was about to decide how large a force it would take to invade New Mexico and move on to occupy the isolated land of Alta California. At this critical moment the president received an appeal from Jesse C. Little, the "Agent of the Church of Jesus Christ of Latter-day Saints in the Eastern States."

Little's petition was not the first time the young religion had looked to the national government for help.[5] Shortly before his murder, Joseph Smith had proposed federal legislation authorizing him to build a string of military posts along the Oregon Trail and to raise a force of one hundred thousand volunteers, independent of the U.S. Army, to defend American interests on the frontier. Although Smith had no military training or experience, he nonetheless commanded the four-thousand-man Nauvoo Legion as a lieutenant-general, a grade not used in the U.S. Army since the death of George Washington. Not surprisingly this proposal, apparently linked to Mormon plans to move west, found few supporters in Washington, D.C.

Amid growing strife in Illinois, Smith's successors turned to the federal government for assistance to move their people to the Far West. On orders from Brigham Young, Samuel Brannan, a Mormon editor at New York, had gone to Washington in 1845 to solicit government help to finance a journey of the faith's eastern members by sea to the West Coast. Instead he became involved with power brokers close to the Polk administration in a questionable contract to trade prospective Mormon lands for unneeded political influence before sailing in February 1846 for San Francisco with some 230 Mormons on the ship *Brooklyn*.[6] Young himself had sought federal contracts to construct a string of block-houses and stockades on the Oregon Trail, but was told it was customary for federal troops to build such posts.

As the first Mormon companies prepared to evacuate Nauvoo and

---

[5]Little to Polk, 1 June 1846, reprinted with Little's report and diary in Watson, ed., *Manuscript History of Brigham Young 1846–1847*, 216–17.

[6]For another look at these events, see Bagley, ed., *Scoundrel's Tale: The Samuel Brannan Papers*, 75–130.

cross the Mississippi River, the Quorum of the Twelve Apostles early in 1846 named Jesse C. Little to head up the religion's eastern operations, replacing the departed Samuel Brannan. As time grew short, they handed the thirty-year-old New Englander the urgent mission to embrace any help Washington might give in making the westward move. The letter charging Little with this difficult assignment closed with a plea that hinted of desperation, "Be thou a savior and a deliverer."[7] And Little, acting "promptly upon my own judgement," got the job done where others had failed.[8]

The key to his success came in the form of a feisty five-foot-six new friend who took up the Mormon cause after hearing Little preach in Philadelphia on 13 May 1846. Twenty-four-year-old Thomas L. Kane was the son of an influential Democratic judge and a disciple of Auguste Comte, the founder of "scientific socialism." A self-appointed humanitarian, he was also a gifted political operative with a burning desire to "be *the* man of the Western West." Kane went to Washington "to help the Mormons to my utmost, principally—but also to help myself."[9] It was undoubtedly Kane who advised his new Mormon friend to play on Polk's fears of a British plot to take over California. When all else failed, Little wisely decided to take Kane's timely advice.

Little's respectfully worded, but not so subtle, threat to President James Polk of a possible shift of Mormon allegiance to Great Britain is among the most important documents in the history of the Mormon movement during the nineteenth century (see Chapter I). Its consequences were not only far-reaching, but they would make this spokesman one of the most significant, if still largely unsung, heroes of early Mormonism. On the very day that Polk received Little's ominous letter, the president decided to allow "a few hundred" Mormons to serve in the California occupation forces. The reason, he wrote in his journal, was to prevent the singular sect from turning against the United States and upsetting the delicate international balance of power in western North America.

Little's suggestion was no idle threat. A "memorial" to the British

---

[7]Journal History, 6 July 1846.

[8]Little to Brannan, 16 March 1886, Harold B. Lee Library, Brigham Young Univ., Provo, Utah, cited hereafter as BYU Library.

[9]T. L. Kane to Mother, 3 July 1846; and T. L. Kane to Elisha K. Kane, 27 May 1846, American Philosophical Society. Kane planned to write a book about his western experiences.

government in the *Latter-day Saints' Millennial Star*, 28 November 1846, revealed that the Mormons were actively courting British support. Their petition requested permission to settle on Vancouver Island, noting "that the Government of the United States is doing much to favour the settlement of its territories on the Western Coast, and even to settle territory now in dispute between it and the Republic of Mexico." The memorial noted that the "United States do manifest such a strong inclination, not only to extend and enlarge their possessions in the West, but also to people them," and asked, "will not your Majesty look well to British interests in those regions, and adopt timely and precautionary measures to maintain a balance of power in that quarter—which, in the opinion of your memorialists, is destined, at no very distant period, to participate largely in the China trade."[10]

While Polk responded to Little's coercive tactics, he held firm on his policy that no members of the faith should be enrolled in the U.S. Army before they reached the West Coast. His directive was unintentionally nullified, however, by a carelessly drafted order from the War Department that appeared to approve the immediate enlistment of a battalion of Mormon infantry to serve in the Army of the West.[11]

So it was that an officer from Fort Leavenworth appeared in June 1846 at Mormon refugee camps in Iowa. Capt. James Allen of the U.S. Army's First Regiment of Dragoons had little trouble signing up the five hundred recruits he was authorized to enlist. Many failed to come within the age limits of eighteen and forty-five, but with the active support of Brigham Young, Captain Allen soon had plenty of "volunteers" to fill the muster rolls of five companies.

The enlistment returned many benefits to the young religion. It provided urgently needed permission to settle for a time on Indian lands west of the Missouri River, giving the Mormons time to prepare for the larger move west. It opened a way to move five hundred followers to California at government expense. Most importantly, however, the soldiers' pay provided desperately needed cash for the dispossessed LDS church. Never in their history was the Mormons' "physical situation more ten-

---

[10]Munro, "Mormon Colonization Scheme for Vancouver Island," 280.

[11]First to recognize the misunderstanding that led to the premature enlistment of the Mormon Battalion was W. Ray Luce, whose article, "The Mormon Battalion: A Historical Accident?" appeared in *Utah Hist. Quarterly* in 1974.

uous, their economy more fragile, and their very survival more in question than in the fall of 1846." Before leaving Nauvoo the faithful had "entered into covenant to assist one anothe[r] till all the Saints got out of that place." This apparently justified Brigham Young in using part of the soldiers' pay and clothing allowances to help finance the church's migration to the Salt Lake Valley in 1847. Young also cajoled thousands of dollars from the few wealthy churchmen who had followed him to the Missouri, and the Mormons received charitable donations—in October 1847 even James K. Polk and James Buchanan would each give $10 to Mormon missionary Charles R. Dana.[12] Yet much of the cash used to finance the trek to the Great Basin came from the battalion.

In return, what Col. Stephen W. Kearny got for troops was a rough slice of the ragged and hungry refugees who filled the Mormon emigration camps scattered across Iowa that summer. The recruits ranged in age from fourteen to sixty-eight, with the average about twenty-seven. Some rode in wagons, too sick to walk, and one died on the short march from Council Bluffs to Fort Leavenworth. According to battalion historian Norma Baldwin Ricketts, more than thirty brought wives (Jefferson Hunt brought two) and at least forty-four children accompanied them, in addition to other family members and assorted camp followers. By the time it marched west from the Rio Grande, however, the command had been reduced by regular officers to an efficient, if untrained, body of some 336 muskets, accompanied by only a handful of civilians and relatives.

From such exceptional and unpromising beginnings, these chosen few would inscribe their names in the annals of the American West in ways only now beginning to be understood and fully appreciated. Even at that time many American citizens felt that the United States unjustly acquired New Mexico, Arizona, and California from its weaker neighbor to the south. Yet the march of the battalion demonstrates that the Mexican claim to the Southwest was as problematic as that of the United States, which purchased this vast territory at the war's end in the Treaty of Guadalupe Hidalgo. In 1846 Mexico's power in the region was in decline. Powerful independence movements in New Mexico and

---

[12]Bennett, *Mormons at the Missouri, 1846–1852*, 113, 120; Journal of Albert Smith; and Bennett, *We'll Find the Place*, 305.

California challenged the authority of the remote central government. Bands of Navajo, Apache, Piman, and Quechan Indians actually controlled most of the country east of California and west of the Rio Grande. At the time they were generally friendly to the American newcomers, but many of the Apaches and Navajos were implacably warlike toward Mexican residents. Following independence from Spain in 1821, Mexico's inability to protect its northern provinces had exposed its colonies in present New Mexico and southern Arizona to prolonged bloodletting by hostile Indians. As Lt. Col. Philip St. George Cooke noted in his December 1846 letter to the governor of Sonora, the Mexican government had done nothing to defend his province against this incessant attack. Despite the remarkable courage of a handful of local Hispanic soldiers, by 1846 the actual dividing line between Mexican authority and control by hostile Indians lay far to the south of any borders drawn on maps of the period.

Without opposition or firing a shot, the Mormon infantry tramped across the width of what was then northern Mexico and even built a wagon road as they went. The invasion of Kearny's little Army of the West made real James K. Polk's vision of a continental nation. However troubling the ambitions of an expansionist American president might appear to some from the comfortable distance of 150 years, both the United States' purchase of the Southwest and the Spanish conquest that was the source of Mexico's title were based on military force. Resting on European conventions, each nation's claim was at least as good as the other, and neither was as strong as that of the oldest native inhabitants, who were themselves being displaced by Navajo and Apache invaders. The American claim gave Mexican colonists not only a promise of political freedom but the hope of protection from hostile Indians. If easily proffered, this commitment would take some forty years to fulfill.

In opening a more direct route to California, Cooke and his Mormon command constructed a new thoroughfare known as Cooke's Wagon Road that cut almost straight across the north-south flow of commerce and travel on existing Mexican trails. Bypassing Janos, Mexico, they headed west from the Rio Grande, near present Derry, New Mexico, to San Bernardino Spring, a historic oasis on the present border between Mexico and the United States in southeastern Arizona. The audacious move tempted disaster but yielded abundant rewards in later years. In

1849 their road became part of the Southern Trail to California, followed by thousands hurrying to the gold fields on the west slope of the Sierra Nevada.[13] Cooke's map and report and subsequent gold rush travel pointed up the importance of the Gila River's southern tributaries, the San Pedro and Santa Cruz rivers, as avenues of transportation and commerce. This influenced the decision in 1853 to acquire for $10 million this region in southern Arizona under the Gadsden Purchase. Seldom has the nation gotten so much for so little. The roughly 30,000-square-mile section, taking in Tucson, proved to be a natural railroad corridor and a treasure house of silver, gold, copper, and other valuable metals.

In California the command arrived too late to take part in the last battles of the American occupation, but just in time to carry out President Polk's orders to treat the people of the region as fellow citizens, not as subjugated enemies. Polk had authorized Kearny to establish civil governments in New Mexico and California, but had cautioned him to "act in such manner as best to conciliate the inhabitants." Unfortunately, glory-seeking countrymen had gotten to California first and grossly violated the spirit and intent of the president's instructions.

Before Kearny arrived, Com. Robert F. Stockton, commander of the Navy's Pacific Squadron, combined forces with John C. Frémont and a rough mix of freebooting mountaineers, Indians, and emigrant volunteers known as the California Battalion, to occupy strategic points and set up their own government. The proud people they presumed to control, who lived at the far end of a long trail from Mexico City, had been largely independent for decades. They saw at first little to gain from opposition to the change in sovereignty. But oppressive measures by Stockton and his ambitious underlings soon provoked *Californios* to take up arms against the Yankee intruders. Before the revolt was put down, it would claim the lives of several of the U.S. Army's most promising officers and leave a legacy of bitterness among the former citizens of Mexico.

The subsequent arrival of Lieutenant Colonel Cooke and his Mormon infantrymen put military weight behind General Kearny's assertion of his lawful authority to command U.S. forces and establish a civil government in California. Cooke found himself leading the only "legal

---

[13]Etter, *To California on the Southern Route 1849*, 51, 111.

force in California," the Mormon Battalion, yet he was the only one on the West Coast "not pretending to the highest authority of any sort."[14] The good behavior and industry of battalion members would accomplish far more than the muskets they shouldered in restoring trust in the new government and its intention to defend the rights and interests of all its citizens. They protected the Californian leaders, who had supported the American takeover and were seen as traitors by some of their Mexican countrymen. They defended ranches against raids by hostile natives, once pacified under the Spanish mission system but increasingly warlike since the secularization of the missions in 1833. And they sank wells, manufactured bricks, and built new buildings to improve community life at Los Angeles and San Diego.

Although few in number, the Mormon volunteers were an important reason the United States was able to pacify a region of proud and independent people as large as California. For their "patience, subordination, and general good conduct," Col. Richard B. Mason, who replaced Kearny as military governor, was outspoken in his praise. From local inhabitants "not a syllable of complaint has reached my ears of a single insult offered, or outrage done, by a Mormon volunteer," he reported.[15] Among citizen-soldiers in the War with Mexico, it was a singular feat. In contrast, the campaigns in Mexico, particularly those in northeastern Mexico, were often brutal, with many civilian casualties and the murder of prisoners by both American and Mexican troops. Partisan warfare behind American lines and the settling of old scores by the Texas Rangers, who as scouts and commandos for the American armies matched the brutality of the Mexican guerillas, exacerbated the situation. The Texan Revolution, fought just a decade earlier, had left bitter memories that remained fresh in the minds of *Tejanos* and *Mexicanos* alike. Gen. Zachary Taylor reported that American volunteers had "committed extensive depredations and outrages upon the peaceful inhabitants" in Mexico. "Were it possible to rouse the Mexican people to resistance, no more effectual plan could be devised than the very one pursued by some of our volunteer regiments about to be discharged," he said.[16]

---

[14]Cooke, *The Conquest of New Mexico and California*, 289.

[15]Mason to Jones, 18 September 1847, House Exec. Doc. 17 (31-1), 1850, 336, Serial 573.

[16]Taylor to Adj. Gen., 16 June 1847, "Mexican War Correspondence," House Exec. Doc. 60 (30-1), 1847–48, Serial 520, 1178.

If their good conduct contributed to the peaceful acquisition of California, it was by no means the only notable performance by battalion members during their term of service. Fifteen men chosen from four companies would escort General Kearny and party, including John C. Frémont, to Fort Leavenworth and the trial of the "Great Pathfinder" for insubordination. In the spring of 1847 near Donner Lake in the Sierra Nevada, they would bury the bodies of Donner party members who had perished in the snow over the previous winter. On the way they met companies of Mormon pioneers following Brigham Young's first party to Great Salt Lake Valley in 1847.

On the trail to South Pass, Kearny's Mormon "Lifeguards" almost met the men and families they had left behind in New Mexico. Three battalion detachments wintered near the trappers' post at El Pueblo in today's Colorado in a now-forgotten Mormon settlement on the Arkansas River whose history mixes elements of comedy and tragedy. This company of some 260 men, women, and children missed a rendezvous with Kearny's party by fewer than a dozen days as they marched to Salt Lake. Some of these men arrived in the new Zion even before Brigham Young and immediately began building irrigation systems like those they had seen in New Mexico. The young veterans' transformative encounter with the Mexican Southwest would profoundly influence subsequent settlement in the Great Basin and create a new American character: the Mormon frontiersman.

Months later battalion veterans in California would witness an event of such significance that it would transform the nation almost overnight and touch off a massive population shift west that still continues. As employees of James Marshall and John Sutter, two of these men—and two only—would record the discovery of gold at Sutter's Mill on the South Fork of American River and the day it happened, 24 January 1848. They were a nineteen-year-old New Yorker, Azariah Smith, and Henry W. Bigler, a slender Virginian in his early thirties. Their journals place beyond reasonable doubt the name of the discoverer, Marshall, and the date of his find. These records stamp false on the claims of many self-professed discoverers who have since tried to win for themselves a share of the limelight.

Battalion veterans W. S. S. (Sidney) Willes and Wilford Hudson soon scored the first major gold strike when they discovered the rich placer diggings at Mormon Island, near present Folsom, which became the destination of the 1849 gold rush. Fellow Mormon Samuel Brannan, one of early California's most colorful and controversial characters, claimed ten percent of all gold harvested at this site in return for some undefined services to the finders to lay the foundation of his early wealth. While fortune seekers around the world prepared to risk life itself to get to the gold fields, in 1848 a company of battalion veterans and ship *Brooklyn* Mormons turned their backs on such riches of the earth and headed east over the Sierra Nevada to join their families and faith in Salt Lake Valley. In going they blazed a new wagon road over the Sierra Nevada, known today as the Mormon-Carson Emigrant Trail, which became in 1849 the main thoroughfare of the gold rush to the new El Dorado.

On the Humboldt River in present northern Nevada, this company met Samuel J. Hensley going west with a ten-man pack party after he had testified at John C. Frémont's trial. The California pioneer of 1843 told them about a new shortcut he had found from Salt Lake Valley to the California Trail near present Almo, Idaho. The eastbound Mormons, including Ephraim Green, Henry Bigler, Israel Evans, James S. Brown, James Allred, Azariah Smith, Samuel Rogers, the Corays, William and Melissa, and missionary journalist Addison Pratt, then rolled the first wagons over this new route, now known as Hensley's Salt Lake Cutoff, one of the California Trail's major branches.[17] Later that summer, a second party of some sixty men, women, and children under veteran sergeant Ebenezer Brown would follow their comrades' tracks to Utah. Reflecting the surprising diversity of Mormon emigration companies, the party included one Pedro and a woman who had been California land baron José Castro's cook. Young Jane Tompkins, who would later marry former battalion Capt. Jesse D. Hunter, recalled, "we took them to Salt Lake with us, where later the girl died, but Pedro remained with us, a faithful servant."[18] This forgotten couple would probably become of the first Mexican-American citizens of Mormon Utah.

In the beginning the Mormon volunteers formed an unhappy command, one that seethed with discontent and outright rebellion. Not only

---

[17]For the story of this trail, see Bagley, ed., *A Road From El Dorado: The 1848 Trail Journal of Ephraim Green.*
[18]"From the Record of Jane E. Hunter," in Jenson, Manuscript History of the California Mission.

did they assign their allegiance to a higher authority, they instinctively rebelled against the U.S. Army discipline that was notably harsh in those years. They also gave little thought to the significance of the events in which they took part. They only wanted to return to their families and get on with the business of making homes and establishing God's kingdom in the American West. In later years they came to take great pride in their service and what they had accomplished—and for good reason. Yet only in recent times have historians begun to recognize those achievements and the important role the Mormon soldiers performed in California and Western history. The narratives found in these pages reveal not only the significant part these men and women played in that history, but how much the lands and peoples of the West transformed and defined the Mormon experience down to our own time.

SOURCES

Almost as rich as the Sierra Nevada's gold is the remarkable trove of original documents the volunteers passed on and from which their story can be told. As directed by their church, many battalion members kept a running account of their activities in pocket diaries they later transcribed into larger journals. These records now exist in uncounted number at many locations. Some have been published, most have not. They open a priceless window on the Far West of 1846 to 1848 and its inhabitants. As historian Paul Hutton commented after surveying a few battalion histories, no student of the Indians of the Southwest can afford to ignore these eyewitness reports. The documents provide detailed information about how a nineteenth-century American volunteer unit was armed and equipped, how it marched, enforced discipline, drilled, stood guard, managed its animals, did its laundry and fed itself, and how its officers and men regarded each other. The journals even describe the music the men marched to and the songs they sang. More importantly these records offer eyewitness reports of the great events— the occupation of New Mexico and California, the opening of major transportation routes, the discovery of gold, and the Mormon entry into the West—that make this period one of the most interesting and significant in U.S. history, one that affects in ways unimagined the lives of Americans still today.

Although not as common as accounts by the men, the women they

left behind and those who marched with the battalion as wives, family
members, and laundresses left their own legacy of letters and reminiscences. These powerful documents provide a new perspective on the battalion experience and let us hear the story from the female voices that are
often so sadly lacking in the scholarly history of the American West.

We have chosen some of the best of these personal accounts, with a
preference for those previously unpublished, for this documentary history. Wherever possible we have relied on contemporary rather than
reminiscent sources to tell the story with immediacy and accuracy. Like
Robert M. Utley, we are "creatures of chronology," and have used that
simplest-of-all historical designs to organize the material in as sequen-
tial a manner as possible, believing that "for a meticulous historian,
chronology matters."[19] Many of the best accounts—Philip St. George
Cooke's powerful command journal, Henry Bigler's chronicle of the
West, Henry Standage's record of the march, Robert Bliss' diary (parts
of which appear to be written in blood), English teenager Robert W.
Whitworth's sprightly daybook, Azariah Smith's plainspoken gold-discovery journal, and Abner Blackburn's rollicking memoir, to name but a
few—have already been published. Some of them have long since been
recognized as Western classics. Informed readers may ask, what unpublished material could possibly be left? The life records presented here
speak for themselves. In these revealing documents and eloquent narratives, men and women describe in their own words the signal events they
experienced while marching with the most unusual command ever mustered into the armed forces of the American republic, the Mormon Battalion of the U.S. Army of the West.

---

[19]Utley, "Letters to the Editor," 89.

Chapter I

"To Conciliate Them"
The Enlistment

Founded in 1830, the Church of Jesus Christ of Latter-day Saints (Mormon) had known little peace after the heavens opened and God spoke again to humankind through an earthly spokesman as He had done in the days of the Old Testament prophets. For some sixteen years the members of this fervid religious movement had been hounded by neighbors and driven from New York, northern Ohio, and western Missouri. After the murder of its prophet, Joseph Smith, Jr., on 27 June 1844, the faith braced itself to abandon its latest home in western Illinois, the city-state of Nauvoo, and head west to establish God's kingdom in the mountainous regions of northern Mexico inhabited only by native American bands, not by the enemies of God's rule on earth.

Jesse C. Little: I Will Cross the Trackless Ocean

At this time of crisis Brigham Young and the Quorum of Twelve Apostles instructed Jesse C. Little on 26 January 1846 to solicit help from Washington in making their projected move west in 1846. He proved an inspired choice. Years later Little would say of himself, "It has been the fault of my life to act promptly. It is my nature to think rapidly and act while the thought lingers with me."[1] But his resourcefulness and spontaneity in this vital assignment proved to be blessings, not faults. They were indeed the very qualities that would make him, as his instructions hoped, "a savior and deliverer" of his people.

Little began by obtaining letters of introduction to leaders in Washington, including Vice President George M. Dallas, and other key fig-

---

[1] J. C. Little to S. Brannan, 16 March 1886, Vault Mss 37, Folder 10, BYU Library.

ures, such as influence-peddler Amos Kendall, a former Jackson administration cabinet member and close friend of President Polk. While taking part in church functions in Philadelphia, Little made an important
new friend in Thomas L. Kane, the son of Judge John Kinzing Kane, a
leading Pennsylvania Democrat. But he also became mixed up with
Kendall and his business associates who had conspired with Samuel
Brannan in a questionable California land deal that was later repudiated
by Brigham Young.[2] After spending ten fruitless days in Washington, the
impulsive agent on Kane's advice wrote an artfully worded threat to the
president of the United States.

The manuscript source for this widely quoted letter is a copy made by
Little's brother-in-law, Apostle George Q. Cannon, who probably transcribed the letter in the 1870s from Little's journal. (The original manuscript of Little's 1846 journal was in his family's possession well into
the twentieth century, but it was apparently destroyed in a fire in California in the 1930s.)[3] The Polk Presidential Papers contain a 9 June
1846 note from Little saying "it is not important that I should see the
Sec of War at this moment as you said I should have the papers & be able
to Leave this afternoon," but interestingly, Polk's papers do not include
Little's historic letter.[4]

J. C. LITTLE TO THE PRESIDENT,
BRIGHAM YOUNG COLLECTION, LDS ARCHIVES.

An Appeal to the President of the United States   June 1st 1846.
To His Excellency, James K. Polk, President of the United States.
Dear Sir:

I trust you will excuse me for trespassing upon your time, by troubling
you with the perusal of this note.

I come to Washington not, Sir, as an office-seeker actuated by a selfish
motive, but as the representative of a noble but persecuted people, and Sir,
allow me to say, that had I not more confidence in you as the Father of this

---

[2]For Little's detailed report on these contacts, see Journal History, 6 July 1846, or Berrett and Burton,
eds., *Readings in LDS Church History*, 2:204–13. For more on the Kendall-Benson-Brannan plot, see Bagley,
"'Every Thing Is Favourable! And God Is On Our Side': Samuel Brannan and the Conquest of California," 185–209.

[3]Conversation notes with historian Michael N. Landon, 7 July 1999, copy in editors' possession. The
preliminary register of the Brigham Young Collection at LDS Archives notes that Little's report was taken
from a copy made by Cannon.

[4]Polk Presidential Papers Microfilm, Series 2: Reel 45, Library of Congress, 6938.

great Nation, than in those that have preceded you—I should not have left my home and family to ask favors of you for this people.

I am a Native American born citizen, born in the State of Maine, and bred in the Granite State, New Hampshire. My Fathers fought in the battles of the Revolution for freedom and liberty, and the blood of my Fathers courses through my veins and arouses the spirit of Patriotism and hatred to oppression which characterized my noble ancestors—and, Sir for this cause while I know that this people have been driven from town to town, from City to City, from State to State, and last of all compelled to leave their homes and firesides and seek a shelter in a howling wilderness over the Rocky Mountains amid prowling beasts of the Forest, and the Red Men of the Bush without house to shelter or arm to save but God's; whose property has several times been confiscated by a mob; they have been whipped and stoned, butchered and murdered, and all this for no other cause than that we worship God different from our neighbors and according to the Scriptures. We have not only been robbed of our houses, lands and property, but of a jewel of far more value than all else—our good names and characters. We have been slandered from morning until night by our enemies, and they have been so far successful that even many good men suppose us to be a set of outlaws and thieves, and that crime and immorality is countenanced by us. But Mr. President this is not true—for in all this vast outstretched Country over which you bear rule—you have no subjects who are more willing to obey the laws of the land than we are—but Sir, if we are robbers and thieves as they charge us, why not fill our prisons with those who are guilty, or hang them between the heavens and earth as a monument of our wickedness and not compel twenty-thousand innocent unoffending men, women and children to leave their homes and their firesides, destitute and without the necessary comforts to take their passage over the Prairies and Rocky Mountains to find a new home in the howling wilderness. Look at their behavior when our best and most noble men were *butchered* at the *Carthage Slaughter House* (the *Prison*) and then look at the mobs in the Eastern Country, at Philadelphia, &c. No Sir, these charges heaped upon us are false, and the time will come Mr. President when you shall know that we are good men and that our characters are more enduring than the lasting hills; and Sir, in justification of our cause, permit me to say that notwithstanding the slander heaped upon us, yet my character stands as high as a moral and upright man as any in the Country—and I have the honor to bear letters of recommendation to this City from men of high standing some from his excellency J. H. Steele Governor of New Hampshire, near whom I have lived from my childhood.

And Sir, My character is no better than my brethren whom I represent especially the Twelve of whom all manner of evil is spoken. I have the honor to be personally acquainted with them and know them to be good men; they have eaten, drank, and slept in my house, and I certify that I never received any instruction from them but what was strictly virtuous and moral.

And under these considerations directed as it were by the finger of God, I come to you fully believing that you will not suffer me to depart without rendering me some pecuniary assistance, and be it large or small you shall not lose your reward.

Our brethren in the West are compelled to go and we in the Eastern Country are determined to go and live and if necessary, to suffer and die with them—our determinations are fixed and cannot be changed. From twelve to fifteen thousand have already left Nauvoo for California and many others are making ready to go. Some have gone around Cape Horn and I trust before this time have landed at the San Francisco Bay.

We have about forty thousand in the British Isles and hundreds upon the Sandwich Islands, all determined to gather to this place and thousands will sail this fall. There are yet many thousands scattered through the States besides the great number in and around Nauvoo who are determined to go as soon as possible; but many of them are poor but noble men and women, who are destitute of means to pay their passages either by sea or land.

They as well as myself are true hearted Americans, true to our country, true to its laws, true to its glorious institutions—and we have a desire to go under the outstretched wings of the American Eagle. We would disdain to receive assistance from a foreign power—although it should be preferred— unless our government shall turn us off in this great crisis and will not help us, but compel us to be foreigners. Means for the gathering of poor we must obtain; thousands are looking to me for help and I cannot, yea I will not, give myself rest until I find means for the deliverance of the poor. In this thing I am determined, and if I cannot get it in the land of my Fathers I will cross the trackless ocean where I trust I shall find some friends to help. But Mr. President were you to act alone in this matter, I full well know your course. I am not ignorant of your good feelings towards us—receiving my information from my friend Mr. S. Brannan who has gone to California, and also the Hon. Amos Kendall and others—believe me when I say that I have the fullest confidence in you—and we are truly your friends and if you assist us at this crisis, I hereby pledge my honor, my life, my property and all I possess, as the representative of this people, to stand ready at your call, and that the whole body will act as one man in the land to which we are going and should our territory be invaded we hold ourselves ready to enter the field of battle, and then like our Patriot Fathers with our guns and swords make the battle field our grave or gain our liberty. We have not been fighting men, but when we are called into the battle field in defence [sic] of our country, and when the sword and sabre shall have been unsheathed we declare before heaven and earth that they shall not return to their scabbard until the enemy of our country or we sleep with the pale sheeted nations of the dead, or until we obtain deliverance.

> With greatest respect I have the honor
> to subscribe myself your Obt. Subject,
> J. C. Little, Agent
> of the Church of Jesus Christ
> of Latter-day Saints in the
> Eastern States.

To his excellency Jas. K. Polk President of the United States of America.

James K. Polk: To Prevent Their Becoming Enemies

Little's letter landed on James K. Polk's desk as the president was meeting with members of his cabinet to decide what military forces it would take to occupy New Mexico and move on to invade Upper California before winter. The appeal came as an unexpected threat to his carefully laid design to seize Alta California for the United States. Polk could not know the Mormon spokesman had no authority to "cross the trackless ocean" and negotiate with the British. Nor could he be aware that the numbers Little gave were outrageously exaggerated. To one who knew little about the Mormons or where they were headed, they looked easily large enough to tip the balance of power in that northern province of Mexico from the United States to Great Britain. As he explained in his diary, the president could not afford to ignore this possibility.

From Quaife, ed., *The Diary of James K. Polk*, 1:443–50.

TUESDAY, 2nd June, 1846.—The Cabinet met today; all the members present except the Atty. Gen'l, was detained at his residence by severe indisposition.

The manner of conducting the war with Mexico was the chief topic considered. The expedition against California was definitely settled, the Cabinet being unanimous in favor of such an expedition. In pursuance of a conference on the subject between the Secretary of War and myself on yesterday, the Secretary read the rough draft of an order to Col. Kearney [*sic*] of the U.S. army, who was designated to command the expedition. Upon several points the order was modified upon my suggestion. It was in substance that as soon as Col. Kearney took possession of Santa Fe, he was to leave a sufficient force to hold it, and proceed without delay with the balance of his command & the mounted men ordered out from Missouri some three weeks

ago towards California, if in his judgment he could reach California before
the winter set in. 1000 additional mounted volunteers were ordered out
from Missouri to proceed to Santa Fe, or follow Col. Kearney to California
as he might order . . . It was agreed that Col. Kearney should be authorized
to take into service any emigrants (American citizens) whom he might find
in California or who may go out with these munitions of War and Military
stores. Col. Kearney was also authorized to receive into service as volunteers
a few hundred of the Mormons who are now on their way to California,
with a view to conciliate them, attach them to our country, & prevent them
from taking part against us . . .

WEDNESDAY, 3rd June, 1846.—. . . Held a conversation with Mr.
Amos Kendall & Mr. J. C. Little of Petersborough, N.H. (a mormon) today. They desired to see me in relation to a large body of Mormon emigrants who are now on their way from Na[u]voo & other parts of the U.S.
to California, and to learn the policy of the Government towards them. I
told Mr. Little that by our constitution the mormons would be treated as all
other American citizens were, without regard to sect to which they belonged
or the religious creed which they professed, and that I had no prejudices
towards them which could induce a different course of treatment. Mr. Little said that they were Americans in all their feelings, & friends of the U.S.
I told Mr. Little that we were at War with Mexico, and asked him if 500 or
more of the mormons now on their way to California would be willing on
their arrival in that country to volunteer and enter the U.S. army in that war,
under the command of a U.S. Officer. He said he had no doubt they would
willingly do so. He said if the U.S. would receive them into the service he
would immediately proceed and overtake the emigrants now on the way and
make the arrangement with them to do so. I told him I would see him on tomorrow on the subject. I did not deem it prudent to tell him of the projected expedition into California under the command of Col. Kearney, who
has instructions to make such an expedition this season if practicable. The
mormons, if taken into the service, will constitute not more than ¼ of Col.
Kearney's command, and the main object of taking them into service would
be to conciliate them, and prevent them from assuming a hostile attitude
towards the U.S. after their arrival in California. It was with the view to prevent this singular sect from becoming hostile to the U.S. that I held the conference with Mr. Little, and with the same view I am to see him again
tomorrow . . .

FRIDAY, 5th June, 1846.— . . . I had a special interview with Mr. Amos
Kendall and Mr. Little of N.H. (a mormon) by previous appointment at
their request (see this diary of the 3rd Instant). I told them that I had consulted the Secretary of War, and that the conclusions to which we had come
was that the battalion of Mormons of which mention was made on the 3rd

Instant, could not be received into the service of the U.S. until they reached California, but that on their arrival there (if the war with Mexico still continued) they would to the number of 500 be mustered into the service of the U.S. as volunteers for 12 months, placing themselves under the command of a U.S. officer who would be there ready to receive them. Mr. Little desired to follow the emigrating party now on their way to California, and on overtaking them to have 500 of their number, mustered into the service of the U.S. so that their pay might commence from that time. This proposition I declined. After Mr. Little retired I explained to Mr. Kendall what I did not think it safe to communicate to Mr. Little, VIZ., that Col. Kearney was ordered to proceed from Santa Fe with a part of his Regiment of dragoons and the mounted volunteers called out from Mo., and it was hoped would reach California this season, but this was not certain; that when Col. K. reached the country he was authorized to receive 500 of the mormons into the service so as to conciliate them and prevent their becoming the enemies of the U.S., but if the mormons reached the country I did not desire to have them the only U.S. forces in the country. I told Mr. Kendall that the citizens now settled in California at Sutter's settlement and elsewhere had learned that a large body of mormons were emigrating to that country and were alarmed at it, and that this alarm would be increased if the first organized troops of the U.S. that entered the country were mormons. To avoid this and at the same time to conciliate the mormons, Col. K. to receive mormons into the service after he reached the country not to exceed in number one fourth of his whole force. Mr. Kendall assented to the wisdom of concealing these views from Mr. Little . . .

W. L. MARCY: A LARGE BODY OF MORMON EMIGRANTS

When President Polk approved the enlistment of a battalion of five hundred Mormons, there was no shortage of men to serve in the Mexican War. His call for fifty thousand to volunteer for twelve months was being overwhelmed by the outpouring of young Americans who rushed to enlist that summer. The president simply caved in to Little's threat. At the same time, Polk steadfastly refused to allow the Mormon soldiers to be enrolled before they reached California. As he explained, he did not want to alert the Mexicans that an American army had been ordered to invade California before winter. Nor did he wish to alarm Americans on the West Coast with news that the first U.S. troops to arrive would belong to the controversial faith. Yet Polk's intentions were overruled by an ambiguous order that failed to convey clearly the decision so firmly agreed upon by both the president and the secretary of war.

MARCY TO KEARNY, HOUSE EXEC. DOC. 60 (30–I), 1847–48,
SERIAL 520, 153–55.

[CONFIDENTIAL]   WAR DEPARTMENT,
                                                   Washington, June 3, 1846

Sir: I herewith send you a copy of my letter to the governor of Missouri
for an additional force of one thousand mounted men.

The object of thus adding to the force under your command is not, as
you will perceive, fully set forth in that letter, for the reason that it is deemed
prudent that it should not, as this time, become a matter of public notori-
ety; but to you it is proper and necessary that it should be stated. It has been
decided by the President to be of the greatest importance in the pending
war with Mexico to take the earliest possession of Upper California. An
expedition with that view is hereby ordered, and you are designated to command it. To enable you to be in sufficient force to conduct it successfully
this additional force of a thousand mounted men has been provided, to follow you in the direction of Santa Fe, to be under your orders, or the officer
you may leave in command at Santa Fe.

It cannot be determined how far this additional force will be behind that
designed for the Santa Fe expedition, but it will not probably be more than
a few weeks. When you arrive at Santa Fe with the force already called, and
shall have taken possession of it, you may find yourself in a condition to
garrison it with a small part of your command, (as the additional force will
soon be at that place,) and with the remainder press forward to California.
In that case you will make such arrangements, as to being followed by the
reinforcements before mentioned, as in your judgment may be deemed safe
and prudent. I need not say to you that, in case you conquer Santa Fe, (and
with it will be included the department or State of New Mexico,) it will be
important to provide for retaining safe possession of it. Should you deem it
prudent to have still more troops for the accomplishment of the objects
herein designated, you will lose no time in communicating your opinion on
that point, and all others connected with the enterprise, to this department.
Indeed, you are hereby authorized to make a direct requisition for it upon
the governor of Missouri.

It is known that a large body of Mormon emigrants are *en route* to California, for the purpose of settling in that country. You are desired to use all
proper means to have a good understanding with them, to the end that the
United States may have their cooperation in taking possession of, and holding, that country. It has been suggested here that many of these Mormons
would willingly enter into the service of the United States, and aid us in our

expedition against California. You are hereby authorized to muster into service such as can be induced to volunteer; not, however, to a number exceeding one-third of your entire force. Should they enter the service they will be paid as other volunteers, and you can allow them to designate, so far as it can be properly done, the persons to act as officers thereof. It is understood that a considerable number of American citizens are now settled on the Sacramento river, near Sut[t]er's establishment, called "Nueva Helvetia," who are well disposed toward the United States. Should you on your arrival in the country, find this to be the true state of things there, you are authorized to organize and received into the service of the United States such portion of these citizens as you may think useful to aid you to hold the possession of the country. You will, in that case, allow them, so far as you shall judge proper, to select their own officers. A large discretionary power is invested in you in regard to these matters, as well as to all others in relation to the expeditions confided to your command.

The choice of routes by which you will enter California will be left to your better knowledge and ampler means of getting accurate information. We are assured that a southern route (called the Caravan route, by which the wild horses are brought from that country into New Mexico) is practicable; and it is suggested as not improbable that it can be passed over in the winter months, or at least late in autumn.[5] It is hoped that this information may prove to be correct.

In regard to the routes, the practicability of procuring needful supplies for men and animals, and transporting baggage, is a point to be well considered. Should the President be disappointed in his cherished hope, that you will be able to reach the interior of Upper California before winter, you are then desired to make the best arrangement you can for sustaining your forces during the winter, and for an early movement in the spring. Though it is very desirable that the expedition should reach California this season, (and the President does not doubt you will make every possible effort to accomplish this object,) yet, if in your judgment it cannot be undertaken with a reasonable prospect of success, you will defer it, as above suggested until spring. You are left unembarrassed by any specific directions in this matter.

Should you conquer and take possession of New Mexico and Upper California, or considerable places in either, you will establish temporary civil governments therein—abolishing all arbitrary restrictions that may exist, so far as it may be done with safety. In performing this duty it would be wise and prudent to continue in their employment all such of the existing officers as are known to be friendly to the United States, and will take the oath

---

[5]Marcy's apparent reference to the Spanish Trail through today's Colorado, Utah, Arizona, and Nevada did not acknowledge the difficulty of using "the Caravan route" as a wagon road.

of allegiance to them. The duties at the custom-houses ought, at once, to be reduced to such a rate as may be barely sufficient to maintain the necessary officers, without yielding any revenue to the government. You may assure the people of those provinces that it is the wish and design of the United States to provide for them a free government, with the least possible delay, similar to that which exists in our Territories. They will then be called on to exercise the rights of freemen in electing their own representatives to the territorial legislature. It is foreseen that what relates to the civil government will be a difficult and unpleasant part of your duty, and much must necessarily be left to your own discretion.

In your whole conduct you will act in such a manner as best to conciliate the inhabitants, and render them friendly to the United States.

It is desirable that the usual trade between the citizens of the United States and the Mexican provinces should be continued, as far as practicable, under the changed condition of things between the two countries. In consequence of extending your expedition into California, it may be proper that you should increase your supply for goods to be distributed as presents to the Indians. The United States superintendent of Indian affairs at St. Louis will aid you in procuring these goods. You will be furnished with a proclamation in the Spanish language, to be issued by you, and circulated among the Mexican people on your entering into or approaching their country. You will use your utmost endeavors to have the pledges and promises therein contained carried out to the utmost extent.

I am directed by the President to say that the rank of brevet brigadier general will be conferred on you as soon as you commence your movement towards California, and sent round to you by sea, or over the country, or to the care of the commandant of our squadron in the Pacific. In that way, cannon, arms, ammunition, and supplies for the land forces will be sent to you.

Very respectfully, your obedient servant,

W. L. Marcy,
Secretary of War.

Col. S. W. Kearny,
Fort Leavenworth, Missouri

STEPHEN W. KEARNY:
THEY WILL BE MARCHED TO CALIFORNIA

Ordered to invade New Mexico, Hispanic Arizona, and Alta California with fewer than three thousand men, including five regular dragoon companies, two regiments of mounted volunteers, and two companies of horse artillery, Col. Stephen Watts Kearny welcomed an opportunity to add more infantry to his Army of the West. Repeated appeals for footmen had barely produced two companies from western Missouri. While plenty of young men were eager to go to war mounted on a horse, there was "an aversion" in that part of the state "to the foot service," as Gov. John Edwards explained.[6] Kearny lost no time in sending James Allen, a senior captain of his regiment, to Iowa Territory to recruit a battalion of Mormon infantry.

KEARNY TO ALLEN, KEARNY SELECTED PAPERS, MIC A139,
NATIONAL ARCHIVES.

Head Qrs. Army of the West
Fort Leavenworth June 19th 1846

Sir:

It is understood that there is a large body of Mormons, who are desirous of emigrating to California, for the purpose of settling in that country, & I have therefore to direct that you will proceed to their camps and endeavor to raise from amongst them 4 or 5 Companies of Volunteers to join me in my expedition to that country—each company to consist of any number between 73 and 109—the Officers of the Companies will be a Capt, 1st Lieut & 2d Lieut who will be elected by the Privates and subject to your approval and the Captain then to appoint the Non-Com'd Officers, also subject to your approval—The Companies upon being thus organized, will be mustered by you into the service of the U.S. and from that day will commence to receive the pay, rations and other allowances given to other Infantry Volunteers, each according to his rank. You will, upon mustering into service the 4th Company, be considered as having the Rank, Pay, Emoluments of a Lieut Col. of Infy and are authorized to appoint an Adjt, Sergt. Major and QMr Sergt. for the Battalion.

The Companies, after being organized, will be marched to this Post, where they will be armed & prepared for the field, after which they will under your command follow on my trail in the direction of Santa Fe, & where you will receive further orders from me.

You will, upon organizing the Companies, require Provisions, Wagons, Horses, Mules, &c—You must purchase every thing which is necessary, & give the necessary drafts upon the QrMr & Comm Dept. at this Post, which drafts will be paid upon presentation.

You will have the Mormons distinctly to understand, that I wish to take them as Volunteers for 12 months—that they will be marched to California,

---

[6]Edwards to Marcy, 11 August 1846, in Golder *et al*, eds., *The March of the Mormon Battalion*, 97.

receiving Pay & allowances, during the above time and at its expiration they
will be discharged and allowed to retain as their Private Property, the guns
& accoutrements to be furnished to them at this Post. Each Company will
be allowed 4 women as Laundresses, who will travel with the Company,
receiving rations & the other allowances given to the laundresses of our
Army.

With the foregoing conditions, which are hereby pledged to the Mormons & which will be faithfully kept by me & other officers in behalf of the
Government of the U.S., I cannot doubt but that you will, in a few days, be
able to raise 500 young & efficient men for this expedition.

<table>
<tr><td></td><td>Very Respectfully</td></tr>
<tr><td>Capt. James Allen</td><td>Your Obt. Servant</td></tr>
<tr><td>1st Regt. Dragoons</td><td>S. W. Kearny</td></tr>
<tr><td>Fort Leavenworth</td><td>Col. 1st Drags.</td></tr>
</table>

James Allen: At the Expense of the United States

On the last day of June 1846, Henry Bigler and his cousin, Jesse
Bigler Martin, were hunting lost stock near the Mormon camps on the
Iowa side of the Missouri when they met an army captain "accompanied
by a guard of five dragoons" and a baggage wagon. The officer asked "if
we knew whether Brigham Young was in camp. We replied that there was
a man in camp by that name, but where he was we could not tell. We gave
that kind of an answer," Bigler wrote in his journal, because they did not
know the officer "or what his business was, though we [knew] President
Young perfectly well and where his quarters were but did not wish him
taken by mob authority under the cloak of law."[7] What Bigler could not
know was that the officer had not come to arrest Brigham Young, but to
deliver a message that was an answer to the Mormon leader's prayers.

To Captain James Allen, Company I, First Dragoons, the order to

---

[7]Wood, ed. "John W. Hess: With the Mormon Battalion," 50; and Journal of Henry William Bigler,
Typescript, Book A:21–22, 30 June 1846, cited in Black and Hartley, eds., *The Iowa Mormon Trail*, 140–41.
The Mormons suspected Allen's motives; their militia general Charles C. Rich directed Hosea Stout on 28
June "to keep a sharp lookout" for Allen. Wilford Woodruff "Had some reasons to believe them to be
spies" and Rich "supposed that he might be looking for" the public arms the Mormons had taken from
Illinois. Woodruff sent Thomas Grover to Council Bluffs to warn the main camp "to conceal all cannons
and artillery from Allen's view"; Grover arrived at the Missouri only a few hours ahead of Allen. Hosea
Stout thought the government was testing Mormon loyalty and suspected they wanted "500 of our men
in their power to be destroyed as they had done our leaders at Carthage." See Brooks, ed., *On the Mormon
Frontier*, 172; and Bennett, *Mormons at the Missouri*, 51–52.

enlist a battalion of Mormons offered a rare chance to advance two full grades, from a company captain to lieutenant colonel of a semi-independent command. Since graduating from the U.S. Military Academy in 1829 with such renowned classmates as Robert E. Lee and Joseph E. Johnston, the forty-year-old Ohioan had served seventeen years on the frontier and had learned that the peacetime army held few prospects for promotion. Now he enjoyed a shining opportunity, and he moved to make the most of it. Four days before his encounter with Henry Bigler, Allen pointed up the benefits of enlistment, adopted a conciliatory attitude toward the religious movement, and did his best to solicit the favor and confidence of Mormon leaders. Allen began his recruitment campaign at the Mormon emigration camp at Mount Pisgah, Iowa, where on 26 June 1846 he issued his announcement.

"CIRCULAR TO THE MORMONS,"
FROM TYLER, *A CONCISE HISTORY OF THE MORMON BATTALION,* 115–16.

I have come among you, instructed by Colonel S. W. Kearny, of the U.S. Army, now commanding the Army of the West, to visit the Mormon camps, and to accept the service for twelve months, of four or five companies of Mormon men who may be willing to serve their country for that period in our present war with Mexico; this force to unite with the Army of the West at Santa Fe, and be marched thence to California, where they will be discharged.

They will receive pay and rations, and other allowances, such as volunteers or regular soldiers receive, from the day they shall be mustered into the service, and will be entitled to all comforts and benefits of regular soldiers of the army, and when discharged, as contemplated, at California, they will be given, gratis, their arms and accoutrements, with which they will be fully equipped at Fort Leavenworth. This is offered to the Mormon people now.

This gives an opportunity of sending a portion of their young and intelligent men to the ultimate destination of their whole people, and entirely at the expense of the United States, and this advanced party can thus pave the way and look out the land for their brethren to come after them. Those of the Mormons who are desirous of serving their country, on the conditions here enumerated, are requested to meet me without delay at their principal camp at Council Bluffs, whither I am now going to consult with their principal men, and to receive and organize the force contemplated to be raised.

I will receive all healthy, able-bodied men of from eighteen to forty-five years of age.

J. Allen, Captain 1st Dragoons
Camp of the Mormons, at Mount Pisgah
one hundred and thirty-eight miles east
of Council Bluffs, June 26, 1846

NOTE.—I hope to complete the organization of this battalion in six days after my reaching Council Bluffs, or within nine days from this time.

BRIGHAM YOUNG: ALL ARE READY TO GO

Even as James Allen made his way to Council Bluffs, on 28 June Mormon leaders issued their own call for recruits to go "over the mountains to set up the Kingdom of God or its Standard yet this year." Despite their church's poverty and disarray, they hoped to send between two and five hundred "able and effective men" to accompany the apostles to "the Bear River Valley, Great Basin or Salt Lake, with the least delay possible."[8] Captain Allen's arrival and the government call for men to join the army would profoundly alter the plans of the Camp of Israel.

Brigham Young would later claim that Allen's call for volunteers was part of a plot by Missouri Sen. Thomas H. Benton and the Polk administration to exterminate the young religious movement as it headed into the wilderness.[9] The alleged conspirators expected him to reject the "tyrannical requisition" at which Polk would call on the governors of Iowa, Missouri, and Illinois for enough troops to "massacre us all."[10] Young claimed to have seen through this wicked design and foiled it with a ringing show of patriotism. At Council Bluffs on 1 July 1846,

---

[8]Ibid., 50–51.

[9]Young made this claim as early as 29 July 1847; see Bagley, ed., *The Pioneer Camp of the Saints.* He often repeated it; see Tyler, *A Concise History of the Mormon Battalion in the Mexican War, 1846–1848,* 117, 344, 352. Cited hereafter as Tyler, *A Concise History.* The absurdity of this charge would become self-evident. As the Mormons prepared to leave Nauvoo, President James K. Polk on 31 January 1846 told Senator James Semple of Illinois that he "possessed no power to prevent or check their emigration; that the right of emigration or expatriation was one which any citizen possessed. I told him I could not interfere with them on the ground of their religious faith, however absurd it might be considered to be; that if I could interfere with the Mormons, I could with the Baptists, or any other religious sect; & that by the constitution any citizen had a right to adopt his own religious faith. In these views Mr. Semple concurred with me." See Quaife, ed., *The Diary of James K. Polk,* 1:205–06.

[10]Tyler, *A Concise History,* 351–55.

BRIGHAM YOUNG in the uniform
of a Nauvoo Legion general
about 1844. From an oil
painting by William W. Major.
*Courtesy, International Society,
Daughters of Utah Pioneers.*

however, he saw things differently. Polk's offer then looked like a gift
from heaven to a leader who had abandoned any hope to cross the
mountains that season, as shown by the following excerpts from the
LDS church's chronological history.

JOURNAL HISTORY, 1 JULY 1846.

Wednesday, July 1, 1846
    Forty-five minutes after eleven, the Council adjourned to the wagon
stand where Pres. Young introduced Captain James Allen, who addressed the
people.
    He said, he was sent by Col. S. W. Kearney [*sic*] through the benevolence

of James K. Polk, President of the U.S. to enlist five hundred of the Mormon men to take part in the war with Mexico and remarked that there were hundreds of thousands of volunteers ready in the States.

He read his orders from Col. S. W. Kearney and the circular which he issued at Mount Pisgah and gave further explanations.

At noon, Pres. Brigham Young addressed the assembly; he wished the brethren to make a distinction between this action of the general government, and their former oppressions in Missouri and Illinois, and remarked: The question might be asked, Is it prudent for us to enlist to defend our country? If we answer in the affirmative, all are ready to go.

Suppose we were admitted to the Union as a State and the government did not call on us, we could feel ourselves neglected. Let the "Mormons" be the first men to set their feet on the soil of California. Capt. James Allen has assumed the responsibility of saying that we may locate at Grand Island, until we can prosecute our journey. This is the first offer we have ever had from the Government to benefit us.

I *proposed* that the five hundred volunteers be mustered, and I would do my best to see all their families brought forward, so far as my influence can be extended and feed them when I had anything to eat myself.

Twenty minutes after twelve, P.M. Captain James Allen said, that he would write to President Polk to give us leave to stay on the route where it was necessary; the soldiers' daily rations would be eighteen ounces of bread and twenty ounces of beef, or twelve ounces of bacon, and they would be paid every two months.

Elder Heber C. Kimball moved that five hundred men be raised, in conformity with the requisition from the government; the motion was seconded by Willard Richards and carried unanimously.

Pres. Young walked out as recruiting sergeant, with his clerk Willard Richards, and took several names as volunteers.

The Twelve and Capt. James Allen repaired to John Taylor's tent. Pres. Young asked the captain if an officer enlisting men on Indian lands had not a right to say to their families, You can stay till your husbands return. Captain Allen replied, that he was a representative of President Polk and could act till he notified President Polk who might ratify his engagements, or indemnify for damage; the President might give permission to travel, through the Indian country, and stop whenever circumstances required.

Half an hour past one P.M. Captain James Allen left camp and the twelve continued to converse on the favorable prospects before the people.

It was voted that Pres. Brigham Young, Elder H. C. Kimball should go to Mount Pisgah to raise volunteers. Pres. Young said, he would start soon, and he desired the companies to be organized, so that it could be ascertained who could go and make camp at Grand Island, and who must remain after raising the troops: the Twelve to go on westward with their families.[11]

About four, Pres. Young and Elder Willard Richards returned to their encampments at the river, whither the teams had gone, and found that some of the President's company had crossed. Elder Heber C. Kimball moved forward with his encampment to the ferry. Pres. Young turned back and informed Brother Kimball that he could not cross; consequently he turned and encamped three quarters of a mile west of the trading point, whither Elder Willard Richards took his family and teams.

BRIGHAM YOUNG:
THE THING IS FROM ABOVE FOR OUR GOOD

With the Mormon emigration scattered across three hundred miles from Nauvoo to the Missouri River, there was only one way to meet Captain Allen's July 6 deadline for mustering the new command at Council Bluffs. This was to recruit teamsters from wagons then on the road or at Iowa emigration camps at Mount Pisgah and Garden Grove, regardless of age, and call forward replacements from Nauvoo and other points. To replace the teamster volunteers without delay was vital to the establishment of a temporary settlement in present Nebraska before winter set in. The urgency of these conditions is reflected in Young's letter from Mount Pisgah, where he met Jesse C. Little on his return, to followers at Garden Grove and Nauvoo.

YOUNG TO BENT, FROM WATSON, ED. *MANUSCRIPT HISTORY OF BRIGHAM YOUNG 1846–1847,* 221–23.

Mount Pisgah, July 7th, 1846

President Samuel Bent & Council, and
the Saints at Garden Grove:

Beloved Brethren:—We write and send by a special messenger at this time, that you may be apprized [*sic*] of the situation and welfare of the church, and what will be for the good of the saints at your place. Brother Young, Kimball and Richards arrived last evening, direct from Council

---

[11]At this time the Mormons planned to build their main winter camp on the Platte River. In late July Young directed Bishop George Miller to send an advance party west to Grand Island. Young changed his mind and on 8 August instructed Miller to move closer to what became the main emigration base on the west bank of the Missouri River. Now a historic site, Winter Quarters was located at Florence, Nebraska, within the city limits of what is now Omaha.

Bluffs (where they left about eight hundred wagons, passed about the same number on the road, besides the hundreds here and between here and Nauvoo,) for the purpose of raising five hundred "mormon" volunteers to enter into the service of the United States, under the command of Captain J. Allen of the U. States army, who will be Lieut. Col. of the Regiment; each company electing their own officers under Col. Allen to be marched forthwith to Fort Leavenworth, there receive their arms, ammunition, camp and hospital stores, follow Col. Kearney's trail to Santa Fe, join his standard, pass through the upper provinces of Mexico, into California, where they are to be disbanded at the expiration of one year from the day they leave Council Bluffs, receive the fit out and pay of regular soldiers of the U. States army, and have their arms and equipment given them in addition, that they stay, look out the best locations for themselves and friends, and defend the country. This is no hoax. Elder Little, President of the New England churches, is here also, direct from Washington, who has been to see the President on the subject of emigrating the Saints to the western coast, and confirms all that Capt. Allen has stated to us.

The U.S. want our friendship, the President wants to do us good, and secure our confidence. The outfit of these five hundred men costs us nothing, and their pay will be sufficient to take their families over the mountains. There is war between Mexico and the U.S., to whom California must fall prey, and if we are the first settlers, the old citizens cannot have a Hancock or Missouri pretext to mob the saints. The thing is from above, for our good, has long been understood between us and the U.S. Government, but the first blow was struck sooner than we anticipated, the Church would not help the Twelve over the mountains when they wanted to go, and now we will help the churches.

We must take these five hundred men from among the teamsters, and send them without delay. If there is any one among you over eighteen and under forty five that wants to and can go, let him be at Council Bluffs forthwith. Drummers and fifers are wanted. Where is bro. Hales and the rest of the band?

The places of these five hundred teamsters—soldiers—must be immediately supplied, and we want you to gather up all the old men and boys and all the others who are capable of going into the army, driving oxen, herding cattle and sheep, milking cows, chopping wood, drawing water, cutting grass, pitching and stacking hay, etc., from the farms, and those who may be in Missouri at work and all others within your call and dispatch them to Council Bluffs forthwith, or five hundred teams must be left without drivers. Captain Allen guarantees to us the privilege of staying anywhere we please on Indian lands, if we send these five hundred men to California, but recommends Grand Island, in the Platte river, as the best place. This is the spot we had before contemplated for to winter.[12] There is a salt Spring at the head of the Island, where buffalo resort and we can make our own salt. Thither we want to go without delay, with all the teams of the camp, unload from five hundred to one thousand of the wagons, to return immediately to Nauvoo, Garden Grove, etc., and before spring carry to the Platte every poor but honest soul that has no means to go, or every saint who wants to go and cannot. The fifteen or sixteen hundred teams west of this are mostly loaded with one year's provision, and Garden Grove and Mount Pisgah, we expect will yield a valuable harvest to be conveyed forward by the teams that will return after the poor.

It is an important item to cut hay for our stock; we have teams enough in the church, and they must be fed, and every team and man that does not return from Grand Island, must go into the grass field without delay. But "Can't I go now?" says one sister; "Do take me," says another. "If my son or my husband goes, I shall go, you are not going to leave me here till you come back," says fifty more. All right, sister, we are glad to see the spirit of western emigration prevail. We have long heard your cries and listened to your entreaties, and we now listen again in anticipation and if you must come, clothe yourselves in appropriate garments, straddle your mules and horses, come on and drive teams and pitch hay; if you cannot do this make yourselves as comfortable as possible till your husbands can go to Grand Island and get a good wagon or carriage to take you on your journey and no whining about it, and when you come up with us in this style of ladies, we will be glad to see and bless you, and we bless you now.

The demand we are making on you for every man and boy (only enough left to watch the farm crops and herds), we shall make immediately in all the regions of Nauvoo, and there must be no deafness on this subject. If the brethren back do not leave all and come immediately, what will become of our cattle next winter? And if we let them die, what will become of us? Where is our milk and beef? But, say you, what shall be done with Garden Grove? Sell it, i.e. the improvements, as soon as you have a chance, and give possession when the crops are removed, and sooner too, if you can get pay for the crops, and come on. Some of the Missourians ought to be glad to give a handsome sum for Garden Grove, to get rid of their neighbors.

We want the Bros. Hales in the army as musicians.[13]

For the Council,

W. Richards, Clerk   Brigham Young, President.

---

[12] Allen was familiar with Grand Island from his experience with the First Dragoons, but George Miller learned from the Poncas that "our big captain knew nothing about Indian customs, that the Pawnee wintered their horses at Grand Island "[and] they would kill all our cattle and drive us away." See Bennett, *Mormons at the Missouri*, 262n98.

[13] Brothers Charles and Stephen Hales were members of Captain Pitt's Brass Band, but neither joined the battalion.

GEORGE WASHINGTON TAGGART:
GOODBY FANNY AND ELIZA ANN

At Mount Pisgah twenty-nine-year-old George Washington Taggart was typical of hundreds who had to make an agonizing choice between faith and family. In the vanguard of the emigration, he had left his wife and daughter behind at Nauvoo five months before. Now the slender New Englander penned the heartbreaking news that he would not see them again for months, maybe years, possibly never. They would have to shift for themselves in the Mormon move west across an unknown wilderness without a husband and father.

GEORGE W. TAGGART TO FANNY PARKS TAGGART, LDS ARCHIVES.

Mrs Fanny Taggart
Camp of Israel—this to be delivered on Her
arival at Mount Pisgah

Mount Pisgah July 8th 1846

Beloved and respected Wife, it is with grief, and disapointment although mingled with bright prospects of the future that I sit down to pen a few lines to you concerning the sudden change that is about to come across My calcu-lations. I expect the disappointment wil be as great to you as to Myself, I have calculated from the time that I stoped at this place until this morning that I should see you and Eliza Ann before I left, but Brother B Young and Kimball came here yesterday from Council Bluffs for the purpose of raising out of the Camp of 500 young Men to send over the Mountains this summer as united States troops under U.S. Officers the object of which you wil learn when you arive here. I went to the Council this Morning and stated your situation as near as I could calculate that it might be at this time and asked Council con-cerning the disposal of Myself and the council to Me was that I had better go. Brother Brigham says that the families of those that go shal be taken care of. My faith is that you wil not murmur at My volunteering to absent myself from you for so long inasmuch as I go by council of the church, you may be asured Fanny it is a great disappointment and a wound to My natural feelings to tear Myself as it were away from My Family that I have not seen for five months, and when I have been immagining to Myself for the last week that you were almost in sight, but I believe that the God of Israel will order all things right for those that act through a pure desire for the welfare of his Kingdom this is the motive through which I hope always to act. My health is good and I hope the Lord has blessed you and Eliza Ann with this blessing since I last heard from you which was by your letter of the 2d of June, take good care of Eliza Ann and tell Her that Her Father is sorry to go away and not see Her and Mother, but tel Her to be a good girl and not forget her Father. The articles of clothing that I left do not dispose of except the coat and that you may keep unless needcesity requires. Sister Julia is well and wishes Me to give Her love to you and say that She wished to see you very much. William is wel also, they expect to start from here soon, when you arive here go to Father [William] Huntington or whoever may be the Councelers tel them your situation and they wil tel you what to do and help you if you need help which I expect you wil, I shal leave My tool Chest with the Council of this place I shal leave the things that you sent with Julia with some others in the to[o]l Chest, it is now night and I must close for I have to start tomorrow morning. If I go with the expedition We probably shal not see each other for at least one year. This wil seem a long time but the work and the will of the Lord be done. I now say goodbye Fanny and Eliza Ann and may the Lord bless you with life and health and with every nesecary blessing and keep you stead-fast in the principles of truth and virtue until We meet again, this is and shal be the prayer of your absent but afectionate Companion

George W Taggart to Fanny Taggart

Ps—if you can I wish you to keep the Chest of tools along with your other things, since I comenced William has concluded to go with Me, kiss Eliza A for Me G W T

When you arive here you wil find Sister Julia about 2 miles Southeast from Father Huntingtons. If She is not gone She wil be with Father Parishes folks.

BRIGHAM YOUNG:
SAINTS WOULD GO INTO THE GREAT BASIN

As directed by the faith's hierarchy, the first four companies publicly enrolled at Council Bluffs on 14 July 1846 before Brigham Young and other leaders, including Captain Allen and Thomas L. Kane, who had arrived, via Fort Leavenworth, as efforts continued to fill out the fifth. The election of officers went according to the practice of an authori-tarian form of church government. Young named the men he wanted to serve as leaders and the members unanimously sustained him. Elected senior captain was a forty-three-year-old Kentuckian, Jefferson Hunt of Company A, whose rugged looks and beard gave him a commanding patriarchal appearance.[14] Also chosen captains were Jesse D. Hunter, 41,

---

[14]Hunt took his whole family with him, including his first wife, Celia, a second wife, Matilda, two sons, Gilbert and Marshall, who enlisted in his company, four other sons, and three daughters. Captain Hunt was among those who practiced the Mormon doctrine of plural marriage, revealed by Joseph Smith in Nauvoo but not publicly embraced by the LDS church until 1852.

Company B; James Brown, 44, Company C; Nelson Higgins, 39, Company D; and Daniel C. Davis, 42, Company E. Other officers were chosen by the same method.

On 16 July Captain Allen mustered at Council Bluffs some 450 volunteers into the U.S. Army for twelve months and took command of the battalion. Apostle Wilford Woodruff watched and "considered I was viewing the first Battalion of the Army of Israel engaged in the United States service for one year And going to lay the foundation of A far greater work even preparing the way for the building of Zion."[15] The strung-out Mormon emigration had required Allen to spend a few days more than he had expected. Not all of the men met his age and physical specifications; there were more women than the limit for laundresses allowed, many with children, but he had more than enough new recruits to qualify as a lieutenant colonel. Two days later, Young revealed that the destination of his followers would not be California on the Pacific Coast, as President Polk had been led to think, but the Great Basin of North America.

JOURNAL HISTORY, 18 JULY 1846.

Forty minutes after five, the Presidency met the commissioned and non-commissioned officers in council in the Cottonwoods near the bank of the river.

Complete lists of families and property and amount of wages to be drawn at Fort Leavenworth were called for, but were not ready. Council suggested that persons be selected to receive the money.

President Young instructed the captains to be fathers to their companies and manage their affairs by the power and influence of their Priesthood; then they would have power to preserve their lives and the lives of their companies and escape difficulties. The President told them he would not be afraid to pledge his right hand that every man would return alive, if they would perform their duties faithfully, without murmuring and go in the name of the Lord, be humble and pray every morning and evening in their tents. A private soldier is as honorable as an officer, if he behaves as well. No one is distinguished as being better flesh and blood than another. Honor the calling of every man in his place. All the officers but three have been in the Temple. Let no man be without his under garment[16] and always wear a coat

---

[15]Kenney, ed., *Wilford Woodruff's Journal*, 3:60.

[16]Before leaving Nauvoo, at least 5,615 members of the faith received their endowment, which included all rites necessary to gain eternal salvation, in the newly completed Mormon temple. A one-piece undergarment received during the ceremony represented the garment given to Adam and Eve in the garden of Eden and provided protection to those faithful to their convenants.

and vest; keep neat and clean, teach chastity, gentility and civility; swearing must not be permitted, insult no man; have no contentious conversation with the Missourians, Mexican, or any class of people; do not preach, only where people desire to hear, and then be wise men. Impose not your principles on any people; take your Bibles and Books of Mormon; burn [playing] cards if you have any.

Let the officers regulate all the dances. If you come home and can say the captains have managed all the dancing, etc., it will be all right; to dance with the world cannot be admitted; all things are lawful, but not expedient; never trespass on the rights of others; when the Father has provided that a man will be his friend under all circumstances, he will give to that man abundantly, and withhold no good thing from him. Should the battalion engage with the enemy and be successful, treat prisoners with the greatest civility, and never take life if it can be avoided.

Elder Heber C. Kimball concurred in what had been said, and exhorted the brethren to humility and prayer, that God might lead them in paths, and before the people in a manner to get as great a name as any people since the days of Moses; advised them to hold their tongues and mind their own business; if they were sick, they had the privilege of calling the Elders, and rebuking all manner of diseases.

Elders John Taylor and Parley P. Pratt concurred in what had been said.

President Young spoke of President Polk's feelings towards the Saints as a people,—assured the brethren that they would have no fighting to do; told them the Saints would go into the Great Basin, which was the place to build Temples; and where their strongholds should be against mobs. The Constitution of the United States was good. The Battalion would probably be disbanded about eight hundred miles from the place where the body of the Church should locate.

Bishop Newel K. Whitney, Daniel Spencer and Jonathan H. Hale were proposed as agents to go to Fort Leavenworth and receive the pay of the soldiers for their families.

After much conversation and explanation the meeting adjourned and the brethren returned to camp about sunset. President Young and Brother Kimball retired to Ezra Chase's and Brothers [Willard] Richards and [Jesse] Little to Brother [David?] Boss' tent.

JAMES ALLEN: TO PASS THROUGH THE INDIAN COUNTRY

To Brigham Young probably the most important benefit of the enlistment was permission, however legal, for his people to settle for a time on Indian lands. Having given up any hope to cross the mountains that season, he urgently needed a place for his followers to settle and get ready for a later move. Further complicating the problem was that a final decision had not been made on whether this place would be on the Missouri River, where the U.S. had recently purchased Potawatomi lands in Iowa, or at Grand Island in the Platte River. Lt. Col. James Allen took on himself the debatable authority to grant the required permission.

JOURNAL HISTORY, 16 JULY 1846.

Head Quarters, Mormon Battalion Council Bluffs
July 16, 1846.
The Mormon people, now enroute to California, raised and furnished for the service of the United States a battalion of volunteers to serve with the army of the West in our present war with Mexico, and many of the men composing this Battalion having to leave their families in the Pottawatomie country, the within permission to a portion of the Mormon people to reside for a time on the Pottawatomie lands, obtained from the Indians on my request, is fully approved by me, and such of the Mormon people as may desire to avail themselves of this privilege are hereby authorized to do so, during the pleasure of the United States.

James Allen Lt. Col. U.S.A.
Commanding Mormon Battalion

THOMAS L. KANE: APPLAUSE THAT IS POSITIVELY DEAFENING

Like hundreds of other privileged young men in the American republic, Thomas L. Kane dreamed of winning glory in the American West. Although only twenty-four and lacking any practical experience, Kane hoped to support himself by writing a book about his adventures, but he did not consider his age a bar to public office or high military rank. He believed that his father, John K. Kane, could use his influence to have his son granted a field officer's commission or appointed governor of California. In May 1846 Kane contemplated joining "some of Fremont's expeditions or emigration parties Oregon." He decided instead to visit Nauvoo "and then join one of the parties going westward" to the Mormon camps "in the rude Missouri valley," whose inhabitants Kane presumed would "exhibit much of queer life: yankee & fanatic; I will see their neighbour Indians and will be able to live cheap on deer meat in the open air." He could then "descend to California" or return home, "having at least seen Indians and forests and queer enthusiasts to

ELISHA K. KANE, THOMAS L. KANE, AND JOHN K. KANE, CIRCA 1842. According to Kane relative Robert Gray Taylor, this image is from a miniature painting on ivory by an itinerant Chinese artist that was based on a Daguerreotype. *Courtesy, LDS Archives.*

satisfaction."[17] With "a little tact and patience and a little maneouvring," Kane had won the friendship of Jesse C. Little, "who rules all the Church east of the Mississippi with despotic sway." Having "got completely round the members of the sect" in Philadelphia, who gave him "letters of genuine strength" to "the great men, too—to Brigham Young and Orson Hyde and the other notables," this aspiring romantic conceived a "wild dream":

> The Mormon party carry to California the first news of War with Mexico—and to the American settlers in the Sacramento valley. These itch for the signal to declare independence of the Mexicans—the war news will probably amount to such—a rising, or rather flag raising (for *no* fighting is to be done) will *certainly* take place upon the arrival of Commodore [James] Biddle's squadron on the coast two months later. At one time or other a government representative may be wanting. Who so fit for one as I?—above all

[17]T. L. Kane to Elish [Elisha K. Kane], undated letter ca. May 1846; T. L. Kane to Elish, 17 May 1846; and T. L. Kane to Mother, 3 July 1846, American Philosophical Soc.

if on the journey I shall have ingratiated myself with the disaffected Mormon army before it descends upon the plains. I could carry my commission in my money belt, and according to the promptings of occasion, be *or be not* the first U.S. Governor of the new territory of California. There would be no difficulty in obtaining some sort of government agency of Polk, if Father would only work for it.[18]

Mormonism was only one of the many causes he espoused in his long life, but Thomas L. Kane did more to insure the survival of the religion in nineteenth-century America than any other single non-Mormon. The following letter, composed shortly after the enlistment of the battalion on 16 July 1846, not only provides surprising new information about Mormon plans in the West, but says much about the mind and motives of the young man who would become the faith's most influential advocate.

T. L. KANE TO MY OWN DEAR FATHER, & MOTHER, 18–22 JULY 1846 (INTERNALLY DATED), THE PAPERS OF THOMAS LEIPER KANE (1822–1883), MARRIOTT LIBRARY.

After you read this [father], let only Pat [brother Robert Patterson Kane] besides—except of course Mother—what you think worth her reading thoroughly.
My Own Dear Father, & Mother,
    This must be my only chance to get a letter to you on which I can rely— for at least two months to come. It needs not this though to make me make it long. I have had, before now no moment when I could open my heart to you since I last wrote, and the dear God knows that this is to me a luxury that needs no sin branding to give it relish. So much I have seen and done and thought and endured since I left home! . . . [19]
    In the first place, you know the importance I attached to the enlistment by the United States of volunteers from the Mormons, and of the great benefits I believed would accrue from the measure to our country as well as that poor people. My presence has been of great service in promoting the measure. Owing partly no doubt to Elder [Jesse C.] Little's delayed arrival (he came you know by the Nauvoo route & thus by overland)—the relief

---

[18]T. L. Kane to Elisha, 16 May 1846 and 17 May 1846, American Philosophical Soc. This letter indicates that the Kane family was remarkably well-informed about Polk's plans in California.
    [19]Here Kane discussed money, noting he would soon need $100 to supplement the $400 his father had already provided. "I know you and Mother never begrudged money thus bestowed." The financial concerns that had filled much of the Kane family's 1846 correspondence had disappeared with J. K. Kane's appointment in June as a federal judge, which let him appoint Thomas to a well-paid sinecure as a court clerk.

was imperfectly understood by some of the leaders and much suspected by the great mass of the people. Captain Allan [*sic*] when I arrived was fidgetting discouraged, mad [?] at being misunderstood—and declaring that if, within a time really too brief, the men were not raised, he would return without them—which only increased the distrust of the Mormons. I went at once into the matter. Within twenty minutes after my arrival in the main camp I held a council there for three and a half hours with the Twelve that were there, and arranged with them that a grand meeting of the people should be held the very next day at Eleven, though Sunday. Short as was the notice, a thousand people met. The right course was voted by acclamation of those present—and I improved the advantages of influence which I was happy to find my words had with the people, by speaking to them at various camps—making it the end of my Sabbath to harangue after nightfall the farthest advanced of all. I had a most enthusiastic audience to be sure, gathered in a five hundred ring around my horse; and altogether enjoyed my evening's romance—but for the ill finale of bugs in my blanket—which considering I slept in a full hut of Indians, whites, dogs & children, and went contentedly supperless to bed after a ride of four miles through the Omahaw country to seek it, was no more than I had a right to expect. After this two days efforts, the matter was decided. I went to live in Captain Allan's tent to show perfect sympathy of feeling between us and did considerable work afterwards—as I have told you having been honestly leisureless till this hour—but I knew that the matter *was* decided and my mind was at ease— "Lord, grant us peace at heart and if no other earthly good, the riches of a good conscience."

In the tent of the American Fur Company where I now am, is a poor wretch to whom I act as Doctor, and who is this afternoon without any other nurse. He is a Frenchman and, as I thought when well, an honest though reckless free and easy fellow—but I fear that he has committed some dreadful crime. He has on him the fever of this region [malaria] and at present he's on a pile of Mackinaw blankets at my right hand crazy with heat and pain. Every now & then he swears fearfully, blaspheming God & cursing every earthly thing. After this, he maybe kicks at his blankets in a rage or beats his head board (on the old trunk that serves him as such) or spits fiercely at a spot of sunshine on the floor at his side. Then he always seems relieved. He talks to me and makes me compliments, and tries to convince himself through me that man can do no good because Fate orders all things good & evil, after which he generally sinks into a doze. After Ten or Fifteen Minutes after however he begins to mutter & rage—at first of things I cannot understand after of things plainly intelligible—but horrible [enough] to curdle ones blood. I actually am in fear of his friends out of doors who neglect him, hearing his secrets.—I may perhaps never return to you, Dear

Father,—and if I do it will be as the poor invalid of old times—but if I sink under sickness it will be in peace, and if I return sick I will return contented. I will return poor as an insolvent can be, too but I trust in God I may be rich in that which this unfortunate will never have, a good conscience and an upright heart.

I will devote much of [my] time when I come home to the Mormons. The book I purposed for my profit I have not the materials to make, but I will write one for their vindication—but I cannot write any more with this man in the room with me. I write unconnectedly—and I lose all the pleasure I looked to from my letter to you. It is a disappointment that I bear ill—but he is very sick I fear, and perhaps I am neglecting him.

And now let me give you an important piece of news for our poor clients that I picked up by mere accident from Col. Campbell in St. Louis and that will be a godsend if they are *hauled over the coals*. Brooker L. is his authority . . .[20]

I wish I were back at my law again. I am dreadfully homesick, having harder work to do than it ten times. Keep for me the clerkship. I want it for an especial reason now. I am going to work for the Mormons, and want all my leisure to manoevure the newspapers and write a book in their vindication. At the Bar, I would be called upon for severe study and uncertain in quantity—there being no limit to studying up for cases. Having a post, however, with fixed duties and a fixed salary, I can feel assured when my days work is over that there is nothing more for me to do, till the morrow, and in the interval I can freely devote to my main task. This must be accomplished now, as soon as possible. If public opinion be not revolutionized before the Sacramento Country fills up with settlers, the miserable dramas of Missouri and Illinois will be acted over again, with the alteration that there will be no country left to which the persecuted can fly. They will be beyond the walls of the Sierra Nevada and on the edge of the last western water. They cannot pass over the Pacific Ocean as their homotypes [*sic*] the Israelites did the Red Sea; they must remain without aid from their American Jehovah. There is none to help them.

You must make up your mind to aid me. They, poor creatures, think my influence omnipotent, and expect that I can save them—with your help. I will perhaps not disappoint them. Your judgeship luckily places you above any vicious popular feeling and you can afford to give it. When I return, we will concert together what is to be done. At present, I want you to do one kindness to me. Try and write to the President an account of what I have written to you, at once, and at some future convenient period, go to Wash-

---

[20]Kane had visited fur-trade entrepreneur Robert Campbell, who would soon decline the post of assistant U.S. treasurer at St. Louis. Campbell later provided Kane with a horse and rifle. The "poor clients" appear to have engaged Kane to investigate land or railroad investments. Kane's "queer story" of political intrigue is here omitted.

ington and have a few words with him in person.[21] All that is private and *personal* had better be spoken to him—indeed, all that you understand as relating—to persons I don't want you to transcribe in writing (upon this I am express, having particular reason for its observance). I have written a letter to the President and to Mr. [Secretary of the Navy George] Bancroft, which I enclose to you, that you may send them on at once, if you think they are fit, for they are miserable things, being written like this letter of yours with a crowd jostling around me and overlooking me except when I have had some moments in the sick room of a raving fever patient—and on detached pieces of paper stuffed away in this blanket or that pair of boots—or in my saddle cover, to keep them out of sights. The President ought to have my letter at once—then if it is not convenient for you to leave Philadel. or Cape May for some time,—*you* ought to write: afterwards you can visit at any time before my arrival speak to him of what is privatest [*sic*].

There are three things to which your letter may if you think fit make allusion. I. At Grand Island on the Platte the Mormons will build a block house to protect their people from the Indians. This is a post where the United States must necessarily make one, in their claim contemplated to the Pacific country. The Mormons will apply through the next winter for the contract of building *all* the blockhouses &c. along this line; and they hope that if the block house they build at Grand Island this winter, is approved in construction and location by Government, that it will be taken off their hands. With their traveling train of Mechanics they can contract cheaper than any competitors for this sort of Jobs.[22] 2. They will apply for the contract for carrying the Mail through to Oregon & S. Francisco being able to do this cheaper than all others. —It would be well merely to make allusion to these matters prealably [*sic*] to future action. — I suppose of course nothing can yet be done with regard to them. 3. I forward to the President by the same opportunity that carries this, a permission on the part of the Pottawotomie Indians to the Mormons to pass the winter on their lands near the place approved by Captain Allan, Agent [R. B.] Mitchell,[23] and myself. He ought to be informed that this is all right. The Mormons are the most reasonable people in the world. The Indians like to have them. The fall is so much later—the spring so much earlier, and the rush pasture for cattle so much better on the Missouri bottom than elsewhere that they will be greatly benefited by staying there. There need be no apprehension that they will

---

[21]James Polk's journal does not mention a visit from Judge Kane on his son's behalf.

[22]This proposal demonstrated how resolutely Brigham Young worked to implement the policies originally laid out by Joseph Smith. Smith had petitioned Congress in 1844 to pay the Mormons to build a string of forts along the trail to Oregon.

[23]Indian Subagent R. B. Mitchell signed the agreement on 2 July 1846, and did "willingly certify that it is for the apparent good of both parties, and there is no prospects of evil arising therefrom." See Watson, ed., *Manuscript History of Brigham Young*, 276, which dated the document 20 July 1846.

remain after Spring opens. I guarantee their departure just as I have advised their sojourn.[24] It will be only a part of the people that will avail themselves of the privilege. A great body starts in a day or two (July 20) westward that will go at least as far as Grand Island. On no account then, ought their right of tarrying be interfered with.

It is with this body that goes on the Oregon trace that I start as soon as this letter and the troops raised leave here. I have been very eager to see these safe off—fearing to the last some slip between cup & lip. Long ill treatment has made the poor Mormons distrustful even of kindness and at first news of the good intentions of the U.S. they were incredulous—though General Young and those (as Little) parties to the application to Washington, were zealous in favor of the enlistment. I came in the nick of time. I spoke to those of influence, and in haranguing the masses, made the more zealous, Mr. [John] Taylor of *England*, Mr. Orson Pratt of New York & Mr. [Wilford] Woodruff & Mr. [George A.] Smith—particularly Messrs. Taylor and Woodruff, who went about with me, and far eclipsed me in their heartfelt praise of the United States Government & the President of the United States as the true friend of the persecuted. So the men were levied in a jiffy—married men left their wives & children & goods in the charge of the church—and four hundred were raised without regard to sacrifice of feeling in two days work. I feel it a personal battle [?] & fought for its completion accordingly.

The most delightful relations subsist between the Twelve and myself. They are without any exaggeration a body of highly worthy men and they give me their most unbroken & childlike confidence. I am admitted with all their consultations as though an Elder of the 1st class—and have held with them two councils of great importance since my arrival. I honestly believe that they would not disobey my advice in any important matter unless it touched their creed: and so long as they do so I feel it my duty to look the more closely to their interests. Elder Woodruff brings with him from England, which he left in March last, news that the Government is even more willing to befriend the Mormons than our own. Besides other marks of kindness, he was directly informed, that the Colonial Department would defray the expenses of a large number of emigrants from the British Islands to California of his religion, upon his making application. He did not do so, not being empowered to state confidently when the American Saints (and where) would be established in California; and in the opinion of some of the twelve the offer would not continue open, now that I had brought

---

[24]These promises were made in good faith, but the Mormons remained at Winter Quarters until as late as the summer of 1848, when they moved to "the place hitherto known as Miller's Hollow, [now named] Kanesville in honor of Colonel Thomas L. Kane, who had ever been as true friend to the Saints," at today's Council Bluffs, Iowa. See Bennett, *Mormons at the Missouri*, 166–67.

them your news that Matzatlan had been taken and that California was in the possession of the U. States.[25] I advised that the application be made, nevertheless,—on the ground, though England since her new Treaty with the U.S. would not have in her power to aid in settling emigrants in California she would *no doubt* be *just* as glad to have the help of the Mormon Church in establishing a colony on Vancouver Island! This, too, I easily showed would be a good thing for the Church to be namely in the two Great Harbors of the Pacific Coast—that of V.'s Isld. and of St. Francisco, and asserting a good influence by its cofellowship in fraternizing upon the Pacific Ocean the long parted trading wealth [?] of England & America. All the Twelve present seemed convinced of my exposition of the case—for indeed men more open to reason and truth plainly stated I have never seen.—I am treated too, in every other respect as I could wish. Servility is not found among such simple hearted people but every other mark of kind feeling is shown me. Poor as they are nothing is too good for me. I dare not eat with them, because the little store of sickness diet is brought out for my table—and quite a show of dainties appears upon my plate while the good woman of the tent will be munching on a crust of dry bread—out of "preference." The people meet me with a, hat's off, and, "How is your health?" or "God Bless you, Colonel," that does my heart good like a cordial. If I speak in public they make histarial [?] responses to every round sentence, of applause that is positively deafening. Make up your mind and tell Mother to do so too, that you need fear nothing for me on my prairie trip. I go with an immense party headed by Brigham Young & Kimball and accompanied among others, by a regularly educated Elder Doctor Richards.[26] If I am sick, I will be nursed as zealously as in health I would be defended—in fact, I may say I am idolized by my good friends . . . [27]

I love more & more this suffering people and am determined to befriend them. I should not wonder if I found I found [*sic*] in this the mission of my life. It is certainly one unworthy of no philanthropist to save some fifteen

---

[25]Although accurate in regard to California's ports, Judge Kane's news was premature. It presumed that Com. John Drake Sloat had acted on Polk's orders of 24 June 1845 to seize Mexican ports on the Pacific upon receiving word hostilities had begun. The cautious sixty-eight-year-old veteran waited until 8 June 1846 to weigh anchor at Mazatlan (which remained in Mexican hands) for Monterey. Secretary Bancroft rebuked Sloat on 13 August 1846, while "believing in the purity of your intentions. But your anxiety to do no wrong has led you into a most unfortunate and unwarranted inactivity." See Harlow, *California Conquered*, 118–21.

[26]Apostle Willard Richards' six weeks of study with Samuel Thompson, founder of a naturalistic school of medicine, made him about as qualified a physician as could likely be found on the frontier in 1846.

[27]Kane described his plan to return home after the malarial season ended and asked his father "to publish at once my nomination to Colonelcy," apparently an honorary state appointment, and to speak "of the perfect order & good behavior of the 15,000 people" in "their dwelling in the wilderness."

thousand souls from misery, if not extermination, and make the happiness of perhaps fifty thousand. I myself cannot rate by any depreciating calculation the number of Mormons in the United States East of the Mississippi less than five thousand nor those in England Scotland Wales and elsewhere less than twenty thousand. These will all strive to join the fifteen thousand now west of the Mississippi, when they reach the Pacific, making them a body of full forty thousand whose welfare is to be looked after. If the Mormon estimate of sixty thousand—(I split the difference between my own calculation and theirs) is wrong now—it will not be so in a few years more—so great is the progress which is daily made by their missionaries. If God spares my life, I will save them from the dangers which now menace them—as great as those which they have gone through.

And how great these have been, and how undeserved and still more how great and undeserved have been their actual sufferings, you will be startled when I tell you. For the sake of what we call impartiality, we always like to find each party in the wrong and I have tried hard to do so—but the damndest Pilate in the world could not help saying I find no fault in this people. On the contrary, to see them as I have seen them, honest and pure hearted, guiltless seemingly of evil thoughts, ennobles ones opinions of our poor human nature, as much as it degrades the same to think that any as innocent, should for conscience sake in our 19th. century, be beaten, robbed, ravished and murdered, and driven from post to pillar and pillar to post, till the solicitudes of the wilderness where famine howls like the prairie wolves round their miserable shelters, seem to them a blessed refuge. They thank God in prayer for it day and night, and sing a song of Miriam[28] to congratulate themselves on having abandoned for ever their pleasant homes where their industry had surrounded them with every luxury and comfort: but which their enemies had made to them a land of Egypt.—When I come home prepared to go to work, I will pray to god for health to labour in their cause, and to tell the world and the people of the Union who these [people] are who have been chased from hearths and altars—from the bosoms of their friends and the graveyards of their parents and children. "The forces of the . . ."[29]

I ought to say that both of the Brothers Pratt, elders, went about with me speaking. We had the most delightful enthusiasm, upon our addresses—and you ought to tell the President that his name was never cheered on earth more heartily. In speaking to the President on the Indian matter, I thought I had best send you a copy of my approval to the Mormon sojourn which General Young sends by this steamboat to the Prest. Captain Allan whose paper I have not time to copy for you has given his *permission* absolute to the

---

[28]"Miriam the prophetess" was the sister of Moses who guided his cradle in the Nile. She sang the Lord's praises when Pharaoh's army drowned in the Red Sea. See Ex. 2:4, 15:20–21.

[29]Here at least a page appears to be missing from the manuscript letter.

Mormons, which I suppose is a little stretch of his power as his instructions from Col. Kearney [*sic*] with regard to raising his regiment & nothing else were very limited.—Stop. I may as well give it:[30]

The real date ought to have been July 2d, which is the date of the Pottawatamies *talk* of permission. The fact is the whole affair was, as you may gather from the false reason assigned for the tarrying of the Mormons marked by me with Brackets a bonus to enduce the poor people to enlist. *Having* enlisted their five hundred, he promised them *then*, his permission &c. This was just before my arrival and was *no go*. It has answered just as good a purpose, however. And now the Volunteers are raised by us, perhaps Mr. Polk ought to know the reasons, as I imagine them, for the act—in vindication of measures by Captain Allan, who is one of the most honest good souls I ever have liked (and bye [?] that he submitted his broleon [?] to be modified by me, and I would not let him change it. The reason the Pottawatamies want the Mormons, is to have to the North of them—so good a barrier against their enemies the Sioux. Besides they are as innocent of conduct as children.

In whatever way convenient, I would like kindness shown to the good prolatary Little who will call on you at Philadelphia; but by no means be familiar with him. He is a very rising man in the Church, possessing Mr. Youngs full confidence and being withal ambitious, but it is necessary to impress him with the heaviest sense of your *omnipotence* (nothing short of it) and our family dignity & wealth. On no consideration, let him have more than five minutes talk with you and that a very short one. Let him not take a meal with the family nor see the children or Mother, except with her bonnet on and "going out after a minute" (if at all). When he calls, wine & cake on a *silver* waiter or anything of the style, brought to the Parlour or Long Room pear table would be an investment more gratifying to me than even him. Let no one else. These my directions are of some importance in their literal observances . . .[31]

And now, dear Father, the sun having gone down behind the dreary hills over the River it is rapidly growing dark . . . Hope for me everything there is to be hoped for . . . what is the greatest comfort to me, the knowledge that already, I have not lived in vain— . . . Farewell—

July 22, 1846   Thomas L. Kane

---

[30]Kane inserted a variant on the James Allen statement that appears in the Journal History, 16 July 1846 (see above). The last line of Kane's version (with his brackets) read: "The Mormon people [*having on due application raised* & furnished for the service of the United States a Battalion of Volunteers] . . . are hereby fully authorized to do so, during the pleasure of the President of the United States."

[31]Beyond impressing Jesse Little, the purpose of this ritual is a mystery, but it is ironic that Kane should remain oblivious to the Mormons' similar manipulations of his own impressions. Kane then asked that someone "write to dear Elish," his older brother, "all about me as soon as possible."

WILLIAM MEDILL:
GOVERNMENT WILL INTERPOSE NO OBJECTIONS

Settlement on Indian lands again became an urgent question when James Allen died suddenly less than six weeks after making these promises. Again Thomas L. Kane came to the rescue. He had already sent copies to President Polk with his own endorsement and later interceded to see that favorable action was taken. It was no doubt Kane who sent a copy of the following dispatch from the commissioner of the U.S. Office of Indian Affairs with his own letter on 11 September 1846 addressed to "General Young."

MEDILL TO HARVEY, SUPT. OF INDIAN AFFAIRS, ST. LOUIS, MO.
MANUSCRIPT HISTORY OF BRIGHAM YOUNG, LDS ARCHIVES.

War Department
Off. Indian Affairs
Sept. 2, 1846

Sir:—Since my letter to you of the 27th July and the 22nd ult. in relation to the Mormons and the desire expressed by them to remain for a time on the lands recently purchased by the United States from the Pottawattomie Indians, and which lie within the limits of Iowa, the subject has been brought to the immediate notice of the president and secretary of war.

The object and intention of the Mormons in desiring to locate upon the lands in question, are not very satisfactorily set forth, either in the application to the president or in the letter transmitted to this office, which contained the assent of the Indian chiefs. If their continuance is really to be temporary and for such length of time only as will enable them to supply their wants and procure the necessary means, for proceeding on their journey, the government will interpose no objections.

The want of provisions and the near approach of winter, which will have set in before they can reach their proposed destination, would necessarily expose them to much suffering, if not to starvation and death; while on the other hand, a location and continuance for any very considerable length of time near Council Bluffs, would interfere with the removal of the Indians, an object of much interest to the people of that region of country, delay the survey and sales of the lands in question, and thus in all probability bring about a difficulty between Iowa, now about to come into the union as a state, and the general government. Both these extremes, in the opinion of the president, should be avoided. The rights and interests of Iowa, now that the Indian title has been extinguished, may not be jeopardized, while the laws of humanity and the rights of hospitality should not be disregarded.

You will ascertain, if possible, the real intention of these people in desiring to remain, and if you are satisfied that they will leave and resume their journey in the spring, or at such period as the season for traveling will justify, and that no positive injury is likely to arise to the Indians from their stay among them, you will instruct the subagent and give notice to any other officers of the general government in that quarter, to interpose no objection to the Mormon people remaining on the lands referred to, during the suspension of their journey, or to their making such improvements and raising such crops as their convenience and wants may require; taking care, however, at the same time, to impress upon them the necessity of leaving at the earliest moment their necessities and convenience will justify, and of observing all laws and regulations in force upon the territory for the time being.

Very respectfully, your obedient servant,

W. Medill
Major Thomas H. Harvey,
Supt., etc., St. Louis, Mo.

OFFICERS: AUTHORIZE YOU TO RECEIVE THE PAYMENT

Before leaving Council Bluffs, the officers as a last duty authorized the agents appointed by Brigham Young to collect the $42 clothing allowance that would be paid to each of the enlisted men and assign it as specified by the soldier. The Mormon leaders justifiably looked upon this aid as their financial salvation, but the diversion of the money that many of the soldiers directed to be sent their families would create unanticipated problems.

JOURNAL HISTORY, 21 JULY 1846.

Council Bluffs, east side
Missouri River,
July 21, 1846

Messrs. Newel K. Whitney, John H. Hale and Dan Spencer.
Gentlemen:—

We, the undersigned officers of Company A of the Mormon Battalion of the U.S. Army, on behalf of the members of said company, hereby authorize you to receive the payment of the cheques returned by the members of said company, and apply them to such uses as may be specified thereon, or as specified on the return list already tendered to you. You will thus confer a favor on us.

> Jefferson Hunt, Captain
> George W. Oman, 1st Lieut.
> Lorenzo Clark, 2nd. Lieut.

MARGARET L. SCOTT: BELOVED BROTHER

As the command prepared to march, Cpl. James Allen Scott, Company E, on 16 July wrote to his sister about his decision to enlist. Although his letter does not survive, much of its content can be derived from her impassioned reply. Margaret Scott's letter reflects the tumultuous conditions of the Mormon diaspora following the faith's departure from Nauvoo. She expressed doubts about the battalion's enlistment shared by many Latter-day Saints, and described the work of a swindler representing himself as a missionary—not a rare problem on the Mormon frontier. Her letter eloquently expressed a woman's justified concern about the human cost of war.

MARGRETT L. SCOTT TO J. ALLEN SCOTT, LDS ARCHIVES.

Tennessee Dyer City August the 30th

Mr. J. Allen Scott

Dear brother I received your letter bearing the dates of July 16 to August the 5th on the 25th inst and with mingled emotions of sorrow and admiration I perused its content. I would have written by the next mail, but my mind was to[o] much agitated to write. James you are aware that it is a hard trial, but I have no alternative, but to submit and calmly resign myself and my beloved brother, into the arms of our heavenly father for protection, and preservation.—You speak correctly when you say, that I do not understand the present movements of the church (would that I did) they are indeed strange to me. For the Church to start to leave the U.S. and stop on the way, and send 500 of her members, to bear privations, and encounter danger, in the service of this government, is, I acknowledge, beyond my comprehension. As to protecting the church, perhaps she [the government] will, and perhaps she will not. You know how she has acted in that regard. But, not withstanding my ignorance on the subject, I have confidence enough in your judgment to beleive [sic] that you have good reasons for acting as you have done. Nevertheless I wish it were otherwise. When you write again cant you put some of the whys and wherefores on a scrap so as to give me some insight. You promise to come back after me when you are discharged. I should like to know how the matter can be arranged, wont the emigrants be all gone from their present station before that time. I have seen an item from the Hancock eagle stating that the church would collect all her scattered members that wished to go this fall and winter and continue their journey next spring—

The sickly season has arrived . . .[32]

I wrote you an account of an imposter or apostate or perhaps both that passed through this country in June by the name of Jett.[33] He said he was an elder and the tythe gatherer. Mr. Mc[Corkle][34] lent him Vic to ride to Dyersburg, where he swapt her to Mr. Thos Saunders and made his escape by getting in a boat and leav [tear]. Mr Mc. got Vic by some trouble & expense. Jett stated he was from the camps which I think is probably true, and if he has not shewed his vile practices there, he may no[t] be there or in your Battalion. If you should meet with him beware for he is a villian *sure*. He is a large man with sandy hair round shoulders and very much sunburnt. He is a tolerable scholar and has practiced law in state. He is son-in-law to Mr. Seth Utly[35] who is a member of the church and a respectable man—Jett was at Roberts when he received your letter and he heard it read (which I have been sorry for) as it made him acquainted with you[r] name and opinions—I want you to be careful with regard to your companions—I know your disposition, you are naturally free and rather unguarded in your Conversation, which gives designing men an oppertunity to take advantage of your simplicity. You have placed yourself in [a] tight place and I know it will require more self control that you are accustomed to to get along

I scarce know what to say to you, you have acted so differently to what I expected. But I would not discourage you now. I want you to stand to your resolution, viz., to act uprightly and acquit yourself honorably—you tell me that your Battalion is the army of Israel and I trust it is and also that you are the Servants of God. Well is it not strange to see an army of Christians sent [?] out Voluntarily with muskets and bayonets (in appear . . .[36]

I may have asked questions which it is not wisdom for you to answer, if so, lay them over.—I suppose that letters will pass between you and some of the brethren in the camps if so perhaps you could arrange it so that Br.

---

[32]Ellipses denote the omission of brief personal discussions of family, health, and the weather.

[33]Jett was probably Hamilton Jett, who appeared as "Hemileton" Jett on the Nauvoo List of Members.

[34]This was R. A. H. McCorkle, cousin to the Scotts. Dyersburg is fifteen miles east of the Mississippi in north-central Tennessee, while Dyer, Margaret Scott's Dyer City, is some twenty miles farther east.

[35]According to Nauvoo Temple Records, Seth Utley was the father of Mary Amanda Utley, who was born 17 November 1821 in Humphreys County, Tennessee. Miss Utley received her endowment on 18 December 1845 and was sealed to John Taylor on 17 January 1846.

[36]Here a square tear along the folds of the sheet destroyed the middle section of page three of Scott's letter. Still legible on the left side of the letter are the phrases "blood of their fellow"; "What General Kear"; "nor why he called on"; and "President order him." The rest of the missing text apparently discussed the weather.

McClellan or Rainy could give me information, that it would not be prudent for you to give at present.[37]

The winter is coming be sure to procure under clothing if possible and take good care of your health as circumstances will admit of, be temperate in all things. You know that nature has her laws which if transgressed you will be punished—I rejoice in what H. C. Kimball has told you and hope it will prove true . . .[38] I have been reading Josephus lately and [he] gives an account of some pious Jews that the whole company was preserved—And I pray our heavenly father that his choicest blessings may rest on your Battalion collectively and on you individually. I am much pleased that you have prayers so regularly in your Crowd. If prayer is attended to throughout the campaign in faith and humility I think you *will* be preserved—

I peruse your letters [with] satisfaction and profit. I am pleased with the manner in which you write. But my dear brother the more I see to admire the harder it is to part with you but I am determined with the aid of the holy spirit to try to bear up under it, hoping that it will be all for the best, though I can't understand it now . . .

Sarah has continued firm and has been looking for your posts, but like me is doomed to disappointment.[39] When I consider the dangers to which you are exposed and the hardships you must undergo and the length of time before you are free, it is almost insupportable, but when I reflect whose you are, a gleam of hope inspires me with courage, and I feel like we'll meet again and spend some happy hours together; if you write often it will help to support me.

Next to your God e[n]deavour to gain the good will of your officers if they try to be good men and obey them you must w[h]ether good or bad. Are your Captains all Elders. I want a particular account of your captain.[40] May our heavenly faither direct and protect you and in due time return to safe home is the prayer of your sister who loves you with undimmed affection—

Margrett L. Scott[41]

[To] J. Allen Scott

---

[37]Probably James McClellan, who married Cynthia Stewart on 19 January 1826 in Bedford County, Tennessee, and died in Utah in 1881. Tennessean David Pinkney Rainey, 28, was a corporal in Co. B who died in Richmond, Utah, in 1888. Scott's concern reflected her awareness that both Mormons and their enemies habitually read other people's private mail.

[38]William Hyde reported that church leaders, including Apostle Heber C. Kimball, in a meeting on 18 July 1846 gave "a firm promise that, on condition of faithfulness on our part, our lives should be spared." Brigham Young had already predicted "that not one of those who might enlist would fall by the hands of the nation's foe." See Tyler, *A Concise History*, 118, 128.

[39]Sarah would appear to be James Scott's sweetheart.

[40]Scott's captain was Daniel C. Davis.

[41]The odd spelling for "Margrett" was perhaps a family nickname. For Cpl. James Allen Scott's diary and fate, see Chapters 8 and 9. For another Margaret Scott letter that confirms the standard spelling of her given name, see Chapter 12.

Brigham Young: The Thanks of This People

In late 1843 the city council of Nauvoo had sought to escape growing opposition and violence in Illinois by asking Congress to declare the
city a territory of the United States.[42] Among signers of the memorial
was Brigham Young. Now in conveying the gratitude of his people to
President Polk, he reviewed Mormon grievances, reminded the president
of the LDS church's political support during the election of 1844, and
promised to renew the bid for territorial status. Later Young would
come to see this as a mistake and create instead the "free and independent government" in the Great Basin named the State of Deseret.[43]

Young to Polk, 9 August 1846, LDS Archives.

(Confidential)

To James K. Polk, President of the United States[44]

    A large portion of The Church of Jesus Christ of Latter Day Saints hav-
ing passed from the nation of our nativity and the Republic over which you
have the honor to preside, and finding ourselves on the western shores of
the great Missouri while others of our friends are following close on our
rear, beg your Excellency's indulgence for a moment while we pour out the
pure feelings of our souls before you.

    The cause of our exile we need not repeat, it is already with you, suffi-
cient to say that a combination of fortuitous, illegal, and unconstitutional
circumstances have placed us in our present situation, on a journey which we
design shall end in a location west of the Rocky Mountains and within the
basin of the Great Salt Lake or Bear River Valley, as soon as circumstances
shall permit, believing that to be a point where a good living will require
hard labor and consequently will be coveted by no other people, while it is
surrounded by so unpopular but fertile country.

    While on our way thither and beyond the borders of the states we were
met by Capt. J. Allen of your army of the west proffering us ~~to~~ the enlistment of 500 men to be marched into California via Santa Fe, there to be
discharged at the expiration of one year, receiving the pay of regular solders
and other valuable and unusual emoluments: To this proffer we promptly
responded, though it has left 500 of our loaded teams standing on the
fringe of the Poduwidemie and Omaha Nations and nearly as many families
destitute of their head and guardian only as they are counseled and nour-

---

[42]Smith, *History of the Church*, 6:132.

[43]Morgan, *The State of Deseret*, 121.

[44]The original of this letter, now at LDS Archives, was presented as a gift to the Mormon church
before the establishment of the National Archives.

ished by their friends who were already overborne with cares, and worn out with anxiety and fatigue; but, in the midst of this, we were cheered with the presence of our friend, Mr. Little, of New Hampshire, who assured us of the personal friendship of the President in the act before us, and this assurance, though not doubted by us in the least was made doubly sure by the testimony of Col. Kane of Philadelphia, whose presence in our midst, and the ardour with which he has espoused the cause of a persecuted and suffering people and the testimony he has borne of your Excellency's kind feelings, have kindled up a spark in our hearts, which had been well nigh extinguished: not a spark of Liberty or democracy, *that cannot be*! but love of a country or rulers from whom previously we have received but little save neglect or persecution.

We also received assurances from Lieut. Col. Allen of the "Mormon Battalion" that we should be safe, and that it would be proper for us to stop on any Indian lands, while it was necessary, considering our hindrance [*sic*] in filling his command, and during the pleasure of the President, which we fully anticipate, will be during all necessary time; and in view of all things here referred to, and many more, which the hurrying duties of the camp will not permit us to mention at this time:

Resolved; that as children of the United States, we have not been disappointed in our anticipation of a brighter day and a more righteous administration in our endeavors for the canvass [election] of his Excellency James K. Polk to the presidency.[45]

Resolved that the thanks of this people be presented to President Polk for his friendly offer of transferring 500 of our brethren, to the land of their destination under command of Col Allen.

Resolved, that should we locate within the territory of the United States, as we anticipate, we should esteem a territorial government of our own; as one of the richest boons of earth; and while we appreciate the Constitution of the United States as the most precious among the nations, we feel that we had rather retreat to the desertes [*sic*], islands or mountain caves, than consent to be ruled by Governm[ent] and judges, whose hands are drenched in the blood of innocence & virtue, who delight in injustice & oppression and whose greatest glory is to promote the misery of their fellows, for their own aggrandizement or lustful gratification.

Resolved that we have heard from various sources, and have the same confirmed by Col. Kane that the friends of ex-gov Boggs are endeavoring to make him governor of California, &c, and that we, as a people are bound to

---

[45]Brigham Young felt he had a great claim on the president's support, for he believed the "Mormon vote in the State of New York, carried that state in favor of Mr. Polk; without which, his election would have been defeated." See Watson, ed. *Manuscript History of Brigham Young 1846–1847*, 221. Nothing in Polk's papers indicates that he was aware of any political debt to the Mormons.

oppose said Boggs in every point and particular that shall tend to exalt him in any country where our lot may be cast; and that *peace* and *"Mormonism"* which are always *undivided*, and *Lilburn W. Boggs cannot dwell together*; and we solicit the attention of President Polk to this important item in the justice prosperity and welfare of the newly acquired territory of our Glorious Republic.[46]

Resolved that as soon as we are settled in the Great Basin we design to petition the United States for a territorial Government bounded on the north by the British and on the south by the Mexican dominions; & east and west by the summits of the Rocky & Cascade mountains.

Having received the strongest assurances of assistance and protection from President Polk through our highly esteemed friend, Col Kane, and that he will continue to use all constitutional power at his disposal for our good, regardless of popular clamor and cabinet intrigues, to establish us in a land where we can sustain our wives and children; to help us to a territorial government "so that we may dwell in peace under our own vine, and eat the fruit of our own labors that he will defend us against every aggression; by the strong arms of twenty millions of freemen, & all their immence [*sic*] resources; that he will ward off the scourge of oppression, the rod of Tyranny, and the sword of death, by all the means that Goes [*sic*] and his country have placed at his disposal"; Therefore, Resolved; that we have the fullest confidence in the friendly protection of President Polk; that our own hearts are with him to do good, and sustain the best government on earth; that he may depend on our warmest gratitude, and our cordial co-operation in all things that shall tend to exalt him, and our fellow creatures, and that our faith, prayers and blessings shall rest upon him so long as he shall magnify those glorious principles, he has espoused, which, we trust, will be eternal.

Done on the west bank of the Missouri River, near Council Bluffs, Omaha Nation, August 9th 1846, in general council of the church afforesaid, & camp of Israel.

Willard Richards, Clerk   Brigham Young, President

P.S. Please give us your views of Lieut. Col. Allen's permit for us to stop on Indian lands as soon as your convinaince [*sic*] will permit.

Direct to N. K. Whitney, Johnathan H. Hale, and Daniel Spencer.

Mormon Camp

Near Council Bluffs

via—Fort Leavenworth, P.O.

---

[46]As governor of Missouri in 1838, Lilburn W. Boggs issued a notorious extermination order that earned the enduring enmity of the Latter-day Saints. Boggs went to California in 1846 and was appointed Alcalde, or mayor, at Coloma during military rule.

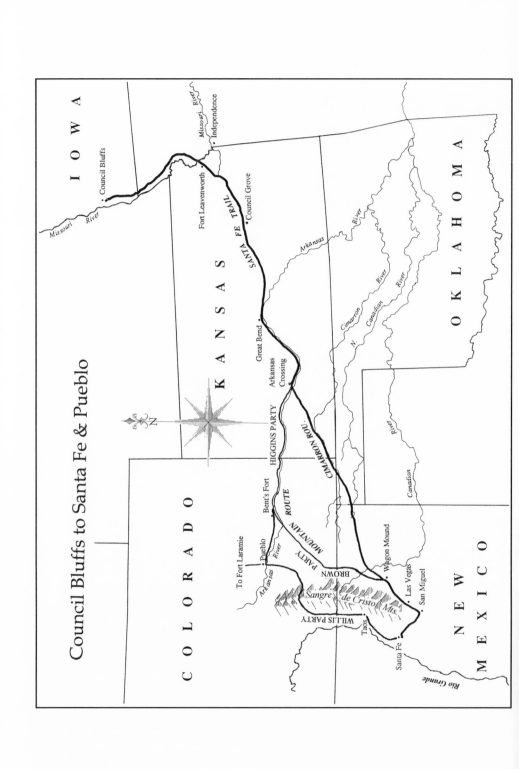

Council Bluffs to Santa Fe & Pueblo

Chapter 2

"THE ROLLING OF THE MORMON DRUMS"
Council Bluffs to the Arkansas Crossing

On 21 July 1846 the Mormon Battalion began the first leg of its historic journey to the traditional marching tune of American soldiers, "The Girl I Left Behind Me." Otherwise, reflecting the permissiveness of recruiter James Allen, now a lieutenant colonel, the make-up of the command was unlike any other body of volunteers ever to serve in the U.S. Army. Age requirements first specified by Allen were shattered by a number of the volunteers. Twenty-two years over the ceiling was the oldest soldier, sixty-seven-year-old Samuel Gould, a Company C private.[1] The youngest recruit was Alfred Higgins, barely fourteen, a member of Company D, commanded by Capt. Nelson Higgins, his father.[2] The number of women accompanying their husbands also exceeded by about sixteen the limit of twenty allowed to serve as laundresses, four to each of the five companies. One man, Lt. Elam Luddington, even took his mother along. Another, Samuel Boley, a Company B private, was so sick he died on the second day. The procession also numbered more than forty children as well as a dozen or so teamsters and other family dependents. All told it came to about six hundred souls.

---

[1] A native of Connecticut, the indestructible Samuel Gould apparently knew the secret of longevity. Born 15 August 1778, he fathered seven children by his first wife, Sally. He returned to Winter Quarters from Salt Lake in the fall of 1847 and was back in Utah in time to join Parley P. Pratt's exploration of southern Utah in 1849. At age 71 he married Fanny Ward Lister and became the parent of four more children. Later he married Cynthia Wright, who gave him one child. Gould died at Parowan at age 91. See A History of Samuel Gould, 1.

[2] Among the underaged was a sixteen-year-old New Yorker who enlisted as Luther Smith but who became famous as Lot Smith. As a Nauvoo Legion major (and later, brigadier general), Smith destroyed three army supply trains in the Utah War of 1857–58. See Larson, *A Data Base of The Mormon Battalion*, 2, 159; and General's Commission, 19 May 1866, in Lot Smith Papers.

LEVI WARD HANCOCK: ALL WAS SILENCE

From Council Bluffs the command would travel about 180 miles over the next twelve days down the east bank of the Missouri River to the crossing at Weston, Missouri. Here they came within a few miles of Jackson County, the center of Mormon millennial expectations and scene of conflict in 1833 between members of the faith and old settlers which spread to neighboring counties and culminated in the so-called Mormon War of 1838. Levi Hancock, a Company E musician, was the only Mormon general authority in the command.[3] Hancock described the march and the reception the Mormon soldiers received as they paraded proudly through the western Missouri towns with music at the head and camped near the Fort Leavenworth ferry.[4]

LEVI HANCOCK, MORMON BATTALION JOURNAL, 20 JULY TO 1 AUGUST 1846, LDS ARCHIVES.

July 20, 1846. I enlisted into the Army of the United States Mormon Battalion, Fifth Company. D.C. Davis, Captain; Jefferson Hunt, First Captain; Jesse D. Hunter, Second; James Brown, Third; Nelson Higens, the Fourth. I was chosen Musician; Jesse Earl was Drummer. James Pace was First Lieutenant and Andrew Little [Lytle], Second Lieutenant.

These men I messed with. Nothing done, but organizing for some time.

22 day. Marched out four miles. Tune: "Girl I Left Behind Me." 7 o'clock, marched again by the request of Colonel Allen. Played: "The Girl I Left Behind Me." Muddy road. Traveled 18 miles and camped on a small stream beside the bluff.

23 day. Continued our line of march and camped beside the water of the Merom.[5] Soldiers generally in good spirits. Some was weary and complained.

24 day. Marched out of camp with music, some had to ride. Crossed Nis-

---

[3]In the complicated hierarchy of the LDS church, general authorities included the First Presidency, the Council of the Twelve Apostles, the Patriarch, the Presiding Bishopric, and the leadership of the Seventy. The Seventy was a priesthood office organized into seven quorums; the First Council of Seventy and eventually the First Quorum of Seventy, were considered general authorities. See Allen and Leonard, *The Story of the Latter-day Saints*, 80–81. As "one of the First Seven Presidents of Seventies," Hancock was the highest ranking church official in the battalion. See Jenson, Andrew. *Latter-day Saint Biographical Encyclopedia*, 1:188–89.

[4]This section of Hancock's diary is based on *The Life of Levi W. Hancock*, as transcribed and corrected for spelling and punctuation by April Hancock. To appreciate how much her editing improves its readability, compare this section with the literal transcriptions of Hancock's diary in Chapter 10.

[5]Actually Mosquito Creek. The waters of Merom refer to the place on the Jordan River, north of the Sea of Galilee, where Joshua defeated a coalition of Canaanite kings. See Josh. 11:5, 7.

LEVI WARD HANCOCK.
A native of Springfield, Massachusetts,
Hancock joined the LDS church in the
autumn of 1830. He was forty-three
when he enlisted in the Mormon
Battalion. In his autobiography
Hancock recalled that "Parley
P Pratt whispered to me, and said
you are chaplain." His journal
is filled with songs, poems, and
sketches of the battalion's march.
*Courtesy, the Museum of
Church History and Art.*

hanybotany[6] and the Colonel was very kind to us. Made us ride and tried to administer consolation to the men. Nothing was too good for his men, he would say. We camped in Anderson, Atchison County, making 20 miles.

Saturday, 25th. Crossed over the Torkeyou Creek. Traveled 20 miles. Not a word of complaint from any man.

26th day. My feet became sore. My pain was severe. The sore had been of long duration. Opened it with my knife. Brother Galley [Samuel Gully] and Brother Lytle and Pace were very kind to me and done all they promised to do, to see that no hardship was placed on me, as I told them my health was poor. Marched 20 miles. Camped by a good spring.

27th day. Crossed the Little Tarkeyou. In the evening, a man was brought in camp called "Colonel." This was one of our men who had palmed himself off upon the people as Colonel of the Mormon Battalion. Had got the people to feed him by the way. Colonel Allen asked him why he done so. He said he wanted a good living, authority and by so doing, he got it. The Colonel smiled and told him to do so no more.[7]

---

[6]This was the Nishnabotna River, which rises in central Iowa's Carroll County and reaches the Missouri River in the northwest corner of Missouri.

[7]Zadock Judd recalled that the "colonel" was "one of the boys rather an eccentric character [who] had procured an odd kind of hat with a feather in it, similar to an officer's uniform." The "much yelling and cheering" that greeted the man's arrival at camp brought him to Colonel Allen's attention, and he "also had a hearty laugh over it." See Autobiography of Zadock Knapp Judd, 18–19.

Next morning, it being Monday, marched out of camp. Tune: "Over the River to Charley." Traveled 25 miles and camped.

28th day. Marched through the country beautiful to behold. 25 miles. Camped on the Nodaway Creek.[8]

29. Continued our line of march at six A.M. Tune: "Girl I Left Behind Me," then changed to "White Cockade" through St. Joseph and camped in Mount Pleasant, making 16 miles this day.

30 day. Marched. Tune: "D. B. Huntington's Favorite."[9] Passed through Bloomington and camped in the woods. Some time in the night there was a high wind. The trees fell every way from us, but none in the camp. One ox was killed out of camp by a limb.

31 day. At 7 o'clock marched. Tune: "Jefferson's Liberty." Passed through Weston. Played the tune: "Over The River To Charley." The whole town looking at the doors. The musician had not kept so good time before. The people looked astonished while Elisha Averet, Allen, Jackson seemed to receive fresh breezes, as it were from the mouth of the Father of Spirits which inspired them with the most perfect sounds on the fife, while sprge [inspiring?] Earl, Smith and Day[10] with listening ears that catched the sound with hands and fingers clenched tight around the drumstick, beat the accents with most tremendous strokes, which were even and handsomely measured with left foot down at the beginning of every bar. All was silence while five hundred Mormons passed and turned three corners in the heart of town.

Camped one mile out of town.

August 1st. Marched to the river opposite the ferry. 7 miles today. Crossed over in town Fort Leavenworth.

ROBERT W. WHITWORTH:
A LARGE CAMP OF LITTLE WHITE TENTS

From bluffs overlooking the Missouri River, Fort Leavenworth had guarded the Santa Fe Trail for nineteen years when the Mormon soldiers on 1 August 1846 marched up the hill from the ferry and camped on the west side of the fort.[11] Three days later two young English travelers

---

[8]Nodaway River was another Iowa waterway crossed by the Mormon Battalion trail.

[9]Although not a musician with the battalion, drummer Dimick Baker Huntington, 38, a private in Co. D, taught martial music in Utah Territory, where he served as Indian interpreter for his brother-in-law, Brigham Young. Huntington became Young's most trusted ambassador to the natives of Utah.

[10]These men were musicians Elisha Averett, Co. A; Henry Wells Jackson, Co. D; Ezra H. Allen, Co. C; and drummers Willard G. Smith, Co. D; and Justice (Jesse) Earl, Co. E. Abraham Day, Co. E, was not officially enrolled as a musician.

[11]The oldest active U.S. Army post west of the Mississippi River, Fort Leavenworth was established in 1827 on the west bank of the Missouri River by Col. Henry Leavenworth, Third U.S. Infantry, to protect the Santa Fe Trail.

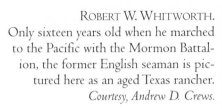

ROBERT W. WHITWORTH.
Only sixteen years old when he marched
to the Pacific with the Mormon Battalion, the former English seaman is pictured here as an aged Texas rancher.
Courtesy, Andrew D. Crews.

came looking for work or adventure. Robert W. Whitworth and William
Beddome decided on the spot to enlist in the battalion and go to California. Over the next twelve months the sixteen-year-old Whitworth
kept a diary of his experiences. In 1913 it was plucked from the gutter
in San Antonio by Texan Joseph J. Brown, who later gave it to historian
Helen J. H. Rugeley for publication. In it Whitworth described the Fort
Leavenworth Mormon encampment.

GRACY AND RUGELEY, EDS.,
"AN ENGLISHMAN IN THE MORMON BATTALION," 134.

The Fort is beautifully situated on a high comanding situation not far
from the River in a beautiful country. It is built in the form of a square with
a Parade ground in the centre. Here we wandered about with our hands in
our pockets (though we had no need for there was but little in them). There
was a large camp of little white tents on the outside of the fort, where we
were greatly amused by the antics of some young fellows of about our own
age. They were running races, wrestling & appeared in high glee. We were
informed that they were part of the Battallion that lay encamped before us.
We had never thought of volunteering before, but we were almost immediately seized with a desire to live in one of the little white tents, so we entered
into conversation with one of the men, who was very talkative, he told us
that they were all Mormons and that they had enlisted for 12 months to go
to California, there to be discharged with their Arms and Ammunition, and

that their pay was 10 dollars per month and find their own clothing. He said they wore no uniform, which suited us so well that we told him that we should like to volunteer, upon which he took us to the Orderly Sergeant of his company, who put down our names and ages, places of birth &c, and we were regularly enlisted in the American Service. The Fort was very crowded at the time I write. Besides our Battallion there was a regiment of Infantry and a regiment of the Missouri Volunteers,[12] who were encamped about a mile from the Fort. We stayed here about two weeks, having nothing to do but to answer to our names morning and evening.[13]

BRIGHAM YOUNG: A PECULIAR MANIFESTATION

On 4 August the men lined up to receive their annual clothing allowance of $42. The Mormon leaders who came next day to pick up the money, apostles Orson Hyde, Parley P. Pratt, and John Taylor, were not those authorized earlier by the volunteers to receive it. To Brigham Young's later displeasure, they got only a small part of the total payment, $5,860 out of as much as $21,000, and most of what they did obtain was earmarked for families. Even so, the following letter suggests these funds were used for the general welfare of the Mormon camp rather than specifically to support battalion dependents. Young indicated he might "send one or two brethren to receive your remittances" along the trail, and renewed the commitment he had first made on 1 July to do his best to bring the battalion families "forward with the camp" in 1847.

BRIGHAM YOUNG TO THE MORMON BATTALION,
JOURNAL HISTORY, 20 AUGUST 1846.

Camp of Israel, Cutler's Park
Omaha nation, Aug. 20, 1846

Capt. Jefferson Hunt and the Captains
officers and soldiers of the Mormon battalion.

Beloved brethren:—Several letters were this day received by Joseph Matthews who has just returned from Fort Leavenworth. The Council of

---

[12]The Second Regiment of Missouri Mounted Volunteers shared the trail to Santa Fe with the Mormon Battalion, although the commands were usually kept separated due to the animosity that existed between them. Many of the Missourians, like their commander, Col. Sterling Price, had taken part in the state's 1838 military campaign against the Mormons. Price later became a governor of Missouri and Confederate general during the Civil War.

[13]Whitworth next described crossing the Missouri on a horse-powered paddlewheeler to visit Weston, where he and a companion passed the day sightseeing and "refreshing ourselves with ice cream."

the Twelve and High Councils of Cutler's park and Council Point were in joint session on his arrival, and we were cheered with his report of your excellent outfit, and the good feelings which appear to prevail at the Fort, and among the officers and soldiers of the Battalion.

Bro. Matthews expressed your feelings and wishes, concerning your families and that you desire your families to be brought forward with the camp. This is all right, and nothing shall be wanting on our part to accomplish this desirable object;

We consider the money you have received, as compensation for your clothing, a peculiar manifestation of the kind providence of our Heavenly Father at this particular time, which is just the time for the purchase of provisions and goods for the winter supply of the camp. After hearing your views concerning the remittance of future payments, from Bro. Matthews, and Bro. Dykes' letter of the 15th inst., we consider it wisdom for you to retain the funds which you may hereafter receive, until you can bring them yourselves, or deliver them to our Agent; for if circumstances permit, and it is wisdom we shall send one or two brethren to receive your remittances; whom you will know by their credentials; otherwise you will retain them till further instructions; and we would again urge the importance in all good faith, of the officers being as fathers to their soldiers and counseling them in righteousness in all things, that they remember their prayers continually, and that they be kind and courteous in all their deportment, showing all due deference and respect to their officers and all in authority over them, using no profane or vain language or doing anything that tends to debase them in the eyes of beholders; remembering the ordinances in cases of sickness, and keeping themselves pure and unspotted from surrounding elements and combinations, so that they may win the respect and confidence of the whole world; and that they, and especially the younger brethren, do not spend their income for things of no value, or that might as well be dispensed with, but lay it up and keep it safe against a day of need, and send to the poor of Israel when opportunity presents and in so doing they will be laying up treasures in heaven, and on earth in the days of their youth; we give counsel upon counsel because it is our duty, and because we love you, and want to exalt you to the highest glory, and not because we have no confidence in you, far from it. It will require all the means the battalion will have to spare, with the united exertion of the camp, to carry out all your wishes, though by the wisdom of heaven we will make every dollar sent us count as good as two or three at ordinary traffic, and especially let every one send all they can by our agent at next payment, for it is very uncertain whether you will have an opportunity to make any more remittances before the close of the year or some distant period. A company of monied men, late from the East, is now forming in Camp to purchase all the materials necessary to put in immediate operation a flouring mill, when we get over the mountains; and nothing will be wanting on our part to make a good and pleasant retreat at the end of our journey.

Since writing you yesterday we have heard that about thirty wagons will winter at the Pawnee village, and Bishop Geo. Miller with about one hundred and sixty wagons at the Punca village, one hundred and twenty miles above.[14]

Let the officers be diligent in enjoining the above counsel.

Col. Kane is convalescent. We regret to hear of the illness of Col. Allen; please present him with our kind feelings and hopes of his health and prosperity.

Those brethren who remembered the counsel in the distribution of their mites, shall receive the blessing of the council; and we bless you all, feeling that you are doing well and trying to do better; and may our heavenly Father preserve you blameless unto the end, is the prayer of your brethren.

Done in behalf of the council.

Brigham Young, president,
Willard Richards, clerk.

P.S. A neglect on the part of two companies of the battalion to make me a return of a copy of their muster roll etc. has caused much trouble to me and their friends. Shall this be removed? I wish it to be understood by every member of this battalion, that on account of the imperfectness and nonappearance of the muster rolls of the different companies of the battalion at my office, the brethren in the army are liable to lose or not receive letters which might arrive for them, from foreign offices, for I know only some of the names that are among you.

Willard Richards, Postmaster.

MARIA RAWSON: I NEVER GOT THE MONEY

The women the soldiers left behind in the Mormon camps on the Missouri now had to prepare to survive a Midwestern winter under primitive conditions. Samuel Turnbow recalled that after the departure of the battalion, "one woman in her distracted state throwed herself in the creek of a shallow stream . . . and I fetched her out dead."[15] Effectively widowed by their husbands' enlistment, these women found themselves dependent on their religious leaders. In exchange for the financial salvation the soldiers' sacrifice offered to his church, Brigham Young had assured the men "that their families should be cared for, and that they

---

[14]George Miller took his followers north to winter with the Ponca tribe on the Niobrara River, and in mid-September Young recalled the wagons sent to the Pawnee village on Loup Fork.

[15]Turnbow, Genealogical and Blessing Book, 41.

should fare as well as he did, and that he would see they were helped along."[16] These promises would prove difficult to redeem.

Most of the battalion families were in the camps in Iowa, and in a deviation from standard practice, the church called special bishops to "take care of the families who were left by the soldiers."[17] Young asked for a report on the soldiers' pay on 18 July, and when they marched off three days later he complained that the rolls the officers had submitted did not report how much money each man would send back to the church.[18] Young convened a meeting of battalion families at Council Point on 14 August and outlined his plan to appropriate the soldier's Fort Leavenworth pay "so no portion of the money shall be squandered without doing the company good." Making collective purchases at St. Louis, Young said, would allow the church to buy "twice as much goods with the funds than the people could buy themselves." Though approved, the motion was not passed by the typical unanimous vote, even after Young said that he would be released "from all obligations that we are under to see that they are provided for and taken care of" to those who chose to keep their husbands' pay. After the meeting, bishops compiled lists of "such things as wanted by the soldiers families." Offered few choices, most battalion dependents went along with the plan, but four days after the meeting fifty-seven Saints on the Iowa shore refused to support the measure.[19]

Writing to her husband from Council Bluffs, Eliza Hunsaker explained her situation:

> you stated that you had sent me twenty five dollars in money but as yet I have not received any for the day that I got your letter there was one came from B Young from the other side of the river stating that their council was to keep the whole of the money that came from the Soldiers together and those that has money sent to them are requested to make out bills of of [*sic*] the goods and provisions that they want and then men will be sent to St Louis and there purchase wheat and storegoods and bring them up here and each one draw their share, and thus be more beneficial to the whole than otherwise divided out into small parcels.

Abraham Hunsaker "wrote that you sent back for me to come on and

---

[16] Tyler, *A Concise History*, 118.

[17] See Watson, ed., *Manuscript History of Brigham Young 1846–1847*, 261–62, for a list of eighty-eight of the men called to care for the families.

[18] Crockett, *Saints in the Wilderness*, 38, 45.

[19] Bennett, *Mormons at the Missouri*, 122–25, 283–84; and Crockett, *Saints in the Wilderness*, 117.

go with you if it was council," but it was not to be. His wife replied, "glad would I have been to have gone with you for long and lonesome seems the time we are to be separated."[20]

The financial acumen and managerial skill later apparent in Brigham Young's business career was not in evidence during that trying winter on the Missouri, where several practical undertakings were bedeviled by a hard run of bad luck. Supplies were low and prices high on the Missouri frontier, and freight charges combined with an unseasonably low river effectively eliminated the advantages of bulk purchases. After Young applied an average markup of sixty-four percent on the goods over their cost at St. Louis, families found that prices at Peter Sarpy's nearby trading post were ten to twenty percent lower than the church's. Young also spent some of the battalion cash on the troubled construction of a grist mill that would never justify the expense.[21]

The battalion's officers apparently did not share Brigham Young's decision to appropriate their pay with their men, many of whom tried to send money directly to their wives. Bulah Clark appealed to Brigham Young to acquire what every woman in the Mormon frontier camps considered the most important item to insure survival: a cow.

BULAH A. CLARK TO YOUNG & COUNCIL,
BRIGHAM YOUNG COLLECTION, LDS ARCHIVES.

Council Point   August 19th 1846
Bro Young & Council
    I wish that you would send me ten Dollars that I may be enabled to buy some things that I need at the present time which will leave in the council's hands twenty-five Dollars and I should like for those that go to buy Cattle to buy for me out of the twenty five Dollars a good new milch Cow and the balance they can buy what they see fit. And by doing so you will Oblige me.
Bulah A. Clark
Wife of Lorenzo Clark

Mary Compton wrote a particularly interesting letter to her husband that listed the supplies she considered necessary to survive a winter on the frontier.

---

[20]Eliza Hunsaker to Abraham Hunsaker, 24 August 1846, Mormon Battalion Correspondence Collection, LDS Archives.

[21]Kelly, ed., *Journals of John D. Lee*, 52; and Bennett, *Mormons at the Missouri*, 124–28, 284–85. Bennett, 127, found Kelly's charges about management of the mill "difficult to substantiate," but by any standard the venture was not a success.

MARY BETTS COMPTON TO ALLEN COMPTON,
MORMON BATTALION CORRESPONDENCE COLLECTION, LDS ARCHIVES.

Camp of Israel August 26th 1846

Dear Husband   I now take this oppertunity of writing to you to let you Know that me and my Little family are all Enjoying good health at this time hopeing that these few lines may find you Enjoying the same like Blessings. I have received two letters from you one dated August 6th the other the 8th which gave me much satisfaction to hear that you was Enjoying good health. You wanted me to Let you Know my Present Situation and who I was in the care of. I am in the care of Brother [Charles] Bird and he under the direction of the twelve. The money that you sent me is in the hands of the twelve and they are going to send it Down the River all to gether in the hands of one man. I have talked with Brigham my self and he says that such Artickels can be bought Cheaper than I could have them bought my self. The church are generaly sending in this way and Each one sent a bill of such Artickels as they want. I have sent my Bill for 4 Barrells of flour 25 lbs of coffee 1 Bolt Cotton cloth 12 yds Lindsey 8 yds of Blue Driling 6 yds of janes [denim] 16 yds of calico 5 pair of Shoes and one Cow. You wanted me to Let you Know whither there would be a chance for me to come on in the Spring or not. I talked with Brigham and he says there will be a chance to come on in the spring.[22] I would like for you to send me about ten Dollars moore and I want you to send it in a letter to me. You wanted me to let you know whether I was in a house or not. I am in a house. I want you to write me as often as you can as I am anxous to Know how you are gitting a Long and how your health is. We think the time Long to see you again.

But I feel in hop[e]s that the Lord will Preserve our health and prepare a way for us to get to calleforny next fall where we shall Enjoy Each others Sosiety as in former Days. I have nothing moore at this time to send you But Ever Remain you Affectionate Wife untill Death

From Mary Compton to
Allen Compton
[flourish]

Camp Cutlers Park Sept
To Mr. Allen Compton, Mormon Battalion

The situation of the families did not improve as winter approached. In late September, Maria Rawson wrote her husband describing her plight, suggesting that he find a way to send money to her directly:

I have to go along to winter [in Missouri] on account of not gitting any

<hr>

[22]Like most of the battalion wives, Mary Compton was left behind in 1847. Her husband, Pvt. Allen Compton, served in the Willis detachment and joined the first 1847 company to leave Salt Lake for Council Bluffs, where he died in 1854.

money. They sent the money down to St. Louis to git goods up before the river closes. I never got the money nor none of the rest of the women. They kept all the money to gether to send down the river after goods to pay the women. Some women got some of the money and them that contend for it all got all their money and i did not git any be cause they said it would be for the better to send down to git good[s] so much Cheaper . . . so you may act your own pleasure except you can send it by some private hand that will give it to me.[23]

When Parley P. Pratt returned from Leavenworth with only a fraction of the hoped-for windfall, Young's frustration mounted. In December he "told the Sisters that they ought not to grumble & complain about the Twelve for not having a sufficiency to live on." Their "dear husbands," Young explained, "had only sent them about 5,000 dollars out of 22,000 they received at Fort Leavenworth, reserving to themselves only [$]17,000 for the Grog Shop, Ball room & card Table." This showed "their great love for their Families, but their greater love for the pleasures around them."[24] Young was similarly blunt with other wives who personally petitioned him for help. Fanny Taggart recalled that the promise that the families would be cared for "kept up my courage on the way" from Nauvoo, but at Winter Quarters the "answer I received from President Young made me feel like bursting into tears." Yet while the families left behind on the Missouri suffered through the grim winter of 1846–1847, one of the bleakest episodes in Mormon history, most of the prominent families "never went hungry."[25] Young's inability to keep his pledge to the departing soldiers was a constant bone of contention for the next two years and would leave a bitter legacy.

ZADOCK JUDD: COVERED FROM NECK TO WAIST

Eighteen-year-old Zadock Judd from Ontario, Canada, had suffered from weak ankles before he joined the battalion with his brother, Hyrum, 21, both in Company E. Even so, he enjoyed the short march from Council Bluffs to Fort Leavenworth. The men, he said, were

---

[23]Maria Rawson to Daniel Rawson, 23 September 1846, Mormon Battalion Correspondence Collection, LDS Archives.

[24]Bagley, ed., *The Pioneer Camp of the Saints*, 106. Historian Richard E. Bennett calculated that Pratt returned with $5,835 for the battalion families, who turned over $4,375.19 to Bishop Newell K. Whitney. See Bennett, *Mormons at the Missouri*, 116.   [25]Ibid., 122.

"happy and cheerful, singing and dancing." But when the recruits were issued their arms and accoutrements, he found out why western Missouri volunteers preferred to make the journey to Santa Fe on a horse. As Sgt. Albert Smith complained, the arms and equipment they received would make "A hevy load for a mule."[26] Here Judd complained about it, but he never had weak ankles again.

AUTOBIOGRAPHY OF ZADOCK KNAPP JUDD, UTAH STATE HIST. SOC., 19–20.

In due time we arrived at Fort Leavenworth. Here we were armed with flint lock musket[s].[27] It was said to carry an ounce ball one mile. Its weight was twelve or fifteen pounds. Its accouterments were a large cartridge box with heavy leather belt two and one fourth inches wide to carry over the left shoulder, a similar belt with bayonet and scabbard attached to carry over the right shoulder and then a waist belt correspondingly wide and heavy all white leather, and we were required to keep them clean.

Our muskets had to be cleaned often. Also a knap-sack in which to carry our clothing and any other little necessities. It was so arranged that a strap came in front of each shoulder and under the arm with a long strap to reach around our bedding. With all these straps in front and the filled knap-sack behind, we were nearly covered from neck to waist. We were required to carry all these fixtures, our clothing and bedding and a few rounds of ammunition and then a canteen in which would hold three pints of water, and then a small cotton sack called a hover-sack, in which to carry our dinner and sometimes a day or two rations. These also were made to swing over our shoulders.

But to ease up on us a little the officers allowed each company to club together and buy a four mule team and wagon, in which to haul our knap-sacks and bedding, each man to bear an equal share of the expense. This was a great relief for a while, but when hard times came on, [the] wagon broke down or teams gave out, we had to shoulder our knap-sacks and bedding.

Here in Fort Leavenworth we were given cooking utensils, a camp kettle, frying-pan and coffee pot. Here we drew our clothing money for the entire year, $42, which as I have said was mostly sent back to needy friends and relatives.

Here our commander, Colonel Allen, laid in a supply of provisions to

---

[26]Journal of Albert Smith, LDS Archives, 5 August 1846.

[27]According to firearms expert Charles Cresap, a descendant of Mormon gunsmith Jonathan Browning, the battalion received Springfield U.S. model 1821 flintlock muskets manufactured in 1826 and 1827. Tyler, *A Concise History*, 136, recalled that companies A, B, and C received "a few cap-lock yaugers for sharpshooting and hunting." The Co. A invoice of ordnance in Ricketts, *The Mormon Battalion*, 38, indicates these "Jaegers" were actually half-stock 1803 Harpers Ferry rifles of the type issued to the Lewis and Clark Expedition.

last the Battalion one year, but by a mishap it was sent the wrong road.[28] After a few days rest and a little drilling and learning to use our guns and properly form ourselves into ranks and getting baggage, wagons ready we took up the line of march. Our Colonel being unwell at the time was not able to go with us, but it was expected he would overtake us in a few days.

Levi Hancock: Operations of the Spirit

Six weeks behind Kearny, the first three companies, A, B, and E, on August 13 marched from Fort Leavenworth in step to the music of their bands, following a branch of the trail to Santa Fe that met the main route in Douglas County, Kansas. Taken suddenly ill, Lieutenant Colonel Allen ordered senior captain Jefferson Hunt to lead the command to Council Grove, jumping off place for caravans on the road to New Mexico, while he remained behind at the fort to recover. Traveling separately the companies maintained a distance between them of as much as five or six miles. The last two, C and D, caught up six days later as Levi W. Hancock continued his daily account of the march.

Levi Hancock, Mormon Battalion Journal,
13 August to 29 August 1846.

13 [August 1846] day. Marched 4 miles down the Missouri River.

14 day. Marched 6 miles. John Allen that [was] baptized at the fort. Confirmed on the 15 day and marched southwest, crossed the valley of Clearwater, making 15 miles.

16 day. Crossed the Caw River,[29] about one fourth of a mile wide. Full banks. Raises some times very high and flows over much land and bottoms. Came on 4 miles and camped by some springs. This side of the river was the Shawnees, on the north was the Delewares. Making twelve miles today.

17 day. Some cattle lost. Hunters were sent out and found them all. One horse not found, belonging to a mover.[30]

---

[28]Allen had sent the provisions over the Santa Fe Trail's Mountain Route, the road taken by Kearny, to Bent's Fort on the Arkansas River, near present La Junta, Colorado. From this point, the Mountain Route headed south over Raton Pass on the line now followed by I-25 to Santa Fe. The battalion was ordered to take the Cimarron Route, a more direct trail, which left the Arkansas River near present Ingalls, Kansas, and cut across the Oklahoma panhandle, while its supplies wound up at Bent's Fort.

[29]Actually the Kansas River. The crossing was near Fish's Ferry, a few miles east of present Lawrence, Kansas.

[30]Hancock's company camped on Coal Creek, a tributary of the Wakarusa River, near its junction with the Kansas River. His comment on Delaware and Shawnee Indians reflected the lands assigned to these tribes in the loosely organized "Indian country" of today's Kansas following their removal from the Eastern states.

18 day. Baptized Leonard M. Scott into the church.[31] Also, some for their health. Passed over some beautiful land, but little timber. Only a small groves [*sic*] between here and the fort.

19 day. Morning found that our cattle had broken in an Indians cornfield and destroyed a considerable corn, which made us sorry, as it appeared to be all his living. I believe the officers made him whole or satisfied him and then we concluded to move on our camp accordingly. In the course of the day, we prepared to take our departure from this place and dried our clothes as they had been washed here and guard the corn at night.

We left here for the prairie on the 20th day, at an early hour. Marched about 4 miles and camped on a hill.[32] Some water and near another company on the east side of a valley, in plain sight. About five o'clock, a storm arose. The wind blew with hail that pelted my right foot that had no shoe on, until it was sore. My shoe had been lost out of the wagon. This storm continued for about an hour. Every tent was blown loose from the bottoms and we had to lay hold of the standards with all our might. We called this "Hurricane Hill," for it was so severe and wind blew so hard, it would run a wagon off without a team, for it was done with a woman in one.[33]

In the night, I had a dream. I thought I saw some [of] the Mormons who had cut their own throats and more was going to do the same. I tried to stop them, but could not. I saw two draw the knife across their own throats, commencing at one jugular vain and cut to the other side of their necks, until their own heads would lop over back. I thought I jumped back and looked to see if any had hit me. I was sick to my stomach to see them behave so and waked up. I did not know what to do. I felt so bad, I thought I should die. I tried to think what I had done. I could think of nothing.

I called on Brother Andrew Lytle and Thomas Wolsey and James Pace to administer to me. They did and it appeared to do me good for a short time.

[31]Leonard M. Scott, a brother-in-law of battalion member Henry Standage, joined the command at Council Bluffs. Both men were privates in Co. E.

[32]Companies C and D joined the rest of the unit on 19 September, and the next day the battalion camped at the crossing of the Oregon Trail, which parted from the Santa Fe Trail two miles west of Gardner, Kansas, on today's U.S. Highway 56. Both trails started at Independence, Missouri.

[33]The woman was Melissa Coray. Her husband estimated that over a hundred tents were "blown flat to the ground. Several waggons were upset. The wind blew my small wagon about 10 rods. I attempted to hold it as it started but finding the attempt was in vain, I reached for my wife, seized her by the arms & brought her to the ground on her hands and [k]nees. As we recovered I took as I supposed the last look of my old waggon whole & sound." The couple took refuge in a second wagon as "Hats, caps, handkerchiefs, fragments of tents & waggon covers could be seen flying in every direction." See Journal of Sgt. William Coray, 5. Elam Luddington's carriage "was overturned with his Wife & Mother in it." See Alter, ed., "The Journal of Robert S. Bliss," 69.

I called on Father Pettigrew and he administered to me and then prophesied that Satan would leave me.[34]

I, about this time, saw D. B. Huntington who told me that some of the brethren had defiled themselves and many witnesses had seen it with their own eyes and could witness against two. "That's my dream," said I. And it is this that makes me feel so bad and as I had warned them before of all approaching danger and told them how the Twelve had warned us to keep ourselves clean and now that they were sick and would call on the servants of God to pray for them in time of trouble. I felt to come out against all sin and disorder and let each man bear his own sin. If he would not repent of his swearing and adultery, I would not lay hands on them to bless them, for if I did, I should be ceased [seized] with the same spirit as I had been before and then be called to lay hands on a clean brother and he not receive no blessing nor benefit from the same. I concluded I would ponder upon the subject and see if there could not be some measures taken that would prevent more of such trouble in the camp.[35]

I therefore called on Captain Hunt and told him we had ought to have some meetings. He then appointed me to take charge of the same. I then call on Brother William Hyde and Taylor[36] to assist me and Father Pettigrew to open the meeting. I there talked to the Battalion as well as I knew how. I told them they must not swear and take the name of God in vain and told them that he that had sinned, to do it no more and for a long time I hoped they would watch over themselves and try to break off from the habit entirely. They said they would try to do as I had told them and all held up their hands to observe the things that I had said. Taylor and Hyde addressed the Battalion upon the necessity of giving heed to all of the requirements of Heaven. After which, the senior Captain addressed the same handsomely.

21st [August 1846] day. Some pieces of artillery pass by and many sol-

---

[34]James Pace, 35, from Tennessee, and Pennsylvanian Andrew Lytle, 33, were the first and second lieutenants, respectively, of Hancock's company. Kentuckian Thomas Woolsey, 39, was a private in Co. E whose adventures carrying mail for the battalion enabled him to become a member of Brigham Young's 1847 pioneer company. Pvt. David Pettegrew, Co. E, at age 55 was the oldest battalion member to complete the march to California. The zealous Vermont native had joined the command at Brigham Young's request to keep an eye on the moral conduct of the troops. He and Levi Hancock led an extremist faction that often disputed the authority of Mormon officers and kept the command in turmoil.

[35]Hancock's "trouble in the camp" apparently involved taking the "name of God in vain," but the unit's officers were simultaneously involved in a venomous dispute. Lt. Robert Clift asked Capt. James Brown's wife to persuade her husband to resign his commission. The night of the storm, Clift and Lieutenant Rosecrans held a "toast meeting" that called for Brown's discharge, "having disgraced himself as an officer," and for the replacement of Nelson Higgins in the command of Co. D with Lt. Cyrus Canfield, "to who it rightfully belongs." Jefferson Hunt on 20 August gave Clift, Rosecrans, and Brown a "complete dressing out." See Ricketts, *The Mormon Battalion*, 44; and Christiansen, "The Struggle for Power in the Mormon Battalion," 53–54.

[36]New Yorker William Hyde, 27, was second sergeant of Co. B. Twenty-one-year-old Joseph A. Taylor, a private in Co. A, was a native of Bowling Green, Kentucky.

diers [on] horseback going to Santa Fe, belonging to Colonel Price command, as I understand.[37]

22. At half past 7 o'clock, marched off from Hurricane Hill and continued our journey. Met a man that I have give[n] some rushes and olemack to the night before and it relieved him of his gravil complaint.[38] He appeared to be thankful. About seven o'clock, our pilot, whose name is Thompson, was taken sick.[39]

Here on the right was a point of timber, but no water. We continued our march south west and about 12 o'clock reached the old Jackson County Road leading to Santa Fe.[40] Traveled until 4 o'clock and put up near half mile from the road, left hand side. A mud hole afforded us all the water that we used here. A few trees and bushes was all the timber we had. All of it being green and no wood to kindle with. This day traveled twelve miles.

23 day. Traveled 25 miles through the prairies without much water and what we had was poor. This night we camped on the northeast side of a creek called 110, as it received its name because it was this distance from Fort Leavenworth. I have made my calculations, according to my own judgment, making all the inquires I could on the way, so I cannot tell how my journal will agree with 110.[41] This stream affords good water. Springs all along the bank. Good timber on the bottom—walnut, hackbury, pignut and mulberry and a considerable of a variety of timbers grow here. This grove is about 5 miles long, ae [?] wide. Other groves further down and some up this stream.

24th day. Marched through the timber and crossed Switzlers [Switzer] Creek. 8 miles from 110. Timber like it. Six miles further is Beaver [Creek],[42]where we camped.

25 [August 1846] day. Crossed several small streams with small skirts of timber. Made 12 miles and put the teams out to feed on this stream, lightly timbered. Two Caw Indians met us here and came on with us until night making 15 miles this day.

---

[37]This was the Second Regiment of Missouri Mounted Volunteers that shared the trail to Santa Fe with the Mormon Battalion. The commanders did their best to keep the Missourians and Mormons apart.

[38]"Gravel" is an old term for kidney stones. Hancock's "rushes" may have been similar to the purgatives of Dr. Benjamin Rush used by Lewis and Clark.

[39]Philip F. Thompson, about 36, first appears in the annals of the fur trade in 1837 at Fort Davy Crockett at Brown's Hole in today's Utah. Thompson, who had led horse raids at Fort Hall and into California, could have provided the Mormon soldiers with a wealth of knowledge about western geography. Thompson was later a captain in the Cayuse War and died of tuberculosis in Oregon on 22 January 1854. See LeRoy Hafen's life sketch in *The Mountain Men and the Fur Trade*, 3:339–47.

[40]At this point, two miles north of the intersection of U.S. highways 56 and 59, near Baldwin, Kansas, the battalion took up its line of march on the main Santa Fe Trail from Jackson County, Missouri.

[41]Hancock's numbers would not agree with this mileage since the distance to Hundred Ten Mile Creek was measured during the so-called Sibley Survey in 1825 from Fort Osage, not Fort Leavenworth. Fort Osage was located on the Missouri River near present Lexington in Ray County, Missouri.

[42]The battalion crossed this stream, now known as Dragoon Creek, just west of Burlingame, Kansas.

26 day. Having an opportunity, I now finish recording the operations of the Spirit upon me. On the 21st day of Hurricane Hill, I thought the Lord spoke to me and told me that my sins was all forgiven and what was done at the meeting was according to his Spirit, which overjoyed me so that I lay sometime in the Spirit, praising my God who is so good and kind as to manifest himself to me in such a manner.

I come to and Brother Wolsey told me that he had a dream at the same time that I was in the Spirit and I told him to prophesy and he obeyed and woke up. I fell asleep again and the Lord spoke again and I saw that I was made happy by the instrumentality of Brigham Young and Heber C. Kimble.[43] I glory to God in the Highest and on Earth, peace to man. The Lord is good and merciful. He has shown himself so to me. Let me ever praise him and do all the good I can for His kingdom. Keep me from sin, said I, and let me never forsake thee and turn from thy commands. Let me praise thee. Let me love thee all my days. Thy wisdom is great. Thy love is great. Forever let me serve thee and in this way did I shout in my heart.

26 day. Morning. Ordained Samuel M. Chapin[44] at 8 o'clock and continued our journey from Bear Creek until we had found water to drink. Some skirts of timber along the valleys sufficient for fuel to do our cooking and also water. The soil of the land is decently good. If there was timber to fence it, there might be some plantations on the right and left as we came along. We continued our march until we come to another creek, making 12 miles. Here we took dinner, baited our teams and then marched to other timber passing over some good land, other not so good and camped here for the night, making 5 miles further.[45]

27th day. Morning. Ordained Matthew Caldwell[46] into the Seventies, to be placed into some quorum when there was a convenient opportunity and marched 7 miles and put up at Council Grove.[47]

28th day. In the morning, before "Reveille" was beat at break of day, I dreamed that a nighthawk flew over the camp and cried, "peek," over all the tents, back and forth and then turned as bright as the sun, which waked me. I looked and behold there was one saying, "peek." Said I to some that was

---

[43]Apostle Heber Chase Kimball, 45, was a loyal associate of Brigham Young. In 1847 he became first counselor to Young in the LDS church First Presidency and served until his death in June 1868. The two men were the same age, both born in Vermont.

[44]Little is known of Pvt. Samuel George Chapin of Co. E except that he was wounded in the battalion's only hostile encounter in California and later worked for John Sutter.

[45]This camp was located on Bluff Creek.

[46]Matthew Caldwell, 24, was a private in Co. E from Illinois.

[47]Council Grove on U.S. Highway 56 takes its name from the talks held here in 1824 with the Osage tribe to ensure safe passage of the Neosho River for wagon trains on the Santa Fe Trail. Later it became a popular stopping place because it provided not only abundant grass and water, but also the last hardwood trees to cut for spare wagon axles. The scenic location is one of the most historic on the trail.

near me, I dreamed just now that that nighthawk looked like the sun for brightness a few minutes ago to me and said, "peek."[48]

I then called for the musicians and beat the "Reveille" and then I heard that there was a letter for the Battalion from the Twelve.[49] I then had a "peek" and it said that we must be careful not to take medicine from the Doctor. Some had been taking sick and Andrew Lytle said, "Brother Levi, this is your nighthawk." I then after this told the sick to peek at that letter when they would ask me what they should do when they were sick and then pray for them and lay hands on them and surely there was many healed at this time. Come on the doctor, Mr. George Sanderson, and surely Death and Hell followed after this man gave his charge to McAntyre,[50] our Doctor, and muckary was crammed down the Saints against their will. We had a new order of things all together. Lieutenant Smith had the command now by the consent of our officers. All power had been given up into the hands of wicked men altogether and all Mormons must submit to it. "Oh," said I, "when will men learn wisdom? God puts power into the hands of our brethren and they will give it away." This is proved out.

On the 29th day, when this man [Lt. A. J.] Smith come on from the fort after the death of Allen, who was a good man and an officer who loved to see our people enjoy themselves and had taken much pains to provide all things as comfortable as possible for the Mormon Battalion.

30 day. He was told that he as excepted [accepted] as our leader to General Corney [Kearny]. This being done, he issued his orders for marching at 7 o'clock tomorrow.

SAMUEL GULLY: IT BECOMES MY PAINFUL DUTY

Three days before arriving at Council Grove, Captain Hunt sent lieutenants Samuel Gully and James Pace, both of Company E, back to Fort Leavenworth to learn the condition of Lieutenant Colonel Allen. They

---

[48]The nighthawk is actually not a member of the hawk family, but is related to the whippoorwill. Its nocturnal feeding habits and monotonous, repetitious song, "peent," gave it superstitious significance in early American folklore.

[49]Delivered by Lt. Samuel Gully, this letter advised the soldiers to "live by faith, and let surgeon's medicine alone if you want to live, using only such herbs and mild food as are at your disposal." It marked the start of a bitter revolt against Dr. Sanderson, whose favorite "cure-all" was the mercurial purgative, calomel.

[50]Dr. William L. McIntire, 35, was a graduate of the New York College of Physicians and Surgeons, who healed mainly by herbal medicines. In recommending him to be assistant under Dr. Sanderson, Lt. Col. James Allen wrote that he appointed him because he was recommended by Mormon leaders, but "I do not consider him qualified to perform all the duties of his profession that are now and will be required in the Battalion."

arrived just in time to attend the officer as he died.[51] As decided by the fort's commanding officer, Lt. Col. Clifton Wharton, Pace carried the report of Allen's death to Brigham Young at Council Bluffs while Assistant Quartermaster Gully delivered the news to the battalion just before it arrived at Council Grove.

GULLY TO YOUNG, BRIGHAM YOUNG COLLECTION, LDS ARCHIVES.

Fort Leavenworth Sunday Morning Augt 23rd 1846

Prsdt B Young

My dear Sir

It becomes my painfull duty to announce to you the death of Lt. Col. Allen; he died ~~just~~ at 6 oclock this morning, with congestive fever, as the doctors say.[52] He was sick eight days. This Sir is to us a very great loss in our present situation, as he was a good friend to us, as well as to our people.

The companies are now ten days in advance of us. Lt. Pace is with me & 8 others who were detailed to take the staff waggons along. It is impossible for me to express to you my feelings on this occasion. We are here alone, and no one to counsel with. Whose hands we are to fall in, is yet to us unknown. Our men having left this post, makes it our right to make our own officers, but as to its policy for us to so, is to me doubtfull, until we get to Genl. Kearney. Coln. Allen never spoke to any person on the Subject; he requested me yesterday Morning to call on him in the after noon alone, that he had some private business with me, but wished to take a little sleep first, as he had had a restless night of it; in the evening I called but he was so much worse he could not make his business known. I sat up with him last night and in the night he requested me to lift him & called me by name, and that was the last word he ever spoke.

The Coln. has many warm friends here and many more in the Army.

It was my wish for Lt Pace or myself to return to the Bluffs this morning, but Lt Smith, a Gentm [gentlema] in the regular service, and Doctr Sanderson, the Surgeon in the Battalion objects to it and Mr. Smith seems to be inclined to assume some authority over us; if he should it will only be temporary, as we shall act decidedly, and as we hope wisely, considering our

---

[51] James Allen was one of the first buried in Fort Leavenworth National Cemetery. Special services at the Veterans Administration in 1977 replaced his gravestone, which had listed him as a captain, his regular Army rank, with a new stone listing his rank while commanding the Mormon volunteers as a lieutenant-colonel. See Harold Schindler, "Rites Honor LDS Friend," *The Salt Lake Tribune*, 16 September 1977.

[52] Capt. Henry S. Turner, Kearny's adjutant general, said that Allen was "a man of a few unfortunate habits which doubtless was the cause of his death." The most common harmful habit of frontier officers was an addiction to alcohol. Turner also said "there never breathed a man of a higher sense of honor; liberal to a fault, and just in all his opinions of and dealings with men." See Clarke, ed., *The Original Journals of Henry Smith Turner*, 3 October 1846.

situation for the future and accomplishing the thing we set out to do. We hope to act wisely and be governed by the dictates of the Spirit of the Lord.

We shall doubtless go through to California without having any difficulty to contend with from the Mexicans, & hope to see you all Safe there with us early in the next season. I hope if you should send us any person to return with the funds we might be disposed to send to our friends [and] that you will write some one in the Battalion, and give us all Necessary Council for our future welfare. We re[ceived]d news from the Command yesterday Morning & it is favourable there [being] but few sick none dangerously sick & most recovering. In haste your Servant

Samuel Gully

GEORGE B. SANDERSON: THE DEATH OF OUR FRIEND

Lt. Col. James Allen appointed Dr. George B. Sanderson battalion surgeon on 1 August 1846. Born in England, the assistant surgeon had been a U.S. citizen some twenty-four years when Allen recommended his presidential appointment. Called "Dr. Death" by his Mormon patients, men such as Elijah Allen complained that the surgeon "said he would rather Kill the Damed [sic] Mormons than cure them." William Johnstun recalled that the doctor's medicine "would kill a dog on short notice."[53] Despite the many protests about the doctor in the battalion journals, Sanderson was trusted by the battalion's regular army officers and was probably as capable as most military physicians of the time.[54]

SANDERSON TO YOUNG, BRIGHAM YOUNG COLLECTION, LDS ARCHIVES.

Fort Leavenworth August 22d
1846

Mr. Brigham Young & others
   Council Bluffs
      Gentlemen
   I have the painful task to perform informing you of the death of our

---

[53]Allen, Autobiographical Sketch, ca. 1848; and Johnstun, Reminiscence, 14 July 1898.

[54]Details of George B. Sanderson's life have long escaped historians. Local records reveal that Sanderson bought land in Platte County, Missouri, in June 1844 and married Ellen Johnson on 25 November 1845. Tax records report him living in Platte County in 1847 with eleven slaves, four horses, and fifteen cattle. In October 1847 he became a charter member of the Weston Royal Arch Chapter No. 4, a Masonic organization. Sanderson sold his large farm, Hazelwood, to Dr. G. W. Bayless in 1850 and apparently moved to St. Louis, where the 1860 census noted him living at age sixty as a private banker. See Annette W. Curtis to Will Bagley, 29 March 1999, copy in editors' possession. We are indebted to Ms. Curtis and the Mid-Continent Public Library of Independence, Missouri, for this information.

friend Lt. Col Allen of the Mormon Battallion [*sic*]. He died this morning about 6 oclock after a confinement of about 10 days to his bed. He died of Congestive Fever [and] was indisposed for many days previous to taking to his bed. Your people have lost a devoted friend and good officer. I am in hopes in fact I have no fears nor you need not entertain any [for] your people will be care taken of. The most perfect harmony has been preserved among themselves since their arrival at this post and every one speaks to their praise. Lt. Smith of U.S.A. will go out with them until they overtake Genl Kearny who will take them on in his official care. I am going out myself as Surgeon to the Battalion—I was appointed by Col Allen on the 1st Inst. and every thing that I have in my power shall be extended to them for their Comfort. Please to give kindest regards to Col Kane and had it been in my power I should have visited him during his illness. I have just learned he is much better. I am the honor to be your obt. Servt

Geo. B. Sanderson Surgeon M. B.

Without any evidence beyond his own suspicions, during the Civil War Brigham Young said concerning Allen's death, "I then believed, and do now, he was nursed, taken care of, and doctored to the silent tomb."[55]

Andrew Jackson Smith: I Deem It My Duty

Lieutenant Colonel Allen's sudden death ignited a controversy over his replacement that would embitter some battalion members for years to come. With Gully's report, Pace also delivered to Brigham Young an offer from Lt. Andrew Jackson Smith,[56] First Dragoons, to take command until the force overtook Kearny, plus Dr. Sanderson's assurances that the soldiers would be well cared for. Whether Smith acted out of ambition or a sense of duty is an open question. At that time, his orders were to escort a "large train of ord[nance] stores"[57] from Fort Leavenworth to the Second Missouri Regiment of Mounted Volunteers. Sanderson had outfitted a hospital wagon and was about to leave the fort to assume his duties as surgeon. He had been chosen by Allen as "a gentleman of the first respectability and of accomplished skill and

---

[55] *Journal of Discourses*, 8 March 1863, 10:104. For Young's reply to Sanderson, see Tyler, *A Concise History*, 154.

[56] A native of Pennsylvania, Andrew Jackson Smith, about 30, graduated from the U.S. Military Academy in 1838. He became a major general during the Civil War and was cited for gallant and meritorious service in the battles of Pleasant Hill, Louisiana; Tupelo, Mississippi; and Nashville. After the war he served as the first colonel of the new Seventh Cavalry, until succeeded in 1869 by Samuel D. Sturgis. The unit rode to fame on the Little Big Horn in 1876 under its second in command, Lt. Col. George A. Custer.

[57] Smith to R. B. Mason, 26 July 1847, S. W. Kearny Selected Papers, 1846–47, Utah State Hist. Soc.

attainments in his profession."[58] In the meantime, without waiting to hear from Young, Lieutenant Smith with the consent of Lieutenant Colonel Wharton, post commander, hurried to take charge.[59]

A. J. SMITH TO R. JONES, S. W. KEARNY
SELECTED PAPERS, MIC 139, NATIONAL ARCHIVES.

Camp Near Ft Leavenworth
Augt 25th 1846

Sir:

I was requested by Lt. Col. Allen of the Mormon Batallion, a few days before his death, to take charge of & select such papers as were directed to the Adj. Genl. U.S.A. & forward them to Washington. The enclosed are all I can find. The Batallion [*sic*] left the Fort several days before the death of Lt. Col. Allen & are now encamped at Council Grove, about 150 [miles] on the road toward Santa Fe. I am now on my way to report to Genl. Kearny and having his instructions to Capt. J. Allen 1st Drags. in relation to the Mormons, in my possession, I deem it my duty as an officer of the Government to have these instructions carried out. I will therefore with the consent of the Mormons, take charge of the Battalion at Council Grove & conduct it to Genl. Kearny, or until I receive further orders from him in relation to them. As no officer has been assigned to the command of the Batallion I am in hopes that my course will be approved of by the department.

I am Sir

Very Respectfully

To Genl. R. Jones
Adjt. Genl. U.S.A.
Washington D.C.

Your Obt. Servt.
A. J. Smith
1st lt. 1st Drags

BRIGHAM YOUNG: ONLY FROM AMONG OUR OWN PEOPLE

Young's response to Lieutenant Smith was courteous but non-committal, saying only that "Col Allen settled that matter at the organization of the Battalion."[60] But in his reply to Samuel Gully, pointedly addressed to the entire battalion, he made it clear that only the senior captain, Jefferson Hunt, should take Allen's place. Young also wrote

---

[58]Ibid., Allen to Adj. Gen., U.S.A., 1 August 1846. "Negro servants," probably personal slaves, accompanied both Dr. Sanderson and Lieutenant Smith. See Tyler, *A Concise History*, 150.

[59]Capt. Philip R. Thompson, First Dragoons, was subsequently appointed to command the Mormon Battalion. He set out from Fort Leavenworth on 29 September 1846 to overtake the command with three wagons and a small escort of dragoons. Thompson arrived in Santa Fe on 31 October, too late to reach the battalion. See Barry, *The Beginning of the West*, 647.

[60]Tyler, *A Concise History*, 155.

directly to Colonel Kearny to express courteously but forcefully the same opinion.

YOUNG TO GULLY,

IN TYLER, A CONCISE HISTORY OF THE MORMON BATTALION, 155–56.

Camp of Israel, Omaha Nation,

August 27, 1846.

Samuel Gulley, Quartermaster, and the "Mormon Bzattalion."

Beloved Brother,—Your letters of the 21st and 23rd inst., per Lieutenant Pace, we received, and feel to mourn the loss we have sustained in the death of Lieutenant Colonel Allen, who, we believe, as a gentleman and officer, had the affections of all his acquaintances. To such dispensations of Providence, we must submit, and pray our Heavenly Father to guide your steps, and move in all your councils.

You will all doubtless recollect that Colonel Allen repeatedly stated to us and the Battalion that there would be no officer in the Battalion, except himself, only from among our people; that if he fell in battle, or was sick, or disabled by any means, the command would devolve on the ranking officer, which would be the Captain of Company A, and B, and so on, according to *letter.* Consequently the command must devolve on Captain Jefferson Hunt, whose duty we suppose to be to take the Battalion to Bent's Fort, or wherever he has received marching orders for, and there wait further orders from General Kearney, notifying him by express of Colonel Allen's decease at the earliest date.

From the great confidence we had in Colonel Allen's assurance of the order of making officers in command, and the confidence we have in General Kearney and the officers of the United States, that they will faithfully perform, according to the pledges made by Colonel Allen as an officer on the part of the Government, we consider there is no reasonable chance for a question on the future command of the Battalion, and as to expediency, we know of none worthy of consideration. But should General Kearney propose any other course, we presume the Battalion would not feel disposed to act upon it until they had notified the General of the pledges they had received from the Government through Colonel Allen, and received his answer, and we know of no law that could require the brethren to act contrary to those pledges, or under any circumstance contrary to their wish. We trust there is not a man in the Battalion who would let pass the first opportunity of procuring the rules and regulations of tactics of the United States Army and making himself master of the same before the close of the year.

For the Council,

Brigham Young, President

W. Richards, Clerk.

BRIGHAM YOUNG:
YOUR REPUTATION AS A GENTLEMAN & OFFICER

The corrections and misspelled words in the following version from LDS Archives of Young's letter to Kearny mark it as a rough draft, but the Mormon leader's point comes across plainly enough. A copy of the final version has not survived. On 26 August Young instructed his adopted son, John D. Lee, to deliver this letter to General Kearny as part of Lee's secret mission to pick up the battalion payroll.

YOUNG TO KEARNY, BRIGHAM YOUNG COLLECTION, LDS ARCHIVES.

Cutler Park
Camp of Israel Omaha Nation
Near council Bluff August 27th 1846

General Kearny
   Sir,
   Having this day received intelligence of the death of Lieut. Col J. Allen, Commander of the mormon [*sic*] Battalion, and having understood that Col. Allen has had no personal interview with you, & but little opportunity of communicating in any wise since the enrolment of his command the council of the Church of Jesus Christ of Latter Day Saints take the liberty of addressing you at this time, to express to you their feelings & that of the People they represent, & we assure you sir that we deeply sympathize with you in the loss of an able assistant in your arduous calling in the death of Lieut. Col. Allen, as well as our brethren in the Army, in their loss of an able commander, one who had endeared himself to them by his kind, gentlemanly, officer like and fatherly deportment and secured their confidence & best wishes.
   If you have been apprised of the fact, it is not necessary though there can be no harm in our repeating that we were very favorably impressed towards Col. Allen, at our first interview, & that many were ready to enlist under him, but others hesitate[d] & question[ed] whether he might not be promoted, fall in batle, be sick or disable[d] from any casualty or circumstances, & the command devolve on some one of whom they were ignorant, & in whom they could not repose confidence. To Silence these fears & expedite the enrolment, that ~~no one officer of the army~~ the council refered the subject to Col. Allen, who on the honor of an officer of the Army pledged himself for the government, that no one officer should ever exist in the Bat. except, himself, only as they were created out of the Bat. & that the captain of Company A, would be the ranking officer in case of absence or failure of the Lieut Col, next capt. of Co. B[61] & so on through the commanders, &

---

[61]That is, Jefferson Hunt of Co. A and Jesse D. Hunter of Co. B.

repeatedly enjoined it on the several companies, & our People to be careful in their Selections of officers & to put their officers in such order as would Secure the best talents to the Bat. & their country, Should he not continue with them to the end of their enlistment. With these assurances, we gav[e] our fulest council to our Brethren to enlist & the command was Specially filled according to your wishes.

Having been apprised that an attempt would probably be made by some one, though not verry deffinately understood by us—to Suspend/precede the ranking officer in command, we thought it wisdom that you Should ~~certainly~~ be apprised of Col Allen's declaration, having the fullest confidence in yourself, grounded on your reputation as a gentleman & officer, that you would see that his pledges to us & the Battalion, were honored/redeemed, & fearing that the sucess [*sic*] of any one to the contrary might tend to a dis-union of feelings among our Brethren in the army which is so essential to their happiness and prosperity, & that success of any enterprise which you might require of them. We labored day & night increasingly to collect our Scatred [*sic*] Friends, & prepare them for your orders, and thus far we are happy to Say, we are fully Satisfied with the action of the government & officers towards them, as they have now lost a Friend to whom they were most devotedly attached. We would Solicit you, Sir to stretch out to them the same Strong arm of Fatherly Friendship Protection & care as was man-ifest in Col Allen and we can assure you that you will recieve in return the confidence & affection of the Same warm hearts.

Done in behalf of the council at the time & place above specified.

     W. Richards clerk   Brigham Young Pres.

P.S. The council would be please[d] to receive a communication from Gen Kearny at his convenience.

                     W.R.

We have unintentionally omitted to say that our esteemed friend, Colonel Thomas L. Kane of Philadelphia, who [you] have doubtless know[n] has been very sick at our camp is convalescent, & I think he will be able to ride in a few days.

                     W.R.

JEFFERSON HUNT: SMITH SHOULD LEAD US TO SANTA FE

Given Brigham Young's authority over his followers, which was virtu-ally absolute in all things, spiritual and temporal, his letter to battalion members was almost an order to mutiny if an officer not of their choice or faith were placed over them. But it came too late to influence the res-olution of the command problem. Three weeks before his letter arrived, Lieutenant Smith reached the Mormon camp at Council Grove on 29 August and moved at once to assume command. For practical reasons, the Mormon captains accepted Smith's offer. A chastened Captain Hunt later explained to Brigham Young how it all happened.

HUNT AND HUNTER TO YOUNG, BRIGHAM YOUNG COLLECTION, LDS ARCHIVES.

Santa Fe, Oct. 17th 1846
Letter No I

To President Brigham Young & His Council.—

We received your letter on the 28th of Aug.[62] and was much satisfied with the intelligence we received that the Church were in good health generally, but felt uneasiness on account of the news of Col. Cane's [sic] sickness. We were also well pleased and thankfull for the Council concerning the course we should pursue in order to preserve our lives and health. Our health's at this present time are good, although we have had a tiresome march and much sickness, with one death, that of Br Felps [Phelps], which we believe was caused by calomel & other poison;[63] although we have had much sickness and but one death our surgeon gains much credit from those possessed with the same spirit of himself, but we feel thankfull to our God that he has preserved our lives. The sick have not taken medicine only as they were obliged to by the doctor, and under the rules and regulations of the army of the United States which we were obliged to obey. We shall now take the liberty to inform you of our condition and circumstances in life, and the difficulties and troubles which we have had to encounter, also the distress and trouble which was given us hearing of the Death of Lt Col. Allen. When word came of the death of Lt. Col. Allen a query arose in the minds of some of the Bat [as to] whose wright it was to take command of the Bat. Therefore I called together all the officers together to council together what was best to do, as word had also come from Fort [Leavenworth] that Lieut. Smith was calculating to come and tender his services to us to lead us to Santa Fe. Now the question was, whether we should accept his services or not, or whether I should go ahead as I had done. The question was partially discussed and finally we concluded to lay it over till the next evening and that Capt. Hunter & Adjutant Dykes should examine the Law on the subject that we might be better prepared to decide on the matter, for there appeared to be some devission amongst us. Circumstances forbade us meeting the next evening, but the day following we met in Council Grove to investigate the matter. Capt Hunter produced the law on the subject—which went to show in every respect that it was my wright to lead the Bat. & that no

---

[62] This refers to the letter dated August 19 which instructed battalion members to rely on faith healing, such as the laying on of hands, herbs, and mild food, to cure illness, not the medicines given by Dr. Sanderson.

[63] Thirty-two-year-old Private Alva Phelps, Co. E, died on 16 September after the battalion surgeon "with some horrid oaths" forced some "strong medicine," probably calomel, down his throat with an "old rusty spoon," according to Sgt. Daniel Tyler. He was buried at the Arkansas River crossing.

other could lawfully do it, unless the parties were agreed & then by appointment of the department of war. So after the matter was all talked over it was
agreed that I should lead the Battalion and go ahead. The next day Smith came
up and I was made acquainted with him immediately. He immediately told me
what he desired and that it was to lead us to Santa Fe,[64] referring to the benefits we should receive from having a U.S. officer at our head. I told him it
might or it might not be so, but for myself I was willing to risk marching the
Mormon Battalion myself to Gen. Kearney. I was, however, but one and could
only act as such; if he wished, I told him, he could see all the officers together
and lay the matter before them and if a majority of them wished that he
should lead us to Gen. Kearney I would consent. Accordingly, I notified all the
officers and they were present in the evening, when Lieut. Smith laid his
propositions if our battalion were gone ahead, that the provision master was
not acquainted with any of our officers and if we should overtake him and
make out a requisition he could not officially know us, inasmuch as we had
neither commissions nor certificates that we were officers. Major Walker, the
paymaster general, addressed us; he candidly advised us to let Smith lead us,
referring to the many difficulties we should have to meet if we undertook to
go by ourselves. Our pilot informed us that it was the intention of Col.
Price,[65] who we all knew was our inveterate enemy, to attach us to his regiment
if we did not accept of Smith.

There was nothing said by our officers one way or the other in the presence of Smith and the other officers, save by Adjutant G. O. Dykes, who
stated our inability to make out correct pay rolls and other documents now
wanting without some instruction and I gave his views in favor of Smith. I
questioned Smith very closely on his intentions, if he calculated to carry out
the designs of Lieut. Col. Allen, stating that I would, under no consideration, resign my command to him, if he did not intend to carry out these
designs; he answered that such was his intention. When they were all
through, I requested that Lieut. Smith, the paymaster, pilot and doctor
should withdraw. I then told the officers that it remained with them, after
hearing what they had, to decide the question. The matter was talked over a
little, when Capt. Higgins moved that Lieut. Smith should lead us to Santa
Fe, which was seconded by Capt. Davis and carried unanimously. Smith was
apprised of this and took command the next morning.

Our commander, I have no doubt, would have acted well with us, had it
not been for a bad influence which the Doctor and pilot use with him. We
had an opportunity of seeing two or three times the benefit derived from
having him our commander. We had not provisions to last us more than half
way to Santa Fe and should consequently have had to go on one fourth or

---

[64]Here the handwriting changes, apparently from Hunter's to Hunt's hand.
[65]Col. Sterling Price was commander of the Second Missouri Mounted Volunteers regiment that
shared the trail with the Mormon Battalion.

one half rations, but he made a requisition on Col. Price and made him give us about twelve days' rations. This Price would not have done for us under any consideration had we been alone. It is true we have had a forced and wearisome march; there was for the better part of the time, however, occasion for this, as we would soon be out of provisions and were now past the time Gen. Kearney had expected us at Santa Fe. We have, however, with much anxiety got thus far, and shall continue our journey under Lieut. Col. Cooke. There are other matters which cannot all be included in this letter. I shall therefore write you another.

In the meantime, I am your obt Servt,

Jefferson Hunt
J. D. Hunter

LEVI HANCOCK: I HAD RATHER DIE A NATURAL DEATH

At Council Grove the battalion held memorial services for its fallen commanding officer, Lt. Col. James Allen, and buried John Bosco, a teamster for Captain Hunt, and his wife, Jane, who had died only two days apart. Several of the men gathered stones from a nearby hill and constructed a low wall around the graves ten by seven feet square and filled it up level inside. Under their new leader, Lt. Andrew Jackson Smith, the command then resumed its march to Santa Fe as recounted by Levi W. Hancock.

LEVI HANCOCK, MORMON BATTALION JOURNAL,
VOL. I, 30 AUGUST TO 16 SEPTEMBER 1846.

31 day. Traveled this day from Council Grove fifteen miles to Diamond Springs.[66] This spring is the best water I have seen on the route from Council Bluffs to here. Water in abundance, but no timber between Council Grove and here.

September 1st [1846]. Marched at 7 o'clock and saw scattering timber at the left. Three miles further saw some scattering trees at the left. Five miles is more. All about the same distance from the road. Grasshoppers now and then, one as big as my little finger. Wild Sunflowers, three inches diameter. Milkweed, white tops resembling white blows, but are nothing but leaves, green all below one third its length. We marched until we came to what is called the Lost Springs, it being at the bottom of the main stream, which stream is now dry. Here we camped. Here we had no wood, but good grass for our mules and oxen and horses. Making 15 miles traveled.[67]

---

[66]Diamond Springs is located in the southwest corner of present Morris County, Kansas. It takes its name from the sparkling quality of the water.

[67]Lost Springs, one of the more scenic spots on the eastern stretch of the Santa Fe Trail, is located near the little town of Lost Springs in the northeast corner of Marion County, Kansas.

2nd day. Marched 18 miles to what is called "Cottonwood Fork." All Cottonwood, some a few trees—walnut and plum. Some scrubs of other bushes. A few wild grapes. Here, Father Pettigrew told me he had ordained William F. Ewell[68] an Elder on the first day of September.

3 day. Marched 26 miles. Camped where there had once been running water by the looks, but now nothing but mudholes. Poor mud at that. It being made of buffalo urine, a good part of it. About twelve at night, the wind blew a shower of rain until day break. [4 September 1846] When the "Reveille" was beat and we prepared to move on. Started at 7 o'clock and marched until 11, when we came to a raise of ground and saw timber on our left, which our pilot informed us was the timber on the Arkansas,[69] at a distance of about 10 miles. Fine prospect here all around, but barren land, light grass. This 4th day made 20 miles. Still water poor.

5th day. At usual time of "Reveille," we awoke and prepared to leave at the hour appointed. When the "Assembly" was beat and all hands was on a march and soon made 10 miles, where we found wood and water. We marched on with a long halt until we made what we called "Little Cow Creek" where there is timber scattering, but the stream was not there, but a good place for it where it comes again.[70]

Four miles further is Bigelow Creek, where the mobbers or robbers killed the Spaniard. I was informed here the man offered them five hundred a piece if they would spare his life, but they would not and by doing the murder, they lost their own lives.[71] This is lightly timbered. I traveled up the stream and found where it looked as if there had once been a garden here. I found some parsley growing. I got my arms full and carried down to camp and it went first rate, it being boiled and tender. We put on some vinegar and it came a rarity. Not many thing[s] here to entice anyone to stay long.

Six day. Traveled over the sand and barren prairie for 12 miles and came to a high sand bank which overlook[s] a large space of desert all around. On the north, at the fork, was a basin which our pilot informed me was often filled with water. Here we had hope to find drink, as we was thirsty and found none. On the top is plum bushes, but no fruit.[72] They had been pick[ed] by the Army that had gone ahead, as we supposed. Marched three

---

[68]William Fletcher Ewell, 30, was a Virginian with a medical degree who served with his brother John in Co. E.

[69]Actually the Little Arkansas River, which joins the Arkansas River near Wichita, Kansas.

[70]The Cow Creek crossing is near Lyons, Kansas.

[71]Near here in 1843 Texan John McDaniel and a gang of Missourians waylaid and murdered New Mexican merchant Don Antonio José Chavez who was on his way to Independence with five servants, more than fifty mules, and two wagons loaded with furs and as much as $10,000 in money and silver bullion. McDaniel and his brother, David, were soon after tried in Missouri and hanged for the crime. Eight others were sentenced to prison.

[72]This was Plum Buttes, low sand hills with plum bushes around them where wagons on the Santa Fe Trail often rested in midday.

miles further and found grass but no water. Here we encamped, being dry. Our teams suffered for water much.

Seventh day. "Reveille" at break of day. Camp marched before breakfast 13 miles. Camped and took dinner. Camp killed a buffalo, poor enough. I saw many that were dead by the road, eaten partly by the wolves. I thought of what the Lord said through Joseph, his Seer. "Woe [to] him who wasteth flesh and hath no need. Every thing hath the Lord ordained for the good of man, both fowl and beast and things that climbeth upon the tree to be used sparingly."[73]

The land that we passed over today is poor and hardly fit for nothing, save it is a harbor for wolves and wild animals. Two o'clock, the Mormon sutlers killed a bull buffalo. It was good eating. These men were appointed to go with us for our merchants. They had many goods with them, very dear.[74]

8th day. Morning. We beat the "Assembly" and marched through the prairie, passed by some timber and found no water. Continued five miles further and came to Pawnee Fork, which made 28 miles. Here we camped for the night.[75]

9th day. Crossed the creek and marched five miles further and camped on the same stream off at the right, about one mile off from the road. As I turned out, I spied a paper done up, a string around it. A man handed it to me and there was a rag around another paper. In it was enclosed these words:

> Look for Indians. We had a man killed here last night by the Com-maches, as is supposed. May thirty first, 1846.
>
> Signed, Bramford[76]

This creek afforded us good water and a plenty of it for the teams. Feed not good, but better than some places that we have seen on our route.

10 day [September 1846]. Morning. Met some men returning from Santa Fe. Said we was wanted there about this time.

I began to feel sorrowful for the Battalion to hear some swear and some was sick and then see the men flock around the black wagon.[77] Some com-

---

[73]Thomas Bullock recorded on 25 August 1847 that Apostle G. A. Smith also invoked founding-prophet Joseph Smith's instructions "not to kill any of the animals or birds, or any thing created by Almighty God that had life, for the sake of destroying it," to the Mormon pioneer company.

[74]The sutlers, who joined the battalion from Fort Leavenworth on 18 August, were not Mormons. They were merchants who had been approved by the Army to follow the command and sell food supplies, water, clothing, and other items to the soldiers.

[75]At Pawnee Fork Lieutenant Smith "met an express from Santa Fe with a circular from Genl. Kearny directing all troops, wagon trains &c. to proceed to Santa Fe by the Semirone route." Rather than follow Kearny on the Santa Fe Trail's Mountain Route via Bent's Fort, the battalion would take the Cimarron Route across today's Oklahoma panhandle. See Smith to Mason, 26 July 1847, National Archives, copy at Utah State Hist. Soc.

[76]Details of this encounter do not survive, but the note was left by Santa Fe trader William Bransford, who in September 1846 was returning west in company with Lewis H. Garrard as clerk of Ceran St. Vrain's train of twenty-three wagons. See Barry, The Beginning of the West, 645.

[77]Dr. Sanderson's medical wagon.

pelled to take calomel or be drove out of their wagons and forced to walk or have medicine fed to them. The "Sick Call" must be beat at sunrise and then all that was not able to do duty must appear before his majesty, the Doctor, to be examined. Who would give them his poison to them according to his own mind. Who had been repeatedly [heard] to say, "I don't care a damn if half of them die."

Our would be Colonel said about the same. Sometimes threaten to cut any man's throat who should presume to give anything that had not been previously prescribed by the Doctor. This I thought to be too hard and as our Captain had previously told me to do on religious matters as I thought best in the Battalion. I considered it a principle of my faith to detest calomel. I came out against it and Brother [Edmond Lee] Brown, our Orderly, told the Colonel that our people did not believe in taking much medicine. "Well I do," said our Adjutant Dikes. Which showed how much he regarded or cared for the apistle of the Twelve.

Still, the nighthawk sounded in my ears, "peek." I told this to the Brethren and they said many times I had rather die a natural death than to be poisoned. Our people had been assembled a short time before to hear the military law read to them, which was death at every sentence or other punishment as the officers might see fit to inflict.

On the 11th day, morning. "Sick Call" at sunrise. Then other beats to answer the law. Then the "Assembly" and "All Hands Ready." March tune often played is: "California March."

This day we ascended the river bluffs and marched until we made 13 miles and camped on the Arkansas River. Here we found good feed, but no timber. Some flood trash made our fuel for cooking. This river is a curiosity in creation. It appears to be a river of sand with now and then a drizzling of water breaking out and then loosing itself again immediately. Dig in the sand and find fish. Sometimes deep holes of water with large fish. I killed some with my sword. Some men killed very large ones, perhaps four or five pounds.

On the 12th day, we ascended this river 20 miles. Some footmen walked in the midst of the river. Some rode horseback. I saw the tracks of five panthers. I saw where one had jumped all of 18 feet.

13 day. Traveled 23 miles further up the river.

On the 14 day, we marched at 8 o'clock. Ascended the river 19 miles and camped. Here was poor feed.

15 day [September 1846]. Marched 10 miles and crossed over on the west side. Here we were detained for some cause or other. Here some families was sent up the river to Bents Fort. I told the officers that I wanted it distinctly understood that it did not agree with my feelings, for it was told to us that we must take the Cimmerone Route.[78]

---

[78]At present Ingalls, Kansas, about twenty-five miles west of present Dodge City, the battalion crossed the Arkansas River to take up its line of march on the Cimarron Route. Before entering this waterless

16 day. We rested. Alvah Phelps died the night following. He had been sick for some time. He said that he knew he would live if he did not take medicine. I know that it was plainly shown if we obeyed Council, not one man would die. But, Satan strove against this principle.[79] There appeared to be an exertion used in favor of the Devil's ruling altogether. Phelps was buried in the night and we was surrounded by Missourian volunteers on both sides, up and down the river.

After the "Tattoo" was beat, Brother Brown, our Orderly, said, "look here and see this star." I looked and I saw a star moving up and down, between two stars as if dancing. I said this is a sign of something and this is what was meant when the Savior said that there should be signs in the heavens. Something will follow soon.

Accordingly, in the morning I looked upwards where the star was and to my joy, I saw James Pace, John D. Lee and Howard Egan about a mile off, as I supposed. I soon met them and had them by the hand. I told them that the camp was on the move or about to move. When they hurried on to let them know the news from the Bluffs, when to their said disappointment, they was treated coolly and no tarrying, but we forced on with rapid strides through the sandy desert, 50 miles without water.

I then repeated I wish we could go to Bents Fort. Our provisions are gone. There Brother Pace and Lee was of the same mind. I heard that the Colonel was willing to give up the command. We thought that the Mormons was capable of leading their own men as God had put it in their power to lead. But no, as the Adjutant said, when Smith came to us, we have no men who understand military discipline and so the power [was] given into the hands of an enemy. However, these brethren started on with us, trying to alter their minds and have them give ear to the Council of the Twelve.

FRANCIS PARKMAN: THESE ARMED FANATICS

John D. Lee, Lt. James Pace, and Howard Egan were not the only ones who met the battalion that day at the Arkansas River crossing. Coming down the river from the opposite direction, young Francis Parkman was on his way home after touring the prairies that summer. Suddenly he

---

region controlled by Comanche Indians, Lieutenant Smith ordered forty-year-old Capt. Nelson Higgins and ten enlisted men to escort ten women and more than thirty children over the trail's Mountain Route up the Arkansas River, via Bent's Fort, to join other Mormon families at Fort Pueblo. They were the first of three detachments of family members and disabled soldiers to be sent to the trappers' settlement in present Colorado. For the story of the detachments, see Chapters 8 and 9.

[79]Sgt. Daniel Tyler blamed Dr. Sanderson for the death of Alva Phelps, 32. "Many boldly expressed the opinion that it was a case of premeditated murder." See Tyler, A Concise History, 158. Phelps was buried on the south bank of the river.

came upon a wholly unexpected sight that he described in his classic work on the early West.

FRANCIS PARKMAN, *THE OREGON TRAIL*, 402–03.

The next day was extremely hot, and we rode from morning till night without seeing a tree, a bush, or a drop of water. Our horses and mules suffered much more than we, but as sunset approached, they pricked up their ears and mended their pace. Water was not far off. When we came to the descent of the broad shallow valley where it lay, an unlooked for sight awaited us. The stream glistened at the bottom, and along its banks were pitched a multitude of tents, while hundreds of cattle were feeding over the meadows. Bodies of troops, both horse and foot, and long trains of wagons, with men, women, and children, were moving over the opposite ridge and descending the broad declivity before us. These were the Mormon battalion in the service of government, together with a considerable number of Missouri Volunteers. The Mormons were to be paid off in California, and they were allowed to bring with them their families and property. There was something very striking in the half-military, half-patriarchal appearance of these armed fanatics, thus on their way with their wives and children, to found, it might be, a Mormon empire in California. We were much more astonished than pleased at the sight before us. In order to find an unoccupied camping-ground, we were obliged to pass a quarter of a mile up the stream, and here we were soon beset by a swarm of Mormons and Missourians. The United States officer in command of the whole came also to visit us, and remained some time at our camp.

In the morning the country was covered with mist. We were always early risers, but before we were ready, the voices of men driving in the cattle sounded all around us. As we passed above their camp, we saw through the obscurity that the tents were falling, and the ranks rapidly forming; and, mingled with the cries of women and children, the rolling of the Mormon drums and the clear blast of their trumpets sounded through the mist.

Chapter 3

"Under the Command of the Devil"
The Cimarron Route to Santa Fe

Of all first-hand battalion accounts, one of the most revealing was written by a man who was not even a member of the command. An adopted son of Brigham Young under a now-discontinued rite, he called himself at this time John D. Lee Young. But by any name, he was a major figure in the Mormon movement, a member of the ultra-secret Council of Fifty,[1] and one of Young's most capable lieutenants. Lee had volunteered to enlist, but Young had a more important mission for him to perform. This was to pick up the first service pay of the soldiers at Santa Fe and return the money to the faith's leaders at Winter Quarters in present Omaha, Nebraska.

On his thirty-fourth birthday, 6 September 1846, Lee left Fort Leavenworth with Irish frontiersman Howard Egan and his own adopted son, battalion Lt. James Pace, to overtake the command on the Santa Fe Trail. They carried Brigham Young's 27 August letters to General Kearny, Samuel Gully, and Lt. Andrew J. Smith on the command controversy; letters from family members to the soldiers; dispatches from Fort Leavenworth to Army headquarters at Santa Fe; and a message from Young advising Capt. Jefferson Hunt and the other officers of Lee's orders to pick up the payroll and instructing them to keep his work secret.

---

[1]The Council of Fifty, also known as "The Kingdom of God and his Laws, with the Keys and power thereof, and judgment in the hands of his servants, Ahman Christ," was a secret organization that included a few trusted non-Mormons. Created at Nauvoo by Joseph Smith, its purpose was to establish the Kingdom of God as a literal earthly state that would rule the world after the second coming of Jesus Christ.

JOHN D. LEE: TAKING MY SWORD IN HAND

It seems perfectly appropriate that Levi Hancock would link a celestial phenomenon with the arrival of John D. Lee, perhaps the most star-crossed of all Mormons. Thirty-one years later a firing squad would execute Lee for his role in the massacre of some 120 California-bound emigrants in 1857 at Mountain Meadows, Utah. A zealot, Lee fanned the fires of resentment and rebellion and joined battalion believers who disputed the authority of U.S. Army officers to discipline the men. Caught in the middle were Mormon officers who found it difficult, if not impossible, to reconcile their military duties with their religious loyalties. Lee's diary of this mission, annotated by the late Juanita Brooks and published by the *New Mexico Historical Review* in 1967, exposes the incompatibility of temporal and theocratic rule that lay at the heart of most conflict between Mormons and their neighbors during the nineteenth century. In it Lee shows why he was one of the best Mormon journalists of the day. His richly detailed account covers many subjects, from animals to weather to the order of march, all from a true believer's perspective. His battalion mission diary finds him at the Arkansas River crossing, near present Ingalls, Kansas, where he overtook the command on 17 September 1846 at the start of its march over the Cimarron Route of Santa Fe Trail.[2]

BROOKS, ED., "DIARY OF THE MORMON BATTALION MISSION, JOHN D. LEE,"
17 TO 27 SEPTEMBER 1846.

Commancha Indians
Desert Encampment
Thurs. Sept 17th, ë46

Morning clear. By day break we resumed our travel & at the distance of 5 ms the Bat. & Col Price's Reg appeared in open view—on the opposite bank of the Arkansas River.[3] Their sight produced no smawl degree of comfort & satysfaction to us & our faces was eaquely pleasing to the Bat.— on reaching the camp ground we found a part of the Bat. on the move. Feel-

---

[2]Brooks' complete work, "Diary of the Mormon Battalion Mission, John D. Lee," appeared in the July and October 1967 issues of the *New Mexico Historical Review*. The version presented here includes only a few of her excellent notes. Original notes by Brooks, with minor changes such as standardization of capitalization and the format of dates, are identified with her name.

[3]Lee and his people despised Col. Sterling Price and his Missouri Volunteers for the role they played as state militia in driving the Mormons from Missouri in 1838. In 1848 Price would mount an invasion of northern Mexico during the closing days of the War with Mexico.

ing anxious to have the Bat. stop until they could hear the decision & feelings of the council of the church at Headquarters, Capt Hunt, the ranking Capt, to my astonishment informed me that he & the officer[s] of the Bat. had Submited the command to Lieut Smith.[4] I asked him if the Bat. approved of that move; he replied that they had nothing to do with that appointment—I then requested an introduction to Lieut Smith—

After I presented him the letter from the council of the church, also read in his presance the views of the council in relation to the situation of the Bat. & the right of command[5] & requested him to Stop the Bat. & let them rest a day or 2 as they had been under a force march for 3 weeks traveling from 20 to 30 ms per day when the law under ordinary circumstances only requires 13 ms per day & allows 1 day in each week to wash; their feet worn out as well as their bodies—their sick suffering in the greatest extreme—one of the soldiers was burried a few hours before our arrival. (Alva Phelps) in the beginning of his sickness plead that no calimal should be poored down him that he would get well without it but to take it was death instantly. Notwithstanding his entreaties, the Dr. poored an even spoonfull of calimal down him & about twice that amount of the Spirits of Turpentine—which soon ended his career.[6]

Not adhearing to my reasoning he [Lieutenant Smith] refused to call the Bat. to a halt though great was the anxiety of the Bat. to hear, not only from their wives & children but hoping to be releived from the bondage & oppression in which they were involved;—feeling indignant at such oppression I was determined to free my mind & rid my garments of his sins. So I invited him to my little carriage to have some conversation with him. (Capt Hunt was present.) Said I, Lieut Smith the men of this Bat. are my Brethren we have (the most of them) suffered to geather for the Sake of our Holy Religion sufficient by the hand of ungodly men—without having everything now that tyrants & oppressors can inflict upon them to make them miserable. When I came up with the Bat. & saw the suffering & oppression of these Soldiers my blood boiled in my veins to such an extent; that I could scarce refrain from taking my Sword in hand & ridding them of such Tyrants. Lieut Smith replied that he did not designedly oppress any man; said I, you are the man that made one of the soldiers get down of[f] his horse & damn him threatening to tie him to the waggon, there drag him like an ox (when he was scarce able to stand alone—

[4]Lee's later report, using his diary as evidence, that Hunt, the senior captain, and other Mormon officers had failed to take command of the battalion after the death of Lt. Col. James Allen reflected unfavorably on these men. Perhaps for this reason, Hunt and others never fully realized their leadership potential in the church.

[5]The letter to Smith was Brigham Young's reply on 27 August to the officer's offer on 23 August 1846 to "take charge of the Battalion." It said simply that "Col. Allen settled" the issue of command when the battalion was organized. Lee apparently then read aloud either Young's letter to Quartermaster Samuel Gully, which said that Colonel Allen had promised there would be no outside officers in the battalion, except himself, or his letter to Kearny, both written the same day. See Chapter 2.

[6]Assistant surgeon Sanderson was applying methods used by most military physicians of his time.

burning with fever), unless he would report himself to the Dr. (Death) & take
what ever he should prescribe, & when the sick man begged the liberty of
being nourished with food & mild herbs by one of his Brethren—who was
verry skillful in bafflling deseases, your reply Sir was that if you ever knew of
our Drs administering medicines to any man in this Bat. that you would cut
his throat; the sergeon was the man to prescribe & administer medicine, when
you were knowing at the same time that he gave double portions of calomel
through spite, saying that he did not care a dam whether it killed or cured &
the more it killed the better, that the dam Rascals ought to be sent to hell as
fast as possible,—such conduct is incredible & more than what I can bear &
should I see him or your honor itself impose upon & abuse one of my
Brethren as you have done in times past I dont know but I would cut your
infernal throats. Those men are men of feeling & sensitive to the rights of each
other and understand human nature & to bear such treatment they will not.
They are now ready to revolt & it is with much difficulty that they can be con-
strained from rising up & bursting off the yoke of oppression. When Col
Allen had the command, the Bat had no cause of complaint. When any of his
men was sick he endeavored to nourish them & make them as comfortable as
circumstances would allow—if they chose to have their Brethren lay hands on
them & Pray for their recovery or administer herbs & mild food it was granted
& even went so far as to forbid any man attaching himself to the Bat. without
being Baptized first.[7] Col Allen was a man of feeling & regarded the suffering
of his soldiers, thereby Endeared himself to them & they would lay down their
lives for him & were you to take a similar course with them they would respect
& stand by you to the last moment. I consider the oppression here as great as
it was in Mo. They would say if you dont renounce Mormonism dam you I'll
kill you. You say to them if you dont take calomel I'll cut your damed throats.
I see no difference at all. I speak of these things for your benefit as well as the
welfare of the Bat. You certainly can accomplish more with love than what you
can by ruling with an Iron hand, & all would be better; for my part I would
not stand at the head of a people that was not fully satisfied with me as an
officer.[8] To all of which he confessed to be right & said would endeavor to
make the Bat as comfortable as possible. I expected that he would have

---

[7]Lee was incorrect. At least three and possibly as many as six non-Mormons joined the command at
Fort Leavenworth, but only one was reportedly baptized. He was John Allen, a private in Co. E, who was
drummed out of the service in 1847 at Los Angeles for desertion. The two English recruits, William Beddome, 17, and Robert W. Whitworth, 16, also in Co. E, may have been baptized, but there is no record of
it. Thomas Bullock's list of the Pueblo detachments listed Marcus Eastman, Schuyler Hulet, Richard D.
Smith, Madison Welch, and Maxie Maxwell as being "not in Church." See the Appendix.

[8]Lieutenant Smith's reputation for being short-tempered makes it highly unlikely that he would have
suffered this alleged tirade. Henry Standage noted that Adjutant Dykes "would not listen to Bro Lee" and
"said there was no time to counsel now." See Golder *et al*, eds., *The March of the Mormon Battalion*, 165. Lee's
story was likely colored for later recitation before Brigham Young and the Council of Fifty at Winter
Quarters.

chalenged me for a Duell but instead of that he never resented the first word—at this juncture of time we came to some water in the Desert for our teams which broke up our conversation—the day was very warm & dusty & water scarce—none in fact for 50 miles with the exception of 2 mud holes ½ buffallo urin[e] at least. Notwithstanding the famishing Brethren would rush into the midst of it & suck and strain the water through their Teeth to keep back the live as well as dead insects & mud from being swallowed by wholesale & after quenching their thirst they filled their canteens out of the tracks of the oxen & mules—others not having strength to reach the Swamp were prostrated by the way—Some of their friends would carry drink to them & as much as they could they would be put into the waggons privately, risking the consequences not withstanding the threats of the commanders—I had in our little conveyance from 3 to 4 sick which was in reality more than our little carriage was able to bear up with safety. There was some water hauled by a gentile & sold the same to the famishing Brethren for 50c a pint—This scene of suffering, oppression & distress was enough to rend the heart of a stone or admantive.[9]

I thought that the Letters from the council of the church togeather with my arguments & the oppression of the Bat. would certainly stir up the [Mormon] officers to stand up for their rights & free themselves from such lamentable Tyrany—when every pledge that had been made on the part of the acting Col was forfeited, saying nothing about the ilegality of submitting the command in which they not only refused to send out express to Gen Kerney informing him of the Pledge made by Col Allen &c according to the discussion of the council, but appointment of Capt J. D. H [Jesse D. Hunter], [Daniel C.] Davis, & L[orenzo] Clark Lieut to wait upon me & inform me that I had no right to abuse their commander Lieut Smith whom they had appointed. Neither the Seargeant, & in fact Capt Hunt was heard to say in the presance of his Co— A when Bro E Averett insisted that the command should rest in the Bat. at least, until Lieut Pace should return that they might have the mind of the council—on the future command of the Bat. (Thought nonsense, what do the 12 have to do with counceling this Bat. They may council in spiritual matters at home but with us they have nothing to do.) & adjutant Dykes[10] also at the

---

[9]This account of the march over the fifty-mile stretch of the Cimarron Route to the first watering hole is contrasted with that of Azariah Smith, who described the region as "a beautifull Prairy," but said "a good many mules and oxen gave out to day, and some of the men had to go without their supper." See Bigler, ed., *The Gold Discovery Journal of Azariah Smith*, 27.

[10]One of the most important posts held by a Mormon in the battalion was that of battalion adjutant. George P. Dykes was recommended by Brigham Young and appointed by Colonel Allen. Perhaps because he was influential, several of the men in the ranks spoke disparagingly of him. Dykes served until 1 November, when at his own request he was returned to take charge of Co. D in the absence of Capt. Nelson Higgins.— *Juanita Brooks*.

Bluffs said he wondered if the President was so foolish as to think that this Bat would stop 2 hours at his request to make him out a Muster Roll. Hunter replied that Allen would stop 2 weeks at the request of Pres B Young. When quartermaster Gully came up with the Bat. he also wished to wait the return of Lieut Pace—before an action should take place & urged the propriety of sending an express to Gen Kerney fourthwith, Andrew Lytle[11] concurred But was over ruled by Shelton[12] the officers assistant commissory & adjutant Dykes who were the ringtail leaders— they appeared to know more law than all Iseral [sic]. Plead entire ignorance to the law on the part of the Bat. saying there was not a man in the Bat. that could make out a correct report return or requisition, therefore urged the necessity of submitting the command to Lieut Smith who was an efficient officer & skilled in the military requirements, that it would be a great advantage to the Bat. & thus intimidates the officers; Lieut Gully replied that he had no objection to the adjutants pleading his own ignorance but never never wanted him to say ignorance about this people again while he had breath—to a gentile—he would be ashamed to acknowledge that the world knew more than the Saints holding the Priesthood. Lieut Smith said that Col Price would attach this Bat to his regiment—unless they would yeild the command to him, neither could they draw rashons as the officers had no commission, hence could not make out a requisition officially to draw provisions. But he (Smith) being a United States Officer could sign & receipt officially & would carry out Allens Pledges, preserve them from impositions & would lead them to Gen. Kerneys. He in this way together with A G Dykes Com. Shelton on law speeches intimidated the officers until they suffered Lieut Smith to impose himself on the Bat. as their commander. As soon as he had gained his point he put the Bat. under a forced march, run down the teams of Families—then sent them to Bent Ft—detached 12 men to guard them to that Point, taking the Bat. [over] the Simeroan [Cimarron] rout direct to Santefe, thus violating the first Pledge [not to divide the Battalion]; & continue so to do to the greatest extreme, however he had policy in taking this course which was to reach Gen. Kerney before the messenger should return from Head Quarters for [he] well knew that our People would not approbate the course that he had taken. Traveled 26 ms & encamped in the Desert without wood or water. Dis 26 miles, total 400 Ms.

---

[11]Second Lt. Andrew Lytle of Co. E, like Samuel Gully and James Pace, was an adopted son of John D. Lee. Lytle led a party of battalion veterans to Winter Quarters in 1847 and was a captain in the 1851 Mormon emigration to southern California. He served as a colonel in the Nauvoo Legion in Utah and as a ranger in the California state militia. Lytle died in San Bernardino in 1870.

[12]Sebert C. Shelton, quartermaster of Co. D, was accompanied by his wife and five children. He and his family were sent with Captain Higgins to Pueblo where they wintered.

New Mexico, Shian Nation
Fri, Sept 18th, 1846

Morming clear, wind S—at 4 A M Tattoo was beat, all was rallied, teams up & on the march. Through the day I obtained a promise that when we got to the Simerone [Cimarron] Springs that we should draw their pay. About 4 P M we reached a water course in the plain where we encamped for the night. Here for the first [time] was grass in abundance but of a harsh nature. I called this creek (Skull Creek) as there were several human skulls and bones with all the teeth in them where probably a battle had been fought.[13] Dis 24 ms, Total 424 m.

Skull Creek Encampment
New Mexico, Shian Indians
Sat, Sept 19th,'46

At 3 morning Tattoo was beat for all to be on the march & about 11 we reached the Simerone Springs[14] & formed the Encampment on the North where we remained till 6 the following morning—the setlers [sutlers] came & demanded the letters that I had for them and for individuals in Santefe.[15] I told him for $10.00 he could have the mail without I would keep it & take it back to Ft Leavenworth. Upon these conditions he took the mail—The Bat. were engaged in writing to their Friends—expecting to draw [pay] & that an oppertunity would [be] presented to send back letters (to their Friends) but in this we were again disapointed. The pay master said it was unlawful to pay in checks or in any larger amount than what is due each individual, & they had no Smawl change—but would have it when they would get to Santefe—This I supposed as usual was a Pretext to put of[f] the payment—at this place I concluded to make an other effort to have Gen Kearney's letter from Head Quarters post-haste before an express would be sent from Lieut Smith—[16] & in order to effect this without Suspicion—I offered to bear it in co with Br Egan—which we would have done without Lieut Smith's knowledge until it was accomplished—Capt Davis said that he would notify the officers to meet at Lieut Gulley's Tent.[17] Bro Hancock,

---

[13]The correct name then and today is Sand Creek.

[14]At this place, properly named Wagon Bed Springs or Lower Springs, a Comanche war party fifteen years before had ambushed and killed thirty-two-year-old Jedediah S. Smith, perhaps the most renowned explorer in Western history. It is located near the confluence of the normally dry Cimarron River forks, near Ulysses, Kansas.

[15]The sutlers sold their goods, including water, at exorbitant prices to all U.S. troops on the trail to Santa Fe, including the Missouri regiment with which the Mormon Battalion shared the road.

[16]Lee now proposed to deliver personally Brigham Young's letter to Kearny without Lieutenant Smith's knowledge, telling the general that Col. James Allen had promised that only Allen or a Mormon officer would ever command the battalion. If Allen made such a commitment, he clearly exceeded his authority. Young's letter to Kearny is presented in Chapter 2.

[17]The Mormon officers were nearing the end of their patience for Lee and the "numerous revelations, visions, and prophecies" he and his fellow zealots claimed justified their conduct. See Christiansen, "The Struggle for Power in the Mormon Battalion," 61.

Dykes, Lyttle, Parke,[18] & myself met, waited till about 10 when we were told
that a Private council was convened at Capt Hunt's tent but for what cause
we were ignorant. Yet the Spirit manifest[ed] that all was not well—we
united our hearts (after A J Dyke returned) in prayer to him that hears in
secret & asked him to have compassion on this afflicted and oppressed People, to heal them of their sickness that they be not compelld to report themselves to the devilish infernal old Dr. & to comfort the hearts of his
Saints—& went to our Rest. Dis. 12 ms—436.

Province of Texas, or of Mexico
Commancha & Shiane Naitions
Sept, Sund 20th, 1846

Morning clear, W S. About 6 Capt Hunt informed me that a council
would be held at Lieut Paces, Lytle's & Gully's Markee the place where we
lodged at 7 eve. At 7 the Bat took up the line of March, traveled up the
Symeroan [Cimarron] Creek the dis of 15 ms—over a broken barren sandy
gravely Desert—over the face those plains are a variety of wild herbs—such
as Sage, Rue, Tanzy, Hysop, & wild Symblins [cymblings]—& Buffalloo, Elk,
Antelopes, different species of wolves, Prairie Fox, one of which I shot—it
was almost white—Hairs. Those animals are about 3 times as large as our
common Hairs or rabbits & are black grey & white—There are an other animal found in great abundance here of the dog specia—they burrow in the
earth & are about twice as large as the wharf rat—but resemble the common
cur fiste[?][19]—About 3 encamped on the North side of the Simerone River.
At this as well as at all the streams in & through those Deserts we have to dig
for water & sink barrels to prevent sand from caving in. Water can be had from
2 to 4 ft. as a general thing. At 7 the officers met agreeable to appointment.
Lieut Pace & myself were visiting the sick as there were many sick and the
most of them would rather do any[thing] consistantly than to be reported to
Sanderson. We were at last sent for—Capt. Hunt said it [was] customary for
the man that appointed the Ball to open it—then proceeded & said that Bro
Lee considered he was insulted by not being permitted to meet with us,
according to appointment. The reason we did not me[e]t at Bro Lee's quarters
was the Capt's wished to meet alone; Bro Lee said that he wasn't offended for
that move—but his feelings were injured when the comitee were sent to wait
upon him—when the Capt's or some of them at least verry [well] knew—that
his views & feelings were not as the committee represented.

---

[18]Juanita Brooks identified Parke as Pvt. William A. Park, Co. E, who later wintered at Pueblo and died
in Knobnoster, Missouri, in 1915. This may have been one of two James P. Parks, both of whom apparently marched to California in Co. B.

[19]Lee described the common prairie dog, *Cynomys ludovicianus*, which despite its name is a burrowing
rodent and not a canine. Five similar species of these close relatives of marmots and ground squirrels were
once common on the Great Plains from Saskatchewan to northern Mexico.

ANDREW LYTLE as a ranger in the California state militia. John D. Lee shared Lytle's "Markee" (or tent) on the march to Santa Fe. *Courtesy, the Norman F. Feldheym Central Library, San Bernardino.*

J. D. Hunter, Capt,[20] said that Bro Lee had not as sound [a] right to be hurt as we have. He came here & assumed the right to dictate [to] this Bat. & even went so far as to light on our commander & Seargon [surgeon] whom we have appointed—& abuse them which we considered to be an insult, & that he was out of his place, & if he bore that express to Gen Kearney he must wait till we give him the liberty of having this honor, if we have got in a bad scrape we are the Boys that can get out of it our selves & when we want help we will call on him & now we will have a drawn game & if Bro Lee will confess that we have as good reason to be hurt, at his conduct; as he has at ours we will drop it. Bro Lee replied that they had no right to confer that honor on him as they had submited the command to Lieut. Smith & should it reach his ears he would veto it. Father Petigrew[21] said that it was [his] mind to send an express to General Kearney immediately to carry out the Pres. (Young) council. Pres. L. Hancock was of the same mind & said he believed there was a good spirit in the council. Capt Hunt—said that he knew better that there was not 5 men in the council of the same mind.—& that Bro Lee & Egan [had] been stirring up the Bat to revault [revolt], that

---

[20]Forty-one-year-old Jesse D. Hunter was a native of Kentucky and captain of Co. B. His second wife, Lydia, one of the four women who traveled with the command to California, died in 1847 at San Diego. After his discharge, Hunter was appointed U.S. Indian agent at San Luis Rey and remained in California, where he died at Los Angeles in 1877.

[21]David Pettegrew was a leader of the faction that sided with Lee and opposed Lt. A. J. Smith and most Mormon officers.

they had no right to council this Bat., that he must (Lee) be put down. The
soldiers are now saying if we had a commander to stand up for our rights as
Bro (Lee) does we would not suffer and be oppressed as we are unless this
influence is stoped he will be our commander & here is Lieut Pace come
here full of the devil & has been ever since, & Bro Hancock he gets up &
spouts round & I have to put him down. No one has a right to council this
but myself & my authority I will exercise in the Name of the Lord & no
man shall take it from me.

Bro Lee said that he did not want the command of the Bat & had Capt
Hunt been as willing to have used his authority in behalf of the Bat. as he
is to exercise it over his best Friend & Bro—there would have been no cause
of complaint—& as for Bro Egan he did not wish to have his name calld
in question as he has had nothing to say Pro nor Con & if there is blame
to be attached let it be on him (Lee). Lieut Gully said that he didn't think
that Bro Lee intended to cause any feelings in the Bat. or do any thing
wrong—Lieut G W Rosecrance[22]—Lytle— Ludington[23] & several others
concurrd in the same—Lieut Pace said the course taken by the officers
reminded me of the circumstances of Moses slaying the Egyptian because
of the oppression of his Brethren—The next day when he saw some of his
Brethren contending with each other he told them that they ought [not] to
strive with each other—they replied will you sley us as you did the Egyptian yesterday & Moses had to flee; The Brethren without [exception] said
that Bro Pace's remarks were too true—& if the officers could get out of
their own scrapes—they would be glad to take them out of the difficulties
which they had got them in—Cap't Hunt said that [he] had the best feelings for these men & we will pay our Portion for their board while they are
with us. Bro Egan was invited to speak in as much as he had not said anything either way,—Bro Egan said that the reason he was silent was because
he saw that they did not want any council. So he thought that in as much
as they had burned their backsides they might sit on the Blisters, that he
had been on board of a man of war for 3 years & has seen the time that all
was wanting to throw every officer over board was for some one to give the
word & this was the situation that we found the Bat in when we came;[24] So
I evaded answering the question of the Brethren & told them to be united
that the times would be better &c. Meeting disolved leaving several persons

---

[22]Forty-four-year-old George W. Rosecrans was a native of Ohio, a Seventy, and first lieutenant of Co.
C. He went to Utah in 1847, but settled in northern California and ran a hotel at Dolores Bar and may
have owned the Rosecrans Quartz Lode mine. Otherwise little is known about him.

[23]First Lt. Elam Luddington, Co. B, 39, went with his family to winter at Pueblo. He was a native of
Connecticut.

[24]One of the most colorful of Mormon frontiersmen, Howard Egan gained a reputation as an "Aveng-
ing Angel" from his service as a Nauvoo policeman and the murder of his wife's lover, but he earned enduring renown as an overland captain, Indian missionary, and Pony Express agent.

to regret the jealosy & ungarded expressions of falible man. Dis. 15 m. Total 451ms.

New Mexico, Comancha Nation
Mon., Sept 21st, 46

Morning clear, W. S. At 4 Tattoo was beat & the roll calld—at 7 the Bat was on the march—traveled over a broken Sandy Desert, nothing of note transpired, only in the morning Capt Hunt was seen riding with Lieut Smith & was heard to say that he submitted the entire command to him till the Bat came up to Gen Kearney's; that he wished him to exercise his author-ity, that he had the right given Lee, Pace, & Egan their orders, telling if they did not hold their peace that they would be put under guard—Encamped about 3 P.M., dug & found water. Dis 18 ms. Total 470 ms.

New Mexico, Simeroan River
Commancha Nation
Teus. Sept 22nd, 1846

Music call by Revelee was beat at 4 A.M. the Roll was calld & all in motion at 6—The sick call was beat, tune Jimmy long Jo—immediately after the call, the sick are ordered to the Seargeant or Death & Hell, which is represented by the Black waggon which is under the controll of the Black Spirited destroying angel—1st Guard mounting is beat at 7, at this call the guard is appointed to gather in Co's. 5 m from this call is beat the Adjutant call, when the Adjutant appears before the music followed by the quick step march. At this call the several guards march to their posts on the left of the music in double files. This being done, the A. J. will say rear rank open order march, 2nd commissioned & non commissioned offices to your Post, march. The officers of the Guard is posted in the right of the front Rank & the Seargeant of the guard on the right of the rear rank (who may be 2nd Lieut). The officer of the day may be the Capt or 1st Lieut & has command of the guard. He may be stationed from 6 to 10 paces directly in front. The A. G. will then say about face (to the officers).[25]

New Mexico, Simeroan River
Commancha Nation
Wed, Sept 23d, 1846

Morning clear W. S. cool. About midnight Sharp lightning, Heavy thun-der, wind high accompanied with rain. About 8 the Bat was on the march. Traveled over a Barren Sandy desert up the Simeroan River—this Stream if a stream it can be called, is a perfect couriosity. It is called in the Spanish language Simeroan which being interpreted is Lost River[26] & derived this

---

[25]Lee's detailed description of the military procedure here is evidence that some attempt was being made to transform the volunteers into soldiers and to establish a military decorum. — *Juanita Brooks.*

[26]Lee is mistaken. The word Cimarron is an Americanism which in Spanish refers to wild things in general and bighorn sheep of the Rocky Mountains in particular.

Title from the fact, that it has no fountain or outlet, runs through a desert the distance between 3–400 ms. without a single tree, or very few at least to be seen on it—In traveling up this stream we frequently found running watter—but the greater portion of the rout, we had to dig for water. I have been told by the traders, that water would rise & run from 2 to 3 feet deep in the short space of ½ an hour and would sink again & leave the bed almost dry within an hour & what is still more strange when this water rises up out of the Sand or even by diging till water is found. Fish are frequently found from 2 to 3 inches in length—About 10, clouds began to obscure the atmosphere. At 11 we discovered the sculls of 90 mules lying in a row alongside of the road. Our guide Mr. Philip Thompson told us that about a year since Mr. Spires a Santefe Trader lost 180 head of mules by the cold wind & snow that drifted to such an extent that it burried up all the animals & but 3 or 4 survived[27]—it is no strange thing for snow to fall in this month to the depth of 18 inches—Equnotical storms are dreaded more than any other storm in this country; the earth is said to be 1400 feet above the surface of the Sea. While I am speaking of curiosity I will mention of an other, those litle Santafe Dogs that Burrow in the Earth have for associates a smawl owl resembling that of a Screech Owl & a large Rattlesnake those companions all reside in the same mansion—there are 2 Specia of the reptile or Serpent kind, There is a smawl dark ruff snake about 3 inches in length calld by the citizens or Natives Massasogos [massasaugas] which are very numerous & poisonous—another kind resembling the rough black lizzard are here known by the name of Santefe Millions—on account of the immense No that are over the face of the plains.

There is a Specia of the Spider that supass any thing that I ever before saw. They resemble our common black spider—though much larger—some of them are as large round as a common tea Saucer & have a white spot in the forehead & on the black-legs wooly & are said to be poisonous & are called the Tyland Tuly or the Asp.[28] Struck camp about 4. Wind N. W., heavy clouds N. W. & occasional thunder & lightening. Dis 14 ms, T 485 ms.

---

[27] At Willow Bar, also known as Hundred Mule Heads, Santa Fe trader Albert Speyer two years before had lost a hundred or so mules in an unseasonable snow storm. For years after, travelers on the Cimarron Route would arrange the skulls of Speyer's mules in patterns created to astonish or entertain those who followed them on the trail. Willow Bar is located in the Oklahoma Panhandle, some ten miles north of Keyes.

[28] The preceding description beginning with "while I am speaking of curiosity," is reproduced almost verbatim in the Journal History of the LDS church, but without Lee's name attached. Lee's record, in fact, is the basis for much of the Santa Fe Mission as given in the Manuscript History of Brigham Young. The living arrangements of the hawk, prairie dog, and snake are similar in southern Utah, where the burrowing owl and prairie dog bunk together. Snakes have also been found in the same underground house, but whether as regular tenants or as foraging for food has not been determined. The large black spider is clearly a tarantula.— *Juanita Brooks*.

New Mexico, Commancha Nation
Simeroan Valley
Thurs, Sept 24th, 1846

Morning clear, W. N. E., mild & pleasant. At 20 ms to 8 the Bat. was on the move. Some mules horse or oxen are left either dead or unable to travel daily. Last evening the Orderly Sergeants & Lieut Smith had quite a Spat, (LS) urged the necessity of having all the sick reported to the Seargeon, the Orderleys details the Treatment of the sick as well as the drug adm. by the Seargeont when the Sick is brought. They all agreed that he administerd Calimal for every disease, Rheumatic pains, boils, lame backs &c by G–d said (L.S.) you must be mistaken. Not so replied the orderly, our statements are true. Well Said (L.S.) you don't no what to prescribe, Neither do I & if the Seargeon kills any man he is accountable for that mans life—See here men by g–d was I to report 450 men able for duty & when General Kearney would examine them & find 400 only fit for service I would be put in Irons—then I would put the Ad G. in irons & he the Capts & they the Lieuts & they the orderleys & by g–d we would all be in Irons—the conversation was laughable & gratifying to me to see the off[ic]ers stand up for their rights—near 4 we took up quarters for the Night, near a large co of Traders, found water in abundance. Wind E high—strong symptoms of a Storm. About midnight turned remarkably cool, about the same time I was taken verry unwell, Seviere pains through my Bowels. Dis 15 ms, T 500 ms.

New Mexico, Simeroan R
Commancha Nation
Friday, Sept 25th, 46

Morning cool & cloudy, wind North, fuel scarce. The country So barren that buffallos scarce could subsist or were hunted out, for the Spaniard & French came even 50 ms East of this to hunt Buffallo; about 8 the Bat. received marching orders—about 11 we left the Simeroan River & on ascending the ridge—Several Peaks & Spurs of the Mountain hove in sight, I in co. with several of the Bat assended several of those Spurs—on the top of one was a cave the mouth of which was about 3 by 4 feet the stone around the cave were perfectly smoothe, of a sand cast, about the door of the Stone, were a great no. of singular characters—representing the Egyptian Hyroglifics. I would have penned some of them down—but the Teams were on the move—between 2 of those Spurs formed a smawl valley in which was a few Trees; the most beautiful for cottonwood & Hackbery that I ever saw, their green foilage appeared so fresh & tender, that it brought forcible to my mind the sayings of the scriptures—shall flourish like a tree by the side of the fountain that is well watered,[29] the country around is

---

[29]See Ps 1:3, Jer 17:8, and Rev 22:1,2.

parched up, at this place we haultd to water our teams—Several antelopes were killed & brought into camp, Some few Deer also—traveled 5 ms more & came to the Cold Springs—where we encamped for the Night—feed scarce, Buffallo dung also. Dis 19ms, Total 519 ms.

New Mexico, Commancha Nation
Cold Springs, Sat., Sept 26th,46

Morning clear, but little wind, Frost in the valley. At 8 took up the line of march & traveled over a Much more fertil country than we had the last 200 ms. the health of the camp improving. I have been called to administer to the Sick so frequent, that I became quite feeble myself—calling Father Petigrew Pace & Lyttle to administer [to me] which raisd me up immediately & but rear [rare] that I laid hands on & prayed for the sick of the Bat. without immediate relief—about 10 we met an express from Gen. Kearney to Ft. Leavenworth, also a Co. of waggons—from them we learnd that Gen Kearney intended to leave for California on the 25 inst, travel by way of Chewawwa [Chihuahua]—that he expected the Bat on [10 October]—At 2 P.M. another Spur of mountains appeared covered with cedar shrubs. At ½ past 4 we reached the valley called the Cedar Springs—but little for so many—it was with much difficulty that water enough could be had to do our cooking, no feed scarcely. About 7 Lieut. Smith started an Express to Gen Kearney by L. A. Stoner of Co. K U.S. Dragoons & Mr. Swington a Spaniard—Pres Youngs letter was sent, Quarter Master Gully wrote a letter for Capt H. [Hunt] in behalf of the Bat. requesting instruction, Stating our situation & soliciting the prevelege to winter North of Bent Fort & not going over till spring etc. Dis 15 ms, T. 535 ms.

GEN. STEPHEN W. KEARNY: COMPLY IN GOOD FAITH

Letters from Brigham Young and Jefferson Hunt reached General Kearny at the Rio Grande on 14 October, twelve days after he learned of James Allen's death from Col. Sterling Price. Kearny ordered First Dragoons Capt. Philip St. George Cooke to return to Santa Fe and take command of the Mormon Battalion. His adjutant's reply to Jefferson Hunt made no mention of any request, as reported by Lee, that the battalion winter near Bent's Fort, probably at Pueblo, but Kearny did pledge to carry out "so far as circumstances will admit" the promises made to the Mormons. Kearny expressed his confidence that Cooke's "prudence & skill" would make the battalion's new leader "acceptable to them in every respect."

TURNER TO HUNT, DIARY AND LETTER BOOK OF S. W. KEARNY (1846–1847),
KEARNY PAPERS, 18 OCTOBER 1846, MISSOURI HIST. SOC.

Head Qrs Army of the West
Camp on the Rio del Norte
Below Fray Christobel Oct 14, ë46

Sir:

I am instructed by Brig Genl Kearny to acknowledge the receipt (this day) of your letter of the 16" ulto, from Cedar Spring, relating to the Battalion of Mormons & the promises made to them by the Gen'l & their late commander Capt Allen, 1st Dragoons—the Gen'l will most assuredly comply in good faith with all the promises made by himself, & also by Capt Allen so far as circumstances will admit & will see that full justice is done to the Battalion in every respect—On the 23d Sept. Orders No. 30 were issued at Santa fe directing that on the arrival of Capt Allen with his command, he should be joined by a mounted Co[mpany] under Capt. Hudson,[30] & the whole under Capt Allen shd then follow the Gen'l on his route to California—And on the 2d Inst. when the Gen'l learned [of] the death of Capt Allen he selected Capt Cooke of the 1st Dragoons (who was then serving with him) & caused Orders No. 33 to be issued directing him to return to Santa fe, & take command of the troops which had been previously assigned to Capt Allen. The Gen'l tho' deeply regretting the death of Capt. Allen [as] a loss to his Country & to the Service—cannot entertain a doubt, but that the Battalion of Mormons will find in Capt. Cooke a commander who will conduct them on their march with great prudence & skill & who will prove acceptable to them in every respect.

Very Resp. Yr. Ob. Serv.
H. S. Turner

Capt Jefferson Hunt
Mormon Battalion

JOHN D. LEE:
KNOCK OUT THE BRAINS OF EVERY DAMNED RASCAL

As the battalion clipped the corners of today's Colorado and Oklahoma and penetrated New Mexico, the rigors of the march clearly

---

[30]Capt. Thomas B. Hudson commanded the Laclede Rangers, Co. E of the First Regiment of Missouri Mounted Volunteers. Before leaving Santa Fe, Kearny ordered Hudson to organize a mounted company of seventy or eighty picked men from the Missouri volunteers. These "California Rangers" were to accompany the battalion to California, but Cooke noted that Hudson's horse company "cannot mount themselves, and it has been broken up by order of Colonel Doniphan." See Cooke's Journal, 13 October 1846.

affected morale. John D. Lee righteously chronicled the conflicts between the unit's officer and men, which sharpened when A. J. Smith ordered fifty men and the best teams from each company to make a forced march to Santa Fe to comply with orders from General Kearny to reach the town by 10 October or forfeit the opportunity of continuing on to California. Lt. George Oman was left to bring up the rear guard as Lee and the advance party forged ahead to encounter the ruins of ancient pueblos and the first Mexican settlements.

BROOKS, ED., "DIARY OF THE MORMON BATTALION MISSION, JOHN D. LEE," 28 SEPTEMBER TO 8 OCTOBER 1846.

New Mexico, Commancha
Nation, Ceder Springs
Sund, Sept 27th,46

Morning clear, W.S.E. On the move at the usual hour, traveld the distance of 12 ms. over a broken Sandy deseret [*sic*]. Encamped about 3 P.M. on the left of the road in a flat near a creek called McCleeses Creek.[31] This creek derived its title from 1 of the traders that was killed supposed by the Indians. Water sufficient for the Bat. Dis 12 ms., Total 546ms.

New Mexico, Comancha Nation
McCleces Creek
Mon, Sept 28, 1846

Morning clear, W.S. After ceremony of soldiers were on the move, traveled 14 ms. Through the day sever[al] smawl Mountains were seen at a distance from about ½ to 3 ms in height, 2 of which were rather South of our route & known by their singularity & calld by the traders Rabbiteers[32]— Those mounds present a sublime appearance, especially of a clear still day—at the first glance I have frequently mistook those mountains for blue clouds—tinged with red. On these mounds (that is the larger ones) are abundance of game, such as Antelope, Deer, Bear, Foxes, Elk, Hairs, Rabbits, Turkeys &c which come to those mounds or rather resort among the shrubs which is the only growth of timber with the exception of a few scatering Trees & willow brush that appear once in a great while on the ravines & water courses. About 3 P.M. we came to the fork of the Rabbit ear creek— found abundance of good water & wood—but no feed. Traveled 2 ms S. W. & encamped in the valley of another Smawl Ravine, grass good for a

---

[31]They actually camped near McNee's Crossing of Corrumpa Creek, a tributary of the North Canadian River, named after a young trader who was killed here in 1828 by Comanche raiders. This scenic place is almost two hundred miles from Santa Fe, near present Seneca, New Mexico.

[32]These landmark buttes known as Rabbit Ears, or Rabbit Ear Mountain, can be seen for great distances.

Desert—Some water—could the insects be sepperated from it. Dis 14 ms., Total 560 ms.

New Mexico, Commancha Nation
Middle Fork
Teus, Sept 29th, 1846

Clear, W. S. W. About 1 P.M. came to the W Fork R [Carrizo] Creek, water & wood—but feed scarce, Traveled 4 ms on & encamped on the left at a smawl ravine—feed midling but had to dig for water—land some better. Dis 17 ms, Total 577 ms.

New Mexico, Desert Commancha Nation
Extra Valey encampment
Wed, Sept. 30th, 46

Morning clear & Smoky, W. E. Traveled over a roling sandy Stony plain mixed with Iron oar—in the fore noon quarter master Gully killed 3 Buck antelopes, however there is not less than from 10 to 20 of those animals brought into camp Daily—after a travel of 17 ms we stoped, watered our teams & cooked our dinner (4) & at 6 we roled out the distance of 7 ms turned out our teams to graze. Dis 24 ms T 604 ms.

New Mexico, Commancha Nation
Barron Encampment
Thur, Oct 1st, 46

Clear, W. S. W. About 5 the Bat. was on the move & at the distance of 3 ms. we came (to) Stillbetter Creek, called a hault, grass good. Orders was given to graze 3 hours during which time our victuals was to be prepared. Marching order was given, traveled 12 ms, Encamped in a valey—that was completely encompassed on the 3 sides with a chain of Rocks—called the Point of Rocks,[33] Water & willow wood, but grazing short. Dis 16 ms. T 620 ms.

New Mexico, Commancha Nation
Bason Valey or Point of Rocks
Fri, Oct. 2nd, 46

Morning clear, W. W. At 5 g[u]ard Montain [mounting] was beat, this call soon put the whole Bat on the march, 3 ms. calld ahault to refresh our teams & men with water which came out at the foot of the Mountain. We were here detained about 1 hour on acount of the Stream's not being sufficient to admit of the whole Bat. getting save it were by twos. Bro. Levi Hancock —J King & Session[34] assended this litle Mountain which was about 300 feet in heighth, while on the Summit they saw 36 other little mountains

[33]Point of Rocks, a noted Santa Fe Trail landmark, is a rock mound rising from the prairie in present Colfax County, New Mexico, from which flows a clear spring.

[34]John H. King was a private in Co. B. There were three battalion men named Sessions—John, Richard, and William B. —*Juanita Brooks.*

at a distance around them, on the top of this M. they erected a pile of
Stone—taking each other by the hands—at the same time offered up a
prayre—then called the place 3 Friends—reaching to the taulest ceder
broke of a twig—brought it down & gave a twig of the lightest to myself
then to Samuel Gully his Friend. At this place the Litle Tyranicle [who]
would [be] Lieut Col. [A. J. Smith] commanded Seargeant Jones[35] to take
his gun & knock out the brains of every damned rascal that disobeyed his
orders—this order was general—Seargent Corray[36] reported Bro. Wm. Follett[37] to the Litle Tyrant for insulting him, calling him a Negro driver;
because of his oppression, having been put on guard 3 days in Succession &
ordering him the 4th—& after receiving a Stiff damning from the T
[Tyrant] was put under guard, telling him damn him he would learn how to
insult his Superiors & that no officer should ever ask a Soldier to do anything but order him & should he refuse to obey the 1st order—shoot him
down or report him to me (the Lieut. T.) & have him court martialed for
mutiny & should any officer fail to do this, he would shoot their damned
brains out. Bro. Wm. Walker[38] was put under guard & drove along before the
Point of the Bayonett into camp because he was sick & unable to walk all
day, keep up & drive cat[t]le. The same day in the evening Bro Jacob Butterfield[39] was put under guard by Lieut Oman & Clark,[40] because he refused to
get up & travel—saying that he was sick & not able to travel—they however
forced him up with their bayonetts. Butterfield said that some of our
Brethren were a d–d site more tyranicle than the Jentiles were—Clark &
Oman then ordered the Sergeants guard to put the lash on him—they
instead of obeying, advised him to hold his peace & travel on as fast as he
could.

   This Sudden manifestation [of] Tyranny & oppression, was renewed
from the fact that the (L.T.) saw that the leading officers would suffer themselves duped & drove about at his pleasure; & instead of standing up for
their rights & that of their soldiers—they would order every man to bear it

---

[35]Nathaniel V. Jones was first sergeant of Co. D. Born 13 October 1822, at Brighton, New York, he
joined the Mormons in 1842 and came to Nauvoo, where he became a lieutenant in the cavalry of the
Nauvoo Legion. Large of stature, strong, fearless and wholly dedicated to the Mormon cause, he filled
many posts of leadership. He left his wife and two children behind to join the battalion; he would be
placed in charge of the guard that accompanied Col. John C. Frémont to his trial.— *Juanita Brooks.*

   [36]Twenty-three-year-old William Coray was first sergeant in Co. B. His wife, Melissa Burton, accompanied him all the way to California.

   [37]New York native William T. Follett, 37, was a private in Co. B. He lived throughout Utah Territory
and died in Emery County in 1887.

   [38]A private in Co. B, William Holmes Walker, 26, farmed in Cottonwood, Utah, and died in
Lewisville, Idaho, in 1908.

   [39]Pvt. Jacob Kemp Butterfield, Co. A, was born in Maine in 1814 and died in Taylorsville, Utah, in
1889. At 6'2", battalion records indicate he was the tallest enlisted man in the unit.

   [40]George W. Oman and Lorenzo Clark were first and second lieutenants, respectively, of Co. A.

& be in subjection to their Superior officers, saying it was council from the
12—& that they would endanger their own lives & lives of their officers to
resist when they verry well knew that there was not an officer in the Bat. that
had a right to put any man under guard or court martial him legally —from
the fact, that no officer had been sworn into office or recieved his commission since the enrolment, & Lieut Smith himself had not the command of
the Bat. legally, not having the vote of the Same. This I learned from Smith
at the time when he offered his Servis to Command the Bat. saying that they
(the officers) could not draw provisions as they had no commissions &c. &
in the 2nd place the little wolfish Tyrant was fully Satisfied that this Bat
would give their consent willingly for him to remain their commander &
that they knew that the right belonged to them & not the officers alone to
Elect the commander of the Bat. to Satisfy himself fully of this fact. Today
after meeting a co. of Dragoon[s] on their return from Santefe stating that
Gen Kearney had left about the 25th Sept with 400 men for California by
way of Chewauwah & that should the Mormon Bat. reach Santefe by the
10th that they should follow on, other wise be discharged & they loose (of
course receiving 1 yr rashion & pay).[41]

    The lat[t]er was rather kept dark from the Soldiers—they were told that
if they did not reach Santefe by the 10th that [they] would likely be discharged when they arrived without pay or rashions & left to make their way
home that dis of 2000 ms without help, at a time too when those [who] are
ever so well rig[g]ed for traveling, endanger their lives to cross those Deserts
& plains, which are from 2 to 300 ms without timber or settlements of any
size. This information too true, bespoke in every face, the fears of treachery
& oppression which they so much dreaded, not withstanding the fair
promises of the little wolfish Col. This last Scheme however was not
resorted to until after the failure [of] an other which I had forgotten to mention in its proper place which was as follows—3 Capt. Said he to some of
his wire workers whom he knew would figure with the Bat are now wa[i]ting
the arrival of the Bat. to take command (just before [he] acknowledged that
General Kearney was not apprised of the Death of Col. Allen, such report
had reached Santefe but he did not believe it). However this Bat. may retain
Smith as their commander if they choose, & thought it would be to their
interest to do so—in preference to a man with whom they had formed no
character—carrying the Idea that 1 of the 1 mentioned must be the com-

[41]Before marching west on 25 September, Kearny left orders at Santa Fe for the battalion to move forward and "follow our trail." To keep the unit within supporting distance, Kearny ordered a forced march
to the New Mexican capital. Lee spread unfounded rumors and engaged in speculation aimed to stir up
resentment and rebellion.

[42]Lee repeated the unlikely rumor that Lieutenant Smith warned friends in the battalion that three
U.S. Army captains were waiting at Santa Fe to claim the right to command at the higher rank of lieutenant colonel, but that the soldiers could keep him, if they chose, and would be better off to do so.

mander; I replied that the Bat had the right to elect any man in their ranks to take Command.[42] Seeing that ignorence would no longer bear up their impositions—they resorted to this last scheme—which was to reach Santefe by the 10th under the pretext that if they did not reach there by that time that they would not have the gloious prevelege & honor of being marched to California—through hunger fatigue & cold this winter under command of a litle Wolfish would-to-be Col.—to be discharged perhaps some 800 ms. from the destination of the church[43] & then be under the necessity of spending a part of their means to take them to their Friends and Families,—when they might just as well had 12 months pay & 6 months Provision, besides having the liberty of assisting & being with their Friends & Families to the place of their destination—which was worth at least 6 mo. pay more—4 of the capts were presant (Higgins yet absent) who cheerfully responded to the little (W T) Sham & said it was firstrate policy. Capt Brown in particular remarked that would be carrying the very things we startd for—Adj Dykes one of the principle wire workers in order to carry out this Scheme—proposed dividing the Bat., drawing 50 able bodied men from each co—together with waggons & teams Sufficient for bagage—& put them under a force march—in order to reach Santefe by the 10th to entitle them—as they said—to the liberty of marching to California—leaving the 11th. Remainder (which is the sick and lame) to come when they can, leaving with them the 1st Lieut of each to take command & the ranking Lieut to command the divisions—6 days rasions were arrainged for these that were selected to go ahead.

At 5 the division took up the line of March—The feelings on this occasion were almost indescrib[a]ble. The Idea of being sepperated, leaving the[m] behind—perhaps never to meet again in the flesh was more than many could bear—bursting into tears as they parted with each other—saying that they went; but not willingly for the council of the 12 was to them never to Sepperate. Quartermaster Gully begged the liberty of Staying back to take care of the sick, which was granted, Lieut Pace—Lyttle—Gully & Clark were uterly opposed to the project—Pace in particular was ready to revoult against such a measure. Many of the brethren came to me saying that they would obey the council of the Church, or loose their lives in the attempt. Come, tell us what to do. I replied, do as you think proper, your officers are over you.[44] Feeling almost over come—with Sympathy—I could no longer hold my peace—Said to Capt Hunt notwithstanding that he and

---

[43]This entry shows that Lee knew the destination of the Mormon migration would be the Salt Lake Valley.

[44]After stirring up resentment against Smith and some Mormon officers, Lee apparently remembered his assignment to obtain the payroll and backed away from leading a mutiny. Instead he advised the men to obey the leaders placed over them.

his Capts had banned against me, saying that I had no right to council them & they had got into a bad Snapp, they were the boys that could get out of it &c—yet as a duty that I owe to my Brethren & suffering humanity, I will tell you words by which you may here after preserve the feelings of your Brethren. Keep out, elude, or rather thwart all plans, snares, or Schemes that may be laid for the injuery of this People. 1st when any thing of this kind is proposed—I would as a mater of Policy beg the liberty of a few hours to reflect before giving an answer—then calling all the officers of the same grade—with the old wise men—that hold the Priesthood—making no distinction amoung them becaus of partiality, convene togeather with humble Spirits in prayer before the Lord that his wisdom might be in your midst— to direct you in your deliberations—while confering with each other— never disdaining or considering it condescending to recieve council or wisdom from any one man in the Priesthood; who may advance or propose.[45]

At the distance of 20 ms came to Salt Creek [Chico Creek], the 1st water from the P of Rocks. Traveled 5 ms more, came to red River where we found a part of 2 divisions encamped.[46] We too encamped on the S W ½ ms. from the river—wood scarce, feed good, eve[n]ing clear. Dis 25 ms, Total 645 sm.

New Mexico—Red [Canadian] River,
Commancha Nation
Sat. Oct 3rd,'46

Morning clear. At day light the Bat. was on the march, traveled to Oho Geauge [Ocaté Creek] the dis of 7 ms—called a hault, watered— cooked & divided the Bat acording to the arraingement. Fri 2nd started at 5 A M, came to the wagon Mounds,[47] dis 21 ms, found water & grass in abundance—the rear arrivd at 1 morn. Here we camp. Left Prices regiment at this Point. Met some Spaniards retailing liquors, cakes &c. The Mounds here are natural curiosity. Some of them resemble waggons covered, another the cuppulow of a Public Building &c. W—high S W, roads dusty, night cool. Dis 28 ms, Total 673.

New Mexico, Waggon Mounds
Wooharapahoo [Arapaho] Nation
Sund, Oct 4th,'46

Morning clear, cold, W S W. At 7 Guard Mounting was beat at which Signal the Bat. was put on the march—through the day several groves of

---

[45]The rest of the page is blank. Apparently Lee was interrupted and did not complete the entry. — *Juanita Brooks.*

[46]Units of Col. Sterling Price's Missouri troops.

[47]Wagon Mound was the last great prairie landmark on the trail to Santa Fe. As the name indicates, it is shaped like an overland wagon and is located near today's Wagon Mound, New Mexico.

Pine & Spruce were seen. Traveled the dis of 20 ms & encamped on the East branch of the river Morough [Mora River][48] excellent feed & water. At this is—a singular chain of Rocks & is said to be Mill Stone grit of the best quality, over the face thereoff is covered with Santefe Chinchapin Shurbs & Cedars—between sun down & dark 5 or 6 Spaniards came into camp with pies & cakes—to sell— told us that it was 4 ms to the 1st Settlements on the Moree river. W S W clear. Dis 22ms, T 667.

New Mexico, Warapahoo Nat.

E. branch of R. Morough

Mon, Oct 5,'46

Clear, W S W. At 6 we were again on the road—at the dis of 5 ms came the river Morough, a smawl clear river, beautiful flush running Stream fed by springs from the mountains—on this stream large heards of cattle, sheep, & goats principly Sustained by grazing through the winter, yet it would appear to a traveler a thing in credible—especially one who had been raised in Illinois or Mo. As to me there seemd scarce grass enough in summer season to keep Sheep alive. The grass in this country though Short & dry is remarkably Strong. At this place are a few setlers, one an Englishman by the Name of Jones. All others are chiefly Spaniards—through the [day] we crossed several clear handsome running Streams, Smawl ceder & pine on the mountains & creeks, yet not well calculated for rails or lumber—rather schrubby. After a travel of 27 ms we encamped in a vally near a Spanish town called Bagoes [Las Vegas][49]—situated on the head waters of the Guena [Gallinas] River,[50] good feed. The population of this place is about 500. Their houses are built of a kind of sun dried brick laid in mud sides bottom & top generally 1 story high. The ruff [roof] has but little slant & is not raised above the wall. The ruff and outer walls are covered over with a kind of cement made of rosin & sand which is said to be waterproof—the whole city at a glance resembles that of a brick yard—their Houses that of Brick Kilns unburned—only larger. The inhabitants are of a dark, swarthy, dirty, lazy, filthy, indolent, rag[g]ed & naked, uncivilized, miserable looking beings. However I suppose those living on the frontier are of the lower class, I hope so at least. They rase some wheat, Squaw corn, onions, red Peper Squashes &c. Their fields are without fences—yet they have large herds of cattle, sheep, goats, mules & some horses all of which are hearded day &

---

[48]A Canadian River tributary. Near this camp the Cimarron Route, followed by the battalion, joined the Mountain Route of the Santa Fe Trail that followed the Arkansas River on the present line of U.S. Highway 50 to Bent's Fort, then headed south over Raton Pass to this junction. Lee was traveling with the advance party.

[49]At Las Vegas nearly two months before, Kearny had proclaimed New Mexico to be part of the United States and administered to the local citizens the oath of allegiance. Kearny issued the proclamation from the roof of an adobe building that still overlooks the old town plaza.

[50]A tributary of the Pecos River.

night to prevent them from destroying their subsistence—Some feed their
stock of Nights. They cultivate the valley only & are under the necessity of
watering all the stuff they raise. I am told that there is no rains in this [val-
ley] from about the 10th of Sept till about the 10 of July—leaving them a
season of 2 months only for making their crops. To day the face of the
country is changed from a plain to a Barren wilderness—Rocks & mountains, but little land situated for cultivation & that is found in smawl vallies
between the mountains. Dis 27 ms, T 694 ms.

N M, Bagas or Spanish Town
Tues, Oct 6th,'46

Morning clear, Frost (Black) as there is but litle dew in this part of the
world. W.W [west wind]. Traveled over a broken Mountainous country—
about noon we came to the Town of Taucaulute [Tecolote], dis 12 ms. This
town was about the same size of Bagus, traveld 6 more ms & encamped in a
vally at another smawl settlement. This evening on the Top of the mountain—where we decended to encamp—we met Mr. Simington with 25 yoke
of oxen from Santefe sent by Gen Kearney for our assistance,—he also
brought a dispatch to Lt Smith saying that Gen Kearney had not heard of
the death of Col. Allen before the express came—only by rumor—that he
left for California on the 20th of Sept—leaving orders with General
Donethan[51] the commander at Santefe to have all troops that should arrive
by the 10th to follow on his trail to California—as he would be detained in
cutting a way through the mountains at a certain Pass—which would make
it much neyher [nigher] to California than the usual travel—about sunset
wind blew strong from the W which brought up quite an angry cloud rain
commenced about 30 mi to 8. It is now 9 & I am in Adj. Dykes Markee
[tent] bringing up my Journal. Dis 20 ms, T 714 ms.

Spanish Settlements N M
between the Mountains
Oct 7th, 1846

About 4 faired away. W[ind]. still W[esterly], quite cool. Started about 7
traveled between the Mountains all day—about 10 we discovered large beds
of snow at the dis of 80 ms or more—we were told by our guide that those
bodies of snow were seen all season of the year. Through the day I made it
to have a conversation with Adj Dykes, Lieut Smith & some others as a
mater of warm familiarity, the better to carry out the thot that I fell upon
to prevent the Bat. from being divided. Passed through St. Magill[52] (a Span-

---

[51]Gen. Alexander W. Doniphan had participated in the Mormon troubles at Far West, Missouri, in
1838, but refused to carry out orders to execute Joseph Smith. When in 1846 he was put in charge of this
section of the Army of the West, the Mormons felt that they had a friend.— *Juanita Brooks.*

[52]The town of San Miguel del Vado, or Ford of St. Michael, on the Pecos River was established about
1795 at the southernmost point on the trail that skirts the mountains to enter Santa Fe from the south.

ish Town) about 11, dis of 3 Or 30 miles from Taucaulute [Tecolote] or 45 from Santefe. At this place I traded some calico for corn—on entering the village I saw about 5 Spaniards engaged in hauling wood, they had 2 yoke of oxen hitched to some thing resemblng what is by backwoods setlers in Ill. called a wooden go cart, the wheels were not more than quarter round— their oxen were riged with a pole fastened to the back part of the Horns by Straps raw [hide] tugs—their manner of driving was still more strange to me—one man stood at the head of the catle with a stick perhaps 2 feet in length & gave the word of command, 2 more men were placed on each side with a pole in their hands, Something smawler than a common rake handle, & were made some what pointing at the end which they used as we would Spears; this However was more than an ordinary circumstance, the load was remarkably heavy & road bad. Their ploughs are made entirely of wood yet not resembling any thing that I ever before saw. In this village is a regular built Catholic Chappel & the only resemblance that I saw was the cross on one of the cupeloes—as there was one on each corner fronting to the East. All buildings here are built of untempered mourtars. Arround the chapel, the Priest residence, & some of the Public houses were enclosed by mud walls from 10 to 12 feet high—their pounds or enclosures for their stock, when penned are built in like manner—There is certainly less enterprise, industry, or economy manifestd among these beings than any others, who pretend at all to civilization—Their principal way of conveyance is upon Mules asses & smawl horses—it is truly astonishing to see the immense loads that are carried by these beasts of burden. It is nothing uncommon to see a barrel of salt or whiskey beside other loading fastened upon one of these animals, the barrel is placed on a frame made for that purpose & set lengthwise on the back. When ever we would hault near their settlements (as they all settle in villages) our lines would be filled with them coming to trade—their principle trafic to travelers is corn (which in their tongue is Mice [maize]—onions, Peper, Squashes, whiskey, apples & mellons & in fact they will trade any thing they have—nothing is measured among them but Whiskey & a quart with them is but little more than a pint of our mea- sure—at 5 we encamped at one of their settlements at a beautiful stream of water I mi North of the Road. Evening clear & cool, W S W. Dis 20ms, T734 ms.

Spanish Settlements, River, N M

Thurs, Oct 8th, 46

Morning clear, W S W. The Bat was on the march in due season, at the distance of 13 ms came to first rate Spring of water that gushed out of N bank of Paco Creek (which is the name of creek that runs between the mountains—on our route). Arround this Spring are Silver ore in abundance—near the same Stands the walls & many of the rooms of a large ancient Mexican or Nephite building—built entirely of clay, sand & rosin cemented together. Some of the walls were about 50 feet in heighth. I should think there were about 40 rooms & apartments. The most of the [wood]work were carved & exhibit far more art & ingenuity than the present race who now inhabit those regions can produce. I was told by the Pilott (who has been in the Spanish trade for 25 years) that this Building was discovered about 250 years ago—which was about the time Santefe was Setled—the whole structure at a glance exhibits great antiquity.[53] We traveled 2 more ms stopped & fed, & while my mules were eating improved the time in writing. Along in this valley are additional growths of timber the Palm trees & the Balm of Gillead or rather Satefe [sic] in this valey—while I was sitting here an Express passed from Gen Kearney instructing the Mormon Bat. that as soon as he heard of the death of Col Allen—& that Lt Smith was at their head he appointed Capt Cook to the office of Lieut Col. to take command of the Bat & to lead them on to California as soon as they would reach Santefe—This information struck Lieut Smith and Adj Dykes as well as many others of the officers almost speechless as they had been anticipating some thing verry different, yet it was just what I predicted to Capt Hunt & the officers of the Bat. when they refused to send Pres's Young's letter immediately to Gen Kearney apprising him of the Death of Allen & of his pledge to the Bat.

What favorable impression might have been made in time—but instead of doeing this—I was overruled & the letter was delayed untill Smith's Express reached him & in fact it is doubtful whether Kearney has yet received the letter referred to. Kearney is now about 150 ms from Santefe & I look for nothing else than to see the officers [agree] to the preasant arraingments without ever assertaining whether Gen Kearney was apprised of the pledges made by Col Allen. About 5 the division came up & emcamped for the night. Dis 15 ms, total 749 ms.

John D. Lee:
To Mingle With the Children of Darkness

Capt. Philip St. George Cooke observed in 1843 that Santa Fe was "probably the most abandoned and dissolute community in North America," one of the few opinions John D. Lee would have shared with

---

[53]The ruins of Pecos pueblo, which was abandoned about 1838. It is now a National Monument. The term "Nephite Building" comes from *The Book of Mormon*, which speaks of ancient cities on this continent.—*Juanita Brooks*.

the battalion's new commander.[54] The oldest continuously occupied seat
of government in North America, Santa Fe was founded in 1610 by
Don Pedro de Peralta on Santa Fe Creek, which flows twenty miles into
the Rio Grande. Since Mexican independence, the city had been a
bustling frontier trading center with a varied population. In 1846 the
settlement was "about 4 miles long, situated in a beautiful valley with a
fine stream of water running through it." Pvt. Robert Bliss observed that
"the city is built of Dried Bricks one story [with] high flat Roofs"
whose houses resembled "thousands of Brick kilns unburnt." Bliss noted
that a silk "American Flag waves gracefully here" and the work at Fort
Marcy "now being built will make it a strong place."[55] John Steele
thought that "all went merry as a marriage bell" during his stay, but Lee
was outraged that some of the Mormon soldiers spent money on drinking, gambling, and fandangos rather than give their pay to him. Lee carried this negative report back to Brigham Young, who told the battalion
wives "they ought not to grumble & complain" about their poverty, for
"their dear husbands who were in the Army" only sent "their *dear* Wives
and children and the Camp of Israel" a small fraction of their pay, "thus
shewing their great love for their Families, but their greater love for the
pleasures around them."[56] The soldiers would not soon forget "the evil
deeds" of the man "who carried news from Santa Fe, disrespectful of
the Mormon Battalion."[57]

BROOKS, ED., "DIARY OF THE MORMON BATTALION MISSION, JOHN D. LEE,"
9 TO 22 OCTOBER 1846.

Spanish Settlements, N M
Valley of Repentance[58]
Friday, Oct 9th, 1846

At 4 morning Revellee was beat that all might be up & make an early start
in order to reach Santefe before night. Cloudy & warm, W S. at 31 mi[nutes]
to 6 the Bat received marching orders—at the dis of 6 miles we met an express
to Ft Leavenworth under the protection of 15 men having in co 2 baggage

---

[54]Young, *The West of Philip St. George Cooke*, 132.
[55]Beckwith, ed., "Journal of John Steele," 10; and Cecil, ed., "The Journal of Robert S. Bliss," 76.
[56]Bagley, ed., *The Pioneer Camp of the Saints*, 106.
[57]Long, *Report of the First General Festival of the Renowned Mormon Battalion*, 35.
[58]Lee evidently blamed himself for his failure to carry out Brigham Young's orders, hence his "Valley
of Repentance." All the conditions they specifically ordered have been set aside: the battalion will not be
led by one of its own men, the group has been divided and separated, the Priesthood is not supreme. —
Juanita Brooks.

wagons—this move I considered to be a pecular manifestation of the Kind Hand of Providence especially should we be so fortunate as to accomplish our mission in time to fall in co with them.[59] About noon we came to a beautiful spring at the foot of the Mountain—in this & the water that runs from the Spring are smawl particles of gold apperently thick—5½ ms further we came to another, where we saw quite a no. of Spaniards collected &—5 ms from this to Santefe—about 3 P.M. the city hove in view—& as all other villages in the Spanish dominions resemble Brick Kilns—Santefe is immediately situated in a valley or Basin, Surrounded on the E N & W by a chain of Mountains. The valley is quite narrow & runs a S W direction & immediately around the city—on the south especially—is a broken Barrow covered with Pine & cedar Shrubs for the dis of 8 ms. In those mountains are found a superior quality of Marble in large bodies—on entering the city we found a part of 3 divisions encamped. The American coulours we seen waving over the city at a considerable distance.[60] The Bat marched into the Town in Military order & encamped on the East boundary of the Main encampment—Gen Donethan received us with peculiar friendship—which was a rear [rare] thing to the Bat. for the last 6 weeks. Wood, feed & provisions were hauled to our quarters immediately which once more revived the spirits of Desponding Brethren hoping that there were better times ahead. About 3 P M just before the Bat. arrived we had quite a heavy storm of Hails which lasted about 30 mi. The valley in which Santefe is situated runs down to the River Rio de Grand which [is] about 25 ms distance from Santefe—& is by some [said] to be the line between Texas & N. Mexico. A stranger at the first glance would conclude that there was [not] a room in the Whole city that was fit for a white man to live [in], but to the contrary some of their rooms are well furnished inside—Floors excepted—The Population is about 25000 about 300 of that No. left the city & fled with their governor Armeho at the time General Kearney entered the city.[61]

About 1½ ms North of the main tracks about 6 ms west of what is called by the guide the Point Rocks & 620 ms W of Ft Leavenworth & 150 ms E of Santefe Stands an ancient Nephite building[62]—built of stone & cement 198 feet in length & 138 feet in width with a hall of 6 feet running through lengthways on the N Side, at the E end are 2 columns about 6 feet square—the North wall is about 6 ft thick & from 9 to 12 feet high & from the amount of stone that is heaped up on the North wall which once stood

[59]For his own safety, Lee hoped to finish his mission in time to return with this party. Comanche raiders made it dangerous to travel over the Cimarron Route alone.

[60]Mexican Governor Manuel Armijo fled just before Kearny's Army of the West occupied the city on 18 August 1846, fired a thirteen-gun salute, and raised the American flag over the Palace of Governors.

[61]In listing the population, Lee put down one too many ciphers; in 1846 it was about 3,000. His description otherwise is excellent.

[62]Lee is bringing his journal up to date. He passed this ruin northeast of Wagon Mound on 1 October.

erect—I would suppose it to have been some 45 or 50 feet in height, for the rubbage was about as high as the presant wall. The whole constructure represents that of a Fort or a strong Fortification—from the fact that on the North is another strong enclosure—enclosing about 3 acres of land. The N wall of the Edifices above spoken of—compose a part of the South wall of this enclosure. The highest part of this last wall is about 3 feet, the remainder having crumbled down—From this building to the enclosure is [a] gate or entrance about 10 feet in width. The structure strongly insists that it was erected in a day when art & science was known, ingenuity—Enterprise & industry was encouraged, though many a century has doubtless passed & fled away since, leaving the ruins or remains of this Monument to testify that once this country was inhabited by an enlightened race of beings that far surpassed the present.

Santefe, N M
Sat, Oct 10th,'46

Morning clear & cool. The first thing when I arose was to urge the payment & get that matter on foot—Capt Hunt & Hunter went immediately to see the Paymaster & Gen Donethan, learned decidedly that Gen Kearney had appointed Capt. Cooke the ranking officer of that Grade to take of the Bat. without the knowledge of Col Allens pledges to the Bat. as the letter had not reached him before the appointment of Capt Cook; that Maj McCloud[63] was appointed paymaster of the M Bat. & that he would pay the soldiers in checks for the term of 1½ months, the officers for 2½—all in checks with the exception of clothing—money—& that would be done as soon as the rear of the Co would come up.[64] Through the day Lieut Lytle & myself walked around the city & was in some 25 or 30 stores, purchased 3 Mexican blankets & some other articles for our Journey. While standing on the walk an other curiosity caught my attention, I saw 4 Gennys drawing wood,—the manner in which they were riged for buisiness was the Rick. Each ass was loaded Sepperately and apart with 12 poles about 10 foot long with the buts of each fastened across the weathers on a fraim made after the manner of a Sadle with straps around the breast to draw by. The top ends were draging on the ground. They were driven by one man without bridle or lines. Around the walks in all public places are found Pine nuts, apples, peaches, pears, large grapes, bread, onions, boiled corn, mellons &c sold by Women & girls—goods are sold remarkably cheap in this city on account of competition running so high among the Sutlers & Traders. About 4 P M the

---

[63]Jeremiah H. Cloud of Missouri was appointed paymaster of volunteers on 2 July 1846.

[64]Since the army lacked cash to purchase even needed supplies, the battalion would be paid largely in treasury drafts. Andrew J. Shupe wrote, "We got $2.60 in cash and the balance was in checks." Shupe gave fifty cents to Lee "for to pay him for his time and trouble coming to take our money to the Bluffs." See Carter, ed., "Women and Children of the Mormon Battalion," 504.

Command of Col Mitchell[65] arrived & encamped on our left. The following
day they received orders to march to Touse [Taos] for winter quarters. Several
of the Bat. were on a sprey [spree], some were put under guard, others in the
caliboose. Some of the Mo. cos determined to release their comrads, broke
down the guard house. In the struggle one of the sentinels fired and killed 2
of them—evening cool—I paid 1.00 for a pint of whiskey to put biters in—

Santefe, N M
Sund, Oct. 11, 46

Morning clear & cool, W S W. About 9 I had my mules shod by Bro
Chapen [Samuel Chapin] the price of shoeing Mules here is about 4.00—
a great many of Co D for the want of proper instructions went to the setlers
[sutlers] & took up all their wages, for fear it would be sent back, partaking
of the same Spirit of C. Canfield[66] the acting Capt. I conversed with some
of the Boys & advised them to send or lend to those that would send back—
they readily consented. About 5 eve an express arrived from Gen Kearney.
Capt Hunt, Hunter, Brown, Lieut L. Clark, Egan & myself visited Lieut
[Col.] Cook who received us with much courtesy & conversed freely—read
us the express from Kearney which was as follows in substance, Having
learned by private Per. Col Price, of the death of Col. Allen & that the Mormon Bat. is on their way to Santefe—there to await my orders, reposing
Special trust & confidence in your courage, good conduct & ability, I therefore appoint you Lieut Col in place of Col Allen to take command of the
Bat. when they arrive at Santefe[67] —Fit them out with 60 days provisions—
not to encumber your selves with baggage as a part of the route will be difficult for the passage of waggons & follow on my trail—Mr. Fitz Patrick the
Pilot that I sent will conduct you to the Pacific, where you will wait further
orders & if necessary I will have a vessel meet you to convey the Bat to Mon-
terae—as their probable destination will be the Sacramento Valley, which is
probably 1000 ms distance from this place,—I have sent Mr. Fitzpatrick
(the bearer of this) who will conduct you through.[68] He was with Capt Fre-

---

[65]In charge of ten of Col. Sterling Price's fourteen mounted companies, Lt. Col. David D. Mitchell led
the Second Regiment, Missouri Mounted Volunteers, which had shared the trail with the Mormon Battalion from the Arkansas River crossing.

[66]Even before they received them, some of the men apparently promised their checks to the sutler in
exchange for cash or spent the money on credit rather than give their pay to Lee to take back to Winter
Quarters. Lt. Cyrus C. Canfield was acting as commander of Co. D in the absence of Capt. Nelson Higgins and the detached George P. Dykes.

[67]On 2 October Kearny received the report of James Allen's death at La Joya, New Mexico, about 130
miles below Santa Fe. Kearny at once ordered First Dragoons Capt. Philip St. George Cooke to return and
take command of the Mormon Battalion.

[68]Thomas "Broken Hand" Fitzpatrick, one of William Ashley's legendary fur hunters, later received
an order from Kearny to claim the twenty-one best mules in Santa Fe for the general's advance party, which
deprived Cooke's command of the finest animals. Fitzpatrick was replaced as a guide by Pauline Weaver,
Antoine Leroux, and Baptiste Charbonneau, son of Sacagawea of Lewis and Clark fame.

mont as a pilot through his exploring expedition. The American Flag has been hoisted & the American coulours waving over California for the last 3 months.[69] Capt Fremont by the assistance [of] American Man of Warr subdued the whole country & Fremont claims to be governor of that province. Until my arrival Gen Donethan & Col Cook proffered to Send all the sick the Women & children of those belonging to the Bat.—to Touse (where there is a branch of the church)[70] there to winter under an escort of our Brethren & in the spring intersect the main body of the church & go with them at the expense of government. This I considered to be a fair & liberal proposal, for I was well persuaded that neither the Sick, Women & children could stand the fatigue & exposures of the Journey to go around with the Bat. Returned to our quarters about 9—eve. clowdy & cool, much more so than what I expected to find in this part of the world.

Santefe, N M
Mon, Oct 12,'46

Morning cool & clear. Early in the day I went with a French Bro. Markse Mcwell[71] & procured about 3 bushels corn—for our Journey. Corn is worth from 6 to $10.00 per bushel. Bro Alburn Allen[72] browned and ground our coffee while I brought my Journal. Bro Egan was walking about to the groceres with some of the officers—apperently unconcerned about the things that I thought should immediately concearn us both, but I submitted the whole arraingment to him that rules the destinys of men. At ½ past 2 P M the rear of the Bat. that was left back—arrived with much rejoicing—part of our divisions met them at the edge of the city & escorted them in—We were escorted by a Horse Co. of Mo'ians [Missourians] when we entered— I must say that I seldom saw the same No. of men greet each other with the same warmth of feelings as did this Bat. Every Spirit was elated with the hopes that the dark clowd of gloom that had hovered over the Bat & threatened them with despairation was about to be blown over & that the Smiles of Freedom would again gladden the hearts of the oppresd Sons of Liberty, but alas in this we were Sadly disapointed—the Serpent (that little Wolfish Lieut Smith) which the officers contrary to the wish of the Bat. took into their bosom as a counsellor to lead them to Santefe—Some of the officers

---

[69]On 6 October Kearny on the Rio Grande met Kit Carson on his way back from California with dispatches from U.S. Navy Com. Robert F. Stockton and Lt. Col. John C. Frémont who reported, somewhat prematurely, that they had already conquered the Mexican province. In a move he would come to regret, Kearny reduced his mounted force to only two dragoon companies, about one hundred men, and hurried on with pack mules to take charge of events in California as directed by President Polk.

[70]Lee is wrong here. Not knowing his geography he calls the place Taos instead of Pueblo, where the Mississippi Saints and the battalion detachments would spend the winter.—*Juanita Brooks.*

[71]Pvt. Maxie Maxwell of Co. A was probably a French-Canadian, but Thomas Bullock's August 1847 Names of Pueblo Soldiers listed "Maxy Maxwell" as a "Deserter" who was "not in Church."

[72]New Yorker Albern Allen, 44, and his son, Rufus Chester Allen, 19, were privates in Co. A.

were not satisfied with the sting of his enmity allready endured by the Lord's anointed or many of them but worked the Wires secretly—in behalf of this Serpent until they prevailed in removing the Most active & true friend to suffering Humanity, that the Bat. could afford,—a man who had in his station the good will & confidence of 9 tenths—of the Bat. & loss of his service is sorely lamented (as well as being sevierly felt).[73] Two of the most bitter enemies to our people now are appointed & the Bat. must take them in exchange for a man whoes real work & worth but few ever realized.[74]

Santefe, Teus, Oct. 13th,'46

Morning clear, W E. At 10 A M the Bat. was called togeather to lay before them the proposition [of] Gen Donethan, with reference to the Sick and the Laundry women of the Bat. which as a general thing met the feelings of the Bat.[75]—Capt Hunt also laid before them the propriety of Sending back all they could [of their pay] to the Poor of Iseral [Israel]—as it would probably be the last opportunity that would present. Also to assist those men to return home—The Bat. almost unanimously consented to the above propositions. At 6 eve the Bat. was again calld together & Adj Dykes read the appointment of A. J. Smith to the office of commissary & quartermaster & Lieut Stoneman[76] assistant of Subsistence. Our little new Wolfish commissary was present—so drunk that he couldn't stand alone—evening clear & pleasant.

Santefe, N M
Wed, Oct. 14th, 46

Morning clear & pleasant. At 6 I traversed the city in co with Br R. Stephens[77] in search of my Mules that strayed of[f]—found them with one of their hobels broken or taken off—also the Haulters—returned about 10—assisted to draw up a petition to lay before Lieut Col. Cook and Gen

---

[73]Lee's adopted son, First Lt. Samuel Gully, Co. E, had been appointed assistant quartermaster to the battalion by James Allen at Fort Leavenworth. He served in this capacity until Cooke removed him at Santa Fe. Other Mormon officers later blamed his dismissal on Adjutant George P. Dykes. Gully died of cholera on his way to Utah in 1849.

[74]Lee apparently referred to Cooke's appointment of Lt. A. J. Smith as commissary of subsistence and Dr. George B. Sanderson as battalion surgeon.

[75]Colonel Doniphan and Cooke ordered ninety-one soldiers, including those pronounced unfit to march to California and the husbands of the laundresses, most of the women, and ten children, more than 120 in all, to join the little Mormon colony at Pueblo on the upper Arkansas River. They left on 18 October 1846 under Capt. James Brown and Lt. Elam Luddington.

[76]Having just graduated from West Point, Lt. George Stoneman saw his first active duty in the Army of the West. He served in Texas in the 1850s with Albert Sidney Johnston's elite Second Cavalry beside Lt. Col. Robert E. Lee and Maj. George Thomas, the future "Rock of Chickamauga." During the Civil War Stoneman led a spectacular but ineffective cavalry raid on Richmond in 1863 during the Battle of Chancellorsville. Twenty years later he became fifteenth governor of California.

[77]Lee had persuaded Cpl. Roswell Stephens, Co. E, to return to Winter Quarters with him to safeguard the money he was carrying.

Donethan, showing the pledges of Col Allen to the Bat. & begged to have
Samuel Gully reinstated to his former office—as he was appointed by Col
Allen—after which I was confined to my waggon—bringing up my jour-
nal—through the day. Br Allred[78] presented me a flannel shirt.

Santefe, N M
Thur, Oct 15th,'46

Morning clear, pleasant & calm. We are yet detained and how much
longer we will have to wait the slow opperation of the officers I no not—
Last evening 9 of the officers received their pay—at Night the Capt's &
Lieut all but G. [George] W. Rosecrance of Co C Lieut [Sylvester] Hulett
of co D & Lieut Pace, Lytle & Gully of co E & Adj Dykes went to a ball
that was got up by some of the Spaniards & Mo volunteers. About ¾ths of
the Bat. also attended. The bill was $2.00 per Head—I had several inverta-
tions to attend & have my bill Paid—but I refused—on the grounds that
our covenants to the House of the Lord prohibited me at least from associ-
ating with unbelievers, much more to take the Daughters of Zion in among
prostitutes—& to mingle in recreation with men whose hands & garments
are stained with the blood of martyred Saints in Mo.[79] I consider it a disgrace to the Priesthood for the Saints of light to mingle with the children
of darkness saying nothing about $1000 spent foolishly—which had better
been sent to the poor in Iseral. Some of the Brethren considered the council good & proposed sending the amount 2.00 that others spent extra to the
Poor in Iseral & risk the consequences—Capt Hunter & Hunt & many
other officers said there was no harm in the Soldiers going into any thing
that their Capt's encouraged—as they had power to control the Spirits—
Lieut Barnes & Omen were as drunk as sots. Oman acknowledged to be at
the gambling table, said that he won $5.00 gave me 50 c[ents], said it was
his tithing—sat down to eat—but was so far gone that he could not desern
between his waiters finger (a little boy), & a piece of meat plunged his fork
through I of the little fingers into the table. After dark Br. David P Rainey
& Wm Hyde and myself walked down thinking to look on privately but
could not get within 10 feet of the entrance for the throng of ruffians that
stood around using the most vulgar language—we were soon Satisfied so
returned with disgust from the scene—About 50 of Co H Mo volunteers
some of our old Friends (mobbers) composed a part of the party—The
Capt of Co H said that it was with much difficulty that he could keep his
men from kicking up a row. Said that the Mormons had the same oppressive spirit that they had in Mo. No more than what would be expected when
Lambs fondle or play with Wolves—the commanders said they took this

---

[78]Reddick Newton Allred, third sergeant in Co. A, was born in Tennessee in 1822. He lived throughout Utah Territory, served as a colonel in Utah's Black Hawk War, and was buried at Spring City in 1905.

[79]Lee's attitude here is characteristic. Years later he refused to join in a dance where there were men who
had spoken disrespectfully of Brigham Young.—*Juanita Brooks*.

course to gain friends, but I am certain the Bat. lost ten lbs of influence to where they gained one ounce of credit or pleasure.

Santefe, N M
Friday, 16th,'46

Clouds rising from the East, accompanied by wind. Last evening about 25 persons were brought up into the ranks, condemned by the Dr & ordered to be discharged—forthwith—contrary to their wishes—without even the privileges of conveyance back to the States or pay for their enrolment. This move certainly mortified my feelings as much if not more than anything that was got up before. I told Adj Dykes that I would consider it more honorable to command those men (sick) to be shot & thereby put an end to their Suffering—than to discharge and leave them here to rot among prostitutes—without a friend to assist them & that the man who raised his voice or assented to this move would have to atone for the sufferings & lives of those men—I also went to the Capt—the thing was soon carried to Gen. Donethan—who upon the honor of a gentleman & Philanthropic went immediately to Lt [Col.] Cook & countermanded the order—saying that Gen Kearney would never discharge a man under like circumstances—to perish—and ordered them to be sent to Perbelo—with the other sick & Laundry women with an out fit—set the time of their enrollment.[80] Said if the Pres. [Young] wished to discharge them he might—when he learned of their Situation—About 9 a guard was placed around each tent to keep all within the guard intill a Search could be made for the Pilot's Gold watch worth $180, also the old Dr's, worth $300, which was stolen out of his trunk the evening before,[81]—no discovery was made—Shortly afterwards Capt Brown's Co was organized & ordered to march on the 17 to Purbeloe.[82] About 2 P M Sergeant Major Ghlines was removed from office & reduced back to the ranks.[83] I made a request of the Capt's for 2 men

---

[80]Lee again is remarkably accurate. According to Cooke, Dr. Sanderson and the military department's senior medical officer, Dr. Samuel De Camp, recommended "a large number" of men for disability discharge, but were overruled by Colonel Doniphan, the commanding officer at Santa Fe, who decided to keep them in service and send them to Pueblo. Cooke did refuse to permit wives to go to California, but later relented and allowed five to go at their own expense. Four completed the journey.

[81]Years later Lee said that Howard Egan, his partner in the secret mission to pick up the soldiers' wages, and Roswell Stephens stole the gold watches and also snatched two mules. See Bishop, ed., *Mormonism Unveiled*, 187.

[82]The detachment under Capt. James Brown, Co. C, left Santa Fe for Pueblo on 18 October 1846. Cooke said it numbered eighty-six men, but battalion historian Norma Ricketts puts the total at ninety-one soldiers, Dr. William L. McIntire, seventeen wives, two other women, and ten children. See Ricketts, *The Mormon Battalion*, 238–40.

[83]Sgt. Maj. James H. Glines, battalion staff, was reduced to private and sent to Pueblo at the request of Capt. James Brown "for the purpose of makeing out the morning reports, provision returns, etc. for the company." See Glines, Autobiography, 6. To fill this important staff position, Cooke selected eighteen-year-old James Ferguson, a native of Belfast, Ireland, who had enlisted as a private in Co. A. During the next decade this extraordinarily talented actor and writer would serve as adjutant general of the Nauvoo Legion, Utah's territorial militia.

on detached Servise—to return back with us. Day after day passed away without effecting the object I desired—said I to adj. Dykes & some others of the officers, I shall be under painful necessity of saying to the Council—that the Bat. at the time I left it,—had not power or influence enough in it to command or controle one man as a messenger on detached Servis—on business of the greatest importance & benefit to the Bat. without breaking him of his commission. However this I hope will be a schooling to the officers of this Bat. & will learn them never to harbour a serpent in their busom or take the Devil as a counsellor. Evening cold, W N E.

Santefe
Sat, Oct 17th, 46

Cold & cloudy. Ice about an inch thick. Santefe I am told is a remarkable cold Place, More so than many deg. further N. Last evening I conversed with the Pilot—he said that he conclud'd to winter in Santefe—thought it unsafe to venture through the desert at so late Season.[84] This morning, got the promise of having Br Roswell Stevens return back with us. Fortunately through stratigem having [gotten] on the sick list to go to Purbelo—which throu [him] out from under the command of the Devil[85]—I spent the major part of the day—in making out a roll of the Bat., regulating their checks to send back. Most of the day Lieut Rosecrans, Thompson & I left quarters. Just before sup[p]er I arranged my things in the Waggons, filed in a bill of an outfit. Rec'd about 100 letters & several litle Preasants from the Brethren. G. W. Rosecrans Liet. presented me $5.00 in gold—the Brethren are very liberal in assisting us to what ever we asked them—it is now about 9 & I have just closed my Journal for the day. Evening cool, clear.

Santefe
Sund Oct. 18th 46

Morning cool. Frost. This morning I was closely engaged assisting Lieut Samuel Gully close his accounts. The night previous we wrote till about 2 morn—about 10 A M Capt James Brown with his detatchment left—for Purbeloe, there to take up winter Quarters. Adj. Dykes reported Seargeant Major Glines to the Col for not handing up his sword & other equipage of his office, whereupon Col Cook sent a file of men after them—or rather took them from him & ordered him to be marched to Bents Fort under guard. Sgt [Lt.] D[ykes] has succeeded in running Seargeant Major from his office as well as the Quarter master or Commissary on whom he for a long time looked with a jealous eye—because they were friends of the Bat. Not yet being satisfied he is trying to reduce Lieut Gully to the ranks—in this

---

[84]The guide who stayed at Santa Fe was probably Philip F. Thompson.

[85]Roswell Stephens took the first step in his planned escape from the battalion by getting himself named to the detachment sent to Pueblo under James Brown. Brown then put Stephens "on detached servis [sic] to Council Bluffs."

however he will doubtless fail, as Bro Gully by my council proposed—agreed to take $250 for his office—from Edmond L. Brown[86] for the remaining term of 9 months & presented his resignation the following morning. This we did for the reason that the Bat. had not retained influence enough among the officers to detach a man on Servis—without braking him of his commission—no matter how important the case might be. It is now 12, air chilly.

Santefe

Mon, Oct 19th, 46

This morning is quite a bustle in camp. The Dr Riding Mule is Missing.[87] About 7 the commandants of Co's togeather with the commissioned officers, that is, those that were opposed to carrying out the Pres council—came to my quarters, wished me to report the amount of money that I had raised from the Bat. as donated—I told Capt Hunt, Hunter & co—that I received nothing from them. Rosecrans, Brown & Lytle Presented me $5.00 each—that the Brethren drew but little money but out of that they were liberal—when I say Brethren I dont mean Puffed up officers—I told them that I called on no woman in the Bat. for money, neither was that my object. I came because the [Lord] sent me & if he has opened the way before me I am thankful—they then withdrew & sent me a Note—authorizing us to use for our out fit of the money sent back & to make due return to the council of the 12—this however was entirely useless—as that I should have done if necessity required.[88] About 9 the co began to move of[f] the ground for California. Adj. Dykes remained on the ground for fear that I should get something that belonged to Uncle Sam & to satisy him with the delay I remained some 2 or 3 hours longer. Bro Steavens started the previous evening. Bro. Gully finding it too great a task to wind up his affairs alone in time—requestd me to wait till morning & assist him—which I did—Bro Egan remained in the city around grogshops till after midnight—came to our quarters about 1—found Bro Samuel Gully and my self writing, asked for a place to lie down. We fixed a bed for he & Bro. Clift.[89] Soon after laying

---

[86]There is no evidence that this deal was consummated, for Edmond L. Brown re-enlisted on 20 July 1847, for an additional six months' service. He was first sergeant in the Mormon Volunteers.

[87]As mentioned, Lee later concluded that Howard Egan and Roswell Stephens stole Dr. Sanderson's gold watch and mule.

[88]According to Mormon Battalion historian Norma Baldwin Ricketts, Lee returned to Council Bluffs with $2,447.32 in checks, currency, and coin from members of the command. In his confessions, Lee said Howard Egan "was given one-half of the checks and money, donated by the soldiers for Brigham Young and Heber C. Kimball, and the remainder was given to me to carry back to winter quarters." See Bishop, ed., *Mormonism Unveiled*, 186. This indicates the two delivered nearly $5,000.

[89]Robert Clift, 22, was third lieutenant, Co. C. After serving as alcalde of San Diego in 1848, Clift was elected the first sheriff of San Bernardino County. Ranger Horace Bell thought the Mormon posse Clift led in 1853 "the best fellows I ever had anything to do with." Clift was killed by Indians in Ruby Valley, Nevada, while carrying mail in 1859. See Lyman, *San Bernardino*, 27–28, 90, 195–96, 418–19.

down he vomited like a sott. It is now I and I am just closing my journal for the day—3 more men were buried just before Sun Set, one of whom was murdered in a Spaniards House the night before—which has made me somewhat uneasy. . .[90] for fear of his being rob[b]ed while I am yet writing I . . . [heard] the feet of horses—arose from . . . in co with Bro Gully went out . . . that it was Lieut Canfield & Bro . . . who had come to bring my . . . mule. Also brought a horse for Lt. Clift to ride back into camp. I went to the waggon to wake up Lt Clift, found Egan was gone which caused a search to be made. Found him lying in the midle of the street flat on his [back], hat & shoes off unable to help himself. I picked him up in my arms by the assistance of Bro Layton,[91] carried him to the waggon, put him in bed—Now I thank the Lord for sending those messengers back—for had it not been for them—he probably might have been Robbed and murdered without our knowledge & I am obliged to acknowledge the hand of the Lord in all things. Messengers returned at 2 morn.

Santefe
Tues, Oct 20th, 46

. . . daybreak, we riged up the mule . . . Lt. Rosecrans & Layton brought . . . in the night . . . placed Bro Egan . . . his back but was unable to ride . . . he [the mule] bounded like an antelope [throw]ing the rider twice. He however took [the mule] some 3 miles distance and secreted him in a private place till we came up. This we had sooner than difficulty or trouble. The mule was honestly mine but Capt Hunter was disposed to cheat us out of him.[92] About 4 P M we left the city of Santefe—traveled 12 miles—& encamped at the foot of the Mountains under a large pine—an attempt was made through the night to robb us by 3 men but was detected by Little Trip[93] who gave us timely Notice to be ready for what might follow. Dis 12 ms.

Foot of the Mountains, N M
Wed, Oct 21st, 46

Morning clear. By sunrise we were on the road—the day was warm & fine. About 3 we came up with Capt Browns Mormon detachment—learned by Bro R Steavens was expecting us—left them in good spirits—traveled 3 ms East of St McGill [San Miguel] & encamped for the night. Dis 38 ms, Total 50 ms.

---

[90]Pages 167 and 168 of the original are damaged. This is the reason for the omissions at the end of this entry and the beginning of the following one.—*Juanita Brooks.*

[91]Christopher Layton, born in England in 1821, was a private in Co. C. Layton, Utah, is named for him.

[92]However he or Egan and Stephens acquired this mule, it showed Lee's characteristic resourcefulness, since Kearny had taken for his own use almost every animal in northern New Mexico fit to pack or ride.

[93]Lee does not mention having a dog by this name, so Little Trip may be his mule.

Near St. Magill, N Mexico
Thur, Oct 22,'46

Morning fine. About sunrise, fearing that something had befallen Bro Steavens, Sent Bro Gully back & we went to the foot of the Pilot Mountain (which can be seen 50 ms), Stoped, fed & got Brakefast & brought up my Journal—about 10 Bro Gully & Steavens came up[94]—which again gladdened our hearts & made us think of home notwithstanding a journey of 1000 ms was before us & that almost a wilderness waste—at ½ past 10 started—passed through the town of Tauculute [Tecolote] about 2 P M, & about 4 we came to the town of Bagas [Las Vegas] where we laid in our corn for the journey—traded them Larriets, old clothes, sackes &c for corn, onions & eggs & the addition of 7 sacks of corn made our load quite heavy. Traveled 4 ms (after cooking our supper in Bagas—while trading) & took up for the night after a distance of 43 ms, total 73.[95]

---

[94]Lee later said he took Stephens with him because he had been discharged for ill health; Stephens was in fact on detached service arranged by James Brown.

[95]Lee and his companions returned the way the battalion had come over the Cimarron Route, arriving at Winter Quarters on 15 December 1846 where he turned the payroll over to Brigham Young.

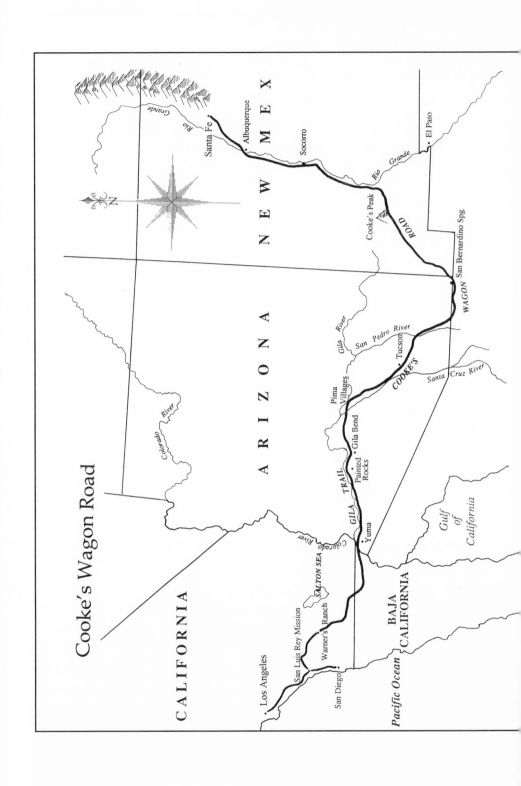

Cooke's Wagon Road

Chapter 4

"WHERE WAGGONS HAD NEVER BEFORE PASSED"
Cooke's Wagon Road

The day Philip St. George Cooke took command of the Mormon Battalion at Santa Fe, 13 October 1846, saw the end of rebellion over calomel and who would be Captain Allen's successor—and the beginning of a historic association. The dragoon captain's leadership left no doubt who was in charge. One of West Point's youngest graduates, the six-foot-four Virginian at age thirty-seven had already served nineteen years in the frontier Army. He was a stern disciplinarian, but a fair one, who understood that nature could be a deadlier threat to survival than hostile Indians. A stickler for details, he tracked provisions to the ounce, gave maintenance of tools and equipment a high priority, and when water was scarce saw to it that the mules and oxen drank first. At the same time, he worried every day about the welfare of his men and agonized over decisions that might put their lives in danger.

Cooke was also known to swear a lot, a habit hardly allayed by the "extraordinary undertaking" Kearny had handed him, even if the senior rank of lieutenant colonel did go with it. For over two centuries the lines of travel in the Southwest had run from south to north in keeping with the course of Spanish expansion in the New World. Now Cooke was expected to cut across the historic flow of colonization and open a new wagon route to California that went the way of a younger nation's "manifest destiny," east to west. To do it, he would have to march "eleven hundred miles, for the much greater part through an unknown wilderness without road or trail."[1]

---

[1]Cooke, *The Conquest of New Mexico and California*, 91, 92. For Cooke's distinguished career as a soldier and writer, see Otis Young's brilliant biography, *The West of Philip St. George Cooke*.

PHILIP ST. GEORGE COOKE,
Lieutenant-Colonel Second Dragoons,
serving with the Army in Utah. "As
Major of Second Dragoons he
served in California and in the
Mexican War, and conducted
the 'Mormon Brigade' across
the continent."
From *Harper's Weekly*, 12 June 1858, 372.

Faced with this daunting assignment, anyone but Cooke might have
despaired at the meager resources with which he was expected to accomplish it. He could see that his new command had been "enlisted too much
by families"; some of the men were too old, others too young, and the
whole outfit was "embarrassed by many women."[2] In addition, Kearny had
taken all the best mules in northern New Mexico when he abandoned his
wagons on the Rio Grande and pushed west by pack train. Cooke also
thought his Mormon footmen demonstrated "great heedlessness and
ignorance and some obstinacy."[3] Cooke would change his mind after he
and his men had taken each other's measure. What his men learned more
than justified mutual respect, if given grudgingly by some.

The spare professional soldier was not a man easily turned from his
duty, and he moved quickly to get the most from what he had to open a

---

[2]Ibid.

[3]Bieber, ed., "Cooke's Journal," in *Exploring Southwestern Trails*, 69. Bieber's transcription of Cooke's Journal is preferred because it was made from the original document in the National Archives. The version
published in Sen. Doc. 2 (31-Spec. Sess.), 1848, Serial 547, is not always accurate.

new southern route to the Pacific Ocean. First he combed the command and sent the sick and disabled and most of the laundresses under Capt. James Brown and Lt. Elam Luddington to the small Mormon colony at Pueblo. At the "earnest" request of two captains and three sergeants, he reluctantly allowed five wives, Melissa Coray, Lydia Hunter, Susan Davis, Phebe Brown, and Sophia Gribble, to accompany the command at their own expense.[4]

Cooke appointed Lt. A. J. Smith to the important task of commissary of subsistence and gave him $800 in treasury drafts to purchase cattle and sheep. As Smith's aid, he named Bvt. Lt. George Stoneman, a new West Point honor graduate, assistant quartermaster. Arriving from Kearny's camp to serve as guide was Pauline Weaver, the son of an English father and Cherokee mother, who had trapped the Gila River from New Mexico to the Colorado River and knew the country. In a fortuitous move Cooke hired as interpreter Dr. Stephen C. Foster, a twenty-six-year-old adventurer from New England, who would also do double duty as scout or surgeon as needed.[5]

Not as ready as he would like to be, less than a week after taking command Lieutenant Colonel Cooke started the battalion by companies on 19 October 1846 over the old Spanish road between Santa Fe and Mexico City. According to his own count, its overall strength came to 397 officers and enlisted men. The expedition also numbered six large ox wagons, three mule wagons to each company, four other mule wagons for the field and staff, quartermaster, hospital, and paymaster, and four or five private wagons for wives. In addition to twenty-eight beef cattle, there was enough flour, sugar, and coffee for sixty days; salt pork for thirty; and soap for twenty.

SAMUEL ROGERS:
THE BATTALION TOOK UP ITS LINE OF MARCH

Marching with Company B as the battalion left Santa Fe was twenty-

---

[4]Sophia Gribble later went with her husband, Pvt. William Gribble, to Pueblo. She parted ways with him in what appears to be Utah's first divorce, granted in Salt Lake in August 1847, and married battalion veteran William Tubbs. The other four women completed the journey to California.

[5]A New Englander, Foster had graduated from Yale, studied medicine in Louisiana, and traded in New Mexico before joining the command at age 26. He later became mayor of Los Angeles.

seven-year old Pvt. Samuel Holister Rogers from Portage County, Ohio, who had left his family behind in Iowa to join the battalion at the request of his spiritual leaders. Rogers told the story of the great journey across the northern provinces of Mexico to the Pacific Ocean in a daily record he faithfully maintained of the adventure.

THE JOURNAL OF SAMUEL HOLISTER ROGERS,
SPECIAL COLLECTIONS, BYU LIBRARY.

Mon. 19 [October 1846]. Last night after roll call the old messes were all dissolved, and new messes organized of ten men in each. A little before noon the Battalion took up its line of march on the tenth day after arriving in Santa Fe. The inhabitants of this country have but few conveniences around them. No furniture in their houses, and but little ingenuity to make any. They nearly all belong to the Catholic Church and are an ignorant class of people.

We traveled 5 miles passing some good farms for this Country.

Tues. 20. Passed over rolling rocky ground and camped on a small creek. After roll call the Colonel's orders were read. We are to have only ¾ of a lb of flour per day and only ¾ rations of sugar and coffee per day with 1½ lbs of beef to the man. A non commissioned officer of each company is to deal out the rations and to have charge of all the teams in the Company and will be known as the Company Quartermaster.

Wed. 21. Traveled 24 miles camped after dark near the Rio Grand del Norte.[6]

Thur. 22. Passed three or four villages also large farms with peach and apple orchards. These farms and villages are in better style than those before seen, the inhabitants are mostly Indians.

Fri. 23. On guard, still passing villages, farms and orchards, also vineyards, the grapes of good quality, large and sweet. The apples also are sweet. The country improves as we go lower down the river valley. Saw three ten mule teams. The Mexicans do not work animals much in harness.

Sat. 24. Passed several villages and one large town called Albuquerque,[7]

---

[6]The command followed Galisteo Creek to the Rio Grande where it camped on the east bank across from San Felipe Pueblo.

[7]Albuquerque was founded in 1706 by Don Francisco Cuervo y Valdez, New Mexico's twenty-eighth governor, who named the villa after the Duque de Alburquerque, the thirty-fourth viceroy of New Spain. The command camped near Capt. John Henry K. Burgwin and two First Dragoons companies that Kearny had ordered to remain in New Mexico. Here Cooke "succeeded in exchanging thirty of my mules, broken down and utterly worthless to the expedition, for fifteen good ones, and also in purchasing ten at forty dollars." He also met Baptiste Charbonneau, son of Sacagawea, who had been sent by Kearny as a guide. After buying other animals, the command crossed the river and headed down the west bank on the Chihuahua Trail. See Cooke's Journal, 24 October 1846.

followed down the river, here a large stream. Here a man and a woman ride on the same horse, the woman rides in front.[8] Passed a small distillery.

Sun. 25 [October 1846]. Continued on passing some villages, camped near Isleta,[9] an Indian village, they have two very handsome vineyards. The Battalion was paraded when orders No. 12 were read. Sergeant E. Elmer of Co. C. was reduced to the ranks.[10]

Mon. 26. Passed a number of villages. We heard that Indians drove off 800 sheep belonging to the Mexicans yesterday.[11] Wood has been quite scarse of late, we bought some of the Mexicans at very high price.

Thur. [Tuesday] 27. Detailed to bring in the ox wagon. It rained a little. Passed a number of Mexican villages. There is a [false] rumor that Gen. Wool has fought a battle at Chihuahua losing 1000 men, but capturing the City. Camped early near a village, wood very scarce.

Wed. 28. Last night it rained moderately nearly all night. This morning we saw snow on the tops of some distant mountains. Passed some towns in one of which there was a distillery. Camped about middle of the afternoon, wood about out of the question.

Thur. 29. At first the road was muddy, afterwards very sandy Crossing some high points that came down to the river. Crossed to the opposite side of the river. Some Cottonwood trees and a large village here.[12]

Fri. 30. Hilly and very sandy road. Camped near the town of Socorro.[13] Saw a cotton patch, the first cotton I ever saw growing.

Sat. 31. On guard, passed two towns with abundance of fruit trees and vineyards which are still green, but snow is near by on the mountains.

---

[8]This practice, which John D. Lee called the "Spanish Rusty," would outrage Mormon leaders when battalion veterans practiced it in Utah. See Chapter 12.

[9]Originally an Indian pueblo, Isleta was located on a small island in the Rio Grande, hence the name given by the Spanish, "Little Island." By 1846 changes in the river channel had placed the town on high ground on the right bank.

[10]Cooke reduced Sgt. Elijah Elmer to the ranks for not forming his company at reveille and "giving the excuse that it was not light enough to call his roll." He also "earnestly exhorted" the battalion "to lend me a more efficient assistance in requiring the mules to be properly grazed and fed, or else the expedition must very soon fall through." See Cooke Journal, 25 October 1846. Cpl. Thomas Dunn said, "Col. Cooke favored us in marching though he was more strict with us than any of our commanders before him. But in this I considered him right, doing justice to all his men." See Dunn, Private Journal, 25 October 1846.

[11]Navajo Indians killed two shepherds and stole more than ten thousand sheep in an audacious foray near the town of Valencia, one of the oldest Spanish settlements along the river. All the able-bodied men of the village had gone after the raiders and left the women unprotected, but Cooke was unable to help them.

[12]This was La Joya, a farming community and stopover town for caravans along the Rio Grande about twenty miles north of Soccoro.

[13]The name Socorro, or "succor," was given to an Indian pueblo by Don Juan de Oñate, first New Mexico colonizer. Oñate's 1598 expedition found relief here after traversing the waterless *Jornada del Muerto*, "Journey of the Dead Man."

Camped near the ruins of an old town, after which general muster. Light dew the past two nights.[14]

Sun. Nov. I. [1846] After guard mounting, general parade, Orders 13 read returning 1st Lieut. Dykes to Co. D. to command the same in the absence of Capt. Higgins[15] and appointing 2nd Lieut P. C. Merrill of Co. B. to the office of Adjutant of the Battalion.[16] The pilot states that we are now 151 miles from Santa Fe, which I learned from Lieut. Barrus.[17] Passed two towns near the the [sic] river, grass and wood plenty. A flock of sheep were driven into camp for our use.

Mon. 2. Left the main road to Chihuahua[18] and instead of crossing the river continued down the right bank in Kearney's trail. Camped in a fine grove of Cottonwoods. Some Indian traders passed our Camp.

Tues. 3. More Indian traders passed. Camped again on the river. We are now reduced to half rations of flour, sugar and Coffee. About half past 4 P.M. James Hampton of Co. A died.[19] 180 or 190 miles from Santa Fe.

Wed. 4. He was buried this morning on the bottom near the river, being rolled in his blanket without a coffin. Two men of Co. D were last night ordered on extra duty for 5½ hours, because they failed to salute the officer of the Day G. P. Dykes upon the rounds. Afterwards they were tied behind a wagon the whole day for indulging in some light minded remarks. Thomas

---

[14]Henry G. Boyle, 22, described the journey to date: "We marched 105 miles down this Stream over an almost continual bed of Sand. The fatigues of the Journey have been great Since we came on this Stream. following this river we have traveled a little west of South. & evry day the Snow had been visible on the *Sieras*, or mountains to our right. We have passed through towns or villages nearly every day. There are considerable many Spaniards or rather I may Say *Mexicans* living on this River. Thier [sic] mode of living & farming is singular enough to me but they Seem to get along. & seem to be happy enough. Thier land for cultivation is enclosed by ditches, hedges, & *adoba* Walls. On account of the dry Seasons in this country, they have to irrigate all this farming land all thier vineyards & orchards which is done by leading the water from the River through ditches through all their grain & every thing else that is raised or produced." See Boyle, Autobiography and Diary, 24–31 October 1846.

[15]On resigning as adjutant, George Dykes rejoined Co. D to fill the vacancy left when Capt. Nelson Higgins failed to return in time to join the march from Santa Fe. Higgins and his men, who had escorted the first family detachment to Pueblo, were permitted to return to Pueblo.

[16]Lt. Philemon C. Merrill's replacement of Dykes as adjutant lifted morale but gave no help to Cooke, who said, "A dumb spirit has possessed all for the last twenty-four hours, and not one of my orders has been understood and obeyed. All the vexations and troubles of any other three days of my life have not equalled those of the said twenty-four hours." Cooke's Journal, 1 November 1846.

[17]Twenty-four-year-old New Yorker Ruel Barrus was second lieutenant, Co. B.

[18]About nineteen miles south of Soccoro, near the Valverde trading post, the historic Spanish route crossed the river to begin the dreaded ninety-mile *Jornada del Muerto* while the command stayed on Kearny's trail down the west bank. This day the force was joined by the renowned Southwest mountain man, Antoine Leroux. Other guides sent by Kearny arrived later that night, Cooke said, "more or less drunk." See Cooke's Journal, 2 November 1846.

[19]The death of Co. A Pvt. James Hampton, 43, was "very sudden," Cooke said; "he walked to the surgeon's tent this morning." See Cooke's Journal, 3 November 1846. Sgt. Daniel Tyler, always ready to blame the surgeon, said Dr. Sanderson had pronounced him "ready for duty" when he was "far from well." See Tyler, *A Concise History*, 186.

Wolsey overtook us, he being one who left us on the Arkansas River to go to Pueblo.[20] He reported that Norman Sharp shot himself accidentally and died on that river.[21] Traveled over a very rugged road today. Camped on a ridge half a mile from the river.

Thur. 5. Remained in camp. Washed and patched my clothes. Soap being scarce I substituted a root called Arinola by the Mexicans, which makes good suds. An ox that tired out yesterday was brought in and butchered.

Fri. 6. Continued our journey over a very hilly road. I was detailed to push wagons up the hills. Camped near the river in a hollow formed by a creek coming down from the bluff. Here Kearney left his wagons and went on with pack mules.[22]

Sat. 7. Made a new trail over hills and a cross valleys and all of the way very sandy. Was detailed on the same duty as yesterday. Camped close to a creek and near the river.

Sun. 8. On rear guard, saw a Mexican trapper who said there are bears in the mountains and beavers in the river. Camped near the river.

Mon. 9. Continued on over hills and hollows as usual. Pioneers have been sent forward to look out the road. White frost seen for several nights past. We have got into a land of dew again. Camped on a bench or table land where Kearney left the river.[23]

Tues. 10. A detachment of 50 men, ten from each Company was here sent back to Pueblo under command of Lieut. W. W. Willis of Co A. Thomas Wolsey was sent with him as pilot, and was instructed to proceed from there to Council Bluffs Carrying despatches.[24] The detachment started about 2 P.M. taking one ox wagon. We left two wagons on the camp ground

---

[20]Pvt. Thomas Woolsey was courier for the battalion escort of the families sent to Pueblo from the Arkansas River crossing. He returned to Pueblo and carried mail back to Winter Quarters.

[21]New Englander Norman Sharp, 37, one of the escort under Captain Higgins for the first families sent to Pueblo, accidentally shot himself in the arm on the Mountain Route of the Santa Fe Trail along the Arkansas River. He was left in the care of an Arapaho medicine man at a "friendly Indian village," near today's Kansas-Colorado border, where he died three days later of gangrene.

[22]At this campground, now under Elephant Butte Reservoir, Kearny less than four weeks before had decided to send his wagons back to Santa Fe and pack by mules to California. After taking the best animals and outfits, the general left to Cooke and his command "the task of opening a wagon road." See "Journal of Captain A. R. Johnston, First Dragoons," 9 October 1846, House Exec. Doc. 41 (30-1), 1848, 574.

[23]Several miles west of today's Truth or Consequences, Kearny left the river and headed west to reach the Gila River near present Silver City, New Mexico, and the abandoned Santa Rita copper mine, then held by the Mimbres Apaches. Here began the historic route to the south, known as Cooke's Wagon Road, that ran between the Rio Grande and the Pima Indian villages on the Gila River, north of Tucson.

[24]Cooke ordered fifty-seven of the sick and "least efficient" men and one woman, Sophia Gribble, to go to Pueblo under Co. A Lt. William W. Willis. "I shall thus get rid of 1,800 pounds' weight of rations, and by means of what they leave, particularly the live stock, increase my rations for the remainder, seventeen days of meat and thirteen of flour," he wrote. See Cooke's Journal, 9 November 1846. Even after "these two weedings of the old, the feeble and sickly," he said, "lads and old grey-headed men still remained."

also leaving our tent poles and arranging to hold up the tent with muskets. Our mess was increased to 9 men. We are now according to the pilot 250 or 260 miles from Santa Fe. The loading taken out of the two abandoned wagons was packed on mules and oxen. Quite diverting to see oxen start off with their packs. Ephraim Hanks brought in a deer.[25]

Thur. 12. Detailed to take charge of two pack mules for the day Camped not far from the river about 290 miles from Santa Fe.

Fri. 13. Left the Rio Grande del Norte, traveled 15 miles and camped on a Creek, the country is more level and the land of better quality. From Santa Fe to this place saw very little wood besides cottonwood and that only along the river.[26]

Sat. 14. The forenoon was occupied with cooking as we did not expect to find water under 30 miles. Left camp about 12 noon, we however reached water at 12 miles distance near an old ruined building where the ground appeared to have been cultivated.

Sun. 15 [November 1846]. Lay by. Two rainbows this morning.

Mon. 16. A few scrubby oaks to be seen here and there the first seen since reaching the settlements. Yesterday some of the boys went about 5 miles and got some wild grapes. Marched 15 miles. Camped near some mountains, wood and water scarce.

Tues. 17. Off at the usual time but only traveled about 6 miles when we camped in the bed of a stream. The mescal plant grows here, it is said to possess nourishing properties. We are here surrounded by high mountains. A singularity attends the streams in this country, they lose themselves in the sand as they descend from their fountains.

Wed. 18. Traveled 20 miles on an extensive plain. Camped near a grove of timber on a stream called the Mimbres.[27]

Thur 19. Detained by a broken wagon, traveled till nearly dark making

---

[25]A noted loner, Pvt. Ephraim Knowlton Hanks was in his element as a hunter for Co. B. At age nineteen, he had already served three years at sea on the U.S. man-of-war *Columbus*. He became a legendary figure as plainsman, Indian fighter, and tavern owner at Mountain Dell east of Great Salt Lake City.

[26]Leaving the Rio Grande at present Derry, Cooke headed the battalion southwest across an unknown region to find a wagon route to the San Pedro River, one of the Gila River's two tributaries from the south. The command camped at Foster's Hole, a rock-bound cistern in a deep ravine named after its discoverer, Stephen C. Foster. See Smith, "The Lost Well of the Mormon Battalion Rediscovered," 277–86. David Pettegrew said: "Here was a well formed by nature in the rocks, the depth I did not ascertain but I should judge it was from 20 to 30 feet by the appearance and about 40 or 50 feet in circumference. Above this well hung a large mass of rocks to the height of 120 feet; on this height our Colonel sat for two hours until all the mules and other animals were watered, cursing the men almost all the time, it being very cold and chilly. The well was called the Lost Well." See Journal of David Pettegrew, 13 November 1846.

[27]The Mimbres River rises in the Black Mountain Range west of the Rio Grande and flows south toward Deming, New Mexico.

20 miles over an almost unbroken plain. Camped near the Copper mine and Sonora road at Cow Springs, but little wood or water here.[28]

Fri. 20. Last night after dark the pilots came in and could find no water ahead. This morning the Colonel caused a smoke to be raised on the top of the highest mountain near us, which is understood to be a sign of distress.[29] In a few hours two Mexicans were seen coming on horseback at a gallop. Each of them had a spear on a long pole. Our pilot met them and brought them into camp. They informed us there was water at a distance of 12 miles, and again at 20 miles from here. That it was 60 miles to the Gila river with a good road.[30] Shortly after their arrival a company of traders came to us. Our rations were increased to ten ounces of flour and 1¾ lbs of beef per day.

Sat. 21. Marched at the usual time, started on the road to Sonora. Travelled about three miles when we halted, and turning to the right traveled 12 miles and camped near a mountain.[31]

Sun. 22. Went 3 miles to get an ox out of the mire, returned to the camp ground but the Battalion had marched on. Ate my dinner and followed on, travelled 18 miles and came up with the Battalion encamped without wood or water. We have traveled to day a south course. The two last bakings of bread has been salt rising [without yeast].

---

[28]Here Cooke faced the most agonizing decision of the entire journey. He could follow the Spanish road that ran south from the old Santa Rita copper mine to Janos, Mexico, then take an existing road, via Fronteras, to his destination, the historic San Bernardino Spring, some fifteen miles east of today's Douglas, Arizona. But this choice would take him more than 120 miles, about six days' travel, to the south and bring the command into a possible confrontation with a Mexican garrison at Fronteras. The only other choice was to go almost due west some sixty miles across an untracked region, direct to the abandoned San Bernardino Hacienda.

[29]Cooke climbed the 8,408-foot mountain, now named Cooke's Peak, to study the trackless region to the west that was unknown to his guides. The peak stands to the north of Deming, New Mexico.

[30]This route was the existing copper mine road that would have taken the command north to the Gila River and placed it on Kearny's trail, an unacceptable alternative as it was impassible for wagons.

[31]After thinking "long and anxiously," Cooke heeded his guides' advice and took the copper mine road south. After a few miles, he suddenly changed his mind when he saw that the road to Janos ran east of south. Risking disaster, he turned west toward San Bernardino. David Pettegrew's fanciful account shows that the Mormon soldiers misunderstood Cooke's dilemma: "Our officers, with Doctor Sanderson, were very anxious to go to Old Mexico (down the copper-mine road). I believed they wanted whiskey, tobacco, wine etc. Seeing their determination and influence with the Colonel I felt disturbed in my mind and had some evil fore-bodings. In the evening I told Bro. Hancock that we would go to every tent and tell the head of every mess to have prayers and pray to God that we might not go Mexico but to California, so we visited all the tents making that request of them, and I believe they prayed. In the morning after I had got through with my commissary business, I started after the battalion who were on the road to Mexico. After a while I saw the Colonel had made a halt. I came up to where the Colonel was and heard him say, 'By God, I don't want to go home again' (as the road rather turned back the way we had come) 'I don't want to go there and be under General Wool's command, my orders were to California.' He looked back to the trumpeters and said, 'Blow that trumpet.' The trump sounded aloud and we turned square to the west. I said aloud . . . 'God bless the Colonel.'" See Journal of David Pettegrew, 11 December 1846.

Mon. 23. On guard. Off at Sunrise traveled 15 miles where we found sufficient water for the men to get a drink. Here the ox wagons belonging to Cos A and B. remained over night with men to guard them. The remainder of the Battalion continued on 15 miles further, arriving after dark found a plenty of good water near a dry lake. Some Mexican traders camped near by.

Tues. 24. Remained in Camp. The Colonel bought a number of mules of the traders to supply the place of those that were tired out.[32] One mule in the team belonging to Co B having failed that Co bought one of Sergeant Coray for $20.

Wed. 25. Continued on, two antelopes were killed and one of the pilots killed a grizzly bear. We traveled southwest for 20 miles and camped near a stream of water. This day observed specimens of the maguey plant[33] in great perfection. The stalks of some of them were near 25 feet high and from 4 to 6 inches through at the butt, all of the growth of one year.

Thur. 26. Traveled 15 miles and camped near a creek. There is a mountain with timber on it. The most of the mountains lately passed are destitute of timbers. This country seems very barren of timber. The Creeks also soon sink in the sand in their descent from their fountains. There are high rocky mountains with with [sic] gravelly and loamy plains.

Fri. 27. Same kind of country and same direction as yesterday, a great abundance of prairie dogs. Camped near a mountain and a creek. Bro. [Thomas] Kirk killed a deer.

Sat. 28. Got on a wrong track and turned back for a short distance. After going 8 miles camped on a plain and dug for water.

Sun. 29. Last evening the pilots brought in an Indian Chief but he was very timid, the Indians having been tricked so much by the Mexicans were very suspicious.[34] The Col. tried to get an Indian pilot as our pilots do not know this country. This morning all the provisions of the Battalion were taken out of the wagons and carried back to the place where we turned back yesterday, thence about 8 miles further where they were left under guard.[35]

---

[32]Cooke purchased twenty mules from a Mexican party for $666.66 and another for $50. They reported the Apaches had plenty of mules, stolen from a Mexican settlement.

[33]The common fleshy-leafed century plant from which the Apaches made mescal, a mild intoxicant used in various ceremonials.

[34]The wary Apache was Chief Manuelita, from whom Cooke hoped to obtain fresh mules. Several days before the colonel had sent Leroux and a newly hired Mexican guide to reconnoiter the route to San Bernardino and return with some Apaches willing to trade. See Cooke's Journal, 29 November 1846.

[35]Misled by its guides, the command seemed hemmed in by the seemingly impassable Guadalupe Mountains on today's border between New Mexico and Arizona. Unloading the wagons, Cooke sent baggage and supplies forward on 140 mules and lowered the wagons by ropes. Henry Bigler said, "I think no other man but Cooke would ever have attempted to cross such a place, but he seemed to have the spirit and energy of a Bonypart." See Gudde, ed., Bigler's Chronicle, 29. Afterward to Cooke's mortification, Stephen Foster discovered Guadalupe Pass on the Spanish trail from Fronteras a short distance to the north. See Ibid., 30 November 1846.

The remainder of the men, I being one, returned to camp. The route is very rough and rocky, never saw one more so. A large number of pioneers out preparing the road. It rained last evening. I sold my butcher knife to Azariah Smith for 37½ Cts. We divided our mess, I sleeping with Lawson[36] in the wagon.

Mon. 30. The tents and cooking utensils were packed on mules and 4 mules were hitched to each wagon and started after the provisions where we arrived and camped. Co. A left a wagon and so did the Staff.

Tues. Dec. 1 [1846]. On guard traveled 7 miles in a westerly direction camped in a small valley having timber of different kinds, sycamore, oak, apparently an evergreen, cottonwood and blue ash. We are on the waters of the Pacific Ocean.[37] The appetites of the men have become so sharp that they now eat beef hides, tripe, feet, heads and entrails, in fine everything that can be eaten.

Wed. 2. Left the valley and entered a plain traveled 10 miles and camped at a deserted village in another valley. The place had been occupied by Mexicans who had been driven out by the Apache Indians. The place was called San Bernardino Ranch and was built like the other Mexican houses we have seen;[38] this was the 31st day since we saw a house. A number of Indians in camp for the purpose of trading. Our course to day was a little north of west.

Thur. 3. One of the Pilots, Mr. Weaver informed me that we are now in the State of Sonora, Mexico, and will be until we cross the Colorado river.[39] Wild cattle abound in this section, some hunters have gone out. They returned bringing in the carcasses of 4 wild cattle, having killed 4 others also. The Indians have brought in some mescal ready cooked, which is sweet and good. The Indians seem friendly they are hearty, robust and intelligent. I have remained in camp all day, waiting the return of the pilots, they returned in the evening and reported favorably on the route,[40] but it was 30

---

[36]New Yorker John Lawson, 41, was a private in Co. B. A blackmsith, Lawson settled at New Harmony, Utah, where he died in 1884.

[37]The battalion on 25 November crossed the continental divide for the last time in the Animas Range in today's southwestern New Mexico. The command was now on the southeastern border of present Arizona where waters drain to the Gulf of California.

[38]The abandoned San Bernardino Hacienda was the center of a ranch established in 1822 as a buffer against the Apaches by Lt. Ignacio Perez on a Mexican land grant of more than seventy-three thousand acres. By 1846 the natives had driven the Mexicans out and made the ranch and another spread along the San Pedro River into a hunting ground for about one hundred thousand cattle which, said Cooke, "support the Indians, just as buffalo on the plains." Before 1822 scenic San Bernardino Spring, now located just south of the border between Cochise County, Arizona, and Mexico, had served for more than a century as a favorite campground on the road between Janos and Fronteras. The John Slaughter Ranch, now a historic site, lies across the international border from the original oasis.

[39]Today's Arizona south of the Gila River (which later became the Gadsden Purchase) was part of the Mexican state of Sonora.

[40]For some miles the battalion would now follow the Spanish road from Janos to Fronteras.

miles to the nearest water, also that there is a Mexican garrison ahead and that we shall pass through or near the town it occupies.[41]

Samuel Rogers made no journal entries over the next four days as the battalion traveled from San Bernardino Spring to the San Pedro River. On 5 December the command camped at a spring, just across the border from present Douglas, Arizona, so overrun by wild cattle that Cooke thought it a "perfect cattleyard in appearance." The entries of William Coray of Company B, one of the battalion's best journal keepers, provide a description of the typical conflicts and new concerns that occupied the men as they marched north through Sonora toward the garrisoned town of Tucson.[42]

JOURNAL OF SGT. WILLIAM CORAY OF THE MORMON BATTALION, 4 TO 7 DECEMBER 1846, NORMA B. RICKETTS COLLECTION.

On the morning of the 4th of Dec. Cook came out with an other order stating that we had wasted 6 days rations and there was enough left to take us at 10 oz. [of flour] per day which statement was a lie indeed. We marched at 1 o'clock and gained 6 miles. The orders were to kill no more beef cattle till the 9th in consequence of their having so much on hand. This evening the Lt. Col. told the Adjt. not [to] receive any guard who had not their knapsacks on, neither should they ride if they had horses. This I call tyranny in the extreme.

The 5th of Dec. 1846. We marched 15 miles. Passed through another range of mountains & camped at a sulphur spring. There were many wild cattle here and Capt. Hunter, Lts. Merrill & Barrus & myself went out to kill a bullock or 2 for ourselves by permission of the Col. We succeeded in killing 2 and bringing the stake into camp though not till after dark some time.

On the 6th we marched 14 miles over a plain of sand as usual among the mountains and encamped at a place we named Maple Grove, it being the 1st maple timber we have seen since we had left Santa Fee. It was very tedious travel here this P.M. as it snowed & rained during the whole afternoon. The cattle and horses are very plenty here. As the teams were soon faged, we laid by on the 7th and I went a hunting again with Capt. Hunter & Barrus. We saw nothing but bulls. We suppose the Indians had selected out the cows & calves as they were tender. When we got into camp, the sol-

[41]A reference to Tucson.

[42]Coray's manuscript journal is said to be in the possession of family members. The material used here is from a typescript provided to the editors by Norma B. Ricketts, who has ably summarized most of Coray's journal in *Melissa's Journey with the Mormon Battalion* and *The Mormon Battalion*.

diers were making preparations for an early start. The pilots had returned & said the San Pedro Rio was within 30 miles. The Pilot Weaver professed to be acquainted all the way. After we got to the San Pedro we had some reason to entertain some fears from Sonora as we were drawing near her borders. We are now within 12 miles of the Spanish Garison and one of the sheep drivers ran away on the night of the 6th, being a Spaniard.[43] We have some reasons to believe that he has gone to inform them of our approach and numbers. Sonora Numbers near 5000 strong. We could expect nothing less than capture if we go among them or their thickly settled country.

JOURNAL OF SAMUEL H. ROGERS, SPECIAL COLLECTIONS, BYU LIBRARY.

Tues. 8. This morning Elisha Smith died after an illness of ten days. He was a waiter of Capt. Davis of Co. E.[44] We took water for two days and started traveled 20 miles in a northwest direction, where we camped without water. Very cold and windy.

Wed. 9. We started shortly after Sunrise and continued northwest for 10 miles and reached the Rio San Pedro.[45] Crossing we traveled north down the stream 7 miles further and camped. A beautiful stream flowing into the Gila River. I bought two pairs of half soles cut from saddle skirts, of Sergeant Green for 50 Cts.

Thur. 10. Traveled down in a northerly direction for 15 miles and then camped on a bluff. The mountains have kept their white mantles the past 4 days.

Fri. 11. Traveled 13 miles down the stream to the north, camped on low bottom lands. During the march today the command was charged upon by a herd of wild cattle. Sergeant Smith of Co. B. and Private [Levi] Fifield of Co. C. were run over and the former was considerably injured, and two mules were gored by the bulls so their bowels gushed out. One of the mules was harnessed in a team at the time. Considerable shooting was done. Lieut. Stoneman accidentally shot a ball through one of his hands. He had a slide

---

[43]Coray wrote this entry about 15 December, for the command was still more than a week's march from Tucson on 7 December.

[44]Forty-eight-year-old Elisha Smith was not a battalion member, but served as a teamster and servant to Capt. Daniel Davis. Levi Hancock recalled that the night of his death it "seemed that all the wolves in the Rocky Mountains from Backbone Ridge to the Gila River had assembled to salute the Battalion. With one mighty exertion did they raise their yells and kept it up all night." See Hancock to Brigham Young, 12 May 1847, Journal History. Smith was buried on the bank of a "beautiful little stream of water running through an ash grove." See Gudde, ed., Bigler's Chronicle, 31.

[45]The San Pedro River flows north from Sonora as one of the Gila River's two main southern tributaries It is probably the stream Francisco Vasquez de Coronado referred to in 1540 as "Rio Nexpa" during his expedition down the river in search of the fabled Seven Cities of Cibola. For the next fifty miles or so the command would follow Coronado's trail.

gun, or fifteen shooter. Two loads exploded at the same time on[e] ball passing through his hand. Several bulls were killed.[46]

Sat. 12. Off at the usual time. Traveled west of north for 15 miles.
Crossed and recrossed the stream. Passed an old evacuated fort this morning.[47]

LT. COL. PHILIP ST.GEORGE COOKE: WE WILL MARCH THEN TO TUCSON

As the command neared the Mexican Presidio of Tucson, Cooke held
an arms inspection and a long drill, "drilling them myself, first a company in front of the others, and then the battalion, principally at loading and firing, and in forming column from line and line from column."
Sonora had refused to support the Mexican government in its war with
the United States, a fact acknowledged in the orders then read to the
battalion.

ORDER NUMBER 19, COOKE'S JOURNAL, 13 DECEMBER 1846.

Headquarters Mormon Battalion
Camp on the San Pedro, December 13, 1846

Thus far on our course to California we have followed the guides furnished by the general. These guides now point to Tucson, a garrisoned town,
as our road, and they assert that any other course is a hundred miles out of
the way, and over a trackless wilderness of mountains and river hills. We will
march then to Tucson. We came not to make war against Sonora, and less
still to destroy an unimportant outpost of defense against Indians. But we
will take the straight course before us and overcome all resistance. But shall
I remind you that the American soldier ever shows justice and kindness to

---

[46]In the "Battle of the Bulls," wounded animals ran up from the river bottom and found battalion
marchers "in the way of thare retreat." The animals injured several, including Sgt. Albert Smith who said,
"one chased me & as he came up threue me & run over me & tho there was no bones broke yet I was hurt
vary Seriously." See Albert Smith, Journal, 11 December 1846. Henry Boyle said, "We wounded Some &
killed ten or twelve & while we were Shooting among them they became desperate. the Smell of blood
Seemed to fill them full of fight ... They wounded two or three of the boys, killed three mules & upset a
wagon. The Indians have killed nearly all the cows, & the bulls are as dareing & Savage as tigers." See Boyle,
Autobiography and Diary, 11 December 1846. The site is near present Tombstone, Arizona.

[47]The Santa Cruz de Terrenate Presidio was constructed on the San Pedro River in 1775–76 to guard
the road between Fronteras and Tucson. It was abandoned in 1780 after Apaches killed two commanding
officers and many of the men stationed at the exposed outpost. The ruins of the early Spanish fort can
still be seen two miles north of the San Pedro River crossing of Arizona Highway 82. See Williams, "The
Presidio of Santa Cruz de Terrenate: A Forgotten Fortress of Southern Arizona."

the unarmed an unresisting? The property of individuals you will hold sacred. The people of Sonora are not our enemies.

By order of Lieutenant-colonel Cooke,

(signed) P. C. Merrill, Adjutant

SAMUEL ROGERS: WE CLEANED OUR GUNS

Although Brigham Young had promised they would do no fighting, battalion members accepted the prospect of action without grumbling and prepared for it like veterans, as described in the continuing account of Samuel Rogers.

JOURNAL OF SAMUEL H. ROGERS,
SPECIAL COLLECTIONS, BYU LIBRARY.

Sun. 13 [December 1846]. Off at the usual time, traveled 10 miles camped at noon. Each man received cartridges up to 20. We cleaned our guns and mustered and drilled.[48] Orders No. 19 were read, stating that so far we had followed the guides furnished by the General, that they pointed to Tucson a garrisoned town as being nearer by 100 miles than any other route, that the Fort is for a defence against the Indians, that the people of Sonora are not our enemies, that as American soldiers we should treat defenceless men and women with mercy and hold private property sacred. We would go to Tucson and conquer all who opposed. The guides went ahead some days ago to gather information, one of them, Foster, went to Tucson and did not return with the others. We supposed he is taken prisoner.

Mon. 14. On advance guard, traveled 20 miles and camped, leaving the San Pedro on our right.[49] Dark before we camped near a distillery belonging to the Apache Indians, who make whiskey from mescal. Here we were met by 3 or 4 Mexican soldiers.

Tues. 15. Traveled 15 miles, this morning one of the Mexican soldiers returned to the garrison, two of our men went with him to buy provisions. On our march today we took 3 Mexicans prisoners, as hostages for Foster.[50] Today saw a squaw grinding wheat by rubbing or crushing it between two stones.

Wed. 16. Last night at midnight 3 Mexican officers came into our camp

---

[48]Pvt. Azariah Smith, Co. B, said that the afternoon muster "was somewhat awkward which made the Colonel swear very much." See Bigler, ed., *The Gold Discovery Journal of Azariah Smith*, 57.

[49]The command now left the San Pedro River near the present town of Benson and headed on the line of today's I-10 for Tucson, the walled presidio on the Santa Cruz River, some fifty miles to the northwest.

[50]Cooke took four Mexican dragoons prisoner to guarantee the safe release of Stephen C. Foster who had gone into Tucson and been disarmed and put under guard. The colonel sent one of the dragoons back to the presidio with an offer to release the other three in exchange for Foster's freedom.

bringing Foster with them when the 3 prisoners we had were released. Started at 8 A.M. the Battalion consolidated in front of the teams and marching in quick time. We reached the garrison a little after noon. The soldiers were gone and also the substantial men of the place, leaving their property behind. At the edge of the town we were formed into line, when the Colonel repeated his last order about meddling with private property, threatening to punish those who failed to observe it. We then marched through town and camped about 1 mile below, 13 miles in all. The town is built in the Mexican style. We took what public property could be found. Some tobacco and wheat. Here are some fine farms. The people seem more intelligent than at Santa Fe. They came into our camp to trade, our advance guard took possession of the Fort without opposition for which the Lord be praised.[51]

Thur. 17. Remained in Camp. The Col. with a party of volunteers from all of the companies made a reconnoitering expedition and returned.[52] Our mess bought some flour and beans of the Mexicans. We are cooking for two days owing to the scarcity of water ahead.

Fri. 18. Last night at midnight the Battalion was aroused from sleep by the sound of trumpets, an alarm had been given by the picket guard who saw a number of Mexicans approaching.[53] We all paraded, the tents were taken down and the fires extinguished inside of 15 minutes. Co. A. was sent to the town to ascertain the whereabouts of the enemy, if any could be found, while the remainder of the Battalion stood in readiness with flanking guards and loaded muskets. Co. A soon returned after having found nothing of the enemy. We were then dismissed and erecting our tents went to bed again. Off at 9–30 A.M. northwest in march until 9 P.M. 25 miles. Camped without water.

Lt. Col. Philip St.George Cooke:
I Did Not Come As an Enemy

Before marching the battalion from Tucson, Colonel Cooke left a

---

[51]With a population of about five hundred, mostly soldiers and their families, Tucson was an island of Spanish colonization in a region controlled by hostile Apache Indians. Its garrison of some 130 men with two brass cannons had fled to the nearby Mission San Xavier del Bac. Founded in 1776 to guard the mission and other Spanish settlements in the Santa Cruz Valley, the presidio in 1846 was virtually isolated and in need of repair after years of neglect by the Mexican government.

[52]Cooke led a reconnaissance toward the mission, but cancelled it fearing an ambush in the dense mesquite brush. Henry Boyle said, "This morning our Colonel called for 40 vollenteers, accordingly 40 of us vollenteered. My self in the number. We were then marched up the country through the wood Some five or Six miles with ev[e]ry precaution that could be taken. The Colonel Staff acted as though they expected to encounter an enemy at evry turn of the road. We were halted & after a Council among the officers we were ordered to about face & march back to camp."

[53]The nervous picket guard thought he saw a double column of Mexican cavalry approaching the encampment.

note in Spanish to the commander of the presidio and a letter for delivery to the governor of Sonora. They illustrate why the United States was able peacefully to occupy the Southwest with barely a handful of soldiers during the Mexican War.

COOKE TO COMADURAN, 18 DECEMBER 1846, COOKE'S JOURNAL.

Battalion Headquarters
Camp at Tucson, Sonora, December 18, 1846

Sir: Having received no orders, or entertained an intention to make war upon Sonora, I regret that circumstances have compelled me to break up your quarters at this post. Making forced marches for the want of watering places, and finding no grass or other forage here, I have found it necessary to use about thirty *fanegas* of wheat from the public granary. None has been wasted or destroyed, and no other public property has been seized. Herewith you will receive a letter for his excellency, the governor of Sonora, on the subject of my involuntary invasion of the state. I respectfully request that you send it to him with your own dispatches. With high respect, your obedient servant,

P. St. Geo. Cooke, Lieutenant-colonel
commanding battalion U.S. volunteers

To Don Antonio Comaduran,
Commandante, Presidio of Tucson

COOKE TO GANDARA, 18 DECEMBER 1846, P. ST. GEORGE COOKE
SELECTED PAPERS, 1846–47, MIC A139, NATIONAL ARCHIVES.

Camp at Tucson, Sonora, December 18, 1846

Your Excellency: The undersigned, marching in command of a battalion of United States infantry from New Mexico to California, has found it convenient for the passage of his wagon train to cross the frontier of Sonora. Having passed within fifteen miles of Fronteras, I have found it necessary to take this *presidio* in my route to the Gila.

Be assured that I did not come as an enemy of the *people* whom you govern: they have received only kindness at my hands.

Sonora refused to contribute to the support of the present war against my country: alleging the excellent reasons that all her resources were necessary to her defence from the incessant attack of savages; that the Central government gave her no protection, and was therefore entitled to no support. To this might have been added that *Mexico supports a war upon Sonora.*

For I have seen New Mexicans within her boundary trading for the spoil of her people, taken by murderous cowardly indians who attack only to lay waste, rob, and fly to the mountains; and I have certain information that this is the practice of many years; thus, one part of Mexico allies itself against another.[54]

The unity of Sonora with the States of the north,—now her neighbours,—is necessary effectually to subdue the Parthian Apaches.

Meanwhile I make a wagon road from the streams of the Atlantic to the Pacific Ocean, through the valuable plains & mountains rich with minerals, of Sonora: this, I trust, will prove useful to the Citizens of either republic, who if not more closely—may unite in the pursuits of a highly beneficial commerce.

With Sentiments of Esteem & respect
I am your Excy's most obt. Servt.
[signed] P. St. Geo. Cooke
Lt. Colonel
Comdg. U.S. Forces.

To His Excy.
Sn. Dn. Manuel Gandara
Governor of Sonora
Ures Sa.

SAMUEL ROGERS: STRAGGLERS SCATTERED FOR MILES

The battalion now took up its line of march on the historic trail to southern California opened in 1774 by Juan Bautista de Anza, then Tubac Presidio commander, and Father Francisco Garces, the Franciscan missionary and founder of Tucson.[55] Samuel Rogers resumes his account as the command headed for the Gila River. He tells the story of the arduous march across the deserts of Arizona and California with powerful simplicity.

JOURNAL OF SAMUEL H. ROGERS, SPECIAL COLLECTIONS, BYU LIBRARY.

Sat. 19 [December 1846]. Off at 7 A.M. Continued in the same direction over these dry, dusty and level plains, covered with bushes armed with thorns, every vegetable growth is guarded with thorns against all comers that may assail. The teams are fed on wheat, taken from Tucson for there is no grass. Traveled 30 miles. The march continued until 11 P.M. The stragglers scattered for miles, because of fatigue. Still no water.

Sat. [Sun.] 20. On advance guard, still to the northwest, 15 miles brought us to water, the first since Friday noon.

---

[54]Cooke referred to the *Comancheros*, New Mexican traders from Taos and Santa Fe who exchanged firearms and whiskey to the Comanches and Kiowas for the spoils of their raids into Chihuahua and Sonora. Cooke had undoubtedly seen this illicit trade firsthand during his service on the frontier.

[55]In 1775 Colonel Anza led a company of 240 men, women, and children over the Gila River trail to the San Gabriel Mission, near Los Angeles, and established the following year the presidio and mission that became San Francisco.

Mon. 21. Off at the usual hour continuing to the northwest, reached the Gila river [in] 15 miles.[56] Camped among scores of Pima indians, who had meal and corn and beans for sale. I traded an old shirt for some beans. These Indians are large, robust and healthy. We here came again upon General Kearney's trail.[57]

Tues. 22. Last night a mule was drowned in the river. Off at the usual time down the river here running west. 10 miles, camped at noon in an Indian village. Saw a squaw suckling a papoose in a singular manner, it was in a round basket with a hole in the side of the basket through which the child sucked as she held the basket under her arm. The squaws were naked except a breech clout. As soon as we camped the Indians, Squaws and Children all came into camp with corn, beans, meal, dried and green pumpkin and bread to trade for Clothes or other articles. They have also water melons; the land appears very dry and barren. They have good horses and poneys. It is said that this tribe of Indians have never shed the blood of white men neither do they war with other Indian tribes but obtain their living by agriculture, having large farms.[58]

Wed. 23. Traveled 20 miles passing through a number of Pima Indian villages.

Thur. 24. Remain in camp preparing for a two days march across the Gila Bend. Many are washing their clothes. A host of Indians of both sexes here to day having the products of their industry with them to trade. Their blankets made from cotton raised by themselves are of excellent quality. Their appliances for spinning and weaving are of the most primitive character, and it is wonderful how they attain such proficiency with such rude implements, and it would almost seem the labor of a life time to make one blanket. Their cooking utensils consist of earthenware made I think by themselves as they have a great deal of earthenware which is used for various purposes. Ate a piece of watermelon today which was very good. Their houses are thatched with straw. The most of them are shaped like the crown of a round top hat, others are square. The Colonel has bought considerable corn of them.

Fri. 25 [December 1846]. Off at 10 A.M. Course South by West passing

---

[56]The command reached the Gila River near the present town of Sacaton on today's Gila River Indian Reservation.

[57]Kearny's mounted command had followed the Gila River all the way from New Mexico. At this point its trail was five to six weeks old.

[58]The Pimas made a favorable impression on the entire command. Thomas Morris wrote, "Here, for the first time in my life, I was introduced to a tribe of Indians unadulterated by the immoralities of the civilized white population where there were drunkards. Here no degrading vulgarity, no pinching poverty, no tippling loafers, no prodigal aristocrats imposing taxes and titles on the communities." See Morris, Autobiography and Journal, 16–22 December 1846.

to the left of a mountain, the river flowing to the right of it. Camped without water at 8 P.M. 20 miles.[59]

Sat. 26. In advance guard, off at day break, course North west 30 miles where we again struck the Gila river.

Sun. 27. Off at 9-30 A.M. Travelled north by west 12 miles, camped on the river at 2 P.M. Some grass for the teams which is unusual in this part of the Country.

Mon. 28. Last night two men came into camp from California. General Kearney had given them passports to Sonora. They reported a skirmish between Kearney and the Californians in which he gained the victory. They also report a quarrel between two of the leading Mexican Generals, and that the people of California are fleeing from there. This morning an express was started to Gen. Kearney and we resumed our journey.[60] Traveled 18 miles down the river.

Tues. 29. The Col. gave orders that no private provisions be hauled in the Battalion wagons. Traveled 14 miles over a very sandy road.[61]

Wed. 30. A very rugged road to day, made 20 miles, but traveled until after dark.

Thur. 31. General muster at 7 A.M. After which marched 10 miles, the ground shows signs of late rains. Camped on a slough of brackish water. The sun shines clear and the weather is fine.

Fri. Jan. 1. 1847. Cool last night. Pleasant today. Marched 10 miles and camped on the bank of the river at 2 P.M. Near by were some Californians fleeing from the turmoils of that country.[62] We are preparing to send some of the baggage down the river in a boat, thereby releiving the teams.[63]

---

[59]Henry Bigler noted that some men bought "watermelons to eat on Christmas day," but like Rogers most diarists did not mention the holiday. Here the trail took a fifty-mile shortcut across the base of the river's great bend to reach its banks again near present Gila Bend. The desert ran to the south of the Sierra Estrella.

[60]This was apparently the first report to reach Cooke of Kearny's disastrous encounter on 6 December 1846 with a body of Californian lancers at San Pasqual. Cooke sent his "useless guides," Leroux, Charbonneau, and three others as an express to inform Kearny of his approach and request that fresh mules and beef cattle be sent to Warner's Ranch in present San Diego County by 21 January. Cooke also considered rushing ahead with two hundred of his best men to reinforce the general, but decided against it.

[61]Rogers neglected to say that the battalion this day passed a large pile of massive boulders covered with Indian petroglyphs of animals, men, and mystic figures, possibly marking a prehistoric boundary between tribes. Increasingly defaced, the petroglyphs can be seen today at Painted Rocks Historic State Park about fourteen miles west of Gila Bend, Arizona, between I-8 and the river.

[62]This company included William Money, a Scottish-American, and his Mexican wife, who had given birth two days before and ridden ten miles on horseback the day after. They were on their way to a mining town in Sonora, some sixty miles south of the Pima villages, where Mrs. Money's father lived. The party provided some additional information about the "sharp engagement" between General Kearny and Mexican forces that gave Cooke "much anxiety." See Cooke's Journal, 1 January 1847.

[63]Having more wagons than needed and too few strong mules to pull them, Cooke at Stoneman's urging attempted to float more than a ton of provisions and luggage down the river on a makeshift barge made by caulking two wagon boxes and lashing them together, end to end, between two cottonwood poles.

Sat. 2. On camp guard last night. Three wagon loads of provisions are to be boated down the river from this point.[64] Marched 12 miles and camped.

Sun. 3. Again marched 12 miles and camped.

Mon. 4. Traveled 7 miles camped at the base of a high mountain. Some of the men climbed to the top of it and rolled down big rocks which descended with tremendous noise. I bought a buckskin of John Lawson for which I am to pay him $1.—with which I faced my pants.

Tues. 5. 1847. Traveled down the river 12 miles. Our rations were again reduced to 9 ounces of flour and 8 ounces of pork per day. We learn that they failed to boat the provisions down the river because of the low stage of the water, so they were left behind.[65] This cuts down the rations of flour for Co. B [to] 7 days.

Wed. 6. We left two men and a mule to recover a part of the flour. Marched 15 miles and camped. Walter Davis[66] shot a Pelican. Our mess bought a beefs head which we dressed in the regular manner. We scalded the skin and pulled and picked the hair off, and boiled it with the rest of the head.

Thur. 7. Traveled over points of mountain and across bottoms for 14 miles. The mules and oxen were swum across the river to where there was some brush for them to browse upon.

Fri. 8. Traveled 15 miles. Camped near the junction of the Gila and Colorado rivers,[67] the whole distance from the point where we left the Rio Grande del Norte to the mouth of the Gila is 686 miles, according to my judgment of an unmeasured road. We have found no timber to speak of, a little Cottonwood on the Gila, though there is plenty of brush such as is common on the plains of Sonora.

Sat. 9. Traveled 10 miles down the Colorado in a southwest course when we camped upon its bank.[68]

Sun. 10. Remained in camp, some of the Companies took their provi-

---

[64]The load included enough pork for thirteen days, flour for some eighteen days, seven or eight bushels of corn, some tools, and assorted baggage.

[65]Despite his "indomitable perseverance," Stoneman's amphibious experiment failed because the water was only three or four inches deep in places, too shallow to carry the loaded vessel over sandbars. Cpl. William S. Muir, 24, from Scotland, and five Co. A men were left behind with pack mules to recover at least some of the flour from the ill-fated effort. Lamented Cooke: "Thus two feeds of corn, which I had brought so far, is lost! And when most needed! The loss of the flour straightens me a little, as I have but fourteen days more, not allowing for wastage. I have reduced the rations to nine ounces again." See Cooke's Journal, 4, 5 January 1847.

[66]Walter L. Davis, a private in Co. E, was born in Upper Canada in 1821.

[67]The mouth of Gila River, where the camp was located, is near the eastern outskirts of present Yuma, Arizona. From this point the Colorado River runs west about ten miles before again turning south toward the Gulf of California.

[68]They camped at the crossing on the left bank of the Colorado River, opposite the present city of Algodones, Mexico, where three members of Corporal Muir's pack mule from Co. A party returned the next morning with 420 pounds of flour. They reported that the determined Muir and two others had stayed behind to look for other deposits of provisions.

sions and baggage across this p.m.[69] The river here is about half a mile wide, with rich bottoms along its banks.[70]

Mon. 11. The remainder of the Battalion crossed the river. One wagon was left on an island and some mules got so chilled in the water that they drowned. Some of the men waded the river.[71] Prosecuted our journey west for 15 miles, but left 4 wagons on the way. We obtained water by digging.[72] The Sheep did not come in and our rations of flour were now reduced to 8 ounces of flour a day per man.

Tues. 12. Early this morning some men were sent ahead to dig for water at our next camping place. Did not start till near noon. The wagon left on the island came up as did also the Sheep. Marched 20 miles to the west camped without water except what we brought with us. One or two wagons were left behind.

Wed. 13. Traveled 16 miles north by west and camped. The men who went ahead obtained water in three wells from 12 to 16 feet deep.[73] One of the beeves tired out and was butchered, some of the rear guard ate some of it, before reaching camp owing to excessive hunger.

Thur. 14. A number of men were detailed to draw water from the wells for the mules. This was kept up all night. Pioneers were sent forward early this morning to dig for water. The march commenced at noon. On rear guard, did not start till 3 P.M. Just before starting a number of Mexicans from Tucson came up. Traveled north west 22 miles and reached camp at 10-30 P.M. when I stood on camp guard 2 hours more. On this day's march three wagons were left behind. One of them was our blanket wagon. The mules and harness were sold to the highest bidder.

---

[69]The men used watertight wagon boxes, built to serve as boats when needed, to float baggage and provisions across the river.

[70]Cooke wrote, "The Rio Colorado here resembles the Missouri in size and color of the water. It has immense bottoms difficult to pass; they are of rich soil. I believe it to be the most useless of rivers to man; so barren, so desolate and difficult, that it has never been explored; running through volcanic mountains and sand deserts, at places through chasms of vertical rock perhaps five thousand feet deep." See Cooke's Journal, 9 January 1847.

[71]The water in places was up to their necks and very cold.

[72]Here Cooke knew "the most trying hour of my long military service" when his tired men found a dry well with a dead wolf in the bottom. Digging deeper, they struck only quicksand that caved in before a puddle could form. To keep the sides from collapsing, the men confiscated a wash tub hauled all the way from Nauvoo by Susan Davis, Captain Davis's wife, who at first refused to give it up even if their lives depended on it. They knocked the bottom out and placed it in the well. Some water formed, but not enough. Cooke then ordered a second well dug, and "a radiant glow of light" came over him when enough water at last flowed to "be dipped with a camp kettle." See Cooke's Journal, 11 January 1847, and "Report," 558.

[73]This camp was at the Alamo Mocha Well, location now unknown, but about six miles south of today's line between Imperial County and Mexico. Of the Imperial Valley crossing, Co. B Sgt. Albert Smith said, "Some went A head with [pick] & Shovel in hand & dug wel[l]s in low places So that we did not quite parish." See Journal of Albert Smith, 11 January 1847.

Fri. 15 [January 1847]. Early on the march 12 miles to the northwest brought us to the well,[74] but there was not enough water for the men. At this place a part of the men who went on express to Kearney met us on their return with 6 Indians, 40 mules and 10 beeves.[75] After resting a little we continued on in the same direction for 14 miles further which occupied the time till 7-30 P.M. when we cooked and ate a little beef.

Sat. 16. We were aroused at 1 A.M. when the march was resumed and continued almost without a halt for 25 miles to the West when we reached running water Called the Cariza.[76] This last has been a forced marched [*sic*] performed without water. Some of the animals were completely tired out and some killed themselves with drinking.

Sun. 17. Started at the usual hour. Traveled west 15 miles over a very sandy road. Midway there were some Palmetto or Cabbage trees.[77] Here the last pork was issued.

Mon. 18. This morning the last flour was issued. Remained encamped, a general muster in the P.M.[78]

Tues. 19. The Battalion consolidated marched ahead of the teams; helped them up a mountain, then marched through a deep valley as before,

---

[74] This was the Pozo Hondo, or "deep well," location unknown.

[75] They also gave a full report of Kearny's defeat on 6 December at San Pasqual, near present Escondido, where the general and two dragoon companies on worn-out mules, their firearms made useless by rain, foolishly charged a larger force of Californian lancers. The Californians, superb horsemen, fell back until the attack was spent, then turned and cut the dragoon force to pieces. The unequal contest, swords against lances, lasted but a few minutes, but in that time twenty-one Americans were killed or mortally wounded, including First Dragoons officers Capt. Abraham R. Johnston, Capt. Benjamin D. Moore, and Lt. Thomas Hammond, Moore's brother-in-law. Hardly hurt, the Californians proudly rode off with one of Kearny's two mountain howitzers, hauled all the way from Fort Leavenworth, an embarrassing loss. Lamented Cooke, "What a loss to my regiment! Ah! who but loved Johnston—the noble, sterling, valued Johnston! And who had warmer friends than poor Moore! Peace to their ashes! Rest to their souls! May their country honor the memories of its heroic champions, who, serving her, have found their graves in distant and desolate regions!" See Cooke's Journal, 15 January 1846.

[76] After fifty hours without water for their animals, the command reached Carrizo Creek, an intermittent stream on the southern trail. The name means "common reed grass," which is often found in Imperial and San Diego counties.

[77] This was Palm Spring, now in Anza-Borrego Desert State Park in eastern San Diego County, not to be confused with the well-known resort city east of Los Angeles. Emigrant vandalism destroyed the original native California fan palms described by Rogers, but they were later replanted when the historical significance of the place became apparent. The little oasis on the Southern Emigrant Trail and Butterfield Stage Road is located on the southeast edge of the park about two miles east of County Road S2, which follows the line of the emigrant and stage trail to Warner's Ranch. The editors are indebted to G. J. "Chris" Graves of Newcastle and L. Louise Jee of Borrego Springs for information on the trail through this region.

[78] The command reached Vallecito Creek after marching over "the worst fifteen miles of road since we left the Rio Grande; and that it was accomplished, under all the circumstances, by mules or men is extraordinary," Cooke said. Vallecito, or Little Valley, once the site of a Butterfield Stage station, is a scenic green spot in the desert. At this camp the colonel received word from John B. Montgomery, commander of the U.S. sloop-of-war *Portsmouth*, that California insurrectionists were expected to march for Sonora over the same trail the battalion was on. See Cooke's Journal, 17, 18 October 1846.

no bugle call being sounded. We then passed through a narrow defile where we helped the teams to get through.[79] Traveled 15 miles. Camped without water.

Wed. 20 [January 1847]. Off before breakfast. Crossed another valley and a ridge of mountains, 10 miles halted for refreshments. Here I was placed on the advance guard and marched 10 miles farther and camped. Observed some evergreen oaks with acorns from 1 to 2 inches long, and from ¼ to ½ an inch in diameter. Vegetation is already starting. Our course today has been west.

Thur. 21. Off at the usual time, 12 miles brought us to Warner's ranch where we camped in a very gentle valley, the best I have yet seen in this country.[80]

Fri. 22. Laid in camp. Washed my clothes. The men are trading their clothes to the Indians for provisions, some even traded off their last shirts from their backs. These are Indians which stay around Warner's ranch. Went to see the hot Springs near here. The water comes out of the rocks, and is too warm to hold one's hand in with comfort. Warner has some fine vineyards. The Quartermaster bought some cattle of him.

Jan. 23. Our rations of beef are increased to 4 lbs per day to each man. Off at the usual hour, marched west for 25 miles. Quite rainy, the first for some time. Our route was over hills and sloping valleys. Some men remained behind to get some flour, they came in with 300 lbs.[81]

Sun. [2]4. Last night it rained all night and continued this morning. At 10 A.M. we started, marched west in the rain 4 miles. Camped near a creek. The rain continued till near sun set.

Mon. 25. Marched west 18 miles entered a beautiful valley where we dis-

---

[79]Rogers' entry failed to describe the hard labor it took by all hands, including Cooke, to hack a passage for wagons through solid rock and widen a narrow defile between the Oriflamme and Vallecito mountains with axes and a pry bar. Even then they had to dismantle and carry some wagons and turn others sideways to get them through Box Canyon, now a historic site in Anza-Borrego Desert State Park.

[80]Established in 1844 by Jonathan Trumball Warner on a Mexican land grant, the 49,000-acre Warner's Ranch was to travelers on the Southern Emigrant Trail as Johnson's Ranch and Sutter's Fort were to California emigrants on the northern route. Warner came to California in 1831, took out Mexican citizenship, and became one of the largest landowners. He was among the earliest advocates of U.S. annexation of California and worked as a confidential correspondent of Thomas Larkin, the American consul at Monterey. Even so, the New Englander was arrested during the oppressive Stockton conquest on suspicion of disloyalty. The ranch building ruins can be seen today on San Diego County Road S2 less than a mile from its junction with State Highway 79, some thirteen miles north of Santa Ysabel.

[81]In a remarkable feat, Corporal Muir and two others overtook the command with four hundred pounds of flour from the ill-fated attempt to float provisions down the Gila River. When Cooke blamed him "for going so far and staying so long," Muir said "he did not dare to come without it, and would have expected to have been sent back if he had." See Cooke's Journal, 23 January 1847.

covered an army of Indians who prepared to dispute our advance.[82] They paraded in battle array and looked quite grand and formidable, but when a despatch was sent to them, they withdrew to their quarters and we encamped. An express came in from General Kearney informing us that he had taken Los Angeles and was on his way to San Diego, to which place he ordered us to march. We had directed our course towards Los Angeles, from Warner's ranch.[83] Snow can be seen on the mountains.

Tues. 26. On guard in the advance, marched towards San Diego. Waded the San Luis river, 18 miles. Camped in a valley. Vegetation starting, especially mustard which appears to grow spontaneously.

Wed. 27. Traveled in the rear of the Staff wagon, towards the south to the town of San Luis Rey, which had been evacuated. The town is pleasantly situated on the bank of the San Luis river, and has a Catholic Church building roofed with tiles, which is the best building I have seen since entering Mexican Territory.[84] Halting a short time we proceeded on our journey. Our course turned a little to the east. Ascending a hill, I beheld for the first time the Pacific Ocean.[85] Marched 22 miles. Camped within hearing of the

---

[82]These natives were the Luiseños, or Temecula Indians, who had come to bury the remains of some thirty-eight members of the tribe who had been killed in an ambush some days before by Californians and their allies from the Cahuilla tribe. Named after the San Luis Rey Mission located in their tribal grounds, the Luiseños were friendly toward the battalion because Cooke had hired a chief and twenty warriors to drive cattle and serve as scouts. See Parker, "The Temecula Massacre."

[83]Ordered to march to San Diego, Cooke had learned that Kearny was advancing against a Californian army at Los Angeles and decided on his own initiative to head northward in support of the general's attack and move against the enemy's flank from the east. But Kearny on 9 January 1847 defeated the insurgents in the Battle of Los Angeles with a mixed force of sailors, dragoons, and marines that included Frémont's mounted "Life Guards" under Capt. Samuel J. Hensley, who would later open Hensley's Salt Lake Cutoff of the California Trail from Salt Lake to City of Rocks, near Almo, Idaho.

[84]Named for Louis IX of France, San Luis Rey de Francia was the "king" of California's missions and the largest in the Americas. When dedicated in 1798 it raised to eighteen the number of missions that formed a chain, about one day's travel apart, from San Diego to San Francisco Bay. San Luis Rey had been looted by government officials and occupied by local Indians after the secularization of the missions in 1833. Now restored, this magnificent historic site can be seen on Mission Avenue about five miles east of present Oceanside.

[85]After marching for four months across the southwest desert, battalion members marveled at their first sight of the Pacific Ocean. Said Henry Boyle, "I never Shall be able to express my feelings at this enraptured moment. when our colums were halted evry eye was turned toward its placid Surface evry heart beat with muttered pleasure evry Soul was full of thankfulness, evry tounge was Silent, we all felt too ful to give Shape to our feelings by any expression. It has been many a weary day, and we have traveled many a long mile Since our eyes have been permited to gaze upon as lovely a Scene. The Surrounding hills are covered with wild oats & grass nearly a foot high, green & luxuriant as midsummer and how Sweet and refreshing is the breeze that is winging its way from the ocean up to this fertile valley which Stretches itself from the Shore back to the 'Sieras.' What an expansive view! how bright and beautiful evry thing looks!!" See Boyle, Autobiography and Diary, 27 January 1847.

ocean waves, near an evacuated house where we obtained some salt, an article much needed by us.

Thur. 28. Traveled east by south 15 miles and camped.

Fri. 29. Reached old San Diego, 20 miles, marching about southeast.
This place is evacuated except by Indians.[86] According to my estimate of an
unmeasured road, by the route we have taken we have traveled 1287 miles
since leaving Santa Fe. Here are some beautiful gardens, with olive trees and
vineyards. Col. Cooke and the officers of the regular army who were along
with us, took up their quarters in the lower town.

Sat. 30 [January 1847]. Some men were detailed to clean out some
rooms connected with the Catholic meeting house, with a view to them
being occupied by the Battalion, but in the evening the regulars marched in
and occupied them.

Lt. Col. Philip St.George Cooke:
High and Essential Qualities of Veterans

For more than three months Lt. Col. Philip St. George Cooke and the
men under his command had taken each other's measure under conditions that put leadership and endurance to the ultimate test. Not all the
men had come to love their hard-driving leader, but many recognized
Cooke as a man of great character. "Had it not been for the cool head-
edness and sagacity of our stern commander in turning everything to a
good account we must have all perished before reaching our destination," John Riser recalled. "There is no doubt in my mind but what
Colonel Cooke was one of the ablest officers then in the Army to undertake such an enterprise with such scanty supplies at his command."[87]
The day after the battalion's arrival at San Diego, 30 January 1847, the
professional frontier officer wrote the now-famous Order Number 1, a
tribute to his Mormon soldiers in which battalion veterans would justly
take pride for the rest of their lives. Five days later, Lt. Philemon C.

---

[86]Rogers referred to the Mission San Diego de Alcala, where the battalion camped, the mother of California's Spanish missions, then "dilapidated and full of Indians and dirt," Cooke said. Dedicated in 1760
by renowned Franciscan Father Junípero Serra, the mission was moved five years later to its present location, six miles up the San Diego River. In its prime, the San Diego Mission numbered nearly fifteen hundred Christian Indians and included vineyards, a school, gardens, and grazing lands. It has also been
restored. See Cooke's Journal, 29 January 1847.

[87]Riser, Autobiography, 1887.

Merrill, the command's twenty-six-year-old adjutant, read the special commendation during roll call at San Luis Rey Mission. The men cheered and threw their hats in the air. Said Henry Boyle, "He is a man too that was Strongly prejudiced against us in the start."

COOKE'S JOURNAL, 30 JANUARY 1847.

Order Number I
Headquarters Mormon Battalion,
Mission of San Diego, January 30, 1847

The lieutenant-colonel commanding congratulates the battalion on their safe arrival on the shore of the Pacific ocean, and the conclusion of the march of over two thousand miles. History may be searched in vain for an equal march of infantry. Nine-tenths of it has been through a wilderness where nothing but savages and wild beasts are found, or deserts where, for want of water, there is no living creature. There, with almost hopeless labor, we have dug deep wells which the future traveler will enjoy. Without a guide who had traversed them, we have ventured into trackless prairies where water was not found for several marches. With crowbar and pick and ax in hand we have worked our way over mountains which seemed to defy aught save the wild goat, and hewed a passage through a chasm of living rock more narrow than our wagons. To bring these first wagons to the Pacific, we have preserved the strength of our mules by herding them ever over large tracts, which you have laboriously guarded without loss. The garrisons of four *presidios* of Sonora, concentrated within the walls of Tucson, gave us no pause. We drove them out with their artillery, but our intercourse with the citizens was unmarked by a single act of injustice. Thus, marching half naked and half fed, and living upon wild animals, we have discovered and made a road of great value to our country. Arrived at the first settlement of California after a single day's rest, you cheerfully turned off from the route to this point of promised repose to enter upon a campaign, and meet, as we believed, the approach of the enemy; and this, too, without even salt to season your sole subsistence of fresh meat. Lieutenants A. J. Smith and George Stoneman, of the First Dragoons, have shared and given valuable aid in all these labors. Thus, volunteers, you have exhibited some high and essential qualities of veterans. But much remains undone. Soon you will turn your strict attention to the drill, to system and order, to forms also, which are all necessary to the soldier.

By order of Lieutenant-colonel P. St. Geo. Cooke,

P. C. Merrill, Adjutant

LT. COL. PHILIP ST.GEORGE COOKE:
UNITY AND DETERMINATION OF SPIRIT

A day after his congratulatory order was read at San Luis Rey Mission, Philip St. George Cooke completed his official report to General Kearny. Virtually unnoticed by historians and only published in 1848 by Congress and in 1954 by the *Utah Historical Quarterly*, this document is without doubt the best review of the historic march.[88] The report reveals how much Cooke's unbending discipline rested on his own faith and self-control. It explains decisions that some complained about at the time and exhibits the stresses imposed by his determination to carry out his assignment while protecting the welfare of his men. In so doing, this eloquent narrative imparts needed perspective to this story. In it Cooke finally displayed his disappointment that he had been given "more humble labors" while fellow officers were winning fame and promotion on the battlefield.

"REPORT OF LIEUT. COL. P. ST. GEORGE COOKE OF HIS MARCH FROM
SANTA FE, NEW MEXICO, TO SAN DIEGO, UPPER CALIFORNIA."

San Louis Rey,
California, February 5, 1847

Sir: In obedience to Army of the West Order, No. 33, of October 2d, I returned from La Joya, N. Mexico, to Santa Fe, to take command of the Mormon battalion; I arrived there on the 7th October.

I found that the paymasters, from whose arrival you anticipated a plentiful resource of money for the quartermaster department, had brought so little specie that no payment of troops could be made. The consequence was, that Captain Hudson's company of volunteers for California, which you had assigned to my command, could not mount themselves; and the quartermaster's department, which scarcely commanded a dollar, could hardly have furnished the transportation. Owing to these difficulties, the captain's new company was broken up by Colonel Doniphan, commanding.

A portion of the battalion of Mormons arrived the evening of the 9th October, under First Lieutenant A. J. Smith, 1st dragoons, who had, in the capacity of acting lieutenant colonel, directed its march from Council

---

[88] The original report is in Kearny Selected Papers, National Archives, MIC A139, copy at the Utah State Hist. Soc. With minor corrections to wording and punctuation from the manuscript, this transcription follows "Report of Lieut. Col. P. St. George Cooke of His March from Santa Fe, New Mexico, to San Diego, Upper California," 5 February 1847, House Exec. Doc. 41 (30-1), Serial 517, 551–62. See also Hamilton Gardner's excellent treatment in *Utah Hist. Quarterly* 22 (January 1954), 15–40.

Grove. The rear of the battalion arrived the evening of the 12th. On the 13th, I assumed command with the rank of lieutenant colonel, by virtue of your appointment. Its aggregate present was 448. I found that their mules were entirely broken down, and that as many as sixty men had, from sickness and other causes, been transported in wagons much of the march; and that there were twenty-five women, besides many children. The assistant surgeon of the battalion, Dr. Sanderson, and the senior officer of the department, Dr. De Camp, reported on the cases of a very large number, as subjects for discharge for disability. But the colonel commanding determined, under all the circumstances, to retain them in service, and ordered them to be sent to winter at "Pueblo," on the Arkansas river, above Bent's Fort. There the Mormons have a temporary settlement, and there Mr. Smith had sent, from the crossing of the Arkansas, a party of ten, commanded by Captain Higgins, in charge of a large number of families, which had theretofore been attached to the Mormon battalion. This detachment had orders to join the battalion at Santa Fe. (They arrived after its march, and, I learned, obtained permission to return to the Pueblo.) About this time, I learned that you had left your wagons, in consequence of difficulties of the country; and was anxious, for the benefit of all, to disencumber the expedition of the twenty laundresses. Learning that the most of them wished to go with the detachment to the Arkansas, I ordered them all to be sent there. With a sufficient number of able-bodied men (husbands of the women) to take care of it, the detachment amounted to eighty-six, and was placed under the command of Captain Brown.

I urged every preparation for the march, but it was impossible to complete them before the 19th of October; the battalion was paid, with treasury drafts, on the 16th and 17th. There was no salt pork in Santa Fe, and a sufficiency did not arrive until the evening of the 16th. Beef cattle, furnished under a previous contract for the battalion, were received the night of the 17th; and a quantity of pack saddles the same evening. On the 19th of October, I marched out of Santa Fe, and encamped at Agua Frio. At the earnest request of two captains and three sergeants, their wives were permitted to accompany the expedition; having their own wagons and mules, and provisions.

The rations had been issued to the companies, and each had three mule wagons, and one drawn by oxen; (these were to be sent back on leaving the river.) The rations were sixty days of flour and salt, sugar and coffee; thirty days of pickled pork, and twenty of soap.

The mules furnished me were mostly poor and worked down; the half of them were utterly unfit to commence an ordinary march. A number, as well as of oxen, were left behind, unable to walk, in the first forty miles. Thus I was obliged to exchange them two for one, and to purchase many others. For the first 150 miles, on the Rio Grande there was at that season no grass deserving the name. I purchased, when I could, corn and fodder, but in very small quantities. I had 380 sheep purchased, near Socorro, and beeves, to make up the sixty days' rations.

About 75 miles below that point, I became convinced that the march must fail, unless some improvement was made. I was marching about eight miles a day, in as many hours, through the deep sand; the mules overworked, growing poorer, giving out, dying and left behind each day.

From the opinions of the guides, there was also reason to apprehend that the supply of provisions was inadequate; and the ox wagons were then to go back. There were twenty-two men on the sick report, who, with the arms and knapsacks of others, encumbered the wagons. I called on the assistant surgeon and company commanders for lists of those they believed worthless for the march; fifty-eight names were soon given to me. Captain Burgwin's camp was 58 miles above. I resolved, then, to send back these fifty-eight men, with twenty-six days rations, with one ox wagon, and to leave the other two there, to be sent for, retaining the teams; and to make another reduction of baggage. Many tents and camp kettles were left in the wagons, and all the upright poles, for which muskets were used as substitutes. (The backs of the tents were opened, and a piece inserted, so as thus to become very large and nearly circular, in which ten men were accommodated.) The oxen I used in mule wagons; packed those unfit for draught, and also, though very lightly, the poor extra mules. The detachment went in command of a lieutenant, who received orders to report, for ultimate instructions, to the officer commanding in the territory. A calculation showed that by these measures, with increased means of transportation, the loads were reduced 20 per cent: and also that the rations (or half rations) of the battalion were increased by eight days. Then, and only then, could I begin to see my way to the end with confidence.

After these two weedings of the old, the feeble and sickly, from the battalion, lads and old grayheaded men still remained.

The numerous guides and hirelings you sent to me, I found at the lowest village; they had been idle for weeks; and I found I was to venture, with my wagons, into a wide region, unknown to any of them.

The river route improved greatly, and, opposite, was apparently a practicable gap in the mountain barrier, between mine and the Chihuahua road, (the fine but badly watered stretch known as the *Jornada del Muerto*.) About thirty miles lower, and in the vicinity of a point called San Diego, the mountains, which so far had confined the road to the river, break off, and then I turned short to the right, on the arid table land of Mexico, which I found studded with a profusion of isolated mountains, of volcanic origin.

My method, now, was this: Leroux, with five, six or seven others, would get a day in advance, exploring for water, in the best practicable direction; finding a spring or a puddle, (sometimes a hole in nearly inaccessible rocks) he would send a man back, who would meet me, and be the guide. This operation would be repeated until his number was unsafely reduced, when he would await me, or return to take a fresh departure. This was the plan, but ever varying and uncertain, attended of course, with much anxiety; and, sometimes, the inconvenience of neglect or tardiness on the part of the guides, making the road, once or twice, to vary from the better course, which a more thorough examination in the first instance would have discovered.

Such, with some vicissitudes of risk and suffering, and the accidental aid of a little confused information from a trading party we encountered, was the manner of my progress for about 250 miles, from the Rio Grande to the San Pedro, a tributary of the Gila; but I anticipate.

Thus I reached the Ojo de Vaca, about 26 miles south from the copper mines, on an old road to Yanos, used for transporting the ore. To the west appeared a vast prairie opening, between the mountains; it was the course; but the principal guides had each his dread of it, founded upon vague information, from Indians, of its destitution of water; and watering places might exist, and not be found by us. They had explored about 25 miles of it, finding an out of the way and insufficient hole of water, ten miles distant.

I ascended a high peak, and there taking the bearings of distant landmarks, which they professed to know, earnestly consulted with them and the interpreter,[89] who had lately passed through Sonora, as to the best course to be taken. They were deceived themselves, as I believe, and so deceived me, as to the direction of Yanos; and gave a decided opinion as to the unsafety of venturing into the prairie; and, also, that it would be best to take the Yanos road, and thence, by an old trail, a road formerly used to connect the presidios or frontier garrisons, Yanos, Fronteras, Tucson, &c.

The next morning, having reluctantly assented, I took the Yanos road. A mile or two convinced me (and them) that its general direction was very different from their representations; and *east of south*. I then took the responsibility of turning short to the right, and ordered them to guide me to the water hole. I had some confused information of water to be found in the direction of San Bernadino. Mr. Leroux had been very decided that it would be necessary to go by this southern point, even if I ventured that far on the unknown prairie. I then marched 40 miles without water, except a drink for part of the men, where I had hoped to find enough for encamping. The battalion were not prepared for it, and suffered much. These were anxious circumstances, and the responsibility I had taken weighed heavily upon me;

---

[89]Stephen C. Foster.

their safety and my success seemed both doubtful. Fortunately a large spring was reached the second night, after a continuous march of thirteen hours; and when men and mules were at the point of exhaustion, for the weather was quite warm.[90]

I was joined here by a party of New Mexicans, who had been trading with the Apaches. I purchased twenty-one mules of them, giving a check on the assistant quartermaster at Santa Fe. I also hired one of them to conduct Leroux to the mountain valley, where they had left the Apaches, and sent him to seek an Indian guide. A day or two after, we found a trail leading toward San Bernadino; and the fourth day, early, just after Chabonnaux [Charbonneau], the only guide then present, had very unwarrantably gone off hunting, we fell into what was believed to be the trail or road from Yanos to Fronteras; and it immediately led us to a precipitous and rocky descent, of perhaps a thousand feet, amongst broken, wild and confused mountain peaks, which extended as far as could be seen from our great height. I soon found the trail could not be made passable for the wagons; and I hunted myself for a more promising descent, and, in fact, saw a part of the proper one; but very inaccessible from the mountain height on which I then was. My next care was to seek the nearest ground suitable for a camp; fortunately I found water about a mile off. All pronounced the country before us impassable for wagons; I, nevertheless, immediately organized a large work-ing party, under Lieutenant Stoneman, and sent him to make a passage. That night Leroux arrived, bringing an Apache chief, whom he had got hold of with difficulty, and probably great address; so shy were they found. Next morning, it was owing to Leroux's decided assertions and arguments that there could be and was no other known pass but the horse trail, that I did not *insist* on his thorough examination. He even asserted, but was mistaken, that he *had* examined the opening I had seen and described, and believed might be a wagon road. Meanwhile, the party continued the second day hard at work with crowbar, pick &c.; whilst I sent one company and about half the baggage, packed on mules, to the first water on the trail, in a deep ravine below. It was about six miles, and the mules were brought back in the evening. Next morning they took the rest of the loading, and I succeeded that day, with much labor and difficulty, breaking one, in getting the wagons to the new camp. Dr. Foster accidentally found the outlet of an old wagon

---

[90]As noted, Cooke's practical decision to head west became a miracle story among the veterans. "We would attend to prayers at night, that the Lord would keep us from the hands of our enemies and that the Colonel might be stopped by an angel before we should go to Sonora," Levi Hancock recalled years later. "Our prayers were answered. The Colonel called a halt and said he was not commanded to go that way, but to go west. Then spoke to our Lieutenant James Pace, who answered him to his satisfaction. When it is said he burst into tears to think the soldiers so readily obeyed his orders." See Hancock to Daniel Tyler, Type-script, LDS Archives.

road, (into mine,) and, following back, it led him to the verge of the plain, about a mile from our point of descent. He says this is called the pass of Guadalupe; and that it is the only one, for many hundreds of miles to the south, by which the broken descent from the great table land of Mexico can be made by wagons, and rarely by pack mules. I hold it to be a question whether the same difficult formation does not extend north, at least to the Gila. If it is so, my road is probably the nearest and best route.[91] But if the prairie, to the north, is open to the San Pedro, and water can be found, that improvement will make my road not only a good but a direct one from the Rio Grande to the Pacific.

San Bernadino is a ruined ranche, with buildings enclosed by a wall, with regular bastions. It overlooks a wide, flat and rich valley, watered by a noble spring, which runs into one of the upper branches of the Huaqui [Yaqui] river, which is but a few miles distant. Here I succeeded in meeting a few of the Apaches, and obtained a guide, who went about 20 miles, and described the rest of the route to the San Pedro. He was afraid to venture further, and return alone over the plain; the point where he turned back was within fourteen miles of the presidio of Fronteras. It was in the mountain pass that we first saw the wild bulls, from which the command obtained their exclusive supply of meat for about two weeks. They are the increase from those abandoned, when the two ranches of San Bernadino and San Pedro (on the river of the same name) were broken up, in consequence of incessant Indian attacks. They have spread and increased, so as to cover the country; they were as wild and more dangerous than buffalo.

I made the next 62 miles, to the San Pedro River, with little more difficulty than cutting my way through dense thickets of mesquite and many other varieties of bushes, all excessively thorny. I was but 27 miles without water over the last divide; there was snow one day, and for about two weeks, at that time, we suffered with cold. I descended the San Pedro 55 miles, to a point whence a trail goes to Tueson [Tucson]. The guides represented that it was 85 miles of very difficult, if practicable, ground to the mouth of the San Pedro, and one hundred miles from there to the Pimos; also, very bad, and little or no grass; and, on the other hand, that it was only about 90 of a good road, with grass, by Tueson to the same point. I reflected that I was in no condition to go an unnecessary hundred miles, good or bad; and that, if their statements were true, the future road must go by the town. I had previously sent Leroux, Foster and others to examine if there was water on the 30 miles, which was the estimated distance to Tueson. Leroux had just returned; he had found water at a "still-house," 20 miles from the river; and

---

[91]The thousands of gold rushers who followed Cooke's Wagon Road to California over Guadalupe Pass soon demonstrated that Cooke was right.

had encountered there a sergeant's party of dragoons. He had made up a story to get off; but, to give it color, Dr. Foster fancied it necessary to go on to the town. Leroux was told, by Indians, that 200 soldiers, with artillery, had been there concentrated. I reached the water next day, and probably surprised the sergeant's party. I found them cutting grass; but the sergeant, as if the bearer of a flag, delivered me a singular message from the commander, which amounted to a *request* that I should not pass his post. Next morning, I made prisoners of four others, who had come, probably, with provisions; and as Dr. Foster's long stay had made me uneasy for him, I dismissed one of them with a note, stating that I should hold the others as hostages for his safety; and promised to release the prisoners if he was sent to me that evening. Deceived as to the distance, but expecting to encamp without water, I marched late; and having made twelve miles on a road very difficult in places, I encamped at sundown, on the high prairie. At midnight, Foster reached me; with him came two officers; one as a "commissioner," with written instructions to offer a kind of truce, by the terms of which I was to pass the town by a certain point, and to hold no communication with the people. I rejected them, and demanded a capitulation; which the commissioner, with great form, wrote, after his own fashion, in Spanish, and I signed it. The terms bound the garrison not to serve against the United States during the present war; and, as the only further tokens of surrender, to deliver to me two carbines and three lances; my men to enter freely and trade with the inhabitants of the town. After a tedious conference of two hours, in which we had been very friendly, but very cold, the officers departed, assuring me my terms could not be accepted. Believing I was eight or nine miles from town, I took measures to march at daylight; but unfortunately the mules being herded in mezquite bushes, and without water, the half of them, in the darkness of night, escaped the guard; and I could not possible march, with any prudence before 8 o'clock.

The distance proved to be sixteen miles. About five miles from town I was met by a dragoon, or lancer, who delivered me a letter, simply refusing my terms. I told him there was no answer, and he rode off. I then ordered the arms to be loaded. Immediately afterward, two citizens rode up, and reported that the place had been evacuated. I arrived at 1 o'clock, and, having passed through the fort, encamped in the edge of the town. Two small field pieces had been taken off, and all public property of value, except a large store of wheat.

The garrisons of Tubac, Santa Cruz and Fronteras had been concentrated, and, I understood Dr. Foster, there were altogether about 230 men; but I have lately learned that he only estimated them at 130. I remained in camp the next day, December 16. There was very little grass, and I fed my mules, cattle and sheep, on the wheat, (and brought off enough for two more days, in the adjoining desert.) That day, to cover some small parties of mule hunters, I made a reconnoissance [*sic*], with about sixty men, marching half way to an Indian village, ten miles off, where the enemy were stationed. (I intended attacking him under favorable circumstances, but the path led me through a dense mezquite forest, very favorable to an ambush. I learned, however, that this demonstration caused him to continue his retreat.)

The garrison attempted to force all the inhabitants to leave the town with them. Some of them returned whilst I lay there, and I took pains that all should be treated with kindness. The day I arrived there, a detachment of twenty-five men, who had been posted at the Pimos, to observe or harrass my march, having been sent for by express, passed unobserved round a mountain, near town, and joined the main body. (I afterward learned that they had made a threatening demand for the mules and goods left for me with the Indian chief. He refused, and expressed his determination to resist, by force, any attempt to take them.) On leaving T., I sent to its late commander, Captain Commaduran, by a citizen messenger, a letter for the governor of Sonora, (and I afterward received an answer that it would be transmitted.) It is appended. All things considered, I thought it a proper course to take toward a reputed popular governor of a State, believed to be disgusted and disaffected to the imbecile central government. It was intimated to me, whilst in Tueson, that if I would march toward the capital of the department, I would be joined by sufficient numbers to effect a revolution.

On the 17th, I marched late, as I did not expect to find water. At 8 o'clock, P.M., I encamped 24 miles from Tueson, with no water or grass. Ten or fifteen miles further there is a little water, in a mountain, close to the road, but it could not be found, and I marched, the second day, *thirty miles*, and, at 9, P.M., again encamped, without water; but the men, about sundown, had a drink from a small puddle, too shallow for the water to be dipped with a cup. On the *third* day, I marched, early, eight or nine miles, and encamped at rain water pools. The next day, I found it ten miles to the Gila, at a small grass bottom, above the Pimo villages. The mules were forty-eight hours without water; the men marched twenty-six of thirty-six consecutive hours, and sixty-two miles in rather more than two days, (in one of which no meat ration was issued).

Thus the 90 miles of the guides turned out to be 128 *to the village*; 57 miles nearer than the reputed distance by the San Pedro. Excepting four or five miles, the road was excellent; but over a true desert. There is, however, a better watered road from Tueson, which strikes the Gila higher up. I believe this route can be well taken for six months in the year; and, that like much of the road on this side, it is impassable in summer, unless for travellers. It is a great gold district; rich mines have been discovered in many of the mountains in view; but it is so barren and destitute of water that even a mining population can scarcely occupy it.

I halted one day near the villages of this friendly, guileless and singularly innocent and cheerful people, the Pimos. There Francisco met me with your letter from Warner's ranche; he brought with him seven mules found on the Gila; and, altogether, I obtained, at the villages, twenty, which had belonged to the dragoons. They were not sufficiently recruited to be of much service. I traded the Indian goods, and every spare article, for corn. After feeding it several days, I brought away twelve quarts for each public animal, which was fed in very small quantities.

With the aid of a compass, and closely estimating the distances, I have made a rude sketch of my route from the point on the Rio Grande, where our roads diverged, to their junction, near the villages.[92] It is herewith submitted. I have good reason to believe that, even with pack mules, better time can be made on my route than yours; and the *mules kept in good order*, for mine improved on the greater part of it. On the 27th December, (after making the forced march, without water, across the head of the Gila,) in consequence of the information received in your letter, I determined to send my useless guides express, to give you information of my approach, &c; hoping thus, as I said, to meet orders at Warner's ranche on the 21st of January, and to be of service to your active operations. I also sent for assistance in mules, understanding that you had placed a number of them in that vicinity.

Sixty or seventy miles above the mouth of the Gila, having more wagons than necessary, and scarcely able to get them on, I tried the experiment, with very flattering assurances of success, of boating with two ponton wagon beds, and a raft for the running gear. I embarked a portion of the rations, some road tools, and corn. The experiment signally failed, owing to the shallowness of the water on the bars; the river was very low. In consequence of the difficulty of approaching the river, orders mistaken, &c., the flour only was saved from the loading, and the pontons were floated empty to the crossing of the Rio Colorado, where they were used as a ferry boat. I passed that river on the 10th and 11th of January. On the first day and night, the loading of the wagons, and many men, were boated over. On the morning of the 11th, the mules were driven two miles, from grass; then drew the wagons through the long ford of a mile, nearly swimming. The wagons were then loaded in the willow thicket, and I marched 15 miles over the sandy road, to the first well, the same day; a great effort and labor. But as there was *no feed* for the mules on this side, I deemed it so necessary that I forced it, against every obstacle; marching, in fact, when one company's wagon was in a hole in the middle of the river; the sheep and rear guard on the opposite

---

[92]For a copy of Cooke's map, see Roberts, *The Mormon Battalion*, 147.

bank. In the well I found *no water*; and, when obtained by digging deeper, it was in quicksand, and quite insufficient for the men. I had another well dug; and, against *hope* almost, when considerably below the water level of the old one, that of the river water suddenly boiled up.

I viewed this, as in other instances, a Providential deliverance. It was the most trying hour of my long military service. That water failing, the next well would also; and *all the circumstances well considered*, it will be found that on obtaining it not only depended my military success, but the lives of very many, who justly could hold me responsible.

When of no real use to me, some wagons, which were broken on the march, were left, in order to save the mules. At this first well I left three, because the mules were unequal to drawing them. I had then remaining one for each company, and two others. I sent forward a strong party to the next well to prepare it and dig another. I arrived there the second day, soon after noon; and, during my stay, until 11 A.M., the following morning, I could not obtain enough of water. There I left two more wagons. (Arrangements were made for sending for all these wagons, the moment I arrived at the first ranche.)

I then took the direction of the "pozo hondo," the *deep well*; sending a party through the first day, and arriving, before noon, the second. Although a second deep well had been dug, the water was insufficient even for the men to drink. I had spent the night without water, and thirty miles of desert were still before me; the men way-worn and exhausted, half fed, and many shoeless. But I met there a relief of mules and some beeves. Mr. Leroux had sent back fifty-seven mules, which were chiefly young, unbroken, and as wild as deer, and the cattle, in one body, (and by poor hands.) So a day's time had been lost, and twenty of the mules.

I immediately had a beef killed, for a meal; a drink of water *issued* to the men; the wild mules caught, by their Indian drivers, with the lasso, thrown, haltered and harnessed; the poor animals, which *then* had not drank [*sic*] for thirty-six hours, struggling desperately during the whole process, which lasted above two hours, under a hot sun. Then I marched until an hour after dark, and halted to rest, until two o'clock in the morning. I had chosen a spot where there was some large bunch grass, which was cut for the mules. There was no moon, but, at two o'clock, the battalion marched again; and, at mid-day, having come 18 miles more, after long ascending its dry bed, met the running waters of the Carizita [Carrizo Creek]. The most of the animals had been without water about fifty hours. Here there was but little grass; and I marched, next day, 15 miles, through the sands, to the bajiocito [Vallecito]; the poor men staggering, utterly exhausted, into camp. At this time there should have been half rations of flour for nine days; but, owing probably to inevitable wastage, the last of it was eaten here. I rested a day, and received, at evening, a letter from Commander Montgomery. It advised me of your march to Pueblo [de los Angeles]; of the tardy arrival of my express, and of communication with you being cut off.

Next day, I encountered extraordinary obstacles to a wagon road, and actually hewed a passage, with axes, through a chasm of solid rock, which lacked a foot of being as wide as the wagons. Two of them were taken through in pieces, whilst the work was going on. So much was I retarded that I encamped, at dark, on the mountain slope, making but seven miles, without water, and without being prepared for it. San Philippi was six miles on this side, but there was a ridge between, so rough with rocks, that, after much labor, it took extreme care to get the wagons over in daylight. At San Philippi I met one of my express men, who had returned, according to instructions, to guide me. Though direct from San Diego, he brought neither orders nor news. I encamped that night near the summit of the beautiful pass, overlooking the valley of Agua Calienta. On the 21st day of January, I arrived and encamped at Warner's ranche; the very day, as it happened, I had promised, in my letter of December 27.

This was seven miles off the road to San Diego; but I had resolved, the night before, to march for the Pueblo de los Angeles, where the enemy had concentrated, unless I met orders or fresh information. That which I had, placed your forces approaching it on the south, and Lieutenant Colonel Fremont's from the north. Thus, I should advance from the east, and from the only pass leading to Sonora. I halted at Warner's the 22d, to rest and refresh my men, before commencing, as I hoped, active operations. The day was required, in fact, to obtain beef cattle, and to collect the new mules, many of which had escaped to their wonted pastures in that vicinity.

On the 23d, I marched 18 miles, on the road to Pueblo. That night we were exposed to a drenching rain, and a wind storm, which prostrated every tent. The storm continued the next day; I, however, marched, over a very bad road, three or four miles, to more sheltered ground, and better grass for the animals. (A mountain torrent in front would have forbidden further progress.)

On the 25th, I marched into the Temecala [Temecula] valley, and encamped four days' march from Pueblo. There I received a letter, written by your orders, which had followed me by Warner's. From this letter I could infer that hostilities were suspended, and that I was expected at San Diego. Accordingly, next morning, I left the valley, by a very difficult outlet, and, descending into that of the San Luis, fell into the road leading from Pueblo de los Angeles.

At San Luis Rey I received your instructions, by express, to march to San Diego mission, and there take post. I arrived there, by a very bad cross road,

THE MORMON BATTALION TRAIL,
crossing Vallecito Valley.
Courtesy, G. J. "Chris" Graves.

on the 29th of January, and the same evening reported to you, in person, at San Diego.

This march from Santa Fe has extended, by my daily estimate, to 1,125 miles. It has been made in one hundred and two days, in fourteen of which no march was made, so that the marching days average slightly less than thirteen miles. The rest days have been very nearly one in seven. It is believed, by many who have experience, that the weekly day of rest is advisable on a long march, even for speed. In looking back, I find that the half of mine were unavoidable detentions. I made, also, some twelve marches of less than nine miles, in consequence of extraordinary bad road, or the delays of road making, over difficult ground; and also the necessity, at times, of accommodating the marches and camps to inconvenient watering places.

If I had continued on the most direct route to San Diego, the distance would have been rather under 1100 miles, (about 1800 miles from Independence, Missouri, by Santa Fe.)

The constant tenor of your letters of instruction made it almost a point of honor to bring wagons through to the Pacific; and so I was retarded in making and finding a road for them. From this road, any that may follow will have various advantages. The breaking the track, often through thickets of mezquite and other thorny bushes, although worked on by pioneers, was so laborious that I habitually relieved the front wagons about every hour; but a team on a firm, open prairie, labors much less, if on a beaten track. Much of the difficult ground on the Gila, consisting of light porous clay, becomes a good beaten road. My journal and sketch indicate some points where the road may be shortened; but between the Ojo de Vaca and the point of leaving the San Pedro river, it is probable that between 80 and 100 miles may be saved, and some bad road avoided. It is only necessary for a small experienced party, well provided with water, (with Indian guides, if practicable,) to explore the prairie, and discover the watering places. The direct distance is about 160 miles.

The worst road is on the Rio Grande, opposite the upper and middle part of the *Jornada del Muerto*. It may probably be avoided by coming the *Jornada* road half way down or more, and then crossing to the west side. I have reason to believe that there are gaps in the mountains, and opposite where my road becomes good. This assumes that the great highway will pass as far north as Santa Fe, which may not be the case.

The country from the Rio Grande to Tucson is covered with grama grass, on which animals, moderately worked, will fatten in winter.

An emigrant company may leave Independence, Missouri, from June 10, to late in August, or Van Buren, Arkansas, later. It will subsist a short time on buffaloes, and be able to lay up much of the meat, dried or salted. In New Mexico, it may rest, make repairs, and obtain supplies—particularly of mules, sheep, and cattle—which, in that grazing country, will be found cheap; it may pass through settlements for 250 miles; and they will be much extended in the rich river bottoms to the south, when the Indians shall be subdued.

I brought to California both beeves and sheep; the latter did, perhaps, the best, requiring little water; they gave no trouble; two or three men can guard and drive a thousand. At Tucson, or at the Pimo villages, fresh supplies may be obtained. The Pimos and Maracopas, 15 or 20,000 in number, wonderfully honest and friendly to strangers, raise corn and wheat, which they grind and sell cheaply for bleached domestics, summer clothing of all sorts, showy cotton handkerchiefs, and white beads. They also have a few mules and cattle. I gave them some breeding sheep. Oxen will not do *well* for draught, their feet become tender; and west of the Pimos, their food is not found sufficient or suitable; mules require no shoes; I cached a large quantity on the Gila, having used none.

Undoubtedly, the fine bottom land of the Colorado, if not of the Gila, will soon be settled; then all difficulty will be removed. The crossing is about 100 miles from the mouth, and about 60 above tide. For six months in the year, the river is said to be navigable by steamboats for 350 miles; its bottoms are wide and rich; and sugar, undoubtedly, may be grown. In winter, it is fordable at the crossing; but I think it has at least as much water as the Missouri at the same season, and may be navigable by steamers to the mouth of the Gila at all seasons.

In conclusion, much credit is due to the battalion for the cheerful and faithful manner in which they have accomplished the great labors of this march, and submitted to its exposures and privations. They would have preferred to lighten and abridge them, by leaving the wagons; but, without previous discipline, all was accomplished with unity and determination of spirit. To enable the mules to endure the extraordinary labor of drawing these wagons, without a road, and often without food or water, the duties of guards were greatly increased, to herd them safely, as they did, over tracts sometimes a mile in extent, sometimes two miles from the camp, or beyond a river; and ten times did the battalion encamp without water.

I am indebted to Lieutenants Smith and Stoneman, of the first dragoons, who performed the duties of assistant commissary of subsistence and assistant quartermaster, for valuable assistance, particularly in directing the pioneers. Mr. Willard P. Hall, too, was ever ready to give me aid, particularly in the most active and venturous duties.[93]

---

[93]Congressman-elect Willard P. Hall had enlisted in the First Missouri Mounted Volunteers, helped fellow lawyer Alexander Doniphan write the New Mexico Code of Civil Laws at Santa Fe in 1846, and accompanied Cooke's command to California. He later served as Missouri governor, but his support for General Kearny did not win him the friendship of the state's powerful U.S. Senator Thomas H. Benton. Since Cooke failed to mention him elsewhere, he perhaps paid him this notice for political reasons.

Thus, general, whilst fortune was conducting you in battles and victories, I was fated to devote my best energies to more humble labors; and all have cause to regret that the real condition of affairs in this territory was so little understood. But it is passed! and I must be content with having done my duty in the task which you assigned to me, if, as I trust, to your satisfaction.

Respectfully submitted:

P. St. Geo. Cooke,

Lieut. Col., commanding Mormon battalion.

Brig. Gen. S. W. Kearny,

Commanding Army of the West,

San Diego, Upper California

GEN. S. W. KEARNY: ZEAL & PERSEVERANCE DISPLAYED

Stephen Watts Kearny had enlisted during the War of 1812 and worked his way up through the ranks without benefit of political influence or a West Point education. He held superior performance to be the norm and was not given to bestowing munificent praise on those who served under him. Confronted with a mutinous Fremont and resentful Californians, he was unable for some weeks fully to study Cooke's report and supporting documents, including the colonel's day-to-day journal and an excellent map, made only by compass and estimated distances, of the 444-mile track from the Rio Grande to the Gila River, known as Cooke's Wagon Road. Then his response was as generous as it ever could be.

TURNER TO COOKE, RECORDS OF THE 10TH MILITARY DEPT., 1846–1847, NATIONAL ARCHIVES, LETTERS SENT MARCH 23, 1847–JULY 8, 1851.

Hd Qrs 10th Mil Dept

Monterey (California) April 13th 47

Sir:

I am directed by the General to acknowledge the receipt of the Journal, Maps & Report of your late expedition from New Mexico to California. The General was highly gratified at this perusal of these interesting papers & instructs me to express his approbation of the successful & officer like manner, in which the expedition was conducted by you. Your discovery of the best & most practicable route for the march of troops from New Mexico to California, will be productive of great advantages to the public interest: and the entire success with which your dismounted command was marched through a wilderness unexplored and 1200 miles in extent, justly entitles you to the thanks of the Government. Great credit is also due to the

officers & men under your command for the zeal & perseverance displayed
by them in the performance of an arduous Service.

Lt. Col. P. St. G. Cooke.	I am Sir Very Respectfully
Comdg Southern Mil. Dist.	Your Obt Serv.
Pueblo de los Angeles	(signed) H. S. Turner
California	Capt. & A. A. A. General

GEN. S. W. KEARNY:
A MOST EFFICIENT SOLDIER & DISCIPLINARIAN

Later that year, General Kearny followed up a personal visit to President James Polk on 11 September with a written commendation of
Cooke, by now a major in the Second Dragoons, and recommendation
for his further promotion.

KEARNY TO JONES, KEARNY PAPERS, MISSOURI HIST. SOC., ST. LOUIS.

Washington Sept 20. 1847

Sir

I have to call the attention of the Hon. Secy. of War & thru' him that of
the Presdt of the U. S. to the Services rendered by Major Cooke 2d Dragoons—Capt Turner 1st Dragoons, & Lieut Emory of the Top. Engrs., all
serving under me in the Expedition from Missouri to California, & I have
most respectfully to recommend that the first named officer be honored
with the Brevt Rank of Lieut Col, & the two others with that of Major.

Major Cooke was assigned by me in October 1846 to the Command of
the Mormon Battn., (5 Comps. of Infy.) with the Rank, Pay &c. of Lieut
Col, & took command of that Battn. at Santa fe—marched it over to the
Pacific, where he arrived in January 1847 having left the Del Norte about
250 miles below Santa fe carrying his Baggage Waggons with him, the whole
distance, & over a Country where Waggons had never before passed thus
solving the Problem of the possibility of their doing so, which is to be a
subject of much importance to the U.S. Maj. Cooke at the head of his
Battn., marched on a portion of the frontier of Sonora, passing thru' Tueson, from which place he drove off a considerable Mexican force which was
collected to oppose his progress—He is highly talented, a most efficient
Soldier & Disciplinarian, educated at West Point & has been in the Army
since 1827 . . .

Brig. Genl R. Jones	Very Resp'y Your Ob. Servt
Adjt. Gen'l	S. W. Kearny
U. S. A.	Brig. Gen'l

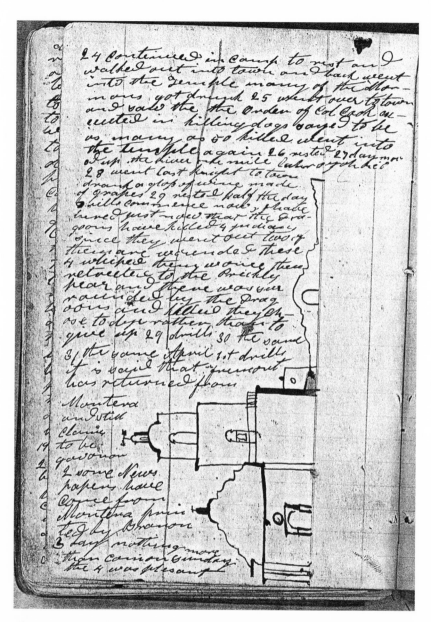

The San Luis Rey Mission as sketched by Levi Hancock (see page 190). Other sections of Hancock's journal intertwined sketch maps and drawings of horizons within its text, making it a difficult manuscript to transcribe.

Courtesy, LDS Archives.

Chapter 5

"Its Protection & Defense"
California Peacekeepers

After one of the longest marches in military history, traversing some two thousand miles, the Mormon Battalion arrived in California expecting to defend U.S. interests in the region against the Republic of Mexico.[1] Instead it found itself a key player in a dangerous confrontation, not between *Californios* and Americans, but one in which the commanders of U.S. army and naval forces in the province were squared off against each other. If it had not proved so threatening to American policy, the standoff would bear an absurd, even comical, look.

Gen. Stephen W. Kearny held the lawful authority to occupy and "establish civil governments" in New Mexico and California under 3 June 1846 orders from Sec. of War W. L. Marcy. On learning from Kit Carson in New Mexico that U.S. Navy Com. Robert F. Stockton and Lt. Col. John C. Frémont had already conquered California, the prudent general sent three of his five dragoon companies back to Santa Fe and hurried on by mule train to carry out his instructions on the West Coast. In the Battle of San Pasqual, *Californios'* lances had further reduced by one third what little command he had left. So he was a general with orders to govern the conquered province, but with no army to back them up.

Commanding the U.S. Navy's Pacific Squadron, Com. Robert F. Stockton possessed plenty of military might, but no mandate to establish a new

---

[1]Historian Stanley B. Kimball concluded "Cooke was generally correct when he made his famous remark" that history "may be searched in vain for an equal march of infantry." Kimball noted that Alexander Doniphan's two–thousand–mile march from Fort Leavenworth to the Gulf of Mexico post-dated "but actually exceeded that of the Mormon Battalion," and modern historians must consider Mao Zedong's six–thousand–mile Long March across China. See Kimball, *The Mormon Battalion on the Santa Fe Trail*, 61. Arguably the honor belongs to Alexander's Macedonians, but by any standard, the battalion's march was a remarkable achievement.

government. Even so, the wealthy grandson of a Declaration of Independence signer, eager to launch a political career, had sailed in ahead of Kearny to claim the prize. The aspiring commodore occupied San Diego and Los Angeles with sailors and marines and announced to the world, somewhat prematurely, that he had defeated the Mexican army and restored peace. He then proclaimed himself by right of conquest supreme commander and governor, afterward bestowing these titles on his occasional subordinate in these exploits, Lt. Col. John C. Frémont.

Known as the "Great Pathfinder," Frémont had arrived at Sutter's Fort on 10 December 1845 ostensibly to conduct the third of his highly publicized explorations of the Far West. His actions and the military makeup of his well-armed, oversized command, however, suggested that his real purpose was to overthrow Mexican rule. His questionable conduct during the Bear Flag revolt would disgust the professional army officers who had to deal with its consequences.[2] At age thirty nine, the explorer and son-in-law of powerful U.S. Senator Thomas Hart Benton had accepted Stockton's appointment as commander of the California Battalion, formed in 1846 from American emigrant and Indian volunteers, but at times he seemed mainly to serve an illusion of himself as liberator of the province and ruler of a new nation on the West Coast.

Seemingly upstaged by these ambitious and well-connected countrymen, the self-disciplined Kearny bided his time and avoided giving Mexican leaders any appearance of dissention among American ranks. When the repressive measures of Stockton and his subordinates provoked a revolt in the south, the old dragoon placed himself under Stockton's overall command to lead the American ground forces that defeated the insurgents in skirmishes around Los Angeles. But with the arrival of the Mormon Battalion, Kearny began to assert the authority that was lawfully his. His first move was to order the Mormon Battalion to San Luis Rey Mission at present Oceanside. From this strategic location it could move quickly against insurgents at either Los Angeles or San Diego as well as confront any enemy incursion from Sonora. He then established his own headquarters at Monterey while awaiting orders from Washington to straighten out the farcical standoff that egotistical military leaders themselves had created.

---

[2]Clarke, *Stephen Watts Kearny*, 345.

Lt. Col. Philip St. George Cooke, whose sense of humor had some-how survived his battalion's long march, now found himself command-ing the only "legal force in California," at the same rank as the alleged governor, John C. Frémont, yet the only one "not pretending to the highest authority of any sort." Said he, "General Kearny is supreme—somewhere up the coast; Colonel Fremont supreme at Pueblo de los Angeles; Commodore Stockton is Commander-in-chief at San Diego, and we are all supremely poor; the government having no money and no credit; and we hold the Territory because Mexico is poorest of all."[3]

DAVID PETTEGREW: THE MISSION IS PLEASANTLY LOCATED

Pvt. David Pettegrew of Company E, the oldest member of the bat-talion to make the entire march from Council Bluffs to San Diego, no doubt took motivation from the calling he shared with his company's fifer, Levi W. Hancock, as spiritual advisor to the command. Always on the lookout for wrongdoing, the fifty-five-year-old Vermont native described the march to San Luis Rey Mission and left a pen portrait of the "king" of the California missions.

JOURNAL OF DAVID PETTEGREW, UTAH STATE HIST. SOC.

February 1st [1847]– We left San Diego to go to San Louis [*sic*] Mission as the quarters were better there than at San Diego. We travelled 18 miles and encamped.

2nd – We again took up the line of march, travelled 21 miles and encamped. We passed a hill called Mule-Hill. At this place General Kearney and his men were surrounded with Spaniards until all their provisions has failed. They ate 16 mules while they were on the hill, which gave the name to the hill which is 8 miles from the San Pasqual battle-ground.[4]

3rd – We travelled 13 miles and came to the San Louis Mission. Here we took up our quarters. The Mission is pleasantly situated on a elevated piece of land about four miles from the coast. There is a church in the southeast corner built square and on the front or south side is a row of pillars that supports an arch on which was a walk that went around the top of the build-ing. In the middle was a square and in the center of this was a sun-dial, an

---

[3]Cooke, *The Conquest of New Mexico and California*, 289.

[4]With a third of his command dead or wounded, Kearny encamped for three days on this rocky sum-mit after the Battle of San Pasqual awaiting relief from American naval forces at San Diego that arrived on 11 December 1846. In the meantime, his men killed and ate the best of their trail-worn mules.

orange tree and two black pepper trees. In this square we were drilled and paraded every day two hours and sometimes more during our stay at this place. On the south and north are two large gardens enclosed by a wall around each of them. In the north is a vineyard and some olive trees with five or six black pepper trees. On these were peppers ripe and green and some in blossom. There were also two cocoanut trees and several other kinds of trees that I have no name for at present. On the south may be seen peach, pear, pomegranate and quince trees.

JAMES PACE:
TO BE TREATED WITH A LITTLE MORE RESPECT

For the first time since its enlistment, the battalion would know a period of tranquility and relative abundance at San Luis Rey Mission. The officers and men had served for seven months and marched two thousand miles without the benefit of formal training in their duties or the arts of soldiering. "The first time that I ever was taught how to turn around" was more than halfway through their period of enlistment, wrote Azariah Smith.[5] Having undergone one ordeal in marching across the Southwest, the Mormon volunteers would now be introduced to a new tribulation—drill and more drill under the hardest of taskmasters, Philip St. George Cooke.

Thirty-five-year-old Lt. James Pace of Company E came from a family with a proud military tradition, for his father, a "captain of the Light horse cavalry," died on 23 December 1814 in a skirmish that preceded the Battle of New Orleans. A native of Tennessee, Pace was a former member of Joseph Smith's life guards and an adopted son of John D. Lee under an ordinance performed in the Nauvoo Temple and later discontinued. He described the six weeks the command spent at San Luis Rey Mission, the last time its companies would be together prior to discharge, and how its members felt about Cooke's training methods.

AUTOBIOGRAPHY AND DIARY OF JAMES PACE, 1811–1888, BYU LIBRARY.

Friday 5th [February 1847]. Spent in Policeing & resting. The weather was faverable & pleasant. All preperations was making to commence the drill AM Monday.

Saturday 6th was clouday. In the afternoon it misted rain sum little. I

---

[5]Bigler, ed., *The Gold Discovery Journal of Azariah Smith*, 8 February 1847.

walked down to the Coast to the Great waters & Saw the rouling [sic] waves assend & decend up & down the shoar which was vary amusing to me besides the pleasant breese that gently blew from the southwest that seamed to give fresh vigor & animation to boath Earth animell Fowl & vegitation which was all in the bloom of life. Seamingly Here I should of said was natur[e']s glory had. Should I of seene the sum of the fair sent & aspecially those of the acquaintance of my youth who could so completely of fil[le]d the space of perfection So fare as the Eye could behould had they been pre-sant But little Could have been added or wis[h]ed for. Yet the mind of Man is like the rouling Seas allways Roveing Either riseing or falling in to the most deep reflections Through which bringeth perfection Preparing the mind of recieveing & disposing of greait & glorious principles As gradual as the Mighty deep rouls her mighty waves up her up the shoar & decend again to bring sumthing grater & more noble; These ware my reflections when a moments thought asked me whare I was & what bro[u]ght me thare. I v[i]ewed the brawd water again & Said suerly [sic] I am on the shoar of the greait western waters & I will return & bring my Famuly to the shoars of the wist [west] whare insted of labour we could rest.

Sunday 7th. B[ea]utiful & pleasant. At 9 AM The Battalion was inspected. The remainder of the day spent in rest.[6]

Monday 8th. Butiful weather. At 9 AM the drill commenced. The officers was drilled one [h]our by the Colenlo [colonel]. The Battalion was one half of them paraded in squads of Ten & drilled one [h]our by there own offi-cers. The remainder of the Battalion in the afternoon by the saim [sic] offi-cers on the first lesson without arms.[7]

Tuseday 9the [sic]. The Morning was foggy the afternoon was fine. At 9. AM the officers was Cal[le]d to the drill again for one [h]our & then The Souldiers in the saim manner as before & on the Same lesson.

Weddensday 10th. Cleare Cule & butifull day. The officers cald to the drill again for the space of one [h]our & then the three first squads of the Dif-ferent companys from 10 to 11 oclk AM. From 3 to 4 in the afternoon the rema[i]nder of the Battalion [drilled] in the same manner.

---

[6]While Pace rested, Co. B Pvt. John Borrowman was arrested for sleeping on watch. He explained, "Last night, being worn down with sickness and our long journey on half rations and having nothing but beef to eat, I was so weak I could not well stand my two hours at a time and sat down to rest a little on a square built of brick, whereon is placed a sun dial, and before I was aware I was caught asleep on my post by the sergeant of the guard who reported me and put me under guard so that I am this day in guard quar-ters a prisoner." See Journal of John Borrowman, Extracts, 1846–1860, 7 February 1847. His excuses won no sympathy from Cooke, who seemed determined to make an example of him for a major offense in time of war.

[7]In the morning Cooke taught military evolutions to the officers who drilled the men on the same exercises during the afternoon. Samuel Rogers said, "The Companies are now divided into squads, the first two of which sweep the Square and others are to do so each day, preparatory for drill. We were drilled in separate squads in the rudiments of military tactics."

Thursday 11th. The morning Cleare & butifull. The drill was attended as before. The officers & soldiers give there utmost attention to the drill.

Friday 12the. Morning butifull & clare [clear]. Drill again at 9. AM. The officers turned out with arms. Comemed [commenced] on the Mannel [manual] lesson # Co—

Saturday 13th. Morning cule & Cleare wind in the North. Drill again as usual. In the afternoon receved sum instruction from Lt Stoneman relative to the formation of a Company, officers places & Co—

Sunday 14th. Cule & clouday in the afternoon a little rain. In the four noon G. P. Dikes give a lecture on Nebecutser [Nebuchadnezzar's] dream[8] foloed [followed] by Capt Hunt which was all a co[m]bustible of wind & but little Matter or a greait cry & but little wool—

Monday 15th [February 1847]. Cleare & butifull. This morning I started a letter th to Bro J D Lee. After I wrote the letter I retiard [retired] to bed at past 2_AM. Whilst I reposed I dreamed of labouring in a greait work & whilst I was ingaged I be came well acquaintid t with the principle Man who was of common stacture [stature] dark complected tho pleasant & Fatherly look[ing]. His wife was fare complection fair hare [hair] & vary harty looking common h[e]ight for a woman & rather moore fleashy than common. Tho pleasant & familiar The gentleman seamed to under stand a siance [seance] Something like Freenology[9] or rather had a gift. His performance was different from a Freenologist. He performed on me by examineing my teeth one by one which he did by feeling & by a notched bone which he placed to my teeth in different positions. The bone was about 3 inches in length & about the brea[d]th of a Mans four[th] finger. On one side was cut four shouldiers [shoulders] or horns & on the other three. After the examination he looked at me with astonishment. He then turned himself towards his wife. She asked him what was the mat[t]er. He said he never had examined one a Man that had the same marks that I had & said he can it be posible that you are to live so long. Said I my Blessing sayed [said I] should see the work accomplished. He then said my age would be as the age of seven Men. He then ra[i]sed the bone before him in his right hand & here said he these shouldiers are horne & are the age of Man. He held the bone directly in frunt of his person in a perpendicular position hauling [holding] it with the right hand below the lowest notch or horn & then commenced counting by placing the finger of his left hand on the first horn below counting up.

---

[8]As interpreted by the Prophet Daniel: "And in the days of these kings shall the God of heaven set up a kingdom, which shall never be destroyed: and the kingdom shall not be left to other people, but it shall break in pieces and consume all these kingdoms, and it shall stand forever." See Dan. 2:44. Mormons at this time believed this prophecy referred literally to them and their plan to establish the Kingdom of God as an earthly state in the American West; see Orson Pratt's "A Prophecy and Its Fulfilment," *The Seer* 2:7 (July 1854), 304.

[9]The supposed science of phrenology held that mental faculties and traits of character are shown by the conformation of the skull. Its practitioners often used the dramatic techniques Pace described.

Explaned he whilst his finger was on the first this represents the age of one man & so on up to the seven & then closed by sa[y]ing youre age will be equal to the Seven—

Tuseday 16th. Butifull & fair. Drilled as usuall nothing of importance through the day.

Weddensday 17th. Cule & sum cloudy. Drilld as usuall on the Manu[a]ll lessons.

Thursday 18th. Cleare fine Morning. Drilled as usual. The day pas[sed] & nothing uncommon ~~too~~ transpiard. The Col[o]n[el] busined all the time with his small business but seldom ~~lt~~ transsended bounds.

Friday 19the. Clear & fine. Driled again as usual. In the afternoon Lt Oman returned from ~~the~~ near Purble [San Diego] with 2200 lb of course [coarse] Flour & six bags of banes [beans]. This was the first breadstuf we got in Calaforn[i]a Making 36 days subsistanc[e] on Beef alone & without salt a part of the time. The 17th Janury our F[l]our was out. We marched untell ~~the~~ Febra 3th before we closed our March to the west or reached quarters to rest from so grate a fatiegue as we had b~~oun~~orn[e].

Saturday 20th. Cleare & fine. Driled as usual. The day pased away & all seamed well. At night word came That a vessell had landed at Sandiego with suplyes for the Battalion which gave us hope that we should not suffer as we had done.

Sunday 21th. Cleare & fine. This morning two waggons was started to Sandiego in hast[e] to get suplyes—at 9. Oclk AM the Battalion was paraded for inspection. At. 11.ock Brother [Daniel] Tyler gave us an exentation preach. At 5 Retreat was beeat. The Battalion formed in frut [front] for inspection.

Monday 22the. Clear & fine. Drilld as usual.

Tuseday 23the. Fine weather. Drilled as usual.

Weddensday 24th. Cleare & fine. This morning three of Company C. Men was sent to the guard house for killing a beef without permition [permission] one Corporal & two privats. Corporal Peck [and] John Moury.[10] There excuse was that they had not enough to eat ate & they had starved long anough in a plentifull cuntry.

~~Sa~~ *Thursday 25the.* Butifull & cleare. Drilled as usuall. At 11. Ock AM a co[u]rt martial was cal[le]d to set on the cases of the three prisners for the beef. The court consisted of Capt Hunt Lt Oman Lt Clift. Cort ajourned untell tomorrow without a decision on there cases.

Friday 26the. Cleare & fine. Drilled as usuall. In the afternoon our waggons returned from Sandiego with provisions. At 5. Oclk. PM The Battalion was formed in frunt of the square for drill parade. The Prisners were Marched in front of the Battalion to receive there Sentence which was Ten days Confinement two [h]ours each day in the dangeon [dungeon] & two

---

[10]Isaac Peck, John Mowrey, and Ebenezer Harmon, all of Co. C, were arrested for stealing and butchering an Indian's cow.

dollars reducted from there wages. Barimor [Borrowman] was released by the Col[o]n[el].[11]

Saturday 27the. Butifull & fair. The day was spent Poleceing [policing] & washing.

Sunday 28the. Weather good. At 10. AM the Battalion was Musterd & inspected by the Coln. Also a detached Company was started back to the Colerada [Colorado River] for waggons that we left consisting of one [officer], 2nd. Lt Thompson & privates 9 or 10—[12]

March 1th [1847]. Cloudy & cule. This morning commenced drilling by Companys. The day spent in the drill.

Tuseday 2th. Cleare & fine. Driled by Company. The day spent in the drill as usual.

Weddensday 3th. Cleare & pleasant. Driled as usual in Companys.

Thursday 4th. Pleasant & fair. The day spent in drilling. The Coln instructed occationally & abusively as the Companys chanced to pass him.

Friday 5th. Cleare & fine. Driled again as usuale. In the four noon the Coln instructed Co A. but was abusive to boath officers & soldiers seaming to drive around as tho he was before a set of wild goats. In the afternoon he presented himself before Comp E. He prisented [presented] us with sum few evalutions [evolutions] that was entierly new to boath officers & Men & with the most unbecoming language & abusive also to officers as well as privates. He drove us through in greait fury. I felt myself highly insulted & could sciercely [scarcely] contain my feelings tho I did until morning. I then let him know I was misstreated & that I was allways willing to be instructed by him but not abused.

Saturday 6th. The morning cleare. Wind from the west & cule. The business of the day commenced as usual. At guard Mounting I reported to him the faithfulness of the guard I being the officer of the day which he received in his usual man[n]er. I then sent him a few lines of which the folowing is a true coppy of the original—

San Lois Rey March 6th 1847

Sir

With all due respect to your official capacity I take this method of requesting you if you have any instruction to give in regard to drill dicipline

---

[11]Cooke had allowed the Mormon officers to court martial Borrowman, but considered the punishment they imposed, six days of imprisonment, two hours of each of the first five days in a dark cell, and pay stoppage of $3.00, "excessively lenient." The case should have been tried before a general court martial, "whose power of inflicting punishment extended, for this crime, to the life of the criminal," he said. He disapproved the proceedings, remitted the sentence, and vowed never to trust a battalion court martial again. To Borrowman the outcome was "in answer to my prayers." See Tyler, *A Concise History,* 268, and Journal of John Borrowman, 26 February 1847.

[12]Cooke had abandoned three wagons at the first well after crossing the Colorado River because there were no mules strong enough to pull them. This party under Lt. Samuel Thompson was sent to retrieve them.

&c that I am ready and Willing at all times to obey your commands but would like to be treated with a little more respect than I was on some occasions yesterday While on drill. I am aware sir of our awkwardness and that it is enough to Worry your patience but that all men have to learn that. That they do not know your judgment and experience will doub[t]less admit.

I am sir you[r] most obedient and
Most humble servant
James Pace 1st Lt Co (E)

To Lt. Col. P. St Geo. Cooke
Commanding
Mormon Bat. of volunteers
A true copy of the original
Attest William F. Ewell

At ten. ock the dril[l] was cal[le]d. The Coln presented him self before Company E again to instruct as he had done the evening before but to the suprise of the company he was a diferent Man. He treated officers and men with respect which he had not done for a week privious. It was evident to [us] he had changed & for good. How long he may continue is doutfull.

Sunday 7the. Cule & cleare. Inspection at 10. AM dress Parade at 5. P.M. Order re[a]d by the agitent [adjutant] stating the reduseing [reducing] Ephrigh [Ephraim] Green to the ranks & the promotion of D P Rany [Rainey] to the office of Sargant.[13]

Monday 8th. Drilled as usual. Weather cule.

Tuseday 9the. Drilled as usuall.

Weddensday 10the. Cule. Drilled as usual.

Thursday 11the. Cleare & cule. Drilled as usuall. In the afternoon dress parade.

Friday 12the. Cleare & warm. Drilled as usual.

Saturday 13th. Cleare & fine. This day the Battalion was thro[w]n together & driled by the Coln Cook.

Sunday 14th. Butiful & Cleare. At 9. ock. Parad[e] inspection. Guard mounting at 10. AM. At 4. ock. PM. Captain Turner came in from Montera [Monterey] with word from Genl Carny [Kearny] to Coln Cook giveng him the command of the southe part of the c[o]untry.

W. B. SHUBRICK, S. W. KEARNY:
SEPARATE & DISTINCT POWERS

The arrival of Capt. Henry S. Turner, Kearny's adjutant general, at San Luis Rey followed a dramatic improvement in the general's position

---

[13]Sgt. Ephraim Green, Co. B, was reduced to the ranks, "having failed to learn his duty and drill as a Sergeant, and thus shown his incompetency for his station." Cpl. David P. Rainey was promoted to sergeant of the company. See Orders No. 23, 6 March 1847, Records of the 10th Military Dept., 1846–1851.

in relation to his two ambitious countrymen, Robert F. Stockton and John C. Frémont. On 8 February 1847 Kearny had arrived at Monterey to find the U.S. warship *Independence* in the harbor. On board was the self-disciplined Com. William B. Shubrick with orders to replace Stockton as commander of the Pacific Squadron. As the two mature commanders exchanged notes, all friction between Army and Navy evaporated. Four days later the foolish confrontation ended for good when Col. Richard B. Mason, First Dragoons, arrived at San Francisco on the storeship *Erie* with new orders from Washington. Kearny and Shubrick captured the essence of these directives in a joint announcement.

"TO ALL WHOM IT MAY CONCERN," STEPHEN WATTS KEARNY LETTERBOOK, MISSOURI HIST. SOC.

Be it Known

That the President of the United States desirous to give & secure to the People of California a share of the good government & happy civil organization enjoyed by the People of the U. S., & to protect them at the same time from the attacks of foreign foes & from internal commotions has invested the undersigned with separate & distinct powers, civil & military, a cordial cooperation in the exercise of which it is hoped & believed will have the happy results desired.

To the Commander in chief of the Naval forces, the Presdt. has assigned the regulation of the import trade, the conditions on which Vessels of all Nations, our own as well as foreign, may be admitted into the Ports of the Teritory [*sic*] & the establishment of all Port Regulations.

To the Commanding Military Officer, the President has assigned the direction of the operations on land, & has invested him with administrative functions of government over the People & Teritory occupied by the forces of the United States.

Done at Monterey Capital of California this first day of March A D 1847

S. W. Kearny   W. Branford Shubrick
Brig. Genl. & Governor of California   Com in chief of the Naval forces

GEN. S. W. KEARNY:
LOOK TO ITS PROTECTION & DEFENSE

His authority at last confirmed, General Kearny moved at once to exercise his indisputable powers as governor and supreme military commander. First he established the 10th Military Department, encompassing all of Upper California. He then sent Capt. Henry S. Turner to Los Angeles with orders to the defiant Frémont either to muster his California Battalion volunteers into the regular service or discharge them and to surrender "with as little delay as possible" all state papers in his possession at Monterey, the new "Capital of the Teritory" [*sic*].[14] Having carried this unwanted news to the former capital, Turner rode south to San Luis Rey where on 14 March 1847 he handed Cooke orders to take command of the department's Southern District. For the next four months the Mormon Battalion would keep the peace in the province's most populous and important region.

KEARNY TO COOKE, KEARNY LETTERBOOK, MISSOURI HIST. SOC.

Head Qrs. 10th Mil. Dept.
Monterey (U.C.) Mar. 1. '47

Sir

By Dept Orders No. 2 of this date, you will see that you are entrusted with the command of the Southern Military District, & required to look to its protection & defence, for which purpose the California Volunteers (now at the Cuidad de los Angeles) the Mormon Battalion, & Co C 1st Dragoon are placed under your orders.

The Southern Dist. is the most important one in the Dept, & the one in which (for many reasons) difficulties are most to be apprehended. The Route between California & Sonora leads from the frontier of that District, & that is the only one by which Mexican troops can be brought into this country.

With the knowledge of this fact, I advise you to have the pass near Warner's Rancho (agua Calliente) well guarded, & the Road from it in the direction of San Felippe & the Desert reconnoitered & examined as frequently as circumstances may render necessary. Troops sent for these purposes should be kept much in motion. The friendship & good will of the Indians on that frontier can easily be secured & it should be done.

It is highly important that a very discreet officer should be in command of the troops you may station at "the city of the Angels," which has been for so long a time the Capital of the Teritory & the Head Qrs. of the Mexicans & Californians when in arms against us. Great discontent, & animosity on the part of the People there towards the Americans have existed & in consequence of complaints ~~on their part~~ made by them of the Volunteers engaged

---

[14]Kearny to Frémont, 1 March 1847, Kearny Papers, Missouri Hist. Soc.

in our cause![15] It is not necessary to enquire if these complaints are well founded or not. The fact that the people have been unfriendly & opposed to us is sufficient to make it our duty to reconcile & make friends of them, & this most desireable object may be effected by a mild, courteous & just treatment of them in future. I urge this subject upon your attention & trust that you will impress it upon those officers & troops you may station there.

In my letter to you of the 11th. Ult. (a copy of which is enclosed herewith) I directed you under certain circumstances to send a Compy. of the Mormon Battalion to San Diego. I have now only to add that should the circumstances alluded to, occur, you will send a Comp'y or more, as you may deem necessary.

The selection of a Place for your Head Qrs. is a matter of some consideration & importance. I suggest that it be the "Cuidad de los Angeles," but leave that subject for your decision, and am unwilling to embarrass you or place any impediments in your way that might prevent you from performing the high duty expected of you.

Lieut. Col. P. S. G. Cooke   Very Respectfully,
Comg. Southern Mil. Dist.   Your Ob. Servt.
San Luis Rey   S. W. Kearny
                                            Brig. Genl.

Capt. Henry S. Turner:
They Will Be Continued in the Service

When Captain Turner left San Luis Rey on 17 March, he carried a letter to General Kearny from the battalion's senior captain. Jefferson Hunt told the general that his men intended to settle near San Francisco and wished to remain in government service. It was the first of repeated efforts by Hunt over the next year to create a Mormon force with himself in charge at the grade of lieutenant colonel. Hunt's overture included a petition for a leave of absence to go to Council Bluffs, Iowa, no doubt to obtain Brigham Young's blessing. Kearny rejected this request, but his reply would encourage Hunt to keep trying over the next year.[16]

---

[15]A reference to Frémont's California Battalion. These poorly disciplined emigrant volunteers refused to be mustered into the regular service and were discharged in April 1847.

[16]Hunt's letter to Kearny is missing from the correspondence of the 10th Military Department, but is listed in a register of letters as received on 21 March 1847. It is summarized: "Capt. J. Hunt Mormon Battln. Signifies the intention of the Mormon Battalion to settle near San Francisco, & wishes to work for Government. San Luis Rey, March 17."

TURNER TO HUNT, RECORDS OF THE 10TH MILITARY DEPARTMENT, 1846–1851, ROLL 1, NATIONAL ARCHIVES.

Head Qrs. 10th Mil Dept.
Monterey (California) March 27th. 1847

Sir:

I am instructed by the General Commanding to acknowledge the receipt of your letter of the 17th inst. and to say in reply that he does not doubt but that the services of the Mormon Battalion will be needed longer than the period of their present enrollment, and that they will be continued in the service of the U. S. should they desire it. The General does not approve of your going to Council Bluff at this time as suggested by you.

I am Sir right Respectfully

Capt. J. Hunt
Mormon Battalion
San Luis Rey (California)

Your Obt. Servt.
Signed, H. S. Turner
Capt A. A. A. Genl.

JAMES PACE:
THE BATTALION MARCHED FOR PUEBLO [DE LOS ANGELES]

To cover a vast region with fewer than four hundred men, not counting Frémont's unreliable volunteers, Lieutenant Colonel Cooke placed his troops where they would do the most good. His decision to detach Company B and send it to San Diego as a largely independent force recognized the quality of this unit and the leadership of its commander, Capt. Jesse D. Hunter. He assigned regular dragoons to guard the pass on the trail from Sonora at Warner's Ranch. Thirty-seven men from four battalion companies, many on sick call, were left at San Luis Rey under Lt. George W. Oman to guard public property there.[17] With the rest, some 225 men, Cooke marched for the point of greatest potential danger. The Mormon Battalion would again be divided, not to be reunited until its members were mustered out of service. In the meantime, Lt. James Pace continues his narrative as he makes ready to march with the largest segment of the command to Los Angeles.

AUTOBIOGRAPHY AND DIARY OF JAMES PACE, 1811–1888, BYU LIBRARY.

Monday 15the [March 1847]. Butiful & cleare weather. This morning Co.

---

[17]This detachment rejoined the command at Los Angeles on 12 April 1847.

B was ordered to Sandiego to reliev[e] a part of the dragoons that they might go to Purbelo [de los Angeles] with the command.[18]

Tuseday 16th. Cleare & pleasant. Drilled in the forenoon. At 3. ock Lt Thompson returned from the Colerado with one waggon. [He] reported the others to of been burned up.[19]

Weddensday 17th. Cleare & fine. Driled in the forenoon by companys. In the afternoon Batta[l]ion drill. A part of a part of Company Ds men refused to drill a in consiquence of not haveng rations sufitient [sufficient]. Those that refused was sent for by the Coln & March[e]d in frut [front] of the Battalion back & fourth & then unit[e]d in the Battalion drill. When the parade was dismissed they was sent to guard quarters & thare confined in the du[n]geons in the Stocke by turns.[20]

Thursday 18th. Fine weather. The Battalion spent the day in fit[t]ing up as well as they could to March to Parbelo [Pueblo de los Angeles] which was making another devishion [division] in the Battalion.

Friday 19th. The morning was dark & foggy. The Battalion Marched for Purblo [de los Angeles] leaving the sick & a few others at the Bay under the Commdmand of Lt Oman. We Marched a distance of 20 Miles. Encamped on the seashore.

Saturday 20the. The morning was fogy. We Marched as usual travel[ed] along the co[a]st a distance of 10 Miles then turned to the right past the St John Mishion.[21] Encamped at a Mishion the names I did not get. The days travell was about 20 miles.

Su[n]day 21the. Clear. Marched at 7. Trav[e]led over a butifull plain a distance of 20 miles.

Monday 22th. Clear & fine. Travled over a butifull plain. Reached the River at St Gabriel 2 Miles below whare Carny was attacted by the Spanyards.[22]

Tuseday 23. Clear & fine. This day we Marched in to Pu[e]blo [de los Angeles] a distance of 10 miles. Marched back one Mile & Encamped on the plain.

Weddensday 24th. Weather pleasant. Nothing of importance. Drunkenness was common with sum of the Mormons.

---

[18]Co. B marched for San Diego on 15 March 1847.

[19]Abandoned wagons made good firewood on the desert.

[20]The next day Sgt. Nathaniel V. Jones and Cpl. Lewis Lane, Co. D, were reduced to the ranks for "insubordination, and conduct disgraceful to them as non-commissioned officers." See Orders No. 25, 18 March 1847, Southern District, Records of the 10th Military Dept., 1846–1851, National Archives, Roll I.

[21]San Juan Capistrano in present Orange County was the seventh of twenty-one missions founded in Alta California. It was formally dedicated by Fr. Junípero Serra in 1776.

[22]The San Gabriel River flows to the ocean at Seal Beach. The command camped near the site of Kearny's final battle on 8 January 1847 before occupying Los Angeles. The nearby San Gabriel Arcangel Mission, fourth of the Spanish missions, was founded in 1771 and moved four years later to its present location in San Gabriel.

Thursday 25th. Weather pleasant. Remain[e]d~~ng~~ in Camp. In the afternoon the seanry [scenery] of drunkenness was lamentable. The screams & yells of drunken Mormons would of disgraced the wild Indian mutch moor a Laterday Saint. This drunkenness was on the 23 & 24. The 25 The Battalion was sober & began to act like they began to know themselvs.

Friday 26th. Pleasant. All was peace. Nothing uncomon occurd.

Saturday 27th. Weather pleasant. A new camp was selected. In the afternoon the Battalion removed to it one mile North East of the Town whare we had good water & a pleasant place for camping.

Sunday 28th. Cloudy & cule. The day spent in soberness. Brother Jeremiah Willy[23] give [*sic*] a short exortation & so ended the day the 28 March 1847.

Monday 29the. The morning cule. The forenoon spent in washing. In the afternoon drilled.

Tuseday 30th. The w[e]ather pleasant. Drilled in the afternoon.[24]

Weddensday 31th. Weather pleasant. Drilled as usual.

Thursday April 1th [1847]. The morning rainy. In the afternoon pleasant & fair. In the course of the day ~~word came from St Louis Ray~~ a letter reached the Command from St Louis Ray informing us of the death of David Smith a private in com[pany] E. He died 23the March.[25]

Friday 2th. Pleasant. Drilled in the afternoon.

Saturday 3th. Weather fine. The day spent in washing up.

Sunday 4th. Weather pleasant. Parade inspection at 7. AM. In the afternoon a dress Parade was cald. Capt Hunt presented himself before the Battalion as Coln but soon shoad [showed] to ev[e]ry observing Eye that he was not a Commander. The Parade [was] to his shame.

Monday 5th. The day pleasant. This day we had two drills in the co[u]rse of the day by the order of C[a]pt Hunt. He stated that the officers as well as soldiers war [were] ~~geting~~ forgeting there drill because he could not go through the Manuel of Arms himself.

Tuseday 6th. The day pleasant. In the afternoon we had a Batta[l]ion Parade. Coln Cook drilled the Battalion.—

Weddensday 7th. Clear & fine. This day the soldiers petitioned the Commanders of Companys to petition Genl. Carny [Kearny] for a Honerable [*sic*] discharge which petition was not answer by the Commanders. There

---

[23]Forty-two-year-old Jeremiah Willey from New Hampshire was a private in Co. A.

[24]Later that day, Jefferson Hunt tried to dispel resentment toward him by some battalion members. Said Henry Standage, "Cap Hunt preached this evening to the Battalion relating over the circumstances connected with Lieut. Smith's taking command of the Battalion and his (Cap Hunts) resignation to the same. Also the different Councils called on that occasion, endeavoring to show that he was not to be blamed and that the prejudice of the Battalion was ill-founded." See Golder *et al*, eds., *The March of the Mormon Battalion*, 216.

[25]Always ready to blame the battalion surgeon, Sgt. Daniel Tyler said twenty-six-year-old David Smith died "as the result of medicine given him by Dr. Sanderson previous to the command leaving that post, as he got worse and so continued from the time of taking the medicine until death relieved him." See Tyler, *A Concise History*, 274.

petition seamed to do good all tho ~~the~~ sum of the officers was quite [w]rathy & thretened punishment to those who si[g]ned it but all did not answer. Upwards of two thirds sighned it. This petition was in direct opposition to what sum of the offitials had been seeking for & they could not swallow it so well. It was learned by a leter to Capt Hunt that he with sum other officers had been seeking for a second enlistment unbenone [unbeknown] to the soldiers.[26]

Thursday 8th. Was pleasant. Drilled as usual.

Friday 9th. Warm & still drilled as usual—

Saturday 10th. Warm ~~&~~ as usual. This was washday.

Sunday 11th. Vary warm. Nothing of importance transpiard [transpired] through the day.

Monday 12th. Clear as usual. This morning Company C was ordered to March to a gap in the Mountain to guard ~~a~~ the Indians from pasing a distance supposed to be 50 Miles.[27] Lt Smith with the Dragoons & a number of volunteers Spanyards was sent to quell the hostiletys [hostilities] of the Indians towards the Spanyards. Here again was witnesed another devision of the Battalion which was the ~~fourth~~ fifth since we Enlisted & which allways give us cause for reflecting [k]no[w]ing the councel [*sic*] of the Twelve was to the officers never to suffer the Battalion to be devided. In the afternoon Coln Cooke & Mason visited the Battalion. Coln Mason inspected the Battal[io]n & give them the pra[i]se of any volunteers he ever saw & inspected.[28] ~~At~~ After inspection Lt Omen arived with those left in his command at St Louis Ray.

Tuseday 13th. Weather pleasant. Drilled as usual.

Weddemsday 14th. Clear & pleasant. Drilled as usual. Nothing of importance.

Thursday 15th [April 1847]. Weather fair. Drilled in the afternoon.

Friday 16th. Clear & pleasant. Driled in the afternoon.

Saturday 17th, Clouday & cule. Nothing of importance transpiard [transpired].

Sunday 18th. Pleasant. This morning at 11. AM The Seventys meet on the River above the Camp. [We] Organised & resolved to ~~p~~ use all posable means in rightousness to stop Drunkenness [w]horedoms & ev[e]ry other abominable practice.[29]

---

[26]An apparent reference to Capt. Henry Turner's reply, presented earlier, to Hunt's bid on 17 March 1847 to enlist a Mormon force under his command.

[27]Co. C under Lt. George W. Rosecrans marched on this date for Cajon Pass on the Spanish Trail, east of Los Angeles, to guard against incursions of Indians who raided the stock of California ranches.

[28]Col. Richard B. Mason, First Dragoons, watched the battalion "go through the manual and firings" and reported the men "acquitted themselves with a good deal of credit." See Sen. Doc. 18, (31-1), 1849–50, 9:272.

[29]Those who had been ordained as Seventies in the priesthood of the LDS faith organized themselves into a formal priesthood quorum for the purposes indicated. James Pace was chosen one of the seven presidents of the quorum.

Monday 19th. Clouday & cule. This day we had no drill. Rece[i]ved & pitched sum five Tents to the Company apiece.

Tuseday 20th. Cule and winday [*sic*]. Drilld in the afternoon.

Weddensday 21th. Weather pleasant. Drilled as usual.

Thursday 22th. Morning clear & cule. This morning I receved an order from Co[l.] Cook to take the command of Twenty four Privat[e]s & one Sargant [&] Two Corporals & prepare for Marching on the 23 to the Calhoon [Cajon] pass to relieve Lt Rosecrants & to perform the same dutys in guarding against all hostil Indians.

Friday 23the. The morning was Cule. The detatchment being fit[t]ed Marched for the pass. Travled 18 Miles on this day. Encamped at Mr workmans Ranch.[30]

Saturday 24th. Weather clear & warm. Marched a distance of 20 Mil[e]s. Encamped near a Ranch. Purch[as]ed a fat Calif for Mete [meat].

Sunday 25th. The morning Clear & warm. Marched this day a distance of 25 Miles. Reached the pass about sunset. Found Lt Rosecrants command in good health.

Monday 26th. Weather pleasant. ☩ This morning I receved of Lt Rosecrants seven public Horses six sad[d]les & one bridle on which I mounted six privat[e]s & one Corporal & Detached them to join Mr Wilson in defending a pass near his Ranch.[31] Soon after Lt Rosecrants left for Purbelo [de los Angeles] the detachment left for Willsons leaving 18 privats & two No[n] comisiond officers with me. We commenced fit[t]ing up saids [sheds] for our comefort & for home in the Mountains for one Month as we supposed But before Lt Rosecrants had Marched 3 Miles an Express Meet [met] him with an order for him to wait & for my Detachment to March weth [*sic*] his to Purblo as thare was sume appearance of trouble from the Spanyards.[32] Lt Rosecrants returned back to camp with the Order. The Detachment was sent for that was on the way to Wilsons. As soon as they returned Tents was struck & a March taken up for Purblo. We Marched in the afternoon a distance of 15 Miles.

Tuseday 27th. Morning foggy. Marched early trav[e]led this day 30 Miles. Encam[p] at Mr. [William] Workmans Ranch.

Weddensday 28th. Morning Clear. Marched Early Reached Purblo in the

---

[30]A naturalized citizen of Mexico, Englishman William Workman left Taos, New Mexico, in 1841 with John Rowland for Los Angeles, where they established extensive ranching operations on a huge land grant in the San Gabriel Valley.

[31]Benjamin Davis Wilson of Tennessee, also known as Don Benito, came to Los Angeles with William Workman in 1841 and created over the years a vast ranching and agricultural empire. A noted Indian fighter, Wilson named Big Bear Lake and was Gen. George S. Patton's grandfather.

[32]The appearance of trouble came not from Mexican loyalists, but from rumors that members of Frémont's California Battalion might attack the Mormon troops. Cooke alerted battalion officers to be ready for battle at a moment's notice and recalled Co. C from Cajon Pass. The rumors proved unfounded.

afternoon. Found the Battalion Engaged in fortifying Tho nothing definet or sertain of war with the Spanyard.

Thursday 29th. Weather clear. Wind high from the west. The labour fortifying continued.[33]

Friday 30th. Clear & pleasant. Color [Colonel] Stevensons ~~about~~ Troops came inn with amunition.[34] A detachment of Thirty of them. They brought about two thousand rounds.[35] At 5 oclk PM. The Battalion was musterd by Coln Cooke.

May 1th 1847. Cleare & fine. The soldiers continued to work on the Fort nothing transpiard [transpired] verry spetial [special].

Sunday 2th. [Today] was pleasant. Work continued this day. The Spanyards spent [it] in Horse raseing [racing]. The excitement is wareing [wearing] off & ~~non~~ apperance of intiruption. Mr Freemont [*sic*] is here & is sho[w]ing himself more frequent.

Monday 3th. Cleare & pleasant. This morning Company drill Commenced again. I road out by permition of the Capt—Road up the River 5 Miles. Bro. Everatt [36]rodd [rode] with me. We v[i]ewed a number of Herds boath Horses & Cattle. We returned to Camp in the afternoon & then walked down through Town v[i]ewing the vinyards. Bro Alread[37] was with us in the afternoon. We returned to camp before retreat. On our return we cal[led] at a stoar [store] & bought each one of us a shirt. Price $2 _ a piece. The best we could find in Town.

Tuseday 4th. Clouday but pleasant. This morning Brother Everatt Allread my self & Byram[38] Sit [set] out for a pleasant ride. We Started from Camp betwen 9 & 11. Road out towards Montera [Monterey] a distance of 7 Miles. We Saw hundreds of Horses but could not find any owners for them or we should of baught [bought] some of them. We returned to Camp in the afternoon.

Weddensday 5th. Clouday & cule & rain all day long. This day I spent in my Tent. No drill nor work in consequence of the rain.

---

[33]Battalion members at Los Angeles labored on building a fort on the hill overlooking the town. Dedicated on 4 July 1847, the redoubt was named after Capt. Benjamin D. Moore of Kentucky, who was killed in the Battle of San Pasqual. The Fort Moore Pioneer Wall was dedicated at the site in 1958.

[34]Forty-seven-year-old Col. Jonathan D. Stevenson had little military experience when he and his regiment, the First New York Volunteers, arrived by sea in March. The former New York politician would replace Philip St. George Cooke as commander of the Southern District in June 1847.

[35]The ammunition was welcome. When Col. Richard B. Mason inspected the battalion at Los Angeles on 12 April, he said, "I saw the battalion go through the manual and the firings, without cartridges, having on hand only thirty-one rounds." See House Exec. Doc. 17 (31-1), 1850, Serial 573, 309. Officers had prepared to meet the rumored attack by Frémont's California Battalion several days before with fixed bayonets.

[36]Probably Elisha Averett, a musician in Co. A.

[37]There were four Allreds in the battalion, all related: Pvts. James R., James T. S., Reuben W., and Sgt. Reddick N., all in Co. A.

[38]This was probably Pace's fifteen-year-old son and aide, William Byram Pace.

Thursday 6th. Still clouday but not rain so mutch as to stop drill or work—

Friday 7th. Cule & windy. Drill in the forenoon. At retreat a number of Orders wer[e] read Specifying General Co[u]rt Martials in diferent Ridgements [regiments] at Montera [Monterrey, Mexico] and other places giving charges against individuals with the Decision of the Corts which was an evident case to me that the Mormons was not the worst beings on the Earth for we had no sutch conduct in our Battalion.[39]

Saturday 8th. Clouday & cule sum Rain—Governor Carney ~~C~~ landed at ~~Sai~~ St ~~Pedro~~ Pedro. The day was spent in policeing & washing. In the afternoon an order was given for Lt Thompson to take Twenty privates & march North a distance of 12. Or 15 Miles to ~~Sup~~ Stop som[e] hostilety of the Indians against the Spanyards.

CHARLES BRENT HANCOCK: KING OF THE MOUNTAINS

An odd—and overlooked—contribution to the history of the Mormon Battalion is Charles Brent Hancock's 1884 recollection of his service in California. This nephew of Levi Hancock recorded meeting the celebrated chief of the Utes (or Utahs), Wakara, near Los Angeles in the spring of 1847. No other source mentions the presence in California at that time of the warrior and raider who whites called Walker, and only Hancock referred to him as "Jim Walker." The old veteran recalled these events while on a mission to California in 1885 as the "History of the Utah Indians as gleaned from a Spanyard in California July 1st, 1847." Though recorded almost forty years after the events described, Hancock's colorful story paints a compelling portrait of this significant leader that appears to be accurate in many of its details.

CHARLES BRENT HANCOCK, REMINISCENCES AND DIARY, 1884–89,
LDS ARCHIVES.

About May 1847 while in Los angeles Cal. there came a large camp of Indians from the east and Pitched their tents near the river of Los angeles. I

---

[39]The Mormon soldiers were models of good behavior compared with other American volunteers during the Mexican War. Gen. Zachary Taylor on 16 June 1847 said, "Many of the twelve months' volunteers in their route hence of the lower Rio Grande, have committed extensive depredations and outrages upon the peaceful inhabitants. There is scarcely a form of crime that has not been reported to me as committed by them; but they have passed beyond my reach, and even were they here, it would be next to impossible to detect the individuals who thus disgrace their colors and their country." He requested that "no more troops may be sent to this column from the State of Texas." See House Exec. Doc. 60 (30-1), 1848, Serial 520, 7:1178.

had the Curiosity to go to their Camp and take a look at them. I had heard from some Spanyards that they were a hostile set of Braves that enhabited the mountains and was [held] en dread by all other tribes and even the People of California and northern Mexico much feared them and dreaded their visits as they made their means and living by Robbing and Stealing, taking captives of children from other tribes and selling as Slaves and if they could not trade to suit they would take by force horses and Cattel and drive them from the country. I saw from their looks and their behavior that they were as Booldoggs [bulldogs] for the many Scars Showd that they had endured many hard struggels for victory. This Indian force ware the Utahs. Their War Chief was Jim Walker, known as king of the mountains. A thousand dollar reward was offerd for his head in California.

His Brother Aropine was a Piece Chief and Honerable in his Position.[40] They did not stay long in California but made their way out by way of the Cowene [Cajon Pass] trail near Sanbernardino. They took many Horses and Cattel with them. Although the mountain was [a] very steep trail narrow and Spanyards in hot Persuit yet through their Stratigem and bravado they made good their retreat.

This trail was guarded by the Mormon Battalion some two months but they did not come back as usual for a new supply.

The Old Spanyard informed me that he had traviled much in the mountains, going up the Rioghilia [Gila River] to Santafe and then taking a trail North and West Crossing the headwaters of the Collorado, over a mountain, down a Canyon, to a lake of fresh water [Utah Lake] and there was a river called Spanishfork, and on further north as the trail led to Oregon there was a large lake vary Salt watter and in going southwest toward Sanbernardino there was rivers and lakes and one small salt lake.[41]

These valleys Lakes, Rivers and mountains the Utahs claimed as theirs. The Country used to be well supplied with Buffalo Elk moose, Deer and other game but not many years ago the Big Snow and hard winter killed them and there was but little game now and fish for their support. The Utahs ware a roaming tribe allways at war. The Shoshonie on the North and the Utahs have many hard fights. I told him we ware Soldiers and soon would be discharged from Service and wanted to go East to our friends and asked which way we had better go. He said go now North to Sacramento. There we would find a road going East to the States. He said it would be only half as far to go across the Desserts this way but we could not cross the sands this time of year. We bought two mules from him. He offered to go

[40]One of many Ute leaders identified as Wakara's brother, Arapeen was both an ally and opponent of the Mormons until his murder during Utah's Black Hawk War.

[41]Though confusing, the geography of the "old Spaniard" is recognizable. The "lake of fresh water" was Utah Lake; the "large lake very salty water" was Great Salt Lake; and the "one small salt lake" was the now-vanished Little Salt Lake west of today's Parowan, Utah.

and Piolet [pilot] us through for Pay if we would agree to find him company to git back and we wait until Oct before starting.

LT. SAMUEL THOMPSON:
HERE WE FOUND THE ENEMY AMBUSHED

Lt. Samuel Thompson of Company C, one of the natural leaders who emerged during the battalion's military service, commanded the only combat action by Mormon volunteers during the Mexican War. The thirty-four-year-old New Yorker received orders on 8 May 1847 from Cooke to stop attacks, apparently by Tulareños Indians from California's Central Valley, on ranches in the hills north of Los Angeles. Thompson's concise report tells how promptly he carried out this assignment.

THOMPSON TO COOKE, RECORDS OF THE 10TH MILITARY DEPARTMENT, 1846–1851, LETTERS RECEIVED, ROLL 2, NATIONAL ARCHIVES.

Camp in the town of the Angeles
May 9th. 1847.

Sir,

By your instructions I marched on the afternoon of the 8th. Inst. in Command of a detachment of twenty men from the Mormon Battalion guided by a California Spaniard named [blank].

We marched to the rancho de los Sanches, where we retired, as I thought, for the night. In About three hours we were awakened by our guide who had found the encampment of the Indians against whom we had set out. We then marched to the rancho del Feliz[42] and from hence to the pass of the Bendayos making in all about eighteen miles from the Pueblo [de los Angeles].

Here we found the enemy ambushed. When they were discovered so as to admit of successful action I ordered the attack which they returned with a warm and continued shower of arrows. The combat lasted on account of the advantage of ambush they had for two hours when they retreated. I found six dead Indians on the field, from only five of whom, however, the California Spaniards that accompanied us took scalps. I had one man rather severely wounded with an arrow, another slightly.[43]

---

[42]The 6,647-acre land grant to Jose Feliz was located just north of today's downtown Los Angeles. It included present Griffith Park and was generally bounded by today's Ventura Freeway, Golden State Freeway, and Western and Fountain avenues.

[43]Privates Benjamin Mayfield and Samuel Chapin were only slightly wounded, "one of them in the privates the other in the Cheak bone." See Elijah Elmer, Diary, 9 May 1847. Sgt. Nathaniel Jones wrote, "The Spaniards used the Indians very brutally, scalped them and cut off their ears and nose before we knew what they were about or we would have prevented them."

P.S. I should have mentioned that a Spaniard who was engaged in the Combat and displayed much bravery was severely wounded, having had three arrows shot into him. He was one of a considerable number who had come of their own accord to witness and, I suppose, if necessary take a part in the affray.

Yr. Obt Servt

To Lt Col Cooke   Samuel Thompson
Comdg   Lt. M. B.

JAMES PACE: A MONSTROUS GOLD MINE

Just before Lieutenant Thompson and his detachment returned from their fight with the Indians, Gen. Stephen W. Kearny arrived to inspect the battalion and announce a change in command before leaving for the United States. The Mormon volunteers were about to bid farewell to Philip St. George Cooke, the professional soldier they had come to respect, some even to admire, and Dr. George B. Sanderson, the English physician they heartily despised. As the fortunate few chosen as Kearny's escort left for Monterey, three by sea with the general and some ten men by pack train under Lt. William Tecumseh Sherman, those left behind settled into a peaceful routine at Los Angeles. They worked to complete the fort overlooking the town, defended nearby ranches against Indians, and counted the days until their time of military service expired in mid-July. Lieutenant Pace continues his daily record of the battalion at Los Angeles as the men neared the end of their initial enlistment.

AUTOBIOGRAPHY AND DIARY OF JAMES PACE, 1811–1888.

Sunday 9th [May 1847]. Clear and cule. About noon the Gove[r]nor arrived in Peublo. He was received with a salute of fifteene guns. A short time after his arrival Lt Thompson arrived or returned from his skouting party with a report of a small skirmish in which two of his men was wounded but not fatal. His report of Indians kiled was five or six. The Govenor came up to Camp. He apeared glad to see us & seamed to congratulat[e] us on geting through. He made us a short visit but said he would return on tomorrow & see us all.

Monday 10th. Clear & pleasant. 9. ock came on. The Battalion was paraded & presented to the Govinor [Kearny] who inspected us closely & remarked that we was a harty sett of boys & that we had accomplished moore [*sic*] than ever had been done by any troops before. He remarked that Napolion done a greait act when he crost the alps but said he you have done a greaiter act in crossing the Contenant [*sic*] through an un[k]nown reagion leaveing a road behind you for the Travler to find his way to the Pacific—he appeard well pleased and said we deserved applause for the conduct of the Battalion saying that he had allways had a good report of us & that he was proud to say to us that we was not the Battalion that had been guilty of anything that was derogatory to the caracter of any man or person. He seamed to chearfooly [cheerfully] complimented [*sic*] us with a greait full hart saying what dose [does] this Battalion wish that I should do for them &c—Teling us that Coln Stevenson[44] would take the command of the Sutherny [southern] part of California & that Coln Cook would return with him to the states—He further moore requested twelve men from the Battalion to go with him to the States for a life guard. The men was soon selected & presented to him. He promised to discharge them if they should meet there Famullys [families] on his return. If they did not they should be discharged at Fort Levingsworth. In the afternoon I bought Ma[tt]hew Caldwells Mayor [mare] & two Laraeets [lariats] for six dollars.[45]

Tuseday 11th [May 1847]. I road out severall miles. Returned & spent the remainder of the day in Camp.

Weddensday 12th. The detachment was fit[t]ed out ready for a start. This day I road out again a few miles up the River [and] seen the plows going [and] Cattle & horses feeding in ev[e]ry direction all most.—

Thursday 13th. Clear cule weather. This morning the generals Detachment left for Montera [Monterey] by land all but two Landers & Willy.[46] They went by water. About two [h]ours by sun an order was sent to Capt Hunt to send a detachment of twenty privat[e]s & one Sargant with a Lt at there head to se[a]rch after som[e] Indians. I was caled to take the command & go in a with two days provision with orders to make prisners of the Indians if I could & not use fir[e]arms & left the camp at sunset. Marched 9 Miles to a ranch whare we camped for the night.

Friday 14th. Marched at 4. oclk in the morning [and] traveled to the foot of the Mountain. Deta[i]led six men to go with the pilot & five or six other Spanyards to search where they ware. I marched with the remainder in to another pass in the Mountains. Stoped & placed two setinals on the highest points & remained thare untell the search was made. About noon the com-

---

[44]Col. Jonathan D. Stevenson of the First New York Volunteers had little in common with the professional soldier he replaced as commander of the Southern District, Philip St. George Cooke. But his political skills paid off when he won commendation for maintaining good relations with the Californians.

[45]For the adventures of Kearny's guards, see Chapter 6.

[46]These men were privates Ebenezer Landers, Co. C, and Jeremiah Willey, Co. A. One other man also sailed to Monterey, perhaps Elanson Tuttle or Lt. Sylvester Hulet, Co. D, who had resigned his commission on 10 April 1847.

pany returned without any discovry. We then kiled a small beefe had a good diner & then proceded to search another range of Mountains. The six that was on the Tramp in the fore noon I sent a near rout[e] taking the remainder with [me] & 5 or 10 Spanyards & searched another range of Mountains affectually but did not discover any fresh sine [sign]. The auld [old] pilot shode [showed] me a monstrous gold mine which is about Twenty miles from Peublo a little ~~west a no~~ North of west & on the side nearist the river & in v[i]ew of it.[47] Our search being over we then Marched to the same Ranch & encamped.

Saturday 15th [May 1847]. We Marched back to Peublo. Reached the camp at 10 ock AM [and] made my report & in the afternoon bought a Hors[e]. Give 8 dollars for him. The day Closed & peace. All the Battalion seamed glad that my Indian hunt pased off as well as it did without sheding there blood.

Sunday 16th. Cule & winday [windy]. Dress Parade at 9. AM. I road out in the forenoon. Returned & spent the remainder of the day in Camp.

Monday 17th. Warm & pleasant. This morning my Mayor [mare] brok[e] away & I had a hard race to get hir [her]. After I caught hir Lt. Roseacrants Lytle & myself rode off in se[a]rch of Rosecrants hors[e]. We returned without finding him.

Tuseday 18th. The morning pleasant. This morning I road out in company with Lt John Bunker Forsgreene White & Brown & Lt Lytle & Byram[48] in search of horses & Mules. We road South & on Ten miles. Could not purchase Mules at a reasonable price. Lt John Forsgreen & Bunker bought four Mayors [mares] at six dollars each. Broke animals. We returned hom[e]. Found all in piece [peace].

Weddensday 19th. Cule & clouday. This day I spent in camp. I bought a horse in the forepart of the day at Ten dollars. [He is] gentle and kind a butifull bay.

Thursday 20th. Weather pleasant. I spent the day at camp & attending my horses. Nothing of importance transpiard [transpired].

Friday 21th. Cule & winday. This day I spent in camp. The boys was bying horses occationally.[49]

Saturday 22th. Clear & warm. This morning I was caled to tak[e] charge of

---

[47]This was probably Placeritas, or "little placers," Canyon where Franciso Lopez, a San Fernando Valley land grantee, discovered gold on 9 March 1842. By December 1843 two thousand ounces of gold had been taken from the San Fernando mines. In 1843 Lopez made a second gold discovery at San Feliciano Canyon, some ten or twelve miles from Placeritas.

[48]Pace's companions on this excursion probably were Edward Bunker; John E. Forsgren; John S. or Samuel White; Ebenezer or Edmond L. Brown; Andrew Lytle; and his son, William Byram Pace.

[49]As their discharge drew near, many battalion members at Los Angeles and San Diego bought horses at relatively low California prices to prepare to rejoin their families

the hands on the Fort. Capt Hunt Davis & Lt. Rosecrants started out for Williams Ranch.[50]

Sunday 23th. Cleare & warm wind high in the afternoon. I spent the day in camp [and] was unwell. ~~Tuesday 24th~~

Monday 24th. Cleare & windy. I spent the day at Camp.

Tuseday 25th. Cleare & windy. This day I spent in camp & was unwell. The Capt returned home from the Ranch.

Thursday 27th. This morning pleasant. This morning I got permition to take a small party of twelve Men & range the c[o]untry [for] four days [and] see all the good country & by all the animals we could. We left at 10. Oclk [and] travled twenty miles. Encamped on the saintabarbre [Santa Barbara] Road near and [an] Indian Ranch where we had butifull water.

Friday 28th. The morning butifull & warm. We left camp at sunrise [and] travled 12 Miles North to Genrl PeCoss [General Pico's].[51] Stoped [and] found the Genul at home. We let him know what our business was. He treated us like a gentleman ~~war~~ furnished us a good brakefast besid[e]s Ouadent [aguardiente or brandy] & beno [vino] plenty & all as free as the water that ran before his door. After refreshment we turned our co[u]rse recost [recrossed] the Mountains travled down near the co[a]st stoped at a Ranch whare we baught sum animals six head in all. I baught two Mules at 36 dollars Broth[er] [Elisha] Averett I Horse 10$. S [Samuel] White I H 9 $ H[enry] Jackson I Mayor [mare] 4 $ [George] Kelly I Mayor 5 $.

Saturday 29th. We left camp at 10 oclk. Travled down the Coast 8 Miles [and] stoped at a Ranch. Encamped & baught a number of animals 8 head in all. I baught I Meyor [mare] 4$ for a brude [brood] Meyor—

Sunday 30th. The morning fine & pleasant. This morning we left camp for Pewblo [de los Angeles] a distance of 14 Miles. Reached Peublo a bout noon with all the animals.

Monday 31th. Butifull weather. This day I spent in camp well a mused seeing the Indians riding the wild animals.

Tuseday ~~th~~ June 1th [1847]. Was pleasant & fine. I spent the day in camp.

Weddensday 2th. This day I also spent at camp.

Thursday 3th. Fine weather. This morning I baught one Mule & two Meyors [mares] for twenty two dollars from a Spanyard. Swap[p]ed the two meyors to John White[52] for one hors[e].

---

[50]This was the Rancho Santa Ana del Chino in present Riverside County, owned by fur trader Isaac Williams, who came to California in 1832 with Ewing Young. It was later a rest stop on the southern trail and a Butterfield stage station.

[51]The Picos were a prominent California family founded in 1776 by Santiago de la Cruz Pico who came from Tubac to California that year with the Anza expedition. This was probably the ranch of Andres Pico who commanded the *Californio* lancers at the Battle of San Pasqual.

[52]John S. White, 29, a native of New Jersey, was a private in Co. C.

Friday 4th. A butifull morning. This day I was on duty. [I] had the charge of the work on the Fort. I gave the men a task & they worked it out by noon. The rema[i]nder of the day we spent with the wild animals.[53]

Saturday the 5. The morning butifull. Brother Averat [Averett] Byram [Pace] & my self road up to wards pecows [Pico's] to a ranch & then returned to Camp do[w]n the River. Bargaded for a Mule to be braught to Camp.

Sunday 6th. Butefull weather. This morning I baught one Mule at 8 dollars & one hors[e] for four & my Trunk. A butifull Rone.

Monday 7th. The day Cule & pleasant. I spent the day in Camp. Baught one Mule in the afternoon for 10 dollars & let Father Petagrew [Pettegrew] have the one I bought on Sunday at the same [price] I gave for him.

Tuseday 8th. Weather pleasant. This day I spent at camp & in Peublo. Sold Leonard Scott[54] one Horse at 9 dollars. I also baught him a Mule for 14 dollars well broke.

Weddensday 9th. The morning clear & warm. Nothing of importance.

Thursday 10th. Warm. I spent the day in camp. [I] was unwell.

Friday 11th. Weather warm. Nothing strange occured.

Saturday 12th. Warm & windy in the afternoon.

Sunday 13th. Cleare & warm. This day I spent in camp.

Monday 14th. Warm. The day spent in Camp.

Tuseday 15th [June 1847]. Cleare & warm. The day spent at camp. I was unwell.

Weddensday 16th. The day spent at camp as usuall.

Thursday 17th. Clear & warm. I spent the day at camp.

Friday 18th. Warm. I spent the day at camp.

Saturday 19th. Warm. I spent this day at camp. Nothing of importance transpiard.

Sunday 20th. Warm. This morning my Horse was gone from his stake. I searched for him during the day but did not find him.

Monday 21th. Weather pleasant. I remaind in camp.[55] I baught a Meyor [mare] from Robert Colens[56] at six dollars.

Tuseday 22th. Weather fine. This morning the Meyor I baught of Collins got away from Byram at water. I followed him [her] six or eight Miles but did not get him. I returned to camp before night. The day closed & without anything special transpiring.

Weddensday 23th. Weather fine. Work continued on the Fort. This day I remained in camp.

---

[53]Many of the horses and mules purchased by battalion members had not been broken.

[54]Leonard M. Scott was a private in Co. E. He is erroneously listed on some records as having died earlier that year at Pueblo, being confused with Cpl. James A. Scott.

[55]While Pace remained in camp, Col. Jonathan D. Stevenson, now commander of the Southern District, left for San Diego to urge Co. B to remain in service. Stevenson's recruiting drive had begun on 18 June when his order was read at Los Angeles calling on battalion members to reenlist.

[56]A native of England, Robert H. Collins, 24, was a private in Co. D.

Thursday 24th. Weather pleasant. This day I remain at camp & attended to my animals.[57]

Friday 25th. Was also cleare & fine. This day I spent at camp. Nothing spetial [special] occurd.

Saturday 26th. Was fine weather. This day I was on duty on the Fort. The hands worked there stent [stint] out before noon.

Sunday 27th. Weather cleare & fine. This day I spent in hunting my horse. I road upwards of Forty miles. [I] was near the Coast at the mouth of the St Gabriel [River].

Monday 28th. Weather good. This day I spent at camp. In the afternoon Capt Hunter reached our camp from Sandiego. [He] had with him sargent Hyde & Corp Alexander.[58]

Tuseday 29th. Weather pleasant. This day I spent at camp. The Battalion was cald on parade & a speech deliverd to them on the policy of a new enlistment by Coln Stevenson which was good & nothing but good reason offer[e]d altho it did not sute [suit] the Battalion to reenlist. After the Coln was through our leading officers cald the Battalion together again in order to urge an enlistment. But by & by the story was told on boath sides & they failed to ra[i]se a briese [breeze].

Weddensday 30th. Weather cleare. This day I spent at camp & attended my animals. At night the officers meet at Capt [Hunt's] qtrs [quarters] in or[der] to draft a co[u]rse for the Battalion to persue on going back as it was the next best thing they thaught [thought] to do as they was under a spetial [special] charge of the Twelve. They the officers had been so strict in there way for the Council of the Twelve. The soldiers seamed to disregard them & chose to take the co[u]rse of Br Levi [Hancock] & Father Petagrew [Pettegrew] which was diferant [*sic*] from the officers.[59]

Thursday July 1th [1847]. Weather pleasant. This morning Capt Hunter [Sgt. William] Hyde & [Horace] Alexander left for Sandiego. In the afternoon the boys raised a fine Liberty pole which the quarter Master had emploid them to do.[60] I spent the day in camp & in Peublo searching for Flour & sugar for those that had given there names to Bro Levi [Hancock] to go back as he & Father Petagrew said.[61] I found Flour in the brand at 3 _ $ a hundred & a bet[t]er article at 4 _ which was preferable.

---

[57]At San Diego this day, Azariah Smith said, "The Colonel has ar[r]ived and is high[ly] [satisfied with] us, and is desirous that we should re-enlist; and the Captain with some twenty men have volunteers for Six months. Some are for him, and some for the council of the Preisthood [*sic*] which we have with us. I am one of the latter." See Bigler, ed., *The Gold Discovery Journal of Azariah Smith*, 86, 87.

[58]Co. B Capt. Jesse D. Hunter openly favored reenlistment, while Sgt. William Hyde and Cpl. Horace Alexander represented those who wanted guidance from Levi W. Hanock, the command's only Mormon general authority, and David Pettegrew, spiritual advisor, both at Los Angeles.

[59]For more on the reenlistment controversy, see Chapter 7.

[60]The liberty pole was raised over Fort Moore in preparation for the Independence Day celebration.

[61]Levi Hancock organized a company of those who intended to head east to rejoin their families.

Friday 2th. Weather plesant & warm for sum[m]er weather. This day I as I did yesterday [and went] searching for a fit out. Learned that Flour could be had out at [the ranches of] Workmans Reads Rolins & williams for 4 $ per Hundred sifted.

Saturday 3th. Weather cleare as usual. The day was spent in Policeeing & cleaning for the 4[th]. I spent the day in camp.

Sunday 4th. The morning foggy but some cleared. At revalee [reveille] the Flag was hoisted. The Battalion was cald to be presant to gether with the [New York] volunteers & Dragoons. A Nationell salute was fiard [fired]. The band plaid & [the troops] then dispersed. At II ock a parade was cald. The command came out under arms & assembled in a squar[e] round the Liberty pole whare a platform had been p[r]ev[i]ously erected to which the officers was cald. Silence [was] ordered & The declaration of Independence was read. [A speech] was oferd and then a patreotic song was sung by Bro Levi Handcoch [Hancock] after which we was dismissed.[62]

Monday 5th. Weather cleare. The morning still & butifull. All remained still untell [until] guard mounting when word came for the Battalion to attend a funerall of one of the Draggoons which we attended.

Tuseday 6th. Weather fine. T[h]is day all was still after the greait celabraition a calm after a storm as within Calaforna usels [itself] whare I remained in camp.

Weddensday 7th. Weather cl[e]ar as usual. This day all was still. Nothing of importance occurd.

Thursday 8th. Morning clear & fine. This day the work commenced again on the Fort Cald by the Coln Fort Moore For the memory of Capt Moore who in the first battle at St Muquall [San Pasqual] fell for his country.

Friday 9th. Weather cleare as usuall. This morning I hunted horses that left the drove the day before but did not find them.

Saturday 10th. Weather fine. T[h]is day I purchased two Mules one for 25$ from Gunl Peco [General Pico] & the other from a strainger from lowar Calafornia for 20$. Boath whites.

Sunday 11th. Weather comon. This day I found two of my lost animals. I also let Bro Averatt have one that I had baught previous for sixteene dollars. A white one.

Monday 12th. Cleare & warm. This morning I paid the Cutler [sutler] 25$ for clothing.

Tuseday 13th. Weather pleasant. This day I spent in camp. Noathing of importanc occurd.

Weddensday 14th. Weather fine & warm. This day I went in search of my Mules that left the drove the day before. I road all the day [and] found all of them & returned to Camp before night.

---

[62]At the ceremonies Colonel Stevenson officially named the new fort. Musician Levi Hancock sang a patriotic song he had composed for the occasion.

THE MORMON BATTALION'S FOURTH OF JULY
This drawing by Charles B. Hancock shows the celebration
held at Pueblo de Los Angeles. *Courtesy, the Utah State Historical Society.*

Thursday 15th [July 1847]. Weather as comon. This day I spent in camp. Nothing of importance occur[red]. Capt Hunter reached peublo [de los Angeles] with his Company ready for a discharge on the morrow.

THOMAS JAMES DUNN: CO. B MARCHED FOR SAN DIEGO

While the main corps of the Mormon Battalion suffered through the tedious duty of an occupation force engaged in military construction, the single company sent south on 15 March to keep the peace at San Diego acted as a largely independent force under much more favorable conditions. The arrival of Capt. Jesse D. Hunter and his soldiers at Los Angeles on 15 July 1847 reunited the five companies of the battalion for the first time since Company B had been detached four months earlier at San Luis Rey Mission. Philip St. George Cooke's selection of this unit to prevent insurrection in such a strategic location paid unmentioned tribute to the reliability of its members. In carrying out this duty, the men more than upheld Cooke's confidence. Its performance in preserving order and earning the respect and friendship of local citizens stands out as exceptional among the battalion's many achievements. Some of the best and most literate journal keepers also belonged to Company B, including Henry W. Bigler, Azariah Smith, and Samuel Rogers. To these is now added the name of twenty-five-year-old Thomas James Dunn, a corporal from New York, whose journal, published here for the first time, provides a vivid account of the Mormon Battalion's service at San Diego.

PRIVATE JOURNAL OF THOMAS DUNN, UTAH STATE HIST. SOC.

Sun. March 14th [1847]—We received an express from Gen. Kearney [sic] in which he did not expect to return to this place. But should start from Monterey to the states. Ordered the Dragoons and a part of the Battalion to Pueblo and one Co. to San Diego. Accordingly on March 15th, Co. B marched for San Diego. Arrived on Wednesday the 17th. About 4 miles from town we met a part of the Dragoons on their return to San Luis Rey. Before our arrival there was some two or three hundred marines landed under command of Comm. Stocedon [Stockton].[63]

Thurs. March 18th—They [the marines] went on board.

Sat. March 20th—The ship "Savannah" anchored two miles from this harbor.[64] Came from Monterey.[65]

---

[63]Before Co. B arrived, San Diego had changed hands several times. Capt. Samuel F. Dupont of the U.S. sloop-of-war *Cyane* in July 1846 captured the Mexican fort constructed on the ruins of the old presidio and named it Fort Dupont. Californian insurgents soon after recovered the position and held it until Com. Robert Stockton came on 31 October in the U.S. frigate *Congress*. He landed about a hundred marines, recaptured the fort, and renamed it after himself. According to Sgt. Albert Smith, the marines and sailors reboarded the ship "a few days after we came." See Albert Smith Journal, 18 March 1847.

[64]U.S.S. *Savannah* was flagship of the U.S. Navy's Pacific Squadron in 1846. The frigate rated forty-four guns, displaced 1,726 tons, and carried a complement of 480. When she fired her guns, said Azariah Smith, "it made the air ring." See Bigler, ed., *The Gold Discovery Journal of Azariah Smith*, 81.

[65]On this date, Dr. John S. Griffin, 31, a U.S. Army surgeon who came to California with Kearny and now directed the hospital at San Diego, wrote, "The prejudice against the Mormons here seems to be wearing off—it is yet among the Californians a great term of reproach to be called Mormon—yet as they are a quiet, industrious, sober, inoffensive people—they seem to be gradually working their way up—they are extremely industrious—they have been engaged while here in digging wells, plastering houses, and seem anxious and ready to work—The Californians have no great idea of their soldier like quallities [sic] and in action would not dread them much—this arising in a great measure from their dress—carriage &c—which is as unlike any soldier—as any thing could possibly be—Yet I think if brought into action they would prove themselves good men—as I am told they are generally fine shots—and they drill—tolerably well—They are barefooted and almost naked—several of them are sick—with Intermittent fever." See Ames, ed., "A Doctor Comes to California: The Diary of John S. Griffin, Assistant Surgeon with Kearny's Dragoons, 1846–1847."

Tues. March 23rd—I went to [the] coast but there was little to be seen. The Frigate "Congress" is now laying in harbor.[66] Two small boats besides. We also received intelligence from San Luis Rey, that the Battalion had all left for Pueblo [de los Angeles] except for 25 who still remained there. There is some few Americans in this place. The most of them have married Spanish women for their companions. But the principle [sic] part of the inhabitants are Spanish. Some of them have pleasant situations. Buildings poor, timber scarse indeed. It has been very dry for some years. Otherwise the climate is delightful and healthful. But very little sickeness. For a few days past it has been rather cool for the country.[67]

April 1st [1847]—We had some rain. Quite cool.

Sun. April 4th—Pleasant. The hours seem to pass slowly the nearer the time of our discharge appears. My mind is almost constantly reflecting on my wife and little ones who are anxiously looking for my return to their embrace.

April 8, 1847—The weather pleasant and fair. This evening we received an express from Pueblo [de los Angeles]. All was well. Also a promise of our pay in two or three weeks. This was good news to us as we are very much in need of clothes. Today a ship landed. Had on board forty barrels of flour for us. Our rations of flour is now raised to 18 oz. per day. By order of Gen. Kearney.

April 12th—For a week past I have been unable for duty by reason of a lame foot.

Thurs. April 15th—A fray between a Spaniard and an American. About a debt of $1.50 which the American, Mr. Russell, owed the Spaniard. Some conversation ensued after which Russell fired a pistol at the Spaniard, but did not hit him. He then caught a stone and threw at Russell but missed him. He next threw a cow's foot which knocked Russell from his horse. The citizenry gathered round the two. They were immediately arrested. Russell was put in irons.[68]

Fri. April 16th—The individuals were brought before the Alcalda for

---

[66]Commodore Stockton's flagship, the 44-gun U.S.S. *Congress*, was the last of the sailing frigates designed for the U.S. Navy and top of the line in its class. The warship displaced 1,867 tons and carried a full complement of about five hundred men. In 1862 the Confederate ironclad steam-ram, *Virginia*, formerly U.S.S. *Merrimac*, sank the wooden vessel in Hampton Roads.

[67]On 29 March Pvt. Azariah Smith described the burial of a child who apparently belonged to John and Anita Warner of Warner's Ranch: "Last evening just before dusk a child of Mr Warners which had died was taken to the grave; two indians carried the corps[e] on their heads and a couple [of] young ladies one on either side with a candle burning. In this way the corps[e] was borne to the grave, and after being placed in the grave the Gentlemen and Ladies help cover it by pawing the dirt in with their hands." See Bigler, ed., *The Gold Discovery Journal of Azariah Smith*, 81.

[68]Richard Dana's *Pilgrim* landed Thomas Russell at San Diego in 1835. Russell led a treasure hunt to the Colorado River in 1836. He worked as a carpenter and became a naturalized Mexican citizen with a proclivity for trouble. Russell apparently headed for the gold fields in 1848. See Bancroft, *History of California*, 5:707–08.

trial. Russell was found guilty on the Testimony of two witnesses. He was again put in irons and the Spaniard was set free. An account of the proceeding was immediately sent to Gen. Kearney at Monterey. A mail route is now being established from this place to Monterrey, commencing on Monday the 18th. A return in two weeks. I now hope for some cheering news to enliven and cheer the mind. Also to pass the time. For more lonesome days I never saw. Nothing to interest the eye and but little the mind. Today I received of the quartermaster, pay for my mule that I sold on the way. During the week I succeeded in getting some clothing.

Sat. April 24th—Pleasant and warm.

Mon. April 26th—Capt. Hunters wife departed this life.[69] [She] was buried on Tues. the 27th. A discourse [was] delivered by Wm. Hyde touching on the resurrection. Mrs. Hunter left an infant a few days old.[70]

Sun. May 2nd, 1847—This evening Major Cloud arrived from Pueblo [de los Angeles].[71]

Tues. May 4th—We received six months of our pay which was gladly received.[72] Though many made a bad use of it in drinking and carousing.[73]

---

[69]Twenty-three-year-old Lydia Hunter died during an influenza epidemic just two weeks after giving birth to a son named Diego. She had been married to Capt. Jesse D. Hunter for fifteen months. One of only four women who completed the journey from Fort Leavenworth to California, she was considered "a most estimable lady" by members of the command.

[70]Dr. John S. Griffin wrote, "Last night the wife of Captain Hunter died of Typhoid fever—or rather I think a malignant form of Quotidian fever. The attack was issued in with severe rigors, some six days ago—with great difficulty of breathing and oppression, followed by high fever. About 11 A M each day the same attack came—with cramps & irregular nervous twitchings—serious diarrhoea—mind affected—purgative of Calomel, Massa ex Hyd &c given until slight ptyalism produced—her breasts became inflamed, and before death suppurated. The nervous twitchings were stopped by the use of small doses of morphia & Assafoetida. The chill checked by Quinine—her brain became very much excited. Delirium for two days previous to death—and deafness—She finally died last night about 10 P M in great pain—This was the first American woman who ever bore a child in San Diego." See Ames, ed., "A Doctor Comes to California," 27 April 1847.

[71]Maj. Jeremiah H. Cloud of the Second Missouri Volunteers, who served as an additional paymaster for the U.S. Army in California, was "a faithful officer, very attentive to his duties, and of sterling integrity," according to Col. Richard B. Mason. He died three months later of head injuries suffered when he was thrown from his horse near Sutter's Fort. See Mason to Jones, 18 September 1847, Sen. Exec. Doc. 18 (31-1), 1849–50, Serial 557, 9:321–22.

[72]Samuel Rogers wrote, "The members of our Company are drawing their pay for six months, deducting what they owe to the sutlers. I drew $40.45, having had $1.55 of the sutler. I paid E[phraim] Green 50 cts. For the half soles, and John Lawson $12.85 and took a receipt in full, for all demands, paid [Thomas] Kirk for the shoes which I had of him. Am now clear of debt, with $24.85."

[73]Dr. John S. Griffin said, "The Mormons after their payment took a little spree—some few men drunk and two or three black eyes—or small fights occurred—but much less drinking gambling &c occurred among them than I have ever witnessed among any troops after a payment—They are extremely industrious—and avaricious. They get all the pelf they can—and keep all they get. They are constantly employed by the citizens, and one is engaged in constructing a horse mill—This is looked upon in San Diego—as the greatest feat that has been ever undertaken in these parts." See Ames, ed., "A Doctor Comes to California," 4 May 1847.

Wed. May 5th—Thurs. Fri. Sat. and Sun.—Nothing of importance transpired. Sun. it rained some. For some time past we have heard rumors of the Spaniards getting a re-inforcement [*sic*] from Sonora, which produces some excitement in the inhabitants of this place.[74]

Tues. morn. The 11th—Albert Dunham departed this life. Was sick only four days before he was interred. The surgeon dissected his head to ascertain, if possible, the cause of death. Found the brain ulcerated, which was the cause of death.[75]

Today we had an express from Pueblo bring word of a battle between twenty of our men and some Indians, in which some of the enemy were killed and three of our men wounded. Also that there had been a battle in New Mexico in which 300 of the enemy were killed and 60 of the Dragoons.[76] This was in the country of Santa Fe. Also that Gen. Kearney and Capt. Cook were going to the states and that Stevens [Col. Jonathan D. Stevenson] is our commander.

Thurs. 13th of May—Doc. Griffin, who had been our physician, left for Pueblo.[77] Mr. French, his steward, remained with us.[78]

Sun. 16th of May [1847]—The mail arrived from Monterrey. Some important from the windward. There had been some 10 or 12 of our men gone as an escort for Gen. Kearney to the states. A small party of the Bat-

---

[74]These rumors proved unfounded.

[75]Pvt. Albert Dunham, who died twelve days short of his nineteenth birthday, was buried on Point Loma near the grave of Lydia Hunter. He had been playing ball on 7 May when he was "suddenly seized with violent pains in the back of the neck & head (he had been subject to Rheumatic Attacks)," Dr. Griffin said. "The brain was carefuly [*sic*] examined about 10 hours after death," he continued. "The veins of the dura Mater much distended with blood, the ventricles full of a bloody serum, and a deposite [*sic*] on the arachnoid resembling coagulable lymph—This could not be removed with a sponge and water—." For his other symptoms and treatment, see Ibid., 11 May 1847.

[76]This referred to the bloody revolt in New Mexico that began at Taos on 19 January 1847, three months after the Mormon Battalion left Santa Fe, when Mexicans and Pueblo Indians killed Governor Charles Bent, Santa Fe Trail pioneer and builder of Bent's Fort on the Arkansas River, and six others. It ended on 4 February when a mixed force of Second Missouri Volunteers, First Dragoons, and a company of volunteers under Col. Sterling Price defeated the insurgents at Taos, killing more than a hundred of them and hanging the leaders. Price lost seven killed, among them Capt. John H. Burgwin, the third First Dragoons captain killed in Kearny's Army of the West.

[77]Dr. John S. Griffin said, "I left San Diego May 13 1847, by order of Lt Col. Cooke—and arrived at the Puebla de los Angeles, in two days and a half. The next day went to duty. Genl Kearny left the day before I arrived—for San Pedro where he would embark on one of the U.S. Vessels for Monterey—from thence he would go to the United States as soon as practicable—I was informed of the *pleasant* news that I might expect to make California my home for some time to come—That is to say if the Californians will allow us to do so—and I think they are great fools if they do—for in a short time our force will be much reduced by the Mormon Battalion being disbanded—and then we leave some points where there is plenty of cannons, San Diego for instance so guarded—that it invites attack." See Ibid., 5 June 1847.

[78]New Yorker Erasmus D. French, Co. C, First Dragoons, was a trained physician. French went to the mines during the gold rush, lived at San Jose and Chico, and in 1869 settled in San Diego as a farmer. See Bancroft, *History of California*, 3:749.

talion were sent out to put down some unruly Indians, who gave them battle. Six of the Indians were killed and two of our men were wounded. This
was about 10 miles from Pueblo.

Mon. 17th of May—I wrote a letter to my wife.

Wed. 12th of May—Our Capt. [Hunter], Lieut. Barrow [Barrus] and
Cliff [Clift] were intoxicated, which was not only settle [a] bad example
before the men but was a departure from the Counsel of the Church and the
Twelve, as will be seen from the commencement of this Journal.[79]

On Sun. 16th [1847]—The Capt. Had changed the hour of guard
meeting from 9 to 8 o'clock in the morning. Of this I was not apprised until
the hour had arrived. When I went to guard quarter, on meeting he said to
me, "It is time you was on hand as officer of the guard." I replied that, "I
did not suppose it to be 9 o'clock yet," when one of the men said the time
of the guard mount had been changed to 8 o'clock. Said I, "This is the first
I have heard of it." I then turned and went directly to my quarters for my
arms. On leaving met the guard at the door. Said I, "What is up?" They
replied, "The Capt. sent us for you." After they had gone I started for the
quarters. On reaching there I met the guard whom the Capt. had ordered to
go and bring me forthwith, but as it happened I was on hand. I met the
Capt., but he said not a word. Such conduct hurt my feelings very much,
because it was taking advantage of me. It manifest to me that he wished to
show his authority, when at the same time it was injury to himself. There had
been many such things happened in the character of our officers, which is
degrading to their profession and to the Council of the Twelve. For to them
we looked for better things. I have not penned anything against them before,
because I have hoped and looked for better conduct and example, but have
looked in vain.[80]

From May the 18th
To
June the 17th

The time was occupied mostly in the purchase and breaking wild horses
and mules.

On the 14th [June 1847]—We received intelligence from Mexico in
which Gen. Taylor had had a Battle with Santa Ana, the General of the Mexican forces, in which Taylor came off victorious. At the time having 7,000
and Santa Anna 18,000.[81] Also that Gen. Scott had taken Vera Cruz, and

---

[79]Lt. Robert Clift of Co. C had been assigned to assist the alcalde at San Diego.

[80]The entries dated 12 and 16 May were added later, apparently to make a written record of Dunn's
grievances against Hunter, Barrus, and Clift.

[81]These numbers were not far off. On 22–23 February 1847, Gen. Zachary Taylor's badly outnumbered but better-led army of about 4,800 defeated a Mexican army of more than twenty thousand under
Gen. Antonio Lopez de Santa Ana in the Battle of Buena Vista, near Saltillo, Mexico.

that the American forces were likely to reach the City of Mexico soon.[82] On Tues. the 21st [22nd] Col. Stevenson and Lieutenant Stoneman arrived in this place.[83]

Wed the 22nd [23 June 1847]—The Co. was called out to ascertain whether there were any who wished to re-enlist, as this was the business of the Col. [Stevenson] to this place. After making his proposition and Capt. Hunter making a little addition which was to enlist for six months to garrison this place, with the privilege of sending an express to the Church and also to ration us to Bear Valley or San Francisco Bay at the end of the months. Under these propositions there was 20 re-enlisted. The Capt. then concluded to go to Pueblo [de los Angeles] to get the Co. made up.

On Thurs. 23rd [24 June]—He, in company with the Col., started for Pueblo. On this day there was an Indian tied to a cannon and whipped severely, by order of the Alealda [alcalde], Lieut. Cliff who succeeded Mr. Fitch in this office.[84]

Sat. 25th [26 June]—There was another [Indian] put in the stocks and came near choking to death. The orders of the Alcalda was to put his head in. These beings suffer most inhumanly and mostly from the sway of the Catholic power, which is and has for a long time been wielded over them.

Sun. the 4th of July—Was celebrated in this place, though nothing of any great or extra performance. Merely the firing of a few guns to witness the great day of our Independence.[85] This evening, the Capt. and those who accompanied him,[86] returned with orders for the Company to March to Pueblo on the 9th.

On their return, they were saluted cheerfully by the Co. in general. Mr. McGil,[87] a much respected citizen of the place, who received a part in the salutes, expressed his great desire for us to remain in the service and garri-

---

[82]Gen. Winfield Scott and an American army of 12,600 captured Veracruz, Mexico, on 29 March 1847. The City of Mexico would fall in September.

[83]Samuel Rogers wrote, "Col. Stevenson came in town to day, he wants us to volunteer for six months longer. Some of the citizens say if the Mormons do not stay they will leave the town, they not having any confidence in any ~~other~~ other troops, to guard the place." See Samuel Rogers Journal, 22 June 1847.

[84]Lt. Robert Clift apparently ordered the Indian punished. In June he replaced Henry Delano Fitch, one of southern California's earliest foreign settlers, as alcalde at San Diego.

[85]Many were apparently recovering from celebrating the night before. Azariah Smith said, "Night before last after midnight, some of the Boys, with their muskets went round to the officers and Don Magill [Miguel Pedrorena], Mr Vansenys [Juan Bandini] and other friendly Spaniards, saluting them by fireing and giveing them cheers; they all treated them and felt well pleased. The boys got pretty high." See Bigler, ed., The Gold Discovery Journal of Azariah Smith, 5 July 1847.

[86]Captain Hunter was accompanied by Sgt. William Hyde and Cpl. Horace Alexander, who were outspoken in opposing reenlistment. Azariah Smith said, "Last evening the Captain returned. I beleave he ran again[st] a snag at Purbelow and is not like[ly] to make out his Company." Ibid.

[87]Miguel Pedrorena, about 38, was an educated Spaniard who came to San Diego via Peru and married into an influential family. During Stockton's occupation, he served as an aide to the commodore and held the rank of captain in Frémont's California Battalion.

son this place, as we had been solicited by the Col. [Stevenson]. But under the circumstances we could not feel at Liberty to do it, in as much as we considered ourselves having to heed the counsel of the Church. Yet there were some who expressed a strong determination to do so. Even Capt. Hunter, Lieut. Barrow [Barrus] and Cliff [Clift], regardless of the Council of the Twelve.

On Fri. the 9th of July—We took up the line of march for Pueblo [de los Angeles]. Arrived there on the 15th.

So ended Company B's tour in San Diego, but the memory of its service lives on. In 1997 Charles and Joan Hackley began searching for the graves of Lydia Hunter, Albert Dunham, David Smith, Lafayette Frost, and Neal Donald. They successfully located the graves of Hunter and Dunham at Fort Rosecrans National Cemetery and determined that David Smith was buried in the garden of Mission San Luis Rey. Frost and Donald, who died while serving in the Mormon Volunteers, were buried in the American Cemetery, which now lies under Interstate 5. Through the efforts of a group of Mormon Battalion enthusiasts three handsome monuments of Cararra marble now mark these historic graves at Fort Rosecrans, Old Town State Park, and the San Luis Rey Mission.

Chapter 6

"OVER A BEAUTIFUL COUNTRY"
Kearny's Life Guards

During the spring of 1847, Gen. Stephen W. Kearny had "no nonsense about him." In just ninety days as military governor of California, Kearny had "brought much order to a vast territory so lately given over to chaos"—an especially notable feat considering the shambles John C. Frémont and Robert F. Stockton had made of politics in the newly conquered province. Kearny was a man of no small insight; he believed "that if left alone," the Mormons would "gradually slide back into an ordinary condition," because only "persecution has kept them together." Finding "the people of California quiet" by the end of April 1847, the general determined "to close my public business [at Monterey] as soon as possible and proceed to St. Louis via the South Pass."[1] Kearny ordered Frémont to accompany him, determined to arrest the insubordinate officer when they arrived at Fort Leavenworth.

GEN. STEPHEN W. KEARNY:
THIRTEEN OF THE MORMON BATTALION

Confirming his high regard for the reliability of the Mormon volunteers, General Kearny chose out of all the troops under his command, volunteer and regular, members of the battalion to serve as his military escort back to the United States. After inspecting the soldiers at Los Angeles, he reported to Washington, D.C., on his plans to leave California for the last time, including what he had in mind for the rebellious John C. Frémont.[2]

---

[1]Clarke, *Stephen Watts Kearny*, 304, 316, 325–26.

[2] Kearny on the same day issued Orders No. 16, which directed Cooke to "select 13 efficient men of the Mormon Battalion to form part of the escort," and ordered these men to "turn in their muskets to the Ordnance Sergeant, & receive from him Rifles in their stead." See Gardner, ed., "Report of Lieut. Col. P. St. George Cooke," 38.

KEARNY TO THE ADJUTANT GENERAL, U.S. ARMY,
RECORDS OF THE 10TH MILITARY DEPARTMENT, 1846–1851,
LETTERS SENT, ROLL 1, NATIONAL ARCHIVES.

Head Qrs. 10 mily Dept.
Ciudad de los. Angeles
California 13 May 1847
No 11

Sir,

My letter No 10. of May 3 informed you of my intentions of coming to this place with Col Stevenson and 2 Compys of his Regt of N.Y. Vols. We reached here on the 9th and I find the people of this part of California quiet, notwithstanding some rumors to the contrary circulated & I fear originated by some of our own officers to further their own wicket purposes.[3]

I leave here tomorrow for Monterey, & will close my public business there as soon as possible, and then proceed to Saint Louis (via the South Pass) where I hope to be by the 20 of August, and where if this reaches you in time (it will go by Santa fe) I shall expect to receive orders for my further movements.

I shall be prepared to go at once, wherever it is deemed my services may be needed.[4]

I this morning started Lt. Col. Fremont to Monterey, to close his public business there before he leaves for Washington. His conduct in California has been such, that I shall be compelled, on arriving in Missouri, to arrest him & send him under charges to report to you.

I shall be accompanied from Monterey by Lt. Colonel Fremont, Maj. [Thomas] Swords (Qrmr.) who goes to settle accounts and bring his family here—Capts. Cooke and Turner 1st Drags, who go to join their Companies, & Assistant Surgeon G. B. Sanderson who has resigned. My escort will be the men of the Top[ographical] Parties who came to this country with Lt. Col. Fremont and Lt. Emory & 13 men of the Mormon Battalion.

Very Respectfully
Your Ob. Servt.
signed, S. W. Kearny
Brig Genl

The Ad't Genl
U.S. Army,
Washington

THROUGH A ROUGH BROKEN COUNTRY:
PUEBLO DE LOS ANGELES TO SUTTER'S FORT

Born in New York in 1822, Nathaniel V. Jones had worked as a ship's

---

[3] An apparent reference to Frémont and his subordinates.

[4] Kearny survived the thrusts of Californian lancers at San Pasqual only to be struck down by a mosquito in Mexico, where he served briefly as military governor of Mexico City before dying of yellow fever on 31 October 1848.

JAMES FERGUSON, JEFFERSON HUNT, AND NATHANIEL V. JONES.
Courtesy, the Utah State Historical Society.

carpenter in his youth. At seventeen, after moving to Wisconsin and converting to Mormonism, he settled in Nauvoo, where he worked on the temple. In the spring of 1847 the naturally handsome Jones was "aged twenty four years, six feet one inch high, fair complexion, dark brown hair, grey eyes, and by profession a carpenter and joiner." As sergeant of Company D he had arranged his discharge on 17 March 1847 "in consequence of the situation of his family needing his assistance and for the purpose of conveying information to the Mormon Community." The release fell through, and Jones was reduced to the ranks the next day, claiming Lt. George Dykes' "false reports broke me of my office."[5] The details of Jones' problems are not known, but they were apparently forgotten when it came time to select Kearny's bodyguard.

Besides Jones, Capt. Henry Smith Turner, First Dragoons, kept the only surviving diary of the journey. A survey of the other primary sources provides a short course in the usefulness of such documents. Apparently sum-

---

[5]Jones, ed., "Extracts from the Life Sketch of Nathaniel V. Jones," 24.

marizing his diary, Thomas Swords submitted a report to the Quartermaster General on 8 October 1847 in Washington, D.C., that seems to
contain several minor lapses of memory.[6] Battalion veterans Joseph Taylor
and Jeremiah Willey wrote brief accounts of the trip in the late 1850s;
Taylor covered the journey in a single sentence, but Willey's more-detailed
recollection confused details of geography and chronology. When
Matthew Caldwell composed his "Short Life's History" some fifty years
after the event, his memory was far from perfect, but he told several great
tales, some of which may well be true. When a relative of Amos Cox eventually told his story, legend firmly supplanted history.[7]

Joseph Taylor recalled that he "was taken to be one of the lifeguards of
Gen. S. Kearney who was ... returning to the US in company with 12 others."[8] The niece of escort Amos Cox proudly related that Kearny:

> ordered the captains of the Battalion to select from each company two of
> the very best all around men: men who could ride the longest and hardest,
> fast the longest [and] live on scant rations the longest, do without sleep the
> longest, load pack-mules the most expeditiously, [and] do double guard
> duty which meant do without half enough sleep.[9]

William Byram Pace noted that the general:

> sent up a Letter requesting twelve men from the Battalion to accompany
> him back to the states as a life guard. The men were selected & sent down
> for his inspection. He told them that if they should meet there familys on
> the Road that he would discharge them & if they did not they should find
> themselves to serve until they got to Fort Leavenworth.[10]

Besides Jones, Cox, and Taylor, the escort included Lt. Sylvester Hulet
and privates John Binley, Matthew Caldwell, Ebenezer Landers, William
F. Reynolds, William W. Spencer, Elanson Tuttle, Charles Y. Webb, and
Jeremiah Willey.[11] Kearny's guards were the most fortunate of the bat-

---

[6]For the contemporary reports, see Clarke, ed., *The Original Journals of Henry Smith Turner*, 125–35, cited
as *Turner Journal*; and Major Thos. Swords, "Appendix E, Report of the Quartermaster General," in House
Exec. Doc. I (30–2), 1848, Serial 537, 226–36, cited as Swords' Report.

[7]See Adelia B. Cox, Biographical Sketch of Sylvester Hulet, Utah State Hist. Soc.

[8]Joseph Taylor, Journal, 1857, LDS Archives.

[9]Cox, Biographical Sketch of Sylvester Hulet, 6.

[10]William B. Pace, Journals 1847–1857, LDS Archives, 50. Punctuation added.

[11]There is considerable confusion about the exact number of men in Kearny's escort, but these twelve are
the men named in the primary sources. Turner reported that fifteen Mormon guards accompanied Kearny, and
his count may be correct, for the Iowa adjutant-general's office muster-out role indicated that Gilman Gordon,
Thomas C. Ivie, and Samuel G. Clark were discharged on Bear River, Oregon, on 16 July 1847, which suggests
they were part of Kearny's escort. See Clarke, ed., *Turner Journal*, 126; and Ricketts, *The Mormon Battalion*, 162.

talion veterans to return east that year, for the long journeys home that discharged battalion veterans made during the fall of 1847 would not be so lucky nor so quick.

Lt. William Tecumseh Sherman led most of these men on a march up El Camino Real, the coastal highway, while Hulet, Willey, Tuttle and perhaps Landers accompanied Cooke and Kearny by sea to Monterey.[12] Sherman recalled that the trip "gave me the best kind of opportunity for seeing the country, which was very sparsely populated indeed, except by a few families at the various Missions. We had no wheeled vehicles, but packed food and clothing on mules driven ahead, and we slept on the ground in the open air."[13] After ascending El Camino Real to Monterey, the escort followed the General Kearny across Pacheco Pass to the Central Valley. Here occurred what could have been a tragedy of major proportions—the loss of the single best account of the march of the Mormon Battalion. The skin boat carrying Philip St. George Cooke capsized while crossing the Mokelumne, leaving him nothing but the clothes on his back. His five-hundred page journal (surely wrapped in an oil-skin) "was carried away on the swirling waters."[14] Fortunately on 9 August 1847 Indians reported finding this invaluable record "on the upper pass on the Muquelemny River." Days before another important discovery, John Sutter wrote on 20 January 1848, "the Nemutchumny Chief has brought me a part of Col. Cook's Journal, which he bought from an Indian for a shirt, and fortunately has not been smoked up."[15]

Perhaps discouraged, Cooke left no record of his trip eastward, and the journals of Henry Turner and N. V. Jones are the best accounts of Kearny's journey. Frémont's attempt during his court-martial to destroy the career of General Kearny, a great American soldier, provides an understated dramatic background to this story. Jones' straight-forward reports on legendary western episodes, such as the Donner party and details of the 1847 overland emigration, make his narrative both colorful and significant.

---

[12]History of Jeremiah Willey, LDS Archives, 30, named "Br tuttle," but as noted, James Pace identified Landers as one of the men who went by sea.

[13]Sherman, *Memoirs of General William T. Sherman*, 1:28.

[14]Thomas Swords reported "our skin boat, which had performed such good service, went down the stream and was lost." See Swords' Report, 230. Thomas Hart Benton later insinuated that Kearny arranged this accident to destroy evidence in the Frémont court-martial, which may have led to the publication of Cooke's journal as an Executive Document. See Clarke, *Stephen Watts Kearny*, 328.

[15]Sutter *et al*, *New Helvetia Diary*, 68, 110.

The location of the manuscript journal is not known, but a version credited to Jones' widow appeared in the *Utah Historical Quarterly* in 1931.[16] The typescript published here for the first time contains about a third again more text than previous versions.[17]

N. V. JONES, TRAVELS WITH THE MORMON BATTALION, 8 MAY–13 JUNE 1847.

May 10. This morning, the General, Col. Stephenson and some others of his officers came out; the Battalion was paraded for him to inspect. He [Kearny] made a great many remarks concerning us, and spoke of us in the highest terms, so much so that I thought it was flattery. He promised to represent our conduct to the President and in the halls of Congress, and give us the justice that we merited. He promised us some clothing and advised us to reenlist into the service for twelve months, and many other things. Today there was an order issued to have three men detailed from each company to go to the States as an escort for him. I was detailed as one of that number.

May 11. Engaged all day in fitting out for the trip.

May 12. Fitting out.

May 13. Left Los Angeles with a detachment of nine men; the other three are going round by water with the Gen. Lieut. Sherman [of Company F, 3d] regiment of [U.S.] artillery has taken command of us. The first day went twenty miles and camped at an Indian ranch where there was a natural curiosity, a spring that was hot, and about six feet from it was one that was cold.

May 14. We started early in the morning, today. We passed through more timber than I have seen in all California before. The country is mountainous and broken with small valleys. We came thirty miles today and camped at an old ranch that had been excavated [evacuated].

May 15 [1847]. We traveled all day over a country very much like that of the day before. Today I purchased a mule. We came thirty miles and camped at the Mission of San Clare.[18]

May 16. We traveled all day on the coast. Came to Santa Barbara at night, a distance of thirty miles. Here I found two men from Rochester by [way

---

[16]See Rebecca M. Jones, ed., "Extracts from the Life Sketch of Nathaniel V. Jones," 6–23; republished in 1946 in Carter, ed., *Heart Throbs of the West*, 7:143–65. These publications were based on a "rather poorly done" typescript created before 1912 and owned by Jones' daughter, Mary Clawson. See Clawson to Riter letters, Nathaniel Jones Collection, Utah State Hist. Soc. Dale L. Morgan had access to a more complete copy of Jones' journal, but neither his version nor the original has been located.

[17]See A Copy of Notes Made by Sergeant Nathaniel V. Jones of His Travels with the Mormon Battalion, Accn. 40, Typescript, Special Collections, Marriott Library, University of Utah. Where the typescript is obviously in error, a logical corrected reading is provided in brackets.

[18]Jones' names for the missions along El Camino Real vary considerably from the Spanish originals. The first three days' journey took the party through the San Fernando and Simi valleys to the Pacific coast at today's Ventura. "San Clare" may refer to either Mission San Buenaventura or to a church in the small community of Santa Clara at the mouth of the Santa Clara River.

of] the Gulf [of Mexico], and I stayed here and had a pleasant interview with them, during the evening.

May 17. This morning we started at nine o'clock and traveled all day on the coast and through the mountains. Camped in the mountains; In all came thirty miles.

May 18. This morning we struck through the mountains. We were in the mountains until we passed through a cloud, where it was raining and the sun shone clear on the top. We traveled all day through the mountains being about thirty-five miles. Camped in a valley near a ranch, just at night. About twelve in the day we passed the Mission of San Tenara. Yesterday we took a prisoner that had deserted from Monterey, and today we took another at the Mission of Tenara.[19]

May 19. Today we crossed a sand plain, all the forepart of the day; very little vegetation upon it. Camped in a valley near a ranch called Capt. Damyrs, a distance of thirty miles.

May 20. All day through a rough broken country until the last twelve miles, we passed through a beautiful valley. Camped in the mountains. All the mountains were covered with wild oats about four miles from the Mission of San Louis.[20]

May 21. This morning we traveled through the mountains seven miles, and came to the Mission of San Margaretha. The rest of the day through a beautiful valley with considerable timber. Some of our party gave chase to a bear. We camped in the same valley, came thirty-eight miles.

May 22. Came down the same valley all day. About eleven in the day we came to the Mission of San Magill. Came thirty miles. Camped in the same valley.

May 23. Still down the same valley. The river is called Monterey river, very little timber. The land is poor. Came forty miles and camped at the Mission of San Obisto.[21]

May 24. Still down the same valley. The country is some better today. Wild oats in abundance; came twenty-five miles and camped on the river.

May 25. This morning we started in very good season. Traveled about fifteen miles through the mountains and came to Monterey about twelve in the day. Quartered in the south part of the town in a building that had been occupied by some of Col. Stephenson's regiment.[22] Today there was sixty

---

[19]From Santa Barbara, the men crossed the Santa Ynez Mountains; Jones' "Mission of Tenara" was probably at Santa Maria.

[20]The party left the coast to camp near Mission San Luis Obispo de Tolosa.

[21]After crossing California's coastal range, the men came to the Salinas River, passed the mission at Miguel Arcangel, and camped at Nuestra Señora de la Soledad, Jones' "San Obisto."

[22]This was the "public barracks, a large *adobe* building, in the centre of the town, much out of repair." See Swords' Report, 229.

ordered out to fight the Indians in the mountains. The General had not come as we expected.

Tonight I saw a great curiosity; two goats on the wharf that belonged on board one of the vessels lying in the harbor and every small boat that landed they came bleating from one boat to another until they found their own boat. It seemed as though they knew every boat as well as if they could talk.

May 26. I was herding mules all day.

May 27. I went on board the Columbus, a seventy-four gun ship. Her length is two hundred fourteen feet, from the top sail to the stern hold, forty-five feet. She has three decks and mounts ninety-eight guns, and has on board seven-hundred sailors and mariners. In every way it is a splendid, well-finished craft.[23] Today the Frigate of war "Congress" came in from [Com. Robert F.] Stockton. Just at evening the Sloop "Lexington" came in with General Kearney and Lieut Col. Cook on board.

May 28. Getting our outfit for the trip.

May 29. We drew seventy-five days' rations and some mules.

May 30. Still fitting out.

May 31. Started. Came fifteen miles and camped with Gen. Kearney.

June 1 [1847]. Came thirty miles through a rough country and camped in a valley.

June 2. This morning we came through a beautiful valley with timothy and clover in their natural state. Came twenty miles and camped in an oat field in the mountains.

June 3. All forenoon through the mountains, camped at night in the valley twenty-five miles. It is called the valley of San Joaquin. This valley from its appearance is some fifty miles in width, with a little timber on the edge of the river.[24]

June 4. Traveled twenty-five miles and camped on the river. Saw numerous herds of wild horses.

June 5. Started very early in the morning, came twelve miles to the crossing of the river.[25] Got across just at night. The river was very high.

June 6. Came one and a half miles. Crossed three branches of the river. One of them we had to ford and carry our packs on our backs to keep them

---

[23]The American sailing navy rated warships by their armament: ships-of-the-line had more than one gun deck and carried at least 64 guns; frigates were rated as 28, 32, 38, or 44 gun ships; and square-rigged sloops-of-war carried at least 18 guns. Columbus was rated as a 74, but as Jones noted, warships typically carried more guns than their rating indicated.

[24]After leaving Monterey, Kearny's party crossed the Salinas Valley. Thomas Swords called it "the richest of any I saw in California—oats and clover, waist high, growing in the greatest luxuriance." See Swords' Report, 229. The men crossed the coastal range along the line of today's Highway 152 over Pacheco Pass, located in 1805 by Gabriel Moraga and named for pioneer rancher Francisco Pérez Pacheco.

[25]Finding the San Joaquin "impassable at the point at which we had struck it," Kearny's men went north to the camp of Capt. Henry M. Naglee's company of New York Volunteers near the confluence of the Merced River. Naglee provided a skin boat to cross the river. See Swords' Report, 230.

from getting wet. Killed four elk. The river is perhaps as big as the Missouri River. The excessive growth has killed the vegetation on the bottoms. There is but very little timber on the river. The probable cause of the river being so very high is the snow melting off the mountains that lie just before us and are covered with snow.[26]

June 7. Started early in the morning; came fifteen miles to the Watonwe [Tuolumne] River. The General crossed and the Major swerved. The Major got one boat load of his things wet.[27] This river is about the size of the Des Moines River and very rapid and bad to cross.

June 8. Crossed early this morning with our mules and got all of our loading across about noon. Started about two o'clock. Traveled fifteen miles and come to another river. Packed our boat on a mule. This river is not so large as the other. The country is poor that we have crossed. The drouth has killed all the wild currants, also considerable timber. The river is called Stameshlan [Stanislaus].

June 9. This morning we prepared for crossing. We had to swim the animals and carry our plunder across in skins. We got across the river at twelve in the day and camped on the opposite side of the river. This morning I learned that there was a settlement of our people some six miles below on the river.[28] We have been passing through the Indians for several days. They are very numerous and are called the diggers. They live upon grass seed and roots, and go naked except a wisp of grass tied around them. This morning the General lost his mules and did not find them until late. We traveled across a very good country, though rather dry. Came twenty miles; camped on a small stream at an Indian village—considerable timber. The village is called the Elebourgis.

June 11. Started early in the morning, came twelve miles over a very good country. About one in the afternoon we came to the best valley that I have seen in California. Here we found some Americans. Here I saw the first field of corn in California. Camped on a beautiful stream; it is called —— [Cosumnes]. Today we learned that there had been an express through from the church and that brother Brannan has gone back to pilot them through the mountains. This evening there was a brother came to see us by the name

---

[26]On the "River San Warkeen," Jermemiah Willey recalled building "a Boat of Green Hides to take over our men and provisions." While "the Boat was Gone up a Large Slue," the men left behind observed "a Band of Indians on the other side of the River," approaching provisions already ferried across. Cooke "told us to swim to the other Side and Guard our Baggage. The River was Vary high and Run Rapid and the water Cold." Four men "Dove into the River with all our Clothes upon us," and Willey almost drowned before "I Gained the Shore with the other three." Having "Crossed the River we Camp for the night But Keept a Close Guard to keep the Indians off." See History of Jeremiah Willey, LDS Archives, 28–30.

[27]Major Swords lost his camp equipment, provisions, and "all the tools I had along for the command" when the skin boat capsized on the Tuolumne "owing to the rapidity of the current." See Swords' Report, 230.

[28]The settlers at New Hope were indeed "our people," being Mormons who had come to California with Samuel Brannan. See Bagley, ed., Scoundrel's Tale, 180–81, 183–86, 189–90.

of Rhodes.[29] He came here last October from Missouri. The brethren are settled in different places through this country.

June 13. We came sixteen miles over a very good country. Came down the American Fork about four miles and crossed the river one and one half miles from the Sacramento. Here we found another man that was a Mormon. This is settled by Americans. Suters Fort is one and one half miles from the crossing; there are twenty-five soldiers stationed at this place. Crossed the river just at night. This is called St. Clare Fort.[30]

THE CURSE OF GOD RESTED UPON THIS COUNTRY: SUTTER'S FORT TO FORT HALL

To honor General Kearny, John A. Sutter paraded the ragtag garrison of his frontier outpost and fired a salute of eleven guns. At 3 P.M. the officers "came to dine at the fort, and left again for camp in the evening."[31] The party that assembled at Sutter's Fort in June 1847 included a few discharged dragoons and Philip St. George Cooke, eager to join the main theater of war in Mexico;[32] Congressman-elect William Preble Hall, who had marched to California with the battalion; Kearny's brother-in-law, Lt. William Radford (USN); Donner party survivor William Graves; a guide identified only as Murphy; and plainsman William O. Fallon, also named as a guide.[33] Journalist Edwin Bryant joined at Johnson's Ranch, carrying in his saddlebags the diaries that would become the classic *What I Saw in California*. "Dr. Death" himself, George B. Sanderson, accompanied the party, none of whom are known to have died from his ministrations.[34] The general's pack-train started with sixty-six experienced frontiersmen, military men, and their servants and traveled from the Sacramento to the Mis-

---

[29]The party had met Thomas Rhoades, a Mormon who had settled between the Cosumnes River and Dry Creek after coming overland in 1846.

[30]The party camped with other soldiers at the ranch of Alcalde James Sinclair.

[31]Sutter, *New Helvetia Diary*, 50–51.

[32]Cooke had been promoted to the rank of major in the regular army effective 16 February 1847. Four days later he was breveted lieutenant colonel for "meritorious conduct in California." See Heitman, *Historical Register and Dictionary of the United States Army*, 1:324.

[33]Bancroft, *History of California*, 5:452; Clarke, ed., *Turner Journal*, 125–26; and Barry, *The Beginning of the West*, 711–12. Fallon's "memoranda" of the "Route Between California and Fort Leavenworth" appeared in the *Saint Louis Reveille*, 4 September 1847. Graves was identified as "one of the sufferers in the California mountains, who returned to the States with Gen. Kearney," in "A Singular Cavern," *Illinois Gazette*, 16 October 1847.

[34]Edwin Bryant noted the presence of "Dr. SAUNDERSON . . . for whose opinion I entertain great respect." See Bryant, *What I Saw in California*, 129.

souri in just sixty-six days. Cooke calculated that they averaged thirty-three miles a day, "every one spent in travel." Riding with a minimum of supplies and a number of horses "to be killed for food, should it become necessary," the skill of their hunters and timely trading kept hunger at bay.[35]

East of the crest of the Sierra Nevada, the veterans found and policed the winter camp of the Donner party. Jones' account is one of the most detailed eyewitness descriptions of the work the battalion escort did to clean up the site of the disaster.[36] Henry Turner wrote, "Reached the 'Cabins,' where 25 or 30 of a party of emigrants, in attempting to pass the last winter, had perished from starvation. Their bodies & bones were strewed about, presenting a revolting & distressing spectacle. The Gen'l directed Maj. Swords to collect these remains & inter them, which having been done we continued our march 10 miles further; and encamped on Greenwood's Creek."[37] Swords reported, "five miles from the lower end of [Donner Lake] we came to the remains of the cabins built by a party of emigrants." He noted, "Stumps twelve or fifteen feet high afforded evidence of the immense quantity of snow by which they were surrounded." Of his burial detail, the major simply commented, "We collected and buried the remains of those that had perished from hunger; some of the skeletons were entire: parts of others were found, the flesh having been consumed by the last survivors."[38] One eyewitness described burying sometime-Mormon Levinah Murphy, whose body was found "lying near one of the huts, with her thigh cut away for food, and the saw used to dismember the body lying along side of her."[39] Jeremiah Willey recalled, "while passing over the moundting [sic] we Came to the Spot where a Company that were Going to California were Caught in the Snow and Could not Git out. Here some died and those that were alive had to Eat those that were dead. Here we found the Bodys of a number of men there fleach being Cut of[f] we Gathered up there remains and Covered them up and past on."[40] Matthew Caldwell remembered:

---

[35]Clarke, *Stephen Watts Kearny*, 335; Swords' Report, 231, 233; and Barry, *The Beginning of the West*, 711.

[36]The only other eyewitness account of comparable detail is Edwin Bryant's, in *What I Saw in California*, 263.   [37]Clarke, ed., *Turner Journal*, 129.

[38]Swords' Report, 231.

[39]A report by "Mr. Peterson" appeared as "California Emigrants—Cannibalism," *Nashville Whig*, 4 Sept 1847. This was probably William H. Peterson, who accompanied Kearny from New Mexico. From a transcription in the C. F. McGlashan Collection, Bancroft Library, courtesy of Kristin Johnson.

[40]History of Jeremiah Willey, LDS Archives, 30.

the place where the Donner Party numbering 300 [*sic*] got belated and snowed in. We, myself and 15 others were the first ones there, after the horrible death of these people. We made shovels, and after clearing out an old cellar, put the bones of 150 [*sic*] persons into it and covered them up the best we could. This was in 1847. This was the most awful sight that my eyes were ever to behold. There was not a whole person that we could find. Neither could we tell the difference between a man and a woman except in some cases by the long hair of the women.[41]

Kearny's men were fortunate in more ways than one: they were traveling early in the season, unencumbered by wagons or families, and they were going in the right direction. As the men ascended the Humboldt River, the country grew more hospitable. Westbound emigrants, already exhausted from crossing the plains and the Rockies, faced exactly the opposite conditions as they struggled across this increasingly "barren unfruitful waste." Leaving the Great Basin, the veterans began to encounter a "great many emigrants" and after reaching Fort Hall found the "road is full of them." Matthew Caldwell's recollected an encounter with "a stalwart woman, much after the masculine order," who asked, "where have you come from?"

"From California, Madam," said I.

"From Californey?" said she, "we don't want to go there, because the Mormons are going to Californey. Kin you raise taters in Californey?"

"I don't know," said I.

"Well, if they can't the Mormons will starve to death, because they ain't got anything but taters."[42]

Caldwell's tale suggests that rumors of a pending Mormon migration reduced California's appeal in 1847 and reveals in part why with "very few exceptions, the entire emigration this year is to Oregon."[43]

N. V. JONES, TRAVELS WITH THE MORMON BATTALION, 14 JUNE–15 JULY 1847.

June 14. Moved one mile and a half down the river. Today we received one horse more to every man. Dried some beef, baled[44] some flour and pork. We are thirty-five miles from the head of the [San Francisco] bay. I think [it is] quite as good [a harbor] as I ever saw in any country. Corn does not do so well unless it is watered. Mechanics wages are very high, also all kinds of common labor.

---

[41]Caldwell, Short Life's History, LDS Archives, 10.

[42]Ibid.   [43]Clarke, ed., *Turner Journal*, 129.

[44]As the men were packing, they loaded these provisions into bales to be carried on horseback.

Land can be bought for twenty-five cents per acre, wheat one dollar per bushel.

June 15 [1847]. We were all day fitting out, baling our packs and effects.

June 16. We started late, came fifteen miles. Camped by a pond of water where there is a stream in the wet season. Some timber. Land poor.

June 17. Thursday, started early in the morning, came twenty miles, camped on Bear Creek at Johnson's ranch, the last house we expect this side of Fort Hall.[45] It is called forty miles from this place to Suters. The country is not very good, some timber.

Foot of California [Mountains]. Bear Creek, Friday, June 18th. Started early in the morning. Came thirty-five miles through the mountains. Wood all the way, and for the last fifteen miles first rate pine. Oak is low and scrubby. Plenty of water. Camped in a small valley of about sixty acres. We passed a place where somebody had been buried.

June 19. Started early; came through the mountains all day. Came fifteen miles, plenty of pine timber, very rough. Plenty of water. Camped in a small valley near the top of the mountain. I must say that this mountain is as good a part of California as I have seen with but few exceptions. The timber is the best I have ever seen.[46]

June 20. Sunday, 20th. Started early; for about eight miles the country was good. The rest of the way very broken. Came through some snow banks. Banks of snow lying all over on the tops of the mountains. The vegetation has just started. This part is the best I have seen on any mountains. Stopped about three hours in bear creek valley, a small valley of about one hundred fifty acres. Here we found a cabin that some emigrants had built last fall. From this place there were five women started for the settlement through the snow on foot, and those who did not die were relieved by a party that came out for that purpose. They left a great many things in the cabin. They were from the state of Missouri.[47] We came twenty miles and camped in a small valley, with snow all around us.

Monday, June 21. Started early in the morning, came six miles, and struck Juber [Yuba] Creek. From here we came about twenty miles through the snow, from two to twelve feet deep and over rough mountains at that. During the day we passed two groves, crossed at the head of Juber over the mountains, and struck the head of Truckie River. Here is a small lake, one mile in width and three in length. We camped near the head of the lake. When we came in camp we found that two of our pack mules were gone.

June 22. Early this morning we started three men back to find them [the

---

[45] William Johnson's ranch on California's Bear River was three miles east of today's Wheatland.

[46] The party camped at Mule Springs.

[47] Jones had seen the remains of a shelter evidently used by the Donner relief parties. He referred to the female members of the Donner party's "Forlorn Hope," who left the lake camp on 16 December 1846. Many Mormon witnesses thought the Donner party was from Missouri, a misconception started in the *California Star* on 10 April 1847, 2/1. All of its members passed through Independence on their way west, but only a few Donner party members had previously lived in the state.

mules]. We came down the lake to some cabins that had been built by some
emigrants last fall. They were overtaken in the snow. There were eighty of
them in number, and only thirty of them that lived. The rest of them
starved to death. The General called a halt and detailed five men to bury the
deserted bodies of the others. One man [Louis Keseberg] lived about four
months on human flesh. He sawed their heads open, ate their brains and
mangled up their bodies in a horrible manner. This place now goes by the
name of Cannibal Camp. While we were stopped here the men came up
with our pack mules. Col. Fremont passed us here, the first time we have
seen him since we left Fort Sutter. After we had buried the bones of the
dead, which were sawed and broken to pieces for the marrow, we set fire to
the cabin.[48] I started about two in the afternoon, came seven miles and
camped. One mile above here there was another cabin and more dead bodies but the General did not order them buried.[49]

June 23. This morning Jigly shot himself through the arm.[50] Started
early in the morning, crossed two bad streams, came twenty miles. Considerable pine, though not as good as that on the mountains. Plenty of water,
road rough. Camped on Truckee River.

Thursday, June 24. We commenced building a crossing. About noon we
crossed over our plunder by hand, swam our animals.[51] About three o'clock
in the afternoon started, came over twenty miles over a rough road. Left Col.
Fremont at the crossing of the Truckee.

Friday June 25. To avoid swimming the river we went around through the
mountains. Very bad all day. Came twelve miles down the river from where we
camped last. Indians plenty. About two miles from here up the river there had
been one wagon and load cached. It was dug up by the Indians. They wasted
everything. We came twenty-five miles around to get twelve miles ahead.[52]

Saturday, June 26. Came across fifteen miles, and struck the river, traveled down it ten miles making in all twenty-five miles. Very rough all the

---

[48]After camping at the head of Donner Lake, Kearny's men stopped at the main camp of the Donner
party. A 1984 archaeological investigation "refuted the common belief that the [Murphy] cabin floor
contained human remains in a mass grave." See Hardesty, "Donner Party Archaeology," 21. The men
burned the Breen cabin, which may lie under the Pioneer Monument at Donner Memorial State Park. See
Hardesty, The Archaeology of the Donner Party, 33–35, 48.

[49]Jones referred to the Donner family camp, whose location remains a mystery. Edwin Bryant wrote,
"a party of men detailed for that purpose" buried George Donner. See What I Saw in California, 263.

[50]This was Robert Quigley, former bugler of Co. C, First Dragoons, who had marched to California with
the Mormon Battalion as Cooke's bugler. See Bancroft, History of California, 4:784; and Gudde, ed., Bigler's
Chronicle of the West, 36. Matthew Caldwell wrote that Quigley "accidentally shot himself. The ball entered just
below the collar bone and came out half way down the back." See Caldwell, Short Life's History, 10.

[51]As the Truckee was "running a perfect torrent," the party found a fallen tree that partially bridged the
river and paid a discharged soldier ten dollars "to swim across, and cut one from the opposite bank." On the
resulting bridge, "our packs were taken over by being passed from hand to hand" and "after many efforts"
their animals, who "were very reluctant to take to the water . . . all crossed safely." See Swords' Report, 232.

[52]To avoid the notorious twenty-seven crossings of the Truckee, Kearny took the party above the river's
twisting canyon east of today's Reno.

way. We camped by an Indian Village (if it would be proper to call it such) for there were no signs of it except some brush which had been cut and stuck in the ground. There were about two-hundred Indians in number, some ran to the mountains and others laid in the brush. Some of them came out after we had been there a short time. Men and women go naked.

Sunday, June 27. Started very early in the morning, came twenty-five miles across a barren desolate sand plain. Then we came to the hot spring. It was a curiosity. It was some two or three miles from the mountain to our right, on a small rise of ground. The water was thrown out by steam in a solid column four feet high and sometimes higher. The steam could be seen three or four miles off. It would discharge one barrel in one minute. The ground all around there seemed to be hollow underneath, and it was hot for half a mile around. There was a mule broke through a half a mile or more from the spring.[53] The stream came up very hot, I have no doubt, from the present appearance of things that two hundred feet from the surface, is a mass of liquid fire. The rock and sand for miles around and the ashes that we saw all look as if they had undergone the action of fire. We came twenty miles from there and camped, making in all forty-five miles, all without wood, water or grass.

The place where we camped is called Mary's River.[54] It is a sunken river. It sinks in the sand where we struck it. No wood and but very little grass. The water is salty and bitter. It seems as though the curse of God rested upon this country. It is all a barren unfruitful waste.[55] Some of our mules and horses gave out today.

Monday, June 28. Started this morning up the river if it could be so called. The same kind or a country. Plain once in a while, a pond of salt water. No grass worthy of note, no timber. Came twenty miles, camped by a slough of water that was less salty than the other.[56] Some grass, no timber.

---

[53]Jones described the Boiling Springs, approximately halfway across the Forty-Mile Desert on the Truckee River route. Many overlanders lost dogs to the searing water, but only Kearny's party appears to have boiled an entire mule. William Graves told of "a very singular cavern" revealed by "the instantaneous disappearance of a mule in the company, which fortunately had on him neither rider nor baggage. On examination it was found that the crust of the earth thro' which the mule disappeared was but a few inches in thickness. The cavern was sounded forty feet, but for aught the party knew its depth might be five thousand feet. The earth for a considerable distance around the hole sounded hollow." See "A Singular Cavern," *Illinois Gazette*, 16 October 1847. Now drained by a geothermal food processing plant, the site can be found at Exit 65 on Interstate 80.

[54]Frémont named the Great Basin stream trappers called Mary's River after German scientist Alexander von Humboldt.

[55]Except for the modern highway that skirts its eastern edge, the Sink of the Humboldt remains every bit as desolate as Jones found it.

[56]The company had reached the Big Meadows at today's Lovelock, Nevada. The Cox family preserved a colorful but unlikely story about such a dry stretch of trail. "Aunt Phrasia" claimed the men had orders that horses were not to "drink and roil the water up" before the men. While Cox guarded a waterhole, "Gen. Kearney rode his horse up and started to water it. Uncle Amos warned him away. He paid no attention until Uncle Amos pulled his gun and threatened to shoot him unless he took the horse away until the men had all drunk and filled their canteens." Kearny later "had Uncle Amos court martialed and strung up by the thumbs for pulling a gun on his superior officer." See Cox, Biographical Sketch of Sylvester Hulet, 5.

Tuesday, June 29. Started this morning tolerably early. Country as usual barren. Came fifteen miles, found grass and water, no timber. The stream is nearly as big as the Truckee and fine running water.

Wednesday, June 30. Started at daylight, came twenty-five miles before breakfast. Stopped at eleven in the morning, started at four in the afternoon, came eight miles; in all thirty-three miles; the country is barren, no grass only in spots and that short salt grass.[57] I have seen one tree in one-hundred fifty miles. We have traveled up the river ever since we struck it. It is a running stream.

Thursday, July 1 [1847]. Still going up the river; started before breakfast, came fifteen miles, cooked breakfast. Started again at three in the afternoon, came fifteen miles farther and camped on the river. No timber yet, very little grass except on the river and that only in places. The rest of the country [is] a sandy desert. Came in all, thirty miles.

Friday, July 2. Started today at daylight, came twenty miles, stopped and cooked breakfast. Started at four in the afternoon, came twenty miles farther, making in all forty miles up the river all the way. The country is sandy and barren, no timber. There are mountains all the way on each side of this river, and some snow on them. On the opposite side of the river, one mile from this place is a boiling spring.[58] I would like to have visited it, but could not cross the river.

Saturday, July 3. Started at daylight, came fifteen miles, ate breakfast, started at two in the afternoon, came thirty miles, making in all, forty-five miles, all the way over a sand plain. We left the river in the afternoon. Camped at night on a small spring brook, plenty of grass, but no timber.

Sunday, July 4. Started early in the morning, came twenty miles over a rough country and struck the river.[59] One of our party by the name of Minek was left back very sick, did not come up till some time after we had camped, which was on the Mary's River.

Monday, July 5. Started early, came fifteen miles, camped, cooked breakfast; started at three in the afternoon, came ten miles. Camped at the big spring seven miles from the river.[60] The country is the same as it has been for a good many days.

Tuesday, July 6. Started at daylight, came seven miles to the river, followed up the river eleven miles making in all eighteen miles, stopped,

---

[57]This camp was near today's Rye Patch Reservoir. Due to the "extremely hot" weather, the party began "travelling by starting before breakfast & laying by in the heat of the day." See Clarke, ed., *Turner Journal*, 130.

[58]Having passed the great bend of the Humboldt, the party reached these hot springs just north of present Golconda.

[59]Turner noted that the route on 4 July from today's Battle Mountain was no cutoff: "Conclude it would have been much better to have kept the course of the river." See Ibid.

[60]Kearny's men camped at Beowawe Geysers, seven miles west of the present town.

cooked breakfast. Started at one in the afternoon. Part of the road was very bad. Came through a very bad canyon. Came twenty miles, making in all thirty-eight miles. The country continued the same, no timber. Still on Mary's River.[61]

Wednesday, July 7. Started at daylight, came sixteen miles, cooked breakfast. Started at one in the afternoon, came sixteen miles further, making thirty-two miles. Camped on the river. This afternoon we found a large quantity of saleratus in some places. It was one and a half inches thick. It is common in this country. Snow mountains [the Ruby Mountains] again to our right. Early this morning we passed a boiling spring on the opposite side of the river. The steam could be seen a great many miles.[62]

Thursday, July 8. Started early, came this forenoon twelve miles. Six miles from camp crossed the main branch of Mary's River, and followed up a small fork on the right-hand side. Last night the Indians stole four of our horses. We followed them to the mountains. This tribe is very bad . . .[63] The country continues the same. The hills and mountains covered with sage. No timber.

Friday, July 9. Started as soon as we could see, came through a pass in the mountains and struck the head of a small stream [Brush Creek] this afternoon. Came twenty miles. To-day there was some few scattering brush on the mountains, sage plains as usual. We are now in Oregon. One mile from camp there was a large hot spring.[64] We came thirty miles and twenty-five of that without water. The country the same. Camped at the big springs. Yesterday we were two day's journey from the Salt Lake by the way of Hasting's cutoff—our day's journey, fifty miles.[65]

Saturday, July 10. Head waters of the Columbia River. Started late, came twenty miles; some scattered cedars on the mountains. Seventeen miles without water. Stopped on a small stream [Rock Spring Creek]; came five miles in the afternoon and camped.[66] Col. Fremont was just behind us.

Sunday, July 11. Started at sunrise, came sixteen miles down the same creek, stopped for noon. Started at one in the afternoon. Came twenty-five

---

[61]The party passed directly up Palisade (or Emigrant) Canyon near today's Carlin, Nevada, and camped at the mouth of the South Fork of the Humboldt, where the Hastings Cutoff rejoined the California Trail.

[62]Trails West has marked this boiling springs, now with a temperature of 88° centigrade, near the Idaho Street exit in today's Elko. See Kaysing, *Great Hot Springs of the West*, 191; and Helfrich and Hunt, *Emigrant Trails West*, 5, 86–87.

[63]Ellipses in typescript. Known as the White Knives, the Tosowich band of the Shoshoni were noted for being "excessively troublesome." See Madsen, *The Shoshoni Frontier*, 48, 214.

[64]Having crossed the stream now named Marys River on 8 July, the party left the Humboldt River and probably ascended Bishop's Creek to camp near the hot springs at the Winecup Ranch.

[65]Given that the party included Hastings Cutoff veteran Edwin Bryant, Jones was ill-informed about the route. In 1846 it took Bryant eight days to reach the Humboldt from the Salt Lake Valley.

[66]After crossing Thousand Springs Valley, Jones arrived at Rock Spring.

miles. Two miles from where we camped, we turned off from this creek. Eight miles from there we came to a fine spring on the mountains.[67] Came fifteen miles without water. Camped in a deep canyon, but little grass and a little water.[68]

Monday, July 12. Started at sunrise, came twenty miles. Eight of the way without water. Camped on a small creek for noon. Col. Fremont travels with us. Snow on the mountains close by us; no timber, country the same. Started at one in the afternoon, came eight miles down the creek, then left it to our right, eight miles across we struck it again and camped.

Tuesday, July 13. Started at daylight, came fifteen miles, sometimes leaving the creek for one or two miles. The country is the same as to soil, the valley is a little warmer. Last night we lost another horse. Camped for noon at the forks of the road, here the old Oregon trail turns off to our left.[69] We came down the stream, crossed over, struck across to the Columbia [Snake] River, eight miles without water. The road is first rate. Came twelve miles, making in all twenty seven miles today. The river is some smaller than the Missouri.

Wednesday, July 14. Started early in the morning, came twenty miles. Met some Oregon Emigrants, in company; forty-three wagons. Camped for noon. In the afternoon met some more emigrants. Came twelve miles, making in all thirty nine miles. Camped a little off the river.

Thursday, July 15 [1847]. Started early in the morning, came fifteen miles to Fort Hall. Here we got some bacon.[70] Started in the afternoon, came sixteen miles and camped on a small creek. The valley at the Fort is very wide, perhaps forty miles. A great many emigrants. The road is full of them.

ACROSS THE MOUNTAINS WITHOUT ANY ROAD: FORT HALL TO FORT LARAMIE

The American emigrants swarming past the wilderness outpost at Fort Hall in 1847 presented the station's commander, chief trader Richard Grant of the Hudson's Bay Company, with both a challenge and an opportunity. Grant had "his own troubles with this travelling mob in their passage at Fort Hall; but contrived with much temper and address to get them quietly off his hands. He sold them Possessions and Goods to the amount of 620 Dollars."[71] Kearny's guards were not the first

---

[67]The party reached the headwaters of Little Goose Creek, a tributary of the Snake River, and were at last in the Columbia River drainage.

[68]Kearny's men ascended Granite Pass to camp at or near City of Rocks.

[69]The party had followed the Raft River to the "parting of the ways" of the California and Oregon trails.

[70]At the fort Quartermaster Swords was "unable to procure any supplies of consequence, and would soon have been reduced to horse meat," but Oregon emigrants "were glad to part with their surplus provisions." See Swords' Report, 232.

Mormons Grant had met at Fort Hall, nor would they be the last. Samuel Brannan and three companions had arrived at the post from California on 9 June 1847, and Brannan returned in mid-August with men from the new settlement at Salt Lake eager to trade for supplies.[72] Grant's first reports about his new neighbors were not encouraging.

> A party of 300 "Mormans," composed of all nations, propose, as Mr. Grant reports, to take up their quarters for the winter at Great Salt Lake, where it is supposed they intend to form a permanent settlement for persons possessing their peculiar opinions. They have the character of being a knavish set, and Mr. Grant is apprehensive that they will give him trouble before long; he however appears to think that the Indians of the place will be a sufficient protection against violence, should any attempt be made upon the establishment.[73]

Some one hundred battalion veterans stopped at Fort Hall on 6 October on their way to Salt Lake, and in early December Grant visited the new settlement to see for himself if the Saints might offer the chance to "Make hay while the Sun Shines."

> In this Wild Mountainous Country great changes are daily taking place, between here and the Great Salt Lake a distance of about two hundred miles, we now see several Mormon Farmers settled down to begin farming and grazing operations. At the Great Salt Lake is already a population of principally I may say all Mormons exceeding 3000 Souls, the work they have done there since their arrival in July last, is hardly to be credited without seeing. They have already built up for their present residences about 600 Adouby or sunburnt brick houses, besides three or four mills under way, with a wall enclosing the place about a 1¼ miles square. From what I have seen and the dealings I have had with a number of those people I have found them the reverse of what they are generally represented particularly by the Folks of the western States. They appear to me to be what I found them, a moral good set of people polite in their demands and ready to pay for what they get.[74]

Timing and geography prevented the Lifeguards from meeting the vanguard of the Mormon emigration on the Oregon Trail. Under the guidance of Moses "Black" Harris, Kearny's men would strike east from Bear

[71]Peter Skene Ogden and James Douglas to Sir George Simpson, Fort Vancouver, 20 September 1847, (Anne Morton transcription), B.223/b/25, in Sir George Simpson, Incoming Correspondence, R3C 1T5, Hudson's Bay Co. Archives.

[72]For Brannan's visits, see Bagley, ed., *Scoundrel's Tale*, 203–05, 221.

[73]Ogden and Douglas to Simpson, 20 September 1847, B.223/b/25, in Sir George Simpson, Incoming Correspondence, R3C 1T5, Hudson's Bay Co. Archives.

[74]Richard Grant to Sir George Simpson, 31 December 1847, D.5/20, 712–15, Ibid.

River across the Greenwood (later Sublette) Cutoff. Kearny reached Hams Fork on 20 July, while Brigham Young's pioneers were some one hundred miles to the southwest, preparing to cross the summit of the Wasatch Mountains. On the trail to the east, however, almost seven hundred Mormon wagons were still struggling up the Platte River road.

N. V. JONES, TRAVELS WITH THE MORMON BATTALION, 16 JULY–2 AUGUST 1847

Friday, July 16. Started early in the morning, came fifteen miles. Rough country. Today our enlistment is out. Camped for noon. This afternoon came twelve miles. Camped in a branch of Bear Valley, on a small stream.

Saturday, July 17. Started early, came down the valley three miles from camp. Crossed without water twelve miles. Found some again, then came fifteen miles to the Soda Pool and five miles to Bear River. Here we camped for noon, making twenty miles. One mile and a half up the river is another Soda Spring, stronger than the other.[75] Came fifteen miles, making in all thirty five miles. Camped on the same valley, considerable timber on the mountains. On the right hand side we go up the valley.

Sunday, July 18. Started early, came twenty miles, six miles being across a cut-off without water. No sage in the country. The nights here are cold, heavy frosts, freezes sometimes. Came twelve miles further and camped on the river. Here we got some more provisions from the emigrants.

Monday, July 19. Came eighteen miles. Six miles to the first creek, the rest of the way plenty of water. Camped on the river; very little timber, plenty of grass. Started in the afternoon, came five miles, making in all twenty three miles. Camped one mile from a trader by the name of Smith.[76] There are about twenty lodges here. They have a great many horses. I saw a man by the name of Smith, who came from California with Brother Brannan, and had been with our emigrants and gave us some valuable information concerning them.[77]

Tuesday, July 20. Started very early in the morning, struck across the mountains without any road. Came twenty five miles and struck the road again.[78] Here were some more lodges. We got some more animals here.

---

[75]The "Soda Pool" the party found at today's Soda Springs, Idaho, is now submerged beneath Soda Point Reservoir, while the second spring may be the one preserved in a city park.

[76]With support from the Hudson's Bay Company, Thomas L. (Peg-leg) Smith ran an emigrant supply station on today's Smith's Fork.

[77]Charles C. Smith was on his way back to California from his visit to the 1847 Mormon Pioneer Camp. For details about Smith, see Bagley, ed., *Frontiersman*, 53, 55.

[78]At the Shoshoni camp on Hams Fork, the party hired Moses "Black" Harris, "an old mountaineer who promised to take us a better & nearer route." See Clarke, ed., *Turner Journal*, 132–33. Harris had met Brigham Young's westbound party near South Pass on 27 June 1847.

Wednesday, July 21. Started early, came fifteen miles, camped for noon. A great many emigrants. The country is brown and desolate, nothing but sage brush. Came twelve miles further and camped on a small creek, plenty of water.

Thursday, July 22. This morning one of our mules ran back, and we went about ten miles before we overtook him. On my way back I met Orlando Strickland, an old acquaintance. Stayed in camp until two in the afternoon. Eight miles to the river; it is called Green River. The road is rough. Left the river about five in the afternoon, traveled nearly all night. Came to the big Sandy, about ten the next morning. The road was rough for the first ten miles. The balance first rate. We came about fifty miles.

Friday, July 23. [Came 25 miles.] Laid in camp for the rest of the day. Here I saw the first thunder storm that I had seen for nearly one year.

Saturday, July 24. Started early in the morning, came five miles on to the Little Sandy. Came nine miles and camped for two hours, started in the afternoon, came through the pass and camped on the Sweetwater, making in all twenty-three miles.[79] Heavy rain during the night.

Sunday, July 25. Came seventeen miles down the Sweetwater and camped for breakfast. Considerable game here. Buffalo and antelope. The country as usual only the sage not so large, but little grass only on the streams. Started again, came thirteen miles over a country like that we came over in the fore part of the day; in all, thirty miles. Camped for the night on the Sweetwater.

Monday, July 26. Started at daylight, came thirteen miles down the river, then left the river and came twelve miles without water. Very little grass on this plain. Camped at a big sulphur spring, distance in all, twenty five miles. This afternoon we came fifteen miles on a good road. We came through the Rocky Buttes and camped on the east side, making in all forty miles. This is called Rose Camp. The mountain on our right has considerable timber on it.

Tuesday, July 27. Came nine miles down the creek, then left the river and came eight miles without water, and camped. Here we bought some flour. Started again some sixteen miles down the river and camped at Independence Rock. The country same as before; distance in all, thirty three miles.

Wednesday, July 28. Started early, left Sweetwater and struck across the plain twelve miles without water. Three miles from there we camped. Started again at one in the afternoon, came twelve miles and camped, making in all twenty seven miles. Very little grass, plenty of buffalo.[80]

---

[79]After rejoining the Oregon Trail at the Parting of the Ways, the men crossed South Pass on the day that Brigham Young entered Salt Lake Valley with the last detachments of the Pioneer Camp.

[80]Camped at Willow Spring, the party met "the rear-most party of Emigrants; who seemed to despair of getting farther than Fort Hall this season." Although he missed emigrants who went by way of Fort Bridger, Henry Turner counted 1,336 men, 789 women, 1,384 children under sixteen, and 941 wagons on the trail—numbers for the Oregon and Calfornia emigration of 1847 that "may be relied on." See Ibid., 133.

Thursday, July 29. Came twelve miles and camped for noon, found water about half way. Started at noon, came twelve miles farther, struck the river and camped, making twenty four miles. Here we found some brethren that were camped and waiting for their families which were behind, and expected every hour. This was the first news that I have had correct, since I left. They left there in March. Here we left one of our party that was unwell, by the name of John Binly.[81]

Friday, July 30. Moved camp early, came down the Platte eighteen miles and camped. The soil is about the same. The surface of the country is more smooth, plenty of Buffalo. This afternoon came twelve miles and camped on Deer Creek near one mile and a half from the mouth. Came today thirty miles.

Saturday, July 31. Started early this morning, came four miles down the river. Left the road, went across four miles further and struck a creek. Came twelve miles from there and camped for breakfast. The road is several miles to the right. Came this forenoon eighteen miles. Started again at two in the afternoon and came twelve miles, making in all thirty miles today. This afternoon Brother [Amos] Cox and I struck across to the road, did not come in at night.

Sunday, August 1 [1847]. Moved camp early, crossed the Platte and went down [the] left hand side of the river. Came fifteen miles and camped. I have seen more timber in the last few days than I have seen this side of the California mountains. Started at one, crossed the river on the right hand side of the river again. Came twenty two miles and camped on the Horse Shoe Fork of the Platte. Hail and rain tonight. Came forty miles.

Monday, August 2. Moved early, came twelve miles and cooked breakfast. Started at twelve N[oon]. Came around about [on a] crooked road of twenty-five miles, making in all thirty seven miles. Camped at the Larmie Fork of the Platte, three miles up from the Fort.

AMONGST THE SIOUX:
FORT LARAMIE TO FORT LEAVENWORTH

The Lakota leaders who met with Stephen W. Kearny during his 1845 expedition to South Pass "apparently paid profound attention to

---

[81]At today's Casper, Wyoming, William Empey, one of the men Brigham Young assigned to manage the Mormon Ferry, sighted a rider "approaching on horse back at full speed riding after me Spanish custom . . . behold it was Br Binley." John Wesley Binley had been kicked by a horse and injured; Empey commented, "it was not until he was within a few steps of [John S. Higbee] that he could distinguish whether [Binley] was a White man or an Indian." Binley received permission from Kearny to stay at the ferry "to wait for his family." See Morgan, ed., "The Mormon Ferry on the North Platte," 144–45.

what the commanding officer said," and it "was astonishing to see what a deep and powerful impression the appearance of troops made upon them." At Laramie in 1847 Kearny did not miss the opportunity to again impress upon the Indians that "Your great father has warriors as numerous as the sands upon the shore of your river."[82] His escorts, however, had learned that the main body of the 1847 Mormon emigration was only a day's journey down the North Platte, and Jones and two companions received permission to visit their encampment.

Following almost two months behind Brigham Young's Camp of Israel, the second division of 1847 was more than ten times the size of the pioneer party. As Captain Henry Turner "passed the whole Mormon Emigration," he carefully counted the company, "numbering as follows: 800 men—750 women—1,556 both sexes under 16 years of age—4,530 head of cattle—142 horses & mules—344 sheep—685 wagons. The great Salt Lake was the avowed destination of the Mormons. We were informed that they had abandoned the idea of going to California."[83] The second division brought Jones a letter from his wife in Iowa, who like most of the impoverished battalion dependents had been too poor to go west in 1847. Of the Mormon escorts, only Sylvester Hulet appears to have met his family.

Crossing buffalo country (Thomas Swords "estimated a million could be seen in one view"), Jones' diary anticipated the end of the journey. He faithfully noted the great landmarks of the Oregon Trail and repeatedly declared his pleasure at traveling "through as beautiful a country as I ever saw." The battalion escort completed their remarkable circumnavigation of today's continental United States on 22 August 1847, reaching Fort Leavenworth on the anniversary of the death of James Allen. They had come 2,152 miles from Monterey "in 83 days; the last 1,905 from the Sacramento in 66 days, without having laid by a day."[84] "The old General," the newspapers reported, "was welcomed

---

[82]Carleton, *The Prairie Logbooks*, 241, 248. How well the Lakotas took Kearny's words to heart is open to question, for these same bands appear to have robbed the returning Mormon pioneers of many of their horses. See Bagley, ed., *The Pioneer Camp of the Saints*, 268–69, 282n38, 288–89, 296.

[83]Clarke, ed., *Turner Journal*, 134. Turner's census reveals an oversight by generations of Mormon historians, for the traditional LDS estimate that the "Big Company" consisted of some sixteen-hundred emigrants failed to count an equal number of children under sixteen.

[84]Swords' Report, 233.

back by friends, and a salute of 13 guns fired in honor of his return . . . He is a great soldier, one who knows no fear, and minds not fatigue."[85]

N. V. JONES, TRAVELS WITH THE MORMON BATTALION, 3 AUGUST–24 AUGUST 1847.

Tuesday, August 3. Having heard from the People, I got permission from the General, to go with the others and meet them. We started this morning at sunrise, and came twenty miles and stopped to graze our horses.

Wednesday, August 4. Started from Fort Laramie early this morning in company with two other men, to overtake the brethren.[86] We rode twenty miles and met them. We found a great many of the brethren, and we heard of our families, and a great deal of other good news. We camped by them at night, when the General came up.[87] This morning we found a great many that I was acquainted with. I received a letter from Rebecca (my wife) the first that I have had since I left Fort Leavenworth— it was written on the 6th of June. Came twenty miles and camped for noon. Started at one in the afternoon, came twenty miles down the river. We traveled down on the left hand side of the river on the trail that our people had made.[88] We are now out of sight of the mountains entirely. The country on this side of the river is broken and rough. We have been amongst the Sioux, since we came to Laramie. Distance today, forty miles. Camped opposite Scotts Bluffs.

Thursday, August 5. We started before sunrise, came down the river twenty miles and stopped about five miles above the chimney rock. No timber, but plenty of grass. This afternoon came sixteen miles, crossed, just before we camped, on the other side.[89] In the night we had a very severe thunder storm. It hailed and rained tremendously, scattered our animals for a long way.

Friday, August 6. Started late and came eighteen miles and camped for noon. The river has raised considerable since last night. It is half a mile wide. This afternoon came eighteen miles, making in all thirty six miles. No timber but plenty of grass.

---

[85]Barry, *The Beginning of the West*, 711.

[86]Kearny reached Fort Laramie on 2 August and "met in Council a number of Sioux chiefs." His men left the fort at 1 P.M. the next day and stopped "a few miles above an Encampment of Mormon Emigrants." See Clarke, ed., *Turner Journal*, 133. The dates in the typescript appear incorrect, for Jones must have reached the Mormon train on 3 August.

[87]Captain Turner noted that Kearny camped only a few miles from "an Encampment of Mormon Emigrants" on the evening of 3 August. Kearny allowed Lt. Sylvester Hulet to accompany relatives to Salt Lake. Here Amos Cox learned of the death of his daughter Loenza at Winter Quarters. See Cox, Biographical Sketch of Sylvester Hulet, 2, 5.

[88]The trail on the north side of the Platte—today often called the Council Bluffs Road—had existed since the early fur trade and was heavily used during the gold rush, but the Mormons made it their own during the late 1840s. It is now popularly known as the Mormon Trail.

[89]Kearny's men crossed the North Platte between Chimney and Courthouse rocks to fall in with the traditional route of the Oregon Trail, which they followed to the South Platte and then to the Missouri.

Saturday, August 7. Another rain last night. Came seventeen miles today. Col Fremont's men killed two buffalo. Camped and cooked breakfast, then came twenty three miles, making in all forty miles. Camped at Ash Hollow. There DeQuigley was very sick and not able to ride. Matthew Caldwell, C. Webb and W. W. Spencer, hospital steward [remained with Quigley].[90] We gave them their rations and one animal a piece and two packs.

Sunday, August 8. Left at sunrise. We here struck across the plain leaving the North Platte, twenty miles and camped on the South Platte. This is larger than North Platte and discharges as much again water as the North Platte. It is three fourths of a mile wide. This afternoon we came twelve miles down the river, crossed the river and camped. Came in all twenty three miles.

Monday, August 9. Left camp very early this morning. Buffalo very plentiful. Came twenty miles this morning and in the afternoon sixteen miles, making thirty miles. Camped on an Island and killed several buffalo.

Tuesday, August 10. Started very early. The buffalo are in innumerable herds. It is marvelous how they subsist in such vast herds. Came twenty miles and camped for breakfast. This afternoon we came twenty miles over a beautiful country. There is considerable timber and plenty of grass. We camped on Big Platte.[91] We made in all today, forty miles. The buffalo was not so plentiful.

Wednesday, August 11. This morning our animals were scattered for several miles, so we started late. Came twenty miles and camped on an island. Started at one in the afternoon, came twenty miles. There were plenty of Buffalo and considerable timber. The country is beautiful. Today we made twenty miles and camped on the river. There is no timber. The river bottom is very narrow.

Thursday, August 12. Started early this morning and came twenty two miles over good roads, some timber and plenty of grass. Camped on a small branch of the river; (the river is from two and a half to three miles wide). This afternoon came twenty miles, about ten miles from camp we crossed Plain Creek. Camped at an old Pony [Pawnee] encampment. Today we made forty two miles.

Friday, August 13. Started early, came twenty three miles and camped at an old Indian camp. Plenty of timber on the river. A good country. This afternoon came twenty miles and camped, making in all forty three miles.

---

[90]"General Kearny determined that we should leave the sick man," Matthew Caldwell recalled. Robert Quigley asked for these men, including the former battalion assistant surgeon William W. Spencer, "to care for him and bring him in." The men got lost and "wandered around for three days and came upon our former camp ground. During this wandering we ran out of food." For seven days they "had nothing but one little turkey hen about the size of a common hen. Talk about hunger—who knows anything about it except those who have borne it." Spencer met five soldiers "on a bee hunt" who directed the men to Fort Leavenworth. See Caldwell, Short Life's History, LDS Archives, 11.

[91]The party had passed the confluence of the north and south forks of the Platte River.

Saturday, August 14. Moved camp early this morning, left the Platte and made a cutoff today of several miles. Came thirty miles and camped on Little Blue Creek; it is fifty miles by the road to the Platte. The country is very good, some timber. Camped at an old Indian camp.

Sunday, August 15 [1847]. Came today, thirty five miles. Twenty miles in the forenoon and fifteen in the afternoon. We were all day on the Little Blue. The country is fair and there is some timber. All along the creek the prairie is good. No Indian signs today.

Monday, August 16. Moved camp early, came sixteen miles this forenoon. Ten miles of it a cutoff and six miles on the river. This afternoon we left the Blue and struck across the prairie. There were small streams every few miles. Fifteen miles to Sandy Creek and ten miles to camp, making in all today forty miles. All the small streams have timber scattered along them.

Tuesday, August 17. Started early and came twenty five miles to Horse Creek and camped for noon. The country the same as yesterday. Came this afternoon ten miles, making in all thirty five miles today. We camped north of the road. There was very little water and but little timber.

Wednesday, August 18. Moved early and came ten miles, crossed a creek, followed down it several miles and left it, then struck for the Big Blue. Arrived there after noon, a distance of twenty five miles. The country is good. There is considerable timber. Moved this afternoon and came all the way across a large prairie. Camped after dark off the road, having come in all today forty five miles.

Thursday, August 19. Left camp early and came through a beautiful country, with plenty of timber and water. Made twenty miles and camped on the Wolf River. This forenoon we overtook a brother by the name of Davenport. He was on his way from the North Platte and traveled with some Oregon emigrants, among them was a missionary by the name of Little-John.[92] This afternoon came twenty miles all the way on the prairie. Camped in a little grove on our right hand. The men from Oregon came in late at night.

Friday, August 20. Left camp early this morning. I bought a horse of the Oregon men for which I gave twenty dollars ($20.00). All this afternoon across the prairie.

Saturday, August 21. Left the road early this morning. Stopped on a small creek at noon. Came eighteen miles this forenoon and fourteen miles this afternoon, through as beautiful a country as I ever saw. Prairie and plenty of timber and water. Camped early on a small creek. Our rations are all gone. We ate the last this morning for breakfast and did not have half

---

[92]James Davenport left the Mormon Ferry on 22 July with a company of ten men, including the suicidal Oregon missionary Philo B. Littlejohn, his wife, Adeline, and two children; the "child not old enough to talk was lashed on to a pony and they drove the pony between them." See Morgan, ed., "The Mormon Ferry on the North Platte," 164; and Barry, *The Beginning of the West*, 710–11.

enough at that. Started at noon and struck the road about three miles from the camp, and followed it to the Independence Creek, which we reached late in the night. Here [Fort Leavenworth] we got some flour from Major Sewards [Swords] for supper.

Sunday, August 22. We drew our pay this forenoon and started for Weston. Arrived there just at night. Stayed at Brother Green's Hotel. Saw the wife of Sterling Davis and Mother Coray.[93]

Monday, August 23. Moved early this morning, traveled eighteen miles and came to Fort Leavenworth. The country is good but broken. Turned over our public property this afternoon. Only received $8.60 (Eight dollars and sixty cents) for our extra service [since 16 July 1847].

Tuesday, August 24. Today we got some clothes for ourselves and started at noon. Came sixteen miles and put up at a house one mile this side of Bloomington. Started, came to St. Joe, traveled some there, started again at noon and met a man right from Waldons Ferry. Camped with Brother Colton at Savannah.[94]

[End of the Journal]

N. V. Jones turned over his public property, including his horses, the very afternoon he reached Fort Leavenworth and the next day left for the Mormon camps on the Missouri River. Jeremiah Willey "Rested a few days and Recevd our Discharge with the Good feelings of our officers." The first of Kearny's Mormon guards reached Winter Quarters by 5 September 1847. Jeremiah Willey arrived on 15 September and "found my family in a Comfortable house and Garden around them." The news spread through the settlement and "the wives of the Brethren I had Left in Calafornia Came to see me and Get the Letters I had Brought to them from the Battalion."[95] Joseph Taylor "found my family in the enjoyment of good health, which I felt very thankful for, having to my entire satisfaction in company with many others proved the truthfulness of Prest. Young's sayings made [to] us prior to our leaving our homes."[96]

Matthew Caldwell's detachment followed Jones to Leavenworth. "Webb and Spencer had the raggedest pants that I had ever seen," he recalled.

---

[93]This was Maria Shumaker (or perhaps Mariah Crosby), wife of Sterling Davis, a private in Co. D. "Mother Coray" was probably Sgt. William Coray's mother, Mary Stephens Coray.

[94]This may have been Charles Colton, father of battalion Pvt. Philander Colton.

[95]History of Jeremiah Willey, LDS Archives, 30. Patty Sessions also noted giving Willey letters on the North Platte on 4 August 1847.

[96]Joseph Taylor, Journal, 1857, LDS Archives. Taylor underlined the moral of this story in 1857: "I was a close observer [sic] in Joseph's day that implicit obedience to council always brought things to bear in righteousness, while the same may be truly said now of Prest. Young."

Our shirts were gone except the collars and a few strips down the back. I was entirely barefoot. My feet and legs were as brown and hard up to my knees as any old digger Indian ever was. You may well imagine our appearance when we reported to the pay-master at Leavenworth, sometime later. There we received some clothing and very much needed back pay—in all, seventy five dollars each as well as our discharge.

Caldwell walked back to Winter Quarters, which "after being used to riding all summer, was very hard on us." Having almost starved on the prairie, it "was watermelon time in Missouri and Iowa and we fared scrumptiously on this trip." As usual, "we took it as we had done through the whole of the Battalion journey as best we could."[97]

Nathaniel Jones found his family in Atchison, Missouri, where his wife presented him a new daughter, "a fine little *girl* in the Image [of] Nathan."[98] He emigrated to Utah in 1849 and subsequently led a colorful life in the service of Mormonism. Jones was bishop of the fifteenth ward in Great Salt Lake City and served from 1852 to 1855 as president of the mission to India. During the spring of 1856 he mined lead at Las Vegas and in March 1857 established a station for the Brigham Young Express at Deer Creek in today's Wyoming.[99] During the Utah War, Jones served in Echo Canyon as a Nauvoo Legion colonel and "suffered many hardships and privations which told very much on his constitution."[100] Jones was one of the men who guarded Great Salt Lake City when Johnston's Army marched through the empty capital in 1858. From 1859 to 1861 he was president of the British Mission. After briefly serving an iron mission to southern Utah, he died in Salt Lake on 15 February 1863, which Juanita Brooks attributed to "overwork and exposure." Only forty, Nathaniel Jones fathered seventeen children and left behind four widows.[101]

---

[97]Caldwell, Short Life's History, LDS Archives, 11–12.

[98]Brooks, ed., On the Mormon Frontier: The Diary of Hosea Stout, 1:272; and Ward, ed., Winter Quarters: The 1846–1848 Life Writings of Mary Haskin Parker Richards, 172.

[99]Mary E. Coray, William Coray's sister, claimed she married Jones during the Mormon Reformation of 1856 after rejecting the advances of Capt. James Brown. She recalled Jones was "a very fine looking man . . . but he was well known to be a hard, cruel man." In her sensational memoir, Coray reported finding a decapitated corpse in Jones' butcher shop. See Winch, ed., Fifteen Years among the Mormons: Being the Narrative of Mrs. Mary Ettie V. Smith, 175–79, 182, 189.

[100]Jones, ed., "Extracts from the Life Sketch of Nathaniel V. Jones," 5.

[101]Jenson, LDS Biographical Encyclopedia, 2: 368–69; and Brooks, ed., On the Mormon Frontier, 2:444n112.

Chapter 7

"A Happier Set of Men"
The Discharge

At the start of every American war, young men have flocked to the colors, full of patriotism and a craving for travel and adventure. But the discipline and boredom of military life have always cooled the volunteering spirit. If the commitment to serve was limited to a specified period, sixty days, six months, or a year, not many have wanted to come forward and reenlist. So it was in the Mexican War when entire regiments deep in the territory of Mexico refused, almost to a man, to extend their enlistment by as much as a day. Instead they turned their backs on the enemy and marched back home.

The outright refusal of American volunteers in 1847 to reenlist gave their usually outnumbered commanders headaches on every front, but nowhere was the resulting need for troops more acute than in California, where a few hundred soldiers occupied an area almost as large as New England, plus New York and Pennsylvania. To replace them, even if trained men were available, was costly and time-consuming. Troops would have to sail around the horn of South America on crowded transports or march overland some two thousand miles from Fort Leavenworth. Either way, the trip would take at least three months and give the enemy in the meantime an opportunity to recover land already conquered.

Faced with these conditions, American commanders in California made an extraordinary effort over several months to get Mormon Battalion members to extend their twelve-month enlistment. Unlike other Mexican War volunteers, they had signed up grudgingly in the first place, less out of patriotism than to obey the "counsel" laid down by the heads of their faith. Given the circumstances of their enlistment, their U.S. Army superiors might have abandoned any hope to achieve a seemingly impossible task. Yet while other volunteer outfits walked off the field in the very face of the enemy, a fourth of the Mormon infantrymen who had made the march to California stepped forward and agreed to serve for at least eight more months.

Ironically the opportunity to enroll an even greater number had come to General Kearny with Capt. Jefferson Hunt's 17 March 1847 letter asking about the possibility of government service in the province. But Kearny fumbled his chance to obtain the troops he needed when he turned down Hunt's request for a leave of absence to return to Council Bluffs and seek Brigham Young's blessing on this proposal. For a man who claimed to know a great deal about the religious movement— Kearny once told U.S. Navy Capt. Samuel F. Dupont the Mormons were "a very sinning people but that they have also been much sinned against"—this was a mistake second only to sending three of his five dragoon companies back to Santa Fe.[1] Young may not have approved the idea anyway, but this was by no means a foregone conclusion.

COL. R. B. MASON: THE AID OF YOUR INFLUENCE

The one who paid the price for Kearny's faulty judgment was Col. Richard B. Mason, his successor as military governor of California. In only a few months the Mormon troops under his command had gained a singular reputation for exemplary conduct and high tolerance to the temptation to desert. Without the benefit of support from higher authority of the faith, he began his effort to reenlist them for an additional twelve months by corresponding directly with their senior officer, Captain Hunt. Showing greater flexibility than Kearny, he suggested tactfully that Hunt might want to take time off, "should you feel disposed to do so," and pay Company B at San Diego "a visit yourself."

MASON TO HUNT, RECORDS OF THE 10TH MILITARY DEPT., 1846–1851, ROLL 1, NATIONAL ARCHIVES.

Head Quarters 10th Mily. Dept-
Monterey. California June 5, 1847

Captain

I am very desirous, in the present condition of affairs in California, to have the battalion under your command continue in service for another term of twelve months, unless sooner discharged.

---

[1]Dupont, *Extracts from Private Journal,* 134.

I hope that you will give me the Aid of your influence with your men to induce them to do so.

If as many as four, or more, Companies of not less than sixty four privates each, with the legal compliment of Officers and Non Commissioned Officers will re-enter for another term, I will give you the command of them, with the rank of Lieutenant Colonel, (unless the Comp[anie]s should prefer to elect their commander from the officers now in service). Should only two, or three, companies re-enter, then, the rank of the commander could only be that of Major.

There will have to be a new organization of those Companies that may re-enter, and a new election of Officers, & Non Commissioned Officers, and it would be well that this new organization and elections should take place *on or before*, the last day of the present term, so as to preserve to those officers who may be re-elected to the grade they now hold, their rank from the date of their *present Commission*.

If the organization & election takes place *after the date* of being mustered out, they must necessarily come in, "de Novo," and take rank with other Volunteer officers from the date of the new commission.

Pay Master, [Maj. William] Rich, will be at the Pueblo, ready to pay off your battalion on the day of their discharge.

Be pleased to Communicate with the Company at San Diego on the subject of re-entering the service for another term; perhaps it would be better, should you feel disposed to do so, to pay them a visit yourself.

I am Sir Very Respectfully

Capt. Jefferson Hunt	Your Obt. Servt
Comdg	R. B. Mason
Mormon Battalion	Col 1st Dragoons
Pueblo de los Angeles	Commanding

COL. R. B. MASON:
THEY SHALL BE DISCHARGED AT THE END OF MARCH

On the same day, Colonel Mason sent an order to Col. Jonathan D. Stevenson, Southern District commander at Los Angeles, enclosing a copy of his letter to Hunt, to exercise his "best efforts" to reenlist the battalion. The law enacted at the opening of the Mexican War did not allow volunteers to be sworn in for less than one year, but Mason possessed the authority to discharge the Mormon soldiers after only eight months and he gave his personal pledge to do so if they requested it.

MASON TO STEVENSON, RECORDS OF THE 10TH MILITARY DEPARTMENT,
1846–1851, ROLL I, NATIONAL ARCHIVES.

Hd. Qrs 10th Mily. Dept-
Monterey. California June 5. 1847

Colonel,

I enclose you a copy of a letter I have this day written to Capt. Hunt of
the Mormon Battalion, and beg of you to use your best efforts to accomplish the object I have therein proposed, and to carry out my views.

You will order up the Company from San Diego in season to join the
Battalion at the Angeles some several days before the expiration of their service, both with a view of being paid and mustered out of service at the same
time, as well as to give those who may choose to do so an opportunity of re-
entering, re-organizing, and being mustered in for another term of twelve
months unless sooner discharged.

The re-organization and mustering in, upon the new term, must take place
on the same day that they are mustered out of service on their present term.

Should you be able to get three Companies to re-enter the service, you
will send one of them back to San Diego or San Louis Rey, as you may
think proper: Or, you may keep the whole of them at the Angeles for a short
time, to assist in completing the fort, but *say nothing* of working on the fort
until after they are mustered into Service.

I have been informed that one of the objections some of the Mormons
express against continuing in service another year, is that it brings them to
the middle of summer before they are discharged, when it is too late to
begin farming; and that if they could be discharged say at the end of March,
that many would re-enter who otherwise would not.

The law of the 13 May last requires that the Volunteers should enter for
twelve months, & therefore, I could not muster them in for a less time, but,
I will pledge that they shall be discharged at the end of March next, if they
desire it.

I am Sir Very Respectfully
Your Obt. Servt.
R. B. Mason
Col 1st. Dragoons
Commanding

Col. J. D. Stevenson
Comdg
Southern Mil. District
Pueblo de los Angeles

COL. R. B. MASON:
MUSTER OUT OF SERVICE THE MORMON BATTALION

Even as he tried to win enough battalion members to make up three
companies, Colonel Mason had to prepare for the probability that few,
if any, would elect to reenlist. To handle their discharge and muster in

any who decided to stay in the service, he turned to a regular officer, the unpopular Lt. Andrew Jackson Smith, who had claimed command of the volunteers at Council Grove and marched with them under Cooke from Santa Fe to California. On arrival, to the battalion's delight, Smith had been ordered back to his own outfit, the First Dragoons, to command the survivors of San Pasqual.

MASON TO SMITH, 7 SEN. EXEC. DOC. 18 (31–1), 1849–50,
SERIAL 557, 302.

Headquarters Tenth Military Department
Monterey, June 7, 1847

Sir: I have sent to Colonel Stevenson an order for you to muster out of service the Mormon battalion when their time shall have expired, as also to muster into service any companies that may wish to re-enter. As there will have to be an entire reorganization of the companies that re-enter, it had better be commenced several days beforehand, so that the officers can be elected, and all the rolls made out, and they be mustered in on the very same day that their time expires—muster out and muster into service all on the same day.

Captain Jefferson Hunt will be mustered in as the major or lieutenant colonel, according to the number of companies, if he wishes the command; but if an election for the field officers is insisted upon, he must be elected by the officers of the new battalion.

I wish you would converse freely with Captain Hunt upon the subject, and urge upon him to accept the command with the increased rank and pay.

I am, respectfully, your obedient servant.

R. B. Mason,
Lieutenant A. J. Smith,   Colonel 1st Dragoons, commanding
1st Dragoons   Angeles, California

COL. J. D. STEVENSON:
MORE VALUE . . . THAN A HOST OF BAYONETS

Jefferson Hunt was the battalion's senior captain, but he could hardly consider himself its commanding officer as the somewhat flattering letter from Colonel Mason named him. Perhaps that is why he chose not to go to San Diego, as Mason had proposed, to urge the reenlistment of Capt. Jesse D. Hunter's Company B. He left this task instead to Col. Jonathan Stevenson who arrived there on 22 June with Lt. George Stoneman. At roll call next day the officer "made a speech respecting the duties that we had performed to his entire satisfaction" and "expressed a very anxious desire for us to re-enlist," noted Pvt. Samuel Rogers.[2] Aware of his strong position, Captain Hunter made a counter offer. Shorten our service time to six months, he said, permit us to send for Brigham Young's approval, and promise after discharge to provide rations either to San Francisco Bay or Bear River in the Great Basin. If these conditions were granted, Hunter and some twenty others agreed to extend their enlistment. But most took the position of Albert and Azariah Smith who wanted first to hear "the council of the Preisthood [sic] which we have with us."[3] To seek this direction, Sgt. William Hyde and Pvt. Horace M. Alexander returned with Captain Hunter and the Southern District commander to Los Angeles.

Stevenson's report of his visit to San Diego is presented in full because it points up the contributions of the Mormon volunteers there and the urgent need to keep them at this post for a longer time. It also describes the Indian trouble near San Luis Rey Mission that would lead to the appointment of Jesse D. Hunter as U.S. Indian agent.

STEVENSON TO MASON, RECORDS OF THE 10TH MILITARY DEPARTMENT, 1846–1851, ROLL 2, NATIONAL ARCHIVES.

Head Qts. Southern Mil. Dist. Calif.
Ciudad de los Angeles
June 28, 1847

Colonel

I have this day returned from San Diego. On my route to and from that Post I made every inquiry into the state of the country, and am happy to be enabled to inform you that all appears quiet and from all I can discover likely to remain so. It is the opinion of the best informed persons in that section who are now and have always been friendly to the United States that the people of the Country will remain quiet unless some powerful aid is offered them from Mexico (or our troops are withdrawn from below) all consider it advisable to keep up a proper and well organized force at the Chief Seaport, towns and especially this Pueblo. Before I reached San Diego it was reported that the Military force was to be withdrawn from that place, at this the inhabitants expressed great dissatisfaction regarding themselves as occupying a peculiarly exposed position and also having incurred the hatred of all friends in Mexico by the prominent stand they took in the early part of the revolution and maintained throughout the contest, and they fear if at no other part of the whole territory, an attempt would be made here to pun-

---

[2]Journal of Samuel Holister Rogers, 23 June 1847.
[3]Bigler, ed., *The Gold Discovery Journal of Azariah Smith*, 86, 87.

ish them if for no other purposes than their devotion to the American interest, and all such men as Capt. [Henry D.] Fitch, [Juan] Bandini, [Miguel] de Pedrorena expressed a full determination to leave San Diego in case some Military or Naval force was not kept there to protect them. I have assured the inhabitants that it is the intention of the officers in Command of California to protect all our friends and that no post will be left exposed even to a sudden attack or surprise. All persons at San Diego are anxious that the Mormons should remain there, they have by a correct course of conduct become very popular with the people, and by their industry have taught the inhabitants the value of having an American population among them, and if they are continued they will be of more value in reconciling the people to the change of government than a host of Bayonets; they have made Bricks, dug and bricked up eight or ten wells and furnished a town heretofore almost without water at certain seasons of the year with an abundant supply. They are about to build a brick Court house, the fees of the Court are already accumulated and the Inhabitants paying for the materials and the Mormons doing the work, in short when within 80 miles of the place the inhabitants of every rancho asked permission for some of the good Mormons to come and work for them, to build an oven, a chimney, or repair the roofs of their houses, and I have been in consequence of this good feeling the more desirous to have them remain.

The Mormons here are generally a very correct set of men and if it were not for the necessity [to build Fort Moore] their constant employment on the public works would be as useful to the inhabitants as their brethrens at, San Diego, they are general favorites here and I am constantly importuned by the inhabitants to employ them.

While on my visit to San Diego I made particular inquiry into the conduct of the Indians who of late have been troublesome at San Luis Rey and between that and Warner Pass and I am clearly of opinion that an Indian agent should be appointed who by a proper course of policy would exercise a controling influence of them; many of the depredations that have been committed by them has been done as they suppose under some color of right on their part. A very large portion of those Indians have at some time been connected with, or are the descendants of those Indians who have been attached to the Missions and especially the Mission of San Luis and they are now advised and believe that all the Mission property of every kind, church furniture and all belong to them and hence they have a right to carry it off for their own use or destroy as they please, and consequently parties of them come to the Mission and its farms and if in sufficient force destroy or remove what they please. Some few weeks since about 50 removed and destroyed considerable Church furniture from San Luis—drove off some Cattle and threatened the life of an old Indian Chief named Samuel who has been for some time in charge of the Mission. Saturday morning on my

way up from San Diego, while at Santa Margarita[4] some six miles from the
Mission, the Indian Samuel and his son called on me, they were not at home
when I passed the Mission on Friday night, and while we were in conversation a party of Antonio's men (the Chief of the Indian Tribe which has
been committing the depredations) actually came to Santa Margarita to take
Samuel prisoner having previously gone to the Mission in pursuit of him;
the moment I was advised of their object I informed them who I was and
that the Chief Samuel was under my protection and that the harm to him
or any further depredation committed upon the Mission property or the
Inhabitants would be followed by the severest punishment, this had the
desired effect as they immediately left and promised to be quiet hereafter.

The Indian Samuel is represented by all our friends at San Diego, here
and in other parts of the Country as being a most trustworthy and honest
man and fully entitled to confidence. I shall unless you direct otherwise give
him charge in writing of the Mission until some other disposition be made
of it and of the property.

The Indian Antonio is represented as a shrewed [sic] but morose,
revengeful fellow, has openly committed depredations and threatened
revenge if interfered with, and on one occasion rude to Col Cooke who
promptly checked him.[5] I will diligently set to work to find out a proper person for Indian Agent who should in my judgement also have charge of all
the Mission property which embraces the most valuable property between
San Luis and Warner Pass. From numerous applications made to me by different individuals on my late visit, very many appear anxious to have any
portion of the Mission property confided to their case that at the permanent [sic] establishment of an American Government they may present some
claim to a preemption right. This property is very valuable and if it belongs
to the Government as from all I can learn it undoubtedly does it must come
in possession of your successor when peace shall be established. It should
therefore be taken care of and if a proper Indian Agent can be found he can
cause to be collected the most industrious and respectable portion of the
Indians, set them to work, and while they provide comfortably for themselves by their labors on the property taken care of it. Until such an Agent
can be found I will if the Mormons reenter place a few men at San Louis to
preserve order and prevent any further depredations. Before Genl Kearny
left this part of the Country he requested Mr. Foster[6] of San Johns to

---

[4]Rancho Santa Margarita was owned by Pío and Andres Pico. For a history of the battle between Pío
Pico and his brother-in-law, John Forster, for the control of the ranch, see Gray, *Forster vs. Pico: The Struggle
for the Rancho Santa Margarita*.

[5]Historian Charles Hughes identified Antonio as Antonio Garra, who later led an attack on a ranch
and was executed in 1852 at San Diego.

[6]John Forster came from England in 1833, married Isidora Pico, and acquired huge land holdings. He
purchased the secularized San Juan Capistrano Mission in 1845 where he made his headquarters. Don
Juan Forster died at age 70 in 1884.

accept the appointment of Alcalde for that District embracing the Ranchos of San Johns [San Juan Capistrano], San Louis, Pala,[7] and some others whose names I do not recollect, he is a highly respectable citizen and will now accept the Office from the necessity of the case there being no other person in the neighborhood that is suitable for or will accept it. If you will send me his appointment for the District to be included I will put it in proper form and forward it. If Mr. Foster [Forster] is appointed he will be of great service to any Indian Agent that may be appointed as all the Mission property lies within this District.

While at San Diego Capt [Henry] Fitch the Alcalde expressed great anxiety to resign his place if not permanently for a short time that he might go north on business of the utmost importance to himself, he applied to me to sanction his appointment of Lt. [Robert] Clift of the Mormon Battalion a A. A. Lt. Master & Commissary of that Post[8] as acting Alcalde during his temporary absence; I was well informed that under Mexican laws an Alcalde has the power of appointing a temporary successor under sanction of the Commander of the District. I endorsed my approval upon Clift's appointment being well satisfied that he was a very proper person and a great favorite in the town, and if he should reenter the Service and he can with propriety be appointed Alcalde in the place of Fitch I would respectfully recommend it. From all I can learn the mode of transacting business by the Alcalde here differs materially from those practiced at San Francisco & Monterey—for instance here there are no trials by Jury; at San Francisco & Monterey there are—this is an important feature and many others of equal importance have been pointed out to me; and as Capt Fitch is on his way North and will stop some few days at Monterey I have given him a note of introduction to you that he may have a conversation with you on all matters touching the public interest at San Diego. In consequence of Don Juan Bandini declining to accept the appointment of Collector I have filled the blank in the Commission with the name Miguel de Pedrorena one of the stanchest [*sic*] friends we have in the Country and decidedly the best man in the town for that important office, he is a native of Old Spain, but from a very early age resided and was well educated in England, he speaks and translates both languages fluently and is the general interpreter of the place, and all the inhabitants united in a favorable expression of his appointment; he held the commission in the American Service under Comd Stockton as you will learn by papers forwarded with this at his request. I have no doubt he will be found a most active and useful officer and that he will be able to make the fees of the office pay expenses. You will observe by the Copies of the papers forwarded you by last mail in

---

[7]Mission San Antonio de Pala, an adjunct of Mission San Luis Rey, was founded in 1815 at the foot of Mt. Palomar to serve the Pala Indians.

[8]Lt. Robert Clift of Co. C was sent to San Diego with Co. B to serve as commissary assistant. He also acted as Captain Hunter's assistant adjutant.

relation to the office of Collector that no salary was named or arrangement made for the contingent expenses of the office, such as rent of office, Stationary, boat, and men, all of which are indispensably necessary. I learned at San Diego that furniture and a boat were purchased for the Collector's office by order of Comd Stockton for a former Collector who was subsequently transferred to Santa Barbara to which place he removed the furniture and that the boat was used by government officers during the War and actually worn out in the public Service. The present Collector does not require any appropriation for office rent or furniture at least for the present or until business increases as he is willing to use his own house and furniture free of charge, but a boat can now be purchased for $50 of a ship about to return to the United States. This boat he purchased upon his own responsibility and with his own funds as I declined giving any such authority leaving it for you to order or not as you should deem proper. My impressions is that he will care very little for a Salary until the emoluments of the office will justify it, if the expenses before enumerated are allowed him. I would therefore request your action on this subject at an early day. I enclose you a Copy of the Oath of office I required him to take and the publication made of his appointment. I have written you a very long and I fear a tedious letter on matters other than Military but I have deemed it my duty to give you all the information I obtained during my journey that you may understand the precise state of this District in a Civic as well as Military point of view which I hope you will regard as a sufficient apology if one be deemed necessary for this long letter.[9]

I have the honor to be
Very Respectfully
Your most obdt. Svt.

Col. R. B. Mason
1st Regt. U.S. Dragoons
Governor of California Col. Comd Tenth Mil. Dist.   J. D. Stevenson

DAVID PETTEGREW: THERE WERE TWO SPIRITS MANIFEST

On 29 June 1847, the day after his return, Colonel Stevenson paraded the battalion at Los Angeles and mustered all the oratorical skills he had acquired as a New York politician to deliver a stirring appeal to reenlist. His eloquence ignited an intense daylong debate between old adversaries that centered, as usual, on the question of who held the right to "counsel," or instruct, the men on what they should do. On one side were most of the officers, led by the captains, Hunt, Hunter, and Davis, who favored reenlistment. They based their author-

---

[9]This letter was first published in Hughes, ed., "A Military View of San Diego in 1847: Four Letters from Colonel Jonathan D. Stevenson to Governor Richard B. Mason," 36–38, along with Stevenson to Mason, 12 July 1847, 38–39; and Stevenson to Mason, 23 July 1847, 41–42.

ity to instruct their men on Brigham Young's order to the captains a year before "to be fathers to their companies and manage their affairs by the power and influence of the Priesthood."[10] On the other side was the same troublesome pair that had so often disputed the military decisions of Mormon officers in the past. David Pettegrew rested his right to interfere on Young's "particular request" for him to join the battalion and the officers' later approval for him "to take charge of the spiritual affairs of the camp," a broad mandate in those days.[11] Levi W. Hancock, a member of the faith's First Council of Seventy, perhaps held the strongest claim. His power as the only Mormon general authority in the command could not be dismissed lightly. "Father" Pettegrew described the final confrontation between these opposing points of faith.

AUTOBIOGRAPHY AND JOURNAL OF DAVID PETTEGREW, 1840–1860,
29 JUNE 1847.

I will now proceed on to the 20th of June, when the battalion was formed in a square and Colonel Stephenson [*sic*] spoke at some length on the propriety of the battalion enlisting again. He said (with all the cunning eloquence he was master of), "you have been looked upon by the States for a long time with a jealous eye, but this noble act of yours in enlisting in the service of your country has removed these jealousies, and if you remain in the service of your country in a few years you will be great and popular. Notwithstanding your families are in a peculiar situation in the wilderness, your country's cause requires your service in the army." And many things he said too hard to bear and grievous to be borne. After a long and tiresome speech of this kind the battalion was dismissed. After this our officers called the battalion together alone, away from the fort. Captains Hunt, Hunter, Davies and Lieutenant Dykes and others addressed them. All concurred with Colonel Stephenson that the battalion should remain in the service and not be discharged on the 16th of July. I, with others, contended or reasoned with them face to face, showing the presumption of such a move. I told them the contract was made by the highest authority on earth that the officers and men were called out for one year and no longer, and if one year would not satisfy twenty would not, and if they were for a further enlistment I was not with them.

Lieutenant Dykes said, "I believe if President Young was here he would counsel the brethren to remain in the war." I arose and said, "I don't believe any such thing, I know better." "Well," he said, "there is so much difference between us." "Time will tell," said I. They then chose a committee to make

---

[10]Golder *et al*, eds., *The March of the Mormon Battalion*, 128.
[11]Journal of David Pettegrew, 1840–1860, 10 July 1846.

the bargain for another year. Captains Hunter and Davies and myself were appointed as committees. The papers were soon made out, but I did not help them much. The meeting was held in the wall-tent and all had the liberty to speak. Captain Hunt said, "Now is the time you complainers crack your whips." Many spoke in turn and there were two spirits manifest, as different as mid-day from Midnight. Some of the officers had warm feelings and made exceptions to my remarks, but afterwards were ashamed.

Lieutenant Cantfield said, "If you go to Salt Lake with all these animals, Brigham Young will kick your asses," etc.[12] Captain Hunter said, "If Levi Hancock hath the word of the Lord, or the old man Pettegrew hath "Thus saith the Lord" let us hear it." We were sorry to see them possessed of such a spirit on the occasion, but notwithstanding all the "whips were cracked" loud enough to unweld the link. The battalion was discharged on the afternoon of the 16th day of July, 1847.

Immediately enlisting papers were brought out they were brought to us by the officers saying, "We want some counsel." We said, "We are going home and all the brethren are at liberty to go home and find their friends in the wilderness. If they want to enlist again, let them, we are going home." He said, "I wish I could get some counsel that I might know what to do," and went out and said that we said it was the best thing for them who were going to stay to enlist again. I contradicted it. The main part of our officers enlisted or set down their names to draw all they could by strategem and wine. They then withdrew their names from the paper. Some good boys were drawn into it to our sorrow. We had counselled as far as we dared to lest the government officers should get occasion against us and make capital against us. Our officers were very much mortified when they saw that the men cleaved to us and to our counsel. We soon organized ourselves into companies of hundreds, fifties and tens, with 500 animals, and on the 22nd of July we began to move off and a happier set of men I never saw.

COL. J. D. STEVENSON:
FROM THE BATTALION SOME FEW MEN

As the argument over the enlistment question raged among the Mormon soldiers, Colonel Stevenson reported further on alleged Indian violations in the vicinity of San Luis Rey Mission and its farm at Pala and the opportunity they opened for Captain Hunter and other battalion veterans to enter the Indian service.

---

[12]Ohioan Cyrus C. Canfield, 29, served as third and second lieutenant of Co. D, as well as the company's temporary commander.

STEVENSON TO MASON, RECORDS OF THE 10TH MILITARY DEPARTMENT,
1846–1851, ROLL 2, NATIONAL ARCHIVES.

Head Quarters, South Mil. Dist. California
Ciudad de los Angeles
12th July 1847

Colonel

On the 6th Inst I had a visit from the principal Chiefs and some Eighty Indians, originally of the San Luis Ray Mission—they numbered in all about 95. They came in—as they said—to present themselves to the Commandant, and to request that the numerous charges made against them of Robbing the Churches [and] Inhabitants might be proved, and also to request that an Indian Agent might be appointed to take charge of them and the Mission property, and they earnestly begged that an American might be selected, as the Californians were their sworn enemies, and they could never be happy or at peace under his [*sic*] orders. When the Indians first made their appearance, the Californians of this town were very much incensed, and alarmed, at the boldness of the Indians coming here, in such force; and soon after the chiefs had called upon me to request an interview the Alcalde and all the public functionaries, called to request that I would order the Indians to leave the town, and break up their camp, which was on the opposite side of the river. They represented the Indians, as being completely armed with Spears, Pistols, Knives, Rifles and plenty of Ammunition. I had agreed to meet the Indians at three o'Clock, but I immediately sent for their chief, Antonio, and directed him, to have all his people, immediately assembled, in front of the Dragoon Barracks, and invited the Alcalde, and the town officers to go with me, and hear what they had to say, as well as my answer; they hesitated but I insisted, and they finally complied—by 10 A.M. the Indians were all present—I asked where their arms were, they said in the camp—I directed 10 men to be sent for them, at the same time requiring the Alcalde to produce the man who informed him that they were so completely armed; in a very few moments the Indians arms arrived, and they proved to be two large bundles of Indian bows and arrows, one lance and one pistol, the lance and pistol, belonging to two of the Chiefs. I enquired if they had not other firearms, and was answered in the negative; about this time the man who made the report of their being so completely armed, made his appearance, and when questioned admitted, that [he] had seen but one lance and two pistols, one of which had since been purchased by a Californian. I then enquired of the Indians what brought them to Pueblo [de los Angeles], and they answered as I have before stated; I told them that an Agent would be appointed within six weeks, and that he should be an American, and as soon as he was appointed I would have the Indians assembled at the Parla [Pala] farm of the San Louis Mission, and place them under his protection; with this they expressed themselves perfectly satisfied; they denied having committed any depredations upon the inhabitants, or church, but admitted having taken some few cattle from the Mission, to feed themselves. I told them that they should be protected from outrage, but they would be severely punished if they violated law, or trespassed upon the property of others, I enquired of the Alcalde, and his associates if they were satisfied, they said they were, and after directing the Quarter Master to furnish them with beef, directed them to leave for their homes at day light the next morning, which order they strictly obeyed. I really do not believe those Indians commit the depredations charged upon them, but that the wild Indians and perhaps some bad Christian Indians do much mischief to the Inhabitants there can be no doubt. I have made diligent enquiry for a proper person to be appointed Indian Agent, but can not find an old resident that is fit for and worthy [of] the place. Capt Hunter of the Mormon Battallion [sic], stationed at San Diego has determined to remain in the country, and will raise a company from the Battallion if possible, failing in that he will accept the appointment of Indian Agent, he is well known at San Diego and its vicinity, and universally esteemed by all; he does not speak the Spanish language, but has been much among Indians, and if permitted would take with him from the Battallion some few young men, who speak and understand Spanish. I have no doubt the wages of these men could be easily paid from the product of their labour and they want no doubt to be thus paid they would be of great service in instructing the Indians how to cultivate the soil, and would at the same time form a strong guard for the Agent; If this plan should meet your approbation, you can send the appointment for J. D. Hunter, with instructions, or you may leave the name blank to be filled up with a proper person. It is of the utmost importance that some agent should be appointed speedily and it is equally important that he should be an American.

I have the honor to be

Col. R. B. Mason   very respy Your Obdt Servt.
Comg 1st Regt U.S. Drags.   J. D. Stevenson
Governor of California   Col Comdg. Southern Military District

DAVID PETTEGREW: VIRTUE IS UNKNOWN TO THEM

While Jesse Hunter would remain in southern California, where he died in 1877, most of the Mormon volunteers prepared to leave the province and rejoin their families somewhere to the east. At about this time, David Pettegrew, the self-appointed religious advisor of the command and its oldest member, penned a word picture of Los Angeles as seen in July 1847 by one of the most zealous members of the camp. It hardly described a city of "angels."

AUTOBIOGRAPHY AND JOURNAL OF DAVID PETTEGREW, 1840–1860, JULY 1847.

[Los Angeles] lies in a valley and at present is the largest town in California. It is inhabited chiefly by Spaniards, but some foreigners keep stores or wine cellars to which the Spaniards resort and most all the people in the place go most of the time to play at the game of Monte. The Spaniards are an indolent race, scarcely ever doing anything but riding. They are all Catholics, consequently are very much bigoted as regards religion. Every Sunday after services they meet for horse racing. The women are, most of them, very fair, especially those of the pure Spanish blood, and beauty is all that recommends them for virtue is utterly unknown to them, and in fact I never saw a people as a nation or heard of any that were sunk so deep in iniquity. The Indians are slaves mostly to them and work the vineyards, which are very fruitful, and at this time in the gardens may be seen pear trees loaded with pears, some ripe and others nearly so; apple trees, peach and quince trees, which bear fruit in great abundance. The fig, the olive and cocoanut trees are also to be seen in the gardens. There are also a number of tar-springs in the vicinity, it has the smell of stone coal and boils up out of the earth. It is used by most of the inhabitants for covering to the houses. When exposed to the sun it melts and becomes soft but in case of a storm it is a perfect barrier. The roofs are flat and when made a layer of cane or small sticks are laid on the poles. After this the tar is broken up from the springs where it becomes hardened when exposed to the sun, drawn in carts and put on the roof. It is there melted down in the process of time and the roof becomes flat.

COL. J. D. STEVENSON:
ALL WERE ENROLLED, AND MUSTERED INTO SERVICE

At mid-afternoon on 16 July, one year to the day after the Mormon Battalion was mustered into service at Council Bluffs, Iowa, its companies lined up in alphabetical order, A in front, E at the rear, and stood at attention for a final inspection at Fort Moore. The absence of marching bands, speeches or military ceremonies of any kind made a dramatic moment even more moving. Slowly Lt. A. J. Smith walked between the long, silent rows of more than three hundred men, then stepped to the front and faced them. For a long moment he stood there as if reluctant to continue. At last he spoke so softly he could hardly be heard by the ranks in back, "You are discharged." The Mormon Battalion entered history as the most unusual command ever to serve in the U.S. Army.

The men cheered three times and all talked at once as they fell out of ranks private citizens for the first time in twelve months. What happened next came as a surprise to the commander of the Southern District who had given up any hope of recruiting any of the Mormon soldiers. The following day the ex-captain of Company E, Daniel C. Davis, and Cyrus C. Canfield, former Company D lieutenant, began taking the names of men willing to reenlist, provided the army met certain conditions, including a pledge to station them at San Diego, the very place they were needed most. Within days the pair had formed a new company of eighty-two members, seventy-nine battalion veterans and three former civilian aides to officers. Said one of the new volunteers, twenty-three-year-old Henry Boyle: "I did not like to reenlist, but as I had no relatives in the Church to return to, I desired to remain in California til the Church became located." A pleased Colonel Stevenson reported on this surprising development as if he had something to do with it.

STEVENSON TO MASON, RECORDS OF THE 10TH MILITARY DEPARTMENT, 1846–1851, NATIONAL ARCHIVES.

Head Quarters Sthn. Mil. Dist. California
Ciudad de los Angeles
23 July 1847

Colonel

I have the honor to inform you, that I have succeeded in organizing one company of Mormons, under the command of Captain Davis, late of Mormon Battallion. Until the day after they were mustered out of the service, there was not [the] slightest disposition evinced to re-enter, but on the 17th in the afternoon, Capt. Davis and Lieut Canfield commenced enrolling, and on the 20th all were enrolled, and mustered into service. I have required them to use their own Arms, agreeing that they should be kept in repair at expense of the government. The company have uniformed themselves completely, from cap to shoe, in the uniform of my regiment [of New York Volunteers]; and they will to morrow at noon take up their line of march for San Diego. Upon the arrival of Captain Hunter, and his company from San Diego on the 15 Inst I learned that my instruction in regard to the Artillery and stores at that post had not been complied with, and also learned that all our friends Californians, as well as Americans, were leaving the town for their Ranchos, and that the hostile portion of the population were preparing to hoist the Mexican Flag. I immediately made arrangements to send a detachment, of twenty picked men under the command of my Adjutant, and Lt Davidson[13] to San Diego, with instructions to remove the stores, and

---

[13]First Dragoons Lt. John L. Davidson came to California with General Kearny and fought in the Battle of San Pasqual.

Artillery, for fortunately a fine Brig commanded by Capt King[14] a patriotic American was at San Pedro—the Capt offered his vessel, to transport the detachment to and from San Diego, without any charge, other than the present of one of the Brace pieces [that] have been receipted for by an officer in our service. I readily agreed to the proposal, and the Detachment sailed on Sunday evening last from San Pedro.

Yesterday I sent forward one of the newly enlisted men to San Diego, as well to advise the inhabitants, as to inform Lt. Davidson that a company was on its way to Garrisson [sic] that Post.

I have the honor to be
very respectfully
Your Obdt Sert
J. D. Stevenson
Col. Comdg Sthn. Mil. Dist.

Col. R. B. Mason
Comdg 1st Regt U.S. Dragoons
and Governor of California

COL. J. D. STEVENSON:
MORMON PLAN OF ACTION IN CALIFORNIA

On the same day that he reported the enlistment of a new company of Mormon volunteers to serve at San Diego, Col. Jonathan Stevenson dispatched a confidential letter to the California military governor to inform him of what he had learned about future Mormon plans. It reveals that Jefferson Hunt and perhaps other officers knew more about Brigham Young's secret design to create an independent theocratic state in western America than either of the religious leaders who had actively opposed the reenlistment. What Hunt did not know, however, was that Young had already determined to establish this unique form of government in the Great Basin, not California.

STEVENSON TO MASON, HOUSE EXEC. DOC. 17 (31–1), 1850,
SERIAL 572, 347.

(Private and Confidential.)

Cuidad de Los Angeles, *July 23,* 1847.

Dear Sir: By the same hand you receive this, I send an official communication announcing the re-organization of one company of Mormons, and their having been mustered into service. Captain Hunt, late in command of the battalion, starts to-day for the north. He will stop at Monterey and proffer his services to raise a battalion of Mormons from those that are coming into the

---

[14]This civilian patriot may have been Ed. A. King who purchased a Mexican brig at Los Angeles in April 1847, about whom little more is known. See Bancroft, *History of California,* 5:580.

country, and I have given him a letter to you on that subject, a copy of which is enclosed. My intercourse with the Mormons has satisfied me that the great mass of them are a simple-minded, ignorant people, entirely under the control of their leaders, and that in every community or association there is some one man who is the controlling spirit, and that all are under the direction and control of some one master-spirit. In the battalion were two men, one of whom was a private soldier, who were the chief men;[15] and but for them, at least three companies would have re-entered; but they opposed, and not a man would enter; and I do not believe we should have succeeded in getting one company, if they had not given it their countenance, or at least made no formal objection. Both before and since they were mustered out of the service, I have conversed with Captain Hunt and some other leaders, and am satisfied they desire to get the military control of the country, and that from time to time they will supply from 100 to 1,000 men for the service, until their whole community shall have had some experience as soldiers, and become furnished with arms; which, by the time the civil government shall be organized, will give them control as well of the ballot-box by their numerical strength, as physically, being a corps of many hundred soldiers, well armed and equipped for service in the field. They look forward to the discharge of my regiment of [New York] volunteers, at the close of the war, as an event that will throw the military defence and control of this country entirely in their hands. This I know to be their calculation, for Hunt and his officers have so expressed themselves to me. This may account for the opposition a re-enlistment of the entire battalion has met from some of their society leaders, as I am well assured they regard an order or instruction from them as paramount to any other power; for at all times I have been told that if a messenger should arrive with but five lines from one of their chief leaders now on the road to this country, all would have re-entered, and all the officers here feel confident that Hunt can raise a battalion if you require it. I have deemed it my duty to give you these brief views of what I conceive to be the Mormon plan of action in California, and you can, no doubt better than I can, judge of the propriety of giving them the military control.

The company that is ordered to San Diego will be sufficient for all military purposes at that post and the surrounding country; and I have no hesitation in saying that the force I have here, dragoons and New York volunteers, will be sufficient to keep this place against any force that can be brought against us, especially if you will authorize the filling up of the two companies of my regiment stationed here. Our discipline is strict, drills regular and rigid, and every point is strictly and vigilantly guarded day and night; and therefore, unless you require them for some other purpose, an additional force will not be necessary here. This place is at the present time

---

[15]An obvious reference to Pvt. David Pettegrew and musician Levi W. Hancock.

quite unhealthy; two of our men have recently died of fever. Our sick list has not, however, increased since my last communication.

It may not be improper for me to remark, that many of the disbanded men are selling their arms to any one that will purchase them. This should prevent any future donation of arms to a company or battalion of Mormons, if mustered into the service.

Very respectfully, your obedient servant,

J. D. Stevenson

Colonel, commanding Southern Military District.

Colonel R. B. Mason,

Commanding 1st Reg't Dragoons, Gov. of California

Stevenson finally submitted to Colonel Mason on 27 July a copy of the agreement he had been required to sign before the new Mormon volunteers would consent to serve for another year. Drawn up on 29 June by a committee of three, Daniel C. Davis, Jesse D. Hunter, and David Pettegrew, this document is of interest because it shows the battalion did not know as of that date where Brigham Young and his followers would permanently land, Salt Lake Valley or northern California, as expected by Samuel Brannan and others. It also indicates the new company held out hope for Jefferson Hunt's efforts to recruit a new battalion of Mormon soldiers to serve in California.

STEVENSON TO MASON, SEN. EXEC. DOC. 18 (31-1), 1849–50, SERIAL 557, 336–38.

Headquarters Southern Military District, California,

Ciudad de los Angeles, July 27, 1847

Colonel: Before the company of Mormons under the command of Captain Davis would consent to be mustered into the service of the United States, they required that the conditions, a copy of which is enclosed, should be signed by me. The only condition upon which I had any hesitation was that agreeing to discharge or pay transportation or rations for the time it would take them to reach Bear river or San Francisco after they were discharged; but upon reflection I became satisfied that it would be much cheaper to obtain them on these terms than to transport a company from the north to San Diego, to supply their place, and that, by way of saving transportation, they could be ordered to Bear river or San Francisco time enough to enable them to reach there before their term of service expired. The promise to disband them in March you had previously made to Hunt; I therefore had no difficulty on that point. There was a strong effort made to obtain for them other arms, that their own might, no doubt, be sent forward or disposed of to the Mormon association; but I positively refused to receive them without arms, except those who were formerly musicians and had now entered the ranks; these, together with some muskets unfit for service, in all about ten, five bayonets, and some few belts, and four non-commissioned officers' swords, were all the arms issued by the ordnance sergeant, and they were receipted for by the captain. I have promised to send them a garrison flag, which you will oblige me by directing the quartermaster to send me, of a medium size, to that post, by the first opportunity. But for the necessity of having troops to garrison San Diego, I should not have subscribed to the enclosed conditions, but have forwarded them to you. The exigency of the case, however, will, I trust, justify the act. The company left here early on the morning of the 25th, and will reach San Diego by Saturday next. The names of the officers are D. C. Davis, captain; 1st lieutenant C. C. Canfield; 2d lieutenants, Inel Barras [Ruel Barrus], and Robert Clift, who performed the duties of acting assistant quartermaster and commissary while that post was garrisoned by Captain Hunter's company; and as he is a good accountant, and has the reputation of being a very correct man, I have directed him to perform those duties at that post, under the command of Captain Davis.

The Christian name of Foster [Forster], alcalde at San Juan, is *John*, which I have inserted in the appointment and forwarded. I have also sent the bond to the collector at San Diego for execution, and I will see that the collectors at Santa Barbara and San Pedro both execute similar ones. In your letter of the 14th instant you name the amount of salary the collector at Santa Barbara is to receive, but omit San Diego. As neither the rate of compensation, nor the office expenses that will be allowed, have yet been fixed for that post, I would respectfully request that you will fix them at your earliest convenience. The mail before last I requested advice as to the extent of my jurisdiction as commander of the southern military district. As your last communication was silent on that subject, I presume it was overlooked. May I request an answer at your earliest convenience.

All is quiet here as when I last wrote you.

I have the honor to be, very respectfully, your obedient servant,

J. D. STEVENSON,
Colonel commanding Southern Military District, California.

Colonel R. B. Mason,
1st U.S. Dragoons, Governor of California.

We, of the Mormon fraternity, whose names are herewith subscribed, purpose to enter the service of the United States as volunteers, on the following terms:

1st. That we enrol[l] to serve under the government of the United States for one year, on condition that the authorized representatives of the government in California pledge themselves, if we require it, to discharge us on the first day of March, 1848.

2d. That we, during the period of our service, have the same privileges, pay, and emoluments granted to us that other volunteers in the service enjoy.

3d. That, on our re-enlistment, we may have the privilege of garrisoning the town of San Diego, and not be sent lower down the coast than that post.

4th. That the authorities of California pledge themselves, on behalf of the government of the United States, at the period of our discharge, to furnish us with the rations and pay allowed by law to the Salt lake, into which Bear river empties, or to the bay of San Francisco, if preferred by us.

5th. That we shall all have the privilege of joining the battalion of Mormons, if there should be one raised.

As far as I have the authority, I agree to the foregoing stipulations,

J. D. STEVENSON,
Col. Commanding Southern Mil. Dist. of California.

True copy.							Ciudad de Los Angeles, July 20, 1847

W. T. SHERMAN,
1st Lieut. 3d Art., A. A. A. G.

Capt. Jefferson Hunt: To Raize a Force from among the Fraternity of Mormons

While the largest body of veterans gathered on the Los Angeles River under Levi Hancock, the battalion's former senior captain led a smaller party north over the Spanish mission road, El Camino Real, along the coast toward San Francisco. Jefferson Hunt had not given up his hope to form a new battalion with himself in command. The Kentuckian still imagined California would become the ultimate destination of the Mormon migration and the place his fellow believers would establish the theocratic Kingdom of God as an independent state. He went to Monterey to see the military governor about his plan, but when he arrived, Col. Richard B. Mason was not there. A disappointed Hunt left a note.

Hunt to Mason, Records of the 10th Military Department, 1846–1851, Roll 2, National Archives.

Capital U. C.
August 10th. 1847

Sir.

On my arrival here yesterday I regretted to learn that you had not yet returned. I am so situated in regard to the party that accompanied me that I must leave here to day. From here I shall proceed to the P. de San Jose and there I shall be highly gratified to receive any communications you may wish to make.

If you should conclude to authorize me to raize [*sic*] a force from among the fraternity of Mormons, I should wish you to name the latest period you would wish them raised,—how and where you would wish them mustered into service and where equipped.

Should I find it impossible to raise a force on account of the emigration not having arrived, and you required a mail taken to the States this season, I should be glad to form a party for the purpose and think I could bear it through at as little or less expense to Government than any other.

Hoping to hear from you soon.

I remain Sir
Your Obt Servt.
J. Hunt

Col. Mason
Govr. Of California.

COL. R. B. MASON:
I REQUEST THAT YOU WILL RAISE A BATTALION

Colonel Mason also had good reason to regret the failure to make contact with Hunt at Monterey. Despite the enlistment of a company of Mormons, his need for troops had grown more pressing. Under the Polk administration's plan to seize Baja California for acquisition under a peace settlement, Lt. Col. Henry S. Burton and two companies of Col. Jonathan Stevenson's New York Volunteers had sailed in July from Los Angeles to seize a foothold on the peninsula. With their departure, Mason had gained one company at San Diego, the Mormon Volunteers, but lost two at Los Angeles to hand him an overall drop in the number of men under his command to stop an insurrection or invasion of southern California. He lost no time in pursuing Hunt's offer.

MASON TO HUNT, RECORDS OF THE 10TH MILITARY DEPARTMENT, 1846–1851, ROLL 2, NATIONAL ARCHIVES.

Head Quarters 10th Mily Dept
Monterey California Augt 16. 1847

Sir,

On my return from the South I found your letter of the 10th inst at this place.

I request that you will raise a Battalion of Mormon Volunteers to be mustered into the service of the United States for the term of twelve months, unless sooner discharged.

The Battalion will consist of,
    Field & Staff I Lt. Col
                I adjt—a Lt of one of the Comps but not in addition
Non Comd. Staff,
                I Sergt Major
                I QMrs Sergt
3 Companies, each of which to consist of
                I Capt
                I First Lieutenant
                2 Second Lieutenants
                4 Sergeants
                4 Corporals
                2 Musicians
                75 Privates

Should the number of privates, on being mustered, not fall below sixty four effective men in a Compy it will be received. Some convenient point to be hereafter designated—between Sutters Fort & San Francisco will be named as the place of Rendezvous.

The battalion will be inspected & mustered into service by an Officer of the United States Army, who will, in every case, be instructed to receive no man who is, in years apparently over forty five or under eighteen; or who is not of physical strength and vigor. To this end, the inspector will be accompanied by a medical officer of the Army, and the Volunteer will be submitted to his examination. It is respectfully suggested, that public notice of these requirements will prevent much disappointment to the zealous & patriotic citizens of your fraternity who may be disposed to volunteer.

It may be proper to remark, that the law provides for the clothing (in money) and subsistence of the Non Commissioned Officers, musicians and privates of Volunteers, who are received into the services of the United States.

In respect to clothing, the law requires that the volunteers shall furnish their own clothing, for which purpose it allows to each non Commissioned Officer, musician, and private, three dollars and fifty cents per month, during the time he shall be in the service of the United States. In order that the Volunteers, who shall be mustered into service under this requisition, may be enabled to provide themselves with good and sufficient clothing, the commutation allowance for six months (twenty one dollars) will be advanced to each non commissioned Officer, musician, and private, after being mustered into service, but only with the express condition that the volunteer has already furnished himself with six months' clothing—this fact to be certified to the paymaster by the Captain of the Company—or that the amount, thus advanced, shall be applied, under the supervision of his Captain, to the object contemplated by law. In this latter case, the advance commutation for clothing will be paid on the Captain's Certificate, that he is satisfied it will be so applied.

When discharged an allowance of fifty cents will be made for every twenty miles distance from the place of discharge to the place of Rendezvous.

The Mormon Company at San Diego will be added to the three which it is proposed that you should raise, making the Battalion to consist of four companies—the command of which you shall have with the rank of Lt. Colonel, but should you not be able to organize three new Companies, then your rank can be only that of Major.

The Sergt Major & QrMaster Sergt will be appointed by yourself and should be good business men.

The Captains, Lieutenants, and Non Commissioned Officers of Companies to be elected by their respective Companies, and I would suggest the *extreme importance* to the public service, that the Officers be judicially selected.

The Battalion will be armed & equipped either at San Francisco or this place, but the Arms &c, will not be given to the men when discharged as was done when the Mormon Battalion was recently discharged at Los Angeles.

When your people arrive in the country you can inform me whether the companies can be raised and at what time. The pay & allowances will be the same as those received by the late Mormon Battalion, unless Congress shall have changed them by some new law of which we have no intelligence.[16]

I am Sir Very Respectfully
Your Obt. Servt.

Capt. J. Hunt   R. B. Mason
Late of Mormon Battalion   Col. 1st Dragoons
San Francisco   Commanding

As Jefferson Hunt set out to find Brigham Young in the Great Basin, he could not know that his people's leader had "damned President Polk" in Salt Lake and was now portraying the enlistment of the Mormon Battalion as part of an evil plot aimed at the religion's destruction. Young's fanciful rhetoric had already effectively precluded any possibility that Hunt would be allowed to raise another "battalion of Mormons," no matter what advantages such an arrangement might offer to the LDS church. At the crest of the Sierra Nevada, Hunt would have a historic meeting with James Brown, the captain sent from New Mexico to command the detachments ordered to winter near the trappers' post at El Pueblo in today's Colorado. Riding hard with a handful of discharged veterans, Brown carried instructions from Brigham Young—and interesting tales to tell about the adventures of the detachments on the Arkansas River.

---

[16]See also Sen. Exec. Doc. 18 (31–1), 1849–50, Serial 557, 9:343–44.

Chapter 8

"The Road to Pueblo"
The Detachments

Although hard on the borders of what Wallace Stegner called Mormon Country, New Mexico and Colorado figure little in the annals of the Latter-day Saints in the West until late in the nineteenth century. The barrier of the Rocky Mountains and the impassible canyon country of southern Utah effectively insulated the territory's eastern neighbors from the incursions of Mormon colonists. A few remote settlements at places like Manassa in Colorado and Pleasanton, Bluewater Valley, and Kirtland in New Mexico marked the limits of their expansion to the east of Deseret. Yet the battalion journals are a valuable, if little-used, collection of sources on these borderlands. The Mormon soldiers' march through New Mexico produced an extraordinary legacy of firsthand reports of the territory immediately after its conquest by the United States. Of special interest are the records of the three battalion detachments sent to winter on the Arkansas River. They tell an essentially forgotten story of life in the four-year-old trappers' settlement at today's Pueblo, Colorado.

Francis Parkman: Blind and Desperate Fanatics

A chance encounter with a remarkable man with a common name led to the first division of the Mormon Battalion on the Arkansas River. Like almost everyone else going overland in 1846, Tennessean John Brown believed Brigham Young would lead his followers west that year. Brown set out from Mississippi on 8 April with fourteen Mormon families he had converted in Monroe County and left Independence, Missouri, the next month with three more families from Illinois. They followed the Oregon Trail almost to Fort Laramie before mountaineer John Richard passed on the rumor that "the Mormons were going up the South Fork of the Platte." Brown's "Mississippi Saints" turned their nineteen wagons south from Goshen Hole to winter at the trappers' post at El Pueblo. On the way they feasted with "the whole nation" of Cheyennes—or at least with the band of Slim Face, who bore a striking resemblance to Andrew Jackson—at Cache la Poudre, but they "searched in vain for the trail of the Mormons." Arriving at Pueblo on 7 August, Brown "found some six or eight mountaineers in the fort with their families. They had Indian and Spanish women for wives." The Mormons "were received very kindly" by the residents, who "seemed pleased to see us." After arranging to trade labor for supplies and giving his party "such instructions and counsel as the spirit dictated," Brown set off down the Arkansas on 1 September with seven men to learn what had happened to their church's hegira. They met the Mormon Battalion eleven days later, which is how Lt. A. J. Smith learned that a band of westering Mormons had taken refuge for the winter at Pueblo.[1]

Returning from his adventures on the Oregon Trail in August 1846, Francis Parkman found the trappers' post "a wretched species of fort of most primitive construction, being nothing more than a large square inclosure, surrounded by a wall of mud, miserably cracked and dilapidated. The slender pickets that surmounted it were half broken down, and the gate dangled on its wooden hinges so loosely, that to open or shut it seemed likely to fling it down altogether." The handful of whites at Pueblo lived at the sufferance of their Indian neighbors, for every year several thousand Arapahoes visited the fort "at the time when the corn begins to ripen." Parkman thought the trappers were "entirely at the mercy of this swarm of barbarians."

While discussing the news of the day at the fort, Parkman found "the doorway was darkened by a tall, shambling fellow, who stood with his hands in his pockets taking a leisurely survey of the premises before he entered. He wore brown homespun pantaloons, much too short for his

---

[1]Brown, ed., *Autobiography of Pioneer John Brown*, 67–70. Historian W. Y. Chalfant suggests that Brown's "Slim Face" may have been Lean Face, brother-in-law of Black Kettle of Sand Creek fame. Lean Face became a council chief of the Cheyenne Wutapiu band in 1854. He may have been with the Ridge People in 1846 as a prominent warrior, but it is unlikely he was their leader. See Chalfant to W. P. MacKinnon, 17 February 1999, copy in editors' possession. John Brown became a member of next year's Brigham Young pioneer company.

legs, and a pistol and bowie knife stuck in his belt." The man's head was wrapped in a linen bandage, and "he came slouching in and sat down on a chest." He had recently surprised a sleeping grizzly bear that "rose on his hind legs, and gave the intruder such a blow with his paw that he laid his forehead entirely bare, clawed off the front of his scalp, and narrowly missed one of his eyes." The man's friends had "raised a shout and the bear walked away, crushing down the willows in his leisurely retreat." Eight or ten more visitors entered the fort's parlor "very coolly" and "began to stare at the company." They reminded Parkman of the hard cases he had met on the Oregon Trail, "though these unwelcome visitors had a certain glitter of the eye, and a compression of the lips, which distinguished them from our old acquaintances of the prairie." They began to "catechise" the young Bostonian, asking where he was from and where he was bound, "and what were our future prospects in life . . . These men belonged to a party of Mormons."[2]

Parkman described "the white wagons of the Mormons drawn up among the trees" on the south side of the Arkansas, half a mile from the fur-trade post:

> Axes were sounding, trees were falling, and log-huts going up along the edge of the woods and upon the adjoining meadow. As we came up the Mormons left their work and seated themselves on the timber around us, when they began earnestly to discuss points of theology, complain of the ill-usage they had received from the "Gentiles," and sound a lamentation over the loss of their great temple at Nauvoo. After remaining with them an hour we rode back to our camp, happy that the settlements had been delivered from the presence of such blind and desperate fanatics.[3]

These early settlers of today's Colorado accomplished little of enduring historical significance, but Sara Emma, daughter of William D. and Margaret C. Kartchner, was the first child born in present Colorado to American citizens.[4] Yet what the history of this little outpost and the battalion's detachments lacks in importance, it makes up in high human drama—and low comedy.

---

[2]Parkman, Jr., *The California and Oregon Trail*, 329–31. The shambling fellow was George W. Therlkill of Illinois. While hunting deer on 6 August, a grizzly attacked William Lay and Therlkill and "knocked them down before they knew it was about." The Mormons "succeeded in killing the bear." See Brown, ed., *Autobiography of Pioneer John Brown*, 70.

[3]Parkman, Jr., *The California and Oregon Trail*, 332–33.

[4]Rickettts, *The Mormon Battalion*, 254, 344n39.

THE HIGGINS DETACHMENT'S MARCH TO PUEBLO

As noted, its commanders reduced the ranks of the Mormon Battalion three times: on the Arkansas River, at Santa Fe, and on the Rio Grande. Capt. Nelson Higgins of Company D led the "family detachment," the first, smallest, and least-documented of these parties. A guard of ten men (plus courier Thomas Woolsey) accompanied the nine women and thirty-three children who left the main command at the last crossing of the Arkansas on 18 September 1846. Smith ordered Higgins to take the families to Bent's Fort and Pueblo and then rejoin the battalion at Santa Fe within thirty days. Pvt. Norman Sharp died on the march of an accidental gunshot wound, despite the ministrations of an Arapaho medicine man.[5] The party arrived at Pueblo on 5 October. Higgins and Quartermaster Sebert Shelton proceeded to Santa Fe, but arrived too late to join the march to California, so Alexander Doniphan ordered Higgins back to Pueblo.

No diaries of Higgins' detachment are known—even battalion chronicler Daniel Tyler "received no journal and but a few items by letter and verbally from members of the party."[6] Perhaps the only surviving first-person account is the brief recollection of Pvt. Dimick Baker Huntington, brother-in-law to both Joseph Smith and Brigham Young. Huntington sketched a year's experience in a single paragraph.

D. B. HUNTINGTON, REMINISCENCES AND JOURNAL 1845–1847, LDS ARCHIVES.

In August 2nd my family came to me at the Fort [Leavenworth] & started for Santa fee by the way of Fort bent   when at the crossing of the Arkansas the familys went to Fort Purbelow & the command went to Santa fe [by] the Semirone rout. Oct 5 arrive at Fort Purbelow. Sick there 30 Days & started for Santa Fee arived there the 27. 29 11 oclock we started for home. Nov 8 arrived at P[ueblo]. (Oct. 1 Betsy Prescindia was born & Died Nov. 9.) Created a set of Blacksmith tools and carried on the business until the 24 of May when we started for California. July 29 Arived in the Great Salt Lake Valley.

Captain Higgins found Pueblo "poorly protected, but it was the best refuge that could be obtained." He set his able-bodied men to work

---

[5]Carter, ed., "Women and Children of the Mormon Battalion," 499.
[6]Tyler, *A Concise History*, 165.

building shelter and fortifications on the south side of the river near the trappers' fort, but lack of food and clothing "occasioned much sickness" among the small command as it prepared for winter on the plains.[7]

THE BROWN DETACHMENT'S MARCH TO PUEBLO

Philip St. George Cooke was appalled at the quality and condition of the volunteer troops whose command he assumed at Santa Fe, but he acted quickly to improve the unit's chances of reaching California. Selecting North Carolinian James Brown as commander, Cooke sent ninety-one soldiers, nineteen women, two children, and Dr. William McIntire to winter quarters at Pueblo. Here Brown's men would be able to use the stores that the Army quartermaster had shipped to Bent's Fort on the mistaken assumption that the battalion would take the mountain route to Santa Fe.[8] This further division of the battalion was not popular with the line troops. Cooke's initial decision to take all the able-bodied men with him would have separated several married couples, but John Steele and John Hess claimed they persuaded Cooke to let them remain with their wives. On the advice of Adjutant George P. Dykes, John Steele asked Dr. Sanderson "to put my name down to go back" with his wife and daughter. Since Steele admitted he was not sick, Sanderson refused to do so and sent Steele back to the adjutant for permission. "I saw there was something wrong," John Steele recalled:

> so I went to all the men who had wives, and asked them to go along with me and see Col. Cooke, but I could not find a man who would go. At last I found John Hess who said he would go. So away we went and when we got opposite where they sold whiskey, John said, "lets go in and get a glass we can face the Colonel better." I said "you can go in and take one but I must be only sober." So he took his glass but I would not taste. We went and found him [Cooke] in a long low cellar in company of about 30 officers. I asked which of the gentlemen there is Col. Cooke. Then there arose a man from the further side of the table, measuring about 6 ft. and 4 inches. I told him I had understood he had issued orders for all the sick men and all the women to go back to Bents Fort. He said yes that was so. I told him I had my wife there and would like the privilege of either having my wife go on to

---

[7]Carter, ed., *The Mormon Battalion*, 117. As is the case in many publications of the Daughters of Utah Pioneers, the source of quotations is not always clear, so this may not be Higgins' phrasing.

[8]Rickettts, *The Mormon Battalion*, 235.

California with me or going back to Bents Fort with her. He spoke very saucy and said he would like to have his wife along with him (but he never had a wife).[9] I told him very likely his wife was in Washington or some other good seaport among her friends, while mine was in Santa Fe among her enemies, and to have her left there with only a guard of sick men, I would not stand it, and the more I talked the more angry I got until at last I could have thrashed the ground with him. Colonel Cooke, seeing that things were becoming serious, said he would go and see General Doniphan. I said I would also, and he walked as fast as his long legs could carry him, but I kept alongside of him and the faster he walked the faster I walked. It made him very angry because I wouldn't fall behind so I stopped outside when he got to General Doniphan's door. They had a small consultation, and in a few minutes Col. Cooke came out, looking altogether another man, and asked me very politely to call his orderly, who was Mr. [William Smith] Muir, a Scotchman. I did so and the Colonel told him to go tell the adjutant to stop making out the returns, and come down to him immediately. Then I knew I had gained my point. The Colonel was very anxious that I should go with him into California. He thought the Mormons were an ugly set as he had taken a bout with Thomas S. Williams just the day before, and the impression made on him was that the Mormons were all fighters, and as we had been used to mob violence but a few months before it did not take much opposition to make us mad at Colonel or General. I then returned to John Hess and told him I would now take a drink with him, and so we came back to camp, and orders were issued that every man who had a wife there had the privilege to go to Bents Fort.[10]

Steele told the story this way in his journal:

There has been many changes since we came to St Afee [Santa Fe]. There was a plan got up to send all the sick to Bents Fort & all the woman and their Husbands to the Bay of St Francisco over the mountains. But to this the husbands ware not willing to agree and every plan was wrought by G. P. Dikes & others to get them to go But John Hess & I went to Lieutenant Colnol Cook, who assumed the command of the Battalion, and after three denials succeeded on account of my Family to get the answer that he would go and speak to Colnol Doniphan who Immediately gave orders for the

[9]Steele was incorrect. On 28 October 1830 Cooke had married Rachel Wilt Hertzog, his wife until his death in Detroit in 1895. See Young, *The West of Philip St. George Cooke*, 55–56.

[10]Beckwith, ed., "Journal of John Steele," 11–12. No manuscript source is known for this version of Steele's journal, published in the *Utah Hist. Quarterly* in 1933. It appears to be a variant of Steele's Reminiscences and Journals, 1846–1898, LDS Archives, which is the manuscript source for the typescript Wanda Steele Cox transcribed as The Journals of John Steele and Mahonri Moriancumer Steele, now at the Utah State Hist. Soc. This version appears to be a recopying of an original daybook, which may survive among Steele's descendants.

JOHN STEELE
as a Patriarch in southern Utah.
Courtesy, LDS Archives.

reports to be stoped and the Agitant [adjutant] to come to him and the
word was that all the married men should go with their families. The agitant
took the Honour of that to himself and told that it was him that got the
men to go when it was John Hess & I as mouthpiece . . . There is a general
bad feeling exists against Agitant G. P. Dikes.

John W. Hess recalled that Dykes claimed credit for the decision
when he climbed upon a wagon wheel and "shouted at the top of his
voice: 'Oh! Oh! All you men who have wives here can go back with them.
I have seen men going about crying enough to melt the heart of a croc-
odile, so I went to the Colonel and had it arranged.'" Hess thought,
"You hypocritical liar; you will take the credit that belongs to others."[11]

James Brown, the least-competent of the battalion's captains, led the
party up the Mountain Route of the Santa Fe Trail. They retraced their
steps over Glorieta Pass and struck out to cross Raton Pass to Bent's
Fort and then go up the Arkansas River. The journal of this young Irish

---

[11]Wood, ed., "With the Mormon Battalion," 50–51.

shoemaker provides a vivid account of the journey John Steele made with his wife and six-year-old daughter.[12]

JOHN STEELE, REMINISCENCES AND JOURNALS, 1846–1898, LDS ARCHIVES.

18 [October 1846] Began our March in Company with 87 men & 20 women that are detached for Purbello undr the command of Captain James Brown, Lieut. [Elam] Ludington, Sargent [Orson B.] Addams & others. Came 6 miles.

Monday 19. Came 15 miles over some of the worst roads. I being a teamster was kept buisy. We traviled the same road we came before.

Tuesday 20. Came 12 miles over Hills & vales. At last camped by Peko [Pecos] River. There is a smal Spanish settlement there.

Wednesday 21. Came 18 miles.

Thursday 22. Came 18 miles and passed the round Bluff between St. Magill [San Miguel] and another Spanish town. John D. Lee & Egan passed by for the Bluffs and Mr. Gulley [was] in their wagon.

Friday 23. Came 25 miles & came to Beijus [Las Vegas] & camped in a valey of Good Grass.

Saturday 24. Came 20 miles and camped by the Moroe where 2 Antilope was shot.

Sunday 25 [October 1846]. Came 3 miles over the Moroe; 12 over the St. Afee road & go on the Bents Fort [road].[13]

Monday 26. Came 18 miles and camped by a stream in a valey of good grass.

Tuesday 27. Came 16 miles through Fine Valeys of good land surrounded by High Mountains & Great rocks. The grass is green all winter. There is a large salt Lake that yields or would yield plenty of saloretice [saleratus] and salt, and the name is the Rione.[14]

Wednesday 28. Came 16 miles. This morning one of our Breathren died about 12 oclock and I helped to dig his grave and caried Him to it and made a bed of rushes for him and helped to cover Him up. His name was Milton Smith.[15]

---

[12]For a colorful account of Steele's later career as a naturopath and astrologer in southern Utah, see Bate, "John Steele: Medicine Man, Magician, Mormon Patriarch," 71–90.

[13]At today's Watrous, New Mexico, Brown's party took the Mountain Route of the Santa Fe Trail, rather than the Cimarron Route, which they had crossed earlier in the month.

[14]Steele's salt lake was probably near today's Cimarron, New Mexico.

[15]An Ohioan, nineteen-year-old Milton Smith had served as a private in Co. C. "We dug his grave and I smoothed down his pillow, got the boys to gather grass and cane and covered him the best we could. Near a tributary of the Purgatory River on the right hand side of the road as we go to Bents Fort there he lies deep in the ground. We also covered his grave with large stones to keep the wolves from digging him up." See Beckwith, ed., "Journal of John Steele," 13.

Thursday 29. Came 20 miles and camped.

Friday 30. Came 10 miles and camped in a valley where there is a good stream.

Satturday 31. Came 10 miles and camped at the foot of the mountains. The weather is very cold. The mountains are of the best kind of sandstone.

November 1 [1846] Sunday. This day came 10 miles through mountains of grait Hight and into deep valeys & rough roads.

Monday, 2. Came 17 miles through some of the Highest mountains and the deepest valleys and camped on a good stream Called the picket wire.[16]

Tuesday 3. Came 8 miles & camped on the same crick. There are good roads all along here. There are plenty of Turkeys & Dear. This day one of our company whose name was Abner Chase died 12 noon and was buried same Evening before we crossed the River.[17]

Wednesday 4. Came 10 miles and camped by the whole in the praeri.

Thursday 5. Came 14 miles & camped beyond the whole in the Rock among the cedars.

Friday 6. Came 12 miles & camped by the willow Springs where there ware 14 yoke of cattle & one mule came up and was distributed among the rest of the Teams.[18] The[y] belonged to accompany of men going to St Fee with provisions for the Army.

Saturday 7. Started and traveled 15 miles & camped by an whole in the prieri [prairie]. This day the owners of the Kettle [cattle] came along & Captain Brown told them to take them and they took seven yok of the[m] back[19] and the rest we brought along and after we came to Puerbello the Captan took 4 yoke of them and the rest were devided among the Favorites of the Captain and many other kettle & mules were picket up & kept.

---

[16]After crossing today's Colorado state line and 7,834-foot Raton Pass, the party camped on the Purgatoire River at today's Trinidad. "Here the prairie commences," wrote Joel Terrell.

[17]A private in Co. D, Vermonter Abner Chase, Jr., was born 18 May 1813. He left a family in Iowa, and his brother, Cpl. John Darwin Chase, was also in Brown's detachment. Reflecting Mormon belief in the imminence of Christ's return, Andrew J. Shupe wrote, "He said all he hated was that he had to be buried in the wilderness, but he said that he would not have to lay very long in the ground." See Shupe diary extracts in Carter, ed., "Women and Children of the Mormon Battalion," 504.

[18]Not to be confused with the better-known Willow Spring at today's Raton, New Mexico, this incident probably took place at Iron Spring in Comanche County, Colorado. John Hess wrote, "It seemed as if we had gone about as far as we could go, when one morning, after the guard had driven the oxen into camp, it was found that there were thirty head of stray oxen, in the herd, all of them in good condition. Captain Brown gave orders to distribute them in the teams of the Detachment." See Wood, ed., "With the Mormon Battalion," 52.

[19]Steele recalled that the animals belonged "to Uncle Sam's fit out. The men came hunting them and the Captain told to take all that they knew to be theirs," but according to John Hess the drivers complained "that each teamster only knew his own team." Hess considered this "a divine interposition of the kind hand of God in our behalf, as it seemed about the only chance for deliverance from starvation." See Beckwith, ed., "Journal of John Steele," 13; and Wood, ed., "John W. Hess: With the Mormon Battalion," 52.

Alexander Brown the Captan son picked up one that had U.S. [branded] on it. He swaped it off for a spanish poney and many other such tricks were played.

Sunday 8. Came 20 miles & camped by the Arcansas River.[20]

Monday 9. Lay still and some went to Bents fort & got 60 days provisions.[21]

Tuesday 10. Crossed the river. Water 3 feet deep and came 12 miles. Camped in shoop valey. Wednesday 11. Lay still.

Thursday 12. Started and came 10 miles & camped in a good bottom for grass and rushes.

Friday 13. Came 15 miles and camped on the bank of the river. Seen an old ruin of an house.

Satturday 14. Came 16 miles. Saw several old ruins of log buildings. Camped by the river side.[22]

Sunday 15 [November 1846]. Came 10 miles and camped within five miles of Purbello.

Monday 16. Lay still all day.

Tuesday 17. Came 5 miles crossed the Arcansas and came to where there ware some 20 Houses. Pitched tent & drew 17 days provisions.

Wednesday 18th. 385 miles from St Afee. Plan was laid out for us to build 18 Houses to winter in.

Thursday 19. We went to work in the woods to get the Timber out. Friday 20. Got our Houses Built [by the] 1st of December and by Thursday 24th we were all into our houses and felt some what comfortable. Nothing of any consequience took place to Monday 22 [December 1846]. There was a detachment of 55 men sent from the Battalion under command of Lieutenant Willis a man [of whom] the Worst report was given of being ill to his men.

---

[20]Steele remembered, "we were very hard up for something to eat." He "had a poor old ox that laid in a mud hole all night and in the morning was not fit to travel, so I held him up while one of the boys shot him, and he was tough. I had the toothache all the way for a month." The party had come "321 miles in 20 days averaging 15½ miles per day. We were all hungry. My wife and myself divided our rations with our little daughter although it was only 4 ounces each per day." See Beckwith, ed., "Journal of John Steele," 13.

[21]Brown left the main party at the Arkansas and went six miles to Bent's Fort for supplies. One of his companions, Sgt. Joel Terrell, wrote, "We took five wagons to the fort and drew rations for 60 days, pork, floour, rice, beans, coffee, sugar, vinegar, soap, &c., it being the forst pork we had since before we got to Santa Fe, no beans since we left there, hence had a feast." Brown, Dr. McIntire, Terrell, and a clerk "got squanderd" at Bent's Fort, and "Capt and clerk laid out the doctor and I." See Joel J. Terrell, Diary, 10 November 1846.

[22]These were the ruins of Gantt's Fort or Fort Cass, built by trader John Gantt in 1832 and abandoned by 1835. See Whiteley, The Cherokee Trail, 7, 44, 45.

THE WILLIS DETACHMENT'S MARCH TO PUEBLO

The unhappy company that arrived at Pueblo shortly before Christmas had endured a hard march from the Rio Grande. As he contemplated striking across the Continental Divide, Philip St. George Cooke dispatched the last of the men judged too sick to make the trip, along with one laundress, Sophie Gribble. Cooke assigned Lt. William Wesley Willis of Company A to lead the party back to Santa Fe. Willis was given virtually no supplies and claimed he "spent $66 of my own private money before reaching Santa Fe."[23] There Col. Sterling Price issued the detachment ten mules and pack saddles and ordered them to Pueblo.

"With this outfit we had to perform a journey of about three hundred miles, over the mountains, and in the winter," Willis recalled. "Packing was new business to us, and at first we were quite awkward." Rather than take the Santa Fe Trail, the party followed the line of State Highway 68 to Taos; why Willis chose the Taos Trail over the Santa Fe Trail's Mountain Route is not clear.[24] It was shorter, but crossing the Sangre de Cristo Range in the middle of winter was a formidable challenge. Probably aware of criticism of his leadership, when it came time to tell the story thirty-five years later, Willis made himself the hero of his tale. He claimed he did his best for the party's sick stragglers and paid "out of my own private funds" for the upkeep of the men he was forced to leave behind. North of Taos, the mountains and "strong fears" about the snow were so intimidating that "some resolved not to attempt it." Faced with mutiny, Willis called the men together and told them he would "carry out my instructions and march to Pueblo to winter, if I had to go it alone." After a difficult trek up the San Luis Valley, the party crossed the summit of the Sangre de Cristos in a "continued cold, piercing wind." Willis detailed a rear guard to "encourage those who began to lag," while he "marched at the head of the column to break the road through the enormous snow banks." Some of the men were severely frostbitten, but presumably shared

---

[23]Lt. W. W. Willis, 35, had been first sergeant and third lieutenant of Co. A before being ordered to Santa Fe. Born in Illinois, he would serve as mayor of Cedar City and die at Beaver, Utah, in 1872. For his account of the road to Pueblo, see Tyler, *A Concise History*, 191–94.

[24]For a description of this route that connected New Mexico with the Oregon Trail, see Whiteley, "The Trappers Trail: 'The Road to Fort Laramie's Back Door,'" 2–16.

"the inexpressible joy [when] we saw the valley of the Arkansas below, where the ground was bare." They had "good weather and pleasant travelling" to their winter quarters at Fort Pueblo.[25]

The battalion's regular army officers do not seem to have selected the best of their militia comrades to command the detachments. Willis faced a tough assignment, but his men complained bitterly that he was not up to the task. Joseph Skeen's criticism was especially pointed. He recalled, "we buried three of the soldiers before we came to santefee which died for want of care and ware used more like niggers by our lutenant then white folks." Skeen claimed Willis did not mourn one of the dead, but "was glad of it he was out of the road. He would threaten to cut their Damned throats and scalp them and to cut them to pieces if they would not keep up when they ware not able to scarcely to walk." Skeen refused to remove sick men from a mired wagon when Willis ordered him to "throw them out in the mud." The lieutenant "would get Drunk whenever he could get it and then he would curse the sick men because they were not able to walk."[26]

Most of the journals echo Skeen's bitter memories, but James A. Scott's diary provides a less-impassioned account of the journey. His tattered daybook contains the most dramatic telling of the unit's crossing of the Sangre de Cristo Mountains, while the diary of his friend, George Deliverance Wilson, fills in gaps in Corporal Scott's record—and paints a more critical picture of their leader. This section of Scott's diary begins with the battalion's march down the Rio Grande, before Willis' men were sent back north.[27]

JAMES ALLEN SCOTT, DIARIES 1846, LDS ARCHIVES.

Monday 9th [November 1846]. Moved on 9 or 10 miles & camped, was corporal of the rear guard. The word came this evening that on the morrow the sick of the Battalion & those who were weakly & not able to stand the fatigue of crossing the Mts should return via Santa Fe to Purbelow, & in the

---

[25]Tyler, *A Concise History*, 192–94.

[26]Skeen, Reminiscences, 1846–July 1847, LDS Archives.

[27]Bad health had dogged Scott all along the trail from Santa Fe. About dusk on 24 October 1846, he "was suddenly taken with a severe pain in the right breast, which caused breathing to be difficult." On 4 November, Scott "Attempted to rise at roll call, but my breast was to[o] painful & sore. Lay down until sun rise, then arose free from pain, but very sore." Captain Daniel Davis carried Scott's musket and he "made my way along in the easiest manner possible, by degrees." The sick man noted, "We have the road to make as we go & rough it is."

Spring proceed on to California. In consequence of feeble health, I was offered the oppertunity of returning, & as it was thought wisdom by my friends I accepted it.

Tuesday 10th. Preparations for returning occupied the day until 3 P.M. when we bade farewell to our friends & commenced retracing our steps, under rather unfavorable circumstances, having only One waggon to haul our provisions, baggage, & sick of which there were 6 or 8 not able to walk. We moved on three miles & camped. Nothing worthy of noting transpired until Sunday 15th when John Green died. He was buried by the side of— Foernout, who died as we passed on.[28]

On the 19th we reached the ruined village 1 mile below Socora. This day John Freeman died after 4 days Sickness. We halted for the night & interred him. During the night Reed Carter died he was sick when we left the Battalion.[29] Thus here were laid two of the victims of exposure & fatigue. Sleep on! No more shall thy peaceful slumbers be disturbed by the shrill notes of the Reveille or the harsh commands of tyrants. By the stupidity of thy leaders, went where they expired [?] & for thy blood will they have to atone. Rest from thy labors for a season, and altho thou art laid in the wild forest in a foreign land, yet thy names shall be remembered & recorded as Martyrs fallen a sacrifice for the sake of thy brethren.[30]

Born in Vermont, George Deliverance Wilson joined the Mormons at Kirkland, Ohio, in 1834, and followed his church on all its subsequent wanderings. His wife died in Nauvoo in 1845, and he left two children behind on the Missouri River after enlisting as a private in Company E. Wilson's diary reflects no reluctance to question the motives of his leaders and describes how these hungry soldiers got along with New Mexico's recently conquered citizens.

GEORGE DELIVERANCE WILSON, JOURNAL, UTAH STATE HIST. SOC.

Nov 18 [November 1846]. This morning we are preparing to move

---

[28]Pvt. John W. Green of Co. C was buried at or near today's Elephant Butte Reservoir next to Pvt. John Hampton, who had died on 3 November 1846. See Larson, *A Data Base of the Mormon Battalion*, 78–79. "This seems to produce no effect on the minds of the brethern," George D. Wilson wrote, "so hardened in trial and sorrow."

[29]Elijah Freeman and Richard Carter, both Co. E privates, were buried together south of today's Socorro, New Mexico.

[30]Scott did not keep daily entries of the two-hundred-mile march back to Santa Fe, but Abner Blackburn described "our loansome trip and not a well man in the lot fit for service." As noted, the conduct of battalion members towards civilians was generally admirable, but when trade with the locals became difficult, Willis' men acted as hungry soldiers have since time immemorial: "we demanded what we needed." In what became an oft-told tale, Blackburn recalled raiding the wine cellar of an "old Padra." See Bagley, ed., *Frontiersman*, 45–46.

ahead in the old stormy way. We yesterday passed 110 trading waggons that had some milions of goods waiting for market after peace is declared.

Nov 19th. This morning my mind is encouraged and we are to move as fast as our teams will go to Santafee and if the team fails the sick are to be left with a man or two to take care of them and the others are to take their equipment and rations, tents and camp kettles on our own backs an[d] go without them. This is Lt. Willis's order, expecting to leave us out at Santafee in the hands of the commander of the post [Sterling] Price, to go at work while he and Br [Thomas] Woolsey goes to the Bluff and from there to Ft. Leavenworth to carry the express to California in the spring, which will be worth 1500 dollars to them. So we are as it were sold again into the hands of the gentiles, for money by our little comdr [commander]. But we will do as best we can. Our Sgt and corp'l mess together and deal out the rations to us but we are in want of bread, while [they] have plenty. We push the waggon through the sand without dinner while they have their haversacks full and make the cry of stolen flour, somebody has taken flour, &c.

The wise judge between us and so forth.

20. This day the destroyer is in the camp. Brother Freemen, who 3 days ago was well and healthy is no more. Brother Carter is now to be buried by his side. Brother Lt. Willis said of Freemen, I'm glad he's dead. This morning Lt. W. threatened to cut their throats if they did not tend to his orders.

This day also corporal [Thomas R.] Burns threatened to without cause to knock a solders God damned Brains out, as he expressed it. There is no time nor strength for faith to be exercised.

Lt. W. cares for something else but his men surely. This day we passed trading waggons to the number of I suppose 100.

21st. This morning we pass General Doniphans command in the river bend where [there] is 250 or 3 hundred men. But he himself has gone where Col Cook intended we should, into the mountains with six hundred men to plunder the Navihoo Indians and obtain mules and resources for Chewaywa when he has already sent his pr[ovision] train of ox waggons.[31]

[22 November 1846]. We are called to halt today on account of teams, which are to be had that belong to our command. Lt this morning orders the sick out of the waggons to walk one mile or else be left at the next town

---

[31]Col. Alexander W. Doniphan commanded American troops in New Mexico. Cooke had noted Navajo depredations on 26 October; Doniphan sent three columns into their country and signed a treaty with the Navajo near today's Gallup, New Mexico, on 22 November. Doniphan's forces returned "much worse by the arduous campaign" and when Wilson met them were on their way to concentrate south of Soccoro in December. After battles at Brazito and Rio Sacramento, Doniphan occupied Chihuahua, leading his men (many of whom had the advantage of being mounted) on an epic 2,100-mile march that "was probably the most difficult trek in a war which saw several American units make long, arduous marches." See Bauer, *The Mexican War, 1846–1848*, 136–37, 150–58.

not caring for the news that there is team and help for us but he is now persuaded by Br Woolsey to take the team which he had already passed. The
design has been to leave us in santafee and there let us labor or stand guard
under the Command of Price there to stay without pay untill spring to grat-
ify his determination to see the bluffs his family &c and carry the express for
1500 [dollars].[32]

Tuesday 24th 1846. We have this day we have traveled twelve miles and
camp near a town. This morning we were called on parade by Lt. Willis and
strictly forbidden selling cartriges under penalty of being whipped over a
waggon tounge with a strap. We were expressly forbidden going in a single
house. Although it was very cold and we had no wood and many wanted to
buy bread on the road this order was to be executed in the most rigorous
manner and the severest punishment—cut to pieces with sword, or (as the
Lt said) There is no God in Israel. This morning one was threatened by the
Lt of being put where the dogs would not bite him. This moment one of
our mess is threatened with extra duty because Br. Skean [Pvt. Joseph Skeen]
was sick and left by the way side and as one of our mess we left two brethren
back to take care of him. For this we are blamed. I choose to loose my years
pay rather than remain in these circumstances if I could only be discharged.

I leave the Brethern this morning to go over the mountain with a return
to the sick Brethren. O God who guidest my way may I find the way through
this value of tears. The Spaniards have already given me some hot gruel.
Thanks to God of Israel for it.

This evening I enjoy a good fire in a Spanish friends house where there is
lice and knits. They give me fitz.[33]

I have learned that they have to water all the land in cultivation so there
is no hurry.

James Allen Scott, Diaries 1846, LDS Archives.

Dec. 1st 1846.

The detachment entered Santa Fe under gloomy prospects of comfort.
The Lieut. Wm Willis had left the Company the day before & came on to
make some arrangements concerning wood, provisions, &c & to have all
things ready, when we should get there. But to our surprise & disappointment nothing had been done. Altho. the day was bitter cold, not a single
stick of wood had been provided, except a nice pile for his Honer's own use.

---

[32]As noted, Pvt. Thomas Woolsey carried messages from Higgins' detachment to Cooke and then
returned to Pueblo. He left Pueblo in December for Winter Quarters with John H. Tippetts (not Willis)
carrying only four days' rations. The detachments would meet Woolsey and Tippetts again.

[33]Farther down the trail, Abner Blackburn recalled the men "managed to get in deserted Mexican
houses at night, but they were stocked with gray backs or body lice." After crossing the Sangre de Cristo,
they "Built a fire and burnt our underclothes with the vermine." See Bagley, ed., *Frontiersman*, 46, 48.

Neither had any provision returns been made. Whether this discomfiture was caused by the Lieut's negligence or not I cannot positively say, but one thing is certain, the Commissary's stores are full & the Government is bound to furnish his soldiers. Near dark we got our sack of flour & some pork. In order to cook the same we were obliged to pay our own money for wood.[34] Slept very uncomfortable in consequence of the cold.

Wed. 2nd. Still cold, spent the day down in town around the fires. 4 O.Clock P.M. went up to the camp. No wood yet, neither was any provisions. Returned to town & slept in the quarters of some of Doniphan's Infantry. Slept very soundly.

Thurs. 5th Drew our rations for 18 days & 10 mules to pack the same, & with this poor outfit the Lieut have orders to prepare for a march on the morrow.

Friday 4th We loaded up & left Santa Fe at 1 P.M. each man whether sick or well having to carry his arms, & napsacky. We marched about 5 miles & camped, Many thro weakness were unable to get to camp until after dark. Used snow for water.

Sat. 5th Moved on 7 miles to where we could obtain feed for the mules & water for our own conveniences & there halted & camped. The road thus far has been N. and directly Over the mountains.

Sunday 6th This morning we determined on leaving those who were unable to march at the first a full days journey & let them proceed slowly to Turley's 13 miles S of Touse[35] & wait until assistance could be procured from Purbelow, so we left 12 men under the charge of Sergt Brazier.[36] The command marched 20 miles & camped. It snowed during the night to the depth of 4 or 5 inches.

Monday 7th 8 Oclock A.M. found us packed & traveling, very tiresome walking. Road lay along the Country of the Del Norte. Settlements thick— Soil better than common. 15 miles brought us to Luissa, we scraped away the snow & pitched our tents. Had a large log heap fire, we rested comfortably until morning.

---

[34]Joseph Skeen charged that Willis "would get Drunk with the money that was given to him to buy us wood," and that when they reached Santa Fe, Willis "was Drunk and would not provide us any thing for us to eat . . . he loved liquor better than he Did his brethren." George D. Wilson "went to the quartermaster and told him our situation and he gave him A sack of flower so we got something to eat." See Skeen, Reminiscences, 1846–July 1847, LDS Archives.

[35]Simeon Turley's mill and distillery was twelve miles north of Taos at Arroyo Hondo.

[36]On his way to Pueblo, George Fredrick Ruxton met "an Englishman, from Biddenden, in Kent, and old Peninsular soldier." This was Sgt. Richard Brazier, 53, of Co. E, whose military experience predated that of any other man in the battalion, for he had apparently served under Wellington in Spain. Brazier had married Elizabeth Annis on 19 November 1843 at Nauvoo. Ruxton "asked what could have induced him to have undertaken such an expedition. He looked at me, and, without answering the question, said, 'Dang it, if I could only once get hoam!'" See Ruxton, *Life in the Far West*, 195; and Cook, ed., *Nauvoo Deaths and Marriages, 1839–1845*, 107.

Tuesday 8. After marching 7 miles we left the bottoms & crossed a point of the Mountains a distance of 8 miles across, then struck the river & took up quarters at the Frenchman's in the village of Limbostha, at which place we remained until Thursday morning.[37] Went on Wednesday night to a Fandango or Spanish dance which was conducted after the American manner.

Thursday 10th [December 1846]. We left early & soon commenced ascending another ridge of the mountains. The ascent was moderate but the descent very steep. At the foot of the mountain was a small village on the Del Norte. We quartered in a very neat house after a day's travel of 10 or 12 miles. Left J. Johnson sick.[38]

Friday 11. Early we left & after crossing another ridge of mountains the city of Touse hove in sight at the distance of 4 miles. At 3 P.M. we passed it, leaving it on right. The town is scattered for a long distance over the Valley & is a place of considerable trade mostly in Whiskey, Flour, & Furs.[39] We quartered to night 3 miles from or above town at a Spaniards. Day's travel 15 miles.

Sat. 12th Sunrise found us on the march. We left another sick man, Geo. Coleman.[40] Marched 8 miles & halted at Turley's, where we took a hour & bought some flour.[41] After resting 1 hour we started & after traveling over hill & dale until an hour in the night, I came in sight of the camp fire which was very agreeable to one who had trudged 20 miles through the snow & over steep mountains. We camped on Red River, lay on the snow.

Sunday 13th At 9 A.M. left the camp & passed thro a town on the river which is the last settlement.[42] Day's travel 10 or 12 Miles.

Monday 14th Our road lay along a considerbale valley entirely destitute of timber except on the small creeks which occasionally broke out from the side of the mountains & after winding their way along the [San Luis] Valley

---

[37]This was the home of Jean-Baptiste Chalifoux at El Embudo. Perhaps the "Baptiste Brown" who gave his name to Utah's Browns Hole/Park, Chalifoux was born in Canada about 1792 and had been in New Mexico since at least 1826. As a "notorious bandit chief," he led horse raids in California with Philip F. Thompson and Peg-leg Smith. Chalifoux married at Taos in 1836 and Ruxton found him at Embudo in 1846 "ending his days as a quiet ranchero." He died in Colorado on 12 December 1860. See Janet Lecompte's sketch in Hafen, ed., *The Mountain Men and the Fur Trade*, 7:57–74.

[38]Ohioan Jesse W. Johnstun, 26, had been a private in Co. C with his brother William. He died at Parley's Park, Utah, in 1860.

[39]Taos was a frontier emporium specializing in the products Scott listed but was especially noted for its "raw, fiery" spirit distilled from wheat, "Taos Lightnin'."

[40]Pvt. George Coleman, Co. A, was born in England in 1817.

[41]Willis recalled that he went ahead to Arroyo Honda "to make arrangements for the sick" and was surprised when Coleman failed to arrive. See Tyler, *A Concise History*, 193.

[42]The northernmost settlement in New Mexico was Rio Colorado, today's Questa, on Scott's Red River. It had a population "of some fifty souls, including one or two Yuta Indians," who told George Ruxton that they allowed the settlement to exist because it was more convenient to raid than Taos or Santa Fe. See Hafen, ed., *Ruxton of the Rockies*, 198.

lost themselves in the Del Norte. The snow was 2 or 3 inches deep. Marched 16 or 18 miles.

Tuesday 15th [December 1846]. Wednesday 16th. Our path still lay along the Valley, the soil of which is sandy & dry in consequence of which there is no Vegetation except a scrubby brush or weed resembling the wild sage, called grease wood. Averaged 18 miles each day.

Thurs. 17th. Left the Valley & turned to the right & commenced crossing the mountains. Our trail lay along a small creek. 18 or 20.

Friday 18th. Commenced crossing the dividing mountain between the Rio Del Norte & Arkansas rivers. The ascent & descent very steep & covered with snow to the depth of from 12 to 18 inches, & being crusted caused the passing of the mountain to be very difficult & fatiguing. We were often oblidged to apply to the bushes for aid in ascending. Supposed the mount. to be 800 or 1000 feet in height.[43] At the foot of the mountain we bid farewell to the Snow. Day's march 16 miles.

Saturday 19th. Our road lay over large hills, barren, marched hard all day & camped with out finding water used snow for water, 25 miles.[44]

Sunday 20th [December 1846]. This morning after travelling 3 miles we came to a small creek named Green Horn upon which is one settlement made by an American named Brown.[45] We pushed on aiming to get to Purbelow which was 25 miles distant. Near noon we fortunately met a squad of [James] Brown's Company who were out on a hunting excursion. They kindly invited us to their camp & presented us with some venison, upon which we feasted heartily. Cooked it on the coals without salt. Our Rati[o]ns having run out the evening before, our appetites had become quite Keen. After dining we Travelled on 8 miles & camped in company with the hunters on the St. Charles, a small creek. Day's travel 18 miles.

Monday 21st. Twelve more miles across a dry prairie brought us to the

---

[43]Willis' party "turned to the right" at today's Fort Garland, Colorado, and followed Sangre de Cristo Creek through El Vallecito, the valley the mountaineers called the "Wind-trap," to cross Sangre de Cristo Pass near where U.S. Highway 160 crosses the La Veta passes at almost 9,500 feet above sea level. See Ibid., 206.

[44]On 19 December John Tippets arrived at "a house where there was some eastern men some of them have Spanish women for wife." He complained, "it seemed as tho our Lieutenant would rush ahead if every man died. No feelings on his part could be shown to poor worn out men."

[45]John Brown, Sr., "the Medium of the Rockies," was born in 1817, fought at San Jacinto, Texas, in 1836, and helped build Fort Pueblo in 1842. He settled on Greenhorn Creek in 1845 and ran a frontier emporium that sold practically everything. See Woodward, "Trapper Jim Waters," 10. With a band of renowned mountaineers, Brown passed through Great Salt Lake City on 4 July 1849 on his way to California. He settled at San Bernardino in 1852 and joined the Mormons, a fact his family later denied. Brown was excommunicated in 1855 and carried the first word of the Mountain Meadows Massacre to Los Angeles. He became a celebrated spiritualist, road-builder, author, and businessman before his death in 1899.

Mormon village or settlement where we were kindly met & welcomed in.[46]
The hearty looks of those who were sick & pale when we parted, assured us
of the healthiness of the place. My heart rejoiced that Kind Providence had,
at last, brought us where [we] could have a respite from our fatigues & privations our selves among our brethren undisturbed by the harsh commands
of Gentile leaders.

    We pitched our tents on the bank of the Ark[ansas] within a few 100
yards of the settlers houses which were built in two long rows & covered
with dirt. Bro [Ebenezer] Hanks kindly offered me the privilege of messing
with him until we could build a house for ourselves. The offer I gladly
accepted as the nights were cool & disagreeable camping out.

    Tuesday 22nd. Lay up and rested, most of the day. Made some prepara-
tions for commencing a house &c. &c.

ON THE HEADWATERS OF THE ARKANSAS: CHRISTMAS 1846

The soldiers at Pueblo built shelters "of cottonwood logs split in
halves and the pieces all joined together in the form of a stockade," John
Hess recalled. "Here we passed the winter in drilling and hunting and
having a good time generally." With "the mountaineers, Mexicans,
Americans and soldiers, Indians, trappers, [and] explorers," Abner
Blackburn remembered, this borderlands crossroads "was an interesting
scenery all the time."[47]

As 1846 drew to a close, the soldiers living in the shadow of the
Rocky Mountains turned their thoughts to their forsaken homes. Many
of the letters written from Pueblo that Christmas ultimately found their
way to Salt Lake and what is, in essence, the Mormon Battalion's dead
letter file. Among the most detailed—and moving—are the letters of
two corporals.

SCOTT TO MCCORKLE, MORMON BATTALION CORRESPONDENCE COLLECTION,
LDS ARCHIVES.

Territory of New Mexico. Fort Purbelow
December 25th 1846

Mr. R. A. H. McCorkle,
    Dear Couisin, friend, & Brother! With a mind full of recollections of the

---

[46]John G. Smith noted that the first of Willis' "haggard and emaciated" men arrived at Pueblo on 20
December 1846. See Tyler, *A Concise History*, 194.
[47]Wood, ed., "With the Mormon Battalion," 52; and Bagley, ed., *Frontiersman*, 45.

past, newly aroused by the ushering in of this Christmas morn which brought to my view the scenes of the last & also which were now enacting at the comfortable mansion at Verdant Grove, I pen these lines for your perusal, believing that they will be read by you with some interest, for I doubt not but that you take an interest in my welfare. Among the first thoughts that persented themselves to my mind this morning, was that of Jimmy, Bobby & Joe, each striving which should rise earliest to get their Pap's Christmas gift, while Granny striving to quell the noise. Aunt Lizah is flying around preparing breakfast. Sarah & Susan are putting everything in the neatest order possible. Pap & Addison are out among the stock. Happiness abounds. Gladly would I exchange my situation which is tolerably comfortable at present for a few days at Verdant Grove. But enough. I have arrived safe & sound at the Mormon settlement which is on the head waters of the Arkansas, within a quarter [mile] of Fort Purbelow, tho on the opposite side of the river which is the boundary between New Mexico & the Indian Territory. Purbelow is on the American side.

After leaving Leavenworth 60 days travel brought us to Santa Fe. Col Allen under whom we enlisted died at Fort L. and the Battalion fell under the control of Col. Smith. When we reached Santa Fe, which was on the 13th Oct. Col. Cook was there waiting to receive us & according to Kearney's command march us to California. On the 19th we left S. Fe with 60 days provisions. Our road lay along the Rio Del Norte. We followed it 22 Days making a distance 250 miles. Near 150 miles below Santa Fe we left the main road & followed Kearney's trail, then commenced hard times living on 8 oz of Flour & 10 of meat per day & pushing waggons over sand hills & having to carry our guns and kampsacks. This was rough fare. *Sure.* After 22 days march, it was found necessary to send the sick & feeble & a sufficient guard back to Purbelow and there let them recruit until spring & then proceed to California. I was detached as one of the guard. We reached Santa Fe on our return on the 1st of Dec. I wrote to Sister M[argaret]. while there. I rec'd a letter from her at Alberkirk 90 miles S. of Santa Fee.[48] We left our waggons at S. Fe & took pack mules to cross the mountains upon which the snow was from 12 to 18 inches in depth. We reached here on the 21st & found Capt Brown's Company, which left Santa Fe on 18 Oct, composed of the then sick & weakly, [now] well & hearty. Immediately on our arriving here we set to make some houses. We have several on hand though none finished.

The Fort is on the American side of the Arkansas river. The Mormon town or settlement is on the opposite side in the newly acquired territory of New Mexico. Touse is the capital of this district. [Charles] Bent of Bents

---

[48]For this letter from "Sister M," see Scott to Scott, 30 August 1846, in Chapter I.

Fort is the Govenor. The land is mostly prairie—tolerably fertile but in consequence of there being but little or no rain the fields have to be watered which is done by means of ditches. I fancy New Mexico & its inhabitants much resembles those of ancient Egypt as respects the mode of agriculture & manner of living. (Their plows are made similar to those represented in the Encyclopedia of Egypt[ian] make, of one solid piece of wood with a small iron point.) They keep large flocks of cattle, sheep & goats, which afford them an abundance of milk cheese & meat. This with a little corn or flour affords their subsistence. They have no fences, there being no timber. They keep their flocks herded during the day & penned at night. If you have read all the letters I have written you're aware that John D. Lee came on with the Battalion to Santa Fe for the purpose of taking back any funds the soldiers should send back. It has been reported here that on his return that he was shot by some Indians, about 40 miles below the crossing of the Arkansas. There were three men with him but the Indians fled & escaped.[49]

ARNOLD STEVENS TO MRS. LOIS STEVENS, MORMON BATTALION CORRESPONDENCE COLLECTION, LDS ARCHIVES.[50]

Fort Pueblo, December 25th 1846

My Dear Wife—

It is with much pleasure and great anxiety I take my pen at this time to inform you of my health and future prospects, through the mercy and blessings of our heavenly Father. I am comfortably situated and I think never enjoyed better health in my life and lack only the presence of my family and the Church to make me happy. You must know my anxiety is very great as I have not heard a word from you since Br. Lee left [for] the Bluffs and as I have not been able to make such remitances as I intended and as your necessities required not having received but a month and a half pay serves to increase my anxiety but still I hope and trust he who has fed us all our life long and hears the young ravens when they cry, will feed and clothe you also and that your lives and health may be precious in his Sight, is my constant prayer.

---

[49]Scott's letter ends unsigned on the third page, suggesting there was another leaf, now lost. Lee encountered no serious problems on his return, but Pawnee raiders attacked Daniel P. Mann's wagons on 28 October 1846. Near the Arkansas crossing Mann's party warned Lee that he "would doubtless fall prey to the Indians." Lee told Indians he met on his return to Winter Quarters "that we were Mormons & friends of the Red men," yet he traveled "fearing the treachery of Indians." See Brooks, ed., "Diary of the Mormon Battalion Mission," 317, 320. Scott's familiar mention of Lee suggests that McCorkle had met him during one of Lee's several missions to Tennessee.

[50]This version of the letter is taken from a copy apparently made by Apostle Franklin D. Richards, who as LDS church historian was interested in the circumstances of his brother Joseph's death. The text from "2 men" is boxed on the manuscript, probably by F. D. Richards.

We are here about 140 of us, of which about eighty-five men and twenty women under command of Capt. Brown, camped here on the 6th November and in about one or two weeks we all got moved into our cabins. I am now dressing dear skins. I and my partner have dressed fifteen and can have all we can do; they are worth about two dollars a piece.

I traded my horse on my way to this place for a good mule. Our horses, mules and cattle live here and keep fat without feeding. It seldom rains here. There has been about two inches of snow twice, but no rain. We are in about twenty miles from the mountains that are covered with about nine feet of snow. They raise some corn here, but have to water their land for a crop, by taking the water out of the river in ditches. The corn is of an inferior quality and is the only thing cultivated here. There are men living here that have lived in California for six or eight years and have been almost in all parts of it and about Bear River and Salt Lake, they say it is a fine country and it rains in some parts, that it produces good crops, that it is mountainous and abound with bear, elk, deer, antelope, &c, and its waters abound with fish, geese, Indian Ducks &c, that the climate is mild. We are about three hundred miles from Fort Laramie and about the same distance from Grand Island. I had a talk with Captain Brown this evening. He thought it likely we would be paid off in the spring and discharged with provisions to last to the Bluffs, or to California.

As I have not been able to send you the means to get teams and provisions, I do not know whether you will be able to come on with the Church or not. If the way should open for you to come with as much provision as the Counsel thinks you will need and can get some one to drive your team, I will foot the bill; if not, make yourself and family as comfortable as you can until I come, and if I have good luck I shall have something to help my family along, only let me know as soon as possible and when you write again let me see your own handwriting and write the particulars. Let Lois Ann write some and Rachel and my dear little son Ransome Abraham. I can read it, if it is nothing but scant marks. My dear Lois, you know my family was always my delight, yet never knew how to prize or appreciate their society. There is scarcely a night passes, but I dream about you. I will tell you one or two of them: I dreamt the other night that I saw you coming towards me, looking very pensive, and Lois Ann and Rachel, behind you, appeared as though they had been crying, but did not see Ransome at all; that troubled my mind a good deal. Again I dreamed of going out of my house where it appeared that I lived, and as I went out, it appeared that I went into a wheat field, where the wheat was cut down and lay as though it had been kept there. I saw Br. Brigham Young and Br. Parley P. Pratt, the latter appeared to be laughing. I cast my eyes to the southeast and saw a wonderful black cloud and it came up with great fury. I said to them, this wheat ought to be took up before it sours, and we all three went to taking it up, but I could bring as fast as both of them. After we had taken it nearly all up, I recollected they had come from the Bluffs, and said, do you know any of my family? Br. Pratt laughed and Br. Young said, they were all well but Nancy and that she was as good as dead. I also saw two men from Perry County, Illinois, which said they had come after me to go and preach to them. So much for dreams. I expect you will have an opportunity of writing soon, I want you to write how soon the Church will start. Whether you can get a fit out, and do not start without counsel, I shall have some clothing for you and the children if I can bring it. I expect we shall be discharged in March. If you can hear anything from Henry or David or the Adamses let me know. I have many things to write and will write every opportunity, and you must do the same. I told you my health was good, I only weigh two hundred and five pounds.

I must now close, the mail will leave this next Sunday. I will send Ransom Abram a Christmas gift. (Yours I will keep until I see you; if I can get anything for the girls I will.) Give them my love, and may the Lord bless you all.

Farewell pray for me.
Arnold Stevens

As John Steele's diary will reveal, neither James Scott nor Arnold Stevens would ever see their families again.

Capt. James Brown: I Have It Imprinted in My Heart

The orders given Capt. James Brown that sent him to Pueblo were less than definitive, leaving open the question of how the detachments would be deployed and finally discharged. Brown wrote Brigham Young shortly after Christmas asking for instructions, while Arnold Stevens sent the Mormon leader a more personal request for advice and news about his family.

Brown to Young, Brigham Young Collection, LDS Archives.

Purbelow Newmexico
December the 27th 1846

To the presidencies of the Church of Jesus Chirst of Latterday Saints

Dear Brethren   I take my pen in hand to address you a few Lines to Let you no where I am and what I am doing. I landed in Purbelow with my Command on the 15 of Nov, Captain Higgins Report[ed] his detachment to me on the 24th Nov. We have all got in Comfortable dwellings for the winter. Lieutenant Willes reported his detachment to me on the 20th of December. They are building [cabins and] which mak[es] 170 Agrigate under my Command. We draw our provisions from Bents fort 75 miles belowe Purbelow. I am Indevoring to govern the me[n] under my Command by the ~~Laws~~ military Laws of the United States and the instructions I received from the presedicies [*sic*] of the Church at Council Blufs for I have it imprentid in my hart for I received it as the word of the Lord and by the power of the preasthood, and [by] the grace of God I will do it and Carry out the principals for which I was sent.

Pray for me brethren that I may be able to do all things that I do in righteousness.

I was Sents [*sic*] with my Detachment to qu[a]rter at Purbelow untell Spring and untell I received further orders. I was sent to this post by Colonel Doniphan who told Captain Hunt and my self that he was going to wright to the president of the United States respecting our further movements and would give me orders as he received them from the president. Doniphan has left the post at Santafee for Chewauwe. The Command at santefe is left with Col Price. I received orders from price to hold my self and Company in rediness for an attack from the indians or to go on to them when Called for. There has bin one train of provisions waggons robed and a grate deal of Government property Stolen by the Indians and it is thought goverment will give them Trouble unless there is a Tretie made.

I[t] is Supposed by some that we shall be Discharged in Purbelow and paid off—I want some Council what we shall do in Case we are discharged hear. My detachment included all the sick and weakly and Landers [laundress] women belonging to the Battalion. When I left Santafeer 2 men dide [died] on [the] march from Santafe to purbe Low, Viz, Milton Smith and Abner Chase. Joseph Richards Dide after we arive at Purbelow. He had knowledge of his death and Cawled me in and Requested I Should seal him up into eternal Life. He was a lovely young man and has gohn home to sleep with his fathers.

The health of my Command is first rate at this time. There is only 4 on the sick list at this time and they are all better. My health is better than it has bin for fou[r] month[s]. I put Roswell Stephans on detached servis to Council Bluffs. I wish him to return as soon as possible for I fear my Superear Officers will tak[e] some advantage of Liberties I have given him.

Give all my respects to all Saint[s]. Yours with respect.

Jas. Brown

STEVENS TO YOUNG, BRIGHAM YOUNG COLLECTION, LDS ARCHIVES.
Presedent B. Yong [*sic*]
Dear Sir I feel happy To have an oppertunity of addressing few Lines to

you and Solicit a Little of your Counsel as I consider my self Subject to your Counsel in all things. As I have not received my pay as was anticipated I have not been able to Send my famaly as much means as they will need. I wish you to inquire into there Circumstances and if it is necessary for me to come there when discharged let me know by the Return of the mail. The Sick among us are getting there health and We are all in good Spirits and expect to get our Pay and Discharge between this and the first of May and we Shall be able to Return to the church and our famalyes. Pray for us. I beg Leave to Subscribe My Self your obedient Son

Arnold Stevens
Fort Peublo December 27–1846

George D. Wilson: Expecting a Revolution Every Day

Part of Lt. W. W. Willis' command remained stranded in New Mexico. On 27 December Willis sent Cpl. Gilbert Hunt "to bring up the sick" left at Turley's Mill. Hunt made good time crossing the mountains and found all the men in good health except George Coleman, who had died of exposure. Sgt. Richard Brazier and Hunt led the men to Pueblo, with adventurer George Frederick Ruxton following their tracks. Ruxton was a brilliant young British Army officer—and perhaps intelligence operative—with a considerable talent for writing descriptive prose. "There were some twelve or fifteen of them," he recalled, "raw-boned fanatics, with four or five pack mules carrying their provisions." He found the men "straggling along, some seated on the top of the mules' packs, some sitting down every few hundred yards, all looking tired and miserable." Ruxton noted "the several piles twigs, of the sagebrush and rushes" the men had used as beds on Culebra Creek, but observed that they had not provided water for their animals. At their camp at the head of El Vallecito, he found two frozen mules, the consequences of this carelessness.[51]

George Wilson's diary described a pleasant stay at Turley's mill at Arroyo Hondo, but he failed to record the most difficult part of the trip—the crossing of the Sangre de Cristo Mountains. Wilson also captured the tension between the native population and their new conquerors that would soon explode into violence.

---

[51]Hafen, ed., *Ruxton of the Rockies*, 105–07, 195, 202, 206.

GEORGE DELIVERANCE WILSON, JOURNAL, UTAH STATE HIST. SOC.

Wednesday [16 December 1846]. I am well and in a house 10 miles above Touse. Governor [Charles] Bent is an old Smugler and not well received by the Spanish. Great talk of an insurrection and retaking Santafee. I expect to go this evening to see a sick brother that is left behind, O God of Salvation have favor and blessing for us in the name of Jesus I pray.

Tuesday 22nd 1846 December. Our brethren are now at Alpasso and there to wait. They are to have 14 pieces [of artillery] to guard and that is all I know about them.[52] As for us we are 14 of us at a place 9 miles north of Touse waiting for assistance from Purbelow to carry the sick.

Crismas Day. 12 miles above Touse. Have the headache to day. Caught cold yesterday and last evening drank whiskey or punch which I think is very unhealthy on it being just from the copper still which made it poisonous indeed and nearly made us all sick.

Crismas Dec. 25th 1846.

Brother Maxey [Maxwell] has gone to Touse to find the truth concerning Br. Coleman which was left there sick and supposed to have been murdered and is heard from today. [He was] found in the mire. The truth is yet to be learned concerning this matter. It is bad policy to divide the brethern, especially to leave the sick behind among the Spaniards as Lt Willis has done in this case. Who must be gilty of this mans blood, God knoweth.

Dec 28 in comfortable quarters this day at turleys being my [thirty-ninth] birth day.

Jan 1st 1847. Our party now in quarters hold a new years feast and drink to[o] much. Expecting a revolution every day.

Jan 2, 1847. This day Corpl [Gilbert] Hunt & [Pvt. Thomas] Bingham arrive to escort us to Purbelow. Brings an order from Lt Willis not to give me any rations but order me to march to Purbelow and Buy my rations [and] carry my rations knapsack and equipage and be there by the time the other men are that have their things carried. This march being 150 miles in the snow was remarkable severe it being very cold. Ordered under threats of being reported a deserter and treated as such altho I had leave to stay behind by the Lt.

Having been sick for one day before they came, I wanted to know if he presisted [sic] in carrying out the order. Yes says Corpl Hunt, I'm bound to. So I start on this journey finding myself every thing And as to rations I had

---

[52]Wilson had picked up incorrect information about Cooke's plans. Writing from Santa Fe on 6 December 1846, R. S. Elliott reported that Willis' men had told him "that Captain C. had given up the idea of going to California at present with the Mormon Battalion, but would march to El Paso del Norte to winter, and endeavor to refit his transportation. But Col. [Samuel C.] Owens and Mr. [Edward] Glasgow think that the report cannot be correct." See Gardner and Simmons, eds., *The Mexican War Correspondence of Richard Smith Elliott*, 125.

no money to buy with but the kindness of heaven provides for all these things [as] necessities.

Jan 5th 1847. On the road to Purbelow not being able to eat my blood weak and my feet frozen and a back load to carry. At 4 oclock I sunk down exhausted on the wilderness Praire the cold winds blowing and no man near but God was my friend and I lived through it. Travelled untill late in the evening and found the camp by the sound of a gun. This was the nearest Death by cold and sickness and oppression and the narrowes[t] escape of my life. My spirit was turned to praying for life and also like David to cursing my enemy That they might fall into the same pit they had digged for my soul. Even so, amen.

Jan 15th. Arrived at Purbelow and glad to get there. I have found friends and Brethern on this trip plenty and also at Purbelow.

Jan 24th. Been kindly received by my old mess mates Skein [Joseph Skeen] [Pvt. William R.] Tubbs and others and have rested in my quarters almost constantly. I hear of the Spanish have revolted and killed all the Americanos Americans at Turleys place and at Touse. Not heard from Santafee yet.

News of the revolt in New Mexico created a sensation in the American settlements on the Arkansas River. Wilson and his companions had made a narrow escape, for on 19 January 1847 the Taos Rebellion erupted. After killing the first American governor of New Mexico, Charles Bent, at Taos, rebels laid siege to Simeon Turley's mill on 21 January 1847, set it afire after a day-long battle, and killed Turley and six of his men.[53] With the arrival of the Brazier and Hunt party, all of the battalion's people who would winter at Fort Pueblo had reached the post. There they would spend a pleasant season disturbed only by the abuses of their inept leaders, and with spring most of the Saints on the Arkansas would decamp for the Salt Lake Valley.

---

[53]For an account of the battle at Turley's mill based on what was known at Pueblo, see Hafen, ed., *Ruxton of the Rockies*, 221–24.

"WE MUST GO TO SALT LAKE"
The Detachments

After visiting El Pueblo in January 1847, George Frederick Ruxton painted a colorful picture of life that winter on the "wide and well-timbered bottom of the Arkansas." The Mormons raised a street of log shanties, "built of rough logs [with] the interstices filled with mud, and rendered impervious to wind or wet." At its end stood "the 'church' or temple—a long building of huge logs, in which prayer-meetings and holdings-forth took place." Ruxton found these people "a far better class than the generality of Mormons, and comprised [of] many wealthy and respectable farmers from the western states, most of whom were accustomed to the life of woodmen, and were good hunters." They were able "to support their families upon the produce of their rifles, frequently sallying out to the nearest point of the mountains with a wagon, which they would bring back loaded with buffalo, deer, and elk meat, thereby saving the necessity of killing any of their stock of cattle, of which few remained."[1]

On a "verry pleasant" 20 January, the Mormons "raise[d] a meeting house 32 by 15," and two days later they "chunked dobed covered and made a door to our meeting house." On the night of the twenty-third, "we chrisened our meeting house by a fandango opened by prayer."[2] Perhaps to celebrate this very event, the Mormons invited a party of mountaineers to join one of their "frequent fandangos," but the guests "were rather taken aback by finding themselves in for a sermon" before the "physical exercises." Ruxton heard "Cap'en Brown," a "hard featured,

---

[1] Ruxton, *Life in the Far West*, 204. Sgt. Joel Terrell noted on 17 November 1846 that his mess arrived at Pueblo with "between 90 and 100 cattle, and some 16 or 18 mules in our care." Ruxton's comment suggests that by January 1847 the Mormons had lost a number of animals.

[2] Joel J. Terrell, Diary, 20 January 1847.

black-coated man of five-and-forty, correctly got up in his black contin-
uations and white handkerchief round his neck, a costume seldom seen
at the foot of the Rocky Mountains," deliver the homily. Assisting was
Absolam Porter Dowdle, the civilian leader of the Mississippi Saints, "a
long tallow-faced man, with black hair combed over his face." Brown, a
former Baptist preacher, felt "like holding forth a little this afternoon,
before we glorify the Lord." He provided his astonished audience with a
remarkable discourse on the doctrine of polygamy and Mormon plans
in the West.

> As there are a many strange gentlemen now-a-present, it's about right to tell
> 'em-a-what our doctrine just is, and so I tells 'em right off what the Mor-
> mons is. They are the chosen of the Lord; they are the children of glory, per-
> secuted by the hand of man: they flies here to the wilderness, and, amongst
> the *Injine* and the buffler, they lifts up their heads, and cries with a loud
> voice, Susannah, and hurray for the promised land! Do you believe it? I *know*
> it.
>
> They wants to know whar we're going. Whar the church goes—thar we
> goes. Yes, to hell, and pull the devil off his throne—that's what we'll do. Do
> you believe it? I *know* it.
>
> Thar's milk and honey in that land as we're goin' to, and the lost tribes of
> Israel is thar, and will jine us. They say as we'll starve on the road, bekase
> thar's no game and no water; but thar's manna up in heaven, and it'll rain on
> us, and thar's prophets among us as can make the water "come." . . . And
> now, what have the Gen*tiles* and the Philis*tines* to say against us Mormons?
> They says we're thieves, and steal hogs; yes, d——— 'em! they say we has as
> many wives as we like. So we have. I've twenty–forty, myself, and mean to
> have as many more as I can get.[3] But it's to pass unfortunate females into
> heaven that I has 'em—yes, to prevent 'em going to roaring flames and
> damnation that I does it.[4]

MARY BLACK BROWN: DAYS OF SORROW

As editor LeRoy Hafen noted, Ruxton's *Life in the Far West* "is fictionalized history. The story is not a reliable historical chronicle, but it is
factual." Ruxton's account of the Mormon sermons at Pueblo appears to
be exaggerated, but a letter by one of James Brown's wives indicates this

---

[3]A descendant recalled that Brown "had a total of thirteen wives" and twenty-four children. See Hill,
Biography of Captain James Brown, 4.

[4]Ruxton, *Life in the Far West*, 204–05.

tale of the Latter-day Saint festival was, as Ruxton said of his book, "*no fiction*."[5] Although the doctrine of plural marriage officially remained a secret until 1852, the Mormons openly practiced it once they reached the West.[6] The journals confirm that polygamy was a main theme of Mormon sermons at Pueblo. John Steele wrote in March that his spiritual leaders were "preaching now prety large" and the "whole Scistom [system] of the Spirritual Wife Doctrine is now unfolded. It is now no longer a secret and six or eight jentiles there from Missoury they know all about it now." George Wilson noted that Captain Brown "preached up the Sprt'l [spiritual] wife doctrine," boasting that he "meant to have 100 wives."[7]

Wife number five was Mary McCree Black Brown, and her story reveals some of the human consequences of these beliefs. Born 28 October 1816 in Mississippi, she was the daughter of a physician "of some note." She married George D. Black in 1837 and gave birth to five children, including a son named after his father. After their conversion by Elder Daniel Tyler in 1843 the family moved to Nauvoo, Illinois. Her husband and two daughters died of malaria in 1845, and the widow went home to Mississippi, where "the angel of death visited her" again and claimed her remaining daughters. Upon her return to Nauvoo, her son "was stricken with malaria." Brigham Young baptized the boy in the Mississippi "for his health," and "he was made well and strong again." The widow Black crossed Iowa in 1846 in James Brown's company and became his plural wife in Council Bluffs on 16 July—the date of the battalion's enlistment—in a marriage of convenience based on her belief that the union would insure not only her own salvation, but that of her dead husband. Mary Brown "was advised to accompany" Brown on the march, and she agreed on condition that "she might be allowed to take her son." She also cared for an unnamed child of Brown's by a previous wife. As one of the official laundresses, "Her duty was to do the laun-

---

[5]Hafen, "Introduction," in Ibid., xvi.

[6]For an overview of the doctrine and its history, see Hardy, *Solemn Covenant: The Mormon Polygamous Passage*, 1–38.

[7]George D. Wilson, Journal, 8 March 1847. The Mormons shared their beliefs with Pueblo's native inhabitants, for on 13 December 1846 James Brown "preached on the resurrection—some of the lamanitish women being present." Both Higgins and Brown on 7 February 1847 testified "verry ablay and emphaticly to what had been secret and several of the lamonites being preasant the meeting went off first rate." See Joel J. Terrell, Diary, LDS Archives.

dry for sixteen men which called for days of hard work that she was not accustomed to do." On the march "the sick learned to bless her gentle hand," and tradition recalls that she "went among them as a ministering angel." She later said, "I wasn't afraid of anything—but the wolves."[8] By the time she wrote this letter to her former brother-in-law, her fate had "turned out far distant from what I fain would have realized."

MARY MCCREE BLACK BROWN TO CURTIS BLACK,
MORMON BATTALION CORRESPONDENCE COLLECTION, LDS ARCHIVES.

Purblow Dec 21[st] 1846

My Dear Brother,

I embrace the present opertunity of sending you this letter to inform you of my present situation as I believe it will be satisfaction to you to know I and my little boy enjoy good Health and have done since we left the bluffs but I have seen menny trubls and days of sor[r]ow since that time. And I expect that I shall see menny more, as things has turned out far distant from what I fain would have realized but I hope the day is not far distant when I shall have the pleasure of sitting down with you and conversing on thing[s] to[o] teadious to mention in this short Communication, but I will mention a few things that you may know the cause of my truble. The treatment which I have received from Mr. Brown fully sho[w]es to me his inability to bring me and my husband that is dead into an Exalted Stetion which is the greatest Blessing that I desire and which alone is worth Living for while here upon the Earth but I intend that when I return to the Church and the Bosem of my Dear Friends that I by the Councell of the Twelve will be enabled to do things in a way that Shall be for My Honour, and the Exaltation of my departed Husband which if I can acomplish threw the blessing of god will be a matter of Everlasting Joy and satisfaction to me and I have no doubt but what you will do all you can to help me that I may obtain the desire of my Hart for in the Dreams and visions of the night it has been shoe [*sic*] me that my Salvation will be obtained threw my Husband's Family.[9] I hope that by this time you are all together with the Church but if not I wish you to write them a Letter and Let them Know from me that I am well. If you see Hendry show him this letter tell him that I had a singular dream about him.

---

[8]Biographical information is from Brown, "With the Camp Fires of the Mormon Battalion," 306–08; Minnie Black Garner's sketch in Carter, ed., "Women and Children of the Mormon Battalion," 481–82; Carter, ed. *The Mormon Battalion*, 100; and Ricketts, *The Mormon Battalion*, 29, 32, 239.

[9]Joseph Smith taught that polygamy was an essential requirement to reach the highest "degrees of glory" and "to learn how to be Gods yourselves." In Smith's theology, a woman's full salvation depended on her husband. The more married a man became, the greater his ability to bring his wives to an "exalted station." See Smith's 6 April 1844 funeral sermon for King Follett, published in *Journal of Discourses*, 6:1–11.

I thought he came here to see me and told me that I was his Brothers Wife and as he was dead it was his Priveladge to have me and it was the order of the Kingdom of god and the god of Heaven had sent him to do his Brothers work, tell him that I shall tell him all about it when I see Him.[10]

I wish none to see this Letter but our own famley. Dear Brother altho I am here my hart is with you and I live in hope of seeing you all together as one famley when I return home. This hope cheers me in my solidtery moments and when I have to stand and here the insults of an unfeeling Mann my Prayer is

> Role fleeting moments role
> Impetious as the Rising Sunn
> That I may see the frends I Love
> When I the Soldiering race have Run

Give my best Love and feelings to sister Melinda and all the Rest if they have come on. No more at Present but with due Respect I remain your Loving Sister in the New and

Everlasting Covenant.
Mary Black

Mary Brown's dream of escape from her new husband was not to be, and she would settle with James Brown in today's Ogden as "the first white woman in Weber County." Seeing her isolated new home, she said, "This is a hard way to serve the Lord." She soon gave birth to a daughter, Mary Eliza. More than fifty years after the battalion march, Minnie Moore Brown asked, "Who can describe her appearance now? We can tell of the whitened head bowed by the years of the toil; of the toilworn patient hands; the sweet tremulous mouth; the bright eyes; but we cannot express the impression of her which we receive when talking to her or sitting in her presence. She is such a cheery little body—has such nimble fingers, and so very much to talk about." She "remained as patient and resourceful as she was forty years ago." Mary Brown died in Ogden, Utah, in 1906. She may have achieved the fondest desire of her heart, for LDS temple records reveal that George D. Black was posthumously sealed to her on 27 March 1877 in the Endowment House in Salt Lake City.[11]

---

[10]Mrs. Brown proposed that her former brother-in-law marry her according to Old Testament tradition.

[11]Additional biographical information is from the George David Black Family Group Sheet available at the LDS Family History Library.

JOHN STEELE:
VERY MUCH TROUBLED WITH THE BIG HEAD

By the time the last stragglers from Willis' command arrived at Pueblo on 15 January 1847, there were some 275 Latter-day Saints assembled on the south bank of the Arkansas River, including about forty-seven women.[12] Made uneasy by the Taos revolt, some of the most colorful mountain men in the West congregated around "Mormon Town" and the trappers' fort, including Joe Doyle, Mark Head, John Hawkins, Maurice LeDuc, Lewis B. Myers, Bill New, George Simpson, "Uncle" Dick Wooton, and Delaware Indians Little Beaver and Jim Swanock.[13] Ruxton noted the "many really beautiful" girls who graced the town, "sport[ing] tall graceful figures at the frequent fandangos," and Wooton recalled that the mountaineers found "inexpressible joy in flirting with the Mormon girls, the first of their race many of them had beheld since they left civilization."[14] Ruxton's fictionalized *Life in the Far West* contained a tale he swore was true of a romance between a hunter named LaBonté and a Mormon girl first called Mary Chase and then Brand. LeRoy Hafen thought the hero might be Lewis B. Myers, who accompanied the Saints to Salt Lake, but Janet Lecompte is probably correct in identifying LeBonté as Bill New, who in 1848 married Mary Gibson, member of one of the two families of Mississippi Saints who stayed behind at Pueblo.[15]

Two of the most prominent local citizens, James Waters and John Brown, Sr., were later sometime-Mormons, but "Old Rube," sixty-seven-year-old Valentine Johnson Herring, "became a convert to the Mormon creed" at Pueblo, holding "forth its wonderful doctrines to such of the incredulous trappers as he could induce to listen to him." Old Rube "was never without the book of Mormon in his hand, and his sonorous voice might be heard, at all hours of the day and night, reading passages from its wonderful pages." He badgered his comrades "and said there

---

[12]Thomas Bullock's August 1847 "Names of Pueblo Soldiers and Mississippi Brethren arrived in Great Salt Lake City" listed 275 names, including those of several deserters and soldiers who died on detached service.

[13]These names are drawn from a number of sources, especially Lecompte and Ruxton.

[14]Lecompte, *Pueblo, Hardscrabble, Greenhorn*, 182.

[15]Ruxton, *Life in the Far West*, 236–40; and Lecompte, *Pueblo, Hardscrabble, Greenhorn*, 183.

never was such a book as that ever before printed; that the Mormons were the 'biggest kind' of prophets, and theirs the best faith ever man believed in."[16] Old Rube's enthusiasm would blow hot and cold for the next ten years.

An Arapaho war party "on their way to fight the Utas" camped briefly at the settlement, "tall, fine appearin[g] wariors armed and equipt for the fray, drest in fighting custom and painted to look like old Nick." Ruxton later met these twenty-one men under Coxo (or Game Leg) on Fountain Creek, "painted and armed for war, carrying bows and well-filled quivers, war clubs and lances, and some had guns in deerskin covers. They were all naked to the waste." Ruxton thought each one "could have sat as a model for an Apollo." They told the Mormons "they were agoing to mash the Utas," but in "about two weeks they come sneaking back. They had found more Utas than they wanted and had lost most of their wariers."[17]

To an Englishman it appeared to be a hard winter on the high plains, "exceedingly severe; storms of sleet and snow, invariably accompanied by hurricanes of wind, were of daily occurrence," but the snow seldom stayed on the ground for long. New England native Henry Sanderson called it the "mildest winter I had ever experienced." The hard-working Mormons found a number of money-making opportunities at the settlement, including irrigating. Sanderson, John Sessions, and John Hess "took a small job of building a canal, and I assisted them, spading and shoveling. I worked steadily and hard."[18] Given the entertaining neighbors, warm quarters, and abundance of food, life at Pueblo should have been good for the soldiers, but their inept officers appeared determined to make it hard.[19] Despite repeated attempts to enforce military discipline, the death of several beloved comrades undermined morale, but the men were unaffected by the general panic that followed news of the Taos revolt. "Excitement and alarm prevail everywhere," George Wilson

---

[16]Bagley, ed., *Frontiersman*, 34–38, 48; and Ruxton, *Life in the Far West*, 206–07.

[17]Bagley, ed., *Frontiersman*, 49; and Ruxton, *Life in the Far West*, 231–32.

[18]Ruxton, *Life in the Far West*, 233; and Sanderson, A History Written by Henry Weeks Sanderson, 29.

[19]James Brown could not control his own officers, for he later claimed that Willis "had his orders from Colonel Price to report to me at Pueblo, but refused to do so, and went on his own hook." See Journal History, 29 July 1847, based on the short history (now apparently lost) that Brown compiled for church historian George A. Smith in 1859.

noted, "Everywhere but among the mormon soldiers who remain totally at ease." Nothing eroded the officers' authority and tried the isolated soldiers' patience like the greed and incompetence of their leaders. At the end of January Wilson wrote, "We were obliged to pay the goverment mules keeping and for our own fire wood and quarters out of our small rations of sugar and coffee rice candles soap vinegar &c. This was hard for the men to submit to. But there was no alternative." Wilson complained about miserly rations and the officers' secrecy. "What next," he asked on 5 February, "God only knows."[20]

JOHN STEELE, REMINISCENCES AND JOURNALS, 1846–1898,
LDS ARCHIVES.

On Thursday 24 [December 1846] it was soposed that two of our men Wm Casto and Jackson Shoop Diserted and on Friday 25 the men were all purraded and the [men] not being here to answer to their name ware seposed to have diserted and old man [Samuel] Gould & son John Knowling [Cpl. Jabez Nowlin] & others, Thomas Williams, Sergent, and others made themselves very busy running to the Captain carying all the news the[y] could rake up and raising all the bad feeling among the men the[y] could, and therefore there was a number of our Boys Tied up and closely guard until the Captain, Sergent [Orson Bennett] Adams & [Ebenezer Joseph] Hanks would return from searching after them men & on Satturday 26 they all returned deserters & all and when the truth was known the[y] ware only out Hunting and on Sunday 27 all peace and Quietness only & deep determination to have satisfaction of our Little petty offisers.[21] There is still grate Harshness used by our offisers and we are purraded three times pr day [and] all privileges are taken from us.

Sunday 3rd of January 1847. There has been told this day that Captain Brown is something above all the men that is here in priestly authority & he has told us often that we do not know who he is he is so high.[22] We all feel the hands of Tyrants. There is not a privilege but what is taken from us.

Nothing of any consequence took place unto Monday the 11. There was a call made for volinteers to build an House to preach in and nearly all the

---

[20]George D. Wilson, Journal, 6 March 1847, 13–14.

[21]Pvts. William Casto and Andrew Jackson Shupe wanted to accompany mail carriers Thomas Woolsey and John Tippets to Winter Quarters and had in fact deserted. Brown with Sgts. Adams and Hanks (and apparently John Steele) "overtook them and brought them back, court-martialed them, fining each one of them to haul 5 loads of wood as punishment." See Beckwith, ed., "Journal of John Steele," 14.

[22]Brown's boast indicates he had received his Second Anointing, a temple rite that "sealed and ordained 'kings and priests' [and] 'queens and priestesses' to God." See Buerger, *The Mysteries of Godliness: A History of Mormon Temple Worship*, 62–63.

compy turned out which caused the captain to say that all our former privileges should be restored to us and Tuesday 13th Captains Brown & Higgans, Lieutenants Luddington & W. W. Willis called the three detachments together and read the *following laws* that there be no Card playing in the company nor Dancing and any soldiers or Laundress that should be found speaking against an offiser should be put under guard and if a woman she should be discharged and that the houses of the soldiers should be cleared of any of their brethren that might be visiting and no one was to be found out of his quarters after 8 oclock at night under the penalty of being sent to the Guard House and tried by a Court Martial next day.

That is the way that our former privileges are restored. That is the way that we have the privileges of Saints. It is Martial Law in the Extreme and he says we are a first-rate set of Boys and is that a way to treat good Boys to curtail them of every privilege?

On Sunday 10/Monday 11 there was a Grand sight seen about 9 oclock A.M. The sun shone out clear and bright and a rainbow back down to the sun another back up to the sun another Clear pale Light shone round the Whole Heavens with the aperance of four artificial suns as you will see from the drawing on the frontpiece.[23] It continued four hours and then disapeared.

Nothing of any consequence took place through the week Except a Tempel to be built opposit to the row of houses that was built for Baracks. The Boys turned out Generaly, but when they found that the[y] were going to Compell them to build a Guard House only 3 or 4 turned out and the House was not put up at the appointed time.

Sunday 17th Jany. All peace. There has [been] 9 waggons arrived from St A. Fee with provisions for 60 days.[24] Tuesday 19th our Boys are nearly all off hunting.

On Sunday Captain B made quite a speech to us on purade. He softsoaped as much as he was able telling us that it was very likely that we would be detained in the service of Uncle Sam after our time (or year) would be out and that he had got the promise (if there would be any more Mormon Battalions raised) that he should be the one that would go and raise them and then said he I shall be a Colnol then and I will help the poor with the pay that I shall get and said he you all look fat & fine and if you all go a Hunting Except 6 [men], 5 must stand guard. I think he is very much troubled with the Big Head. Tuesday 19. One of our Brethren dyed, named John

---

[23]The microfilm copy of Steele's journal at LDS Archives does not include this image. However, Joel Judkins Terrell's manuscript letter to Respected nephew, Mormon Battalion Correspondence Collection, contains a sketch of "This Phenomenon [which] appeared on 9th January 1847." It shows two sets of concentric circles, the smaller intersecting the larger.

[24]Actually "9 wagons came from Bents Fort with 60 days rations." See Beckwith, ed., "Journal of John Steele," 14.

Pirkins and was buried on Wednesday 20 at the root of a large Cotton-wood.[25]

This day Monday Jan 25 as we were about to prepare supper news arrived that Toes [Taos] was in a state of arms and all the white people ware killed and at Turleys 12 miles from Toes the[y] had assembled for protection and shut their gates and put chords of wood behind each gate. This scarcely done when 500 Spaniards hove in sight [and] fought them all day but night being drawing on the[y] did not do any thing to morning. Morning came bringing Death. Eight Americans being at Turleys put the Spaniards to flight but a reinforcement of the Pueblo Indians came to the Spaniards assistance at night then they burned their gates killing all that could not get away. Governor Bent of Bents Fort got killed, Turley got wounded and [is] soposed by this time to be dead. Grait excitement prevails. The man who brought the news said he believed he had killed 8 spaniards himself & got there in two days on foot with a narrow escape several balls being shot through his hat.[26]

Things are a getting ready for to receive the Spaniards up to this date 4th of February Thursday. Monday all the Kettle [cattle] were to be gathered in and be sent to a place of safe keeping with twelve men to guard them and all things are to be in readiness against any immergency whether to fight or flee and all the Horses Mules & other Kettle are being gathered in. We had two Spaniards prisoners one got away the same Evening the other two or three days [later] & to boot taking three mules along. All the families that live around are gathering into safe Quarters.

Friday 5 [February 1847]. This day I am called to relate the death of one of our Beloved Brethren, [James A.] Scott, belonging to Lieut. Willeses detachment. I followed his last remains to the silent tomb. A number of our sisters accompanyed the corps. A company of fine looking soldiers accom-panyed the corpse with sholdered arms under the command of lieut. Willis. When the body was laid in the grave, Brother [John Darwin] Chase had a few remarks upon the Deceased. Said he probably said he [*sic*]—He is gone to the courts above to cary news respecting our Batalion and said he in the morning of the first resurrection he will come forth for he has fell a sleep in Jesus. After that the soldiers fired three volies of musquitry & then retired, leaving the pall bearers to cover up the Grave.

There has been considerable excitement here this last few days. There has been arrangements went into of different sorts. Captain B[row]n & Lieuts.

---

[25]Pvt. John Perkins, Co. C, was born in Bath, England, and died of a lingering illness shortly before his twenty-sixth birthday.

[26]John Albert carried word of the attack to Fort Pueblo, "which threw the fierce mountaineers into a perfect frenzy." See Hafen, ed., *Ruxton of the Rockies*, 219–20. For the Taos rebellion and Albert's account of the battle at Turley's mill, see Hafen, ed., *The Mountain Men*, 2:23–25, 48.

Ludington & Willis went to Bentsfort and at last succeeded in getting a grant from the Quarter Master of four months provisions and sufficient Teams to haul it and to send Lieutnt Willis with 60 men to guard them to such time as the[y] could get away for said they there is no doubt but St. Afee is taken and we will not be able to get any word from that quarter.

The arrangements being made and all being Right and the offisors just having returned there came a messenger & a letter telling that the Spaniards ware routed. St Afee having received the word sent an army to Toes under the command of Colnol Price with a number of pieces of artillery. Colnol P being some distance ahead was taken prisoner but his troops coming up he was soon Rea taken. The Pueblo Indians & Spaniards got into a Spanish Church [and] the artillery began to play but made no impression only cut a hole as big as the Ball. The soldiers rushed fore word and cut a whole in the wall by which an entrance was made. One man got shot through the thigh. The mob rushed out at the door [but] the cannon laid them low. 270 met the fate that the[y] well diserved.[27] This news arrived on the 23 which altered all our calculations.

25 [February 1847]. One of our company died this evening named Melsier Oiler [Melcher Oyler]. He has been sick almost from [the time] we started. There has been two births one Thomas Williams one James Shoope [Shupe] and one marriage, & Corporal Chase married to Captain Higgan's daughter.[28]

JOHN STEELE: A PERFECT MASTERPIECE

William Bird had written to Brigham Young in December that the "conduct of Capt. Brown towards his troops is outrageous and that many of the Bat. were as ungodly as the Gentiles."[29] By early March the Mormon settlement on the Arkansas was in disarray. Ruxton had noted "there was a little rivalry in the way of preaching" between James Brown and the leader of the Mississippi Saints, Porter Dowdle.[30] Brown won the contest when the civilians "agreed to accept the authority of Captn Brown." Brown immediately "cutt off from the church" Joel Terrell "for nought but circumstantial evidence." William Tubbs refused to testify

---

[27] The ruins of the Church of San Gerónimo de Taos, site of this battle at Taos Pueblo, are now off-limits to tourists.

[28] Albina Merrill Williams gave birth to daughter Phoebe Isabell on 15 January 1847. Sarah Coates Shupe, wife of Pvt. James Wright Shupe of Co. C, gave birth to Elizabeth Margaret on 2 March. Cpl. John Darwin Chase married Nelson Higgins' sixteen-year-old daughter Almira. See Larson, *A Data Base of the Mormon Battalion* 48, 154–55, 187–88.

[29] Kelly, ed. *Journals of John D. Lee*, 117.

[30] Ruxton, *Life in the Far West*, 205.

against either Terrell or Thomas R. Burns, who was called to answer charges before Dowdle "for misdoing."[31] What these dramas accomplished is a mystery, but Captain Brown undercut his claims of spiritual authority by abusive behavior, "blowouts and long preaches," and a zealous attempt to build up his polygamous kingdom. General confusion over the detachments' destination led to a further erosion of morale. Brown left for Santa Fe to sort out the fate of his command and Willis went for Bent's Fort to pick up supplies, but the comedy began with renewed vigor on their return.

Nothing better illustrates the leadership crisis at Pueblo than the episode that began when a poem lampooning "a graceless Captains heart" spread throughout the command:

> Old Blaso he would quickly be
> Ass wiper in eternity
> And many a spiritual wife of course
> Be ceiled for better or for worse
> O blessed church maid with you I part
> To cheer our graceless heroes heart

"It all means me," James Brown protested, and both Higgins and Willis pointed to parts of the poem and said, "That means me." The author—George Deliverance Wilson—was correctly "suspected with others of writing it." Wilson believed the insulted parties secretly resolved "he shall die whoever wrote it." On 4 March 1847 the officers secured the camp and ordered their men to form a hollow square. The officers tried to "scare [the] men to see if they could find who wrote" the poem. Claiming they were looking for stolen property, they searched the camp for Wilson's journal, which, he noted, "I took care of. I expected there would be a very bad time of it from the spirit shown by curses oath and other threats so I called in the Lord to give me a strong spirit & calm mind."

Nelson Higgins named Wilson as the versifier and denounced his poetry as "the worst in the world trash of no account." With an unstated but sinister threat, Higgins noted the poem was "of the same spirit that murdered the prophets." If the women wanted to ride such a man "up

---

[31]George D. Wilson, Journal, 6 March 1847, 15. The chronology of this section of Wilson's journal is confusing and its legibility marginal, so its contents are summarized in the following paragraphs.

and down the streets all day" he would not stop them. "Damnable" said
another officer, "over and over." Lieutenant Willis called the poem "the
grandest piece of composition he ever seen" and its "disaffected mutinous spirit entirely unjustifiable." Brown climaxed the spectacle by saying he "had a sneaking spirit ever since he [had] known" Wilson, and
charged "every word was furnished [by] some d–md rascal disappointed
in love. Continuous damning" followed, and Brown again leveled a
deadly charge: the poem showed "The spirit that killed the prophets,
Joseph &c." The officers said there were now two parties at Pueblo—
Brown's and Wilson's. "We'll give them hell in Purbelow," Willis sput-
tered, and if the officers "did not give them hell it would be because
powder wood not burn."

Willis offered five dollars to anyone who would turn in the poet, but
no one betrayed the author. Wilson and William Tubbs decided to leave
their "quarters on account of persecution," and on 6 March Wilson was
"alone in one of the holes of the mountains writing." Two days later he
and Tubbs had apparently returned to camp and were "alone in our
quarters." Sgt. Thomas Burns' "case was had over in private counsel" on
15 March, but "there was some difficulty in determining on which
clause of the Celestial Law they could put him out of the way." Captain
Brown wanted the "tares rooted up immediately." Wilson, Burns, Tubbs,
John Cazier "and others" decided that "if things are pushed to go to
Bents Fort and claim protection under the US laws" due to "the lousy
condition of the camp," which showed "the entire indifference" of the
officers. The officers retreated to a contrite position, and on 17 March
called the men together and said "many fine things" in "soft soap
speeches." Brown left for Santa Fe the next day and Willis went to pick
up wagons and supplies at Bent's Fort. A temporary peace returned to
the camp while its officers were gone.[32] John Steele's diary provides an
entertaining view of life at Mormon Town.

JOHN STEELE, REMINISCENCES AND JOURNALS, 1846–1898, LDS ARCHIVES.
   Nothing of any consequence took place up to this time of any account.
March 1, Monday. All peace. The grait Excitement is a getting over about
the Spaniards and our officers are agoing to St. Afee about the 10 of March.

---

[32]George D. Wilson, Journal, 6–15 March 1847, 14, 16, 17, 20–21. Thomas R. Burns' alleged descent
from poet Robert Burns may have cast suspicion upon him as the poem's author.

March 4 [1847]. This day we were all paraded after 9 oclock. All the guard called out & eight others to assist them in doing the business of the day. No man permitted to leave the ranks. Also a guard was called out to guard the houses that no woman might pass out nor in.

After a Holow square being formed Captain Higgans oponed the meeting by speaking about some poetry that has been soposed to be written by one of Lieutenant W. Willises company containing some slurrs as they say. I did not se[e] the writing myself but as W W Willis says it was a perfect masterpiece. But Captain Higgins says it was not but after a long purramble from all the commissioned officers but one we were dismissed after several names were called such as Wilson who was soposed to be the writer of the poetical verces, and was called a dmd rascal by C[aptain]. B[rown]. and he knew it.

March 7. It is said that all who wish to go to the Bluffs as to the Church are apostates from the true order of Heaven.[33] The Captn = Brown says that we must go to Salt Lake and there put in a crop of corn and wait there for the Church. There has been Letters as we sopose sent to us from the Bluffs for one of Bents Fort men said that there was a paccage rowled up for us & he forgot to bring them but as we soposed our officers would as the[y] ware there at that time trying to get us a fitout for Bear Valey and that he would bring them up to us but to our grait astonishment there were but three one for Captain B and one for Elroy Root the Capt Servant and one for some other one. Orders has now arrived that we must get an out fit and go to California soon.

Mar 18 Thursday. Captain Higgans purraded the men and mad[e] a bungland [bungled?] speech saying that we ought to be kind and have a forgiving spirrit and wanted us to pray for them, and out of a hundred & thirty men six or eight said they would. Then Cap B said he would Confess his sins before the Boys & partly confessed & tryied to smoth it over and asked the Boys if they would forgive him if he had done them any harm and promised to do better for the time to come. But next morning the Tromendious Oaths that came from his mouth was *Horible* & his *Common* word is God Dam their Souls to Hell—But I will have their Goddamned Throats Cut Just as if we were as many Negars in the south.

Things are now in peace since the Capt. & the Lieutenant are gone. There are preaching now pretty large in Pueblo. The whole Scistom [system] of the Spiritual Wife Doctrine is now unfolded. It is now no longer a secret and six or eight jentiles there from Missoury they know all about it now and for oughts I know all other mistreys are revealed and if all reports be true

---

[33]Despite this warning, Daniel and Harriet Brown, Thomas Burns, James Glines, and probably others returned to Council Bluffs rather than go west. See Ricketts, *The Mormon Battalion*, 251.

Widow Sharp[34] is united to Capt B and the Folks are told that none but men that stands high in athority can save them. This for fear the Soldiers would try to practise on the example set by their commander.

March 21. This day, 26 years ago at 4 oclock on a Wednesday morning I was ushered into this world and since that time I have passed through Many Trials both by Sea & Land.

March 28. This day I am called to Record the death of one of our Beloved brethren Arnold Stephans Corporal. He was taken sick on the 21 and continued still worse on to the 26 when a Blud vesal Bursted and he continually spit blud and on Sattarday 27 he called in Ebenezer Hanks & Orson Addams & made His will. His mule saddle & Bridle was to be given to his oldest son and all the rest of his effects to be given to his wife. So after he had finished he spit up a Grait mouthful of Blood and continued to get worse and at half past Seven oclock he gave up his spirrit to that God who gave it. All possible hast[e] was then made for his buireal. His Robes of white was then put on—Cap, shoes, & Apron—and while we ware a dressing Him the Blood oozed out of his mouth & Nose and on Sunday the 28 we interred him about two oclock among the rest. His Breathren marched to the Grave with the Honours of war and left him to sleep to the morning of the first resurrection.[35]

April 9 [1847]. This time the offisers returned from St Afee Bringing us word that there was no one there that had power to discharge us or to give us any orders to leave until Colnol Cairney returnes from California.[36] Things are going on a little better now than they have done for some time. But still there are some blow outs and long prieches of Lieutenant Ludington and Captain Higgans has brought some barrels of whisky from Tous that they payd $2½ dolars and sold it at 8 pr gal and the Boys are ageting themselves drunk as fools. One day when James Oakley was drunk Ludington came up and talked saucy to him and he said he would do as he dammed pleased. With this the Captain came up and said to poot that man under Guard. He said he did not care. With this the Cap got angry and snatched a

---

[34]Martha Jane Sargent Sharp, a laundress in Co. D, was the widow of Norman Sharp. She gave birth to a posthumous daughter, Sarah Ellen, at Pueblo on 28 November 1846. Mrs. Sharp married Pvt. Harley W. Mowrey of Co. C on 4 July 1847, and they were both buried at Vernal, Utah, in 1920. See Carter, ed., "Women and Children of the Mormon Battalion," 498–99.

[35]Corporal Stevens of Co. D "was handling a wild mule when he was dragged over some logs and hurt internally." See Beckwith, ed., "Journal of John Steele," 15. He was buried in the temple robes used in the Mormon endowment.

[36]John Hess recalled that Brown "took a guard of ten men, of which I was one." The party crossed "a high range of mountains" and found "we had to tramp the snow for miles so our pack animals could walk over it." Brown drew the pay at Santa Fe, "and we started on our return trip; got back to our quarters at Pueblo about the first of April, and found spring weather." See Wood, ed., "John W. Hess: With the Mormon Battalion," 52.

gun & baynet & swore he would run him through, and for sometime he was a mind to do it. After a while he got over it and began on the women and told them they were like an old Goose that had wore all the feath[ers] out of His tail and did not know their arce from a hole in the Ground and several very homly Expressions like that.

One day he [Captain Brown] called us out and told us that if we wanted our pay that we must sign the power of atorney and send him & Higgans to Stafe [Santa Fe] and he would charge us two and a half pr cent 2½ on all the moony that was Coming to us and there are over 8000$ dolars coming. That would amount to about 200 dolars that he will speculate out of us Boys. He said that it would tak[e] 13 mules at 10 dolars apiece, and some of the men that went to Stafee with him before said it would not cost him more than two dolars.[37]

Our Boys are all well and harty. More than fifty of them has got Horses and calculate to serve Uncal Sam no longer than the[y] can help. The weather is now warm and pleasant and good for an Express coming from the Bluffs which we are looking for daily. The Captain and Company has arrived from Stafee being gone 18 days and brings word that we are to go to California and to start on the 25 of May with 2½ months of provisions.

JOHN STEELE: ON TO HORSE CREEK

The frozen Arkansas started to break up on 17 March 1847. It soon froze again, but by the twenty-fourth "the ice moved bodily away" and "when the first robin appeared, the hunters pronounced the winter at an end." Brown and Higgins returned from Santa Fe on 18 May with "the soldiers' money and orders to march to California." At noon on 24 May the command began its trek up the Trappers Trail to Fort Laramie on the Oregon Trail.[38] Fur traders, explorers, and military expeditions had traversed the road along the front range of the Rocky Mountains for more than a decade, and it was so heavily used that by 1846 game had virtually vanished along parts of its course. The route would become part of the Cherokee Trail to California in 1849 and a main emigration corridor for Utah-bound emigrants from Texas during the 1850s.[39] The trail connected "a chain of trading posts, where whiskey and gunpowder

---

[37]Brown and Higgins made a second trip to Santa Fe on 1 May to collect back pay and get final orders. Abner Blackburn recalled that "the notorious" Sgt. Thomas Williams "crost the mountain to Taos and stole a band of horses" that he later sold to emigrants. See Bagley, ed., *Frontiersman*, 49.

[38]Hafen, ed., *Ruxton of the Rockies*, 233–34; and Tyler, *A Concise History*, 197.

[39]Melvin C. Johnson's forthcoming *Mormon Voices from Texas Dust* will tell the story of this forgotten Mormon emigrant trail.

are bartered for robes and tongues; it destroys soul and body,—man and beast together," wrote Philip St. George Cooke, recalling his 1845 reconnaissance. "Verily the golden calf of civilization has been raised far in the wilderness!"[40]

Compared with other episodes in the saga of the Mormons' Great Western Measure, the winter at Pueblo was quite pleasant. The Saints on the Arkansas certainly endured less "suffering and exposure" than their compatriots on the Missouri, and many of the Pueblo journals are brightened with hunting stories, cordial fandangos enjoyed with interesting neighbors, and the comic relief provided by the officers' conduct. The soldiers and emigrants did not leave Pueblo empty handed, "for their stay had been highly profitable," both in material goods and "certain ideas and skills" that would prove invaluable aids to survival in the Great Basin.[41]

As Janet Lecompte observed in her study of the trappers' settlement, the winter in Colorado assumed "a woeful image which the Mormons cherished and nourished for years afterward, until the legend of their stay on the Arkansas became as grim as an account of the plague." Yet the reality was not nearly so bleak: of the detached soldiers only fifteen men died (nine of them at Pueblo), some as a result of accident rather than illness, and more than 90 percent of the 159 soldiers in all three detachments survived their military service, a death rate not much higher than could be expected on the frontier. The several detachments gave the battalion's leaders a way to dispose of men too sick to march to California, but the commanders also used them to get rid of trouble makers and reduce the number of camp followers who would impede the unit's progress. While most of the detached men were probably either too sick or feeble to endure the rigors of a protracted march, their general health was remarkably good; when Brown's party reached Pueblo, only six of his men "were still sick." Interestingly the Mormon Battalion suffered only five additional casualties during its enlistment, suggesting that the general health of the unit was remarkably good, given the generally poor condition of its recruits and the cursory nature of their medical examinations at Council Bluffs.[42] These numbers also indicate that the sol-

---

[40]Cooke, *Scenes and Adventures in the Army*, 415–16.

[41]Lecompte, *Pueblo, Hardscrabble, Greenhorn*, 181, 186.

[42]Ibid., 180–81. In 1852 the annual mortality rate in the U.S. was between 1.24 and 1.55 percent of the population, or one death to every seventy-three living persons; see Ibid., 310n17. Total battalion casualties are from the roster in Ricketts, *The Mormon Battalion*, 283–290.

diers' medical care was not extraordinarily deficient—and if Dr. Sanderson was engaged in a conspiracy to murder his charges, he was not particularly successful.

Joseph Skeen found much of what happened at Pueblo that winter "too mean to mention." He recalled, "the officers would steel from us they would take every thing off the soldiers that they could and then curce them be cause the could not get more." Captain Brown was "as big a raskel as ever graced the soil of purbelow he took some of the cattle that belonged to the government and put his own brand on them and many things he done that the Devil is A shamed of." Lieutenant Willis went "hand and hand with brown in every thing that he does." Brown "left a stink behind him when he left purbelow."[43]

One small band of Mississippi Saints left Pueblo about the first of May, but Capt. James Brown delayed the departure of the detachments until after his visit to Santa Fe, presumably to get orders. What those orders were is not clear, but Col. Sterling Price may have directed the soldiers to join the Army of the West on the coast, where they could be paid off and properly discharged.[44] With their ultimate destination still an open question, the detachments took up their march to the Oregon Trail and the Great Salt Lake Valley.

JOHN STEELE, REMINISCENCES AND JOURNALS, 1846–1898,
LDS ARCHIVES.

May 24 [1847]. Started & came 8 miles and camped. A guard was then placed to prevent any one from taking our animals.

25. Started and came 23 miles this day. A severe Hail storm came on us & we had to lay down in the wett. Saturday 29. This day we started & came 18 miles to a place called Jamey's Camp named after that same James that the High peak was named after.[45] We have been lying still since Tuesday to this day.

Sunday 30. Came 18 miles over a most beautiful rolling prieri [prairie] &

---

[43]Skeen, Reminiscences, 1846–July 1847, LDS Archives. Janet Lecompte noted that the Mormons appropriated federal property "besides what they were entitled to, including fourteen wagons that had been sent to them with rations and not returned." See *Pueblo, Hardscrabble, Greenhorn,* 186.

[44]Archivist Michael Meier of the National Archives and historian Floyd O'Neil have searched the old military records for Price's orders. Since the orders did not appear in the Executive Documents, it is unlikely that they were sent to Washington, and they probably no longer exist.

[45]Pike's Peak was actually named after the first white man to climb it, Dr. Edwin James of the 1820 Stephen Long expedition. The camp was Jimmy Camp Creek, named after trader James Daugherty who was killed there about 1840. See Hafen, ed., *Ruxton of the Rockies,* 203; and Whiteley, "The Trappers Trail," 12. Subsequent trail information is from Lee Whiteley's excellent article and Frémont's 1845 map.

through some pine timber to point of rocks.[46] Monday 31. Came from the point of rocks to Cherry Creek a distance of 20 miles. Pine plenty. Tuesday, 1st June 1847. Came 20 miles and camped on Cherry Creek. There are plenty of grass & a good country. Wednesday 2. Came 18 miles and camped. 3. Came 20 miles & Camped on the south fork of the Platt.[47] This evening Dr [William Walker] Rust came up & told us that Sgt [Sebert C.] Shelton lost all his horses. It is now 145 miles from Pueblo. 4. This morning Captn Brown called a vote to se[e] how many men would uphold him & stand by him to carry out all commands that ware Wright. We passed 4 trading houses this day. One of them had a 6 pounder in it.[48] Feed scarce. Camped after coming 20 miles. Saturday 5. Started & came 9 miles to the crossing. There is one old fort here.[49] Crossed the [South] Platt about 12 oclock and came 9 miles and camped on its banks. 18 miles.

6 [June 1847]. Lay too all day. Monday 7. Started & came 24 miles. Crossed the Cashley Poud named so by some Frenchmen that hid some pouder. Crossed Crow Creek.[50] There are neither feed wood nor watter but an abundant crop of prickley pears. Tuesday 8. Lay too all day. Wednesday 9. Shelton come up with 10 oxen & 2 cows which were afterwards sold— one to Captn Brown for 13½ and the other to David Leughland [Laughlin] for 20 dollars.[51] Thurs 10. Came 20 miles and camped on some creek. Friday 11. Came 20 miles and camped on poll creek. There is a good spring here. After we got our tents pitched there was a cry made Wolsy [Pvt. Thomas S. Woolsey] & [Pvt. John A.] Tippets was came with Amas A. Lyman.[52] Satt 12. Same on to Horse Creek, 18 miles.[53]

BRIGHAM YOUNG: BE A FATHER UNTO THEM

The open question of exactly how the Mormon Battalion would be

---

[46]Leaving Fountain Creek east of today's Colorado Springs, the east branch of the trail passed through the Black Forest and crossed the Arkansas/Platte divide to descend to Point of Rocks on West Kiowa Creek.

[47]The party followed Cherry Creek to its junction with the South Platte in today's Denver.

[48]Noted posts encountered going north on the Trappers Trail included Forts Lupton (or Lancaster), Jackson, and Vasquez. The cannon perhaps belonged to West Point graduate Lancaster Lupton.

[49]The party forded the South Platte at Fort St. Vrain, also known as Fort Lookout or Fort George.

[50]After crossing Cache la Poudre River, the soldiers turned north northeast to strike Crow Creek about twenty miles south of today's Wyoming line.

[51]By such creative means the party picked up three hundred head of cattle by the time they arrived at Salt Lake. See Journal History, 29 July 1847.

[52]Amasa Lyman was a Mormon apostle. Joel Terrell wrote that the mail "gave some of us much satisfaction others disstress of mind." For Terrell, it brought "Joy and greif to me," and he dryly commented on the fee Woolsey and Stevens charged for their services: "at any rate it gave us an other chance to part with one dollar more of our hard earnings." See Joel J. Terrell, Diary, 11 June 1846.

[53]The party struck Horse Creek about twenty-five miles above its mouth and turned northwest for Fort Laramie.

discharged resulted in much discussion among the officers and their religious leaders. Brigham Young adopted his own hard line on the issue. At
Fort Laramie on 3 June, Thomas Bullock "Made up the Mail of 349
letters" for Thomas Woolsey and Young "appointed him Deputy Postmaster." Woolsey, John Tippets, and Roswell Stephens returned to the
battalion with Apostle Amasa M. Lyman to guide the detachments to
Salt Lake. Lyman carried a rhetorical epistle from Brigham Young that
directed the Mississippi Saints to "keep a sharp lookout for buffalo,
Indian and bears" and "pray continually," and the following letter. But
Young also "wrote a note in pencil to send at the same time." On the
banks of the Laramie River, he made clear to Lyman that the detachments were to proceed to Salt Lake. His note directed that the soldiers
"must not follow Brown to Mexico" and advised them "to throw all the
Gentile officers out of the Battalion" if they were so ordered. Young was
"very angry with the President" for limiting Mormon enrollment in the
Army of the West.[54] The expiration of the volunteers' enlistment in July
made the question moot, but the Mormon leaders continued to wrestle
with the problem.

YOUNG TO BROWN, BRIGHAM YOUNG COLLECTION, LDS ARCHIVES.

Pioneer camp of Israel June 2d 1847
North bank of Platt River opposite
Fort Laramie

Capt James Brown,

Your Letter of last winter by Bro Tippits was received at winter Quarters
on the Missourie, where we left upwards of 4000 of the Saints on the 14th
of April in the pioneer company numbering 143 men—73 waggons, and
have had a prosperous journey to this point, where brothers Wooley, Tippets, & Stevens will leave, at their first possible chance, to return to their sta-
tions in the Battalion, accompanied by Elder A. Lyman, who will give you
all the particulars of our travels, situation of the church &c which we have
not time to write.

From this hence we shall continue to travel westward, till we find a resting place for the Saints, & as you asked council we say to you, loose [*sic*] no
time in following after us, with your command so as to arrive in California
before the year of enlistment expires, according to the original Stipulation
of Capt. Allen. See that your company has provisions, & is well provided for
as possible. Be a father unto them. Be humble, pray much & teach them to

---

[54]Clark, *Messages of the First Presidency*. 1:322; and Bagley, ed., *The Pioneer Camp of the Saints*, 178–79.

pray without ceasing & in all things give delight. Heed to the council of Bro Lyman, and the remainder shall be made known hereafter.

Read this to your command that all the Saints may know that we remember them most affectionately, and we bless all the faithful in Christ Forever Amen.

from the council

Willard Richards Clerk   Brigham Young Prest

P.S. We expect another company of Saints are on the way from winter Quarters, following our trail, among whom will be as many of the families of the Battalion as can possibly be fitted out, & they will be with us nearly as soon as yourselves.

JOHN STEELE:
THE VALLEY WHERE OUR BRETHREN ARE PLANTING

The battalion detachments missed meeting Brigham Young at Fort Laramie by less than two weeks, but from Laramie to Fort Bridger they gained ground on the Pioneer Camp. At the Mormon Ferry on the last crossing of the Platte, twelve men under Thomas S. Williams "ware detailed to overtake the Pioneers." The scouts caught up with the Camp of Israel on the Fourth of July at Green River. Brigham Young and "some of the 12" met the men at the ferry and escorted them "down to there camp [where] we were received with three cheers of hosanna to god and the Lamb by Brigham and all the rest with amen & amen."[55] The main company did not overtake the pioneers as expected, but some of Williams' scouts entered the Salt Lake Valley before Brigham Young and immediately began implementing the irrigation techniques they had learned in New Mexico. As Abner Blackburn wrote, they had found a "place for the Saints to make a Home in the far west."[56]

JOHN STEELE, REMINISCENCES AND JOURNALS, 1846–1898,
LDS ARCHIVES.

Sund 13 [June 1847]. This day had Elder Amas E. to preach. He said to leave off our card playing & profain swearing and return to God and a grait many other things. He said we ware not as bad as he expected to find us. Capt Bn. then got up and made an acknowledgement & said that he had just played one game and how he had kept publick worship & preaching twice a

---

[55] Terrell, Diary, 27 June and 4 July 1847. See Bagley, ed., *The Pioneer Camp of the Saints*, 218–19, for a list of the scouts.   [56] Bagley, ed., *Frontiersman*, 60.

week.[57] Monday 14. Came 10 miles and camped on Box alder creek. Tues
15. Came 18 miles and camped on cottonwood. Wednes 16. Started & came
20 miles to Larimays Fork. About 50 of us upon horses [set off] to get
some of the Breathrens horses that had been stolon. Got the Horses came
back & camped.[58] 29 men on guard that night. There are about 70 lodges of
Sooes [Sioux] camped here. We came 20 miles this day. Thurs 17. Crossed
the river & came six miles and camped by the North fork. Friday 18th.
Came 18 miles and camped by a warm spring. 19. came 17 miles and
camped by a good spring [Heber Springs]. We are passing some of the mile
boards [on the] 17 of June.

Sunday 20 [June 1847]. Lay too all day. Amas E. Lyman preached & said
he had watched us and to leave of[f] our folly and be men of God[59] and then
Captain Bn got up and made acknowledgements of his faults and said he
had been hit very hard. He then went on to run down his Boys and said one
man had the Ausumption to contradict him in placing out a picket guard
and said it is not worth while to plant them on the top of a high hill after
dark for the[y] cant see and said he was not going to be counceled by any
private soldier. His councellars war officers. I am the man [who contradicted Brown] and I tried it and could neither heare nor se[e]. 21. Came 21
miles and camped on the Massoony [sic].[60] Cattle are dying off with some
distemper or poisoned. 22nd, good water. Came 15 miles and camped by a
fine stream [Deer Creek]. Got our horses, Loaded buffalo. Saturday 26
came 16 miles along the river. Plenty of buffalo and good feed.

Sunday 27. Came six miles to the [North] Platt where we found Brother
Grover and company busy ferrying large companies of Missourians across
from Fort John to the crossing Plat, $1.50 for crossing.[61] 28. Lay too all
day. About 15 of the brethren went ahead to overtake the pioneers.[62] 29.
Crossed over in the evening and camped for the night. 30. Came 8 miles and

---

[57]At the top of the manuscript is a note: "From L Publo to Larimay 293 miles"; and a string of numbers: 187, 58, 245, 48, and 10.

[58]Joel Terrell and ten men left camp on 14 June "to find some stolen horses." The next day they met
"a war party of the Soux Indians who made a very hostile apperasense being monted on horse back well
armed with bows arrows guns spears &ct." The Lakota warriors escorted the scouts to Fort Laramie, where
the men found some of the horses nearby "in the hands of some frenchmen who dwelt in loges." With help
from Steele's reinforcements, on the sixteenth they "took what we could find and returned back a short
distance to camp."

[59]Lyman "gave us all a good whipping at 2 oclock and a great deal of good council." See Joel J. Terrell,
Diary, 20 June 1846.

[60]This was probably Bed Tick Creek.

[61]On 19 June 1847 Brigham Young assigned Thomas Grover and eight men to establish an enterprise
at the site of present Casper, Wyoming, that became known as Mormon Ferry. See Bagley, ed., *The Pioneer
Camp of the Saints*, 174, 194, 196.

[62]Timothy Goodale and other mountaineers had apparently stolen some of the animals Thomas
Williams had himself rustled in New Mexico. Williams and twelve other men set out in pursuit.

camped by an old crossing. Plenty of Oregon emigrants all the way. Thursday 1st of July, 1847—Platt River. Came 30 miles and camped by the Willow Springs. Plenty of wood and water, grass scarce. Plenty of antelope. I came across a place in the mountains that is hollow. I could find no bottom. The lava boils up when you remove the surface. Friday 2. Came 20 miles through the mountains and found several lakes, covered with saleretus. The water tastes like strong epsom salts. Camped by Independence Rock on Sweetwater. There is snow to be seen on the mountains. Saturday 3rd, came ten miles. Camped by Sweetwater.

Sunday 4 [July 1847]. Plenty of feed. Sent a company of hunters out. Towards night on Monday our hunters returned loaded heavy with meat. Tuesday 6th lay too all day to dry our meat. Wednesday 7th, came 18 miles. Good road. Snow to be seen. Thursday 8. Came 14 miles over a sandy road. Met Phenes Young, Brother [Henson] Walker, and others going back to meet the families.[63] Friday 9th, came 23 miles through sand. Camped by Sweetwater. There are a number of sick in our camp. Saturday 10th, came 15 miles over the mountain.[64]

Sunday 11. This day lay too and had a good preach from Amos E.[65] 12. Came this day 25 miles and camped on Sweetwater. Plenty of streams. There was an Indian woman came to us about 120 years of age being left by her tribe. I gathered her about 50 weight [of flour] and left [it] with her. She was thankful. 13. Came 16 miles and camped on Dry Creek. This day we came to the highest point of the mountains [South Pass] from whence the waters run to the Pacific. These are called the Green Springs.[66] They flow Westward. 14. Came 20 miles all way down hill and camped by Sand Creek [Little Sandy]. This evening Elder Brannon left for Green River. Good feed. Thursday 15. Came to Big Sandy. 20 miles. Friday 16. This morning at sun up there ware several shots fired to celebrate the 16 morn that freed us from U: Sam.[67] Came on to Green river 8 miles. Blocked up our waggon Boxes and crossed. The water is about Arms[-length] deep. Satturr 17. Came 23 miles and camped on Blacks fork.

Sund 18. Came 15 miles. Crossed Blacks Fork & Hams Fork then

---

[63]Walker and Brigham Young's brother Phinehas were returning to meet the Mormon companies that were following the Pioneer Camp.

[64]The "mountain" was the arduous stretch of road later dubbed Rocky Ridge.

[65]Apostle Amasa Lyman was one of the great Mormon preachers. Steele's spelling provides insight into the pronunciation of his first name.

[66]The soldiers crossed South Pass and camped at the spot most overlanders called Pacific Springs.

[67]Confusion remained about how they were to be formally discharged, but the anniversary of their enlistment on 16 July 1846 marked the end of the Iowa Volunteers' enlistment. The "salute of small arms" was fired "to let every one of Uncle Sam's officers know we were our own men once more. We still kept up our organization, and respected the words of command as usual, and was rather better than some had been before." See Beckwith, ed., "Journal of John Steele," 16.

crossed Blacks fork & camped. Mon 19. Came 17 miles and camped by Ft Bridgers. Bought some skins.[68] Captn Brown bought 5 horses for 220 dollars for to go to the Bay. Gave U.S. for them. Tuesday 20. Came 13 miles and camped. This day Brother [William] Casto came back to us from the pioneer camp. Tuesday 21.[69] Came 20 miles over the mountains. At Bridgers we are 6665 ft. above the sea. Plenty of springs, iron, ore, copper and sulpher. Camped two miles from Bear River. There is a grease or tar spring here one mile from our camp S.W.[70] This evening I heard from Sgt. Hanks that Captain Brown drew five mens rations, also 340 pounds that was back rations belonging to us the time we lay in Pueblo and 240 pounds of flour that was taken out of the store house. Supposed to be Captain Brown. 22. Came 17 miles this day. About 12 miles from Bear River I came through one acre of flax. Came to Readings [Cache] Cave and camped. Friday 23. Came 16 miles this day. As I was coming four miles from where we camped last night I went and discovered a cave about 300 ft. high 40 ft. long 20 ft. wide. I wrote our names in the rock on the 23rd of July. We then found sugar maple and oak, cedar, cottonwood and pine, ironwood, birch curns [?], etc. Saturday 24. Came 10 miles through willow brush. Plenty of hops. Rained and thundered at night.

Sunday 25 [24 July 1847]. Lay too. Elder Lyman Told us we had got out from jentile persecution and now we would be troubled with Devils in our own midst and said that there was some of the darkest characters here that could be & the officers were run upon and their orders disobeyed, which caused Captain Brown to get up and ask if he had not acted as a Father to us and tell how good he had been. Not a man spoke because we were told when we would get to headquarters all would be right. He is such a Father as the Devil would be to us. 26. Came 15 miles and camped in the willows. Had considerable trouble to gather our oxen. Tuesday 27. This day came 13 miles and camped on a fine bottom. Here Elder Amos E. left for the pioneers. Wednes 28. Came 18 miles all the way through brush & Firs. Came to the Top of a Hill from whence could be seen the valey where our breathren are planting.[71] Camped at the bottom of the hill. James Oakley &

---

[68]Steele recalled that Jim Bridger, "the old mountaineer," said "we could not live in Salt Lake valley for it froze every month in the year and would give us a thousand dollars for the first ear of corn raised there, but if we would give him $1000 he would take us to the G–d–d best valley ever was. I spoke to Captain Brown if it was a G–d–d valley we did not want to go there." See Beckwith, ed., "Journal of John Steele," 16–17.

[69]Here Steele inserted two entries for 21 July, a mistake that advanced his subsequent dates by one day.

[70]This was the spring later famous as the Brigham Young Oil Well.

[71]From Big Mountain summit Joel Terrell "had the most sublime the most commanding and the most glorious view my eyes ever beheld. I was filled with admiration and delite at the grand appearence of the towering mountains of Israel from this summet." See Joel J. Terrell, Diary, 27 July 1847.

others came to us and said it was 12 mile[s]. 29. Lay too all day and gathered lots of service berries to our teams would come up. Friday 30. Came on 12 miles to the valey. All the Twelve come out to meat us and gave us a hearty welcom. When I first came into the valey I killed a wolf.

John Steele did indeed kill a wolf upon entering Salt Lake Valley. He saw "what we thought was a bear, which proved to be four wolves." Steele "took time to put a cartridge in my gun" and "rode up and shot one wolf, and Wm. Bird got off and cut his tail off and stuck it in his cap, and wore it into camp."[72]

Seven of the apostles went to Emigration Canyon on 29 July 1847 to greet the battalion, where they heard a "tremendous roaring" and "suddenly a rise of about 3 feet of water rushed in a perfect head down the Kanyon, washing away the bridges." The deluge left several wagons stranded, but "the Battalion & Council with 3 of the Mississippi Wagons" entered the valley "in Military order: Council & Officers first, Infantry next with martial music, then followed the Cavalry with the Baggage Wagons bringing up the rear." Mary Brown "rode into the Valley horseback, beside her husband, and President Young greeted her with the words 'And the wolves didn't get you after all, did they?'" The next evening Brigham Young "made some very pointed remarks, stating that the battalion saved the people by going into the Army. If they had not gone, Missouri was ready with 3000 men to have wiped the Saints out of existence."[73]

The men set to planting and irrigating crops, and Brigham Young soon had the veterans molding adobe bricks for a fort that by the first of September had a "doby wall nine dobies high." Among the Mormons it was customary "whenever the large camps rested for a few days together,

[72]As Steele's diary is a day advanced, these events took place on 29 July 1847, when "one of the most uncommon rains fell that day imaginable." Brown had sent Steele ahead with twelve men "to make good the crossings in Canyon Creek by cutting birch and tying them in bundles and laying them in the creek." While crossing Emigration Creek "the flood came down as big as a wagon box" and carried Thomas Richardson "several rods down the stream, horse and all." See Beckwith, ed., "Journal of John Steele," 17. The Mormon leaders used this flash flood to justify not sending the soldiers to California for their formal discharge.

[73]Brown, "With the Camp Fires of the Mormon Battalion," 308; and Bagley, ed., *The Pioneer Camp of the Saints*, 243–45. This was the second public account of a conspiracy theory that became a favorite myth in Utah Territory. On 28 July, Young had "damned President Polk" for his "tyranny in drafting out 500 men to form a Battalion, in order that the women & children might perish on the Prairies."

to make great arbors, or boweries as they called them, of poles, and brush, and wattling, as places of shelter for their meetings of devotion or conference." Brigham Young's first assignment to the battalion veterans on 30 July 1847 was to build such a structure on the newly selected temple site.[74]

Two days after his arrival, John Steele "went to the hot spring and bathed," and on 9 August 1847 noted a happy occasion: "This morning before break of day my wife was delivered safely and speedily of a fine daughter, being the *first birth* in this great city, named Young Elizabeth," after Steele's sister Elizabeth and "in honor of President Young." Steele "built the first chimney that ever drew smoke" in Salt Lake and "made the first pair of gaiter shoes."[75]

The apostles had long-since decided that "the troops have not provisions sufficient to go to the western coast," and since there was "no officer short of California" authorized to discharge them, the soldiers would stay in Salt Lake, "either on parole, detached service, or some other important business." With "an escort of 15 or 20 mounted men and Elder Brannan for pilot," Captain Brown could "gallop over to the headquarters, get his pay, rations and discharge and learn the geography of the country."[76] After conducting a hearing for veterans William Tubbs and William Gribble that led to Gribble's divorce, the apostles "decided there has been much wickedness in the Battalion" it would "be the best thing to baptize all of them."[77] City Creek was dammed and virtually everyone in the settlement was baptized.

Brigham Young had only heard the most vague reports of the fate of the main corps of the battalion, and he dispatched Brown and an escort of six former soldiers to Monterey on 9 August, with powers of attorney from the Salt Lake veterans.[78] Their mission was to carry mail to Mormons in California—and to secure the battalion's desperately needed payroll. Brown's party included Samuel Brannan and the redoubtable Abner Blackburn, who kept the only known record of the

---

[74]Kane, "The Mormons," in Tyler, *A Concise History*, 80; and Bagley, ed., *The Pioneer Camp of the Saints*, 245.

[75]Cox, ed., The Journals of John Steele, 24; and Beckwith, ed., "Journal of John Steele," 18.

[76]Council of Twelve to Lyman, 8 July 1847, Journal History.

[77]Bagley, ed., *The Pioneer Camp of the Saints*, 248.

[78]Roberts, *Mormon Battalion*, 61.

trip. The men rode north to Fort Hall to join the California Trail, and on Goose Creek met Com. Robert F. Stockton and his entourage, "orderd to Washington to settle the quarrel between Kerney, Fremont and Stockton." Guided by a Mandan woman and a French-Canadian Blackburn called Lou Devon, Brown's party followed the Humboldt River "until we were tired of it. The scenery is not verry strikeing unles one is desirous to be struck. It appeared like some fervent heat had taken the life out of it." The boredom of the arduous trip was relieved only by campfire tales, Indian scares, and hostilities between Brannan and Brown, who "could not agree on anny subject. Brannan thought he knew it all and Brown thought he knew his share of it. They felt snuffy at each other and kept apart." The scenery grew more stark and the "mountains looked like they had been burnt with some great heat. The rocks would ring like crockery ware, with no timber in sight, only willows on the river." Near today's Reno, Brown wanted to make an early start, but "Brannan said he would eat breakfast first." Brown claimed the horses:

> for they belonged to the goverment and were in his care. They both went for the horses and a fight commenced. They pounded each other with fists and clubs until they were sepperated. They both ran for their guns. We parted them again. Started on and left Branan with his own horse. After we stopt, Branan went past. We thought the savages would get him certain.[79]

Two days later near the Donner party's winter camp, Brown and his veterans met some two hundred of their former comrades, bound for Salt Lake. These were the men who had been discharged at Los Angeles on 16 July 1847, and the messages Brown carried in his saddlebags would change their lives—and the history of the American West—forever.

---

[79]Bagley, ed., *Frontiersman*, 63–65, 101–103.

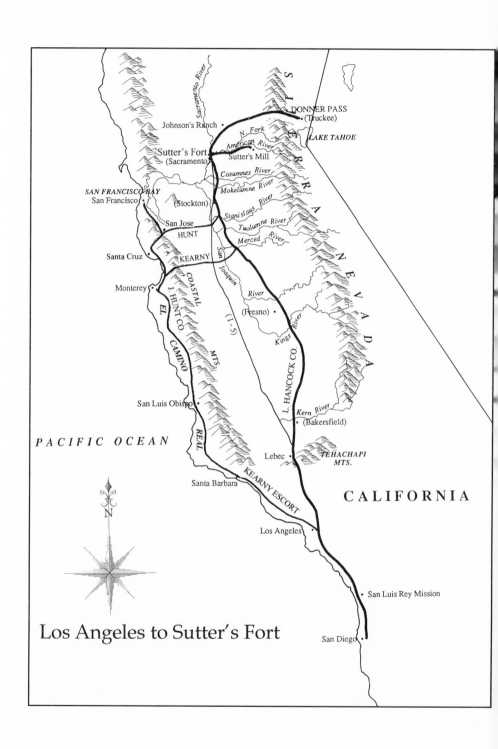

Los Angeles to Sutter's Fort

Chapter 10

THE RETURN

It is impossible to return to a place one has never been, so the discharged Mormon Battalion solders could not return to Utah in 1847, since none of them had previously visited the Great Basin. Yet Mormon annals often class the adventures of these men under the general heading, "The Return of the Mormon Battalion." Some of the veterans did indeed return to their starting point on the Missouri River, but chroniclers such as Andrew Jenson—and even some of the men themselves—used the phrase to mean a return to the LDS church; James Ferguson wrote of the pledge the volunteers made "to return home to the bosom of the Church."[1] In 1847 the church was not connected with any place but was a nomadic enterprise: the Camp of Israel, as Brigham Young called the migrating body of the church.

Long before its discharge, the hope that the battalion would act as a single unit had been shattered, and after July 1847 the California veterans quickly broke into ever-smaller groups. The Mormon Volunteers served under Captain Daniel C. Davis as a garrison for San Diego until their discharge in March 1848. A few of the men who did not reenlist chose to stay in California, finding work with ranchers such as Isaac Williams or taking jobs in San Francisco.[2] Most of the veterans cast their lot with their religious leaders and set out with them to find Brigham Young and the new Mormon Zion.

Although Young had identified the Great Basin as his follower's likely destination while still in Nauvoo, he did not make the information public. Many of the Mormon soldiers believed their church was bound for the West Coast, as James Scott wrote in his lyric, "Come go with me":

> We'll go away, from this vain world
> With freedom's banners wide unfurled
> To a land of peace of liberty
> Beside the great Pacific Sea.[3]

---

[1] See Jenson's Return of the Mormon Battalion, LDS Archives; and Bagley, ed., *Scoundrel's Tale*, 252.

[2] For the experiences of these battalion veterans in California, see Chapter 11.

Much later Reddick Allred recalled, "At the time of our discharge a sealed letter from the Apostles was read saying: 'You will meet the Church in the Valley of the Great Salt Lake, on the east side at the foot of the Mt.'"[4] None of the journals mentioned such a document, and Jonathan Stevenson's letter of 27 July 1847 reveals that Jefferson Hunt was not sure about the church's final destination, so this letter never existed or its contents were kept astonishingly secret. The battalion's religious leaders had a general notion that the main body of the LDS church was going to the Bear River country in the Great Basin, and William Wood wrote to his parents that he would soon leave to meet the church "about 500 miles from here near the Great Salt Lake."[5] Yet Henry Bigler recalled the men only understood they "were going home (and where that was, no one in camp knew)."[6]

WILLIAM CORAY: THIS COUNTRY WAS IN AN UPROAR

Most of the discharged battalion veterans camped a few miles from Los Angeles, where they waited three days to draw their final pay. As civilians the men were at last able to resolve the conflict between their religious and military leaders that had plagued the battalion since the volunteers marched out of Council Grove. The former officers met and appointed Jefferson Hunt to lead one party to Monterey, while Lt. Lorenzo Clark "was to take a company *via* Cajon Pass," with "other leaders in other directions." Due to "dissatisfactions these arrangements were not carried out, and all took their way according to chance or inclination."[7] Only a few men sided with the officers, and most chose instead to follow Levi Hancock. William Coray acknowledged Hancock's "authority over me in spiritual things" and thought that some of the officers "set very bad examples & were somewhat tyrannical," but he felt that Hancock had acted improperly "in getting up an excitement against the officers and destroying their influence with the men whom they should controll according to Prest. Young's instructions."[8] Coray fol-

[3]Scott, Diaries 1846, LDS Archives.
[4]Allred, Mormon Battalion Experiences, 11.
[5]Wood to Father and Mother, July 1846, in Carter, ed., *Our Pioneer Heritage*, 11:381.
[6]Bigler, "Extracts from the Journal of Henry W. Bigler," 62.
[7]Little, *From Kirtland to Salt Lake City*, 151–52.
[8]Coray, Journal of Sgt. William Coray of the Mormon Battalion, 56.

lowed Jefferson Hunt up El Camino Real to Monterey, and his brief account of the trip, written before 1849, described the mission road up the coast, which proved "almost impracticable" for wagons. Coray provided a colorful account of the Mormon community in San Francisco—and insight into the character of its leader, Samuel Brannan.

JOURNAL OF SGT. WILLIAM CORAY OF THE MORMON BATTALION, 57–58.

Meanwhile those who believed the council of Bro. Levi [Hancock] made preparations and started with him to meet the church by way of the Walker Pass [and] near 40 or 50 [men] in Co[mpany]. with Capt. Hunt also marched for the Bay of San Francisco expecting to hear something from the Church, as this was the place the Twelve supposed we would be discharged. As for myself, I had to act for my self, having a wife with me in a delicate situation. I thought it best to make my way as fast as possible to San Francisco, seeing this country was in an uproar and the Spaniards threatening an outbreak after our discharge. I begged Capt. Hunt to wait for me to which he freely consented. As to the rout[e], it was almost impracticable. While going through the gavaote pass I took my wagon apart and took a piece at a time over one place. Had it not been for Capt. Hunt & two or 3 others who came back 3 or 4 miles to help us through I should have been obliged to stand at the mercy of Indians till I could have made other arrangements for transportation. However, we got through the pass and by the assistance of some Indians with their Reatas, they kept the wagon from upsetting til I could drive around sideling places by very careful management.[9] I only upset once in going to Monterey at which place I arrived the 13th of Aug. At this place I considered all things & concluded to stop for a season, expecting my wife to be confined every day. I rented a room and went to work with my team for the Alcalde. Business became very dull with me & I worried more and more about the church, hearing nothing, only that Capt. Hunt with a part of his Co. had gone to meet them. Time passed on as usual until the 2nd Sept. when my wife was delivered of a fine boy, & I named him Wm. after myself as he was my first born. Near two weeks after I went to San Francisco & seeing there was plenty of money, I concluded to move my effects there forthwith that I might gain some to myself. I also saw Mr. Brannan direct from the Church which had located at Salt Lake and laid out a city there, calling the Battn. all back but not forthwith. Capt. Brown had also been through to get the pay for his men, bringing letters to the boys. So as agreed upon, I moved to San Francisco. My health at this time was not good, being troubled by a bad cough. I was disenabled for

---

[9]Coray crossed Gaviota Pass in the Santa Ynez Mountains north of Santa Barbara. Reatas (or riatas) were lariats, while "sideling places" were steep and sloping hillsides.

business for one month or more. I kept my team a going which brought me in a considerable money. San Francisco is a beautiful place. A fine ship harbor, perfectly secure from storm. Also very healthy. The place at this time was improving rapidly, lots selling at a great price & it was all speculation & money making both by the Mormons & the worldings & seemed to me that the Saints here were going to the Devil fast enough. The Mormon girls marrying sailors & drunkerds & he who should be their counselor [Samuel Brannan] was backing them up directly or indirectly, while at the same time he would play Billiards & drink grog with the greatest blacklegs in the place, saying it was policy to do so. Said he to me one time when he was some intoxicated, "Every act of my life is through policy."

Coray and his wife Melissa left California in the summer of 1848 and arrived in Great Salt Lake City on 6 October. Coray was "greatly reduced in flesh" and his bad cough proved to be tuberculosis. A little more than a month after his daughter was born, William Coray died on 7 March 1849. "We had such plans and anticipations, but, alas, how soon our hopes are blasted," Melissa Coray wrote. "I have but one thought to console me in losing my companion. He was willing to go inasmuch as it was the will of the Lord."[10]

Levi W. Hancock: A Great Struggle for Power; Pueblo de los Angeles to Sutter's Fort

The great majority of the battalion veterans who did not reenlist chose to follow religious authority in the person of Levi Hancock. After being paid, the men left in groups for the San Fernando Valley. They were excited at the prospect of returning to their friends and families—wherever they might find them. The men met on the evening of 20 July and chose Elisha Averett "and nine or ten others to act as pioneers by going ahead and selecting the way we should travel." Henry Bigler recalled, "We felt like birds let out of a cage."[11] The scouts left the next morning, while the main camp organized into companies of hundreds, fifties, and tens. The party had both religious and secular leaders, a model that other eastbound Mormon wagon parties would follow in 1848. James Pace recalled that on 23 July, "we organised our company

---

[10]Melissa Coray to Howard Coray, 6 April 1849, quoted in Ricketts, *Melissa's Journey*, 100.
[11]Bigler, "Extracts from the Journal of Henry W. Bigler," 62.

of 163 men, I being elected Captain." Reddick Allred remembered, "Andrew Lytle with Jas. Pace to assist was placed at the head."[12] The confusion over who was captain of the party resulted from both Pace and Lytle being captains of one hundred. Hancock was the company's nominal leader and traveled with Lytle's hundred in Daniel Tyler's Fifty, but he shared the religious leadership with David Pettegrew and had no effective power, a fact that did not please him.

Poorly educated but deeply religious, Hancock placed great faith in his dreams—except those that "must be of satan." He put his thoughts and feelings into rough rhyme, and on 22 July Hancock inserted a long poem in his journal that was a litany of Mormon troubles from the Missouri feuds to the battalion's service in California. In particular the poem attacked Sen. Thomas Hart Benton, an old political enemy of the LDS church, and his son-in-law, John C. Frémont.

> But fremonts name must surely smell
> Mong deasent men as bad as hell
> Let Kearney take him whare he may
> We'r[e] glad that he has gone away

Henry Bigler recalled, "We hardly knew what way to strike out, for we had no guide, except an old California map with very few rivers or anything else marked on it, and a paper pretending to give the route."[13] Yet the Mormons were familiar with Frémont's travels in the Central Valley and Bigler's "old map" was probably a copy of the 1845 map of the second Frémont expedition's journey in early 1844 up the San Joaquin Valley, over Tehachapi Pass, and across the San Gabriel Mountains to the Mojave Desert.[14] The veterans often used native guides, but as soldiers the men had heard a little about ways to cross the Sierra and hoped to locate the pass that Joseph R. Walker had opened in 1843. The Mormons crossed the Tehachapi Mountains by Tejón Pass, following the route of present Interstate 5, and then marched down the Central Valley east of the line of today's U.S. 99. They were not entering uncharted territory, for the men generally followed trails first recorded by Francisco Garcés in 1776, later explored by Lt. Gabriel

---

[12]Pace, Autobiographical Sketch, LDS Archives; and Allred, Mormon Battalion Experiences, 11. Allred recalled "Wm. Hyde was Capt. of the 1st 50, Daniel Tyler, 2nd, and myself the 3rd 50."

[13]Gudde, ed., Bigler's Chronicle, 62.

[14]For a copy, see the map portfolio of Spence and Jackson, eds. The Expeditions of John Charles Frémont.

Moraga and other dimly recalled Spanish parties in 1806, and finally used by Frémont in 1844 and 1845. These routes passed the southern end of the vast drainage called Laguna Grande de Los Tulares, the now-vanished Tulare Lake, crossing the Central Valley to a trail that traversed the western foothills of the Sierra Nevada.[15] The men completely missed Walker Pass, but their passage through the heart of California left a vivid record of a wild country now transformed into an agronomic wonder that would be unrecognizable to the veterans of 1847.

To provide an example of a Mormon Battalion document with minimal editorial corrections, Hancock's journal is here presented in a literal transcription, with extra spaces inserted at likely sentence breaks. We appreciate the original transcription efforts of Robert K. Hoshide and April Hancock. Like other battalion documents, it provides a record of a vanished world. Even discounting its more gruesome passages, Hancock's diary is a colorful account of California and the overland trail in 1847.

LEVI WARD HANCOCK, JOURNALS 1846–1847, LDS ARCHIVES.

The 16 of July [1847] has come and what there has passed I canot tell only there has bin a great strugle for power and to get us inlisted again   I said I would not and many others say the same   such crualty on soldiers I never saw men chained and a ball hung to them and to ware it for 6 8 or 10 months gagued and imprisoned

17   no money drawed as yet

18   drawed

19   the same[16]

20 [July 1847]   moved   my mares are lost

21   Cooking provisions

July twenty second   moved three mile[s] north of the fort and camped on the Rio san gabriel   have not yet found my mares   on the third day morning one mare braught in by a spanyard   payed him two dollars[17]

July 23 started from our Camp 8 miles North of Pubelo same day many horses broke loos & mostly not found   six miles this day   went further very much scatered   agreed to meet at the ranch of the arcaldres and there gather

---

[15]For maps of Central Valley watercourses in 1846, see Bancroft, *History of California*, 2:49, 51.

[16]Henry Bigler noted, "On the nineteenth, the Battalion was paid off all except our transportation money, all of which we never got (to this day)." See Gudde, ed., *Bigler's Chronicle*, 61.

[17]The long poem lamenting the suffering of the Mormons is omitted here.

24 went to Pecoes ranch and found many more and camped   good
water here[18]

25 [July 1847] passed over the first Mt which was 4 miles from camp
last knight and at the head of a canion   the pass left of here is said to be
worse than this   after we had got to the top of what is seen we had not got
half up and we had to go winding our cours around on the tops untill we
had gained the sumit   then turned to the left and went down into another
canion   while on the top the sea breeses blew cool & good   we followed
down an easterly cours and come to the ranch of the Arcaldies[19]   a butiful
stream it is on with two branches   our men we found camped on them both
one company behind yet

26 day bought our cattle which cost us two dollars apiece[20]

27 day 20 men [were] called upon to drive them which we found to be
hard   we went about 2 miles and found an other canion and followed it up
9 miles from last camp   came to an Mt and crossed over and in a hollow
on the top we found timber and water   a good camp it made   27 marched
on through a hollow which went out N East and went winding through the
tops of the Mts & here we found timber land   we followed the trail which
must be many hundread [years] old wore down in some places 3 & 4 ft
crossed over high peaks and down in some hollows   some times the path
not more than one foot wide on the side of the Mt where if the horse had
fell it would have dashed him to death   some times on both sides it was so
steep no creature of cattle kind could stand but we thought if fremont had
bin there we could   Lost 9 cattle they ware very wild & would charge on
any man who was in there way   some was shot and part saved after and
brought in here   met Rusel Brownal & James Miler[21]   came up & told us
that the other company was behind coming & would be able to catch us in
one or two days which caused us to rejoise much and we have peace now
no swaring and cursing each other   all are trying to do as well as they can

---

[18]Hancock arrived at Mission San Fernando, called Pico's Ranch because Andres Pico, the victor of
San Pasqual, leased part of the property. Here the veterans "bought some fine pears and also took a little
wine for our stomachs sake." Henry Bigler thought Pico "a fine specimen of humanity, well dressed, wearing a red silk sash around his body. He bore in his hand a lance and showed us how it was used, maneu-
vering it as if in action with an enemy." See Bigler, "Extracts from the Journal of Henry W. Bigler," 63–64.

[19]The *alcalde*, the local chief magistrate, was Antonio del Valle, at whose 48,600-acre Rancho San Francisco the party purchased cattle. This was the first settlement most of the Death Valley forty-niners
encountered after their ordeal in the desert.

[20]"Some time before our discharge we made contact with the Alcalda of De-los-Angelos for fifty fat
oxen, and to receive them, at his ranch about 30 miles over the High mountains, towards the head of the
river San-wau-kie, so we passed on by companies of tens, and stopped at the Ranch, until we came
together. When we obtained our cattle according to agreement, and started our journey, but, we so[o]n
found them hard to drive, and very dangerous so we concluded to kill them, and dry the beef." See Journal
of David Pettegrew, 86.

[21]Cpl. Russell Gideon Brownell, Co. C, died in 1895 in Fresno, California. His brother-in-law, New
Yorker James Myler, Jr., served with him as a private in Co. C. Myler died in Idaho in 1894.

Brownal went back to inform the men whare we are   many deer seen to day
said to be small   last knight a grisley bear come to our camp & we drove
him off   our horses was much frightened and had have like to brake loos[e]
all around we was glad to have him leave

The water that is found here is salt in the kettle   the timber is mostly
willow in these valies some oak cotonwood sycamore seen two Beach trees
camped here good timber here and water to do for us and animels by waiting patiently

28 day   Mts on each side   I think we should have trouble if we had not
have run [the bear off]. Made 12 miles to day

28 day   we left our camp on the Mts in a butiful vally and took up an
other canion coming in from the N East and crossed over an other Mt continuously asending going some times on the tops and some times on the
sides of the Mts winding our way passing through valies and we have today
passed through some good timber on the hills beside of the dry beds of the
creek   the rodes is narow some times not over one foot wide on the side
hills   there is a considrable variety of timber in these Mts   some hemlock
we have seen on our rout here no timber the like the timber in the states
the leaves are smaller   seeder is the most natural

after we passed into the other canion [on] the 29 day we found a stream
of water running from the East and turning to the N West and winding to
the W through the Mts towards thee sea   we went up it for about one mile
and it turned to the N East and went crooking around untill it we took
another turn nearly North west and at at [sic] wonce we come up to the foot
of a Mt and it tooked looked as if we could go no farther but all at wonce
we saw a light east & we saw that the stream came between the Mts from the
east   we turned and went about one mile & it took another turn turn and
come from the NE   one vally come in from the east   we journeyed NE
and asended the stream untill we came to what used to be called the hot
springs three years ago but now are cold and we have traviled over the worst
kind of road between the Mts and over rocks and between them they would
tare our horses hoofs to peses   the worst going I ever saw   we have now
camped and have good feed & water   this day made 12 miles and the council is to kill all the cattle tomorow and dry [the meat]

Fryday 30 [July 1847] this morning our cattle has bin killed and we lay
by to dry beef   about one oclock I went up on the top of the Mt and drew
a map of the canion   we passed and a head I could see our road for a long
distance a head   I loo[k]ed up the hollow on the left and the NW I saw a
large smoke I suppose raised builded by the Indians   our men have all come
in while I was on the Mt   our cours is through the vally   in two days the
Indian [says] we can get to tulelary vally

31 day   our Pioneers have gone a head to find water and a road with the
indian guide we are drying beef calculating to move on tomorrow

August first 1847 this morning we packed up our beef And started on
our journey   made 15 miles   crossed over some small hills   from last
knights camp we moved north for about 2 miles and turned over a hill [tak-
ing] a diagonal course into a valley or a branch of the same [that] we started
in   here is the hill we passed over and road up this branch runs nearly NW
after we had gon down on over the hill I met two indians and brought a yaw
ah[22] or Mare and continued NW for about 3 miles and crossed over an
other small hill and went down in to a very low vally   on the north was a
high Mt about 3 miles a head   we turned east and still went down and
come to a lake or neare one as it looked and it was white as flower   I can
not tell whether it was dry salt or what it was   we turned north before we
got to it and continued down and passed much timber and butiful land and
grass botoms about one mile wide and soon we decended further down and
came to a butiful spring and woods   very large timber   one tree meshured
25 ft round   an other cloos by had a epitaff on it with a catholic cross
Peter Lebeck killed by a Bear Oct 17 — 1837   his grave was by the tree[23]
our Pioneers stayed here last knight and we found a plenty of fire   I see on
the hill east of here about half a mile 4 antelope

August 2 1847 this morning we took an early start and we went out of
this butiful vally into an other canion and following it down continualy
decending about NW corse following a butiful stream of water big enough
to carry a mill and good wood all down for about six miles and came out
into the Tulearry Vally[24] and we had to crook about some in the canion and
cross the stream several times   after we came into Tularry vally turned about
N and traviled about 14 miles and found that the Rio was so high we could
not cross and turned and took about an east course & traviled six miles and
camped NNW from the mouth of the canion we came out to day

3 day this day an Indian came in camp and others came[25]   some are
going for guides   ~~we came~~ we have to travil North to day   we see the canion we came out of and here is the picture below[26]   we now have camped
and from now have to travil a NNW corse   made twelve miles to day along
by the Kings River or Rio Ra[27]   there is an Indians hut here   we crooked

---

[22]*Yegua* is Spanish for mare.

[23]Fort Tejón in Grapevine Canyon marks the site of the demise of trapper Peter Lebeck. For a facsim-
ile of the epitaph, see Wood, *The Life and Death of Peter Lebec*.

[24]The party crossed the Tehachapi Mountains and entered the southern end of the Central Valley of
California near the bed of Tulare Lake.

[25]Years later William Pace recalled, "We encountered Hostile Indians, though by an effort they were
brought into camp where a general Pow-wow ensued, during which Father Brown, an aged veteran of the
Batalion, spoke in Tongues, at some length, which proved to be understood by the Indians, after which they
could not do too much for us. Guarding our animals and helping us across the San Joakin River which was
swolen and had to be rafted." See W. B. Pace, Autobiography, LDS Archives, 58–59.

[26]A simple line drawing shows, "Road out here," and "Camp here" next to "Lake here."

[27]Hancock was actually camped on Kern River near today's Bakersfield.

About a considrable to day   there is many fish in these waters   last knight
the Indian arcalda came in to camp And he said that we was the best people
that ever passed this way   we made him some presants

Wendsday 4th   we traveled about NN East 8 ~~6~~ miles and crossed the
River   the horses had to swim untill an other ford was found a little below
that ~~nearly~~ crossed or more half mile [*sic*]   we camped on the River some
timber here for fire many flags poplar tree coton wood   it is a butiful country [with] water enoug[h] to water the whole country   This Tulary trybe of
Indians have three thousand waryers and many old men they consider to[o]
old to fight   they often fall on the spanyards and fight them it is said   This
is the Trybe that Lieutenant Thomso[n] fought by order of Col Cook   Lieutenant Col of the Mormon Batalion[28]

Thursday 5 [August 1847] we started early from our camp on the Rio
Ra or Kings River and had a considerable brush and timber and came out on
a place and took up a canion or dry hollow and passed over a high hill at the
head and then went down another crooking around between the lofty hills
and narow path on the botom of a dry stream   no timber for a long way of
any kind untill we came down very low and saw timber still lower down and
soon we came to it and found down the stream runing to our right and to
the east a hole of water   here we had thought to stay and refresh ourselves
and anemils but the Pioneers went a head and to water all of our beasts
would have took till knight   we continued our journey and traviled as we
had 12 miles back a NE corse   the same we continued untill we made 28
[miles] and camped in a hollow nere or in sight of a high Mt east of us
about 4 miles [Mt. Baggett or Rocky Hill?]   we have passed a good deal of
timber and through among the large oaks for Mt oak in the vallys grows the
coton wood and poplar   seen one Buck eye tree   NE corse all day   our
road was crooked and this afternoon we come over some beg [big] hills
poor feed and water to knight

6th day   crossed around and over hills very large down in deep hollows
then up and down dry beds whare water wonce ran   in about seven miles
came down here as steep as 45 degrees in some places   we came down others not so bad   we soon found a little water no grass   soon found grass &
no water   soon found good water and wood & grass   last knight dug for
water in many places   this stream runs some   traviled about N by East to
day   this day made 10 mile

7 day   traviled about N & winding in the valies and on the tops of the
high hills   many of the vallys had large tress and many grew on the hills
we traveled about 16 miles and decended into another vally which looked

---

[28]As noted, on 8 May 1847 Colonel Cooke dispatched Lt. Samuel Thompson and twenty men from
Co. C to make "every effort to destroy" these troublesome Indians. David Pettegrew called them the "Tol-
eraneus" Indians (in Spanish, the Tulareños). See Journal of David Pettegrew, 80.

almost as looking from the clouds and found a plenty of timber and feed & water tho it is in holes   we left 20 men yet behind who have not got in yet we have not seen them since yesterday morning   the low vallys have good land but no water to use   I have put down the hill that we have come over to day and corse of the road and creek   timber here and a butiful country it is[29]

8 day the pilots went and got in some Indians to pilot us over the Mts they apear to be naked all but a brich clout   they fe[t]ched in some deer skins and traded some   last knight I dreamed that Dimic Huntington come in camp and said go ahead all is right   he was hors[e] back   made 6 miles to day and camped on a butiful stream that we have assended about 2 miles from north of last knights camp had to come over hills to day to get to this creek   good fish in this stream which runs about NW

9 day traveled 25 miles NW direction over many hills and pass a little water under some rocks & this side of the hill some 4 miles found some more under a tree at our right   we are on a butiful stream a ~~pten~~ plenty of water deep and runing stream crooked around as before in vallys and on ri[d]ges and up and down the hills[30]

10 [August 1847] day made 8 miles we was detained on the banks of this stream a long time to get over our men   made a raft and crossed our bagage   swam our horses and mules   we come over a few hills and decended onto the botoms and a butiful country it is well timbered and thousands of water [sources.]

11 day made 28 miles NNW corse without water [and] no pilot across the level botoms   many suffered for water   all did not get through untill the next day[31]   many come in the knight [over] the straightest corse we have made   water was sent to the men behind   we have a camp [with] plenty of water and feed   some today have gone to get one man who got hurt last knight the old man Clark[32]   last knight the Indians brought in some roots for us   we gave them some beef in exchange   very friendly

12 day rested while our Pioneers went to serch out a rout for our men[33]

---

[29]Hancock sketched his route on the next two pages. The veterans apparently followed the Tulare Trail along the line of today's Highway 65 to a camp near present Porterville.

[30]The men probably camped on a ford of the Kaweah River about seven miles from today's Visalia.

[31]This camp was on Kings River a few miles east of today's Fresno.

[32]This was probably Joseph Clark, born 15 May 1792, or Samuel Gilman Clark, who would turn forty-seven the next day. Both men had been privates in Co. E.

[33]While camped at the mouth of Kings Canyon, William B. Pace recorded, "Capt Averett in Co. with some four of the Pioneers went up the river in search of A pass through the California Mountains." On 13 August, "the report was that we could not pass and it was thought best to turn for Sutters Fort." It has long been assumed that Elisha Averett was searching for Walker's Pass, which was some one hundred miles to the south, but the men may have heard reports of Sonora Pass, which lay to the north above today's Yosemite National Park.

some of them went out to see the [Kings] River which they found to be
about six rods wide   a butiful place it is here   the Indians ware afrighted
and ran with there women & children[34]   our men disturbed nothing

13 day last knight some men came in and said that they had found a
camping place about 10 mile[s] off   to day made ten miles   we have
lerned we are right   I dreamed last knight that there was a man come in
camp and said that our men that we sent out was returning back & that we
could pass   I asked him if we could pass   he said yes but it will take some
work & it is not the place you intendid to go said ~~he~~   I then [said] let us
call it the Mormon pass   yes said he and there is one below that has the
same name of surgent or surgen   I then awoke and told Andrew Lytle

14 day saturday yesterday we went to the Mts and tryed to cross but in
vane and we will call this the pass and hope that no man may try to go over
again untill much work is done and we found that we had to work to pass
the river   we came down about 5 miles and crossed over in two places and
continued down about 3 miles further and camped   many Indians came in
we found that they was at war with the Mts Indians   when they are at war
with any trybe they take away all there standing monuments which are
pealed poles & painted like barber poles   they are religious here and have
many dances   we told them that we was friends to the Indians and loved
them and did not want to hurt them   we spoke by an interpreter an Indian
who could talk a little spanish   they said we could ~~tolk~~ lay down and sleep
in peace and not be disturbed   they then sang and danced and one had the
power as methodist dus at there camp me[e]tings[35]   then they tryed to
ex[h]ort us   I never saw so fine Indians before   this Rio runs from the N
East to here and to the sw below[36]

15 [August 1847] day sunday   we left the Rio san Joquin [sic]and
journed NW up neare the hills below the foot of the Mts and in 12 miles
made water by diging in the sand at the botom of a creek   the Pioneers
went with ~~the~~ all speed to a Mt and looked at the NW and they thought in
about the same distance there was water   we put on our packs an our anemils and started and in about 13 miles made a river the largest we have
passed and camped[37]   in the morning there was a considrable trouble to
find a ford   at last we found one up the stream about half [a] mile and continued our journey NW for about ~~20~~ 15 miles and camped on a stream
which dus not run above the sand   dug & found water   we have passed
whare we have seen signs of elk & deer or Antelope   stoney going small
stone up and down small hills

---

[34]Robert Bliss believed "this is the tribe [Joseph R.] Walker had a fight with & killed some 30 of them
at all events they are much afraid of firearms." See Alter, ed., "The Journal of Robert S. Bliss," 114.

[35]Members of Hancock's family had become Methodists during a New York religious revival.

[36]Hancock described the course of Kings River.

[37]The company left Kings River and camped on the San Joaquin River north of present Fresno.

~~16~~ day 17 yesterday was the 16th and we had hard times but felt to be patient crossed some dry streams we found the water to do us we have camped again and we have passed over one sand Rio a large one about 12 miles back we have come 22 miles to day we have seen many Antelope on our way none killed yet one of our men saw an Elk

Wednsday 18 this day made 22 miles on a straight line and camped on a butiful stream that the Indians said was in three days journey of sooters fort[38] and one of the end of the sacramento and 1½ miles of Fremonts Rout here we got plenty of watermellons and some muskmelons some of these fellows was intirely naked the women had a brich clout on our rode was bad to day over stone hills and NNW corse our horses was tender footed I find that the streames we passed back are named on the map or some of the largest of them[39] one Antelope just killed much game here we have no guide now and trust in the lord and we find we get along better for when we had one we was always going wrong

19 day we took an North cours and in about 10 miles came to an other river [Tuolumne River] which was butiful and well timbered for this country we have seen many antelope on our way we then turned down and found that the river ran East & west we crossed and went to the N side made 20 miles not so much stone on our way as we had yesterday we soon saw an Indian with a recomend who brought it to one of our captains I read it and found it was from sooter recomending this tribe as friendly people and would not steal as some of the tribes do[40] we here found that there was some Americans on the next Rio a head

20 [August 1847] day we travaled West about 10 miles and turned up NNW crossed in about 4 miles a dry bed of a creek I suppose the water ran under the sand went 10 miles further the same corse and camped on a butiful River the best I have seen water melons and corn was brought in by the Natives to sell us these Rivers are well timbered the trees low but large bodys and tops the water is clear made of the snow from the Mts we have the best of feed for our animels to knight much sacarta an[d] other grass the Indians ses that there are some Americans dow[n] stream[41] some of our men talk of going to see them

---

[38]Like most contemporary phonetic spellers, Hancock pronounced John Augustus Sutter's name as Abner Blackburn spelled it, "Suiter."

[39]This is further evidence the Mormons had a copy of Frémont's 1845 map, which began naming San Joaquin River tributaries with "Rio de los Merced," Hancock's "butiful stream."

[40]The certificates presented by local Indian leaders demonstrate the control Sutter exerted over the native population of his empire, New Helvetia.

[41]The veterans had reached the Stanislaus River near present Ripon, about eight miles upstream from the New Hope settlement Samuel Brannan's *Brooklyn* Mormons had founded the previous summer. Reddick Allred recalled that his brother-in-law, Timothy S. Hoyt, stopped with the family of Charles Clark Burr. See Allred, Mormon Battalion Experiences, 12.

21 Day Andrew Lytle George Rosacrants D P Raney[42] started to go to the American settlement to see if they could here [news] from the church and the company came on North and camped on a creek about 10 miles from last knights camp   good water and feed

22 Sunday we started and took a NN West cours and came to an indian town in about 10 miles on the botoms of a creek or River [Calaveras River] from there we lerned that we ware [with]in 15 miles of the other River   the Pioneers went on and crossed hill after hill   very stony and hard for the Horses hoofs and they became very lame   we passed through much timber land down and up hill [across] baron land and praries   kept Fremonts rout some of the way and sometimes cut off crooks and went as straight as we could and about 5 oclock all or nearly all came in camp on a butiful River [Mokelumne River] and we lern we are in one days march of the big wagon rode that passes over the Mts

23 day yesterday while we was journeying we came to a spring on top of a hill or small Mt of the best kind and it was in a time of need and must have saved the lives of some of our anemals   I had one which was about to give out when all of a suden he jumped out one side into a large crowd of horses and sprang into it and would drink in spite of me while hot   I felt considrable alarmed but it done him no hurt   this day traviled a NNW Course 12 miles and for fere we should find no more water for a long time [we] camped   not much feed or water   our road has bin crooked to day some wild Indians have come into camp and say we are nere the big wagon road which is a little north of us   we cannot find how far   last knight I was troubled in spirit and had the worst kind of dreames seing the dead and bur[y]ing grounds   also I thought that a company of men came on us and one man cryes shoot   I then called for a general rally and awoke   the camp we have to knight resembles the camp I dreamed of last night   I could not sleep much in peace and concluded that it must be of satan and I would not believe it for I had a serting [certain] witness that I could see home and rejoice with my family

24 day 18 miles   we continued our journey and went NNW course and when we came in sight of the river I saw at my right a house and it looked like a home[43]   here we learned that [Jefferson] hunt and others was nere just a head

25 [August 1847] day this day rested on Causumey [Cosumnes] river or Creek while our pilots went on to fort sooters and while here a Mr Jhn P Rodes came to our camp and told us the horable tale of those men and women who eat each other   he states that one Mr Keesburg was a most

---

[42]Henry Bigler wrote that four men made up the party; the other man was either John Forsgren or A.P. Haws. At Sutter's, Jefferson Hunt "connected with the party led by Captain Andrew Lytle." See Little, *From Kirtland to Salt Lake City*, 152.

[43]This was Murphy's Ranch, home of Martin Murphy, Jr., an 1844 emigrant.

horable canable and the tale he states is the most shocking account I ever
read or hered of in my life   this man ses that there was more hands and feet
than one man could carry which this Dutchman eat   he must have murdered many   he had two tin buckets of blood dryed and human bodys all
around   one mans privats with the lower part of the belly lay on the ground
before the fire beside of his child   he states that he had a man and women
boxed up   he would cut of[f] the head of a man and split it open and ate
the brains and when he saw one woman after he got through he told her that
he would like to eat her she looked so good   he knew she would eat well[44]
    26 day Thursday we crossed the river and traveled NW ~~15~~ 20 miles and
camped in about 2 miles east of sooters fort[45]   5 miles   the road around
here is a butiful country but sickly   the people nearly all sick but the time
of year has come when the sicness abates   the Indians are all sick nearly this
day   Jefferson [Hunt] starts out I understand with recruting orders [to
raise] five companys from the Mormons   we think he cant come it   he is
gone ahead of all with his picked company of officers   the old fathers as
the soldiers call them

LEVI HANCOCK: THE WORST LOOKING PLACE I EVER SAW; SUTTER'S FORT TO DONNER LAKE

Although Hancock made little of it in his journal, his party frag-
mented further at Sutter's Fort. Lacking means, some men wintered over
at New Helvetia, while four tens pushed ahead immediately. Hancock
stayed behind at the fort. For the rest of the veterans' march, he would
lag behind rather than lead it, though as the foremost party approached
the summit of the Sierra, they "traveled in slow order that the company
we left at Sutter's may overtake us."[46]

Other veterans' journals and recollections contain detailed accounts
of the crossing of the Great Basin. Since 1847 overland sources are rare,
these documents provide valuable information about the California

---

[44]John Pierce Rhoades, the oldest son of Thomas Rhoades, came to California in 1846. He was a
member of the first and fourth Donner rescues. Louis Keseberg was the most notorious survivor of the
Donner disaster. In May 1847 he sued members of the fourth relief party for defamation of character and
won one dollar in damages. Keseberg made and lost two fortunes, managed a distillery for Samuel Brannan, and ultimately convinced writer C. F. McGlashan of his innocence. Reduced to poverty, Keseberg
died in the Sacramento County Hospital. For the significance of the "dryed" blood, see Stewart, *Ordeal by
Hunger*, 231.

[45]At a meeting that evening Hancock said, "a few might remain and labor until spring and all would
be right," for, as James Pace noted, "a few of our company stoped for want of menes to go futher." See
Tyler, *A Concise History*, 311; and James Pace, Journal, 24 August 1847.

[46]Gudde, ed., *Bigler's Chronicle*, 73.

Trail.[47] Hancock's directions and mileages are usually precise, but his description of crossing the Sierra is thoroughly confusing. A close examination of other sources helps untangle the mystery. The cabin "with many human bones" that Hancock reported on the sixth was the ruin of the first Donner relief camp at the "head of the Yuba," where a brutal winter storm caught James F. Reed in early March 1847.[48] "Fremonts piramid," on whose western side Hancock's party camped in Summit Valley, was perhaps Castle Peak, an extinct volcano. While Hancock was familiar with Frémont's reports, he does not seem to have had a copy at hand, and he apparently confused this site with Pyramid Lake, far to the east.

The timing of the battalion veteran's encounters with Samuel Brannan, coming west "very indignant because of [his] failure"[49] to persuade Brigham Young to settle in California, helps explain Hancock's Sierra crossing. The advance company under Averett met Brannan east of Donner Lake early on the morning of 6 September. Brannan told them that Capt. James Brown was only a short distance behind him, bringing mail from Salt Lake. The veterans returned to their camp near present-day Truckee to wait for Brown to arrive and for Hancock's company to catch up. After an hour's rest, Brannan went west with David P. Rainey, arriving at Hancock's camp in Summit Valley "just at night," Azariah Smith noted, "to hur[ry] us on to [join] the rest of our company." The next day Hancock's men crossed "the back bone," taking a convoluted course that led Hancock to complain, "our course has bin East 25 miles but not less [than] 10 miles from last knights camp." Hancock's erratic route on 7 September suggests he followed the newly opened trail over Roller Pass, arriving at Averett's camp "at 3 o'clock P.M."[50]

---

[47]The letters of Chester Ingersoll in McMurtrie, ed., *Overland to California in 1847*, and the memoir in Camp, "William Alexander Trubody and the Overland Pioneers of 1847," contain almost everything known about westbound 1847 California Trail companies. Mormon journals of 1847 west-to-east Great Basin crossings are found in Alter, ed. "The Journal of Robert S. Bliss," 120–28; and Bagley and Hoshide, eds. "The Last Crossing of the River: The 1847 William and James Pace Trail Diaries." Brief memoirs by Reddick Allred, Edward Bunker, David Pettegrew, and Albert Smith are at the Utah State Hist. Soc. and LDS Archives.

[48]Stewart, *Ordeal by Hunger*, 84.

[49]William B. Pace, Autobiography, LDS Archives, 60.

[50]Bigler, *Azariah Smith*, 102. Daniel Tyler, traveling with Hancock, garbled dates and facts in *A Concise History*, 315, but noted, "We camped overnight with Brannan." Henry Bigler gave the time of Hancock's arrival at the advance camp in a misdated letter to George A. Smith, quoted in the Journal History for 6 September 1846.

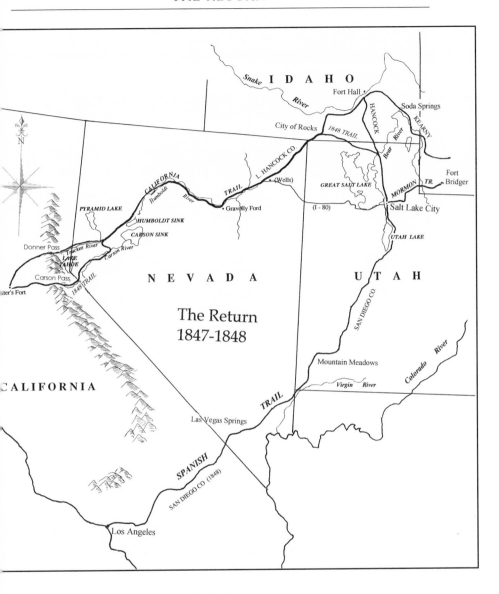

The most sensational element of the Hancock journal is the detail it provides on the Donner party story. Since the last relief expedition came out of the mountains in April 1847, students of the tragedy have argued over whether Louis Keseberg murdered Tamzene Donner. Hancock's story of Keseberg's "two tin buckets of blood dryed" could be considered the definitive "smoking gun" in the case—or simply another circumstantial and hearsay account.

LEVI WARD HANCOCK, JOURNALS 1846–1847, LDS ARCHIVES.

27 [August 1847] fryday stop to get some hors[e] sho[e]ing done and all who are ready push through the Mts

28 day concluded to stay to day and get some more horse shoing done half went yesterday   this ~~at~~ morning bought me a jack saddle & lasso fo[r] 15 dollars   this morning I strained my brest around my hart which gave me the most severe pane and now I feel bad and sore around my hart   I have got shoes for my riding beast paid 125¢

29 day started out of camp about half past 8 oclock and traviled on a North course 18 miles and camped by some holes of very poor water and feed but little   we have had good traviling   last night we had high winds thunder & lightning and just before day a small shower of rain   it seemed like old time   we have seen at our right upon the tops of the Mts clouds that looked like rain   also west of us there is clouds on the Mts but none in the vally   the rivers are kept up by perpetual snow which falls all times of the year and some times thaws which keeps the rivers high and hard to ford and almost imposable to ford   some times we find a place whare the water runs swift and makes it low just above the breast and by bracing well we have [been] able to cross all of them so far

Monday August 30 took an north corse some west but turned and come to us   went a long distance out of way but our corse N was 22 miles and come to Bare creek   here we was told that some of our men left here yesterday morning   this country along this valley must be nearly all under water some times of the year   weeds have floted four or five ft in many places along our way on the level plane   sink holes are common on the Sacramento whare dead water stands   this we had to drink   it must be sicly here   whare we are on the Bear River the water is dead   some timber here not much[51]

31 day we started into the Mts an ~~N&~~ NE East corse over ruged hill & down steep hollows crooking around untill we made 21 miles and camped by a small spring of water which woould soon loos[e] all water   in this place we watered our anemels which was something like 250   to day we

---

[51]Hancock had reached Johnson's Ranch on Bear River. English seafarer William Johnson had married Donner party survivor Mary Murphy, whose family had lived in Nauvoo during 1841–42. Reddick Allred learned she had been "carried out over on the men's shoulders and thus her life was saved. She expressed regret that she was married and said that were she able she would mount a horse and go with us to the Church. We sympathized much with her for her husband appeared to be a heartless sailor." See Allred, Mormon Battalion Experiences, 12. Murphy soon left her husband and had the marriage annulled. Marysville, California, was named for her in 1850.

have passed much timber some pine & oak of many kinds which grows on
the planes here but it is low & bushey tops pines long & slim   poor feed
we take the advantage of it and spread out into a long train

Sep[tember] 1st – 1847 this day is the first day of fall and we cast our
minds back to this time last [year] & whare are we now & whare was we then
now we are on the Mt top camped in among the pine by good water and
grass about 20 miles from Bare valley whare the emegrants eat each other
last winter in among the Siara Mts   one year ago we was under [Lt. A. J.]
Smith in the Mormon Battallion marching towards santafe under a swift
march   had to cary our armes and cartreg box and clothes napsac [and]
standing guard when sick or have to take calomel & be sicker   now we do
as we please and can ride and take our time

Sept 2 this morning we started and left one ten with a sick man one of
the Hoyets[52] who has the gravel   we found some watermellons seeds and
thought that if he had some tea made of them that would be good for him
the rest of us traveled on for about five miles and come to the Mt   we
passed trough 2 very bad hollows before we come to the Mt   here is our
road down and up the steepest [part] of the Mt[53]   this day made 20 miles
and come to the Mule Springs [which has] the coldest water I have seen in
Californa and the best   here we have found the names of many [of] our
breathring [brethren] who went with Carney and wrote on an oak tree   on
the tree there was names and said June 19–1847 and then there names was
wrote on the other side was Capt Pace with 50 men camped August
31–1847[54]   we have a company as large under Capt Andrew Lytle who
camps here to knight Sept 2–1847–

Sept 3 we left Mule springs which lies on the top or nerely of a high Mt
a few rods each side   it looks to be a thousand ft down to the botom   on
the left is Bare Creek where you look west altho here it seems nearly E NE
to SW   we are nere the head of a bend   al[l] along it passes through rocks
we traveled about ENE and [after] croking around in about 8 miles [we]
came down like coming out of the clouds and crossed the creek   folowed
it up about 4 miles and camped   made 12 miles   here we found fee[d] a
plenty   the botoms are half mile wide [with] good grass and water   two
miles from here back was a little [grass] that some of our men found and let
there horses eat   man[y] pea vines are there which the Horses love   this
country is the best timbered of any I have seen in California   I saw one pine
to day I should judge it to be ten feet [in] diameter and 150 high   here is

---

[52]Reddick Allred commanded the men left with Henry Pike Hoyt.

[53]This was Steep Hollow, where the trail left the Sierra foothills. Hancock labeled a line that wandered
from the bottom of one page in his journal to the top of the next as "Mt top steepest part" to sketch his
trek.

[54]James Pace noted that on a cool 31 August, "we crost some lofty mountains and through some very
heavy Pine timber."

plenty of the Redwood or [what] I call seeder[55]   some call it fir some pine
leaves taist like hemlock   we boiled some and it took the hemlock taist out
and made the best kind of drink   the trees are all as large as the pine and
look like hemlock but the wood is considred the best[56]   we are now in the
Bare vally at the head of the creek   camped along down for two or three
miles wating for our men who are back who have not so good horses   some
have come in since we come

Saturday Sept 4th–1847 this next day rest and wate for Capt Alred[57] who
was left back with Henry Hoyt who was left sick with the gravel   the 2 days
of Sept where we stayed one knight an whare I had this dream just before day
I thought I hered brother Heber C Kimble call me   I sayed I will come
directly   I had something that I was doing which I done quick and started
and went and the first man I saw was the Prophet Joseph Smith and the first
words he sayed to me was the field of grain must be attended to first and I
never knew or I did not know that it was with you as it is and I must go & I
will see you again and after he said these words he put his armes around me
and huged me and I awoke and told Andrew Lytle   I did not write it down
untill now considring it a dream but last knight he and I came together again
and I asked him if what I taught was correct   I told him I wanted to be right
and he would know   he looked plesent at me and sayed I do not see but that
you have done right in evry perticular   if there is anything wrong it is here
perhaps   it might have bin betered and arose as he sayed these words and
some others who was with him arose and stood up and Joseph sayed the reason why [James] Strang fell was that he assumes to himself power and ketched
a puppy and turned him around as if he was runing after his tail and could not
ketch it and so it was with Strang and I awoke[58]

Sunday 5th   we started over the Mt   went first up the vally and at the
foot of the Mt was the Irons of some of the wagons that had been left by
some of the emegrants last yeare[59]   last knight brother Alred came with the
sad news of the death of brother Hoyt[60]   we felt to mourn his loss but we

---

[55]Hancock was well out of the range of the redwoods, and his "seeder" is incense cedar, *Libocedrus decur-
rens*. See Graydon, *Trail of the First Wagons over the Sierra Nevada*, 2–3. Graydon lamented the destruction of
these cedars on the south side of Negro Jack Hill.

[56]Trail historian and naturalist LeRoy Johnson identified "pea vines" as a native California clover
(legumes). The pine is Jeffrey, *Pinus jeffreyi*, or Ponderosa pine, *Pinus ponderosa*. Mountain hemlock, *Tsuga het-
erophylla*, is restricted to the highest parts of the Sierra.

[57]According to Azariah Smith, the party awaited Allred's arrival in Little Bear Valley, four miles west
of Emigrant Gap. See Bigler, *Arariah Smith*, 101.

[58]James Jesse Strang claimed that Joseph Smith had appointed him his successor. Strang eventually
founded a colony on Lake Michigan and was crowned king of Beaver Island, where a disillusioned follower
assassinated him in July 1856.

[59]This was probably the campsite N. V. Jones had passed on 20 June 1847, where James Reed had met
Jotham Curtis and his wife in mid-November 1846. The Curtises abandoned their wagon and accompanied Reed to Sutter's Fort. See Johnson, ed., *"Unfortunate Emigrants,"* 176, 204.

have had to part with him   he was buried on the side hill on the top of the
first Mt this side of [the] steep hollow one mile   [They carved] his name
on a tree about half way between him and the road   he dyed by the afects
of the Calomel so said which fell in the Testickles[61]   we turned east at the
head of Bare vally and took the point of ridge and bore of[f] NE untill we
come to a bench about half up the Mt and went up east and over in an other
hollow not so deep by two thirds and saw the road more levil and turned
NE again and passed over some hills and saw at our right a pond of clear
water of about 3 acors   on the tops of the Mt is many ponds here which
burst through the rocks and on the other side of the Mts make springs
which make the rivers   these ponds are made of snow which lie all summer
the water is almost cold enough to freeze here   we turned here to the east
and we have com about that direction untill we come onto Juber [Yuba]
Creek and followed it east untill we came to the falls and turned of our
corse and we camped[62]   not much feed but it will do   made 12 miles   we
have had the worst kind of road to day   many stoney hill[s] we have passed
over and sharp conererd too bad for horses feet

Monday the sixth of Sept   we left our camp and continued our corse &
found that we had to turn east over a Mt about a half mile high and come
down on the same stream and continued our corse about EN East over the
points of Mts crooking around untill we asended a high hill or Mt and saw a
steep Mt suposed to be Fremonts piramid and camped on the west side of it
    this day made 12 miles still through the thick forest   passed one Broken
wagon and one cabin[63]   many human bones there so said   I did not call to
see   we left one man back by the name of Seshons[64] sick with the chills   I
have just came down from the Mt while on the top I counted 9 small lakes
and took the shape of the Mt tops   this Mt stands on the top of the Siara
of Californa Mts in the center of a great baison and is about 600 ft high
and is nearly straight down   here we rolled down large rocks that would

---

[60]Henry Pike Hoyt was born 2 August 1815 in New York. Reddick Allred, Hoyt's brother-in-law, and
eight men waited for three days below Bear Valley for Hoyt to recover. The party laid Hoyt "2 rds. below
the road, having nothing but a hatchet to dig down the side of the hill. We wrapped him in his blanket and
piled rocks around him and covered him with sticks and brush, and marked on a tree, '80 miles from Sutters Fort, Henry P. Hoyt died after 5 days illness of Jaundice, Sept. 3rd 1847.'" See Allred, Mormon Battalion Experiences, 13.

[61]Hancock's odd diagnosis attributed yet another death to battalion surgeon G. B. Sanderson.

[62]Hancock followed the wagon trail from Bear Valley, through Yuba Gap, and past Crystal Lake, his
"pond of clear water." His falls are difficult to identify, but were probably near the Big Bend of the Yuba.
The camp may have been near the present Hampshire Rocks campground.

[63]Although other sources do not mention a wagon or cabin at this site at the head of the Yuba, this
was probably the "Starved Camp," where James Reed and rescued members of the Donner party waited
out a blizzard in March 1847.

[64]Richard Sessions and his sons, John and William Bradford, settled in northern Utah. John Sessions
accompanied James Brown to Pueblo.

mak[e] a tremendious crashing below   this day I have now noticed that we are in a country of the balsam of fir which is a perfect cureosiaty[65]

Sept 7̸ 7th last knight Samuel Branhan came in our camp and had much to say about Capt Brown and had much and told of the difaculty between them and this knight I hered Browns story which was not as he [Brannan] stated and [Brown] called on brother [John S.] Fowler to witness to what he had said & Esquares   both said brown told the truth[66]   I stoped to the place whare the men eat each other   this day the boys said they saw one man lying on the plane up about one mile above us in a hollow   the most horable sight my informent ses he ever saw   some of the flesh was still dryed up like a mumma [with] clothes on   has bin draged about by wild anemels[67] many bones seen skulls backbones [and] thy bones of human beings   Fremont has burned the most of them[68]   our course has bin East 25 miles but not less [than] 10 from last knights camp   the Mtn we crossed is the back bone   we turned to the south and wound around west then south over the Mt down over on the other side of the Mt [and] went into a large vally [Donner Lake]   we passed snow last years   the Mts are covered each side I picked a snow ball out of Andres Lytles hand which he took closs by my horse   we went down in a hollow south for a number of miles and come to where the man eater lived who it is said eat the widow Murphy after he cut her throat[69]   he had two pales of blood when he was found & it was dry he sayed he got it out of dead mens bodys who died of starvation   the people say it cannot be got   it is the worst looking place I ever saw   the creek [Donner Creek] is called now Fether Creek on the account of the distruction of many beds   fethers [were] strung down it

8th day   we left & traviled an easterly course   made 18 miles & camped last night Capt Brown cam   we found [him] with the pioneers and Capt Pace   have good feed now   we have not got threw the Mts yet   last knight had a letter from my wife it done me good to here from her   she has a son born on the first day [of] Feb   Levi she calls it[70]

---

[65]Hancock camped in Summit Valley. Balsam fir is white fir, *Abies concolor*, but Hancock may have confused it with California red fir, *Abies magnifica*.

[66]"Esquares" was William Squires, a member of Brown's party who died at Sutter's Fort in 1850. John S. Fowler came west with the 1847 pioneer company and was bound for San Francisco to meet his wife and children, who had come to California with Brannan. See Bagley, ed., *Frontiersman*, 58, 102, 108.

[67]This was perhaps the body of Charles T. Stanton, one of the heroes of the Donner tragedy. Stanton died 21 December 1846 after he persuaded the "Forlorn Hope" to leave him behind. A monument commemorates his grave at the north end of Cascade Lakes.

[68]Hancock apparently assumed that Frémont had done the job, but as noted, on 22 June 1847 Kearny ordered the burial of the Donner party victims. Clarke, *Stephen Watts Kearny*, 332–34, suggested how historians later came to give Frémont credit for the burials.

[69]The "man eater" was Louis Keseberg. Hancock did not visit the Donner family camp, so this is probably a second description of the lake camp. Mrs. Levinah Murphy, baptized in Tennessee by Apostle Wilford Woodruff, died about 20 March 1847; Keseberg denied he had killed her.

[70]Levi Ward Hancock, Jr. (1 February 1847–10 December 1915), died in Lone Pine, Calif.

Brigham Young: A Location Which Can Not Be Beat

Over Brigham Young's signature, Willard Richards dictated two important letters on 7 August 1847, one appointing Samuel Brannan "President of the Saints in California," and a second containing instructions for the battalion veterans.[71] Aware that not all of the battalion families felt that he had kept his promise to look after them, Young's epistle began with a careful defense of his treatment of the families. It was "hardly to be expected" that "every one of your families" would have been able to travel to Salt Lake, but Young held out the hope that "a great many of them" would be in the new settlement; in truth, only a few of the dependents could afford to make the trip that year. The letter revealed a surprising grasp of western geography, acquired from the pioneers' many encounters with the mountaineers. It contained excellent advice, especially its counsel to avoid the Hastings Cutoff, and indicated that the Mormon leaders were already interested in developing a snow-free route from Salt Lake to southern California. Supplies were short in Salt Lake, so Young did not object to the veterans staying in California, but his epistle expressed a decided preference to have the men gather to the new "stake of Zion." The letter clearly stated that it would "be better for them to come directly to this place," but the recollections suggest he gave James Brown oral instructions that differed from the ones in this letter. Daniel Tyler recalled that Brown directed "those who had not means of subsistence" to "remain in California and labor, and bring their earnings with them in the spring." The events that Brigham Young's letter would set in motion still resonate in California today.

Young to Hunt and Battalion, Journal History.

Camp of Israel
Valley of the Great Salt Lake
Aug. 7, 1847

To Capt. Jefferson Hunt & the officers and soldiers of the Mormon Battalion.

Brethren: As Capt. Brown and escort is about to leave this place for [army] head quarters in California, we improve the opportunity of saying to you, that hitherto hath the Lord God of Israel blessed us and brought us to a goodly land, where we design to build a house unto his name and a city, which shall be a resting place unto his saints.

---

[71]Bagley, ed., *The Pioneer Camp of the Saints*, 252. For Brannan's letter, see Bagley, ed., *Scoundrel's Tale*, 215–20.

In the former part of April we left your families and friends at Winter Quarters (and vicinity), a city which we built last fall on the west bank of the Missouri river, nearly opposite the Liberty pole of your enlistment, consisting of more than 700 houses; and some of your families occupied some of the first that were built, and your families were better supplied with houses, fuel and provisions than the families with us generally, and we say this to you at this time to comfort your hearts and not to boast of what we have done. We will let our boasting be till another day.

The pioneer company with us number 143 men. We arrived here in this valley of the Great Salt Lake on the 22nd (and ~~23rd~~ 24th) of July and the detachments of the "Mormon Battalion" from Pueblo arrived here on the ~~31st~~ 29th, together with a company of saints from the Mississippi, and now we number about 450. Before leaving Winter Quarters we made every arrangement possible for our teams and waggons, and all those within our influence, to be sent on with your families as soon as the season would permit, and come to the place of our location. We have heard that they started in June and have sent back our messengers to pilot them to this place, and we expect them here in a few weeks. We do not know that every one of your families will come in this company; it is hardly to be expected; but if the brethren do as we have done, and we anticipate they will do, a great many of them will be here. Therefore, when you receive this and learn of this location, it will be wisdom for all, if you have got your discharge as we suppose, to come directly to this place, where you will learn particularly who is here, who not. If there are any men who have not families among your number who desire to stop in California for a season, we do not feel to object; yet we do feel that it will be better for them to come directly to this place, for here will be our head quarters for the present, and our dwelling place as quick as we can go and bring up our families, which we left behind this season for the purpose of bringing on yours, that you might meet them here; and we want to see you, even all of you, and talk with you, and throw our arms around you, and kill the fatted calf, and make merry; yes, brethren, we want to rejoice with you once more. Come then and see us, and we will do you good, and we will show you a location which can not be beat upon the Pacific Ocean, and you shall have an inheritance in this goodly land. We do not suppose that you want any urging to come here, but we speak out of the fulness of our hearts.

We are making every exertion to prepare for the families that we expect immediately here, and will spend but little time in writing to you now, as Capt. Brown can tell you a great deal more than can be written. Some few have passed by a new route to California called the Hastings cut-off by the south border of the Salt Lake, but it is not a safe route on account of the long drive without water, and it is not wisdom for you to come that way.

Brethren, cultivate the spirit of kindness and assistance towards another, and do each other all the good you can, and be humble and prayerful, and show yourselves men of God wherever you may be, and God will bless you.

Should this meet you in the southern part of California, or should any circumstance prevent your returning previous to the approach of cold weather, do not attempt to come by the north route, but come on the southern route.

Your arms, equipments, camp equipage, etc., you will retain and bring with you, for you will need them all at this place.

We remain your brethren in behalf of the Council,
Willard Richards, clerk   Brigham Young, President

Levi W. Hancock: The Worst Kind of Road; Donner Lake to Deseret

Captain Brown's mailbags carried a letter from his wife, but Levi Hancock said nothing about Young's letter, perhaps because it was addressed to Jefferson Hunt. In response to Young's directives, about half the company returned to California, and "About one hundred of us went on for Salt Lake over the high mountains where the perpetual snow was plenty. 140 miles and came to the sink of Mary's river. up that river near to the rise, thence to Fort Hall from thence 210 miles to Salt Lake."[72] The men with families were desperate to return to their wives and children. As William Pace noted, the men "thought it best" to "let those that wished to go to the Council Bluffs push through as we had about eight Hundred miles farther to go to get to the Bluffs."[73] The divisions also had practical advantages, for the smaller groups were better able to take advantage of the trail's limited resources, but the continued fracturing of the company aggravated Hancock.

Levi Ward Hancock, Journals 1846–1847, LDS Archives.

9 day   traveled down this river which is called Truckey 26 miles over many rocks & over high hills and steep ones too   this river is swift running water and round rocks & slipry   we have crossed it 5 times   the botoms narow   we came to a slew and had to turn to the right and went around a large scape of wet marshey mudy land and had to pass through much of it to get across it   then went along by the foot of the hill which was very

---

[72]Journal of David Pettegrew, 86.
[73]W. B. Pace, Autobiography and Journals 1847–1857, LDS Archives, 69.

rockey and camped in a good place for grass   these botoms and marshes is
all grass and rushes   last knight the officers called all hands together and
hered them express there feelings concerning pushing forward which all
agreed that on the acount of so many the swift travilers might go ahead with
the blessings of the Lord upon them and if they had time to go to the
[Council] bluffs they could [go with] there prayers and good wishes   here
they asked each others forgivness if they had hurt any one feelings

    10 day [10 September 1847] we went down the river 25 miles and
camped in a place we could not git out and I lost my horse   the Indians
stole it & Lyt[l]es mule and went to the Mts in as bad a place as they could
find   Lytle went to find them and tract them to the Mts   on the 11 day
we stoped on the river and took breakfast [at] nearly 10 oclock   our corse
has bin East ~~N~~ South E

    this 11 day we took around on the hill the worst kind of a road   we
found the Pioneers had gone ahead with many of our breathering on the
desart of 40 m before us and I am left with out an anemil to ride   the river
turns from 6 miles below our camp here NNE and runs winding through
hills   we have spoiled nearly all our catriges   4 oclock we left this river
called Truckey and took an ENE course and traviled until about 10 oclock
and come to the boiling hot springs a perfect curiosity[74]   the water is boiling hot and it boils about 2 ft high in one place   at others it can be hered
for long distance from the holes   they [are] larg enough in some places to
let in a man   I should think there is 30 or forty holes and other places show
they wonce boiled but are now caved in   I have dreamed of this place many
a time and new not what it ment untill I saw them and went in among them
and remembered my dreames   I hope the Lord ment I should take notice
of it by repeatedly giving me a sight   to here the rumbling put me in mind
of the secttarion hell   we camped closs by and found that our anemals
would not drink much   it cooled off in about 12 rods but are called bitter
as soon as morning came we packed up and soon it began to rain but it did
not last long   yesterday and to day made 40 miles no grass and no water
thats good and to knight is poor but our anemils will [make] do   I think it
is called the sink here I suppose of St Marys river[75]   we have come a ENE
course yesterday & today very sandy and in many places must be the worst
of going in wet weather

---

[74]On the way to the Boiling Springs, Robert Bliss noted that the veterans "about dark met Emigrants
for California." This was Chester Ingersoll's party of some twenty wagons, which had left the Humboldt
Sink on 10 September. See McMurtrie, ed., *Overland to California in 1847*, 34, 40. Traveling with the
advance party, William Pace wrote, "Several Boiling Springs where the water is so hot that it boils up several feet and the ground for several feet around shakes and there is holes in the rocks where the water is
seen to bluber up and Boil."

[75]The party reached the dike at the southern end of the Sink of the Humboldt.

Monday 13 we took an NN East cours for 23 miles then NN West one mile and cours NE 1 mile and NE 1 mile   25 [miles] this day   this is a desart & nothing grows on it but wild sage save on the sloughs a little grass we came on one to knight   seen a plenty of wild gees today in the ponds east side of us when we came by   have not hit san marys river yet

Tuesday 14 we traviled NN East up stream through the baron land for ~~20~~ 25 miles and went to our right down on the botoms by the River and camped   Mts on each side of this stream not so high and some miles off

Wendsday 15 day [September 1847] we traviled NNW 4 miles and turned NNE 3 m and then N untill we [went] 15 miles and our Capt showed me an Note left about one mile back which read like camp on st marys river   Capt Lytle sir   Capt Pace & Company arived at this place of encampment at 12 OC this day   since our arival the company has bin called together & it is the minds of all after having taken into consideration the scarcity of feed & the conveinience of traveling in small companies and that we are now where there is no danger of the Indians &c &c to travil on and if we should get to the forks of the road before you over take us & should [we] conclude to take Hastings Rout across the desart we will leave signs &c my camp are genrally well and hope all is well with you &c Yours with respect   respect   Capt Pace D Pettigrew E Averett W Hyde[76]

Thursday 16 started [when the] sun [was] an hour up and went North 4 miles and turned east 2 m then N east untill we made 25 miles and camped on the river st marys   met more movers going some to California and some to Oregon[77]   good feed to knight

Fryday 17 we marched at an hour by sun and made 25 miles NE up the river   good grass & water

18 day Marched East up the river winding our cours around on the banks of the streame   made 25 miles   no timber on this streame but a few willow sticks[78]

19 day made 35 miles East S East   crooked road   good feed beside the river   the Indians have bin troublesom to travilers[79]

20 day [September 1847] we made 25 miles East   after many long turns we have tryed to ketch Capt Pace until we are tired and conclude that if he

---

[76]Hancock learned of Pace's decision to break up into small companies near the point where the southern route to Oregon branched off the California Trail near today's Rye Patch Reservoir.

[77]Oregon-bound Lester Hulin encountered Jefferson Hunt's party on 14 September 1847: "To day we traveled about 18 miles and camped in good grass with some of the Mormon battalion from California." See Hulin, Day Book, 21. Hancock may have met William Wiggins' "lost" party of eighteen wagons, which tried to follow a waybill to the Sacramento River. The party wound up in Oregon, and their disappearance led Californians to fear a repeat of the Donner disaster. See Stewart, The California Trail, 190–92.

[78]Hancock had passed the Humboldt River's "Big Bend" at today's Winnemucca, Nevada.

[79]As Lester Hulin wrote farther west, "These prowling indians are as hard to find as the deer." With their food sources destroyed by emigrants, the natives of the central Great Basin exacted a toll of dead animals.

is a mind to leave us he might go[80]   our anemils are run down   our covenant was to stick together without a common consent and we can not ketch them   they have mules we have maires   we have traveled all of 65 miles in two days with our poor anemils

21 we made 20 miles East   croked around considrable   this river runs among the baron hills or Mts and [is] very levil   here we found the water ran swifter   we have picked up some anamils that have bin run down

22 we traviled NN East 23 miles the most of it Mts[81]   on the left side of the river as we came up stream and in the valies seen many springs coming out of the side hills   wild Indians all along   seen Children tracks there is some Patriges on this streame

23 day made 24 miles N East   passed many Indians naked   what they eat I cannot tell unless it is grass seeds and seeds of weeds

24th made 24 miles EN East in among the hills   this streame is a curious concern   it has cut through the hill here a little below about 3 miles and here it looks as if it was wonce a lake[82]   our cours has bin crooked to day   this morning found another letter from father Pedegroo who is with Capt Pace stating that they was with Capt Hunt on the 20th[83]

25th day [September 1847] went 24 miles east NE many turns   no water runs here now [but there is] some in holes   road appears to leave the river here[84]

26 day made 20 miles [and] passed Haisting cutoff   found that Hunt and Capt Pace had gone there   the letter from the twelve was not to go it we have made 10 miles and camped a little west of the hot springs which makes a considrable of a streame out of a canion a short distance east of our camp   we have seen much good land on our rout for a few days march but no timber   I think by the looks of the grass that anything would grow without arigating   warm springs here in this canion comes out from under the Mt about as dish water[85]   Course ~~NN~~ EN East

27 day left our camp in the mouth of the canion [taking] a ENE cours

---

[80]The veterans were even more widely scattered than Hancock's journal indicates. On 18 September, Robert Bliss, a day or two behind Hancock, noted that he was four or five days ahead of the last companies.

[81]East of Gravelly Ford, Hancock's party crossed Emigrant Pass to camp near today's Carlin.

[82]Hancock had passed the junction of the Hastings Cutoff with the California Trail where the South Fork of the Humboldt "cut through the hill." The men camped west of present Elko, Nevada.

[83]James Pace noted on 20 September 1846, "traveled 10 Miles & over took our Fathers   we past them a bout one Miles   encamped a bout 12 ock   our Fathers did not visit us except one or two of there company." "Our Fathers" was an ironic reference to Hunt's men, many of whom had been officers.

[84]On this day, Robert Bliss reported, "on our way today found the fragments of a letter left by Prest Hancock . . . [We] suppose the Indians found it & tore it in Pieces   they follow our camps for Plunder &c they are a wreched set of Lamanites wild as the deer on the Mts."

[85]Hancock confused the Hastings Cutoff with the 1845 road that Pace's company took to today's Wells, Nevada. Hancock's party camped on the original 1843 trail at the mouth of Bishops Creek near the warm spring that forty-niner John Banks thought "one grand object . . . of the most transparent clearness, gushing from the mountainside. Nothing can surpass it in beauty."

for five miles then turned east and went across the plane and came to the road that we thought was the cut off and saw the tracks of our breathrings horses and after we had made 20 miles we came to the hot springs and found Capt Pace and company and there was Hunt a little a head   Hunt and company leaves   made this day 20 miles   our course back from the forks of the road has bin ENE   we passed a back bone ridge between St marys River and these hot springs[86]   we brought up sevral anemals our breathring left behind

28th day journied N East 10 miles and found water in a well like place good water there is in all these places threw [to] California and many of them there is too   from there we took more north and found that it is NNE for about 10 miles further and found another well   here was a bad place to git to the water   one mare myred but after it was onloded it come out   this day made 25 miles and camped beside good water & grass[87] large Mts and hills on each side yet

29th day traviled N East and found water along for about 10 miles in places   then found none untill we came the waters of goose creek and followed it down NE untill we made 25 miles and camped   had to crook around in among the hills [and] passed over some

30 day went N East 18 ~~15~~ miles and turned North and went 3 miles and took up a canion and went untill we made 25 miles and camped by good water & grass

Our fathers [officers] have left us & gone on before ahead
But nothing consoling unto us have said
And left not fathers there blessings and fathers would of one
When blessing they wonted to rest on there sons

Altho they camp nere us but just on before
But Oh & Alas we can reach them no more
Some times they pass by us but wont crack one smile
But And will not camp nearer us than one half mile

And we cannot tell what it is that we have done
That should make our fathers dispise their sons
O father O father a while Oh do stop awhile
You left us behind you as much as one mile

You say that our Company your mules dispise
And will not stay with us because hes too wise
If he did leave us we are sure he left you
And you for to find him had all you could do

---

[86]After ascending Bishops Creek, Hancock had reached Thousand Springs Valley and found Pace and Hunt camped "encamped on a small creek near a hot Spring" at the Winecup Ranch, owned in the 1950s by film star James Stewart.   [87]The company camped at Rock Spring.

Therefore we do hope that you will not dispise
Your sons any longer if they are not wise
If you are our fathers do treat us as such
And do not dispise us as you do so much

But if you reject us we must give let you up go
And trust in kind providence until wer'e go through
So farewell dear fathers oh do be so kind
As to leave the road you have traviled behind

this day we have seen many gees good land and water & ducks [but] no wood of any account

Oct 1st [1847] we went N east crooking around and over mts and through vallys untill we made 26 miles and we camped by good water and grass   the water here is warm at the springs   we passed some Mts covered with the best of marble[88]

2 day   went NE 10 miles and come over the uplands to the banks [of Cassia Creek] and decended down on the botoms to an other river [Raft River] called [blank]   we then went down it untill we made this day 33 miles   our anemils was tiered when we stoped as well as we ware   this river like others we have passed between this and st marys is small perhaps one rod across and runs crooked sometimes very narow botoms and sometimes wider   sometimes it spreads out wide and would make good plantations traviled 11 hours to day

3 day   traviled down this stream or river 20 miles   a NN East cours not so crooked   we have passed the Oregon rout   seen some graves beside the road [and] some at the turn off back one mile[89]   our horses are almost run down   we have our match to get them along

4 day   traveled NN East about 8 miles and came to big snake [River] and traviled up it untill we made 20 miles & camped   this streame is about ⅙th of a mile across in high water

5 day   traviled up it 6 miles NE and came to the falls and found them to be about 20 ft high called the American falls   we come to two falls yesterday and supposed them to be what these are but they was small   come on the same cours untill we made 20 miles and camped down on the botoms about one mile from the road   here the botoms spread out wide and butiful   not any timber on this River but small brush   on the bluffs is small seader in

---

[88]After crossing the far northwest corner of today's Utah, the veterans climbed Granite Pass to camp near the Silent City of Rocks in present Idaho.

[89]The grave "of Lydia Edmonson, who died Aug. 15. 1847, Aged 25 years" was opened after N. V. Jones passed the Raft River ford on 13 July. See Read and Gaines, eds., *Gold Rush: The Journals, Drawings, and Other Papers of J. Goldsborough Bruff*, 1:113–14, 263. The Oregon-California Trails Assoc. marked the site in 1992 with the help of landowners Lyle and Carol Woodbury. See Duffin and Brown, *Graves and Sites on the Oregon and California Trails*, 80–81.

patches   it looks more like rain this eveing than any time since we left Pubelo [de los Angeles]   we one evening had a small sprinkle and wonce at the hot springs but did not hurt but laid the dust hansomely   last knight I had a dream which gave me great joy if I was a sleep   I thought my wife came to me and asked me [if] I did not wont to go whare she roosted   I thought it was in a great tree top she had found some whare   I told her I did   she took hold of my hand and we traviled a considrable distance and come to an other road and she said I call this Haistings cut off   you must not take it   she then let go of my hand and ran ahead and said here is the way and we traveled on and soon we came to a vally and I saw George and Charles Hancock[90] and an other man   I cannot tell who it was   and they turned and faced east and she said I roost here and I awoke   I thought sometimes I would fly and some time a foot and some times a riding my mare

6 day   went NNE untill we got to the fort   15 miles to day   6th day traviled NE 8 miles and came to the river and crossed it and went 10 miles further [on the] same cours and camped at fort hall   here we bought some bacon and buck skins and on the 7th day morning Capt Pace went ahead[91] I told him [of] the pass which was south from the fort egsactly by the compass and he got on a head and took two anemils a Jack and mare and my Horse   ten men went with him   we followed him untill we got sick of it we was in hopes all the time he would turn but he did not and whare he will go we cannot tell   this is the only pass   we had to travil 35 miles to day

7 [8] day   we got up our horses and went south on this streame about 15 miles and camped on good ground for feed

9th   we followed this creek up and in about 15 miles we went over the divideing part of it untell the ground discended South West   our cours has bin all day SS west and a part of yesterday   made 30 miles to day   no water and not much feed

10 [October 1847] we turned east and took into the Mts through a canion and from last knights camp we are 10 miles   3 in the Mts   found water & paper stating Capt Pace is a head   10 oclock mad[e] this day 20 miles

11   made 20 miles and camped by Reed creek[92]

12   day   28 miles   we have crossed Bare [Bear] River   passed some warm springs which is salt   we are at good water now and feed   Pace is gone ahead again   our anemils are tyred

13   made 30 miles

14th   traviled 25 [miles] five out of our way by mistakeing the man who

---

[90]Levi Hancock's nephews George Washington and Charles Brent Hancock had been privates in Co. C.

[91]James Pace recorded on 7 October 1847, "This day we left the fort [Hall]   a part of our company continued on the road to Fort Bridger but the largest number turned south for the Great Salt Lake City we journed [sic] successfully day after day untell we reached the promised Land."

[92]"Roseaux or Reed Cr" was the name used on Frémont's 1845 map for today's Malad River, which flows from Idaho into Utah along the line of I-15. Pace camped here on 10 October 1847.

directed Capt Pace   he Pace led ahead   Lytle stoped at an Indian town and
I took command of Lytles company and took a shoot for the trail and
found it in three miles and Capt Lytle a standing egsactly against the point
of the Mt I made for

[End of the Journal]

Levi Hancock's 1847 journal ended in the middle of a page. Family
tradition tells that he had a stroke on his trip from Fort Hall, perhaps as
he wrote the last entry. Hancock wintered in the Salt Lake Valley and the
next summer unexpectedly reunited with his family at Cache Cave on the
Mormon Trail. He separated from his wife, Clarissa, in 1850, but
"labored assidiously [*sic*] for the upbuilding of the Kingdom of God"
on the ragged edge of the Mormon frontier for three more decades. As
long as battalion veterans lived, they sang Hancock's songs at their many
reunions. Zealous to the end, Hancock died in Washington County,
Utah, on 10 June 1882.[93]

WILLIAM HYDE:
WEATHER ABOUT AS COLD AS I EVER WITNESSED

"We found Capt. Grant at Ft. Hall, a station of the England Hudson
Bay Fur Company," recalled Reddick Allred. If anyone was an authority on
survival in the northern borderlands, it was Richard Grant, a veteran of
thirty years in the fur trade, and he was not encouraging. "He told us we'de
be unable to raise a bushel of grain in Salt Lake Valley, that it would be a
failure if we attempted to establish a Colony there."[94] Robert Bliss arrived
at Fort Hall eight days after Levi Hancock, where Grant "read his remarks
on our people who had passed him this fall, as recorded in his Journal; He
says they were gentlement [and] payed for all they got of him & he heard
no Oath or vulgar expression from any of them but he could not say so in
regard to Other people who had passed him this season; He is a Gentleman of Inteligence & Observation." A skilled diplomat, Grant perhaps
gave his friends a less complimentary report about the Mormons, for John
McLoughlin had heard "that they are Disagreeable Neighbors."[95]

At Fort Hall the veterans again divided, some taking the Oregon Trail

---

[93]M. L. Hancock, Autobiography of Levi Ward Hancock, 99; and Jenson, *Latter-day Saint Biographical Encyclopedia*, 1:189.

[94]Allred, Mormon Battalion Experiences, 14.

[95]Alter, ed., "The Journal of Robert S. Bliss," 125; and Sampson, *John McLoughlin*, 58–59.

directly to Fort Bridger where they waited for the men who had "struck South (without a trail) for Salt Lake."[96] The bitter division between the officers and the men persisted all the way to the new Mormon settlement and beyond. A small band of officers led the way, for P. C. Merrill recalled, "In company with Captain Jefferson Hunt and seven others, arrived in Salt Lake on October 11th 1847."[97] The parties straggled into the valley until late in the month; Robert Bliss arrived with one of the last contingents on 25 October. Apostle John Taylor helped collect clothing for the ragged men who "presented an almost ludicrous appearance after donning the additions to their wardrobes." Fifteen men "started across the Plains to Winter Quarters" on 18 October 1847 under the command of P. C. Merrill, followed shortly by divisions led by James Pace and Andrew Lytle, who were "determined to make an effort to spend the winter with their wives and children."[98]

Reddick Allred's memoir provides insight into the movements of the party that took the Oregon Trail directly to Fort Bridger.

> A few of us kept on the old Emigrant road by Soda Springs, and up Bear River, which we left near Bear Lake and went over the hills to Ft. Bridger, a trapping post where we waited a few days until the rest of the company came from Salt Lake. Jos. Thorn was camped 4 miles from Ft. Bridger. At Peg Leg Smith's Elisha Everetts [Averett] and myself went and remained over night with them where we had our first supper of warm biscuits, butter and milk, prepared by Smith's wife, an indian squaw. Thorn joined us with his wife (so he said) to go back to the States to secure an outfit with which to go to the Valley. We left Bridger (33 in number) [with] Capt. Andrew Lytle in charge.
>
> I found a give out mule, left by Wm. Hyde who had preceded us a few days with Jas. Pace and a few others. I took the mule along.[99]

---

[96]W. B. Pace, Autobiography, LDS Archives.

[97]P. C. Merrill, Autobiography. Merrill found that two of his sisters, Phoebe Lodema Merrill, "who accompanied the Mormon Battalion as a nurse," and Albina Marie Merrill (Mrs. Thomas Williams), "had come in with [James] Brown" from Pueblo in July. See Ibid., and Jenson, *Latter-day Saint Biographical Encyclopedia*, 4:754.

[98]Little, *From Kirtland to Salt Lake City*, 159–60. Sgt. Daniel Tyler described his "Eastward Journey" traveling with Andrew Lytle's division in *A Concise History*, 318–325.

[99]Allred, Mormon Battalion Experiences, 14. Peg-leg Smith's camp was near Montpelier, Idaho. Perhaps the first of all "back outs"—emigrants who returned east from Mormon Utah—Joseph Thorn joined Lytle's party "with his wife and one or two children, in a light wagon." See Tyler, *A Concise History*, 323. If not an apostate at the time, Thorn certainly was by 1884 when he swore at San Bernardino that he had heard Joseph Smith reprove Brigham Young "for taking and using for his own private purposes church moneys." Thorn contributed one of many affidavits collected by the RLDS church to prove Smith had said, "If Brigham Young ever leads this church he will lead it to hell." See "He Will Lead the Church to Hell," 510.

The diary of William Hyde tells the story of the trip to Winter Quarters with the men who followed P.C. Merrill. The adventures of those led by James Pace are recounted through the journal of his son, William Byram Pace, whose autobiography described the expedition's inauspicious start from Salt Lake:

> Here some of the Battalion Boys found their families or relatives and stopped over, others were compelled to stop, for want of sufficient outfit, to cross the plains, a distance of over a thousand miles, while we had [already] traversed over fifteen hundred miles from Los-Angeles via Sutters Fort.
>
> Finally a company of between 30 & 40 under Lieut. James Pace began preparing to brave the dangers of crossing the plains during the winter months. Provisions being scarce in the valley, we were told we could get supplies at Fort Bridger and at Laramie reasonable, and it would be a great help to the people if we would leave our provisions and replenish on the road. Having a common interest we unloaded our supplies, taking only what was supposed enough to do us to Fort Bridger (one hundred and fifteen miles) and moved out late in October.
>
> At the head of Echo Canyon we encountered our first snow storm, and the cold seemed to have a chilling effect on the Animals as they were from a warmer climate but before 10 o'clock the next morning it cleared up. The snow soon melted and we was on our way rejoicing; arriving at Fort Bridger we found that they had not anything to sell. Here we were as it was over 400 miles to Fort Laramie and nothing to eat. A council was called, consisting of a committee of the whole (camp). Much time was taken up in trying to decide whether the party in Salt Lake who advised us to leave our supplies and depend on getting more on the road acted from sinister motives, whether we were to go back to Salt Lake and fight it out during the winter with the others, or go ahead without anything to eat, however no one thought for a moment but what we could get what we wanted at Fort Laramie so it was unanimously decided to go ahead, and depend on game.[100]

After their discharge at Los Angeles, the eastbound battalion veterans elected William Hyde president of their first fifty. A twenty-nine-year-old New Yorker and former sergeant of Company B, Hyde had been a Mormon since 1834 and was counted "as one of the founders of the city of Nauvoo."[101] At the Sierra crest in September, Hyde had learned of the death of his only sister and the birth of his first son at Winter Quarters.

---

[100]W. B. Pace, Autobiography, LDS Archives, 61–62.

[101]Jenson, *Latter-day Saint Biographical Encyclopedia*, 1:758–63. Jenson summarized much of Hyde's journal from the work of Edward W. Tullidge.

He was one of the men determined to return to his family in 1847, and his party set the pace for the following companies all the way back to the Missouri. Hyde's family published *The Private Journal of William Hyde* in 1956, from which this version is taken. Finding aids date the composition of the document to 1868–1873, but Hyde's battalion account is certainly based on a daybook.

WILLIAM HYDE, THE PRIVATE JOURNAL OF WILLIAM HYDE, 46–49.

On the 3rd of October [1847] we reached Fort Hall, which is situated about 200 miles north of Salt Lake Valley, and over 700 miles by the route we had traveled, from Sutter's Fort.

On the 4th we resumed our journey and without as much as an Indian trail to guide us. Reached the camp of the saints in Salt Lake Valley on the 12th of October. The reception with which we met gladened our hearts and revived our spirits. A small portion of the company found their families here, and consequently had got home. The Presidency and some of the pioneers had returned to Winter Quarters. The saints that were remaining felt very well pleased with the situation of the Valley, and my conclusions were that it was a place of retreat, or a hiding place which God had, in his wisdom, prepared for his people.

On the 15th of October [1847] I left Salt Lake, with 16 in company, for Winter Quarters.

The 19th we reached Fort Bridger, distance 115 miles.

The 20th. Laid by. Snow fell two inches.

The 21st. Continued our journey, and on the 25th camped on Sweetwater.

The 29th. Camped at Independence Rock.

The 30th. Left Sweetwater and traveled 22 miles to Willow Spring. The weather was very cold and windy.

On the morning of the 31st found that one of my mules was missing, and after hunting for some time was obliged to pursue my journey without it. This day the weather was extremely cold. Traveled 15 miles.

November 1st [1847]. Reached Platte River. Two buffalo were killed.

The 2nd. The weather continued cold and disagreeable. Made a short drive.

The 3rd. Camped on Deer Creek.

On the morning of 4th snow fell 1 inch, At 10 o'clock A.M. clouds broke away and we again picked up our traps and rode 10 miles. At this place of encampment I killed a buffalo, some of the meat of which we partly dried and have taken along with us, and was truly a help to us as we had started from Salt Lake with a very small quantity of flour.

The 5th, 6th, and 7th. The weather about as cold as I ever witnessed. Had to run behind our mules with robes wrapped around us to keep from freezing.

The 8th. Reached Fort Laramie. At this place we were very hospitably received and entertained. A substantial supper and breakfast, with mule feed, was furnished us free of charge.

The 9th. Started in the afternoon. Crossed the Platte on the ice. Traveled 6 miles.

The 10th [November 1847]. Traveled 30 miles.

The 11th. Left the timber. Snow from 8 to 12 inches deep, had about 200 miles before us without firewood. At our places of encampment had to poke under the snow for buffalo chips.

The 19th came to timber.

The 23rd. Two of the best horses in camp were stolen by the Indians.

The 24th. Had a snowstorm, Weather very cold and disagreeable. The wind blows hard and the air is full of snow, and the roads are also being drifted full.

The 28th. Reached Loup Fork. We were detained here 6 days as the stream was swolen and so much ice running that it was impossible to get across. After finding [it] impossible to cross at or near the ford, we concluded to go up to the forks of the river, which was some 12 or 15 miles distance through brush and over broken ridges without any road or trail. After reaching the forks we were two days before we succeeded in getting all [our] things across. I was the first person that crossed each fork. I crossed on foot to try the depth of the water, and the last stream I had to swim part of the distance. The water was extremely cold and with much ice running. In crossing the animals, one of the poorest of the horses mired in the quicksand, and as our provisions had entirely failed, and as it was impossible to get the animal out alive we concluded to cut its jugular vein and save the meat, which was done.

The 4th of December [1847] started on our homeward course. Traveled 15 miles.

The 5th. Passed some corn fields belonging to the Pawnee Nation. We went into one of the fields and by kicking up the stocks that lay under the snow we succeeded in finding a few nubs of corn. This we ate raw, but it had become sour by laying under the snow and it did us much more harm than good.

On the 9th we camped within about 15 miles of the horn [Elkhorn River], which place is 30 miles from the general camp of the Saints, or Winter Quarters. But as we were strangers to the route, we were not aware that we were so near our place of destination, and as the snow was deep, and our meat which we had saved from the horse entirely exhausted, we seated ourselves upon the snow around our camp fire and entered into council as to the wisest course to be pursued. Some thought best to send two men on two of the best mules in camp for Winter Quarters. To this I replied that we had now traveled near five thousand miles, and that we had suffered much with hunger, cold, thirst and fatigue, and now to give out on the last hundred miles I didn't like the idea. I then said that in case we could not get through with out [help], we would make a free will offering of my riding mule and we would eat her, as she was in as good order as any in camp. To this proposition all readily agreed.

On the morning of the 10th, we all were united in calling on the Lord to regard our situation in mercy and send us food from an unexpected quarter that we might have wherewith to subsist upon. And here the Lord heard our prayer. Soon after reaching the Horn, the wild turkeys began to pass our camp in droves, and such a sight I never before witnessed. Drove after drove continued to pass through the woods until night set in. We succeeded in getting four, which was one to every four persons, and after this we could not get any more although our shots might be considered ever so fair, and we concluded to be satisfied. Probably it would have been a damage to us if we had got all we wanted as we were then suffering in the extreme with hunger.[102]

The 11th. Went to the camps of the saints at Winter Quarters. The day was bitter cold and the company was well nigh used up. Our clothing being in no wise calculated for winter, we had suffered much with cold, as well as with hunger. Brother Ira Miles, from poor health and extreme suffering, had become as helpless as a child. But the reception with which we met, and the blessings that were poured upon our heads on our arrival, seemed to cause new life to spring up and to compensate us for all our toils. This company, numbering 16 souls, were the first to return from the Battalion after our discharge in California.

December 12th, I crossed the Missouri River and rode to Council Point, a distance of 12 miles, where I found my family and father's house. All were well, and I am pretty certain we were glad to meet again. I reached home on Sunday, and as it was dusk when I arrived, the people of the little burgh had gathered for worship. The news of my arrival soon reached their place of gathering, which proved the breaking up of their meeting. All were so anxious to see me that without ceremony they flocked out of the meetinghouse and gathered into my humble but happy cot[tage] which had been built by my father and brother for the benefit of my family in my absence. This was a joyful meeting, but as the evening began to wear away my appetite began

---

[102]Mormon pioneers often felt "we had a direct manifestation of the mercy and goodness of God, in a miracle." Hyde's experience resembled the famous "Miracle of the Quail" that took place on the Mississippi River on 9 October 1846. See Bagley, ed., *The Pioneer Camp of the Saints*, 34, 76.

most keenly to return, and I was induced to say to the people, that inasmuch as they felt a kind regard for me, they would manifest it by withdrawing that my wife might have the privilege of preparing me a morsel to eat. This love was readily manifest, and a warm supper was soon ready. But as to satisfying my appetite, this was out of the question, as I had suffered too long to have my appetite become natural by eating one meal or in one week.

William Hyde returned to Utah in 1849 and later went on a mission to Australia. He commanded a hundred men in the Utah War and settled Hyde Park in Cache Valley in 1860. There he served as a bishop, judge, patriarch, and militia general. He died in 1874, the husband of five wives and the father of twenty-five children.

WILLIAM B. PACE: THE DANGERS OF CROSSING THE PLAINS

William Byram Pace had served as an aide to his father, Lt. James Pace, during the battalion march. Only fifteen at the time of his return to the Missouri River, ten pages of his journal describe his "900 mile jaunt in mid-winter without anything to eat" in the late fall of 1847.[103] The manuscript journal is a fragment, written on loose pages, beginning on 5 January 1847 on page 19. The section reproduced here was apparently copied from the original daybook, with its concluding section composed after the party reached Winter Quarters. The document consists of daily entries until the first of November, when the rigors of the trip probably prevented diary keeping. The surviving journal was probably copied from original sources shortly after the concluding entry of 25 March 1852. Whatever its origins, Pace's adventurous tale is a classic of youthful overland literature.

WILLIAM B. PACE, JOURNALS 1847–1857, LDS ARCHIVES, 74–77.

The 6th [October 1847] was rainy. We reached Fort Hall and encamped about one mile south at some springs making a travel of fourteen miles. On the morning of the 7th apart of our company took the main road to go to Fort Bridger, and await for the remainder of the company, that wished to go by the City of the Salt Lake. We start early for the valley of the Salt Lake, traveled 15 miles. Encamped on a small river in the mountains.

On the 8th we left this river [and] traveled up a Canion; and crossed a

---

[103]W. B. Pace, Autobiography, LDS Archives, 61–62.

WILLIAM B. PACE.
Only fourteen when he marched
to California as an aide to
his father, Lt. James Pace,
William Pace later served as a
general in Utah's disastrous
Black Hawk War.
Courtesy, LDS Archives.

large ridge. Encamped in a butiful valy (water and grass plenty) making a travel of fifteen miles. 9th This day we traveled 35 miles; encamped in a small ~~creek~~ canion (grass and water scarce). On the 10th—we traveled ten miles to Reeds Creek [Malad River], a tributary of Bare river. The 11th was rainy. We traveled 20 miles, down this Creek, and encamped on the banks. On the 12th morning clear & pleasant; Crost the creek [and] traveled a few miles acrost a plane to Bare River; Crost over and traveled down the foot of the Mountain, past a large Hot Salt Spring, and another spring close by the side of fresh water but Hot. This day we traveled a distance of twenty-five miles, encamped at a nice cold spring.[104] Grass plenty.

13th The Morning pleasant. We traveled down the valley twenty-five miles, the road was good, and we crost a number of streams rushing from the Mountains, and runing down into a butiful large Valley; The Morning of the 14th [was] warm and pleasant; this day we crost several larger Streams. Past the Encampment of Miles Goodgers and some of the Utaw

---

[104]The Hot and Cold Springs, noted on Stansbury's map of 1850, were just north of today's Honeyville at Crystal Springs.

Indians;[105] Here, we learned that we was within forty miles, of the Salt Lake Settlement; we traveled eighteen Mile, and encamped at small creek, near the foot of the Mountains (grass poor and scarce).

On the 15th [October 1847], the weather pleasant, we traveled twenty five miles down the Valley; and encamped at Perygreen Sessions camp, where he was a herding cattle, about ten miles above the Salt Lake settlement;[106] On the morning of the 16th we reached the settlement; found them all well, & busy a building houses & preparing for the winter.

The 17th [was] cold & frosty. It being Sunday at eleven oclock Jetediah Grant & [John] Tailor preached.[107] On the 18th morning we fitted-out and started for the Bluffs. Traveled 11 miles [and] encamped on Browns creek night very cold and frosty;[108] The 19th we traveled over a Mountainous Road about twenty-seven miles. Encamped on Weber River a tributary of Bare River. The 20th Stormy. We traveled 27 miles this afternoon and night we had a large snow storm. We encamped at Cha=cach=chee [Cache] Cave. The night very Cold and stormy. The morning of the 21st Clear and very cold. We packed up our half frozen Animals and traveled to little Bare River a distance of fourteen miles. On the 22nd Clear and Cold traveled twenty seven miles encamped at cold spring. On the 23rd we traveled 6 miles to Fort Bridger. Bought some Bacon and other Articles and then traveled 8 miles farther and encamped on Blacks Fork. The 24th Morning cloudy traveled twenty-seven miles encamped on Blacks Fork. The 25th Traveled a distance of 25 miles. Crossed Greene River [and] encamped on Big Sandy.

On the 26th traveled a distance of 26 miles. Crossed Big Sandy and encamped on Little Sandy 3 miles below the ford. 27th traveled twenty-six [miles and] encamped at the Pacific Springs at South Pass. The 28th traveled 17 miles. Crost Sweet Water and encamped on Willow Creek about five miles below the Sweet Water Ford. 29th Cool. Traveled a distance of eighteen miles. Encamped on Sweet Water. There we had the first Buffalo killed which came in good play as we were out of meat and flour was Scarce. On the 30th traveled 27 miles encamped on Sweet water. Weather very cold and

---

[105]Mountaineer Miles Goodyear built Fort Buenaventura near the confluence of the Weber and Ogden rivers in 1846 at a spot now in the heart of Ogden, Utah.

[106]Perrigrine Sessions camped on the site of present Bountiful shortly after arriving with the second division of 1847. His wife Patty recorded "some soldiers come in" and "more soldiers came" to Salt Lake on 11 and 12 October. See Smart, ed., *Mormon Midwife*, 101.

[107]Jedediah Grant would later be mayor of Salt Lake, second counselor to Brigham Young, and the driving force of the Mormon Reformation until his premature death in 1856. During this sermon Apostle John Taylor appealed for clothes to be given to the battalion veterans. Taylor was sustained president of the LDS church in October 1880 to succeed Brigham Young.

[108]Originally named for John Brown of the Pioneer Camp, this is today's Emigration Creek.

windy. 31st Cold and cloudy traveled twenty miles encamped on Sweet water.[109]

On the 1st of November we started on and after a hard & tedious Journey we reached Fort Larrimie. Here our Provisions being exhausted we procured a little Flour some Hard Bread and some dryed Bufflo meat and proceeded on. After travelling several days down the Platte we had a series of Snow Storms a little below Ash Hollow but as there was no Chance for fuel only Buffalo Chips and no feed for our Animals except what was covered under the snow we were forced to make some Hard Drives to get to the head of Grand Island 200 miles as that was our only chance for firewood & grass. During this travel we had several mules frozen to Death.[110] Besides our provisions began to fail so that we lived on Quarter Rations and by the time we got there we were out of Provisions entirely.

After travelling several days without food and not knowing where we would find the next [meal] one of D. P. Rainy's Animal gave out (I think it was a Jack Ass) and we called a halt but finally drove on and encamped near Wood River. When after considerable consultation we agreed to make a supper out of the Old Jack; So in a few moments a looker on mite have seen Abraham Hunsaker & Elisha Averett & others with a gun and Knives amarching to the field of Battle; Shortly after they returned with a part of the old Jack Dressed & Ready for to be confiscated [sic] into a repast for some ten or twelve half starved Mormon Soldiers. At this I must confess there was feelings of considerable intrest. Some stood off and would not partake while others piched into it like as many ravenous wolves devouring their Prey. After this beds were made down in the grass & weeds and in a few moments, all except the sentinels were sunk into a Sweet Repose that none but a soldier can apreciate, Dreaming of their homes fathers & Mothers Brothers & Sisters Wives & children and ready to welcome them back to their homes again.

At length morning came again and our half starved mules were again Packed up and the Line of march taken. At sun set of the same day we arrived on the Banks of the Loup Fork which we found to be imposible to cross at that point. We contented ourselves by building up a good Fire & Having Nothing to Cook or Eat we Rooled up in our blankets to await the coming of another Day. The next Morning (Sunday) we concluded to travel down on the west side of the River until we came opposite the Pawnee Sta-

---

[109]Here Pace ended daily entries.

[110]Pace's memoir, which contradicted his journal on several points, recalled that the party lost nine mules in "a genuine snow storm" near Scotts Bluff. William Maxwell shot a buffalo so tough "our scientific man decided him to be one of the Buffalo left by 'Noah' from the Ark in an early day." See W. B. Pace, Autobiography, LDS Archives, 63.

tion and there to get a boat and cross over to the station where we expected to get provisions. On the evening of the Second Day (after reaching the River) we came in site of & opposite the old Mission.[111] But to add to our Cons[t]ernation there was no boat to be found & what was worse there did not appear to be any one about the Mission. Everything appeared to be Evacuated and our Last Chance for Supplies turned a hoax.

After encamping Bro Abraham Hunsaker and others tried the crossing of the River but found it unfordable but after a considerable effort was made they succeeded in getting a raft across to an Island. The shore on the opposite side being Frozen so that it would beare the weight of a Man A couple of the Boys went up to the Mission but found it Deserted. They then wint to the field to search for some Frost-bitten Corn that per chance might have been Left in the Hurry of the reapers but found so little that on their return we concluded to try the Beef of a Mule that was worn-out and undoubtedly would not go much farther. Shortly afterwards the identified Mule was led up into Camp and shot down, when the boys went to taking the Hide off and in a few moments more mite be seen pieces a Roasting for supper it being the First supper since we left Wood River. After Supper we set about to Devise ways & means for the Crossing of the River Although it seemed Impossible, For to make a raft Large enough to ferry our effects over was out of the question for we had neither axes Augers nor Ropes and to undertake to swim our animals we should undoubtedly Drown a great portion of them, For the Stream had frozen from its banks on Either side to within fifty yards of the centre & that had cut a channel deep enough to Run a Steamer [through].

After a considerable consultation we concluded to trust in Providence and perchance the River might Block up within a day or two as there was ice runing in large Flakes—

Morning came & with it a tremendous snow & wind storm & [it] continued During the Day. The next day Cold & Windy. On the night of the same Day the River Blockaded and on the Morning of the fifth Day after our arrival at that Point we succeed[ed] in crossing our animals on the Ice. During our Crossing some of the Omaha Indians came to our camp & on observing the mules head Lying by they understood our condition & gave us some squaw Corn and Wolf Meat and other Indian Refreshments that was very thankfully Received. Although they stole enough to amply pay them for their Kindness towards us. The Remainder of this day we employed ourselves in Gleaning over the Cornfields & trading a little with the Indians for

---

[111]The men struck the Loup River at its upper ford and traveled downstream past the lower ford the 1847 pioneer company had used. Even in good weather the Loup was difficult to cross. Presbyterian John Dunbar abandoned the mission, located near today's Genoa, Nebraska, when the Lakota burned the nearby Pawnee village in 1846. See Jensen, "The Pawnee Mission, 1834–1846," 301–10.

supplies to last through to winter quarters a distance of about One Hundred Thirty five Miles.

The next morning we left the Mission And after a tedious travel for several Days through Snow & Storms we arrived safe into Winter Quarters on the 17th Day of December 1847 where we met with Friends & Relatives & exchanged our camping out for the Soft side of a Feather Bed & snug Log Cabbins—

Pace's journal ended abruptly, hastily summarizing the last arduous miles from the Loup to Winter Quarters, but the reminiscences of Reddick Allred and Edward Bunker provide additional information about the journey's end. Allred traveled with Andrew Lytle's company, typically a few days behind Pace's men. Daniel Tyler recalled that shortly after crossing the Loup, Lytle's party "found Captain Pace's company just in time to save them from the danger of being robbed by Pawnee Indians," after which the two groups traveled together.[112] Such recollections are not as reliable as contemporary accounts, but Allred and Bunker told great tales and preserved interesting details of their cold journey.

REDDICK ALLRED, MORMON BATTALION EXPERIENCES OF REDDICK N. ALLRED OF SPRING CITY, UTAH. TYPESCRIPT, UTAH STATE HIST. SOC.

We camped one night about 10 miles above a Sioux Indian Tribe. Many of them came up to see us, one of them urged me to trade him the mule for a pony which I did. But the next day as we passed their camp (about 300 lodges) near the road one of their braves seized the pony (I was riding it) by the briddle and held it fast. I was a little in the rear as I had been fixing a pack, but Jos. Thorn saw it and passed the word that the Indians had taken me a prisoner. Capt. Lytle and [Daniel] Tyler came back but by the time they reached my side the mystery was solved for they brought out the mule to me, which of course I accepted—it being the first arbitration to be successfully made so we moved on in peace.

The traders told us at Laramie that if we killed buffalo on the plains it would make the indians mad—we were told this with a view perhaps to buy from them, but we hadn't the money with which to buy, so after getting well out upon the plains and our meat supply well exhausted we killed some meat and brought [it] into camp. We had no sooner done this than the indians raised a smoke on the opposite side of the Platte River, and remembering the warning we expected an attack that night. So Capt. Lytle called a council of War, in which all expressed the opinion that we should pack up after

---

[112]Tyler, *A Concise History*, 323–34.

dark and escape by flight, but I strongly opposed it on the ground that our animals were weak and that they could soon overtake us and we'd have to fight at a disadvantage, and I preferred to fight on the ground we then occupied to which they yielded. But the indians didn't come and the next day we moved on unmolested.

One night when camped perhaps 100 miles from any timber and without tents it snowed. It snowed about a foot upon our beds and we were obliged to resort to wet buffalo chips to make our fires.

The day before we reached the Loop Fork I found the head of a jack that a company of our boys, one week in advance of us, had left after eating the rest of the animal. I took out the brains and we cooked and ate them.[113]

We made camp on the West bank of the Loop Fork of the Platte River at sundown and next morning it was snowing, the River was full of flood ice and we were unable to cross. It snowed all day and we remained in camp, divided all we had and ate it up, without any prospects for food the next day as we were then out of the Buffalo district. It was 5 days before the ice blockaded sufficiently solid enough to cross, during which time we lived [on] cow-hides from our packing bags. [Illegible] when a mule got so weak it couldn't get up we killed and ate it. Thus we lived until we crossed [the Loup] where we gleaned corn in the Pawnee field. [Illegible] with some indians so we had enough [illegible] to last us into the settlements, at I gill per day. We were exactly 8 days traveling through 18 inches of snow. My old pack mule became so stiffened up that I was forced to leave it and pack my riding horse, which compelled me to tramp snow the rest of the way. When night came the dread of sleeping in the snow with aching bones, I felt like saying, "Would to God it was morning." And when morning came, anticipated a hard day's walk—it would be "Wish to God it was night."

We camped on the Elk Horn River, 30 miles from Winter Quarters, and I told Capt. Lytle I was in favor of going through the next day, but he said, "No, it would be too late as we would not know where to find our friends." I told him I knew I had friends there, (if my folks were not there) that would rather take me in than to let me sleep another night on the snow. The next morning I told the boys to drive the packs that I would walk ahead and for them to keep up with me which took us in before dark. When Capt. Lytle found that we were nearing town he told one of the boys to let me ride his horse. The result was that Pres. Young sent Col. A. P. Rockwood out to tell us to take our animals to the Tithing Yard and that places would be provided for our comfort. But I was fortunate enough to be invited by the first

---

[113]"Captain Allred took an ax and opened the skull," of D. P. Rainey's donkey, "and he and his messmates had a fine supper made of the brains." See Ibid.

man we met, Dr. [Jesse Charles?] Braley, to stop with him. Next Col. [Albert P.] Rockwood asked me to stay with him to which I consented. Than came Sister Henry and told the Col. I must go home with her, which I did. She, good old soul, prepared me a splendid supper and then when I had eaten but a few bites she demanded me to stop, however with not much reluctance. She said, "As you've been without food so long it might hurt you." This I hadn't thought of. She then furnished me with a tub of warm water, a change of under clothes and put me on a good feather bed, and I suffered more than I did on the snow—the change being so great.

This was on the 18th of Dec. 1847 and the next day I crossed the River and went 8 miles to Little Pigeon Creek where I found my wife living with my father. Tears of joys flowed freely at the return of the soldier—a scene never before enacted in our family. T'was several days before I was allowed to appease my hunger and even then I was much distressed after eating it didn't seem to satisfy my appetiate.

I remained with my father all winter in what was called Allred's Camp.

At our arrival Pres. Young proclaimed a Jubilee for the returned soldiers and as Wm. Hyde and I approached the company Pres. Young said to Pres. Kimball (turning to us) "These men were the salvation of this Church."[114]

EDWARD BUNKER, BACK TO WINTER QUARTERS,
UTAH STATE HIST. SOC., 5–6.

When I left the valley, I had sixteen pounds of flour to take me a thousand miles and three mules which I took from California to Council Bluffs. On our journey we bought some buffalo meat from the Indians and killed a few of these animals ourselves. On arriving at Loop Fork on the Platt River, we camped for the night and tried to ford the river, but the ice was running so thick that our mules would not try to cross, so we put up for the night. The next morning found us in as cold a northeastern snowstorm as I had ever experienced in the state of Maine.

We stayed in camp all day and ate the last bit of provision we had, even a pair of raw hide saddle bags which I had brought from California on a wild mule. The next morning there was about ten inches of snow on the ground and we started down the river hoping to find missionaries at the Pawnee Mission. That day we killed some prairie chickens which was all we had. Next day we came opposite the mission houses which were across the river from us. Some of the boys commenced to build a raft when, on look-

---

[114] For another version of Allred's memoirs, see Carter, ed., "The Diary of Reddick N. Allred," *Treasures of Pioneer History*, 5:307–10. It ends, "We all had a free dance and enjoyed it very much . . . In the spring of 1848 . . . I went to Fort Leavenworth and drew 3 months' pay and subsistance by which I was able to clothe myself and family very comfortable, for I had returned quite destitute."

ing down the river, we saw Robert Harris[115] crossing the ice by means of a long pole. We abandoned our raft and followed his example and crossed the river on the ice. We found the mission deserted and the corn all gathered, but we went into the fields and with our feet gathered a few ears of frost-bitten corn which the Indians had left, and which we ate raw. We went into the houses and stayed all night without bedding. One of the boys brought a frying pan and the corn we didn't eat raw, we parched and ate all we wanted and took the rest to camp with us.

On reaching camp the next morning, we found that one of our mules had got into the water and was so badly chilled that he had to be killed, and we ate all the meat except the lights [lungs]. Those I tried eating, but they were so much like Indian rubber that I gave up the attempt.

After getting all the company across the ice, we went to the Mission homes and stayed all day. Having obtained a little good corn from the Indians, we took up our line of march for Council Bluffs, 140 miles distant, with the snow from 8 to 10 inches deep. We arrived in Winter Quarters on the 18th of December, 1847, having been gone 18 months. Three days later the Missouri River froze over sufficiently hard to be crossed by teams and wagons. On reaching Winter Quarters I spent the night with one of my companions thinking my wife was still in Garden Grove where I had left her. Next morning I went to find Bro. [James] Brown's family and they told me my wife was living a short distance from them. This was good news, I assure you, and I lost no time in seeking out Emily and her mother, Abigail Abbott, who was a widow with eight children. Emily, being the eldest, had been able to move to Winter Quarters with the assistance of William Robinson.

It may not be out of place to enumerate the articles I had for a winter campaign: One pair of white cotton pants, a white cotton jacket, an old vest, a military overcoat, which I bought from one of the dragoons, a pair of garments, and a shirt; the latter articles were made from an old wagon cover by Sedric Judd, the tailor of our mess.

I found my wife in quite poor circumstances, but with a boy eleven months old, my eldest son, Edward, who at this writing is bishop of Bunkerville. After resting a few weeks, I got a harness, hitched up my mules and went to Missouri to work for provisions. I found employment splitting rails for fend I earned a fat hog and some corn and returned home. We moved across the river to Mesquite Creek. Sister Abbott moved with us. She

---

[115]Wilford Woodruff converted Robert Harris, Jr., in England and he emigrated to America in 1841 to settle in Nauvoo. Harris was a private in Co. E and took his family to Utah in 1850. Harris served in the Utah and Morrisite wars, colonized the Muddy River, eventually settled on the Malad River, and died in Kaysville, Utah, in 1876 at age 67.

had two small boys and we put in crops of corn together. Next spring Mother Abbott emigrated to Salt Lake City. I assisted her to a yoke of oxen and the following year received from James Brown, the money for the same.[116] With this I bought cattle to assist me to emigrate next season. I also received three months extra pay from the government and a land warrant which I sold for $150. The emigration to California began next year and corn brought from 25 cents to $1.50 per bushel. I raised a good crop and this assisted me very much to obtain an outfit . . . In the spring of 1850, I started to Salt Lake Valley in Captain Johnson's hundred and Matthew Caldwell's fifty, and I was captain of a ten.[117]

Having the advantage of a guide, Ira Miles, the men under P. C. Merrill arrived at Winter Quarters a week ahead of the Pace and Lytle parties. "Sixteen of our Brethren who went in the army returned today from the valley," noted Hosea Stout. "They had an uncommon hard time. Suffered extremly with cold and hunger, was detained ten days at the Loup fork by floating ice. They report more on the way." On 17 December 1847, the last contingent arrived, "Some 20 more of the brethren came in from the valley."[118] They were "pennyless and destitute, having suffered much from cold and hunger, subsisting on their worn out mules and horses."[119] The veterans, "unavoidably dirty and ragged," received a warm welcome at Winter Quarters, but they were often met by bad news. "The little babe I left," recalled Philemon C. Merrill, "died in my absence."[120] A newborn son greeted William F. Ewell, but the "privations in that terrible winter" weakened him. His wife recalled that the next year "he passed away from this life in my arms, leaving me grief-stricken."[121] Levi McCullough's service to his country and his religion

---

[116]Capt. James Brown wrote to Abigail Abbott on 6 August 1847 saying he had been ordered to the West Coast. "You must wait with patience and I will assist you all in my power," he promised. For the letter, see Bagley, ed., *Frontiersman*, 247–48.

[117]Chamberlain, A Supplement to the Life Histories of Edward and Emily Abbott Bunker, 5–6. Bunker reached Salt Lake Valley 1 September 1850 and settled on Canfield Creek in Ogden near James Brown. He was a member of the first Ogden city council and the founder of Bunkerville, Nevada.

[118]Brooks, ed., *On the Mormon Frontier*, 1:290–91. Joseph Thorn's wagon probably slowed Lytle's party. Hosea Stout reported "Thorn had also moved back with his family. He got dissatisfied."

[119]"General Epistle," in White, ed., *News of the Plains and the Rockies*, 3:186. Brigham Young's account somewhat ambiguously stated that the last contingent, "with others, in all about thirty, arrived here on the 18th instant."

[120]Tyler, *A Concise History*, 325; and Merrill, Autobiography, LDS Archives.

[121]Recollections of Mary Lee Bland Ewell, in Carter, ed., *Our Pioneer Heritage*, 8:534.

cost him dearly, for he found his wife and infant daughter dead. McCullough sought food and shelter with friends, and when his son was
brought to the house, the boy asked, "Which one of these ragged men
is my father?"[122]

---

[122]Carter, ed., *The Mormon Battalion*, 109.

Chapter 11

"LOOKS LIKE GOLD"
The Veterans in California

The most remarkable events connected with the Mormon Battalion took place following its disbanding: the Mormon Volunteers provided a police force for the overtaxed army while California's military governor lobbied hard to recruit a second battalion; the discharged battalion men provided a capable workforce that eased the desperate labor shortage in the conquered province's economy; and the veterans proved able trailblazers, opening a number of new wagon roads that still define the path of modern transportation corridors. Some former soldiers also became entangled in a counterfeiting scandal and were peripherally involved in one of Brigham Young's first attempts to secure a mail contract from the U.S. government. Yet certainly the veterans' most legendary activity was the role a handful of former battalion men played in the discovery and opening of California's gold country.

Col. J. D. Stevenson:
Capt. Hunt to Bring in a Battalion

From the perspective of the present, it is hard to appreciate the very tenuous nature of the United States' hold on California in 1847. The situation in the conquered province in July 1847 was every bit as explosive as it had been in New Mexico, where conditions led to the firestorm of the Taos Revolt. William Coray noted in July that "the country was in an uproar" with the local population "threatening an outbreak after our discharge." It was a concern shared by the conquered province's military commanders, and with good reason. They had fewer than a thousand troops to defend a vast territory, and many of the American freebooters who had served in John C. Frémont's militia had not been paid and felt aggrieved. Their watchword, according to Samuel Brannan, was "let the consequence be what they may . . . the Spanyards may take the country and be dam[n]ed!"[1] With the military situation deteriorating in Baja California, it is no wonder that the American officers who governed Alta California looked hopefully to the Mormons to provide them with another battalion of disciplined American soldiers.

Encouraged by Gov. Richard Mason's letter of 16 August 1847 directing him to raise another "Battalion of Mormon Volunteers," Jefferson Hunt rejoined most of the veterans under Hancock at Sutter's Fort. The former captain "had orders for Govt. Horses," and Sutter delivered several "War Horses" that his retrospective diary complained were "not paid for yet."[2] As we have seen, Hunt traveled east following the trail over the Sierra Nevada first opened to wagons in 1844 by the Elisha Stephens party. At the meeting with James Brown in the Sierra, Hunt scribbled a note recommending Brown to the military governor and continued on to Salt Lake. In the valley he learned in October that the emigration had truly arrived, but the only man who could approve his enlistment scheme was not there. After leading the pioneer company west that summer, Brigham Young had gone back to the faith's emigration base on the Missouri River, not to return until the following fall.

A frustrated Hunt now volunteered to lead a small party, including frontiersman Orrin Porter Rockwell, back to California to obtain seeds and animals for some three thousand new Great Basin settlers who faced the winter with a declining food supply. In going they opened a new avenue south to the Spanish Trail near present Cedar City, Utah, and followed the all-season route to southern California. After eating three of their horses, they reached Isaac Williams's ranch near San Bernardino in late December.[3] Hunt hurried to Los Angeles to see Col. Jonathan Stevenson who reported on their meeting.

---

[1]Brannan to Jones, 18 April 1847, in Bagley, ed., *Scoundrel's Tale*.

[2]Owens, ed., "General Sutter's Diary," in *John Sutter and a Wider West*, 20. Samuel Brannan accused James Brown of defrauding the government, and "this surly Nabal" rebuffed Capt. Howard Stansbury when his survey party arrived in Utah in August 1849. Stansbury thought "the ungracious" Brown "had some reason to expect and to dread a visit from the civil officers of the United States, on account of certain unsettled public accounts" and mistook his surveyors for "some such functionaries" sent to arrest him. See Bagley, ed., *Scoundrel's Tale*; and Stansbury, *Exploration and Survey of the Valley of the Great Salt Lake*, 83–84.

[3]For the story of this journey, see Schindler, *Orrin Porter Rockwell*, 169–74.

STEVENSON TO MASON, RECORDS OF THE 10TH MILITARY DEPARTMENT, 1846–1851, ROLL 2, NATIONAL ARCHIVES.

Head qts Sn. Dist Calif.
Cuidad de los Angeles
January 12th 1848.
Sir,

Some few days ago Capt Jefferson Hunt and two chief men of the Mormon fraternity arrived from the settlement of the Salt Lake for the purpose of purchasing horses, and I believe to look out for a place of settlement in this District. Capt H expresses much regret that your terms had not been more liberal and a longer time allowed for him to enroll and bring in a Battalion of his people which he could readily have obtained and which he assures me he can yet do if you desire it.[4] If therefore you consider it the intention of our Government to retain permanent possession of Lower California which I really do not unless their views have changed after the close of the War, and deem it advisable to send Col. [Henry S.] Burton an additional force, I have no doubt an arrangement could be made with Capt Hunt to bring in a Battalion that would relieve some of the Posts in Upper California and enable you to send more of my Regt. to Burton.[5] Hunt will remain in this District for at least a month which will give you time to communicate to me your wishes on this subject.

One of the men with Hunt, a Mr. Rockwell, desires to make an arrangement for conveying a mail from here, Monterey, or San Francisco to Fort Leavenworth or the nearest Post Office. He proposes to leave here about the 15th of February, and immediately upon his arrival at Salt Lake settlement to depart for Leavenworth. This settlement at Salt Lake embraces 2500 souls and he supposes a mail of 3000 letters will be sent from there; if this be so, these letters with a moderately sized mail made up from the different Posts of California would justify his employment at a reasonable rate; for the postage of letters from Leavenworth to the points of destination would pay well; he is anxious to make an arrangement to convey a mail from this Country to the States at stated periods say 3 or 4 times a year, in which he has no objection on Oregon mail to & from the States should be included. He informs me that he has promised his people to convey a mail for them to the States, immediately upon his return and if he can get anything for conveying a mail from California it will be all the reward he receives for his labor, at his request I write

[4]Despite Hunt's assurances, Asahel A. Lathrop carried a letter from the Salt Lake Stake High Council, which governed the settlement in Young's absence, to the Saints in California that read: "We counsel all of you not to re-enlist as soldiers . . . But as fast as . . . your circumstances will permit repair to this place." See Ibid., 170–71.

[5]On 21 July 1847 Lieutenant Colonel Burton and his two companies of New York Volunteers occupied La Paz, a fishing village and capital of Baja California, near the southern end of the peninsula.

you on the subject.[6] These people are destined for some time to come to be the chief reliance of our Government for defence [*sic*] against foreign invasion, and domestic insurrection in this Territory, for at any time their whole male population capable of bearing arms could at a short notice be brought into service and their very fanaticism closely organized as they are make them obedient and devoted Soldiers, and I would therefore respectfully suggest their employment by Government on every proper occasion where it can be done consistent with the public interest.

> I have the honor to be
> Very Respectfully

Col. R. B. Mason   Your Obdt. Servt
1st U.S. Dragoons   J. D. Stevenson
Gov. of California   Col. Comdg. S.M. Dist.

COL. R. B. MASON:
THE MOST LIBERAL & MUNIFICENT PROVISION

Since Mason's reply to Hunt in August 1847, the fighting in Mexico's western provinces had intensified. In November Com. William B. Shubrick landed U.S. Marines to occupy San José del Cabo, a farming center on the southern tip of Lower California, and sailed on to capture Mazatlan on Mexico's west coast. While Shubrick consolidated his foothold there, resistance grew on the peninsula. Capt. Manuel Pineda and a scratch force of Bajacalifornians attacked Lt. Col. Henry S. Burton's little command at La Paz. The New Yorkers fought them off, but Mason was forced to send another company to reinforce them, which reduced further his command in Upper California.

As 1848 began the military governor scrambled "to raise an infantry battalion in California for service in the south." Mason offered a major's commission and command of the outfit to Lansford W. Hastings based on the promoter's "knowledge and extensive acquaintance with the immigrants in this country." That same day Mason wrote Samuel Brannan, still "President of the Saints in California," stressing that it was "all-important to raise a strong force for service" in Mazatlan "with all possible dispatch," since he doubted Commodore Shubrick would "be able to hold it after the hurricane season in those seas sets in." Mason

---

[6]According to historian Harold Schindler, nothing came of Rockwell's proposal because "the military in California decided to deliver their own mail." See Ibid., 173.

was working "to raise one thousand men in Oregon, California, and from the settlement on the Great Salt Lake" and asked Brannan to use his influence "in encouraging and supporting the effort of raising a battalion in California."[7] Mason's hope to raise a battalion from Utah explained why his reply to Stevenson held out every inducement the law allowed for the Mormons to volunteer. Mason directed his young adjutant, William Tecumseh Sherman, who would become one of America's most famous soldiers, to draft his reply to Stevenson.

SHERMAN TO STEVENSON, RECORDS OF THE 10TH MILITARY DEPARTMENT, 1846–1850, ROLL 1, NATIONAL ARCHIVES.

Head Quarters 10th Mil Dept.
Monterey California Janry 25/1848

Sir

Your letter of January 12 announcing the arrival of Captain Hunt, has been received & I am directed by Colonel Mason to inform you that he is at a loss to understand why Captain Hunt should say, that he was unable to bring into California a Battalion of his People because the terms proposed by Colonel Mason in August last were not sufficiently liberal.

Volunteers entering the Service of the United States, are entitled to whatever pay, allowances & bounties may be provided for them by Congress & the promises of no person whatever can increase or diminish these in the least. Any apparent illiberality therefore must have been in the Law of Congress but since the departure of Captain Hunt in August last we have received official information of the passage of several Bills by Congress that make the most liberal & munificent provision for the Volunteer Soldier. These laws are in our possession. Col. Mason is willing to place the most liberal construction on them to favor the Battalion of Mormon Volunteers of whose former services he entertains so high an opinion.

These laws & the orders of the War Department founded on them are in your possession, & in conversation you can explain to him that every non-commissioned officer, musician & private of Volunteers or Militia is entitled "to fifty cents in lieu of subsistence & twenty five cents in lieu of forage for such as are mounted for every twenty miles by the most direct route, from the period of their leaving their homes to the place of rendevouz & from the place of discharge to their homes." See Genl Orders No. 21, A.Q.D. June 19th, 1846. When the volunteer reaches the place of Rendevous & is mustered into service his pay begins & does not cease until a sufficient time after his discharge to enable him to return home at the rate of

---

[7]Mason to Hastings and Mason to Brannan, 28 January 1848, Sen. Exec. Doc. 18 (31–1), 1849–50, Vol. 9, no. 18, Serial 557, 446–47.

twenty miles a day, & during the period of his service he is subsisted, & if sick well cared for at the expense of Government, also for every month he serves the Volunteer Soldier draws the sum of three dollars & fifty cents for his clothing, & finally when discharged he receives a warrant for 160 Acres of land, or if he prefers Treasury Scrip for one hundred dollars bearing 6 p[er] cent interest payable semi-annually. See Gen. Orders No. 17 dated Washington April 15th 1847. At no previous period of our history have such munificent provisions been made for an army. You may inform Captain Hunt that the laws of Congress are thus liberal now & that Colonel Mason is still willing to receive into the service of the United States a Battalion of Mormon Volunteers to be commanded by Captain Hunt, or in case he do not [sic] wish it then such other person as may be properly elected by them. This Battalion should consist of one Major, an acting Adjt. Selected from the subalterns of the Companies (See page 4 General orders no 14 dated Washington March 27th 1847/one Sergeant Major, one Quarter Master Sergt. & a Chief Musician. See Sec. 3 Act of Congress approved June 18th 1846 & four companies each of

One Captain	Four Sergeants
One 1st. Lieut	Four Corporals
Two Second Lieuts.	Two Musicians drummer & fifer
And Seventy five Privates.	

Colonel Mason desires that such a Battalion should rendevous [sic] at Los Angeles, as early in April as possible where they will be mustered & accepted into the Service of the United States to serve "during the war" & to be entitled to all the pay & allowances that are now or may hereafter be provided for. Colonel Mason wishes the Battalion for service on the Bay of San Francisco to releive [sic] the three Companies of your Regt. now there who may be sent to Lt. Col. Burton in Lower California. These should be dispatched early in June, if not before & for that reason the sooner this Battalion of Mormons arrive the better. Please mention this to Captn Hunt that if he agrees to bring into California such a Battalion; he may do so in time, for relief to be sent to Lt. Col. Burton before the Squadron is compelled to withdraw from the Gulf of California.[8]

The instructions of the War Department require some fortification to be constructed at the entrance of the Bay of San Francisco, as yet nothing has been done there & the heavy ordnance lies within a few yards of where it was first landed. It is designed to ~~have~~ place some of these Guns in position during the coming year & if any part of the Mormon Battalion is employed in constructing such a fort, you may assure Captain Hunt that every man actu-

---

[8]The guns of Com. William B. Shubrick's naval squadron had enabled Burton's command to hold off the Bajacalifornians, but if the ships were withdrawn from the Gulf of California to protect American forces at Mazatlan, the New Yorkers would be heavily outnumbered unless reinforced.

ally employed in such work shall receive 18 cents for each days labor in addition to his other pay and allowances.

In relation to entrusting a mail to Mr. Rockwell for the United States I am directed to say that at this time there is not sufficient necessity to make up a public mail for the United States. I send however one package addressed to the Adjutant General of the Army Washington D.C. which Colonel Mason directs to be entrusted to Mr. Rockwell who will be paid by the A. A. Qr Master at Los Angeles what ever may be deemed by him sufficient compensation for delivering such package at any post office in the United States.

Be pleased to communicate at the earliest moment the result of your interviews with Captain Hunt.

I have the honor to be
With much respect
Yr obt. Servt.
W. T. Sherman
1st Lieut 3rd Art
A. A. Genl.

To Col. S. D. Stevenson
Comdg. Srn District
California

COL. R. B. MASON:
PROCEED AS RAPIDLY AS POSSIBLE TO THE SALT LAKE

Renewed Mexican resistance south of California suddenly took the need for more American troops from pressing to urgent. Checked by Burton's New York Volunteers, Capt. Manuel Pineda regrouped his little army in Baja California and moved early in January 1848 against the garrison of seventy-two U.S. Marines under Lt. Charles Heywood at San José del Cabo. Guerrilla raids at Mazatlan compelled Commodore Shubrick to ask Gen. Winfield Scott for five hundred to a thousand men to hold the port. American forces in the West were being stretched to the danger point. So it happened that just six days after his reply to Stevenson, Col. Richard B. Mason decided to take more direct action. He dispatched Lt. William H. Warner of the topographical engineers from his staff to contact Hunt at Los Angeles and go to Salt Lake Valley, if necessary, to obtain a battalion of Mormon soldiers.[9] His orders carried a discernable note of urgency.

---

[9] Lt. William H. Warner came to California in 1846 with General Kearny as a member of Lt. William H. Emory's party of topographical engineers. He was promoted to brevet captain for gallant and meritorious service in the battle of San Pasqual, where he was slightly wounded. After surveying Sacramento City for Samuel Brannan he was killed by Indians in the Sierra Nevada in 1849.

SHERMAN TO WARNER, RECORDS OF THE 10TH MILITARY DEPARTMENT,
1846-1851, ROLL I, NATIONAL ARCHIVES.

Head Quarters 10th Mil. Dept.
Monterey California Jan 31, 48

Sir,

I am directed by Colonel Mason to convey to you the following instructions. In obedience to Dept. Orders No 11 of this date you will proceed to Los Angeles California & procure at the earliest practicable moment an interview with Captn Hunt formerly of the Mormon Battalion & such other Mormons of intelligence & influence as may be with him. You will inform them that the honor & interests of the United States require that a Land Force should occupy Mazatlan, and that Colonel Mason has sent to Oregon for five hundred men, to the Sacramento for three hundred & to the Mormons he looks for four or five hundred more. This Battalion should consist of four or five Companies each consisting of a Captain, one First and two Second Lieutenants, four Sergeants, four Corporals, two Musicians and Sixty four to one hundred privates. The Battalion if consisting of four companies will be commanded by a major or if of five Cos. by a Lt. Col. with a Sgt. Major, Qr Mr Sergt. & Chief musn [musician]. The Battn will have an actg Adjt. Who will be a Lt. In one of the Co.s. & if there be a such able person an Asst. Surgeon will be mustered into service with the Battn. Who will be entitled to the same pay as an officer of the same grade in the Regular Army. I enclose you herewith a table of monthly pay for officers & men of a Battn of volunteer infantry such as is proposed to be raised among the Mormons & pursuant to orders No 14 & 20 of 1846 & Gen Orders No 4 of 1847 which will explain the pay, clothing allowances, pensions & Bounties that the Law at present provides for volunteers. These you will lay before Captn Hunt & inform him that Col. Mason desires under these laws to receive the Battalion for the period of "during the War unless sooner discharged." Or if they are unwilling to engage for such term then for "one year unless sooner discharged." The Law you will perceive allows a Vol. 50 cts for every 20 miles from his home to place of Gen'l Rendezvous that is from the settlement on the Great Salt Lake to Los Angeles California if such place be established as the Rendezvous and muster. It is believed that many Mormons are desirous to come to California anyhow, and may be willing to come to Los Angeles under these terms, there to be mustered & accepted into the service of the United States, but should Hunt insist upon their being mustered into the Service at the Great Salt Lake it must be done, & then the Battalion must be conducted to Los Angeles at the expense of the U.S. In this case you must adopt the best means available for subsisting them on the route. It is believed Hunt is possessed of sufficient influence to command the services of five hundred men in the Settlements of the Great Salt Lake, so if he is favorably inclined you may offer him the command of the Battalion & can entrust to him the Blank Enrollments herewith sent you, provided he be willing to accompany you to the Salt Lake. If not then let him provide you with Letters to his people, and with the names of such men as would be most likely to raise Co's for service.

It may be that Hunt may object to his people going ~~to Maz~~ out of California, then say to him that Col. Mason is still willing to receive a Battalion for service in California which would releive [*sic*] a party of the New York Regt for service in Lower California.

Should none of these proposals meet Captn Hunt's sanction you need not go to the Salt Lake, but will return to Monterey; but should he receive the offer favorably then proceed as rapidly as possible to the Salt Lake, & spare no efforts to bring to Los Angeles as speedily as possible this Battalion, sending in advance Lt. [Christopher "Kit"] Carson back to Angeles to report to Col. Stevenson the probable strength of that Battalion and the probable date of its arrival at Los Angeles, so that he may dispatch a courier here to Monterey, for a ship & supplies to meet this Battalion at San Pedro. Also as early as possible report from Los Angeles if possible the result of your interview with Capt Hunt so that preparations may be made in advance for the Battn's arrival.

I enclose you also Ten Blank Muster Rolls, for you to muster in the Companies of this Battn. Should this duty devolve on you, but should the Mormons consent to come to Los Angeles there to be mustered into Service, then please deliver these Rolls to Capt. A. J. Smith 1st Dragoons, who will be instructed to muster & inspect the Battalion upon their arrival there.

I am with much respect
Your obt Servt
W. T. Sherman
1st Lieut 3rd Art.
A. A. A. Genl

Lieut. W. H. Warner
Top Eng.
Monterey, Cal.

LT. W. H. WARNER:
THEY WOULD CHEERFULLY COME TO UPPER CALIFORNIA

Lieutenant Warner's mission suddenly to produce a battalion of Mormon troops ran into the same obstacle Hunt had faced all along. Members of the faith simply would not volunteer on their own accord out of motives of patriotism or financial reward. They would only do so if they were told to enlist by the one man who possessed the authority to give such direction. And that authority, Brigham Young, was out of contact some two thousand miles to the east at Winter Quarters, the Mormon emigration base on the Missouri River. But Hunt was unwilling to give up. He had seen Salt Lake Valley. Like Samuel Brannan, he thought the religious movement eventually would have no choice but to continue on to California. So anxious was he to provide a new battalion that he even professed to believe that Young would reach Salt Lake Valley "sometime in May" and the Mormon command could reach southern California "by the middle of June." As his report shows, Lieutenant Warner was not at all taken in by these wildly optimistic estimates.

WARNER TO SHERMAN, RECORDS OF THE 10TH MILITARY DEPARTMENT, 1846-1851, ROLL 1, NATIONAL ARCHIVES.

Pueblo de los Angeles
Feby. 14th. 1848

Sir,

In obedience to my instructions from Col. Mason of Jany. 31st. I lost no time unnecessarily, in seeking an interview with Capt. Hunt. I found him at Williams' Ranch about thirty five miles from this place, on the evening of the 12th inst. He said there was no prospect of raising a battalion among the Mormons for Lower California, or the coast of Mexico—That their men would not be willing to be so far separated from their families, who were many of them houseless, & destitute of many of the comforts of life. But he thought they would cheerfully come to Upper California, & that their leaders would give their consent. It will not be possible however to get a battalion of them here by the time the Colonel requires them. Their leaders, (who must be consulted on the subject) are not at the Salt Lake, but east of the mountains, near the Missouri River. Capt. Hunt thinks they will arrive at Salt Lake sometime in May.

Capt. H. is now ready to start for the Salt Lake. He drives cattle. After he gets well on the road with them, he will send forward a man with a small party light to the settlements. The same man will take fresh animals on his arrival at the settlement, & proceed directly, to meet the leaders & will bring back their answer. In the mean time, Capt. H. will have arrived at the Lake, & made all the preparations that he can make upon an uncertainty. When the courier returns, if the answer be favorable, Capt. H. will dispatch another immediately to the Comdg Officer of this place, & in four or five days after, the battalion will be ready to commence its march. He thinks he can get here by the middle of June. I urged that this delay might frustrate the Colonel's plans, & that I feared he would not be willing to receive the battalion into service so late. To meet this contingency, it was agreed that I should report the result of our interview to Col. Mason, & receive his decision, in time to send it by the Mormon Company that is about to be mustered out of Service. A part of all of these men will proceed immediately to the Salt Lake, & will arrive there before the courier to meet the leaders can have returned.

With this arrangement I left Capt. Hunt. He will probably start tomorrow.

Without having expressed to Capt. H. any doubt that he will be able to arrive here with his battalion by the middle of June, I have doubts, for these reasons—

Wherever the Mormon leaders may be on the Platte River, they cannot start before the 1st of May, & naturally will not before the 10th. or 20th. on account of there being no grass. It will then take them at least two months to come to the Lake, unless they leave their wagons & come on light. Also, the courier cannot leave the Lake to meet the leaders until the new grass shall have started. Capt. H. allows himself from thirty five to forty two days to march to Williams'.

Thus I fear the battalion cannot get here before the middle of August, instead of the middle of June.

Col. Stevenson has directed the Asst. Qmr to forward this communication without delay & I shall wait here for farther [*sic*] instructions.

A reply for Capt. Hunt ought to be here by the 5th. of March.

I am Sir—   Very Respectfully
                                           Your Obedt. Servt.
To Lieut. W. T. Sherman   Wm. H. Warner
A. A. A. Genl. U.S. Army   1st Lt. Topl. Engs
Monterey, Ca.

LT. W. H. WARNER:
SHOULD YOU FIND THAT YOU CAN ARRIVE EARLIER

Colonel Mason's answer came too late to reach Jefferson Hunt before he left Los Angeles, and Lieutenant Warner on 11 March relayed it to him at Salt Lake Valley. In it Mason ignored Hunt's extravagant claims on how soon he could return to California with the troops the colonel had called for and took the Kentuckian at his word. He even urged Hunt could arrive sooner, "it is desirable that you should do so." But time was running out on the senior captain's dream to form a new battalion of Mormons.

WARNER TO HUNT, RECORDS OF THE 10TH MILITARY DEPARTMENT, 1846–1851, ROLL 2, NATIONAL ARCHIVES.

Pueblo de los Angeles
March 11th. 1848

Sir,

I have the honor to enclose to you a copy of Col. Mason's answer to a letter from me, in which I gave him the particulars of my interview with you on the subject or raising a battalion of Mormons. In this letter I am referred to a letter addressed to Col. J. D. Stevenson on the same subject, a copy of which, Col. Stevenson informs me you have. From these two letters, you will fully understand Col. Mason's wishes with regard to the Battalion.

I also send you copies of some laws respecting the Army, which may be of service or interest to you, & I shall send in a separate package, some large sheets of paper for you to enroll your companies upon.

I told Col. Mason you thought you could get into California by the middle of June. Should you find that you can arrive earlier, it is desirable that you should do so.

Col. Mason directed me to caution you against the enrollment of men who have any disease or infirmity that will disqualify them for the duties of a soldier. They should be able-bodied men, between the ages of Eighteen & Forty five.

I am Sir
Very respectfully
Your Obedt. Servt.
Wm. H. Warner
1st. Lt. Topl. Engs.

Capt. Jefferson Hunt
Mormon Settlement

Capt. J. D. Hunter: We Should Have the Entire Control of This Country

Governor Mason's campaign to raise a new battalion of Mormon troops even reached to former Company B captain Jesse Hunter who had remained in the occupied province. Hunter had accepted Mason's appointment as the Indian agent at San Luis Rey Mission and its outlying farm without Brigham Young's permission. At Mason's urging, he now requested Young's approval to raise another force on the enticement that it would give the theocratic religious movement military control over the region. In so doing, he expressed his own a preference for southern California as a place to live, a choice shared by many other members of the faith who settled at San Bernardino after they had seen the Great Basin.

J. D. Hunter to Brigham Young & Counsel, Brigham Young Collection, LDS Archives.

San Louis Rey
Feby 20th 1848

President Brigham Young & Counsel,
Dear Sirs:

Esteeming it my duty as well as privelege to let you know the precise situation of the country at this time both as it regards its Gov. and local situation as well as the feelings of the people towards our people. The only Troops now in this country is Col. Stevenson [*sic*] Regiment of N. York Vols. And one Company of Dragoons besides Capt Davis [*sic*] Company at San Diego. The Vol. will be discharged at the close of the War. But the trouble is, They or some other Troops are called upon to go to the South. And the Gov. is very anxious that the Mormons should raise another Battalion to Garison this Country. I have conversed with him upon the Subject in Aug[ust] last and have received Communications since expressing his wish that we would settle in California. He said we should have the privelige to garison all upper California and would be in a short time the only forces left in this Country. As regards the feelings of this people with the exception of a few about the Bay— there is not a Man Woman or Child, but would rejoice at the very idea of our settling in this Country. It has a fine climate and fertile soil, Though the Land is mostly owned by individuals yet it can be purchased on reasonable terms. I am well aware that we will have to have a trading point on the Coast and from all I can learn the Gov. is willing that we should have the entire control of this Country. I have not heard from you since I arrived here. I wrote to you when the Battalion was discharged but have received no answer as yet. I am still acting as Agent for the Indians, having also the charge of San Louis Rey and the Pala Farm which keeps me very busy. I am in hope I will hear from you soon. When Brother [Asahel] Lathrop and his party arriv'd here and delivered unto us the Epistle of the [Stake High] Council at the Lake. We gladly recieved their Council. But as Circumstances always alters Cases, and since we have been so strongly solicited to use our influence in favor of raising another Mormon Force to defend this Country, we have not only consented to this, But have Concluded to try and influence Capt. Davis and his Company to remain in service untill they can hear from you.

I have an extensive influence among the Indians here my word is their law, but if I should be left here alone without any backing, I am aware that jealousy would arise and that Influence which we have gained in this Country would be lost. I believe also that if we should refuse to help them at this time that jealouscies would arise and perhaps we may be troubled or interupted in our trade upon the Coast, if it should be garisoned by them instead of us. These are the feelings of my mind and after laying these things before you, I will leave it with you believing that it will all work right.

Remaining Yours as Ever,

Pres. Young   J. D. Hunter

Col. R. B. Mason: Not a Syllable of Complaint

Even before Hunter's letter reached Brigham Young or Lieutenant Warner's appeal arrived at Salt Lake Valley, events had erased the need for more American troops and blasted Jefferson Hunt's hope to lead a

new Mormon command. Before the end of March 1848 Colonel
Mason received word that a cease-fire agreement had been reached on 29
February under the Treaty of Guadalupe Hidalgo, signed on 2 February,
that ended the war between the United States and Mexico.[10] An even
more momentous event occurred on the South Fork of the American
River in northern California. On 24 January, as six battalion veterans
looked on, James Marshall picked up a nugget of gold at Sutter's Mill in
the Sierra foothills. As these decisive events broke at the same time, it
seemed destined that March would also see the end of the volunteer
company at San Diego. Of the service of this unit and other Mormon
soldiers the military governor was outspoken in his praise.

MASON TO JONES, SEN. EXEC. DOC. 18 (31-1), SERIAL 557, 318–22.

Headquarters Tenth Military Department,
Monterey, September 18, 1847

Sir: . . .

The town of San Diego, the southernmost one of Upper California, is
now garrisoned by a company of Mormons, under the command of Captain D. C. Davis. The company was organized on the 20th of July at Los
Angeles, and on the 25th of the same month marched to occupy the town
of San Diego, which had been necessarily left without a garrison when Captain Hunter's company, of the Mormon battalion, was withdrawn to be discharged. During this temporary abandonment, the good people of the town
expressed great terror of the Indians and of their own countrymen; but
since the return of the company, not a word of fear or apprehension had
reached me, and I infer they are perfectly satisfied.

The time for which the battalion of Mormons had agreed to serve expired
on the 16th of July, on which day they were formally mustered out of service
by First Lieutenant A. J. Smith, first dragoons, at Los Angeles, California; and
as General Kearny had promised them their arms and accoutrements, I caused
this promise to be redeemed, and in addition ordered to be given to such as
really intended to return towards the United States to meet their families a
small quantity of ammunition. Of the services of this battalion, of their
patience, subordination, and general good conduct, you have already heard;
and I take great pleasure in adding, that, as a body of men, they have reli-
giously respected the rights and feelings of these conquered people, and not a
syllable of complaint has reached my ears of a single insult offered, or outrage
done, by a Mormon volunteer. So high an opinion did I entertain of the battalion, and of their especial fitness for the duties now performed by the garri-

---

[10]Under the Treaty of Guadalupe Hidalgo, Mexico renounced its claim to Texas, New Mexico, and
Upper California for a payment of $15 million and an abandonment of prior American claims.

son in this country, that I made strenuous efforts to engage their services for another year; but succeeded in engaging but one company, which, as before stated, is now at San Diego. Certain promises or pledges were made to this company, which you will find amongst the military correspondence sent to you by this same mail.[11] Some few of the discharged Mormons are scattered throughout the country, but the great mass of them have gone to meet their families, supposed to be somewhere in the vicinity of the Great Salt Lake. Captain J. D. Hunter, late of the Mormon battalion, has been appointed sub-Indian agent, to take charge of the mission of San Luis Rey, and the mission Indians in that neighborhood. . .

R. B. Mason
Colonel 1st Dragoons, Commanding.

General R. Jones,
Adjutant General U.S.A., Washington city, D.C.

JOHN J. RISER: THE ONLY FEASIBLE WAGON ROAD

Jefferson Hunt came to a parting of the ways with Porter Rockwell in California, for Hunt left for Salt Lake without the noted scout on 14 February 1848 in company with Asahel Lathrop and about a dozen men. Hunt's party purchased two hundred cattle, plus pack mules and mares from Isaac Williams, and the ranch owner gave them all the bulls they could catch. The crossing of the Mojave Desert proved arduous: of the forty bulls that started the journey, all but one "perished from thirst, half the cattle had died on the drive, and the party had been plagued by Indians."[12] Battalion veteran Elijah Allen wrote the only known contemporary account of the trip:

> went to san gabr[i]el mission and worked till 1848   I left williams ranch about the 15 of february in company of 10 or 12 others with 200 head of catle for the church   I stood guard most every night & drove cattle all day for about 3 months till about the 23 of May I arrived in salt lake valley & commenced farming at the mouth of red Bute Canion.[13]

Jefferson Hunt had sent his son to El Pueblo with Brown's family

---

[11]Among such promises was the commitment to discharge the San Diego volunteers in March 1848 if they requested it, which they did

[12]Schindler, *Orrin Porter Rockwell*, 172. The Salt Lake Stake High Council on 11 June 1848 required Rockwell to explain why he had not accompanied Hunt. See Ibid., 175.

[13]Allen, Autobiographical Sketch, ca. 1848, LDS Archives. Allen's travels were not over. He soon "started for the United States for too see my father mother Brothers & sisters once more & crossed the Missouri River the 23 of Oct 1848 & thus after being Gone over two years I felt I had landed once more on the shores of America."

detachment, but John Hunt met his father in Salt Lake. He joined Hunt's November 1847 return to California, during which they "did what I think no other party of 'Mormon' emigrants ever had to do—we killed and ate our horses." The trip was arduous, but Hunt's men returned to Utah with valuable "seeds and cuttings."[14] More than fifty years later, John Hunt recalled their adventure.

> We were exhausted when we reached the Chino ranch, but Col. [Isaac] Williams was very generous in his treatment of us. He furnished us wild cows which we milked after strapping them down, and plenty of flour from which to make our bread. We remained there five or six weeks, resting up and preparing for the return trip. Finally, on Feb. 15, we started out, with about 200 cows, for which we gave him $6 each, and a few pack animals and mares, also about 40 bulls. He told us he would give us all the bulls we wanted to drive off. They all died but one from thirst, while about 100 cows also perished. Occasionally the Indians would sneak up close enough to kill one of them, but otherwise they did not bother us. We got back to Salt Lake in May, 1848.[15]

Another trail-blazing band of battalion veterans soon followed Hunt's party. Mustered in on 20 July 1847, Capt. Daniel C. Davis' eighty-two Mormon Volunteers had kept the peace in occupied California's southernmost region. "We are comfortably quartered here," said Pvt. Henry G. Boyle, "and have full rations, and nothing to do as far as Soldiers duties are concerned." The following March when their enlistment ran out, Boyle summed up their service: "We have met with nothing of a Serious nature. Since we re-enlisted, I have been at work on company with four others of my brethern making brick. I have also during the winter been engaged white washing, I have whitewashed nearly all the town, & have been otherwise engaged to the best advantage."[16] The company was discharged on 14 March 1848. A month later Captain Davis, his wife Susan and son Daniel, Jr., and most of the men started for Salt Lake Valley, guided by Orrin Porter Rockwell. As they returned to their families, they took the first wagon over the Spanish Trail and the southern corridor in present Utah generally followed by today's I-15.

---

[14]To her "unspeakable joy," Eliza R. Snow "met the California boys, 7 of them," on 10 May 1848 in Salt Lake. Snow recalled that she "gave 75 cts. for 6 or 7 little potatoes, all of which I could hold in one hand." The seed stock produced a bushel "of beautiful, well developed potatoes." See Beecher, ed., *The Personal Writings of Eliza Roxcy Snow*, 32, 223.

[15]"'Mormon' Pathfinders Guests of Senator Clark: Startling Story of the First Trip From Salt Lake to Los Angeles," *Deseret Evening News*, 7 October 1905, 27/6–7.

[16]Boyle, Autobiography and Diary, 15 August 1847 and 7 March 1848.

No contemporary account of this significant trail-blazing venture survives and few veterans gave it even passing attention in their memoirs. Henry G. Boyle's retrospective account has long been known, but John J. Riser's has only recently come to light.[17]

AUTOBIOGRAPHY AND DIARY OF HENRY G. BOYLE, 38–39.

March 14th Today we have been disbanded. Tomorrow we are to receive our last payment.

March 21st To day we leave this Seaport town for Salt Lake. Some of our brethern have come through from there to this place [*torn page*] to Pilot us through.

March 31st Today we arrived here at William's Ranch and from here we visited Los Angeles City at which place and here, we purchased our fit-out of animals provisions &c.

And on the 12th of April, 1848 we commenced our journey across the plains for Great Salt Lake. 35 Souls in the company Porter Rockwell for our guide. We have one waggon in the company & 135 mules & horses. We had a long and arduous journey but nothing of any note transpired on the trip. We arrived at the old Fort Salt Lake Valley on the 5th of June 1848 all Safe & well, bringing through with us the first wagon that ever passed that rout. As the History of this Church will be faithfully recorded, I Shall write nothing in my history but of a private nature, nothing but that pertains to my self.

Sparked by a "great love of adventure" rather than a commitment to Mormonism, John J. Riser had enlisted in the battalion as a private in Company C, attributing his "military Ardor" to his forefathers, "who had seen much service in the wars of Germany." Riser's recollections of the trip are the most detailed eyewitness accounts to survive, but its reference to "numerous and troublesome" Indians suggests participants preferred to forget about what were probably difficult and violent encounters.

The first of Riser's accounts presented here is a brief memoir provided to historian H. H. Bancroft. Apparently inspired by the experience, Riser wrote a much longer account of his service with the battalion that is still in the possession of the family.

JOHN J. RISER. AUTOBIOGRAPHY, 1887, BANCROFT LIBRARY.

Having a great desire for adventure, I joined a company of Twenty-three on a tour to Salt Lake and some even concluded to visit again the Atlantic states, I among the latter. We started on the 12th of April [1848] from the Rancho El Chenno. [We went] through the Tejon [Cajon] pass with one

---

[17]Ricketts, *The Mormon Battalion*, 265.

JOHN J. RISER, who as a young man helped blaze the wagon road from Salt Lake to Los Angeles, is shown here wearing his Mexican War medal. *Courtesy, Lorin Hansen.*

wagon and 135 Mules and Horses. The majority of us of course were packers, but this wagon that we took was the first wagon that ever traveled the route, and this wagon route afterwards proved to be the only feasible wagon road from southern Utah in winter to California. Passing up into the Utah Basin from the Santa Clara River, and through little Salt Lake valley we found the Indians very numerous and troublesome nearly the whole way.[18] We arrived where Salt Lake City now stands on the 5th of June 1848, and here I found my brother George who had arrived the year previous but none of our company felt Inclined to go farther East just then. While looking about at this place I met for the first time my present wife Helen R. Allen, and would have been glad to go either east or west again, but I could not find enough that wanted to leave to make up a safe company for such a journey.[19]

---

[18]San Bernardino pioneer George Crismon recalled that at Virgin Hill near today's Mesquite, Nevada, Captain Davis "had to lower the wagon down in sections with ropes." See "'Mormon' Pathfinders Guests of Senator Clark," *Deseret Evening News*, 7 October 1905, 27/1–4. The Journal History, 5 June 1848, reported the party went "up the Muddy Valley and across the Escalante Desert to Beaver Creek and onward to Chalk Creek (Fillmore, Utah)." Based on this description of the route going "across the Escalante Desert," historian Steven Heath reasoned that Jefferson Hunt was looking for Rockwell's wagon road in 1849 when he turned west at today's Beaver, Utah, a decision that "cost him the confidence of his followers" and contributed to the subsequent misfortunes of the Death Valley forty-niners. See Heath, "Jefferson Hunt, Bad Judgement, the 49ers and the Mormon Battalion," 6–7.

[19]Salt Lake winters caused Riser "to hanker more and more as time passed on for the delightful climate of California and I made a resolve that come what would I would go there as soon as circumstances

JOHN J. RISER, MEMOIR, CIRCA 1887,
ORIGINAL IN POSSESSION OF THE FAMILY, 130–35.

And now just prior to my last discharge from the Army a company had arrived from Salt Lake. They came through the Tejon [Cajon] pass or the southern route as it was called. They came they said to buy cattle and drive [them] to Salt Lake. Among them was the notorious Porter Rockwell, and also one James Shaw. Mr. Shaw went to work for one Colonel Isaac Williams, a rancher, but Rockwell lived by his wits. All the Balance Except these two mentioned above returned to Salt Lake as soon as they had made their purchase of stock but this party when they came to california brought many letter to the soldier Boys from their friends from Salt Lake. I also got one from my Brother George, telling me that he had arrived there in safety, and asking me to come to the valley of salt lake also and describing the valley to me.

Well as I said before we got our discharge, many of us had a longing to see the atlantic states or salt lake. I contemplated that if we could raise a company I would be one that would go. But I had not thought much about staying in salt Lake, but would not stop until I reached Ohio where my Father lived.

But man proposes and God disposes. We Brought a company together of 23 persons, among the number was James Shaw an[d] Porter Rockwell. Some of us Engaged James Shaw for our Guide to Salt Lake, and others Engaged Rockwell. One man Captain [Daniel C.] Davis took a wagon. It was however a question, if we would get it through, as no wagon had ever made tracks in that region before. The rest of us had packmules or Horses. I had two mules and three Horses. We took the Tejon Pass route and made the first wagon road to Salt Lake on that route that was ever made there and [it] was the route taken by Emigrants in after years, the distance being about Eight hundred miles.

We started on the 12th of April 1848 and arrived in salt Lake on the 5th of June, but our route was beset with many hardships and dangers, passing over much desert Country and [through what] was also an Indian Country, and the most of them were treacherous and Hostile, stealing in one Haule from us Eleven Horses and mules. And they were constantly hanging on our trail night and day, but we sometimes paid them dear for their trouble with us.

I found my Brother and his Family and they were highly pleased at my arrival. Most all that came from california at this time found some friends here, and we all concluded to stop for a while at least myself included. Infact I could not help myself as one in those days could not travel alone, on account of Hostile Indians and no considerable number could be found that wanted to travel farther at that time. And the authorities of the church resolved before their High Council, that no member of the church should

---

would allow." Riser and his bride left Salt Lake on 11 April 1850 with the Blackburn-Beatty party that founded Mormon Station, the first settlement in today's Nevada. The company of thirty wagons traveled down the Humboldt "in true Pioneer style and had a splendid time all the way. My wife often refers to it as the Happiest part of our lives." A successful farmer, Riser died in Alameda County, California, in 1910.

be permitted to leave the valley until Brigham Young came in. He had gone East, and had not yet returned but would be in that fall, but too late for any company to leave after that even if permission was then given to go and so things stood at this time. I had not long been in salt Lake before I could dis- covered [sic] great dislike to the soldier Boys. If we were seen walking or rid- ing with a young Lady, the Old Elders looked at us like Hyenas, and made public remarks about us, and the High Council made laws to annoy us in many ways. We should not ride on sunday, and should not walk on sunday with a Lady. But when Brigham Young came in these stringent laws were somewhat moderated, but it was then too late to leave that fall.

And so I had to content myself the best I could for the present.

COL. R. B. MASON:
PURPORTING TO BE THE COIN OF THE UNITED STATES

The San Diego company's reputation for sterling behavior was hurt less than a month after its discharge when at least three battalion veter- ans were arrested in southern California on charges of passing counter- feit money. Former American consul Thomas Larkin wrote from Monterey in April 1848, "Much excitement exists at the Angeles and San Diego in consequence of the circulation of false gold coin, pur- porting to be from the New Orleans Mint." Larkin reported the general conclusion that "the pieces were brought from the Salt Lake and issued immediately after Major [William] Rich paid off the troops at the South. Three Mormons who came in with the last company from the Salt Lake are arrested in San Diego for the circulation of this coin. There was a quantity of it found in their possession."[20] Three of the men arrested on 1 April at Los Angeles were recently discharged officers of the Mormon Volunteers. Governor Mason did not want the men tried in a military court and directed Stephen C. Foster, alcalde of Los Angeles, to organize a special civil court to handle the case.[21]

---

[20]T. O. Larkin to B. R. Buckelew, 14 April 1848, in Hammond, ed., *The Larkin Papers*, 7:225. It seems aston- ishing that Mormons would haul counterfeit gold coins across the plains *and* the Mojave desert, but Larkin was one of the best-informed men in California. Another possible source of the bogus was Samuel Brannan, whose correspondence described the passing of counterfeit in New York by Apostle Orson Pratt. See Bagley, ed., *Scoundrel's Tale*, 120. A local legend tells that Lansford Hastings' Montezuma House near the confluence of the Sacramento and San Joaquin rivers was filled with "numerous appliances for the manufacture of coins" that were "probably intended for the use of the Mormons." See Hoover *et al*, *Historic Spots in California*, 513. While Hastings acted as an agent for the Mormon church in California, this tale lacks credible documentation.

[21]R. B. Mason to J. D. Stevenson; and Mason to S. C. Foster, 18 April 1848, House Exec. Doc. 17 (31-1), 1850, Serial 673, 539–40. Dr. Foster came to California as a Mormon Battalion guide. For

Charges of counterfeiting had long followed the Mormon church. Governor Thomas Ford was visiting Nauvoo to investigate counterfeiting charges when Joseph Smith was murdered in an Illinois jail.[22] In August 1845 a marshal appeared at Carthage, Illinois, "with writs for all the Twelve" based on Dr. Abiather Williams' claim "that the Twelve made bogus at his house in Iowa." The charge sent the apostles into hiding.[23] Upon his excommunication in November 1845, William Smith denounced his fellow apostles as "Powerless Rogues Rascals Scoundrels Counterfiters &c &c." Prominent Saints, including Theodore Turley, were actually arrested on "charges of bogus-making." William Smith promised that "more of these truths will appear to light when a Mr. Turley the head Counterfieter of Nauvoo is sent to Alton *Penatenciary*." Brigham Young repeatedly denied that his followers had anything to do with counterfeiting, but early in 1846 a U.S. grand jury "found twelve indictments against prominent members of the Mormon church," including Orson Pratt and Brigham Young, "for counterfeiting the coin of the United States."[24] Young conceded on 24 January 1846 that a "set of bogus-makers" in Nauvoo were "determined to counterfeit coin here by wagon loads and make it pass upon the community as land office money." He claimed these criminals wanted to "be avenged upon us for not consenting to the establishment of their bogus mints." Tales of bogus making followed the Mormons west from Nauvoo, and during the trek across Iowa, Young mediated a dispute involving Thomas S. Williams over the profits of a counterfeiting operation. President Young "reproved them for dealing in base coin" and warned, "the Lord would be against him and all those who partook of such corruption."[25]

William Coray's disaffected sister Mary believed that the "bogus money" was "mostly made at Nauvoo" with "the personal sanction and *blessing* of the Prophet Joseph, and of the Twelve." She claimed "the press for making bogus money rolled into sight" when a wagon tipped over in

---

Mason's careful assignment of jurisdictions to civil and military courts, see Harlow, *California Conquered*, 285–86. Stevenson's original letter of 10 April 1848 describing the arrests was not printed with the other official documents and could not be located in the National Archives.

[22]Oaks and Hill, *Carthage Conspiracy*, 19.

[23]Roberts, ed., *History of the Church*, 7:491.

[24]Bagley, ed., *Scoundrel's Tale*, 99; and "The Mormons," *Niles' National Register*, 3 January 1846, 288/3. *Niles'* reported the indictment alleged that Joseph Smith "used to work with his own hands at manufacturing those counterfeits."

[25]Roberts, ed., *History of the Church*, 7:525, 574, 609; and Morgan, *The Humboldt*, 216.

Iowa, and she reported that the press was taken to Salt Lake by Council of Fifty member Peter Haws.[26] Orson Hyde's "celebrated bogus sermon" at Winter Quarters on 20 June 1847 denounced "all bogus makers, counterfeiters thieves, &c.," but the apostle's command to "such & all who knew of any such to come forth" carried an odd provisio: Hyde "absolved them from all former acts and covenants to keep secrets."[27] Looking at Nauvoo, one Mormon historian correctly noted that "evidence is lacking to implicate" LDS church leaders in the many crimes attributed to them, and that "the reoccurring allegations of counterfeiting were never substantiated."[28] Yet the persistence of such charges in Illinois, Iowa, New York, California, and ultimately in Utah Territory suggests that counterfeiting, like polygamy, was a publicly condemned but secretly sanctioned activity in early Mormon society.

MASON TO FOSTER, SEN. EXEC. DOC. 18 (31-1), SERIAL 557, 516–17.

Headquarters Tenth Military Department
Monterey, California, April, 1848

Sir: Colonel Stevenson has reported the arrest of Canfield, Barnes, and others, charged with passing counterfeit gold coin purporting to be the coin of the United States. I herewith endorse an appointment of judge for yourself and _____, to hold a special court for the trial of said persons. The court will be held at Los Angeles, on such day as you may appoint, after consulting with Colonel Stevenson. You will cause the prisoners to be tried by a jury of twelve impartial men. It would be well to summon eighteen or twenty jurors, so that, if any are objected to, there may be others on the spot to supply their places. A list of the jurors summoned should be given to each of the prisoners at least two days before they are put upon their trial. Be careful to have each juror, witness and interpreter properly sworn, and that fact entered on the record; and see that the prisoners have a fair and impartial trial. If found guilty, the court will pronounce sentence, which, together with the whole record, will be forwarded to me. The record should present each day's proceedings; the testimony given in should be entered, as near as can be, in the words of the witness, who should accurately state, or near as he can, the day, month, year, and place where the counterfeit coin was passed, together with all the circumstances attending the same.

---

[26]Green, ed., *Fifteen Years among the Mormons*, 28–29, 107. Frontiersman Joseph H. Jackson confirmed many of Mary Coray Smith's charges in his fantastic *A Narrative of the Adventures and Experiences of Joseph H. Jackson in Nauvoo*, 10, 13–15. Devout Mormon historians have long denounced both sources as apostate slanders, but the repeated linking of Mormons and counterfeiting indicates they should not be dismissed entirely.

[27]Brooks, *On the Mormon Frontier: The Diary of Hosea Stout*, 261.

[28]Godfrey, "Crime and Punishment in Mormon Nauvoo, 1839–1846," 220.

Colonel Stevenson will appoint some one to prosecute the cases on the part of the Territory; you will appoint a sheriff and a clerk for the occasion. Be pleased to examine well the Mexican law on the subject of passing counterfeit coin. I am told it is very severe.

The quartermaster at Los Angeles has instructions relative to paying the costs of the prosecutions.

I am, very respectfully, your obedient servant,

R. B. Mason
Colonel 1st Dragoons, Governor of California

Stephen C. Foster
Alcalde, Cuidad de los Angeles.

I, Richard B. Mason, colonel of the 1st regiment of dragoons, United States army, and governor of California, by virtue of authority in me vested, do hereby appoint Stephen C. Foster and _____ judges, to hold a special court at Cuidad de los Angeles, on such day as may be appointed by said judges, for the trial of Ruel Barnes, C. C. Canfield, Samuel Myers,[29] and others, of the company of Mormon volunteers, late in the service of the United States, charged with passing counterfeit gold coin purporting to be the coin of the United States.

Given at Monterey, the capital of California, this 18th day of April, A.D. 1846, and the 72d year of the independence of the United States.

R. B. Mason,
Colonel 1st Dragoons, Governor of California.

WILLIAM KENNEDY: PASSING COUNTERFEIT GOLD

William A. Kennedy, Company G, New York Volunteers, probably befriended his fellow Irishman, Sgt. Maj. James Ferguson, while both men were stationed in Los Angeles. His April 1848 letter to Ferguson at San Francisco began with gossip about mutual friends, but turned to the latest news—the arrest of some of Ferguson's fellow Mormon Battalion

---

[29]In the Mormon Battalion, Ruel Barrus was second lieutenant, Co. A; Cyrus Culver Canfield was second lieutenant, Co. D; and Samuel Myers was a private in Co. B who became second sergeant of the Mormon Volunteers. Myers stayed in California until at least 1850 and died in Reno, Nevada, in 1901. John Steele recalled Canfield as "a rough harum scarum man" who "dearly loved his glass and his lull." Canfield made deposits in the Brigham Young gold accounts in December 1848. He went on a gold prospecting mission to Kern County, California, in 1855, and in 1887 applied for a Mexican War pension at Stillwater, Nevada, where he died in 1889. See Davies, J. Kenneth. *Mormon Gold*, 62n9, 311; and Larson, *A Data Base of the Mormon Battalion*, 43, 128. Barrus served a mission with Parley Pratt in northern California, came to Utah in 1857, and during the "Johnston Army troubles . . . organized a company of militia, of which he became the major." Barrus was elected mayor of Grantsville, Utah, where he died in 1918 at the age of 96. See Jenson, *Latter-day Saint Biographical Encyclopedia*, 312–13.

veterans for counterfeiting. Kennedy's provocative letter sheds light on military activities in California and provides the only source that indicates the bogus operation involved the notorious Orrin Porter Rockwell.

WILLIAM KENNEDY TO JAMES FERGUSON, LDS ARCHIVES.

2 April 1848

Dear Friend

This is the third letter I have written to you since Sergt. [James C.] Low paid us a visit and I have received no reply. I am happy to inform you that my friend W. W. & myself enjoy good health and I hope that I may congratulate you and Mrs. F. on the same.[30] Anderson has been out with a detachment at the Cohone [Cajon] pass for the last month but does not ~~much~~ enjoy a Soldiers life much. Sgt. Falls has completely broken out what with Drink & Women. If he dont get himself into Difficulty before long I am no *Prophet*.[31] We are living in hope that the first Mail from the States will being orders for our Discharge. The Mormon Company has been discharged and yesterday Even[in]g. Lts. Campfield [Cyrus C. Canfield] & Barrett [Ruel Barrus] and another man that come on with the last Emigration called Rockwell were taken prisoners for passing counterfeit Gold. This Rockwell is said to be the same person who Shot the Governor in Missouri and there is a Detachment sent after some more of the same company on the same account. The Gold was Coined into 5, 8 & 16 dollar pieces.[32] The 16 is too large and the 5 & 8 too Rough. The Detachment that went out after the other men are not yet returned but I shall not close this letter till the[y] do come as I shall send you the names of the others (if any). Remember me kindly to the Old Woman and if you have any news I would be glad [if] you would let me know it *a very little of which is valuable*. I am told that Trade in San Francisco is in a very depressed state but I hope it [does] not affect you any. When once I get clear of the

---

[30]"W. W." was perhaps William W. Weirick, a lieutenant in Co. G, New York Volunteers. Ferguson married Lucy Jane Nutting, one of the single women who came to California on the *Brooklyn*, at an undetermined date early in 1848 in San Francisco. They went to Utah that summer with the Ebenezer Brown company.

[31]Anderson was probably Frank P. Anderson, Co. D, New York Volunteers, who would go on to be a printer for the *Californian*, one of William Walker's Nicaragua filibusters, a Confederate colonel, and a San Francisco policeman. Sgt. Richard J. Falls, First Dragoons, was a veteran of San Pasqual; he settled at Napa, overcame his vices, and served with distinction in the Civil War, rising to the rank of colonel.

[32]The denominations Kennedy listed suggest that the coins were copies of Mexican *reales* gold pieces. The late Harold Schindler, the premier authority on O. P. Rockwell, observed, "Only particular U.S. coinage was minted in gold: $5 half-eagle and $10 eagle in 1795 and the $2.50 quarter eagle in 1796; and since Congress did not authorize the gold dollar and gold $20 double-eagle until 3 March 1849, we have to assume the bogus was the 1795–96 variety ($5, $10, $2.50)." Schindler argued it was "highly unlikely that any pioneer Mormon" in Utah or California "had access to dies of that variety." He suspected the coins were "from that crop of counterfeiters" at Kanesville-Council Bluffs where "a gang of bogus makers was holding forth with a coin stamp." See Schindler to Bagley, 8 Aug 1997, copy in editors' possession.

Army you may keep a close look out for me as in my present mind I shall not be 24 [hours] in Pueblo after that event and it is the only one that I look forward to know with any Degree of Satisfaction.

I am My Dear Friend
Yours Sincerely
W. A. Kennedy

P.S. I have just ascertained that the Detachment Brought in [Samuel] Myers second Segt. of the Co[m]p[an]y on the same charge as the others, the passing the Gold and said the[y] got it from the paymaster. What the result will be I dont know but I shall write you as soon as I ascertain it.   WAK[33]

LT. H. W. HALLECK:
THE GOVERNOR IS PLEASED TO MITIGATE THE SENTENCE

Acting as California's secretary of state, Lt. H. W. Halleck informed Stevenson and Foster in July that Mason had approved the proceedings of the trial of "Ruel Barnes, C. C. Canfield, Samuel Myers, and others." Of the alleged bogus-passers, the jury at Los Angeles found only one guilty, the "Ruel Barnes" who was surely former battalion officer Ruel Barrus. The jury convicted Barrus "of the crime of knowingly passing counterfeit coin" and sentenced him to five years' hard labor, but Mason mitigated the sentence "to one year's confinement to hard labor, to date from 23d of May, 1848," the probable date of the trial.[34] The other defendants were apparently acquitted. These letters provide no hint who "the others" tried for the crime might have been, but Orrin Porter Rockwell was not among them. Rockwell had volunteered to carry mail east for the army in January, but as noted Lt. W. T. Sherman only sent "one package addressed to the Adjutant of the Army." The famous scout left California on 12 April to guide veterans of the Mormon Volunteers to

---

[33]J. Kenneth Davies first brought this letter to light in 1984. He suggested that battalion veterans in northern California had turned gold dust into coins "to disguise their mining operations," an interpretation he noted had "no direct evidence." See Davies, Mormon Gold, 53–55, 62. Barrus, Canfield, and Myers would not have had time between their discharge on 14 March 1848 and their arrest on 1 April to travel from San Diego to the gold fields and back to Los Angeles. Harold Schindler long believed the Kennedy letter was a forgery. Its content and a careful examination of the original document convinced Will Bagley that the Kennedy letter was authentic. Bagley believes his observations persuaded Schindler, but Schindler never made his own view clear before his death in 1998.

[34]H. W. Halleck to J. D. Stevenson and S. C. Foster, 20 July 1848, "California and New Mexico," House Exec. Doc. 17 (31-1), 1850, Serial 673, 571.

LT. RUEL BARRUS,
Los Angeles, 1847.
*Courtesy, International
Society, Daughters of
Utah Pioneers*

Salt Lake.[35] Kennedy's charge that Rockwell was among those arrested
may have been incorrect, or perhaps Rockwell was able to resolve his
legal problems with remarkable dispatch.

It is improbable that Colonel Mason would reduce the former lieutenant's sentence because of his youth, for Ruel Barrus was twenty-five
years old. It is reasonable to presume that the stern colonel, known for
his own strict honesty, looked at the evidence and gave him the benefit
of the doubt out of his high regard for the Mormons soldiers who had
served under his command.

---

[35]Schindler, *Orrin Porter Rockwell: Man of God, Son of Thunder,* 173.

HALLECK TO STEVENSON AND FOSTER, SEN. EXEC. DOC. 18 (31-1), SERIAL 557, 547.

State Department of the Territory of California,
Monterey, July 20, 1848.

The proceedings of the special court convened at Los Angeles, California, by virtue of an order of the 18th of April last, for the trial of Ruel Barnes, C. C. Canfield, Samuel Myers, and others, have been approved by the governor. Ruel Barnes having been found guilty by a jury of twelve impartial men of the crime of knowingly passing counterfeit coin, was sentenced by the said court to five years' hard labor in such place of detention as the governor might direct; at the same time, from the palliating circumstances which appeared upon the trial, as well as the youth of the prisoner, the court recommended him to mercy. In consequence of this recommendation of the court, the governor is pleased to mitigate the sentence to one year's confinement to hard labor, to date from the 23d of May, 1848. The sentence will be carried into execution under the direction of the commanding officer at Los Angeles.

By the governor:
H. W. Halleck,
Lieutenant of Engineers, and Secretary of State
Copy sent to Col. Stevenson and Stephen C. Foster.

HENRY W. BIGLER: LOOKS LIKE GOLD

Whatever disrepute the counterfeiting mischief in southern California might have brought upon their co-religionists was soon obscured by the hard work and good conduct of the large majority of their colleagues. Six veterans built a mill at Rancho Santa Ana del Chino for Isaac Williams, near the spot where Mormon colonists would found San Bernardino in 1851. Carpenters and bricklayers from the battalion helped transform the villages of San Francisco and Monterey into cities, while California's most successful empire builder, John Augustus Sutter, the founder of a thriving empire at the confluence of the American and Sacramento rivers known as New Helvetia, needed workmen desperately to fulfill his ambitious dreams. Sutter employed some eighty veterans as shoemakers, blacksmiths, butchers, tanners, carpenters, farmers, herdsmen, laborers, and millwrights—an essential supplement to his traditional labor force of American frontiersmen, hired Mexicans, and indentured Indians and Hawaiians.

Among Sutter's workmen was a slender, unassuming man from western Virginia. The hallmark of Henry William Bigler's life was obedience to the counsel of those placed over him. Bigler followed Mormon general authority Levi W. Hancock over the Sierra Nevada to the fateful rendezvous near today's Truckee, California, where Capt. James Brown delivered the first news most of the men had received from their families in months. There Brown read the letter from Brigham Young advising the single men "to work in California through the winter, so that they could come on with plenty in the spring," that would make Bigler famous as the chronicler of an event so historic it changed the course of American history.[36]

As much as he wanted to rejoin his family, Bigler as always obeyed. A bachelor, the former Company B private headed back over the Sierra Nevada summit with about one hundred others to look for work in California. At Sutter's Fort they found a man who never refused anyone a job who needed one whether he could afford to pay him or not. John Sutter met with three veterans and agreed "to give the whole of us employment." Bigler dug ditches for a flour mill until 17 December 1847, "when a man dressed in buckskin came to our quarters while we were at dinner." James Marshall, Sutter's morose partner from New Jersey, "wanted four men from our crowd to go with him" to "work and help build a sawmill" on the South Fork of the American River, some six miles north of present Placerville.[37] As edited by noted early California historian John S. Hittell, Henry Bigler's journal is one of only two that describes what happened there on a day that would shape the destiny of the nation.

JOHN S. HITTELL, ED., "DIARY OF H. W. BIGLER IN 1847 AND 1848," 241–45.

Sept. 14th[1847] – Reached our old campground near Sutter's Fort about noon. Three of our party went to see Captain Sutter, who said he would employ all of us on the flour mill which he wanted to build.[38]

Sept. 15th. – We made a bargain with Capt. Sutter. He is to pay our wages in money, furnish us with provisions (we to do our own cooking), and take charge of our animals. This afternoon we moved to the mill site, six miles above the Fort.

---

[36]Hittell, ed., "Diary of H. W. Bigler," 240.

[37]Gudde, ed., *Bigler's Chronicle of the West*, 81–82. In later years, Bigler retold his California experiences many times. These variants have appeared in several editions, but only a few pages of his original daybook survive.

[38]This gristmill was located on the American River at the present site of California State University, Sacramento.

Sept. 17th. – This morning all except our cooks were at work on the race with plows, scrapers, shoves and spades, and ox teams. Our bargain was that we should receive 12½ cents a yard, and we found in the evening that each man had earned $1.50.

Sept. 27th. – While we were at dinner James W. Marshall came to our house and said that he was a partner with Sutter in building a sawmill up in the mountains on the South Fork of the American River, and he wanted four of us to go up there with him.[39] Israel Evans, Azariah Smith, William Johnston, and I, of our battalion, and Charles Bennett lately from Oregon, went with him, traveling with an ox team.[40]

Sept. 29th. – We arrived at his mill site, where we found several members of our battalion who had been working for Sutter since August. The only house was a double log cabin one end of which was occupied by Peter L. Weimer, whose wife, the only white woman here, does the cooking for the mill hands.[41] The work to be done consists in getting out mill timbers, erecting the building, making a dam, and digging a race.

Nov. 6th. – I rested from my work today and went out with my gun to look for my horse, found him and also found a large black-tailed deer within reach of my bullet. An Indian with me carried it to the camp.

Nov. 15th. – I have spent much of my time in hunting, for which Marshall pays the same wages as for work at the mill, and he sends an Indian with me to carry home my deer. Sutter had neglected to send provisions and we should have been on short allowance but for my game.[42]

Jan. 1st, 1848. – All hands worked on the mill dam, which is built of brush.

Sunday, Jan. 23rd. – We have had much rain of late, and last week we built a cabin near the mill. Today four of us moved into it.[43]

---

[39]A replica of the sawmill can be seen today at Marshall Gold Discovery State Historic Park at Coloma, California, on State Highway 49, about thirty miles east of Sacramento and six miles north of Placerville.

[40]Ohioan Israel Evans, 20, and New Yorker Azariah Smith, 19, were former Co. B privates; Evans left Coloma to work on Sutter's flour mill before January 1848. William J. Johnstun, usually spelled Johnson, 23, hailed from Ohio. Not a battalion veteran, Charles Bennett, 36, was a former First Dragoon who was hired about the same time as Bigler and his companions.

[41]A "double log cabin" consisted of two separate buildings joined by a covered porch. Also known as a "dog-run" cabin, this design was developed in the American South to cope with the region's heat and humidity. Thirty-six-year-old Peter Wimmer supervised Indian laborers at the mill. He and his wife, Elizabeth Jane ("Jennie"), came to California in 1846, crossing the Great Salt Lake Desert on the Hastings Cutoff just ahead of the Donner party. They and their seven children by former marriages lived in one part of the double log cabin while the hired hands, including six Mormons, lived in the other.

[42]Six days later, Azariah Smith wrote, "Yesterday there came five wagon loads of provision, as the provision for the winter, has to be bro[ught] before the rainy season commences." See Bigler, ed., *The Gold Discovery Journal of Azariah Smith*, 21 November 1847, 106.

[43]Azariah Smith said, "Mr. Marshall having arived we got liberty of him, and built a small house down by the mill, and last Sunday we moved into it in order to get rid of the brawling, partial mistress, and cook for ourselves." The tyrannical Jennie Wimmer's offense was to require the Mormon workers to come to meals when they were ready or she would stop cooking for them. See Ibid., 30 January 1848, 108.

Jan. 24th. – This day some kind of metal that looks like gold was found in the tail race.[44]

Sunday, Jan. 30th. – Clear and has been all the week. Our metal has been tried and proved to be gold. It is thought to be rich. We have picked up more than a hundred dollars' worth last week.

Sunday; Feb. 6th [1848]. – Today Barger[45] and I visited the creek opposite to the mill to look for gold. I found $6 worth.

Feb. 12th. – This afternoon I did not work, being tired and not very well. I took my pan and went down the creek pretending to hunt for ducks, but in reality to look for gold. About half a mile down the creek I discovered some rock on the opposite side that indicated gold. I took off my shirt and pants, crossed over and soon picked up $21.50 worth lying in the seams of the rock. What is worst of it all is that it is on Sutter and Marshall's claim, for after the gold was found in the mill tail, they leased a large scope of land from the Indians, and have sent to the Governor to have it secured. I cannot get a claim on the land.[46]

Sunday, Feb. 13th. – Spent most of the day looking for gold. Found $8 worth.

[Note by H. W. Bigler, 1887]:——

Perhaps it would not be amiss for me to give some additional particulars, which are as fresh in my memory as though they happened last week. The men working at the mill were Alexander Stevens [Stephens], James S. Brown, James [William] Barger, Wm. Johnston, Azariah Smith, and myself, all of the Mormon Battalion, besides James W. Marshall, Peter L. Weimer [Wimmer], Charles Bennett, and Wm. Scott.[47] Before New Year's day the dam was

---

[44]Bigler's unedited diary, preserved in the library of the Society of California Pioneers in San Francisco, said: "~~Sun~~ Monday 24th this day some kind of mettle ~~was discover~~ was found in the tail race that looks like goald." He later inserted in darker ink, "first discovered by James Martial [sic], the Boss of the Mill." See Paul, *The California Gold Discovery*, 62. In a journal entry on 30 January 1848, Azariah Smith, the only other person who recorded the event when it happened, wrote: "This week Mon. the 24th. [date inserted later] Mr. Marshall found some pieces of (as we all suppose) Gold, and he has gone to the Fort, for the Purpose of finding out." See Bigler, ed., *The Gold Discovery Journal of Azariah Smith*, 108.

[45]Thirty-eight-year-old William H. Barger, one of the eyewitnesses of the gold discovery, had been a private in the battalion's Co. D. He died in Iowa in 1858.

[46]Sutter and Marshall ignored the Koloma people at the gold-discovery site and negotiated a three-year lease on a tract ten to twelve miles square with Sutter's old clients, the Yalisumni, who lived some miles downstream from Coloma. See Kenneth N. Owens to Will Bagley, 1 April 1999, copy in editors' possession. The lease payment consisted of some clothing, beads, trinkets, and colored handkerchiefs. When they asked the military governor to approve the lease, Col. Richard B. Mason told them the United States did not recognize the right of Indians to sell or lease their lands to private individuals before the Indian claim had been extinguished.

[47]Thirty-four-year-old Alexander Stephens from North Carolina was the uncle of James Stephens Brown, 19, both formerly of Co. D. Little is known about William Scott, except that he was not a Mormon and worked as a carpenter.

completed, and the race was nearly finished. Some Indians under the super-intence [*sic*] of Weimer worked in the race, and every afternoon, Marshall went to see how they were getting along. They made slow progress because they struck the bed-rock, a rotten granite.

On January 24th while looking at the race, through which a little water was running, he saw something yellow on the bed-rock. He sent an Indian to Brown for a plate, whereupon Brown said, "I wonder what Marshall wants with a tin plate." Just before we quit work for the day, Marshall came up and told us he believed he had found a gold mine. Nothing more was then said on the subject, as no one considered the matter worthy of atten-tion. In the evening he again came round to our shanty, and began talking about the gold he had found in the lower end of the tail-race. He had tried to melt it and could not. He thought it must be gold. He requested Brown and me to shut off the water in the morning and throw some sawdust, rot-ten leaves and dirt above the gate, so as to fill the cracks, and prevent any leakage, so that he could examine the bottom of the race.

The next morning Brown and I obeyed his orders and then went to breakfast, while Marshall was walking along the bank of the race. We had returned to work at the mill when Marshall came up with a gleaming face and said, "Boys I have found a gold mine." And with that he set down his slouch hat, which he had been carrying in his hand, on a workbench. We all gathered round him, and then we saw perhaps a teaspoonfull of gold dust, some particles as large as a grain of wheat, and others in small, thin scale in the crown of his hat. Azariah Smith took out a half-eagle, and we could see that there was a difference in color, and though none of us had seen virgin gold before, we all believed that Marshall was right. On his invitation we went with him to the race, and there we found small particles of the same metal in the crevices of the rock. Marshall requested us to say nothing about it until we should find the extent of the mine. After a little prospecting we all went back to our work. My task at the time was drilling a bowlder [boul-der] in the race for blast. Brown was whipsawing; Stevens was hewing tim-ber with a broad axe; and Bennett, Scott, and Marshall were framing timbers. But from that time we had gold on the brain, and it was the chief subject of our thought and conversation.

As Sutter had failed to send provisions and some of the necessaries of life were in very small stock with us, after several days Marshall went down to the Fort, taking some of the gold along. If my memory serves me right he was gone four days, and after his return, in reply to a question about the test he said with interlarded oaths as he often spoke, "O boys, it's the pure stuff. The old Cap [Sutter] and I locked ourselves up in a room and spent half a day try-ing. It agrees with all the encyclopedia says of gold. Aquafortis don't affect it.

We balanced some of it with silver and when we put the scale in water the gold went down and the silver"—here he gesticulated, raising one hand and lowering the other—"and that told the story. It's the pure stuff." He told us that Sutter would arrive in a few days to see for himself.

Several days after this conversation Marshall came to our shanty and told us that Sutter had arrived and was at the other house, and he added: "Now boys, we all have a little gold and I move that we all give some of it to Henry [myself] so that when he goes in the morning to shut off the water, he can sprinkle it on the bedrock where the old gentleman will find it when I take him down to the race; and he will get so excited that he will treat us all round out of the bottle he always carries with him." This suggestion was agreed to with a hearty laugh. The gold was contributed and put in the race before breakfast, and while we were still at the table in our shanty we saw the captain, a well dressed old gentleman, hobbling along with a cane between Marshall and Weimer. We went out; he shook hands with us all; spoke to all affably, and invited us to go with him prospecting. Just after he had given us this invitation, one of Weimer's little boys came running as fast as he could, and getting into the tail-race, ahead of us, picked up nearly every particle and then came to meet us, and exclaimed, holding out his open hand, with perhaps three ounces of gold, "See what I've got." Not one of us ventured to tell how the boy came to find so much. When Sutter saw what the boy had, he struck the ground with his cane emphatically, saying, "By Jove, it is rich!" We then went into the race where the captain had the pleasure of picking up some particles that the boy had overlooked. Sutter and Marshall soon afterwards called the Coloma Indians together and made an agreement with them to lease a tract ten or twelve miles square for three years, the rent to be a supply of shirts, knives, handkerchiefs, meat, flour, and peas, and Sutter having brought such things with him, paid the first year's rent at that visit.[48]

[*The Journal, 1848*]

Feb. 21st. [1848] – Weather cloudy and cool. I harrowed in three acres of peas for Marshall. Wild flowers of many hues abundant.

Feb. 22d. – Snowed in the night, and the ground is white with snow. This morning I started out to hunt for ducks, but soon changed my notion, and made my way to the gold mine, wading the creek, which was cold and deep. After crossing, I found my feet were extremely cold, so I tried to strike a fire, but my hands were so benumbed I could not hold the flint and steel. I tried to catch fire from my gun, but my powder had got wet and I could not see the yellow pieces lying on the rocks. Finally I got warm, and when I returned to our castle in the evening I had $22.50.

---

[48]See note 45.

[*Note by H.W.B., 1887*]:—

When I got home the boys wanted to know where my game was, and why I was out so late. They evidently suspected something, and I worried them for a while with evasive replies, and finally called for the scale and said we would weigh the game. We had made a pair of scales with wood and string, using a silver dollar for an ounce weight, and a half dollar for half an ounce. Gold was estimated to be worth $16 an ounce. When the scales were ready, I pulled out one corner of my shirt-tail with a knot in it. This, when untied, yielded my yellow game, which was weighed by Stevens and declared to be worth $22.50. This was the first gold they had seen coming from any place outside of the mill-race, and my success in mining filled them with astonishment and pleasure. They were so happy that they repeatedly burst out into loud roars of laughter, and I laughed with them. They talked about quitting work in the mill, but decided not to do so, because it would be unfair to leave the job unfinished, and besides they were not sure they could do better at gold hunting. I had written to my friends at Sutter's Fort that gold had been found.[49]

[*The Journal, 1848*]

Sunday, Feb. 27th. — I took the boys to my gold mine, but the river had risen so that the part of it where I got the gold on the 22nd was under water. However, five of us got nearly two ounces, and of this I picked up more than a third. Barger said Bigler could see gold where there wasn't any. Three of the battalion boys arrived at our shanty from Sutter's Fort to see for themselves about the gold discovery of which I had written to them. Marshall was there when they came in and he sat till a late hour. He was in an excellent humor that evening, and as usual, a very entertaining companion. Hudson,[50] one of the visitors, asked the privilege of prospecting in the tail-race the next morning, and it was granted. The next morning the three, Wilfred Hudson, Sidney Willis, and Fifield,[51] went into the race and Hudson found a piece worth $6. They sojourned with us till the 2nd March, and then returned to the Fort following the course of the river and hunting for gold along its banks. They found some at the place afterwards known as Mormon Island.[52]

---

[49]Bigler recalled, "I had written, about the twentieth," to Jesse Bigler Martin, Ephraim Green, and Israel Evans "that we had discovered gold in the race. It was told to them as a secret." Secret or no, other veterans soon heard the tale. See Gudde, ed., *Bigler's Chronicle of the West*, 103.

[50]Wilford Heath Hudson, 29, had served as a private in Co. A and was a native of New York.

[51]New Yorker W. S. S. (Sidney) Willes, 28, had been a private in Co. B. Former Co. C private Levi Joseph Fifield, 44, hailed from New Jersey.

[52]At Mormon Island, a big sandbar in the South Fork of the American River, Willes and Hudson made the first major gold strike following the Coloma discovery. Soon after Mormon miners used Indian baskets to wash out as much as seven dollars a load. The rich diggings, now under the waters of Folsom Reservoir, became one important destination of the 1849 gold rush.

March 11th [1848]. – We started the sawmill this afternoon, and it was a success, and a great surprise to the Indians, one of whom when previously told by Brown that the mill would saw of itself, said it was a lie. He had helped Brown at the whipsaw and knew a saw would not go unless there was a man at the end of it. Now he lay on his belly for two hours watching the saw cutting boards much faster than any whipsaw, and finally got up, said it was *bueno*, and he wanted to learn to manage a sawmill.

March 12th. – The saw ran all day, but the tail-race was not deep enough. There was so much back water about the wheel that the power was insufficient, so when the gate was shut down, it was with the order that it should not be raised till the tail-race should be deepened.

Sunday, March 19th. – All hands hunted for gold. I was the luckiest one, and found $31. Last week we completed the tail-race and the saw did much better.

Sunday, March 26th. – All last week, I was busy teaching some Indians how to chop down trees for saw logs. They were anxious to learn, but awkward, and they cut some awful gashes in their feet and legs; and then looked at me as if I should have prevented them from wounding themselves. Today I found $6 worth of gold.

Sunday, April 2d [1848]. – Clear and warm. Found a new place for gold, and got $30.

April 7th. – Stevens, Brown, and I, saddled our horses and started for Sutter's Fort for the purpose of settling with Sutter and arranging with the men of our battalion for the journey to Salt Lake. Having started late, we traveled only a few miles and camped in the mountains.

April 8th. – Arrived at the mill site near the fort[53] and were told that Hudson and Willis had gone up the river to hunt for gold, where they found it before.

Sunday, April 9th. – The members of our battalion held a meeting and we resolved to be ready to start for Salt Lake on the 1st of June; excepting those who are to leave next Saturday with an express for Salt Lake and perhaps for the Eastern States.[54]

April 11th. – After dinner Brown and I started on our return trip and camped in the foothills.

April 12th. – In the morning while our horses were cropping the young

---

[53]A reference to Sutter's grist mill on the American River near Sutter's Fort.

[54]At this meeting Samuel Brannan proposed that the veterans open a new road over the Sierra. Brannan had hired six battalion veterans, William Hawk, Nathan Hawk, Silas Harris, Richard Slater, Daniel Rawson, and Sanford Jacobs, to carry to the states two thousand copies of a special edition of his newspaper, *The California Star*, with a six-column article on "The Prospects of California," written to attract immigrants. The paper's brief mention of the gold discovery helped ignite a public frenzy in the East. See Ricketts, *Mormons and the Discovery of Gold*, 24–28.

grass, we prospected a ravine and got about $10. Mounting our horses we followed up the river till we found the mining camp of Willis, Hudson, and party. Here I saw an improvement for washing gold. The boys were using Indian baskets, as tin pans were not to be had, and they say the baskets are as good if not better. They told us they had taken out $250 that day, or more than $41 to the man. We camped with them.

[*This was the first party that washed gold as a regular business, day after day, in the Sierra Nevada. — H. W. Bigler, 1887.*]

April 13th. — Late in the afternoon arrived at the sawmill after prospecting at many places along the road, without finding anything that would pay.

April 14th. — This morning I set out in company with A. Stevens [Alexander Stephens] and J. S. Brown to hunt for *plata*, as the Spaniards call money, half a mile below the sawmill on the north side of the river. As there were not tin pans for all, I used a wooden trough, or tray, made by Stevens for kneading dough. Stevens, Brown, and I, worked together under an agreement with Marshall that he should furnish us with tools, provisions, and Indians when we wanted them, and that we should give him half the gold. The richest dirt today was found 500 yards from the river, and we had to carry it so far in sacks to wash it. We had not sacks enough, and on one occasion, I filled my cap with dirt which yielded half an ounce of gold.

Sunday, April 23rd. — Like Christians we kept the Sabbath day; and for the first time our little camp was visited by gold hunters.

May 12th [1848]. — This day I have made a claim to one mile square of land, and have laid the foundation of a house. In the afternoon I helped Brown lay the foundation of a cabin about a mile below. It is thought Sutter and Marshall cannot hold so much land as they have taken up.

Sunday, May 14th. — Gold hunters arriving every day and the place is filled with people, as much or more than any other in California. It costs 25 or 50 cents to get a shirt washed, and everything is high in proportion.

May 15th. — Planted corn, pumpkins, squash, beans, and red pepper on my claim.

June 1st [1848]. — I have done nothing on my house since the 15th of May. I have no idea that I can hold it. The miners pay no attention to Sutter and Marshall's claim. People have come in so fast that the banks of the river and the ravines are filled with mining camps. It seems as if everybody in California were here. Report says that all business at San Francisco has stopped.

June 2nd. — Spent half of the day getting my oxen across the river. In the afternoon washed out nearly $20.

June 17th. — On account of the heavy snows in the mountains, I did not start for Salt Lake until today. We continued to mine until June 10th. Today I and two others went in advance as pioneers.

June 28th. – Prospected for gold and found some.

June 29th. – Washed out $26.

June 30th. – Washed out $42.

July 1st [1848]. – The whole party started to cross the mountains, except Mr. [Orin] Hatch and myself, who remained behind to search for some missing oxen.

July 4th. – Found the oxen and followed the trail. When we camped alone for the night, we were startled by the roar of cannon from the eastward. It reminded us that this was the birthday of American Independence.[55]

July 5th. – We overtook the party in camp at a valley called Sly's Park on the southern divide between the American and the Macosme [Cosumnes] Rivers. The party included 45 men, one woman, 17 wagons, and 400 head of livestock.[56]

---

[55]The cannonade came from Sly Park, where Ephraim Green noted that the main Mormon party "fired two rounds with the six pounder." The veterans had acquired two brass cannons from John Sutter, who in turn had purchased them from the Russians when they abandoned Fort Ross on California's northern coast. See Bagley, ed., *A Road from El Dorado*, 7, 18.

[56]In going, this mixed party of battalion veterans and California Mormons opened a new wagon road over the Sierra Nevada, now known as the Mormon-Carson Emigrant Trail, that became for several years the main avenue of the overland Gold Rush. More than six thousand would cross the great mountain range by the new route in 1849. A mountain peak on this trail has been named after Melissa Coray, the only woman in the party. Kenneth N. Owens and Michael N. Landon will edit the documents that tell of the Great Basin crossings of battalion veterans in their forthcoming volume in the KINGDOM IN THE WEST series.

Chapter 12

"IN HONORABLE REMEMBRANCE"
The Legacy of the Mormon Battalion

The military contribution of the Mormon Battalion to the outcome of the Mexican War was so inconsequential that credible historians have written entire volumes on the conflict without once using the word "Mormon," let alone mentioning the unique militia recruited from the religion's ranks.[1] A PBS documentary spent four hours on the war but did not find it necessary ever to refer to the battalion.[2] Quite naturally these studies focus on the colorful campaigns in Mexico and tend to ignore the much more enduring achievements of General Kearny's Army of the West. Yet the conquest of the Southwest and California created the continental nation that is the heart of today's United States and left behind a complicated legacy that still invigorates our nation's life. The battalion's part in the war was certainly minor; it fought no battles and won no martial glory, but its presence in California had significant political impact. The Mormons' loyalty to Stephen W. Kearny confounded John C. Frémont's dangerous games and confirmed the American conquest. The good conduct of its men diffused much of the hostility towards the Mormons that was endemic in the Far West, temporarily winning their church much good will.

Utah and the LDS church felt the influence of the Mormon Battalion most profoundly. While the battalion is still widely celebrated in the state and the Mormon church, its complicated legacy is not well comprehended. Yet from the moment its first veterans entered Salt Lake Valley on 22 July 1847, they would have a dramatic impact on the destiny of Mormonism in the West.

---

[1] See, for example, John S. D. Eisenhower's *So Far from God: The U. S. War with Mexico, 1846–1848.*

[2] "The U.S.-Mexican War (1846–1848)," Dallas/Fort Worth: KERA, 1998.

LET NOTHING STOP US: SALT LAKE VALLEY, 1847

Along with the almost three thousand men, women, and children who had reached the Salt Lake Valley by October 1847, battalion veterans faced the difficult challenge of surviving winter in the Rocky Mountains in primitive shelters with few supplies. John Hess remembered arriving "in a country that was untried," a thousand miles from any supply station. He had "only the outfit of a discharged soldier"—a "small tent, a sheet-iron camp-kettle, a mess pan, two tin plates, two spoons, two knives and forks, a pair of blankets badly worn, two old quilts, ten pounds of flour," and his "precious wife, Emeline," the sister of Henry Bigler, "who had been with me through all of the trials and hardships and had endured them all without a murmur." Hess "almost despaired because of the gloomy outlook," but "concluded a faint heart would not buy a baby a frock." He "began to get out house logs to put up a shelter for the winter."[3] The arrival of the second 1847 company aggravated the situation when they failed to manage their loose stock. John Steele complained:

> Company after company came in and turned their cattle loose and devoured about 40 acres of grain in one field and 20 in another and among the rest eat up to me 1¼ acres of buckwheat and corn, beans and peas, and devoured all that I had for to live upon through the winter for my family, consisting of four.

Although "we knew well there were plenty of provisions in our camp," when Steele tried to buy grain, his fellow settlers "all refused saying they have not got enough for themselves." Steele paid $12.50 for a hundred pounds of corn meal, complaining "I was forced to get it to keep my family from starving." Otherwise, they "had to live upon meat or else starve." In desperation, the veterans drafted a petition to the religious body Brigham Young had left to govern the infant colony.

PETITION TO THE STAKE HIGH COUNCIL, GREAT SALT LAKE CITY, 2 NOVEMBER 1847. FROM JOHN STEELE, REMINISCENCES AND JOURNALS, 1846–1898, LDS ARCHIVES.

Great Salt Lake City   November 2nd 1847
Mr. President & breathren of the Councel
    We do hereby present our petition before you becaus of the peculiar cit-

---

[3]Wood, ed., "John W. Hess, With the Mormon Battalion," 53.

uation in which we are at present placed. We left our Winter quarters on 24 of May and have had to live on two thirds rations til all we had was consumed and when two hundred miles beyond fort John, Elder Amesy A. Lyman met us with councel from the president of the Church saying to let nothing stop us but come immediately to him so here was a double command. Well we at last arived in the valey went to work [and] put in our grain thinking by so doing we would be well provided for untill the next season. All done well until the first companyes came in who turned their cattle loos and devoured our crops that would have been fit to harvest in a few days (and of course devoured our means of subsistance). When the president left he told us to stop here and go to work for the wealth of the Church was coming on and we would get breadstuff from them for our labour. With this before us we sent back 70 head of cattle that we would have had to subsist on this winter that we might not starve also waggons and several private waggons & cattle two yoke & [a] waggon from Brother [Sebert C.] Shelton and the same from Brother James Brown 2nd who are now without Bread. Now Sirs to buy is altogeather out of the Question and the little that can be bought the price would stare the Extortiones [extortionists] in the Face with astonishments. 12 ½ dollars a hundred weight for corn meal and the like Ratiew [ratio] for other commodities.

There is yet two or maybe three of U.S. Oxen that may probably do to the wealth of the Church get their hearts oponed—a thing that is as nothing compared with what we have done for them for as Brother Brigham said none could have come here had our Battalion not went and said he you stand as saviours to this people. Now Sirs if the[y] are not willing to devide with those that the pressident says stand as their saviours and if there be suffering all suffer together the[y] are not worthy of the name of Saint or Brother and of course no confidence can exist. We dont crave it as a charatable donation we claim it is our just Wright to be sustained as Breathren with you. Still we are willing to pay for any thing that we may get as soon as we receive our money from [the] Government. But we do want the privelege of living here among the breathren if it is possible. Now Sirs into your hands we commit ourselves hoping you will do some thing for us if possible and if nothing can be done we want to know it.

N.B. we would also wish to remember our brethren that have lately come from Californea[4] who are in the same situation with ourselves.

With feelings of respect we subscribe ourselves your breathren the soldiers.

John Steele
S. Shelton
James Brown, 2nd
D. B. Huntington, &c &c &c

---

[4]This referred to the discharged veterans who arrived with Jefferson Hunt and Levi Hancock.

Steele described the result of the petition:

This petition occupied the minds of the Councel for sometime. They began to mak[e] arrangements to sell some waggons and other things to buy provisions but as they were about to make sale of them Captain James Brown returned from California [on] Novem 17 and nocked all our arrangements in the head making us pay 10 pr cent for our money and wanting us to pay 6 cts per lb. for all the US Oxen that we have eat since the 16 of July.

Like other inhabitants of Great Salt Lake City, Steele and his family survived part of the winter eating thistle roots, and before spring many in the settlement were reduced to eating the hides of their animals.

A CHARGE AGAINST CAPT. JAMES BROWN

Abner Blackburn started east from Sutter's Fort on 5 October 1847, bound for Utah with former Capt. James Brown and three other men on what Blackburn considered "the biggest torn fool erant that ever is known." In his saddlebags Brown carried "about five thousand dollars in Spanish doubloons," the pay of the battalion detachments that he had collected from the army paymaster and almost lost on the trip to Sutter's. Blackburn "found the treasure" on the trail and recalled that Gov. Richard Mason and Brown "had been takeing too much of the needful," and blamed the mishap on the fact that Brown "had brought a bottle of auguedente along with him to keep level." After a harrowing crossing of today's Nevada and the Hastings Cutoff, Brown's men arrived at "the camp of the Saints, the New Jerusalem," on 16 November 1847.[5] Four days later Brown reported to the stake high council, the body governing Salt Lake in Brigham Young's absence, to make the claim that John Steele complained, "knocked all our arrangements in the head."

JOURNAL HISTORY, 20 NOVEMBER 1847.

Capt. James Brown stated he had returned with the authority to act as deputy quartermaster or agent in the disposal of government property in this valley. He was counselled [sic] to conduct the same upon honorable and righteous principles. He also stated that he had been gone three months and seven days and had been to some expense and trouble and thought he should

---

[5]Bagley, ed., *Frontiersman*, 111–12, 118.

charge the boys 10% for getting and bringing their money, and so it was voted by the Council, which also decided that Henry G. Sherwood and Capt. James Brown should purchase the Goodyear place and property, if it could be obtained on fair terms.

Before the end of the month, Blackburn and Lysander Woodworth sued Brown for refusing to pay them for their services during the return to Utah. Again the Great Salt Lake City Stake High Council considered the matter.

JOURNAL HISTORY, 27 NOVEMBER 1847.

[Abner] Blackburn (of the Mormon Battalion) and Lysander Woodward [Woodworth] (also of the Mormon Battalion) preferred a charge against Capt. James Brown for not supplying them with beef according to contract. Willard Snow spoke for the plaintiff and Abraham O. Smoot for the defendant. After the case was duly traversed it was voted unani[m]ously that Capt. Brown should furnish 400 lbs of beef to each and if that is not enough, he should furnish sufficient to last them till next spring.

Before returning east in 1847, Brigham Young had told Henry G. Sherwood that his "council to him about buying out [the] Goodyear property be: $2,000 cash." Young referred to mountaineer Miles Goodyear's Fort Buenaventura on the Weber River in today's Ogden, the only extant land claim in all the Great Basin. The high council had appointed "a committee to see if the means could be raised to make the purchase," but the amount was about $2,000 more than all the cash available in the new settlement.[6] The detachments' pay provided the solution: for $1,950 of the money he had brought back from California, James Brown purchased Goodyear's alleged Mexican land grant, seventy-five cattle, seventy-five goats, twelve sheep, six horses, and a cat. The dairy products produced at Brown's Fort, or Brownsville as the settlement was called until 1850, provided critical supplies for the Mormons' first winter in Utah. Dale Morgan noted that the "money with which Goodyear was bought out did not belong to Brown . . . Mormon Battalion funds were used." Morgan concluded that "only the extraordi-

---

[6]See the Great Salt Lake City Stake High Council minutes in Carter, *Our Pioneer Heritage*, 17:89, 96–97. One early historian concluded that excepting Brown's cash, "there was probably not a cent of money in the country among the Mormons in the years 1847 and 1848." See Tullidge, *Histories*, "Biographical Supplement," 111–12.

nary character" of LDS social organization made possible the "public use of funds which properly belonged to individual battalion members."[7] Brown may have "retained only two or three hundred acres," allowing any Pueblo veteran who wanted to "to settle in the country without price or question of their rights," but few took up his offer.[8]

Brigham Young: The Lowest Scrapings of Hell

The care provided for battalion families left behind in the camps on the Missouri became an enduring controversy. Brigham Young's enemies later told "very hard stories" about his use of the battalion's pay and cited affidavits "of his heartless indifference to the wants of the wives and families of the absent soldiers."[9] Former Sgt. Alexander McCord swore in 1864 that Young "did not fulfil the promises he made" to apply the battalion's pay "for the benefit of their families" and to take their wives and children west "even if he had to leave his own family behind." When the destitute "wives appealed to him, expecting in good faith to receive according to promise, he laughed, mimicked, and made fun of them on the public stand; showing how they cried and whined." The Mormon leader, McCord charged, compelled the battalion wives to accept his terms and ridiculed those who "desired their husbands' share, and some cried for want of it."[10]

The problem boiled over at Winter Quarters in March 1848 when Andrew Lytle refused to pay John D. Lee $56.76 for food and clothing that Lee claimed he had provided for Lytle's family while the lieutenant was in the service. With the backing of her neighbors, Hannah Lytle denied she had ever received the items. The matter was taken before a church court and Lee offered to forgive the debt, perhaps recalling the five dollars Lytle had given him in Santa Fe. But Brigham Young, who was not formally involved in the proceeding, arrived and testified he "knew by the Spirit of God that the acount was Just" and refused to let Lee settle. "There has been no man in this Church that has done as

---

[7]Morgan, *History of Ogden*, 18–19.

[8]Tullidge, *Histories*, "Biographical Supplement," 111.

[9]Stenhouse, *The Rocky Mountain Saints*, 247.

[10]Alexander McCord, Affidavit, 4 May 1864, U.S. Superior Court, Utah, reproduced in Waite, *The Mormon Prophet*, 16–17.

much for the Soldier wives & the Poor widows as Bro. Lee has but my self," said Young. Lee had "run & exposed him self enough to wear him out." Those who chose to "opress & sacrifice" John D. Lee would "go down to Hell." According to Lee, Young then launched into a tirade against the veterans and their wives:

> I know that the lowest scrapings of Hell were in that Bot [battalion], notwithstanding there was some good men among them. The soldiers wives have lied & Tatled about me & Bro. [Albert P.] Rockwood, & Said that we have cheated & wronged them out of their money & thereby Poisoned & soured the feelings of their Husband[s]; in so much that they give way to the Same Spirit & commence finding Fault with their Brethren who has done all they could to Sustain the Soldiers Familys while their Husbands were gone.
>
> Great God! could women Tramel me in this manner? NO! All their council & wisdom (although there are many good women) don't weigh as much with me as the weight of a Fly Tird. Excuse me for my vulgarity. It is not common for me to use such Language, but I know of no Language to mean to suit the case before us. It is not a woman's place to council her Husband & the moment a man follows a woman he is led astray & will go down to Hell unless he retracts his stepts. I could have a perfect Hell with my wives were I to listen to them, but when ever one begans to strut & lead out, I say go it & show your wisdom & soon she gets ashamed & curls down, but still my [wives] stick to me. I Treat them kindly acording to their delicate constitution, but, Elders in Iseral, to stir up strife & contention & to try to destroy the influence of Each other and the Peace & Happiness of Families, it is a shame.[11]

The opinions of neither Lee nor Young improved with their arrival in the Great Basin. "The Battalion Boys since returning from the Army," John D. Lee quoted Brigham Young as saying in January 1849, "have become Idol, Lazy & indolent & with very few exceptions are disapated, indulging in vice & wickedness." Lee wrote on 18 February 1849 that Young added the charge of "corrupting the Morals of the young Females."[12]

MARGARET SCOTT: THE IDOL OF MY HEART

Lingering questions about how Brigham Young had managed the bat-

[11]Cleland and Brooks, *John D. Lee*, 1:5–7.
[12]Ibid., 1:86, 93.

talion's pay and cared for the families left at Winter Quarters helped rouse his resentment against many of the veterans. Arguably he had done his best under trying circumstances to meet his obligations to the unit's dependents, only to be the victim of conditions—such as weather and wholesale prices on the frontier—beyond his control. But for some who had borne the cost of war, such questions were unavoidable.

MARGARET SCOTT TO BRIGHAM YOUNG, 17 SEPTEMBER 1848, BRIGHAM YOUNG COLLECTION, LDS ARCHIVES.

Tennesse Dyer City Sept the 17th 1848

Mr Brigham Young——

Respected brother in Christ.

Can you, though the multiplicity of business necessarily involving on [*sic*] you, by your high station in the Church of Christ, can you I repeat, find leisure to read these lines and reply to them.

My brother James A. Scott, my *only* brother the *Idol* of my heart, around whom was entwined all my sisterly affections, has fallen a victim to the cold grasp of *death*, and now his body rests at *Pueblo.*

In the spring of 1846 br. James went to Nauvoo, in order to become better acquainted with the Latterdaysaints, and learn his duty from the teachings of the Church. (He and I having previously connected ourselves with the church.) He continued at Nauvoo until June, when a party leaving for the west he concluded to accompany them, as far as the Bluffs, and then proceed down the river home. By this time his mind was satisfied relative to the latterday work, and he was only coming after me (his only sister) to go on with the emigrants. When he arrived at the Bluffs the call was made for Volunteers, and he responded to the call. But not until he had consulted you privately on the subject. He informed me by letter that your advice publicly and privately was *go.* Also that Elder Kimball the second in the kingdom said that if they went in faith, they should be like the sons of Moroni, not one of them should fall.[13] And I have since learned that you told *him* that there would be a way provided for his sister.

Well I have good reason to believe that my brother went in faith. I have in my possession five letters written after he volunteered. In them I have evidence, that he firmly believed he was in the path of duty, and that he would be *preserved*, and permitted to return for me—I am informed by letters from those that were with him that his conduct was exemplary and his faith firm.——

---

[13]In *The Book of Mormon*, Helaman reported to Moroni that of "my two thousand sons (for they are worthy to be called sons)" who had campaigned against their fellow Lamanites, "not one soul of them had fallen to earth." See Alma 56:10, 56.

Now brother Young, *Why* has he fallen? and he in the path of duty, under the direction of the church, fallen contrary to his faith and expectations. I repeat *why* O *why* has he *fallen*. He was young, his talents above the common order, his education tolerably good, his conduct exemplary through life. And yet he is gone in the bloom of youth, to try the realities of the eternal world, fallen too in a land of stranger[s] *far far* from those he loved. Will you satisfy my mind concerning his (apparently) untimely end. I ask you to commiserate my situation and to help to alleviate my sorrows, and enlighten my mind. By my brothers death I am left as it were alone in the world, without protector or guide, I have none to console or advise me that holds to the same principles that I do. To *you* I turn for consolation and *light*. Believing that you are in possession of that *wisdom* which cometh from above and that you will take pleasure, in enlightening the darkened mind, and binding up the bleeding heart of a bereaved sister—What course will the church pursue relative to the memory of those that have fallen.

Brother James kept a journal of his travels, this I am very anxious to possess. I have written letters to the brethren asking them to make an effort to get it for me. I am sure it is a valuable work, and to me it would be an inestimable *treasure*. It was in Lieut. [Sgt. Thomas S.] Williams hands.

I think, if you will reflect, that my brother went influenced by your advice, that you will not, you can not, refuse me your *teachings* on the probable cause of his death his future employment &c. And what course I ought to pursue, in order to be received into the same mansion. If you write, any information or advice that *wisdom* may dictate will be gratefully received. If you wish information relative to my br[other']s conduct, I refer you [to] elder Levi Hancock, Capts. Higgins, Hunt, Brown and Davis and many others of the Battalion—I Close by again requesting you to sympathise with me in my bereavment, and grant my request, and thereby dispel the cloud of darkness that envelopes my mind.

May the eternal Father bless you with light and wisdom, and influence you to answer this immediately is the prayer of her whose heart is opprest with sorrow——In the bonds of the new and

Everlasting Covenant
Margaret L. Scott[14]

P.S. Direct to Corkwill P.O. Gibson Cty Ten//

Brigham Young apparently never answered this letter.[15] He would later say, however, that "as true as the almighty lives; if the Battalion had

---

[14]Although she signed herself "Margrett L. Scott" in the letter reproduced in Chapter 1, here Scott adopted the more standard spelling of her given name.

[15]At least no reply survives in the Brigham Young Collection. Brigham Young's office did not start using a letterpress copybook to log all outgoing correspondence until 22 November 1851, so it is possible (but unlikely) that Young sent a reply that was not retained.

done as I told them in every particular, there would not have fallen one man in that service."[16]

John J. Riser: Low Hungry Ragged Soldiers

American veterans have often had a hard time adjusting to life after military service, and the men discharged from the Mormon Battalion were no exceptions. Instead of returning to familiar hearths and families, the veterans faced the additional problem of adjusting to life in a religious society disrupted by a mass migration to the Far West. The soldiers found little appreciation of the contribution they had made to the LDS church, and they often encountered downright hostility. John J. Riser recalled that many of those who went to Salt Lake in the fall of 1847:

> had a hard fate, and were despised by those that should have been their friends, for going on Brighams Call to save the Church from destruction by their Enemies. They were called the low Hungry ragged Soldiers, that knew nothing but blood and thunder. They had been hired and paid for it by the month, and [the authorities] advised the young girls to have nothing to do with the soldiers. This was rather poor consolation to those that had left friends and all behind for the sake of the salvation of the Church, and had soldiered a musket and live[d] a soldiers life and endure[d] all the hardships that we endured, and to send them their small pittance as pay, for services rendered to Uncle Sam, to this same church to be devoured by them, and now return in disgrace to them and be hated and despised by this same Holy people. O Consistancy thou art a jewel.[17]

The former soldiers had brought back habits and attitudes from the Mexican borderlands hardly likely to endear them to some of their elders during the early years of Utah Territory. The rising generation's speech, enlivened with new words such as *cañon*, *corral*, and *vaquero*, and outlandish clothes—"the gay uniform of the Spanish Hidelgo," with its buckskins, spurs, and sombreros—coupled with outrages like the notorious "Spanish Rusty," made many of the young veterans into pariahs. Samuel Rogers noted in New Mexico, "Here [when] a man and a woman ride on the same

---

[16]Long, *Report*, 17; Tyler, *A Concise History*, 353.
[17]Riser, Memoir, 129–130.

horse, the woman rides in front." This was in direct contradiction of proper practice in Mormon society, where a woman sat behind the man while sharing a mount.[18] In Salt Lake the "boys took delight in pestering the leaders with their California customs," Abner Blackburn recalled. "When we went to a dance, the girl rode in the saddle and her pardner rode behind on the same horse. The boys did not care and the girls did not mind it. The authorities gave [us] a severe lecture. They said such indecent procedings must stop."[19] Early in 1849 at Salt Lake some half-dozen battalion veterans "rode into the fort on horseback with women before them" on their saddles.[20] This seemingly harmless prank outraged Mormon officials. John D. Lee described the result:

> 6 of the souldier Boys cut a Spanish Rusty by Riding into the fort with a young Lady sitting in the sadle before, & the man behind with his arms around the woman. One of the men was sawing on the violin. This they called Spanish manners or Politeness. Voted by the council that they all be cut off from the church & fined 25 dollars each & that the marshall collect their fine fourth with.[21]

Hosea Stout reported that the Legislative Council inflicted:

> a fine of 25 dollars each on five young men named, Elias Pearsons, B Brackenbery, John F. Murdoc Jesse Earl & [Thomas L.] Frazier for unbecoming and demoralizing conduct.
>
> They got up a party on the Cottonwood at Fraziers Mothers & they each selected their lady and marched their Spanish fashion with the Lady on before & they behind Staid all night & came home the same way. This and some more calculations of a worse nature still was the cause of their being fined. The subject was spoken of by A. Lyman & E. Snow, who also spoke at some length against all such proceedings & the introduction of other savage Spanish customs also against going to the gold minds, after which W. W. Phelps spoke & moved that those be cut off from the church who were fined as above, which was carried unanimously.[22]

---

[18]Why the opposite arrangement was called the "Spanish Rusty" is a mystery, but the name is a sure indication that the Saints identified it as a Mexican custom.

[19]Bagley, ed., *Frontiersman*, 177, 181.

[20]Journal History, 23 February 1849.

[21]Cleland, *John D. Lee*, 1:96.

[22]Brooks, *Hosea Stout*, 2:343. Abner Blackburn described a similar escapade in 1851, but it is possible that Blackburn was "cut off" in 1849 with the five men Stout mentioned, most of whom were later restored to membership.

THE FIRST GENERAL FESTIVAL OF THE
RENOWNED MORMON BATTALION

Prejudice against battalion veterans persisted for much of the first decade of Mormon settlement in Utah, but the situation changed when Col. Edward J. Steptoe arrived in Utah Territory late in the summer of 1854 with some three hundred soldiers and civilian employees. Steptoe was officially engaged in surveying a military road, but he also investigated the murder of members of Lt. John Gunnison's survey party the previous year. The command had rocky relations with its civilian hosts during the winter it spent in Great Salt Lake City, and the intimate contact between Saints and soldiers had "unpleasant results for the peace of Gentile-Mormon relations." The rumored designation of Steptoe as territorial governor and local sermons denouncing the "wickedness and abominable corruptions" of the soldiers aggravated the situation, as did Steptoe's investigation into Mormon-Indian relations. Steptoe declined to accept the appointment as territorial governor and marched his command to the coast in the spring.[23]

The army's visit compelled LDS leaders to reconsider their military situation, and before the troops departed Brigham Young took active steps to improve his relations with the largest body of experienced military veterans in the territory. The result was the "First General Festival of the Renowned Mormon Battalion," which did much to rehabilitate the reputation of the men who had done such good service for their country and religion in the War with Mexico.[24] The two-day affair opened in "the magnificent Social Hall, Great Salt Lake City" at 2 P.M. on 6 February 1855 and consisted of speeches, feasts, concerts, dancing, and many rounds of toasts. The elaborate bill of fare offered dinner at six and supper at midnight consisting of "elaborate dainties" of beef, mutton, chicken, pork, boned turkey, and fifteen different pastries, including Deseret and Tipsy cakes. Father Pettegrew began the speeches with a stirring review of the

---

[23]Furniss, *The Mormon Conflict, 1850–1859*, 40–44.

[24]Clerk John V. Long's *Report of the First General Festival of the Renowned Mormon Battalion, which came off on Tuesday and Wednesday, Feb. 6 and 7, 1855, in the social hall, G.S.L. City, U.T.*, provided a detailed account of this event. The *Report* was issued in two editions, one "Printed at the Deseret News Office" that was "For Sale by T. S. Williams, at the Deseret Store," in Great Salt Lake City, and a second printed by the *St. Louis Luminary*. Citations are to the St. Louis edition. Daniel Tyler reproduced most of this record in his *Concise History*, 345–363; the selections that follow focus on material Tyler altered or did not reprint.

accomplishments "of those men who were offered [as] a sacrifice for the Church." Dimick Huntington asked the veterans to "remember the ladies dresses" and called on them "for one day [to] deny yourselves" tobacco. "Let us show brother Brigham that we are the boys who are willing to lay down our lives for the cause of truth." Thomas S. Williams, who organized the event, outlined the arrangements and then "one cotillion after another went off spiritedly until 5 o'clock," when Jedediah Grant of the First Presidency gave a rousing speech that reveals how he earned the nickname "Brigham's Hammer."[25] Grant elaborated on a myth that justified the enlistment of the battalion, a tale Brigham Young had first told in July 1847. This view claimed the battalion had acted as Abraham's "ram in the thicket" to save the church from the evil designs of anti-Mormon politicians.

> Mr. Thos. H. Benton wanted to take troops and pounce upon your wives and children when upon the banks of the Missouri river, and sweep them out of existence. And when Colonel Kane argued the case, and said, "supposing you cut off the men, what shall be done with the women and children?" "O," said Benton, "cut them off, men, women, and children, for the earth ought to drink their blood;" and the feeling was so strong that it came within a little of magnetizing the whole nation.[26]

Had the Mormons refused to answer President Polk's call for the battalion, Grant charged, "Israel must have been put upon the alter." He claimed he had heard this story from Thomas L. Kane "in his father's own room; it is not some wild chimera, but it is the truth as I heard it from head quarters." The "authorities of the nation did advocate the doctrine of putting to death all the Mormons, and we know it." Grant encouraged the veterans to "raise up lots of children, good boys to form many more Battalions. Israel is ready!"[27] Heber C. Kimball then predicted that Senator Benton "shall be spiritually and literally damned; he ought to have been damned years ago, and why did we forget it?"[28]

---

[25]Long, *Report*, 4, 5, 7–8.

[26]Brigham Young, in Ibid., 9. Tyler, *A Concise History*, 349, did not name Thomas Kane as the source of this story.

[27]Long, *Report*, 10–11. The summary of Grant's remarks in Tyler, *A Concise History*, 348–51, omitted references to Thomas L. Kane. It seems unlikely that Kane, whose father was a close political ally of President Polk, would tell such a tale.

[28]Long, *Report*, 12.

When "Dinner was announced at 6 o'clock, P.M. Presidents Young, Kimball, and Grant sat down at the first table." Young was immensely pleased and spoke afterwards. Finding "the company full of life and merriment," he declared, "this beats all the parties I have ever seen." The Mormon leader said these men "had a goodly share of my faith, prayers, and sympathies from the time they volunteered," and then the usually blunt-spoken Young used the passive voice:

> Some have imagined, as I have been informed, that the Battalion was not looked upon with sufficient favor, by the balance of the community. Owing to this misunderstanding I will take the liberty of expressing my feelings in part. Perhaps, in a few instances, there may have been remarks made about some members of the Battalion, from which it may be inferred that there might be persons who rather lightly esteemed those who went into the service of the United States. I presume that some of those now present have this idea.[29]

Young elaborated on Grant's story, claiming that Benton "did actually apply for, and receive, papers from President Polk" to call on the militias of Missouri, Illinois, Iowa, and Kentucky "to raise a force strong enough to wipe this people out of existence." Young recalled, "I was moved upon to forestall it. As quick as this idea entered my mind it came to me, I will beat them at their own game. Did we not do it? I think we did." Yet the Mormon leader still gave the men conditional praise:

> The brethren who went into the Battalion went with as good hearts and spirits, according to their understanding, as ever went upon missions in the world, and they manifested a readiness to do anything required of them. I will say to you, that, according to the best knowledge I have of you, the course and conduct of many, were not justified before the Lord, and a knowledge of these facts caused me to weep. But . . . perhaps no other set of men, under the same circumstances, would have done better.[30]

Brigham Young concluded by addressing the rumor "that we have a new Governor." All he knew was that Colonel Steptoe had received a personal letter "stating that he is the governor of Utah Territory"; how such news could arrive "before they could send official intelligence, I cannot tell." Young's four-year appointment would expire in March

---

[29]Ibid., 14–15.
[30]Ibid., 15–16; compare with Tyler, *A Concise History*, 352–53.

1855, but "When I shall be removed I know not, and care not." He remained confident "no man can thwart the plans of the Almighty, for he will, carry them out, and none can stay his hand."[31]

"Cotillions, French-fours, and Scotch reels went off with much harmony and spirit until 9 o'clock," when "Captain Ballo's excellent Brass Band" saluted the battalion "with their sweet music." Five veterans danced hornpipes in "masterly style," and then the Hancock brothers sang "The Mormon Bullfight." Thomas Williams reported that the event had served 532 people. James Brown gave the benediction at 2 A.M. and the festival adjourned for twelve hours. The party was so well attended that Williams asked "those living in the city who have plenty of opportunities of attending parties" to give preference "to those from the country." He issued a special invitation to battalion widows to join the festivities.[32]

The next afternoon "went off briskly," filled with dancing, "songs and recitations." After the Nauvoo Brass Band entertained in the evening, William Hyde said, "I have been looking for a day of this kind ever since we left the service . . . it is a glorious day to me." The men then gave complimentary toasts to James Allen, Jefferson Hunt, Daniel Davis, James Brown, and the "wives and children of the battalion." Others received less favorable notice, particularly George Oman—"A bad omen!"—and John C. Frémont—"A cipher once, now, and forever more, Amen." (D.B. Huntington later wished Frémont "a thousand feet underground, and that it might take a thousand years to dig him up.") General Kearny was "held in greatful [sic] remembrance," and Philip St. George Cooke was saluted as "The man that dare praise us among friends and foes; we will cherish his memory forever." Governor Young received the final tribute as "The bumper of bumpers. May he ever bump his enemies and bumper his friends, and the Mormon Battalion will help him."[33]

James Brown's speech celebrated "the first opportunity we have had of meeting together, since we left Santa Fe, and went some to one place and some to another." The old captain predicted that the "Mormon Battalion will be the means of redeeming Zion in the last days, where the

---

[31]Long, *Report*, 18–19.
[32]Ibid., 20.
[33]Ibid., 22–23, 25, 28.

house of the Lord will be built," a reference to Mormon millennial hopes of returning to Independence, Missouri. The veterans would meet again, and they could mark the time: "We shall know by the Battalion gathering all together, who have got the spirit of revenge, to avenge the blood of the prophets shed in Carthage jail, and we shall do it, or swear our children to never rest, nor give up till the blood of the prophets is avenged upon those who dwell on the earth." More toasts and speeches followed, and Thomas Williams advised the veterans, "let us all rub up our muskets and swords, according to counsel." Williams had some hard words for former lieutenants Dykes and Oman, but Dimick Huntington recommended mercy: "They are dead and damned, and hence I feel to say, leave them alone." Gentiles were apparently fair game, for in another round of toasts Williams recalled the "OLD IRON SPOON" Surgeon Sanderson had used to administer medicine to the battalion: "while he is in hell administering Calomel to our enemies, may he have nothing but the old iron spoon to eat with." The organizing committee also settled accounts with John D. Lee and Howard Egan: "Here's to the men who carried news from Santa Fe, disrespectful of the Mormon Battalion—may they suffer on earth till compelled to repent of their evil doings." Lorenzo Clark ridiculed the president to whom the Mormon people owed more than they realized: "May President Polk ever want a cloak, and always wear a yoke with a poke."[34] Brigham Young took up the theme two years later when he denounced James K. Polk as one of the "poor, low, degraded curses [who] sent a requisition for five hundred of our men to go and fight their battles!" President Polk, said Young, "is now weltering in hell with old Zachary Taylor."[35]

Thomas Williams concluded the event, remarking that about one thousand "had been fed during the festival, at a cost of over $1300,00." He proposed that they make such events a tradition, "having another festival in one year from yesterday." The motion carried unanimously. "About 5 o'clock, A.M., the house was called to order," and David Pettegrew gave the benediction. Battalion veterans would continue to hold such reunions for almost fifty years, though few could be so "pleasing to all who participated in the pleasures "of the first celebration."[36]

[34]Ibid., 24, 29, 32, 35.

[35]Brigham Young, "The United States' Administration and Utah Army," 13 September 1857, *Journal of Discourses*, 5:233.   [36]Long, *Report*, 36.

James Ferguson:
In All Our Rags You Were Proud of Us

The conflict between Mormon theocracy and federal authority so subtly celebrated at the battalion festival of 1855 sharpened over the next two years. Ultimately the American union and its most peculiar territory crossed swords in a political confrontation that came within an ace of exploding into all-out war.[37] Few documents evoke the passions that fueled the confrontation better than the letter James Ferguson, former sergeant major of the Mormon Battalion, wrote to his old commander. Born in Belfast in 1828, Ferguson became one of the most "capable of the younger men" in Utah Territory, where the "handsome, dashing, eloquent" veteran "was equally brilliant as soldier, lawyer, actor and orator." This talented Ulsterman served as adjutant general of the Nauvoo Legion in Utah and was a leading figure on *The Mountaineer*, a newspaper founded in 1859 to oppose the federal presence.[38] The few surviving examples of his work suggest that Ferguson was the most literate enlisted man in the Mormon Battalion.

At Council Bluffs "James Ferguson was appointed Historian for the Battlion by Doct. [Willard] Richards."[39] If his surviving letters are any indication, Ferguson kept a precise and powerful contemporary account of the battalion's service. A note in the annals of the Daughters of Utah Pioneers indicates that the writer was familiar with Ferguson's account:

> His ready pen was serviceable in making up muster rolls, and having been appointed "historian of the campaign," he kept a graphic account of the movements of the volunteers throughout their long and toilsome trek to the Pacific Coast. A prayerful, devout spirit pervades his records from beginning to end. An interesting feature of their camp life was a debating society in which James Ferguson excelled. His wit and humor enlivened every scene and he was a universal favorite.[40]

James Ferguson's journal survived until 1897, when it was mentioned

---

[37]For the continuing adventures of battalion veterans such as N. V. Jones, Lot Smith, and James Ferguson, see William P. MacKinnon's forthcoming *At Sword's Point: A Documentary History of the Utah War, 1857–1858*.

[38]Jenson, *Latter-day Saint Biographical Encyclopedia*, 4:743.

[39]William Willis' Mormon battalion report, 1. The Daughters of Utah Pioneers also preserves this tradition, noting that Ferguson "was known as the historian of the campaign." See Carter, *Our Pioneer Heritage*, 3:565. For another of his letters, see James Ferguson to the Presidency and High Council, 1 April 1848, in Bagley, ed., *Scoundrel's Tale*, 251–53.

[40]Carter, ed. *The Mormon Battalion*, 70.

in the catalog of the Pioneer Jubilee's "Hall of Relics" as the Mormon Battalion's "official record of organization and travel." The Ferguson family collection encompassed "general orders, several in number," including "A letter by Lieutenant Cooke congratulating the Battalion on their arrival on the coast, after the tedious march of over 2,000 miles."[41] The LDS church considered publishing Ferguson's epic history about 1900, but it has since disappeared and, some say, has been destroyed.

Only a few examples of Ferguson's passionate and eloquent writing survive. In the spring of 1858, Brigham Young capitulated to federal power and Thomas L. Kane's political alchemy diffused the crisis that brought Lt. Col. Philip St. George Cooke west with the Utah Expedition. Before the federal army entered Salt Lake, James Ferguson read a *New York Times* letter credited to Cooke that bitterly denounced the Mormons as "a set of cowards, like all assassins and bullies." The *Times* letter, embroidered with flattery and rhetoric alien to Cooke's crisp military style, threatened that if the territory resisted, the army would prove "a more devastating swarm of grasshoppers" than any that had yet assaulted Utah.[42] The letter proved to be a forgery, but it provoked an impassioned denunciation by James Ferguson. Although Ferguson was sergeant major and official historian of the Mormon Battalion, apparently no record of his service in these capacities has survived. As a missionary in Liverpool in 1855, Ferguson had praised "our brave Colonel," but in May 1858 he felt betrayed by his former commanding officer. Few documents provide a better link between the battalion experience and the near-disaster of the Utah War or so passionately invoke the hot passions that inspired the conflict. As also one of the few surviving examples of this talented young man's writing, this letter's powerful prose reinforces the belief that the loss of Ferguson's contemporary history of the Mormon Battalion was a historical calamity.

---

[41] *Catalogue of the Relics*, 29.

[42] "Interesting Information from the Utah Expedition. Col. Cook's [*sic*] Report," *New York Times*, 26 January 1858, 7/2. An authentic letter, entirely lacking invective, appeared as "The Utah Expedition. Lt. Col. Cooke's Report of his March to Black Fork," *New York Times*, 29 January 1858, 3/2–4.

FERGUSON TO COOKE, UTAH TERRITORIAL MILITIA RECORDS,
UTAH STATE ARCHIVES.

Great Salt Lake City U.T.
May 5th 1858

Col Cooke

In looking over some files of eastern papers received by the Southern Mail, I noticed a letter, professedly an official report from you under date "Camp Scott U.T. Novr. 29th 1857." I was not surprised at the long vexed columns of absurdities issuing from the correspondence of that mongrel variety of Army parasites and hot-blooded young Candidates for military honors who invariably make up the material of a military Camp. Nor was I much astonished at the manifestations of vexation and disappointment from officers of mature experience, for whose lack of acquaintance with the Mormons were substituted the misrepresentations of Vagabond Judges, Indian Agents and general loafers whose rotten hearts found no congeniality in our midst. But that you who have known us so well; who had tested our fidelity in the dark hour of our bitterest experience; who had witnessed the tenacity with which we clung to the banner of our country amid the desolation of our own homes, and when our hopes appeared blasted forever; that you who led us from our household treasures, threatened in their peace and honor by red savages and white barbarians; that you should degrade yourself to a level with lying scoundrels and join in the general hound-yell against us, indeed surprised me. That your duty compelled you to advance with the Army intended for our subjugation and extermination might indeed have been true. That armies at best are but scalpels to be used for the torture of the living, the hacking up of the unresisting corpse, or to give relief to the sufferer, at the will of the directing hand, is most true. But that an officer of your rank and reputation was at any time necessitated to justify an awkward position by scurrility and insult I had yet to learn. This however may be among the "moral lessons" the gallant army now croaking upon our borders may have been sent to teach. Perhaps, Colonel, bright associations a mong [sic] the virtues and moral revellings of your peace garrisons may have dulled your memory. Or it may be that the precious laurels won by your brilliant conquest of the poor old Brulés and their trembling squaws may have confused your ideas or whetted your appetite for blood.[43]

Collect your ideas; smooth down your mettle for a few short minutes, while I reprove in kindness your treacherous memory and compare the

---

[43]Ferguson referred to Cooke's role in Bvt. Brig. Gen. William S. Harney's campaign against Little Thunder's band of Brulé Lakota in 1855, which resulted in the killing of more than one hundred men, women, and children and earned Harney the nickname among Mormons as "Squaw Killer."

Cooke of '57 with the brave gentlemen and gallant Commander I knew eleven years agone [*sic*].

Thus, it is said, writes Col. Cooke in November 1857:—"This people design our starvation, our destruction, and there is no device man can resort to which they will not practice, from assassination, murder fire and flood. The robbers and assassins will scatter and form bands of guerillas, and no party, no train, no band of cattle, will pass to the valley, if they can murder, burn or run off. x x x [ellipsis] The Mormons are a set of Cowards, like all assassins and bullies."

Hear now what Col. Cooke once wrote of the same 'Assassins and bullies.' In his official journal under date Decr. 20. 1846. in speaking of the patient endurance of the Mormon Battalion, on quarter rations, while passing the Sonora deserts he says; "They are almost barefooted, carry their muskets, knapsacks &c and do not grumble!"

And hear again his official testimony, in his own autobiography, carefully buried up, no doubt, on the dusty shelves of the blustering Virginia Warclerk: . . .[44]

These were the genuine sentiments of what then I believe was a brave and honest heart. And these sentiments added to the companionship of long continued sufferings on our weary march, I am not even now ashamed to say; endeared you to us. Then Colonel, in all our rags you were proud of us. 'Assassins and bullies' as we were you slept soundly while guarded by our sentinels, and did not blush to wear the honors we gained for you. 'Cowards' as we were you did not hesitate to assure Genl. Kearny of our ability to sustain him against the insurrectionary demonstrations of a late candidate for Presidential honors, nor did you feel yourself dishonored by the compliment paid those same 'Cowards' by that brave, generous old chief, when he refused Capt. Stevenson's request for a detachment to be sent from his corps for the repulsion of the Indians who were then threatening the southern frontiers of California, directing you (to use his own words) to "send the Mormons they know how to march and how to fight."

"The Mormons" you say "have great fear of mounted men." You forget that these are the same 'Cowards' with whom you were not afraid to meet the gallant Cavalry of Genl. Flores on his retreat from Los Angeles. But, by the way, if you wish to know who really are afraid of mounted men I would refer you respectfully to that gallant officer of the 10th. who immortalized himself by his diving retreat through Hams Fork not many years ago.

"This people design our starvation, our destruction." Did you say that for effect, Sir, or are you serious? You cannot mean it. No, Sir. You have had far too much experience in starving and destroying,—your own proper

---

[44]Here followed Cooke's "Order No. 1" of 30 January 1847; see Chapter 4.

trade, not ours, to have indulged the illusion for a moment, that we did not hold your whole army for weeks at our mercy. Had we possessed in our hearts a fractions part of the bitterness that dwells in yours, you would not have lived to scrawl that villainous letter at Camp Scott. We could ourselves have selected the spot for your destruction, and furnished you with a winding sheet in the snows of the South Pass or in the ashes of your own trains on Green River.[45] At whose mercy were the unprotected trains that lay for weeks within our reach and from which you have drawn your subsistence during the winter? What act of ours bears testimony to your base insinuations? Was it the order forbidding our men to fire at your shivering pickets, or the recall of our detachments that you might prepare your winter quarters in peace? Was it the return of your people after a short humane confinement, while you vented your spleen on one poor fellow by abusing him in cold chains during the winter, under the terrors of an illegal gallows?[46] Was it the invitation to the officers of your army to participate during the winter in the hospitalities of our mountain home? Was it the offer of provisions for the whole army when your supplies should be exhausted? Was it the supply of salt to season your fresh meat furnished by us, and spurned with a pretty peevishness by your commander? These, Sir, are your proofs; these are your arguments, to sustain your accusation. Are they not powerful and convincing? How worthy of a gallant mind, matured with the discipline of thirty years. Based upon what tried courage and skill do you assure your "dear Major" that "when spring comes, a more devastating swarm of grasshoppers will never have swept that valley of Salt Lake than will this Army be if our progress is molested." Is it the judgment that scattered your supplies from Laramie to Bridger, rendered Hams Fork immortal for your marches and counter-marches, and strewed the plains with the skeletons of your teams and chargers? Or is it the courage and discipline that prompt your brave troops, to pursue the Squaws of your Indian guests into the thickets and there abuse and violate them? These indeed may be samples of your discipline and skill, and others of the grave "lessons of morality" you are sent to teach, but they do not prognosticate a very serious devastation. Your troops must feel particularly complimented by your comparison. A gallant army, a cloud of grass hoppers. They should vote you a medal, Sir, a medal with the insect on both sides, mounting a pair of huge spurs, string it on your neck, and send you home to share your dignities with your Coun-

---

[45]Ferguson referred to the destruction of three government supply trains by partisans under battalion-veteran Lot Smith in October 1857.

[46]The "poor fellow" was Maj. Joseph Taylor, Nauvoo Legion, who had been one of Kearny's battalion escort. U.S. troops captured Taylor in the fall of 1857 near Fort Bridger and imprisoned him at Camp Scott. A federal grand jury indicted Taylor for treason, but Taylor escaped and the charges were dropped following James Buchanan's general pardon at the end of the Utah War.

trymen [Sec. of War John B.] Floyd, and mingle in his griefs [*sic*] for the disappointment of his favorite schemes. Perhaps after all, Sir, your comparison is correct and just; for it has been too often proved that the armies of a Republic in times of peace, like grasshoppers are only used to destroy or consume the fruits of the labor of industrious, honest men. And it may also be proved in your case they are as short lived and transient.

But finally Sir, upon what principle do you presume to "So hope Congress will declare the Territory in rebellion" &c? What right have you even to express an opinion on any political question? Why do you even dare to reflect on what a freemans rights are? You are but a tool;—the tool of a tyrant Sir; the willing or unwilling slave of a bad administration: a foreman butcher employed to make the free soil of our country a slaughter-house and spread the carved relics of liberty on your bloody shambles.

Oh, Sir, you dealt us out treachery and ingratitude in return for our services and affection. A kind word or even your silence, would have cost you no more than your insults and abuse. How have we ever spoken of you? In terms of honor and respect.

In one of our first celebrations in this city you were termed by the principal speaker "that worthy model of Irish generalship" the highest compliment in my opinion that could be paid to an officer. And one of the battalion you commanded, in addressing a public assembly in Europe, thus speaks of you:—"And our brave Colonel! He was rigid in his discipline and often cross and exacting. But, beneath it all he had a kind manly heart, and while sometimes he would curse us to our face, he would defend us as his own honor in our absence."[47]

These were the feelings of the men towards you, over whose homes you wish to spread your devastating pestilence; and whose wives, sisters and daughters you would place under the moral tuition of your troops. What have we done to you, Sir? What have we done to our country to deserve to be butchered or enslaved? We have fought for and with you. You wear the laurels now that we won for you. Our country's highways are laid upon the tracks of our weary marches. Her treasury has drawn millions from the *wealth that we discovered*. To the suffering Mormon and Stranger alike has the hospitality of our dear-bought homes been extended. In dreary camps did we leave our weeping babes and their heart-broken mothers to march wearily and far for the defense and honor of our Country's flag still red with the blood of our murdered prophets. And thus we are repaid. Think of it, Sir. And if you have a heart not yet frozen up to all the feelings of humanity, blush for your country and your profession. Blush for it and leave it. There is no longer honor in it. The epaulettes of every officer in your army are

---

[47]This was Ferguson himself, speaking in Liverpool on 7 November 1855. See Tyler, *A Concise History*, 364–68.

spotted with dishonor by the act of a cruel despot. Your sabres are sullied with his pestilential breath. Throw your Commission in his teeth and tell him your sabre was given you to defend the rights of freemen, and not gore them into slavery.

I have the honor to remain, Colonel,
The friend of my Country and Soldier
of her Constitution.
James Ferguson[48]

Cooke denounced the *New York Times* letter on 8 June 1858: "I wrote no such letter;—I wrote no letter for publication;—I never wrote or spoke, such a sentence for publication." He thanked Ferguson for "informing me of this mysterious forgery" and recalled his order praising the battalion, "which stands printed in a Senate Document . . . I can only refer to my connection with you on the Battalion Staff, as a satisfactory and pleasant one."[49] Cooke visited Brigham Young on 2 August 1858 and "spoke favorably of the brethren in the Mormon Battalion." Young's clerks referred to the "mean virulent character" of the *Times* letter, "speaking disrespectfully of the battalion," and noted that Cooke "in a polite letter utterly denied ever writing or seeing it, and allowed Brother F. to make what he wished of his reply."[50]

DANIEL TYLER: EXCUSE MY CROOKED WRITING

Brigham Young promised in 1855, "The Mormon Battalion will be held in honorable remembrance to the latest generation."[51] As time went on, Young forgot his own early hostility and during the Civil War recalled, "The boys in that battalion performed their duty faithfully. I never think of that little company of men without the next thoughts being, 'God bless them for ever and for ever.'"[52] While the nation and its historians may have largely forgotten the Mormon Battalion, tens of thousands of the veterans' descendants have not. The state of Utah recently spent more than a quarter of a million dollars to refurbish a

---

[48]Several versions of this letter survive; Ferguson perhaps sent the shorter and more moderate letter printed in Tyler, *A Concise History*, 369, rather than this impassioned statement.

[49]Cooke to Ferguson, 8 June 1858, LDS Archives; see also Tyler, *A Concise History*, 369–70.

[50]"Brigham Young Office Journals—Excerpts, 1853–62," *New Mormon Studies CD-ROM.*

[51]Tyler, *A Concise History*, 354.

[52]See Young, "The Persecutions of the Saints," 8 March 1863, in *Journal of Discourses*, 10:104.

monument to the battalion's memory on the state capitol grounds, and several competing commemorative organizations regularly don anachronistic uniforms to celebrate their heritage. Yet even in the state that still honors its service, the history of the Mormon Battalion is poorly understood.

Early chroniclers helped embed the story as a hero tale in the public memory. In the 1870s Daniel Tyler, former sergeant of Company C, began compiling the material that became *A Concise History of the Mormon Battalion in the Mexican War, 1846–1847.* Tyler became the battalion's unofficial historian "at the insistence of his colleagues and with the encouragement of John Taylor," then leader of the LDS church. President Taylor promised him "full use of available Mormon journals and diaries in Church archives."[53] Tyler wrote numerous letters to his old comrades and assembled an impressive collection of sources "from surviving members of that valiant corps," including personal narratives no longer found in western archives. The old sergeant was a competent chronicler, but he told the tale as a religious epic that celebrated the battalion as "the Ram in the Thicket" whose sacrifice saved the Mormon church. Tyler recognized that the passage of time had limited the scope of his work, noting that "many important and interesting facts and incidents have doubtless been buried with the departed veterans."[54] But his mix of myth and history was accepted as gospel by generations of descendants.

In 1900 the LDS church considered publishing James Ferguson's now-lost history of the Mormon Battalion. This news prompted a moving letter from Daniel Tyler.

DANIEL TYLER TO FIRST PRESIDENCY, ROBERT COLE COLLECTION.

Beaver Utah
Aug. 23. 1900

First Presidency
Lorenzo Snow
George Q. Cannon
Joseph F. Smith

Dear Brethren first of all I must ask that you excuse my crooked writing

---

[53]For Tyler's life and work, see Harold Schindler's 1969 "Introduction" to the second issue of the Rio Grande Press reprint of Tyler, *A Concise History.*

[54]Tyler, *A Concise History,* "Preface." Most of Tyler's own papers and correspondence and all of his journal collection are unfortunately lost.

MORMON BATTALION FIFTIETH ANNIVERSARY REUNION, 1896.
Front row: John Ritter, Edward Bunker, Melissa Coray Kimball, Lorenzo Clark,
Christopher Layton, Mary McCree Black Brown, Charles B. Hancock, Zacheus
Cheney. Second Row: Ralph B. Douglas, George W. Hancock, John M. Bybee,
John C. Thompson, Joseph Taylor, Reddick N. Allred, William Smith [?],
Alexander Brown, Oliver G. Workman, Orin Hatch. Third Row (starting at first
bayonet): Jarvis Johnson, Willard G. Smith, Jesse S. Brown, James W. Shupe,
George W. Boyd, Clinton D. Bronson. *Courtesy, Norma B. Ricketts.*

as my Sight has so far failed at 84 years of age that I canot See to follow the
ruled lines. In a late numbe[r] of the Juvenile Instructor I observed a Photo
of the late James Ferguson and the remark that he was appointed historian
of The Mormon Battalion.[55]

The question with those not Posted would naturally arise if brother Ferguson a well educated bright Lawyer was appointed Battalion historian why

---

[55]James Ferguson's picture appeared on 15 June 1897, *The Juvenile Instructor*, 365, in Scipio A. Kenner's
rambling "The Pioneers and Others: What They Did and How They Did It." The article made no mention of Ferguson's role as historian of the battalion, but the 1 November 1897 installment mentioned
Tyler's "well written" and "interesting" book on page 650.

did Daniel Tyler write a history of said valiant Corps especially would that question arise should this history take the precedence which it would likely to do as his abilities and acquirements were *far* Superior to mine and his story was written at the time of service and mine thirty six years subsequently. I have not the slightest objection to his taking the precedence if the substance of the following statement of facts be stated in a note or Preface to the publication to wit. I did not undertake the intricate labor on my own suggestion altho many times requested by Comrades to do so. I did not feel competent. Elder Israel Barlow an early member wrote me a very lengthy and urgent letter requesting me to undertake the work. I laid his letter a side the same as I had others without a thought of corresplying [*sic*]. Some days after seeing it on my desk, read it again and felt impresed to mail [it] to Pest. Taylor which I did with the remark that I had never felt qualified to under take it. He wrote for answer that if I felt like undertaking it I should have his approval and any assistance he could give and proposed that I get all I could from the historians Office. Under those circumstances I undertook the enterprise. Before publishing I presented the Mss. to him for his consideration. He appointed President Geo. Q. Cannon to examine it remarking that whatever he (Prest C[annon]) approved he would approve which was done with other help from both [men]. I heard of Bro. F's appointment but failed to locate his history 36 years after it should have been in the historians Office.

Your Brother
Daniel Tyler

P.S. My health fluctuates. I am well at present. I Hope [the]] Presidents health has finally reversed. With Kindest Regards to you all and Brother [George] Gibbs.   Daniel Tyler

The LDS church historian's office returned Ferguson's document to the family, and it has since vanished.[56]

It remained for Mormon historian B. H. Roberts to write an accurate assessment of the battalion's story. After Roberts completed his monu-

---

[56]John E. Forsgren's battalion journal met a similar fate. Born Jan Eric Forssgren in 1816 in Gävle, Sweden, Forsgren was a sailor "short of stature but strong, and powerful of frame," who converted to Mormonism in 1843. He marched to California as a private in Co. D and opened the LDS mission to Sweden in 1850, leading the first of many Scandinavian emigrant parties to Salt Lake in 1853. Forsgren delivered his journal, "a large thick, well bound foolscap book of 721 pages containing the history and experiences from his birth until the month of May 1878," to the LDS Historian's Office, where it sat unused in the office until he reclaimed it. By 1886 Forsgren "had evidently become insane over religion." He moved into a tent on Salt Lake's east side and became known as "the Bench prophet." His battalion narrative presumably perished in one of the many fires that bedeviled his career as an oracle. See Journal History, 8 July 1878; *Deseret Evening News*, 21 January 1886; and *Salt Lake Herald*, 9 July 1881. Forsgren died on 22 January 1890 in Salt Lake and was buried in Brigham City.

mental *Comprehensive History of the Church* in 1915, he served as a chaplain in the U.S. Army and directed his considerable scholarly skills to writing *The Mormon Battalion: Its History and Achievements*. Roberts honestly described how "Mormon leaders had appealed to the government to allow them to enlist a battalion in the Mexican War to help get their people to a home in the Great Basin, a much different conception from the one long held by most Mormons that the enlistment was a sacrifice demanded by President James K. Polk."[57] He concluded that "the call for the enlistment of the battalion was not a villainously-designed plot," nor was it a test of loyalty or "a wicked, inhuman plot" to leave women and children "helpless prey to hordes of savage tribes to wipe them out of existence." Without identifying who indulged in "all these evil surmisings," Roberts noted that the creators of the myth had not distinguished between rumors started by "some evilly disposed and irresponsible individuals at Washington, who may have uttered idle threats and boastings" and "the responsible officials of the [Polk] administration." The slandered president "intended to be helpful to the Latter-day Saint exiles, and was helpful to them."[58] When Roberts presented his findings at the unveiling of the Mormon Battalion Monument at the state capitol on 30 May 1927, his "comments, startled his audience, composed mostly of Mormons, in a manner that was quite unexpected. They did not comport well with the traditional views held by most of those present."[59]

Roberts' work rejected the myth that Brigham Young had created to justify the battalion's sacrifice to his people, but Roberts did not venture to explain why the Mormon leader would invent such a story. Young's reasons lie in the contemporary attitudes and anger expressed in many of the documents found in this volume. The tale explained why the Mormon church would "send 500 of her members, to bear privations, and encounter danger, in the service of this government" that had done so little to defend their religious liberties, a decision that Margaret Scott found "beyond my comprehension." It also served Young's subsequent desire to rouse "a bitter vindictiveness against the Government." T. B. H.

---

[57]Madsen, ed., *Studies of the Book of Mormon*, 20.

[58]Roberts, *Comprehensive History of the Church*, 3:372–73

[59]Wells, "The Mormon Battalion," 98–99.

Stenhouse told President U. S. Grant that no other story had been so influential "in shaping the sentiments of the Mormon people against the Government." Stenhouse noted, "Of all the preaching in the Tabernacle against the nation, nothing has ever made such an impression upon the people as Brigham Young's story of the Mormon battalion."[60]

JOHN STEELE: I WOULD NOT HAVE KNOWN MYSELF

The Mormon volunteers' jarring encounter with Mexican culture in the far Southwest profoundly affected their church's culture and prospects in the West. These young men—often impressionable adolescents—left the camps on the Missouri as Midwestern farm boys, most of them with roots in Puritan New England. Their contact with the peoples of New Mexico and California transformed them into something new: frontiersmen. On arriving in Great Salt Lake City, John Steele recalled that even his appearance had been transfigured:

> Our men that looked natural enough when they left Council Bluffs, now look like mountaineers, sunburned and weather beaten, mostly dressed in buckskin with fringes and porcupine quills, moccasins, Spanish saddles and spurs, Spanish bridles and jinglers at them, and long beards, so that if I looked in the glass for the young man who left the Bluffs a year ago, I would not have known myself.[61]

"Went away afoot," Steele remembered, "came home riding a fine horse." On their march through the Southwest these men and boys gained firsthand knowledge of Catholic culture and encountered Indians both civilized and wild. Their adventures conferred upon them a confidence and courage that translated into a striking independence and resilience. James S. Brown remembered, "We had become accustomed to pioneer life," and in 1848 he and his companions thought nothing of blazing a new wagon road over the Sierra Nevada.[62] Many of these men declined to

---

[60]Stenhouse, *The Rocky Mountain Saints*, 237, 241, 249. Stenhouse wrote to Philip St. George Cooke about the matter. Cooke believed that Polk's action reflected "a friendly interest in the misfortunes of that sect" and a desire to "assist their migration." Cooke noted that the usual regulations regarding the age of volunteers and the number of women allowed along "were much relaxed in their favour." Jessie Benton Frémont told Stenhouse that her father "was not the man to seek to reach the Mormons through any covert means, involving another's responsibility." See Ibid., 243, 249.

[61]Beckwith, ed., "Journal of John Steele," 17.

[62]Brown, *Life of a Pioneer*, 107.

settle in Brigham Young's Deseret. Some struck out on their own to California and a surprising number ultimately died in Iowa, but many—perhaps most—remained loyal to Mormonism throughout their lives.

Such experiences made these young men into Westerners, a metamorphosis that was sudden and profound. The Mormons quickly adapted the ancient Indian technology they had seen in the borderlands to their own uses. At Winter Quarters farmers had hauled buckets from the Missouri to water their crops, but on the Rio Grande, James Scott reported, "The soil is watered by means of ditches, by which the water is conveyed from the River & Springs to the fields." He commented that a "Great deal of labor is expended in ditching as many are of miles in length & from 3 to 5 feet in depth."[63] Robert Bliss noted that the farms at Las Vegas, New Mexico, "are watered by ditches cut to carry it in every direction," and at the Pima villages "the Indians filled a ditch with water from the River for our use."[64] Henry Boyle observed that the "land for cultivation is enclosed by ditches, hedges, & *adoba* Walls. On account of the dry Seasons in this country, they have to irrigate all this farming land all thier [*sic*] vineyards & orchards which is done by leading the water from the River through ditches through all their grain & every thing else that is raised or produced."[65] The veterans had seen the pueblos of New Mexico "made of what is called adobe or sundried brick which answers very well for a dry country."[66] In the first meeting in the new bowery, battalion veterans heartily supported Sam Brannan's endorsement of adobe as the ideal western building material.

Out of such cultural collisions a new American West was born. These ancient techniques created to survive in the arid West found immediate application in the Great Basin. Janet Lecompte was among the first to note that "Irrigation and common ownership of irrigation systems first came into the Salt Lake Valley via the Pueblo Mormons."[67] Even before Brigham Young arrived in the valley, the Colorado veterans had built dams and dug ditches to flood the summer-baked fields to prepare the ground for the plow. The reports of men like Abner Blackburn make

[63]Scott, Diaries 1846, 23 October 1846.
[64]Alter, ed. "The Journal of Robert S. Bliss," 74, 81.
[65]Boyle, Autobiography and Diary, 24–31 October 1846.
[66]Beckwith, ed., "Journal of John Steele," 10.
[67]Lecompte, *Pueblo, Hardscrabble, Greenhorn*, 186.

clear that they were implementing technologies they had seen used in New Mexico.[68]

The encounter with Hispanic culture influenced the very bread the Mormons ate. In the fall of 1847, Jefferson Hunt "packed through two bushels of seed wheat" probably purchased at Sutter's Fort, and his men brought "a variety of garden and fruit tree seeds."[69] James Pace "introduced the club-head wheat," while the Pueblo detachments "brought the variety of wheat known as *toas*, [*sic*] common in our Territory." Daniel Tyler left six quarts of California peas with Seely Owens in Salt Lake in 1847, and the next fall Owens told him that "they were the best and most prolific peas he ever saw." When Tyler's peas reaped a bounteous harvest from forty-niners, "every family wanted some of the new variety."[70]

Battalion veterans—Bingham, Davis, Draper, Layton, the Paces, the Slaters, and the Stoddards—left their names on Utah's maps, not to mention the towns of Hatch, Hinckley, Hanksville, Holden, Hoytsville, Hyde Park, Huntington, and Huntsville that commemorate their memory. The former soldiers spearheaded LDS colonization in today's Arizona, Nevada, Idaho, and California. They became, as historian Michael Landon has observed, the mules on whose backs the Latter-day Saints colonized the Great Basin.

Perhaps the Mormon Battalion made its most enduring contribution to the history of the West in blazing wagon roads. As James Ferguson noted, "Our country's highways are laid upon the tracks of our weary marches," and trails opened by the battalion still define several of our nation's transportation lifelines. Philip St. George Cooke claimed that when the federal government investigated "the great problem of the practicability and best location of a Pacific railroad" after the War with Mexico, they had his "map of this wagon route before them" and "perceived that it gave exactly the solution" that "would avoid the Rocky Mountains and Sierra Nevada, with their snows, and would meet no obstacle in this great interval." The appeal of this route led to the Gadsden Treaty and the acquisition of today's southern Arizona in 1853. As B. H. Roberts later observed, "The Southern Pacific Railroad traverses

[68]Bagley, ed., *Frontiersman*, 44, 62.
[69]Little, *From Kirtland to Salt Lake City*, 159.
[70]Tyler, *A Concise History*, 318–19.

practically the route of the battalion."[71] Battalion veterans opened the wagon road over Carson Pass that was the gateway to the gold fields for the majority of the forty-niners, and it was discharged Mormon Volunteers who hauled the first wagon from Los Angeles to Salt Lake over the line now traversed by I-15. That same highway and I-84 follows Hensley's Salt Lake Cutoff north into Idaho over the tracks of the wagons of Henry Bigler, Melissa Coray, and Azariah Smith.

AZARIAH SMITH: BOYS, AND GIRLS AND LADIES

As the veterans aged, their youthful exploits won them a measure of respect from their community and support from their government. The soldiers of the Mormon Battalion were survivors, and even counting the unit's casualties, the average age of veterans with known death dates was an astonishing seventy-nine.[72] As decades passed, the veterans achieved the status of honored pioneers, particularly the majority of the men who settled in Utah. In the 1880s the government began to provide Mexican War veterans a monthly pension of $8.00, which helped ease the rural poverty that was their general lot. A few of the men rose to high positions in Utah Territory, but most lived out their lives as plain farmers and tradesman, and almost a third of them moved to California or the Midwest, outside the borders of Brigham Young's kingdom. Those who lived into the 1890s witnessed a welcome transformation of national attitudes when the LDS church renounced the practice of polygamy. A half-century of vilification of their religion ended with Utah's admission to the union and the dawn of an era of good feeling, during which the battalion's survivors found a new appreciation of their contribution to America's history.

Even in the face of harsh poverty, many veterans maintained an honest dignity. Welshman Thomas Morris, whose "Mormon Battalion Song" graced the pages of Daniel Tyler's history, served his church as a Hawaiian missionary and Brigham Young as a gardner. Morris spent his last days in a home in which "Brigham Young had kindly given him a life

---

[71]Cooke, *Conquest of New Mexico and California*, 159; and Roberts, *Comprehensive History of the Church*, 3:118,n28, 373.

[72]Larson, *A Data Base of the Mormon Battalion*, 208.

possesory interest," working as a "Market Gardener" in Salt Lake. Morris survived by making horseradish every fall. When his store of roots spoiled and deprived him of any possible income at age eighty-five, he hanged himself in January 1884.[73] Most of the veterans came to happier ends, and many went to their graves survived by vast polygamous families. As this volume bears witness, a remarkable number of these men spent their old age writing and rewriting the epic of their youthful experiences.

None of the men left a more endearing record of their lives than the eminently likable Azariah Smith. A tender-hearted New Yorker, Smith began to keep a journal on his eighteenth birthday, 1 August 1846, when he marched into Fort Leavenworth as a young recruit. He became with Henry Bigler one of two men who recorded in their pocket diaries, later transcribed into larger ledgers, James Marshall's discovery on 24 January 1848 at Sutter's mill.[74] Like Bigler, Smith had obeyed Brigham Young's orders for the unmarried men in Levi Hancock's party to return to California and work for a year. Deeply disappointed, he had gone back to Sutter's Fort while his father, Albert, the former orderly sergeant of Company B, continued on to meet his wife and other children in Salt Lake Valley. On 3 October 1847 the lonesome nineteen-year-old wrote, "Sutter sent after some hands to go up in the mountains, about thirty miles; to work at his sawmill and I with several others went."[75]

Following the gold discovery, Smith and Bigler joined the Mormon party that left California in June 1848. As young men across the nation and around the world braced themselves to risk life itself to reach the ground they stood on, they turned their backs on "the root of all evil," as Smith called it, and journeyed east over the mountains to gather with other members of their faith. Henry Bigler went because obedience to the leaders of his faith was the star he steered by. Smith had another, more personal reason. "I was home-sick as well as physically sick," he said. "I wanted to see my mother and did not care whether there was gold in the locality or not."[76]

After traveling more than three thousand miles by foot, horseback,

[73]Morris, Thomas. Autobiography and Journal.
[74]For Smith's account, see Bigler, ed., *The Gold Discovery Journal of Azariah Smith*, 108.
[75]Ibid., 3 October 1847.
[76]*San Francisco Examiner*, 24 January 1898.

and wagon, Smith and his family colonized the town of Manti, Utah, some 120 miles south of Salt Lake. He would not be homesick again. For the next fifty years he would not venture far from his front door, except to make short trips to the Utah capital to attend church conferences and work on a stretch of the transcontinental railroad.

Early on Mormon leaders in Utah Territory began attributing the gold discovery to the Mormon Battalion. Brigham Young proclaimed that battalion members had "exposed the gold of California, and turned the world upside down," and preached that "some of that body first discovered gold there."[77] Orson Pratt speculated that "If it had not been for the 'Mormons' where would have been the gold mines of California? They might not have been opened up for fifty years yet if it not had been for the Mormon battalion."[78] With such encouragement, it is not surprising that battalion veterans developed a strong tradition that they were responsible for the discovery, and there were soon "many conflicting accounts [as to] how it was discovered and by whome etc." Witnesses such as Azariah Smith and Henry Bigler knew the truth, and Bigler wrote, "I have often wondered how it was that the Willises and Hudson never disabused the mind of President Young on that matter."[79]

Early in 1898 Azariah Smith and other surviving eyewitnesses of James Marshall's discovery, including Henry Bigler, received special invitations, round-trip tickets on the railroad to San Francisco, and expense money to take part in California's fifty-year Golden Jubilee as special guests of the Society of California Pioneers. The event would be the most spectacular San Francisco would see prior to the great earthquake and fire, eight years later. Up to fourteen thousand marched or rode in the grand parade, more than eight hundred on horses and fourteen hundred in carriages or floats. Some six hundred musicians performed in thirty bands. Spectators crowded streets and windows. It took two hours and twenty-five minutes for the procession to pass by the Chronicle

---

[77]Brigham Young, 6 April 1853; and 8 July 1863, *Journal of Discourses*, 2:32, 10:229.

[78]Orson Pratt, 6 October 1868, *Journal of Discourses*, 12:304.

[79]Bigler to Alexander Stephens, 5 April 1891. William Johnstun's son-in-law, Samuel C. Young, claimed that about 1897 in Manti, Utah, Johnstun, Azariah Smith, and Henry Bigler told him, "It was the Batallion [*sic*] boys, the three of us being in the bunch that found the gold." See Young, The Discovery of Gold in California in 1848. William Johnstun told the *San Francisco Examiner*, 23 January 1898, "I was working at the construction of the saw-mill when Marshall discovered gold," but John Sutter's *New Helvetia Diary* indicates that "Johnston arrived by land with Horses" at Sutter's Fort on 25 January 1848.

Building. At the center of the great celebration, quite overwhelmed by all the unaccustomed attention, was the sixty-nine-year-old old gentle spirit who described it all with wonder and amazement in his journal, as published here for the first time.

A JOURNAL OR HISTORY, OF AZARIAH SMITH; HIS TRAVAIL &C IN THE MORMON BATTALION, IN THE SERVICE OF THE UNITED STATES, TO CALIFORNIA; AND FROM THERE TO; SALT LAKE VALLEY, LDS ARCHIVES.

Thurs. the 20th [January 1898]. After breacfast, I and Bro. [William] Johnston, rode up to the Depo, and some [Salt Lake] Tribune reporters took our Photo. While there Bro. [James Stephens] Brown also came and at 12 oc. we started, and had a good ride to Ogden, And Bro [Henry] Bigler, soon came to the Depo, and being glad to see each other again. I and Johnston took a long walk up [the] street, getting us some dinner. And after returning we got our sleeping berth ticket, to start at 2 oc 41 min in the morn. And having supper, we went to rest until 1oc. but I could not sleep, but we got ready and at 2oc we went on the cars and being shown our sleeping berth, and going to rest in it, being a good bed for each of us. And in 41 min. we started, giving us a good shaking, but I rested verry well.

And Fri. the 21st. We arose early having our beds folded up leaving two nice seats, for each of us, and having a good breacfast, still Flying on a good job, being somewhat cloudy, and the ground well covered with snow. At 12oc we stoped 20 min. at Elko, and then going on. Bro Bigler is weak and feeble, being 83 years old. We stopped at Collie [Carlin] a few minits, then going on fast, and about 3 oc. we had supper, and our beds being let down, we went to rest, and I slept well. And passing Sacramento, on the 22nd. Also many nice houses and orchards &c. And was met by Almarin B Paul,[80] and Gen. W. H. Pratt,[81] and also two Ladies, that pinned the Silk Jubilee Badge on each of our coats, and upon coming to the Depo, Mr. [John S.] Hittell[82] and others there, pleased to see us. And we were taken in a Coach, to the Russ House, and each of us furnished a nice room, with bed, sopha [sofa], table, chairs, with an Electric Lamp, &c. And many Prominent men were introduced to us, with their good wishes. And Mr. Hittell went with us up [the] street to several large buildings, also the Cal. Pioneer building, with an

---

[80]Almarin B. Paul, 71, general manager of the Calumet Gold Mining Co., came to California in 1849. He wrote for the *San Francisco Bulletin* under the pseudonym "Cosmos," was one of the first fifty members of the city's Vigilance Committee, and later became a banker and mining executive.

[81]At age twenty-two New Englander William H. Pratt arrived in San Francisco in February 1849 on the first run from Panama of the steamer *California*. He later served as a U.S. Indian agent and engaged in the mercantile business until President Harrison appointed him U.S. Surveyor General for California.

[82]John S. Hittell came to California at age twenty-four to seek gold in 1849. He became a writer for the *Alta California*, the author of many histories and guide books, and one of the state's most distinguished journalists and historians.

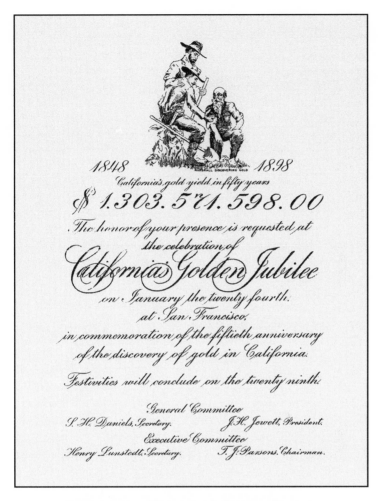

1848   1898

California's gold yield in fifty years

$ 1.303.571.598.00

The honor of your presence is requested at the celebration of

California's Golden Jubilee

on January the twenty fourth. at San Francisco, in commemoration of the fiftieth anniversary of the discovery of gold in California.

Festivities will conclude on the twenty ninth.

General Committee
S. H. Daniels, Secretary.   J. H. Jewett, President.
Executive Committee
Henry Lunstedt, Secretary.   T. J. Parsons, Chairman.

INVITATION TO CALIFORNIA'S GOLDEN JUBLIEE.
Each of "The Companions of Marshall" received this invitation
to attend the commemoration of the fiftieth anniversary of the
discovery of gold in California. *Courtesy, Keith Irwin.*

Asembly room, Library, &c. And then going back to the Hotel, finding our rooms well fixed, and to the dining room having supper. And I got some pen and ink and paper, and wrote a letter home, also sending them a paper. My mind was full of thoughts, and reflections, of the past, and with a thankful heart, and asking this blessing I went to bed.

I rested well, and arose early on the 23d. having breacfast, and I had the barber shave me, and Mr. Hittell came to see us, also Bro. John B. Miller, an Elder came,[83] and I and Bro Johnston went with him to Sun[day] School, at 10 oc. and stoped until after meeting, all being glad to greet us. And after dinner Bro. Miller went with us on a street car, about 6 miles out to the Cliff House, the Seal rock, and Sutro's height, where we could see a great distance out on the Ocean, being verry windy; and soon returning, and resting, geting dark. And on Mon. the 24th. I arose early, and washing myself, and with the others, down to breacfast, and then preparing ourselves for the Procession. Bro. Miller came, aiding us in fixing up for the ocasion. I put on a white shirt, and Mr. Hittell came, wishing us to be ready soon for the Coach, and soon it came, and we were helped into it by an officer of the day.

And on each side of the Coach, were placed in large letters, The Companions of Marshall, and we were introduced to many of the officers, and notable men of the City. And at 10oc. 40 min we were formed in the Procession, and Bro. Johnston was given an American Flag, one side of the Coach, and me, the Cal. Pioneers Flag with a large Bear, painted on it, on the other side. And the Procession made a grand show, with many nice Floats, wagons, coaches &c. also soldiers, with music, and Boys, and Girls and Ladies, &c, extending a long distance, down the street, being verry full of Spectators on either side, also the windows being full, and waving Hankerchiefs &c, with applause, many greeting us on the way. The streets were well lighted, and decorated, making a grand sight indeed.

Bro. Bigler, felling [sic] poorly, was taken to his room at the Hotel. And some officers came, and had us taken to the large Pavilion and leading us through the crowd; up on to the stand, by the side of the pulpit, where there was reserved seats for us. The room, and also the Galery, was well filled with spectators; being beautifully adorned for the occasion.

Many of the officers, again shaking hands with us, with respect and good wishes. Opening by singing, and prayer and some songs recitations, &c, also a long speech. And then one speaking of the Gold Discovery by Marshall in 1848 being the main stay and impetus for the building up of Cal. And a speaker then speaking of the four companions of Marshall, now living, and with them on the Stand, and wishing to introduce us to the asembly and as our names were called to Arise.

And my name being called first, I arose and speaking somewhat of my former life, and being one of the members of the Mormon Batt And also at the building of Sutter's Saw mill, at the finding of the first Gold, in Cal. And introducing me to the large Asembly, amid much aplaus, and then the other three names were also called, and introduced to the Asembly, speaking of us in high terms. And then three Cheers were given for The Companions of Marshall which was hearty indeed. Then a woman and some others spoke

[83]Elder Miller was serving an LDS mission in California.

well for the occasion, and after dismissal; and shaking of hands, with many Gentlemen and Ladies, we were led to the Coach and taken to our rooms, and getting a little refreshment. And in the evening, I and Johnston, went with a guide to a Beautiful Dancing room, seeing some good dancing, mostly waltzing. We were waited upon well, and given some ice cream. And being introduced to many Gentlemen and Ladies. We soon went down to the Russ Hotel, and after having supper and Prayer we went to bed, resting well.

Tues. the 25th. – We were in our rooms, having many visitors, wishing to find out some particulars, concerning, one thing, or another, and treating us with respect. Bro. Miller, also came to see us, and take us out to the Park, but there was too many visitors. Prest. Jewitt came also,[84] telling us to come [to] the Pioneer Society Building any time and welcome. [There] being a fire in Bro. Bigler's room, I go in there sometimes to get warm.

Wed. Jany, the 26th. – I got up early, washing, and having breacfast, and, then wrote another letter to send home. And several Gentlemen came in having conversation with us. And Mr. Hittell came and went with us, up to a large Library, also a Mechanics institute with a ticket to go all day. But we soon went to our rooms, and many calling in to see us. I and Bro. Bigler went up to the Brittish Californian office. They have our photo, and say that they will Publish something of us in the next No. and forward us a copy. Bro. Bigler bought a large record book. And upon coming to our room, finding many to converse with, but my memory is poor and I had supper, and writing some, and, in the evening I and Bro. Johnston went up a long way, where there was some Latter day Saints asembled, and they were glad to see us. They had good singing, and administered the Sac[rament]. And many Brethren, and sisters bearing strong testimony to the truth of the Gospel. And we also had the opportunity of speaking a short time, of the tryals and shifting scenes that we had been called to pass through and giving God the Glory. After dismissal there was a hearty shaking of hands with us, and two Elders, Edwin N. Austin,[85] and Prest. Frank Parkinson,[86] came with us down to our rooms, and one sleeping with me and one with Bro. Johnston, and also taking breacfast with us.

Thur. Jany the 27th. – And after some conversation they went with us, up to the Call House, taking us up on an elevator, to a verry high room, where we could see out on the Bay, and over the City, so far as the eye could extend being somewhat smoky. And after coming down they bade us goodby. And we went to the Hotel, and I went in the Bath room, and then

---

[84]John H. Jewett was an officer of the Society of California Pioneers.

[85]LDS missionary Edwin N. Austin, 57, first came to California in 1846 with his parents on the ship *Brooklyn* and became at age seven the youngest gold hunter at Mormon Island.

[86]Born in Kaysville, Utah, thirty-eight-year-old Franklin C. Parkinson had been called on an LDS church mission to California in 1896.

had dinner. And about 2 oc. Prest. John Jewitt having invited us, sent a
Coach, and took us all four up to a large Hall in the Pioneer building, and
furnishing us seats together, and kindly introducing many of the Gentlemen, and Ladies, unto us. Continually coming, shaking hands and wishing
to talk with us of the finding of the Gold, and also concerning our homes;
good wishes being extended by all. Continuing until 4 oc. fearing that they
would weary us, they led us out, and took us to our rooms. I did not feel
much worried [wearied], but Bro. Bigler, being 83 y. and Bro. Brown, having
to walk on crutches, with loss of one leg.

Fri. Jany, the 28th. – I was early up, and had breacfast; and Capt. John T.
Mc Kensie came with a Coach and driver taking us out to the Park, showing
us many principal parts of the same, being many kinds of large and small
animals, and also the largest Bear, under controll in the world, weighing
2000 lb. Also, Elk, Deer, and many other kinds of Animals, also many trees,
with beautiful green grass among them, Also going out to the Cliff House,
and seeing many boats, and also a Steam Ship just going off. And many
beautiful things in the building that I can not name. And again getting in the
Coach, and going through the Park down to the City, stoping at several of
the most notable buildings in the City and showing us some of the most
beautiful rooms, and scenery that I ever beheld. And again, introduced to
James D. Phelan,[87] the Mayor, and many Gentlemen & Ladies, and in the
Coach we were taken to several prominent places, and being well treated, and
receaved by all, giving us all of the drink we wished. And about 4 oc. we
were brought down to our rooms, and, Capt. Mc Kensie, talking with Bro.
Brown some time, and then, with a shake of the hand and our thanks, he
bade us goodby, saying that he would come and take us out again tomorrow.
I am well satisfied with what I see, and locking the door of my room when
away. The streets are well filled with cars, coaches, &c, and the side walks
with People, passing hither and thither. Prest. Jewitt came, with my ticket
extended for another month. And wishing us to sign a Certificate, Certifying, that we were with Marshall at the first discovery of Gold. J. F.
Pinkham,[88] the Marshall was also with him. After having Supper, with
thanks to our Father, I went to bed.

Sat. Jan,y 29th. – I arose early, and having breacfast. And Capt. McKensie came at 9 oc. with a coach ready and taking us down to the Bay. And getting on a tug ship, and going some distance along the Bay. We passed some
large, and small boats, along some distance to the Navy yard, where there
was ships building and repairing, and also Iron works, making Engines, and
all kind of machinery, and having steel plate an inch thick, to cover war ships

---

[87]San Francisco Mayor James D. Phelan, a banker, had been elected the year before on a pledge to
reform city government. In 1915 he was elected to the U.S. Senate.

[88]J. F. Pinkham was marshal, or sergeant of arms, of the Society of California Pioneers.

with and machinery to lift them out of the water and take the steel plate to its place. Mr. Mc Kensie was showing us many Curiosities, being some 3,000 men at work, and many were pleased to us. And then, getting on the Tug and riding back, the Coach being ready and taking us to the Hotel. Capt. Mc Kensie remained with us, and speaking with us, and kindly of us to many men, and women, that were glad to see us, and wishing us well. And at 2 PM The Coach came and again took us; up to a Photo Office, again getting many greetings. And, after brushing up a little we were placed in a group, and a Photo taken of us. Promising to send us each one. And after being taken to our rooms I wrote two letters, one to my Wife, and to Peter Hansen. And then having supper.

And some of the Pioneer Officers came, and also a band of music, and in two coaches, we were taken through the large Asembly to the stand, being chairs for us. The house was crouded [sic], and the galery full. There was eloquent speaking, and one speaking in high terms of us, had us rise to our feet, and was introduced to the Asembly. And after some speaking, they dismissed, informing us that there were many of the Ladies, and Gentlemen, wishing to shake hands with us, and they passed along, verry many passing, and shaking hands with us, with many good wishes. And also many Children were glad to shake our hands. And thus they passed until satisfied. And then we were taken to the other end of the Hall, to a bar room, and there we were given some refreshment. And some of the Committee, and others, were with us a long time, conversing, and having a pleasant time, with them. And I and Bro. Bigler went down with them to see a variety of the Fair Show, being mineral of all sorts, and a great deal of machinery, and then going back to the bar room. I gave Capt. McKensie a Photo, saying that he would send me one of his. And after a little we were taken in a coach to the Hotel. Mr. Hittell has been unwell, but was down to the Hotel to see us this evening. I was writing until 12 oc.

Sun. Jan,y the 30th. – 98. I arose early, having breacfast, and going in to the barber. Mr. Hittell came in with others to see us, giving us each a Photo. And being sent for, I and Bro. Johnston again went up to the L.D. Saints, Sun. School and meting, being welcome by them. There was good singing, and speaking, and by request, we spoke a short time and after dismissal, we were speaking with, and shaking hands with many. And going, and having dinner, Bro. Miller was in to see us. And Mr. Paul, of the Pioneer Society came, and gave us each twenty dollars, to pay our expences home. Our Tickets are extended, and sleeping berth paid for. And I and Bro. Johnston went with him up to the Palace Hotel, and going through it, being beautiful indeed. And after returning, some of the leading Officers of the Society came, and wishing us to go to a room, where their wives and other Ladies were wishing to see us before we leave. And going to the room, we were introduced to a dozen or so of them with a cordial greeting. And Mr. Jewitt, the executive of the Comittee, in a kind and jovial way, speaking to each of us, and puting a present of money in our hand And it being their wish, we signed 8 or 10 Autigraphs [*sic*] for them. And they also gave us each a book, with a Photo of us, and also many of the Pioneer Society in it. Also a scetch of the finding of the first Gold in Cal. And many nice pictures in it. And Mr. Jewitt, spoke some time, verry truthfully and highly of us. Also Bro. Brown, spoke some time, of the passed [past] scenes that we have passed through, from Nauvoo, and going in the Mormon Batt. And through such hard trials, and also concerning the finding of the first Gold. And by request we signed a paper, Certifying that the first Gold was found on the 24th. of Jan,y 1848.[89] Again they all shook hands with us, and biding us goodby, wishing to see us at another Jubilee, before long. And going to our rooms, Sister Nye[90] soon came and giving us a nice silk Badge, as members of the Mormon Bat. I gave her my Photo. Prest. Parkinson and other brethren were down to see us. Sister Nye was verry sociable, and I gave her a wreath of Flowers, that I had standing in my room, her little girl, also kindly kissing me, and her Mother, sending one to my wife. And in the evening I and Bro. Johnston went to a meting with the Saints, again And being glad to see us, and shake hands. An Elder spoke well, the subject being the Kingdom of God. They had good singing, many expressing their joy and satisfaction, to see us. Prest. Parkinson, told me that the Saints were on the increase, and doing well in Cal. And that our visit will doubtless have a good influence. And wishing me a safe trip home, and good wishes to those working in the Temple, and blessing him in his labours. Bro. Miller came down with us again, stoping over night with us. And I put my things up ready to start in the morning and rested well, having a good pleasant Dream.

Mon. Jany. the 31st. – I got up early having breacfast. Bro. Brown is calculating to stop some time longer. Also, Bro. Johnston could not find his railroad ticket, and will have to stop over night. But Mr. J. F. Pinkham, A. B. Paul, J. S. Hittell, and Capt. McKensie came, and took me, and Bro. Bigler, in a Coach down to the wating room until 8 oc. AM, then went on the train, with us, and showing us our Berth, and biding us goodby.[91]

---

[89]The Society of California Pioneers wanted the signed testimony of the four eyewitnesses to counter a story the day before in the San Francisco *Mining and Scientific Press* that Bigler and Smith were wrong and the true date of the discovery was 19 January 1848 as remembered by James Marshall years after. Bigler's journal, however, has proved convincing in this continuing controversy.

[90]Harriett Nye was the wife of Ephraim H. Nye, president of the LDS church's California Mission from 1896 to 1901.

[91]Azariah Smith kept his journal up to date until his eighty-third year, 1912, when he died quietly at his home. He was burried in the Manti Cemetery, where he lies with the rest of his pioneer family.

Appendix

Names of Pueblo Soldiers And Mississippi Brethren

Shortly after the Mormon Battalion detachments arrived in Salt Lake Valley on 29 July 1847, Thomas Bullock, the "Clerk of the Camp of Israel," compiled a roster of its members and dependants. This roll of 275 names has never been published before and contains a wealth of information about the composition of both the detachments and the Mississippi Saints who wintered at El Pueblo. The list shows priesthood or LDS church membership status for men and ages for women and children. Of special interest is the identification of deserters, non-members, and one African-American, John Edmunds, whose position on the list suggests he was a slave of Sgt. Thomas S. Williams.

August 1847
Names of Pueblo Soldiers
And Mississippi Brethren
Arrived in Great Salt Lake City

[Page 2]				
Milton Smith (dead)		Arnold Stevens (dead)		H.P.
Joseph W. Richards (dead)		Alexander Brown Corpl.		Member
Abner Chase (dead)		Joel J. Terrill		23 Quo
		John D. Chase		H.P.
		James Allred		4 Quo.
James Brown Capt.	Hi Priest	Reuben W. Allred		Member
Elam Luddington Lt.	do.	Joshua Abbott		Member
Orson B. Adams Sergt.	6th Quo.	Franklin Allen		12 Quo
Thomas S. Williams do.	16 Quo.	Judithon Everett [Juthan Averett]		Elder
Ebenezer Hanks do.	26 do.	Erastus Bingham		4 Quo

William Bird	Elder
Jesse S. Brown	Member
William E. Besched [Beckstead]	do
Marvin S. Blanchard (dead)	
Albert Clark	Member
William Casto	26 Quo
George Cummings	Elder
William H. Carpenter	Priest
Isaac Carpenter	Member
James Calkins	do.
John Calvert	do.
James Davis	34 Quo.
Ralph Douglass	Elder
Francilias [Francillo] Durfee	
Philip Garner	H.P.
David Garner	20 Quo
James H. Glines (deserter)	
Samuel Gould	Elder
John Gould	Member
William Gribble	Elder
William Gifford	Member
Luther W. Glazier	Teacher
Schuyler Hewlitt [Hulet]	not in Church
Elijah E. Holden	a 70 in no Quo
James P. Hirams [Hirons]	Member
John W. Hess	22 Quo
Charles Hopkins	Elder
Charles A. Jackson	
Bailey Jacobs	Member
Jarvis Johnson	do
Lorin Kinney [Kenney]	Elder
Thomas Carn	21 Quo
Lisbon Lamb	Member
Thurston Larson	do.
Barnabas Lake	do.
David S. Laughlin	33 Quo.
Peter I. Mesheck [Mesick]	21 do.
Daniel Miller	Elder
Jabes [Jabez] Nowlin	70 do.
Melchir Oiler [Melcher Oyler] (dead)	70
James Oakley	Member
Harmon D. Persons [Pierson]	Elder
Judson Persons [Pierson]	do.
David Perkins	do.
John Perkins (dead)	Member
William A. Park	9 Quo
Jonathan Pugmire	22 do.
Carrotad [Caratat] C. Rowe	Elder
William Rowe	Member

Benjamin Roberts	do.
John G. Smith	22 Quo
Roswell Stevens [Stephens]	28 Quo
Lyman Stevens	H.P.
John Sessions	28 Quo
John Steele	29 Quo
Richard D. Smith	not in Church
Andrew J. Shupe	30 Quo
James W. Shupe	a 70
Abel M. Sargent	21 Quo
Henry W. Sanderson	Member
Albert Sharpe [Sharp]	Member
Dexter Stillman	H.P.
Clark Stillman	Member
Miron [Myron] Tanner	14 Quo
Solomon Tindal [Tindell]	Elder
William Walker	
Almon Whiting	Member
John P. Reeston [Wriston]	Elder
Edmond Whiting	
Charles Wright (deserter)	
David Wilkie [Wilkin]	5 Quo

[*Space left by Bullock, apparently to separate the James Brown and William W. Willis detachments.*]

William W. Willis Lieut.	4 Quo
Richard Brazier	10
Thomas Burns (deserter)	
John Buchanan (Corpl.)	29
James A. Scott (dead)	
William Squires (Corpl.)	
William Burt	31 Quo
Abner Blackburn	Member
Samuel Badham	a 70
John Bybee	Elder
Thomas Bingham	Member
James Bevan	22 Quo
Daniel Brown	20
Lorenzo Babcock	19
John Harimhall [Brimhall]	Member
Haden W. Church	[illegible entry]
Alva C. Calkins	Elder
George Clarke [Clark]	
Josiah Curtis	Elder
James Camp	Member
Allen Compton (Corp.4)	36 Quo
James Cazier	Elder

John [Cazier]	do.	Mis.	
James Dunn	H.P.	Fanny M. Huntington	37 yrs
Eli Dodson (dead)	Member	Clark A. Huntington	16 yrs
Henry Dalton	16 Quo	Lot E. Huntington	14.
Edward Dalton	6 Quo	Martha Z. Huntington	3
Marcus Eastman	no member	Mary Button	
James C. Earl	20 Quo	James H. Button	11
David Frederick	21	Judson Button	9
Eli Hewitt	Member	Louisa M. Button	7
Alfred Higgins	do	Samuel Button	3
Arza Hinkley [Hinckley]	27 Quo	Almira Chase Higgins	17
Lucas Hoagland	Member	Sariah [Sarah] Higgins	41
Jesse W. Johnson [Johnstun]	4 Quo	Alfred Higgins	16
Wm. C. McLellin [McClellan]	Member	Driscilla Higgins	13
Maxy [Maxie] Maxwell (deserter)	not in Church	Nelson D. Higgins	11
Erastus D. Mecham	Member	Heber Kimball Higgins	8
Thomas Richardson	H.P.	Carlos Smith Higgins	5
Wm. W. Rust	10 Quo	Wealthy [Welthy] M. Higgins	3 mos
Isaac N. Wriston	Member	Jane Blivin	43
Benjamin Richmond	34	Mary Eliza Luddington	23
Joseph Shipley	Elder	Angeline Luddington	1
James Stewart	Member	Elizabeth [Mayfield] Shelton	41
Benjamin Stewart	Member	Andrew J. Mayfield	19
Joseph Sheen [Skeen]	18	John Mayfield	16
John H. Tibbets [Tippets]	17	Sarah Mayfield	13
Nathan Thomas	22	Emily C. Shelton	16
		Marion J. Shelton	13
[Page 3]		Abraham C. Shelton	7
Haywood Thomas		Thomas H. B. Shelton	5
Francis T. Whitney	26	Mary Elizabeth Shelton	2
Thomas Woolsey		Celia Hunt	40
George Wilson	3 Quo	Jane Hunt	16
Lisander [Lysander] Woolworth	Member	John Hunt	15
Madison Welch	No member	Peter Ness [Nease]	14
William Tubbs	20 Quo	Joseph Hunt	9
		Hiram [Hyrum] Hunt	7
		Harriet Hunt	12
[Space left by Bullock, apparently to separate the William W.		Mary Hunt	2
Willis and Nelson Higgins detachments.]		Ellen Ness [Nease]	10
		Matilda Ness [Nease] [Hunt]	19
Nelson Higgins (Capt.)	P. 2 Quo	Lidia [Lydia] [Gibson] Hunt	19
Dimic [Dimick] B. Huntington	H.P.	Mary Brown	26
Sebert C. Shelton QM Serg.	H.P.	David B. Brown	6
Montgomery E. Button	14	Eliza B. Allred	25
Arla Morey [Harley Mowrey]	26/	Elzida [Elzadie] E. Allred	19
Gilbert Hunt Serg.	20	Mary Ann Hirons	22
James Hendrickson	Elder	Ruth Abbott	36
Nicholas Kelley	20	Albina Mariam Williams	20
James Brown 2nd.	19	Carline [Caroline] Mariam Williams	4
Norman Sharp (dead)	26	Ephraim Thomas Williams	2

Phoebe Isabel Williams	6 months
Phoebe Lodema Merrill	16
John Edmunds (Black)	30
Catherine Steele	28
Mary Steele	6
Susanna Adams	28
Jane Hanks	26
Emeline [Bigler] Hess	24
Emeline Sessions	25
Malinda Kelly [Kelley]	36
Melinda Cathrine Kelly [Kelley]	6 mos.
Sarah Shupe	25
Elizabeth Margaret [Shupe]	6 mos.
Sophia Gribble	
Harriet Brown	
Martha [Sharp] Morey [Mowrey]	18
Sarah Ellen Sharp	6 mos.
Mississippi brethren	
James Harmon [Harman]	8 Quo
Absalom Porter Dowdle	Elder
Sarah Ann Dowdle	
Sara Catherine Dowdle	Child
Benjamin F. Matthews	Elder
Temperance Matthews	
Sarah Jane Matthews	
Mary Elizabeth Matthews	
Sally S. Matthews	a babe 4 weeks old
George Sparks	Elder
Lovana Sparks	
William Thomas Sparks	
Mary Ann Sparks	
William C. Ritter	Elder
Sarah Ann Ritter	22
Anderson Taylor Ritter	Child
William D. Kartchner	Priest 27
Margaret Jane Kartchner	21
Sarah Emma Kartchner	1 year
Lidia Ann Hunt	
William C. Smithson	Deacon

Lucinda Smithson	
Sarah Elizabeth Smithson	14
John Bartley Smithson	12
Martha Serilox Smithson	under 8
Almira Smithson	under 8
Elvira Smithson	under 8
Elzira [Eliza] Smithson	under 8
Allen Smithson	Member
Lelilia Smithson	
John Bartley Smithson	
Catherine Smithson	Children
James D. Smithson	Children
Mary Emma Smithson	Children
John Holiday	Elder
Cathrine [Catherine] Holliday	
Karon [Keren] H. Holliday	17
Kezia [Keziah] D. Holliday	13
David H. Holliday	15
Thomas N. Holliday	11
Leonora M. Holliday	8
Mary Ann Reer	
Perrill E. Reer	16
James Reer	5
Sally Ann	4
Josephine Reer	3*
William Terrill	

[Page 4]
[Instructions were given] not to sell to the Indians any
Powder or Balls for their Skins, as is it not wisdom to do so

Eunice Brown	39
Neuman Brown	18
Robert Brown	15
Sarah Jane Brown	12
John T Brown	2 mos
Sarah Kelly	27
Raymond Parley Kelly	9
Betsy Kelley	2

---

*Norma B. Ricketts has noted that no family named "Reer" appears in Mormon annals. Florence Cannariato, a descendant of James Harman (not Harmon), suggests a solution to this puzzle, for she reports that names at the end of Bullock's list—Mary Ann, Perrill E, James, Sally Ann, and Josephine Reer—are actually those of Harmon's wife and children.

BIBLIOGRAPHY

This is not a comprehensive bibliography of the Mormon Battalion, but lists only the sources and manuscripts used in *Army of Israel*. Readers interested in additional works on the subject are urged to consult the bibliography in Norma B. Ricketts' *The Mormon Battalion: U.S. Army of the West, 1846–1848.*

BOOKS

Allen, James B., and Glen M. Leonard. *The Story of the Latter-day Saints.* S.L.C: Deseret Book Co., 1976.

Ames, George Walcot, Jr., and George D. Lyman, eds. *A Doctor Comes to California: The Diary of John S. Griffin, Assistant Surgeon with Kearny's Dragoons, 1846–1847.* S.F: Calif. Hist. Soc., 1943.

Bauer, K. Jack. *The Mexican War, 1846–1848.* Macmillan Publishing Co., Inc. N.Y: 1974.

Bagley, Will, ed. *A Road from El Dorado: The 1848 Trail Journal of Ephraim Green.* S.L.C: The Prairie Dog Press, 1991.

———. *Frontiersman: Abner Blackburn's Narrative.* S.L.C: Univ. of Utah Press, 1992.

———. *The Pioneer Camp of the Saints: The 1846 and 1847 Mormon Trail Journals of Thomas Bullock.* Spokane, Wash: The Arthur H. Clark Co., 1997.

———. *Scoundrel's Tale: The Samuel Brannan Papers.* Spokane, Wash: The Arthur H. Clark Co., 1999.

Bancroft, Hubert Howe. *History of California,* 7 vols. S.F: The History Co., 1886–90.

Barry, Louise. *The Beginning of the West: Annals of the Kansas Gateway to the American West, 1540–1854.* Topeka: Kansas State Hist. Soc., 1972.

Beattie, George William and Helen Pruitt Beattie. *Heritage of the Valley: San Bernardino's First Century.* Pasadena: San Pasqual Press, 1939. Second edition, Oakland, Calif: Biobooks, 1951.

Beecher, Maureen Ursenbach, ed. *The Personal Writings of Eliza Roxcy Snow.* S.L.C: Univ. of Utah Press, 1995.

Bennett, Richard E. *Mormons at the Missouri, 1846–1852.* Norman: Univ. of Okla. Press, 1987.

———. *We'll Find the Place: The Mormon Exodus, 1846–1848.* S.L.C: Deseret Book Co., 1997.

Berrett, William E. and Alma P. Burton, eds. *Readings in L.D.S. Church History from Original Manuscripts,* 3 vols. S.L.C: Deseret Book, 1953, 1955, 1958.

Bieber, Ralph Paul, ed. "Cooke's Journal of the March of the Mormon Battalion, 1846–1847." In *Exploring Southwestern Trails, 1846-1854.* Glendale, Calif: Arthur H. Clark Co., 1938, 65-240.

Bigler, David L., ed. *The Gold Discovery Journal of Azariah Smith.* S.L.C: Univ. of Utah Press, 1990).

———. *Forgotten Kingdom: The Mormon Theocracy in the American West, 1847–1896.* Spokane, Wash: The Arthur H. Clark Co., 1998.

Bishop, William W., ed., *Mormonism Unveiled; or The Life and Confessions of the Late Mormon Bishop, John D. Lee; (Written by Himself).* St. Louis: Bryan, Brand & Co., 1877.

Bishop, Guy. *Henry William Bigler: Soldier, Gold Miner, Missionary, Chronicler: 1815-1900.* Logan: Utah State Univ. Press, 1998.

Bitton, Davis. *Guide to Mormon Diaries & Autobiographies.* Provo, Utah: Brigham Young Univ. Press, 1977.

Black, Susan Easton and William G. Hartley, eds. *The Iowa Mormon Trail: Legacy of Faith and Courage.* Orem, Utah, Helix Publishing, 1997.

Brooks, Juanita, ed. *On the Mormon Frontier: The Diary of Hosea Stout,* 2 vols. S.L.C: Univ. of Utah Press, 1964.

Brown, John, Sr. *The Mediumistic Experiences of John Brown, The Medium of the Rockies.* Des Moines: Moses Hull & Co., 1887.

Brown, James S. *Life of a Pioneer, Being the Autobiography of James S. Brown.* S.L.C: Geo. Q. Cannon & Sons, Printers, 1900.

Brown, John Z., ed. *Autobiography of Pioneer John Brown, 1820–1896.* S.L.C: Stevens and Wallis, 1941.

Bryant, Edwin. *What I Saw in California.* New York: D. Appleton & Co., 1848.

Buerger, David John. *The Mysteries of Godliness: A History of Mormon Temple Worship.* S.F: Smith Research Associates, 1994.

Carleton, J. Henry. *The Prairie Logbooks: Dragoon Campaigns to the Pawnee Villages in 1844, and to the Rocky Mountains in 1845.* Ed. by Louis Pelzer. Lincoln: Univ. of Neb. Press, 1983.

Carter, Kate B., ed. *Heart Throbs of the West,* 12 vols. S.L.C: Daughters of Utah Pioneers, 1939–51.

———. *Treasures of Pioneer History,* 6 vols. S.L.C: Daughters of Utah Pioneers, 1952–57.

———. *The Mormon Battalion.* S.L.C: Daughters of Utah Pioneers, 1956.

————. *Our Pioneer Heritage*, 20 vols. S.L.C: Daughters of Utah Pioneers, 1958–77. Includes "Women and Children of the Mormon Battalion." I:457–512.

Catalogue of the Relics, Souvenirs and Curios Associated with the Pioneers of Utah. S.L.C: Geo. Q. Cannon & Sons, Printers, 1897.

Clark, James R., ed., *Messages of the First Presidency of the Church of Jesus Christ of Latter-day Saints, 1833–1964*, 4 vols. S.L.C: Bookcraft, Inc., 1965.

Clarke, Dwight L. *Stephen Watts Kearny: Soldier of the West*. Norman: Univ. of Okla. Press, 1961.

————., ed. *The Original Journals of Henry Smith Turner: With Stephen Watts Kearny to New Mexico and California, 1846–1847*. Norman: Univ. of Okla. Press, 1966.

Cleland, Robert Glass and Juanita Brooks, eds. *A Mormon Chronicle: The Diaries of John D. Lee 1848-1876*, 2 vols. San Marino, Calif: The Huntington Library, 1955. Reprinted S.L.C: Univ. of Utah Press, 1983.

Cook, Lyndon, ed. *Nauvoo Deaths and Marriages, 1839–1845*. Orem, Utah: Grandin Book Company, 1994.

Cooke, Philip St. George. *Scenes and Adventures in the Army*. Philadelphia: Lindsay & Blakiston, 1859.

————. *The Conquest of New Mexico and California, An Historical and Personal Narrative*. N. Y: G. P. Putnam's Sons, 1878. Reprinted Albuquerque: Horn and Wallace, 1964.

Coy, Owen C. *The Battle of San Pasqual. A Report of the California Historical Survey with General Reference to Its Location*. Sacramento: Calif. State Printing Office, 1921.

Crockett, David R. *Saints in the Wilderness: A Day-by-Day Pioneer Experience, Winter Quarters and Mormon Battalion March*. Tucson, Ariz: LDS-Gems Press, 1997.

Cutts, James Madison. *The Conquest of California and New Mexico by the Forces of the United States in the Years 1846 and 1847*. Philadelphia: Carey & Hart, 1847.

Davies, J. Kenneth. *Mormon Gold: The Story of California's Mormon Argonauts*. S.L.C: Olympus Publishing Co., 1984.

Duffin, Reg and Randy Brown, *Graves and Sites on the Oregon and California Trails*. Independence: Oregon-Calif. Trails Assoc., 1991. Second Edition, 1998.

Dupont, Samuel F. *Extracts from private journal-letters of Captain S. F. Dupont, while in command of the Cyane during the war with Mexico, 1846–1848*. Wilmington, Del: Ferris Bros., 1885.

Eisenhower, John S. D. *So Far from God: The U. S. War with Mexico, 1846–1848*. N.Y: Random House, 1989.

Etter, Patricia A. *To California on the Southern Route 1849: A History and Annotated Bibliography*. Spokane, Wash: The Arthur H. Clark Company, 1998.

Farris, William M. *The Crossing of Imperial County, California and Baja California, Mexico, by the U.S. Mormon Battalion.* El Centro, Calif: Imperial Valley College Museum Soc., 1976.

Ford, Thomas. *A History of Illinois from its Commencement as a State in 1818 to 1847.* Chicago: S.C. Griggs & Co., 1854; Lakeside Classics Edition, Milo Milton Quaife, ed. 2 vols. Chicago: Lakeside Press, 1945.

Franzwa, Gregory M. *The Oregon Trail Revisited.* St. Louis: The Patrice Press, 1972. Fifth edition, Tucson, 1997.

———. *Maps of the Oregon Trail.* St. Louis: The Patrice Press, 1982. Third edition, 1990).

———. *Maps of the Santa Fe Trail.* St. Louis: The Patrice Press, 1989.

Furniss, Norman F. *The Mormon Conflict, 1850–1859.* New Haven: Yale Univ. Press, 1960.

Gardner, Mark L. and Marc Simmons, eds. *The Mexican War Correspondence of Richard Smith Elliott.* Norman: Univ. of Okla. Press, 1997.

Golder, Frank Alfred, Thomas A. Bailey, and J. Lyman Smith, eds. *The March of the Mormon Battalion from Council Bluffs to California, Taken from the Journal of Henry Standage.* N.Y: The Century Co., 1928.

Gray, Paul Bryan. *Forster vs. Pico: The Struggle for the Rancho Santa Margarita.* Spokane, Wash: The Arthur H. Clark Co., 1999.

Graydon, Charles K. *Trail of the First Wagons over the Sierra Nevada.* Gerald, Mo: The Patrice Press, 1986.

Green, Nelson Winch, ed. *Fifteen Years Among the Mormons: Being the Narrative of Mrs. Mary Ettie V. Smith* [Mary E. Coray]. N.Y: H. Dayton, 1858.

Gudde, Erwin G. ed. *Bigler's Chronicle of the West: The Conquest of California, Discovery of Gold, and Mormon Settlement as Reflected in Henry William Bigler's Diaries.* Berkeley: Univ. of Calif. Press, 1962.

Hackley, Charles M. III. *A Quest for Sleeping Heroes.* San Marcos, Calif: Jrhagain Enterprises, 1999.

Hafen, LeRoy R., ed. *Ruxton of the Rockies.* Norman: Univ. of Okla. Press, 1950. Third printing, 1982.

———. *The Mountain Men and the Fur Trade of the Far West,* 10 vols. Glendale, Calif: Arthur H. Clark Co., 1965–72.

Hammond, George P., ed. *The Larkin Papers: Personal, Business, and Official Correspondence of Thomas Oliver Larkin, Merchant and United States Consul in California,* 10 vols. Berkeley: Univ. of Calif. Press, 1951–68.

———. *The Adventures of Alexander Barclay Mountain Man.* Denver: Old West Publishing Co., 1976.

Hancock, April S., ed. *The Life of Levi W. Hancock.* S.L.C: Utah Bookbinding Co., 1997.

Hardesty, Donald L. *The Archaeology of the Donner Party*. Reno: Univ. of Nevada Press, 1997.

Hardy, B. Carmon. *Solemn Covenant: The Mormon Polygamous Passage*. Urbana: Univ. of Ill. Press, 1992.

Harlow, Neal. *California Conquered: War and Peace on the Pacific 1846-1850*. Berkeley: Univ. of Calif. Press, 1982.

Harris, Everett W. *The Overland Emigrant Trail to California: A Guide to Trail Markers Placed in Western Nevada and the Sierra Nevada Mountains in California*. Reno: Nevada Emigrant Trail Marking Committee, Inc., 1975. Reprinted 1986.

Hastings, Lansford W. *The Emigrants' Guide, to Oregon and California*. Cincinnati: George Conclin, 1845.

Heitman, Francis B. *Historical Register and Dictionary of the United States Army, From Its Organization, September 29, 1789, to March 2, 1903*, 2 vols. Washington, D.C: Government Printing Office, 1903. Reprinted Urbana: Univ. of Ill. Press, 1965.

Heizer, R. F. and M. A. Whipple, eds. *The California Indians: A Source Book*. Second edition, Berkeley: Univ. of Calif. Press, 1971.

Helfrich, Devere and Helen, and Thomas Hunt. *Emigrant Trails West: A Guide to Trail Markers Placed by Trails West, Inc. Along the California, Applegate, Lassen, and Nobels' Emigrant Trails in Idaho, Nevada, and California*. Reno: Trails West, Inc., 1984. Reprinted 1991.

Henry, Robert Selph. *The Story of the Mexican War*. Indianapolis: Bobbs-Merrill Co., 1950.

Hoover, Mildred B., Hero Eugene Rensch, and Ethel Grace Rensch. *Historic Spots in California*. Stanford: Stanford Univ. Press, 1932. Fourth printing, 1962.

Jenson, Andrew. *Latter-day Saint Biographical Encyclopedia*, 4 vols. S.L.C: Andrew Jenson History Co., 1901.

Johnson, Clark V. *Mormon Redress Petitions: Documents of the 1833-1838 Missouri Conflict*. Provo: Bookcraft, 1992.

Johnson, Kristin, ed. *"Unfortunate Emigrants": Narratives of the Donner Party*. Logan: Utah State Univ. Press, 1996.

Journal of Discourses, 26 vols. London: Latter-Day Saints Book Depot, 1854–1886.

Kaysing, Bill. *Great Hot Springs of the West*. Santa Barbara, Calif: Capra Press, 1990.

Kelly, Charles, ed. *Journals of John D. Lee, 1846-47 & 1859*. S.L.C: Western Printing Co., 1938. Reprinted S.L.C: Univ. of Utah Press, 1984.

Kenney, Scott G., ed. *Wilford Woodruff's Journal*, 10 vols. Midvale: Signature Books, 1983.

Kimball, Stanley B. *The Mormon Battalion on the Santa Fe Trail in 1846*. Santa Fe: U.S. Dept. of the Interior, 1996.

Kissell, John L. *Friars, Soldiers, and Reformers: Hispanic Arizona and the Sonora Mission Frontier, 1767–1856*. Tucson: The Univ. of Arizona Press, 1976.

Larson, Carl V. *A Data Base of the Mormon Battalion.* Providence, Utah: Kieth [*sic*] W. Watkins and Sons Printing, Inc., 1987.

———, ed. *Women the Mormon Battalion.* By the editor, 1989.

Lecompte, Janet. *Pueblo, Hardscrabble, Greenhorn: The Upper Arkansas, 1832–1856.* Norman: Univ. of Okla. Press, 1978.

Little, James A. *From Kirtland to Salt Lake City.* S.L.C: James A. Little, 1890.

Long, John V. *Report of the First General Festival of the Renowned Mormon Battalion, which came off on Tuesday and Wednesday, Feb. 6 and 7, 1855, in the social hall, G.S.L. City, U.T.* Reported by J.V. Long. St. Louis: St. Louis Luminary Office, 1855.

Lyman, Edward Leo. *San Bernardino: The Rise and Fall of a California Community.* Salt Lake City: Signature Books, 1996.

McClellan, Susan Webb. *Charles Young Webb: Mormon Pioneer.* Miami, Okla: Timbercreek LTD, 1991.

McCormac, Eugene Irving. *James K. Polk: A Political Biography.* Berkeley: Univ. of Calif. Press, 1922. Reprinted N.Y: Russell & Russell Inc., 1965.

McMurtrie, Douglas C., ed. *Overland to California in 1847.* Chicago: Black Cat Press, 1937.

Madsen, Brigham D., ed. *B. H. Roberts: Studies of the Book of Mormon.* Urbana: Univ. of Ill. Press, 1985.

Morgan, Dale L. *A History of Ogden.* Ogden, Utah: Ogden City Commission, 1940.

———. *The Humboldt: Highroad of the West.* N.Y: Farrar & Rinehardt, 1943.

———, ed. *Overland in 1846: Diaries and Letters of the California-Oregon Trail,* 2 vols. Georgetown, CA: The Talisman Press, 1963.

Oaks, Dallin H. and Marvin S. Hill. *Carthage Conspiracy: The Trial of the Accused Assassins of Joseph Smith.* Urbana: Univ. of Ill. Press, 1975.

Officer, James E. *Hispanic Arizona, 1536–1856.* Tucson: The Univ. of Arizona Press, 1987.

Owens, Kenneth N. *Archaeological and Historical Investigation of the Mormon-Carson Emigrant Trail, El Dorado and Toiyabe National Forests,* Vol. II History and Appendix A. Placerville: U.S. Forest Service, 1990.

———, ed. "General Sutter's Diary," in *John Sutter and a Wider West.* Lincoln: Univ. of Nebr. Press, 1994.

Parkman, Francis, Jr. *The California and Oregon Trail: Being Sketches of Prairie and Rocky Mountain Life.* N.Y: George P. Putnam, 1849. Reprinted as *The Oregon Trail: Sketches of Prairie and Rocky-Mountain Life,* ill. ed. Boston: Little, Brown, and Co., 1892.

Paul, Rodman W. *The California Gold Discovery: Sources, Documents, Accounts and Memoirs Relating to the Discovery of Gold at Sutter's Mill.* Georgetown, Calif: The Talisman Press, 1966.

Peterson, Charles S., John F. Yurtinus, David E. Atkinson, and A. Kent Powell. *Mormon Battalion Trail Guide.* Utah State Hist. Soc., 1972.

Quaife, Milo Milton, ed. *The Diary of James K. Polk during His Presidency, 1845 to 1849,* 4 vols. Chicago: A. C. McClurg & Co., 1910.

Read, Georgia Willis and Ruth Gaines, eds. *Gold Rush: The Journals, Drawings, and Other Papers of J. Goldsborough Bruff, Captain, Washington City and California Mining Association, April 2, 1849-July 20, 1851,* 2 vols. N.Y: Columbia Univ. Press, 1944.

Ricketts, Norma B. *The California Star Express.* Sacramento: Sacramento County Hist. Soc., 1982.

———. *Tragedy Spring and the Pouch of Gold.* Sacramento: Ricketts Publishing Co., 1983.

———. *Melissa's Journey with the Mormon Battalion—The Western Odyssey of Melissa Burton Coray: 1846–1848.* S.L.C: Daughters of Utah Pioneers, 1994.

———. *The Mormon Battalion: U.S. Army of the West, 1846–1848.* Logan: Utah State Univ. Press, 1996.

———. *Mormons and the Discovery of Gold.* Fourth Edition, Mesa, Ariz: Odyssey Press, 1998.

Roberts, Brigham H. *The Mormon Battalion, Its History and Achievements*: S.L.C: The Deseret News, 1919.

———. *A Comprehensive History of The Church of Jesus Christ of Latter-day Saints,* 6 vols. S.L.C: Deseret News Press, 1930.

———, ed. *History of the Church of Jesus Christ of Latter-day Saints. Period 2. Apostolic Interregnum. From the Manuscript History of Brigham Young and Other Original Documents,* vol. 7. S.L.C: Deseret News, 1932.

Ruxton, George Frederick. *Life in the Far West.* Edinburgh and London: William Blackwood and Sons, 1849. Reprinted Norman: Univ. of Okla. Press, 1951, edited by LeRoy R. Hafen.

Sampson, William R., ed. *John McLoughlin's Business Correspondence, 1847–48.* Seattle: Univ. of Wash. Press, 1973.

Scamehorn, H. Lee, Edwin P. Banks, and Jamie Lytle-Webb, eds. *The Buckeye Rovers in the Gold Rush: An Edition of Two Diaries.* Athens: Ohio Univ. Press, 1965.

Sellers, Charles. *James K. Polk, Continentalist, 1843–46.* Princeton: Princeton Univ. Press, 1966.

Schindler, Harold. *Orrin Porter Rockwell: Man of God, Son of Thunder.* S.L.C: Univ. of Utah Press, 1983.

Sherman, William T. *Memoirs of General William T. Sherman,* 2 vols. New York: D. Appleton and Co., 1876.

Singletary, Otis A. *The Mexican War.* Chicago: Univ. of Chicago Press, 1960.

Smart, Donna T., ed. *Mormon Midwife: The 1846–1888 Diaries of Patty Bartlett Sessions.* Logan: Utah State Univ. Press, 1997.

Smith, Joseph. *Doctrine and Covenants*. S.L.C: The Church of Jesus Christ of Latter-day Saints, 1990.

Spence, Mary Lee and Donald Jackson, eds. *The Expeditions of John Charles Frémont*, 4 vols. Chicago: Univ. of Il. Press, 1970–1984.

Stansbury, Howard. *Exploration and Survey of the Valley of the Great Salt Lake*. Philadelphia: Lippincott, Grambo & Co., 1852.

Stenhouse, T. B. H. *The Rocky Mountain Saints: A Full and Complete History of the Mormons, from the First Vision of Joseph Smith to the Last Courtship of Brigham Young*. N.Y: D. Appleton and Co., 1873.

Stewart, George R. *Ordeal by Hunger*. New York: Henry Holt Co., 1936. Second Edition, Boston: Houghton Mifflin, 1960.

———. *The California Trail: An Epic with Many Heroes*. New York: McGraw-Hill, 1962.

Sutter, John A. *et all. New Helvetia Diary*. S.F: The Grabhorn Press, 1939.

Talbot, Dan. *A Historical Guide to the Mormon Battalion and Butterfield Trail*. Tucson: Westernlore Press, 1992.

Thrapp, Dan L. *Encyclopedia of Frontier Biography*, 4 vols. Glendale, Calif. and Spokane, Wash: The Arthur H. Clark Co., 1988, 1994.

Tullidge, Edward W. *Life of Brigham Young; or, Utah and Her Founders*. N.Y: Tullidge & Crandall, 1876.

———. *Histories of Utah Volume 2: Northern Utah and Southern Idaho Counties*. S.L.C: Press of the Juvenile Instructor, 1889.

Tyler, Daniel. *A Concise History of the Mormon Battalion in the Mexican War, 1846-1847*. S.L.C: 1881. Reprinted Glorieta, N. Mex : The Rio Grande Press, Inc, 1980.

Unruh, John D. Jr., *The Plains Across: The Overland Emigrants and the Trans-Mississippi West, 1840-1860*. Urbana: Univ. of Ill. Press, 1979.

Waite, Catherine V. *The Mormon Prophet and His Harem; Or, An Authentic History of Brigham Young, His Numerous Wives and Children*. Chicago: J. S. Goodman and Co., 1867. Fifth Edition.

Ward, Maurine Carr, ed. *Winter Quarters: The 1846–1848 Life Writings of Mary Haskin Parker Richards*. Logan: Utah State Univ. Press, 1996.

Watson, Elden J., ed. *Manuscript History of Brigham Young 1846–1847*. S.L.C: Elden J. Watson, 1971.

Weems, John Edward. *To Conquer A Peace: The War Between the United States and Mexico*. Garden City, N.Y: Doubleday & Co., Inc., 1974.

Wheat, Carl I. [and Dale L. Morgan]. *Mapping the Transmississippi West*, 5 vols. San Francisco: The Grabhorn Press [vol. I]; and The Institute of Hist. Cartography, 1957–1963.

White, David A., ed. *News of the Plains and the Rockies, 1803–1865*, Volume 3, *Missionaries, Mormons, 1821–1864; Indian Agents, Captives, 1832–1865*. Spokane, Wash: The Arthur H. Clark Co., 1997.

Whiteley, Lee. *The Cherokee Trail: Bent's Old Fort to Fort Bridger*. Denver: Denver Posse of Westerners, 1999.

Winders, Richard Bruce. *Mr. Polk's Army: The American Military Experience in the Mexican War*. College Station: Texas A&M Univ. Press, 1997.

Wood, Raymund F. *The Life and Death of Peter Lebec*. Fresno, Calif: Academy Library Guild, 1954.

Woolf, William L., ed. *The Private Journal of William Hyde*. S.L.C: Privately published by William L. Woolf, 1962.

Young, Otis E. *The West of Philip St. George Cooke, 1809–1895*. Glendale: The Arthur H. Clark Co., 1955.

PERIODICALS

Alter, J. Cecil, ed. "The Journal of Robert S. Bliss." *Utah Hist. Quarterly*, 4:4 (1931).

Ames, George Walcott, Jr., ed. "A Doctor Comes to California: The Diary of John S. Griffin, Assistant Surgeon with Kearny's Dragoons, 1846–1847." *Calif. Hist. Soc. Quarterly*, 21:3–4, and 22:1 (Sept. 1942–March 1943).

Bagley, Will and Robert Hoshide, eds. "The Last Crossing of the River: The 1847 William and James Pace Trail Diaries." *Crossroads*, 4:2 (Spring 1993).

——— and Robert Hoshide, eds. "From Sooter's Fort to Salt Lake: The 1847 Levi Hancock Diary." *Crossroads*, 4:1 (Winter 1993).

———. "'Every Thing Is Favourable! And God Is On Our Side': Samuel Brannan and the Conquest of California." *Journal of Mormon History*, 23:2 (Fall 1997).

Bate, Kerry William. "John Steele: Medicine Man, Magician, Mormon Patriarch." *Utah Hist. Quarterly*, 62:1 (Winter 1994).

Beckwith, Frank, ed. "Extracts from the Journal of John Steele." *Utah Hist. Quarterly*, 6:1 (January 1933).

Bigler, Henry W. "Extracts from the Journal of Henry W. Bigler." *Utah Hist. Quarterly*, 5:2–4 (April, July, October 1932).

Brooks, Juanita, ed. "Diary of the Mormon Battalion Mission, John D. Lee." *New Mexico Hist. Review*, 42:3–4 (July, October 1967).

Brown, Minnie Moore. "With the Camp Fires of the Mormon Battalion." *Young Woman's Journal* (July 1904).

Camp, Charles L. "William Alexander Trubody and the Overland Pioneers of 1847." *Calif. Hist. Soc. Quarterly*, 16:2 (June 1937).

Christiansen, Larry D. "The Struggle for Power in the Mormon Battalion." *Dialogue: A Journal of Mormon Thought*, 26:4 (Winter 1993).

Cooley, Everett L., ed. "The Robert S. Bliss Journal." *Utah Hist. Quarterly*, 27 (October 1959).

Cowan, Richard O. "The Mormon Battalion and the Gadsden Purchase." *BYU Studies*, 37:4 (1997–98).

Davignon, Keith. "Were Mormons Counterfeiters?" *Coin World* (21 September 1998).

Gardner, Hamilton, ed. "Report of Lieut. Col. P. St. George Cooke of His March from Santa Fe, New Mexico, to San Diego, Upper California." *Utah Hist. Quarterly*, 22 (January 1954).

Godfrey, Kenneth W. "Crime and Punishment in Mormon Nauvoo, 1839–1846." *BYU Studies*, 32:1 (Winter 1992).

Gracy, David B., II, and Helen J. H. Rugeley. "From the Mississippi to the Pacific: An Englishman in the Mormon Battalion." *Arizona and the West*, 7:2 (Summer 1965).

Hardesty, Donald L. "Donner Party Archaeology." *Overland Journal*, 10:3 (Fall 1992).

Heath, Steven. "Jefferson Hunt, Bad Judgement, the 49ers and the Mormon Battalion." *Pioneer* (Summer 1995).

Hittell, John S., ed. "Diary of H. W. Bigler in 1847 and 1848." *The Overland Monthly*, 10:57, Second Series (September 1887).

Hughes, Charles, ed. "A Military View of San Diego in 1847: Four Letters from Colonel Jonathan D. Stevenson to Governor Richard B. Mason." *Journal of San Diego History*, 20:3 (Summer 1974).

Jensen, Richard E. "The Pawnee Mission, 1834–1846." *Nebraska History*, 75 (Winter 1994).

Jones, Rebecca M., ed. "Extracts from the Life Sketch of Nathaniel V. Jones." *Utah Hist. Quarterly*. 4 (January 1931).

Kenner, Scipio A. "The Pioneers and Others: What They Did and How They Did It." *The Juvenile Instructor*, 22 (15 June 1897 and 1 November 1897).

Morgan, Dale L., ed. "The Mormon Ferry on the North Platte: The Journal of William A. Empey." *Annals of Wyoming*, 21:2–3 (July–October 1949).

Munro, J. B. "Mormon Colonization Scheme for Vancouver Island." *The Washington Hist. Quarterly*, 25:4 (October, 1934).

Parker, Horace. "The Temecula Massacre." *The Westerners Brand Book*. Los Angeles Corral, Book 10 (1963).

Porter, Larry C. "From California to Council Bluffs." *Ensign*, 19:8 (August 1989).

Smith, Carmen. "The Lost Well of the Mormon Battalion Rediscovered." *Utah Hist. Quarterly*, 57:3 (Summer 1989).

Utley, Robert M. "Letters to the Editor." *Montana*, 49:1 (Spring 1999).

Whiteley, Lee. "The Trappers Trail: 'The Road to Fort Laramie's Back Door.'" *Overland Journal*, 16:4 (Winter 1998–99).

Williams, Jack S. "The Presidio of Santa Cruz de Terrenate: A Forgotten Fortress of Southern Arizona." *The Smoke Signal*, 47 and 48 (combined), Tucson Corral of the Westerners (1986).

Wells, Junius F. "The Mormon Battalion." *Utah Genealogical and Hist. Magazine*, 18 (July 1927).

Wood, Wanda, ed. "John W. Hess: With the Mormon Battalion." *Utah Hist. Quarterly*, 4:2 (April 1931).

Woodward, Arthur. "Trapper Jim Waters." Keepsake of the Los Angeles Corral of Westerners, Publication No. 23 (1954).

Yurtinus, John F. "Images of Early California: Mormon Battalion Soldiers' Reflections." *Hist. Soc. of Southern Calif. Quarterly*, (Spring 1981).

NEWSPAPERS

"A Singular Cavern." *Illinois Gazette*, 16 October 1847. Reprinted *Crossroads* 8:4 (Fall 1997), 4.

[Coray, Melissa.] "Utah Woman's 2,000-mile March Fifty-five Years Ago." *Salt Lake Herald*, 26 May 1901.

"He Will Lead the Church to Hell." *The Saints' Advocate*, January 1885, 510/1.

"Interesting Information from the Utah Expedition. Col. Cook's [*sic*] Report." *New York Times*, 26 January 1858, 7/2.

"Mormon' Pathfinders Guests of Senator Clark." *Deseret Evening News*, 7 October 1905, 27/1-7.

Schindler, Harold. "Rites Honor LDS Friend." *The Salt Lake Tribune*, 16 September 1977.

THESES AND DISSERTATIONS

Clegg, Dennis A. "Levi Ward Hancock: Pioneer, Soldier, Political and Religious Leader of Early Utah." Master's Thesis, Brigham Young Univ., 1966.

Shoptaugh, Terry L. "Amos Kendall: A Political Biography." Ph.D. diss., Univ. of N.H., 1984.

Yurtinus, John F. "A Ram in the Thicket: The Mormon Battalion in the Mexican War." Ph.D. diss., Brigham Young Univ., 1975.

MANUSCRIPTS

Allen, Elijah. Autobiographical Sketch, ca. 1848. MS 5, LDS Archives.

Allen, Franklin. Diaries. MS D 1397, LDS Archives.

Allen, Charles H. Autobiography. MS 6589, LDS Archives.

Allred, Redick. Mormon Battalion Experiences of *Redick N. Allred* of Spring City, Utah. Typescript A-60, Utah State Hist. Soc. See also Mormon Battalion Experiences of Redick N. Allred. Acc 333, Ms 88 Typescript. Special Collections and Manuscripts, Marriott Library, Univ. of Utah; and Kate B. Carter, ed. "The Diary of Reddick N. Allred." *Treasures of Pioneer History.* S.L.C: Daughters of Utah Pioneers, 1956, 5:307.

Bates, Joseph W. Autobiography. MS 11748, LDS Archives.

Bigler, Henry W. to Alexander Stephens, 5 April 1891. Special Collections & Archives, Univ. Libraries, Utah State Univ.

Bingham, Thomas, Jr. History of Thomas Bingham and Thomas Bingham Jr. A 187 MSS B 289, Box 1, Utah State Hist. Soc.

Bliss, Robert S. Journal, 1847–1848. Utah State Archives.

Borrowman, John. Diaries 1846–1853; 1856; 1859–1860. MS 1495, LDS Archives. See also Journal of John Borrowman, Extracts, 1846–1860. Joel E. Ricks Collection of Transcriptions, Special Collections & Archives, Univ. Libraries, Utah State Univ.

Boyle, Henry G. Autobiography and Diary of Henry G. Boyle. Special Collections and Manuscripts, Marriott Library, Univ. of Utah. See also Boyle, Reminiscences and Diaries, 1846–1888. MS 1911, LDS Archives.

Brown, James to Abigail Brown, 1847 Aug 6, Salt Lake Valley. MS d 4308, LDS Archives.

Brown, Mary McCree Black to Curtis Black, 21 December 1846. Mormon Battalion Correspondence Collection, 1846. MS 2070, Folder 5, LDS Archives.

Caldwell, Matthew. Short Life's History of Matthew Caldwell. Typescript, MS 15020, LDS Archives.

Chamberlain, Helen Bunker. A Supplement to the Life Histories of Edward and Emily Abbott Bunker. Typescript, MSS B 289, Box 2, Utah State Hist. Soc., 1980.

The Church of Jesus Christ of Latter-day Saints. Journal History.

Clark, Bulah A., to Brigham Young, 19 August 1846. Brigham Young Collection, MS 1234, Box 30, Folder 18 #2, LDS Archives.

Cooke, Philip St. George to James Ferguson, 8 June 1858. MS 344, LDS Archives.

———. Selected Papers, 1846–47. MIC A139, National Archives, copy at Utah State Hist. Soc.

Coray, William. Journal of Sgt. William Coray of the Mormon Battalion. Typescript provided to the editors by Norma Ricketts.

Cox, Wanda Steele, ed. The Journals of John Steele and Mahonri Moriancumer Steele. Typescript, A 2646, Utah State Hist. Soc.

Dunn, Thomas. Private Journal of Thomas Dunn, 2nd Corporal of the Mormon Battalion, Co. B. MSS A6074, Folder 1, Utah State Hist. Soc. Copied from the original diary of 1847 by Verlaine Larsen. See also Thomas Dunn, Journal, 1846–1849. MS 6217, LDS Archives.

Elmer, Elijah. Diary. Special Collections, Harold B. Lee Library, BYU.

Farnsworth, Julia P. M. Scrap Book for the Daughters of the Mormon Battalion for the Years 1905-22. Mormon Battalion Monument Committee, Newspaper Clippings, B100J3, Utah State Archives.

Ferguson, James. Papers, 1846–1858. MSS A 4349, Utah State Hist. Soc.

———— to Philip St. George Cooke, 5 May 1858. Utah Territorial Militia Records, Folder 44, Item 655; Microfilm Series 2210, Reel 25, Utah State Archives.

Glines, James. Autobiography of James Harvey Glines. A 2956, Utah State Hist. Soc.

Green, Ephraim. Journal, 1848 June–Sept. and 1849 Dec. MS 5606, LDS Archives.

Gully, Samuel to Brigham Young, 23 August 1846. Brigham Young Collection, MS 1234, Box 20, Folder 19, LDS Archives.

Hancock, Charles Brent. Reminiscences and Diary, 1884–89, MS 1569, LDS Archives.

————. Journal of. MS 5228, LDS Archives.

Hancock, Levi W. Autobiographical Sketch, 1878. MS 614, LDS Archives.

————. Journals 1846–1847. MS 1395:3, LDS Archives.

Hancock, Mosiah Lyman. Autobiography of Levi Ward Hancock [ca. 1896]. MS 570:3, LDS Archives.

Hill, James LeRoy. Biography of Captain James Brown, Founder of Ogden, Utah. Donald R. Moorman Collection, WA 86 5, Box 1, Folder 6, Weber State Univ. Archives, Ogden, Utah, 1958.

Holmes, Jonathan Harriman. Diary. MS 1673, LDS Archives.

Hulin, Lester. Day Book or Journal of Lester Hulin, Oregon Trail & Applegate Route 1847. Typescript from Lane County Pioneer Museum, Eugene, Oregon, 1959, from original owned by Wilbur S. Hulin. See also, "Over the Westward Trail." *The Sunday Oregonian*, 3 May 1931.

Huntington, Dimick Baker. Reminiscences and Journal 1845–1847. MS 1419 1, LDS Archives.

Hyde, William. Journal. MS 1549, LDS Archives.

Jenson, Andrew. Return of the Mormon Battalion. MS 4029, LDS Archives.

————. Manuscript History of Pueblo, Colorado. MS 4029:3, LDS Archives.

———. Manuscript History of the California Mission. CR 1316, vol. I, LDS Archives.

Johnstun, William J. Reminiscence, 12 March 1894 and 14 July 1898. Typescript by Joseph Johnston from originals at LDS Archives and the Daughters of Utah Pioneers Museum in editors' possession.

Jones, Nathaniel V. Papers. A54-2A, Utah State Hist. Soc.

———. Papers, 1847–1861. COLL MSS 158, Special Collections & Archives, Univ. Libraries, Utah State Univ.

Judd, Zadock Knapp. Autobiography. A 462, Utah State Hist. Soc.

Kane, Thomas L. Papers. MS 227, Marriott Library. Copies of the Kane Family Papers from the American Philosophical Soc. Library, Philadelphia, Penn.

Kearny, Stephen W. Papers. Missouri Hist. Soc., St. Louis, Missouri.

———. Selected Papers, 1846–47. MIC 139, National Archives, copy at Utah State Hist. Soc.

Keysor, Guy Messiah. Acts & Events of Great Places. A 705–I, Utah State Hist. Soc.

Merrill, Philemon C. Autobiography. Ms 8244, LDS Archives.

Morgan, Dale L. Papers, Bancroft Library. Microfilm copy at Special Collections and Manuscripts, Marriott Library, Univ. of Utah.

Morris, Thomas. Autobiography and Journal. A2613, Utah State Hist. Soc.

Mormon Battalion Correspondence Collection, 1846. MS 2070, LDS Archives.

Pace, James. Journal, 1846–1847, MS 1730:1, LDS Archives; and Autobiographical Sketch [ca. 1862]. MS 1730:2, LDS Archives. See also Autobiography and Diary, 1811–1888. Typescript Mor M270 M82 v. 13, BYU Special Collections. Copied in 1946 from original journals.

Pace, William B. Autobiography and Journals 1847–1857. MS 1658, LDS Archives.

Pettegrew, David. Journal of David Pettegrew. MSS 4278, Utah State Hist. Soc. Typescript by David L. Bigler from the original owned by Mrs. Virginia Kelson of Salt Lake, copy in the editors' possession. See also Pettegrew, David. Autobiography and Journals, 1840–1857. MS 2282, LDS Archives.

Polk, James K. Presidential Papers. Microfilm Series 2: 21 March 1846 to 10 June 1846, Reel 45, Library of Congress.

Riser. John J. Autobiography, 1887. Bancroft Library.

———. Memoir. Copy in possession of the family.

Rogers, Samuel H. Reminiscences and Diary, 1841–1886. BYU Special Collections.

Sanderson, George B. to Brigham Young, 22 August 1846. Brigham Young Collection, MS 1234, Box 21, Folder 2 #2, LDS Archives.

Sanderson, Henry Weeks. A History Written by Henry Weeks Sanderson at Fairview, Sanpete County, Utah, January, 1884. Typescript, Ms 255, Special Collections and Manuscripts, Marriott Library, Univ. of Utah.

Scott, James Allen. Diaries 1846. MS 1398 1–2, LDS Archives.

Scott, Margrett L. to J. Allen Scott, 30 August 1846. MS 1398, LDS Archives.

——— to Brigham Young, 17 September 1848. Brigham Young Collection, MS 1234, Box 21, Folder 14 #2, LDS Archives.

Shupe, Andrew J. Diary Extracts. MS 997, LDS Archives. See also Kate B. Carter, ed., "Women and Children of the Mormon Battalion." 503–05.

Cox, Adelia B. Biographical Sketch of Sylvester Hulet, 1st Lieut. Co. D., Nelson Higgins, Capt. A 425. Utah State Hist. Soc.

Simpson, Sir George. Incoming Correspondence. R3C 1T5, Hudson's Bay Co. Archives, Provincial Archives of Manitoba, Winnipeg, Manitoba Canada.

Skeen, Joseph. Reminiscences, 1846–July 1847. MS 1551, LDS Archives.

Smith, Albert. Journal of Albert Smith. MS 1835, LDS Archives.

Smith, Azariah. A Journal or History, of Azariah Smith; his travail &c in the Mormon Battalion, In the service of the United States, to California; And from there to; Salt Lake Valley. LDS Archives, copy in the editors' possession.

Smith, G. A. and R. L. Campbell to Nelson Higgins, 14 December 1859. A 102, Utah State Hist. Soc.

Smith, Lot. Papers. AZ 186, Special Collections, Univ. of Ariz., Tucson, Arizona.

Steele, John. Reminiscences and Journals, 1846–1898. MS 1847, LDS Archives.

Stevens, Arnold to Mrs. Lois Stevens, 25 December 1846. Mormon Battalion Correspondence Collection, 1846. MS 2070, Folder 26, LDS Archives.

Taggart, George W. A short sketch of His travels with the Church of Jesus Christ of latter day Saints on their journey from the City of Joseph. MS 1184, LDS Archives.

Terrell, Joel Judkins. Diary, July 1846 to July 1847. MS d 1762, LDS Archives.

Tippetts, John H. Mormon Battalion Diary. A 1505, Utah State Hist. Soc.

Turnbow, Samuel. Genealogical and blessing book of Samuel Turnbow with brief sketch of his life, 1804–1876. Brigham Young Univ. Library, 1940.

Tyler, Daniel, to First Presidency, 23 August 1900, original in the possession of Robert Cole, copy in the editors' possession.

Utah Territorial Militia. Correspondence 1849–1875. Utah State Hist. Soc., A-384.

Willey, Jeremiah. History of Jeremiah Willey. MS 1591, LDS Archives.

Williams, James Van Nostrand. Life Sketch. A 1426, Utah State Hist. Soc.

Wilson, George Deliverance. Journal. MS A 1005, Utah State Hist. Soc.

Workman, Andrew Jackson. A Short History of the Life of Andrew Jackson Workman. MSS B 289, Box 11, Utah State Hist. Soc.

Willis, William. Mormon Battalion Report. Brigham Young Collection, MS 1234, LDS Archives.

Young, Brigham to James K. Polk, 9 August 1846. MS 4622, LDS Archives.

Young, Samuel C. The Discovery of Gold in California in 1848. Edited transcription by Joseph Johnstun from typescript at LDS Archives, copy in the editors' possession.

DOCUMENTS

Bullock, Thomas. Names of Pueblo Soldiers and Mississippi Brethren arrived in Great Salt Lake City, August 1847. LDS Archives.

"California and New Mexico." House Exec. Doc. 17 (31-1), 1850, Serial 673.

Cooke, Philip St. George. "Report of Lieut. Col. P. St. George Cooke." 5 February 1847. House Exec. Doc. 41 (30-1), 1848, Serial 517. See also "Journal." Sen. Exec. Doc. (31–2), (1849–50), Vol. 2, 1-85.

Johnston, A. R. "Journal of Captain A. R. Johnston, First Dragoons." 9 October 1846. House Exec. Doc. 41 (30-1), 1848, Serial 517.

"Mexican War Correspondence." House Exec. Doc. 60 (30-1), vol. 7, 1848, Serial 520.

Mormon Battalion, James Brown Detached Company, Descriptive Roll and Soldiers' Pay Record, 1847. MS 9126, LDS Archives.

Pension Files, National Archives, Mexican Department.

"Presidential Message Communicating Information on California and New Mexico." Sen. Exec. Doc. 18 (31–1), 1849–50, Vol. 9, n. 18, Serial 557.

Records of Members 1836-1970. CR 375/8/Reel 6109, LDS Archives.

Records of the 10th Military Dept., 1846–1851. National Archives.

Swords, Major Thos. "Appendix E, Report of the Quartermaster General." House Exec. Doc. 1 (30–2), 1848, Serial 537.

COMPACT DISKS

Infobases Collector's Library '97. Orem, Utah: Western Standard Publishing, 1997.

New Mormon Studies CD-ROM: A Comprehensive Resource Library. S.L.C: Smith Research Associates, 1998.

Utah State Hist. Soc. *The Utah Centennial History Suite: The Most Comprehensive Collection of Utah History on CD.* S.L.C: Utah State Hist. Soc., 1998.

VIDEOS

"The U.S.–Mexican War (1846–1848)." Dallas/Fort Worth: KERA, 1998.

INDEX

THE EDITORS

David L. Bigler was born in Provo, Utah, and served in the U.S. Navy in World War II and Korean War. He graduated from the University of Utah in 1950 with a degree in Journalism. Southern Utah State College, now Southern Utah University, at Cedar City, awarded him an honorary Doctor of Letters degree in 1979. He is the retired director of public affairs for U.S. Steel, now USX Corp. Since 1986 he has devoted full time to the study of Utah and western history. Mr. Bigler is past president, Oregon–California Trails Association and a founder and first president of the Utah Westerners. He has served on the Utah Board of State History and is a former officer of the Friends of University of Utah Libraries. He has won the Utah State Historical Society's Dale L. Morgan Award. His *Forgotten Kingdom: The Mormon Theocracy in the American West, 1847–1896*, the second volume in the KINGDOM IN THE WEST series, won the Best Book Award for 1998 from Westerners International. Although only a distant cousin of Henry Bigler, he is a great-great-grandson of Albert Smith and edited his great-uncle's diary, *The Gold Discovery Journal of Azariah Smith*. Mr. Bigler and his wife, Evah, now live in Roseville, California.

Will Bagley lives in Salt Lake City with his wife and two children. He attended Brigham Young University and is a graduate of the University of California at Santa Cruz. He has edited several historical narratives, including *Frontiersman: Abner Blackburn's Narrative.* With Harold Schindler, he revised Dale L. Morgan's classic *West from Fort Bridger.* With his brother, cartoonist Pat Bagley, he published *This is the Place: A Crossroads of Utah's Past*, a children's book. Mr. Bagley serves as editor of the Arthur H. Clark Co. series KINGDOM IN THE WEST: *The Mormons and the American Frontier* whose first volume, *The Pioneer Camp of the Saints: The 1846–1847 Mormon Trail Journals of Thomas Bullock*, won the 1997 Stephen F. Christensen Award for Best Documentary from the Mormon History Association. The manuscript of his forthcoming study of the Mountain Meadows Massacre, *The Blood of the Prophets*, won a first place in the Utah Arts Council's Original Writing Contest in 1998. Mr. Bagley is not related to any member of the Mormon Battalion, but George Deliverance Wilson is his children's great-great-great-granduncle.

KINGDOM IN THE WEST SERIES

The role of the Church of Jesus Christ of Latter-day Saints in the settlement of the American West has been a subject of controversy and fascination for one hundred and fifty years. KINGDOM IN THE WEST: The Mormons and the American Frontier, a series from The Arthur H. Clark Company, explores the story of the Mormon people and their part in the greater history of the American West. Using primary source documents, most of them never before published, the projected set of fifteen volumes examines the Mormons' religious vision and political ambitions, revealing how they saw themselves and how they appeared to others.

The series' first volume, *The Pioneer Camp of the Saints*, brought the Latter-day Saint people to the Great Basin via the Mormon Trail journals of Thomas Bullock. In Volume 2, *Forgotten Kingdom: The Mormon Theocracy in the American West, 1847–1896*, David L. Bigler provided a narrative overview of the Latter-day Saint movement in the American West. Volume 3, *Scoundrel's Tale: The Samuel Brannan Papers*, told the audacious story of Mormons in California and their larger ambitions in the American West.

Volume 4 uses source documents to tell the story of one of the West's most amazing adventures, the Mormon Battalion. Subsequent volumes will focus on Great Basin overland narratives, the handcart emigration, polygamy, Indian relations, and the Utah War.

Series subscriptions are welcomed. Manuscript proposals of a documentary nature may also be submitted. Address inquiries to the publisher:

THE ARTHUR H. CLARK COMPANY
P.O. Box 14707
Spokane, Washington 99214
(800) 842-9286